"Traditional criminology often eschews the problem of cri criminality. This leaves students and practitioners with nowhe tical techniques to address the crime problems they face. Int *Handbook of Crime Science*, taking an impressively 'broad spe editors have done a sterling job of bringing together emerg the current and future state of crime science. This is a must-have book for crime researchers and practitioners."

Jerry Ratcliffe, Professor in the Department of Criminal Justice and Director of the Center for Security and Crime Science at Temple University, USA

"Richard Wortley, Aiden Sidebottom, Nick Tilley and Gloria Laycock have produced an outstanding contribution to the study and control of crime. Encompassing numerous disciplines, a wide range of crime forms, and a diversity of research methods the contributors to the comprehensive work show how we can make progress against crime. The *Routledge Handbook of Crime Science* should be read by anyone who is concerned about crime."

John Eck, Professor in the School of Criminal Justice, University of Cincinnati, USA

"The walls around criminology have been breached. Diverse scientists are welcome to enter. Hooray for crime science!"

Ken Pease, Professor of Policing, Derby University, UK

"Finally, we have a book that clearly explains the breadth and depth of crime science, philosophically, theoretically and historically positions the discipline, and identifies its role as a unique but interconnected academic enterprise. I highly recommend this book to all practitioners, policy makers, inventors, academics and anyone who has an interest in preventing of crime and increasing security."

Anna Stewart, Professor in the School of Criminology and Criminal Justice, Griffith University, Australia

"This is not a book about criminology. It's more than that. Criminologists have for decades espoused the value of interdisciplinary approaches and the need for the field to inform and guide the reduction of crime and its pernicious effects on society. But, these pursuits have for the most part been unsuccessful because criminology has mistaken empiricism for science, statistics for solutions, and only paid lip service to interdisciplinarity through the repetitive use of a narrow range of social science theories. In boldly defining and presenting to its readers the notion of *crime science* the editors and uniquely curated selection of authors herein identify an expansive path forward for the field in a way that may save it from becoming moribund and irrelevant. It unabashedly draws from scientific topics and approaches of the 21st century – engineering, genetics, architecture, forensics, cybersecurity, etc. – to establish a truly interdisciplinary identity for criminology that respects its potential to enlighten researchers about the causes of crime while informing and guiding the policy and interventions that will be needed in the years to come. Researchers, students, and practitioners need this book, as does the field itself."

Volkan Topalli, Professor, Professor of Criminal Justice and Criminology, The Andrew Young School of Policy Studies, Georgia State University, USA

Routledge Handbook of Crime Science

Crime science is precisely what it says it is: the application of *science* to the phenomenon of *crime*. This handbook, intended as a crime science manifesto, showcases the scope of the crime science field and provides the reader with an understanding of the assumptions, aspirations and methods of crime science, as well as the variety of topics that fall within its purview. Crime science provides a distinctive approach to understanding and dealing with crime: one that is outcome-oriented, evidence-based and that crosses boundaries between disciplines. The central mission of crime science is to find new ways to cut crime and increase security.

Beginning by setting out the case for crime science, the editors examine the roots of crime science in environmental criminology and describe its key features. The book is then divided into two sections. The first section comprises chapters by disciplinary specialists about the contributions their sciences can make or have already made to crime science. The second section of the book comprises a series of exemplary case studies in crime science, showing a wide range of the kind of work that crime scientists do. The editors conclude by drawing on the preceding contributions, as well as germane areas of research, to offer a thoughtful consideration of future directions for crime science.

This book is essential reading for social scientists and scientists alike and marks a new phase in the study of crime and its detection and prevention.

Richard Wortley is Director of the Jill Dando Institute and Head of the Department of Security and Crime Science at University College London.

Aiden Sidebottom is Associate Professor at the Jill Dando Institute of Security and Crime Science at University College London.

Nick Tilley is Principal Research Associate and Professor at the Jill Dando Institute of Security and Crime Science at University College London.

Gloria Laycock is Jill Dando Professor of Crime Science at the Jill Dando Institute of Security and Crime Science at University College London.

Routledge International Handbooks

Routledge Handbook of the History of Women's Economic Thought
ed. Kirsten Madden

The Routledge Handbook of Contemporary Feminism *ed. Tasha Oren, Andrea Press*

Routledge Handbook of Global Populism *ed. Carlos de la Torre*

Handbook of Indigenous Environmental Knowledge *ed. Thomas Thornton, Shonil Bhagwat*

The Routledge Handbook to Museum Communication *ed. Kirsten Drotner, Vincent Dziekan, Ross Parry, Kim Christian Schrøder*

Routledge International Handbook of Sex Industry Research *ed. Susan Dewey, Isabel Crowhurst, and Chimaraoke Izugbara*

Routledge Handbook of Cultural Sociology 2e *ed. Laura Grindstaff, Ming-Cheng Lo, John R. Hall*

The Routledge Handbook of Latin American Development *ed. Julie Cupples, Marcela Palomina-Schalscha and Manuel Prieto*

The Routledge International Handbook of Embodied Perspectives in Psychotherapy: Approaches from Dance Movement and Body Psychotherapies
ed. Helen Payne, Sabine Koch, Jennifer Tantia and Thomas Fuchs

The Routledge Handbook of Teaching Landscape *ed. Elke Mertens, Nilgül Karadeniz, Karsten Jørgensen, Richard Stiles*

For more information about this series, please visit: www.routledge.com/Routledge-International-Handbooks/book-series/RIHAND

Routledge Handbook of Crime Science

Edited by Richard Wortley, Aiden Sidebottom, Nick Tilley and Gloria Laycock

Routledge
Taylor & Francis Group
LONDON AND NEW YORK

First published 2019
by Routledge
2 Park Square, Milton Park, Abingdon, Oxon OX14 4RN

and by Routledge
52 Vanderbilt Avenue, New York, NY 10017

First issued in paperback 2020

Routledge is an imprint of the Taylor & Francis Group, an informa business

British Library Cataloguing-in-Publication Data
A catalogue record for this book is available from the British Library

Library of Congress Cataloging-in-Publication Data
Names: Wortley, Richard (Richard K.), editor.
Title: Routledge handbook of crime science / edited by Richard Wortley [and three others].
Description: Abingdon, Oxon ; New York, NY : Routledge, 2019. | Includes bibliographical references and index.
Identifiers: LCCN 2018032446 | ISBN 9780415826266 (hardback) | ISBN 9780203431405 (ebook)
Subjects: LCSH: Criminology. | Forensic sciences. | Criminal psychology.
Classification: LCC HV6025 .R675 2019 | DDC 364—dc23
LC record available at https://lccn.loc.gov/2018032446

ISBN 13: 978-0-367-58041-4 (pbk)
ISBN 13: 978-0-415-82626-6 (hbk)

Typeset in Bembo
by Swales & Willis Ltd, Exeter, Devon, UK

Contents

Contributors

Martin A. Andresen is a Professor in the School of Criminology and Director of the Institute for Canadian Urban Research Studies, Simon Fraser University; Chair of the Crime and Place Working Group in the Center for Evidence-Based Crime Policy, George Mason University; an Associate Editor for the *Journal of Quantitative Criminology*, and an editorial board member for numerous academic journals. He obtained his PhD from the University of British Columbia (geography) and his BA and MA from Simon Fraser University (economics). His research areas are in spatial crime analysis, crime and place, geography of crime, environmental criminology, and applied spatial statistics and geographical information analysis. Within these research areas he has published three edited volumes, two books, and more than 100 refereed journal articles and contributions to edited volumes.

Kevin M. Beaver is the Judith Rich Harris Professor of Criminology in the College of Criminology and Criminal Justice at Florida State University. His research focuses on the development of antisocial behaviour and the various ways in which genetic and environmental influences work in tandem to contribute to criminal offending.

Gisela Bichler, PhD, is Professor of Criminal Justice at California State University, San Bernardino. A major focus of her research investigates how social networks shape crime opportunities. She explores this topic in considerable detail in a forthcoming book titled *Diving into Criminal Networks: A Methodological Primer*, available from the University of California Press in 2019.

Daniel Birks is the University Academic Fellow in Quantitative Policing and Crime Data Analytics at the School of Law, University of Leeds. He holds degrees in artificial intelligence, computer science, cognitive science, and criminology and has previously held research and teaching positions at University College London, Griffith University, and the Australian Research Council's Centre of Excellence in Policing and Security. His research primarily focuses on the role computational methods can play in better understanding, predicting and disrupting crime problems.

Cashen Boccio is currently a doctoral candidate at the College of Criminology and Criminal Justice, Florida State University. Cashen does quantitative social research. His most recent publication is 'The role of verbal intelligence in becoming a successful criminal: results from a longitudinal sample' (*Intelligence*, 2018).

Hervé Borrion, Associate Professor, UCL, pursued his postgraduate education at the École Nationale Supérieure d'Aéronautique et de l'Espace (Masters) and at University College

London (PhD). He developed a strong interest in the application of sensor-based technology in various research centres including the Commissariat à l'Énergie Atomique (France), Los Alamos National Laboratory (US), UCT-CSIR (South Africa) and Tsinghua University (China). His research activities are situated at the interface between quantitative crime analysis and design/engineering, and include various EU and EPSRC projects examining how crime can be reduced using dedicated technological systems and smart infrastructures. A strong supporter of crime science education, he was the founding director of several pioneering courses in the field of crime science, including the BSc Security and Crime Science, MSc Countering Organised Crime and Terrorism, MRes Security Science and PhD Security Science. He is a board member of the International Collaboration Network for Public Safety Research.

Kevin Chetty is a Senior Lecturer (Associate Professor) at University College London. His research focuses on radio-frequency sensing, and radar micro-Doppler signal processing using machine learning approaches. Applications of his research include exploiting wireless communications such as WiFi for personnel tracking, and behaviour classification for use in operational policing and tele-healthcare. Other research interests include through-the-wall and FMCW radar, and reconfigurable hardware. He is the author of over 60 peer-reviewed publications and has been an investigator on grants funded by both government and industry. Kevin also sits on the Technical Committee for the International Security and Crime Science conference and is a reviewer for a number of highly esteemed journals including: *IET Radar, Sonar and Navigation*, *IEEE Geoscience & Remote Sensing*, and *IEEE Communications* magazine.

Toby Davies is a Lecturer in the Department of Security and Crime Science at UCL. His background is in mathematics, and his research is concerned with the application of quantitative methods to the modelling and analysis of crime. He has particular interest in the spatio-temporal characteristics of crime, and the modelling of these towards the end goal of crime prediction. In addition, his research involves the application of network science in the context of crime, particularly in relation to the role of urban form in shaping patterns of crime.

Itiel E. Dror pursued his interest in expert performance after finishing his PhD in psychology at Harvard. Along with his theoretical laboratory-based research he has conducted fieldwork with a variety of experts (such as with Air Force pilots, investigators and frontline police officers, forensic examiners, and medical professionals). Dr Dror has led to the understanding that the perceptions and cognitions of the human expert play a key role in forensic and scientific testimony. Building on these insights he developed unique ways to combat these weaknesses and improve expert performance. Dr Dror has published over 120 peer-reviewed articles specifically looking at cognitive factors that mediate human expert performance, and he has trained forensic examiners, as well as lawyers and judges in numerous countries.

Helen Earwaker is a Lecturer in Forensic Studies within the Institute of Criminal Justice Studies at the University of Portsmouth. Her interdisciplinary research interests include value within forensic investigations, decision-making within forensic processes, fingermark quality assessment, and fingermark visualisation methods. Helen's research sits within the Forensic Innovation Centre: a collaborative approach to forensic science learning, innovation and research facilitated through partnership with police scientific support. Prior to joining the University of Portsmouth Helen worked as a fingermark laboratory practitioner for Northumbria Police, moving on to complete a PhD at University College London focusing upon decision-making within fingermark submission processes. Helen has worked on reports for the Forensic Science Regulator and Knowledge Transfer Network.

Phil Edwards, BSc CStat PhD, is a Chartered Statistician and Associate Professor in Epidemiology & Statistics at the London School of Hygiene & Tropical Medicine. His main research interests are in Transport and Health, in particular the epidemiology of road-traffic injury. His UK study of the effect of reduced night-time street lighting on road-traffic injury risk and crime was conducted in close collaboration with the UCL Department of Security and Crime Science, which led to further research collaborations in crime science.

Paul Ekblom is Emeritus Professor of Design Against Crime at University of the Arts London, and visiting professor at the Department of Security & Crime Science UCL, and the Applied Criminology and Policing Centre, University of Huddersfield. Formerly a researcher in the UK Home Office, his interests include crime futures, arms races and evolutionary approaches to crime, cybercrime, terrorism and security, and the design of secure products and places.

Paul Fine is Professor of Communicable Disease Epidemiology at the London School of Hygiene & Tropical Medicine. He has a background in veterinary medicine and infectious diseases, and has been involved in research on a variety of diseases and public health interventions in Africa, the USA and UK. He has been involved in teaching epidemiology for more than 40 years, and has a particular interest in the application of epidemiological methods in the social as well as medical sciences.

James C. French is a Teaching Fellow at the Department of Security and Crime Science at University College London, where he has been based since he completed his PhD at UCL in 2013. He teaches undergraduate and postgraduate students and as part of the interdisciplinary UCL Centre for the Forensic Sciences, he is involved in a number of research projects in various fields of the forensic sciences. His principal research interests include trace physical evidence, evidence dynamics and the interpretation of forensic evidence, particularly the use of Bayesian Networks for reasoning about forensic evidence. A major area of interest is the use of gunshot residue (GSR) in forensic investigations and James's experimental work on the secondary and tertiary transfer of GSR has considered the implications of these dynamics for the investigation of firearms offences.

Michael J. Frith is a Postdoctoral Research Associate and PhD candidate at the Department of Security and Crime Science (University College London). His postdoctoral research looks at modelling refugee flows from conflict zones (particularly Syria) and the impact they have on their host countries. His PhD thesis and more general research interests include the applications of discrete choice models and graph theory to the analyses of offence location choices to explain their spatial and temporal distributions.

Jamie M. Gajos is a Postdoctoral Fellow in the Prevention and Methodology Training (PAMT) Program at Pennsylvania State University. She received her PhD in Criminology and Criminal Justice from Florida State University in 2017. Dr Gajos's specific research agenda seeks to understand how substance use, problem behaviours, and mental health outcomes manifest across time within the context of important proximal social environments. Another interest surrounds the role of interventions for preventing/reducing substance use, how person–environment interactions may change intervention effects, and whether interventions affect substance use outcomes via intermediate behavioural/social processes across time.

Paul Gill is an Associate Professor in Security and Crime Science at University College London. He has over 60 publications on the topic of terrorist behaviour. He has conducted research funded by the Office for Naval Research, the Department of Homeland Security, DSTL, the European Union, the National Institute of Justice, CREST, Public Safety Canada and MINERVA. He currently manages the European Research Council Starter Grant project entitled GRIEVANCE. Collectively these grants have been worth over €9 million. These projects focused upon various aspects of terrorist behaviour including IED development, creativity, terrorist network structures, risk assessment and management, and lone-actor terrorism. His doctoral research focused on the underlying individual and organisational motivations behind suicide bombing. This piece of research won the Jean Blondel Prize for the best PhD thesis in Political Science in Europe for 2010. He has published in leading psychology, criminology and political science journals.

Stephen Hailes is Professor of Wireless Systems in the department of Computer Science at UCL. Stephen graduated from Cambridge University in a mixture of natural science and computer science and came to work at UCL as a post-doc, researching in the area of multimedia systems. In that role, he performed the first demonstration of video conferencing over IP networks in the UK – a precursor of technologies like Skype. Stephen's research interests then developed in three main directions: trust and security, in which he was one of the founders of the field of computational trust; networking, in which he has contributed to the development of the next generation internet and to the security of networked industrial control systems; and, latterly, sensor, Internet of Things and robotic systems. Over the past decade, Stephen has built a set of interdisciplinary relationships with the aim of improving the nature of the science that can be undertaken in a variety of fields. This includes the development of systems that can be used to measure data of interest, most often using sets of relatively inexpensive sensors, and frequently in the developing world. Stephen's group designs hardware appropriate to particular deployment domains and writes the software for that; they design data collection mechanisms; and they both tune and use existing data analysis techniques and develop new mathematical tools for the analysis of data, enabling them to conduct novel science in collaboration with others. As a consequence, Stephen publishes in both computer science and more general scientific venues.

Adam J. L. Harris is Senior Lecturer in Experimental Psychology at University College London. His research interests lie in the area of judgement and decision-making. He is also the course director for the MSc in Cognitive and Decision Sciences.

Pieter Hartel is Head of the Cyber Security research group of the faculty of Electrical Engineering, Mathematics and Computer Science at Delft University of Technology. He also holds part-time professorial positions at the University of Twente and at Singapore University of Technology and Design. He has 25 years of research and teaching experience in Cyber Security in the Netherlands, the UK, the US, Malaysia, and Singapore. He is the coordinator of the 4TU Cyber Security Master Specialisation where he teaches a course in Cybercrime science, the Capstone courses on Social, Business, and Entrepreneurial skills in cyber security. His research interests include the human factor in cyber security, cybercrime, crypto markets, and block chain technology. He was the principal investigator of the recently completed €13.5M EU TREsPASS project on socio-technical cyber security risk management.

Shane D. Johnson is the Director of the Dawes Centre for Future Crime at University College London (UCL). He has a PhD and an MA in psychology and a BSc in computer science.

He has published over 120 articles and book chapters and his research has focused on reducing crime through design, predictive policing, understanding spatial and temporal patterns of riots, maritime piracy and insurgency, the application of complexity science to issues of crime and security, and developing the evidence base of what works to reduce crime. His current interests focus on how developing technology and social change are influencing new forms of crime opportunity. He is a member of the UK Home Office's Scientific Advisory Council, sits on the editorial boards of the journals *Research in Crime and Delinquency*, and the *Journal of Quantitative Criminology*, and is an Associate Editor of the journal *Legal and Criminological Psychology*.

Marianne Junger is a Professor of Cyber Security and Business Continuity at the University of Twente. Her research investigates the human factors of fraud and of cybercrime, more specifically she investigates victimisation, disclosure and privacy issues. Why do users trust phishing emails or fraudsters? Why do they comply or not comply with safety rules, why do they disclose so easily personal information and how can they be helped to become more vigilant users in order to protect themselves? The aim of her research is to develop interventions that will help to protect users against social engineering and to increase compliance. She is a member of the Scientific Advisory Council (WAR) of the Dutch Defence Academy. She founded the Crime Science journal together with Pieter Hartel and was an associate editor for six years (https://crimesciencejournal.springeropen.com). Her research was sponsored by, among others, the Dutch Police, an EU grant and ZonMw (for health research).

Daniel Koch is a Researcher in the field of critical morphology and Teacher at the KTH School of Architecture and Chalmers Institute of Technology, and a practising architect at Patchwork Architecture Laboratory. His research concerns spatial configuration as an intrinsic aspect of architecture, and involves examining borders, boundaries, spatial relations, disjunction and heterogeneity, and how this performatively situates people and thus produces social situations and relations. Central to this investigation has been the production of public culture, sociocultural (re)production and training in aesthetics as well as how diagrammatic representations of such relations work to drive research and design forward. He is currently the editor of the *Journal of Space Syntax* and co-editor of the *Nordic Journal of Architecture Research*. His current activities include two research projects funded by Vinnova on social sustainability and urban design (KTH), and theory and method development in the project C-ARC (Chalmers).

Tony Krone worked as a Defender and Prosecutor in criminal law. After obtaining a PhD in law Tony became a research specialist with the Australian High Tech Crime Centre. Tony focuses on cybercrime and in particular, online child exploitation as an Associate Professor in the School of Law and Justice at the University of Canberra. Tony is currently a Chief Investigator on an Australian Research Council grant focusing on demand reduction strategies for child exploitation material (DP160100601).

Dick Lacey joined PSDB (aka Centre for Applied Science and Technology (CAST)) in October 1979 after obtaining a BSc and PhD from the University of London and worked initially on the development of protective equipment for the police. He moved to work on explosives detection after the bombing of the Grand Hotel in Brighton and took responsibility for some of the aviation security research programme in 1989 after Pan Am 103, eventually becoming Chief Scientist for CBRNE at Home Office Scientific Development Branch (note the name change). He was also the head of Public Protection Sector, which included a number of projects to address the prevention of acquisitive crime. Since partially retiring in 2014, he has had responsibility for CAST's futures and innovation work. He is or has been a member of a number of international fora in the field of contraband detection and a fellow of the Institute of Physics and the Royal Society of Chemistry. He has had visiting chairs at Nottingham Trent University, Strathclyde University and University College London. He is chairman of the STFCs Nuclear Security Steering Group.

Anita Lavorgna is Lecturer in Criminology within the Department of Sociology, Social Policy & Criminology at the University of Southampton, UK. She is currently leading research projects on internet-facilitated wildlife trafficking and health frauds. Anita's research pivots around organised crime (especially Italian mafias and online criminal networks), cybercrimes (especially internet-facilitated trafficking activities), and the propagation of fake/fraudulent health information online.

Gloria Laycock has a BSc and PhD in psychology from UCL. She established and headed the Home Office Police Research Group and was founding Director of the UCL Jill Dando Institute. She has carried out research and development in prisons, policing and crime prevention and has acted as a consultant and trainer on policing matters around the world. She is currently Professor of Crime Science at UCL and was Director of Research supporting the What Works Centre for Crime Reduction until 2016. She was awarded an OBE in the Queen's Birthday Honours 2008 for services to crime policy.

Aili Malm is a Professor in the School of Criminology, Criminal Justice and Emergency Management at California State University, Long Beach. She is interested in the assessment and evaluation of policing strategies and intelligence. In this capacity, her research requires an ability to blend theory with advanced methodologies, including social network analysis. She was one of the pioneers in applying SNA to help understand illicit networks and has used social network analysis to examine several different types of markets, including arms, drugs, art, and human trafficking. She has worked as a PI or Co-PI for over $5 million in grants, and has authored over 40 peer-reviewed publications.

Matthew Manning is an Associate Professor at the Australian National University and an adjunct Associate Professor at University College London. He is a microeconomist with degrees in economics and criminology. His work focuses on the economics of crime and security, with a particular focus on financial crime. The aim of this work agenda is to examine how and where to invest finite resources to deal with money laundering and terrorism financing (ML/TF) in a way that maximises the return on investment whilst reducing impact on other economic and social opportunities, including growth, distribution, international trade and access to financial services. In addition, Matthew is developing tools and processes that will assist financial organisations with compliance, auditing, identification of suspicious activity and ultimately mitigating the risks of ML/TF in order to protect the integrity of the financial system.

Zoe Marchment is currently a Post-doctoral Researcher in the Department of Security and Crime Science, University College London, and a research assistant on the European Research Council-funded GRIEVANCE project. Her research examines the spatial patterns of terrorist target selection, with a focus on lone actors and violent dissident Republican activity. Zoe has worked on projects for the UK Defence Science and Technology Laboratory; Centre for Research and Evidence on Security Threats (CREST); FP7 Preventing, Interdicting and Mitigating Extremism (PRIME) and the VOX-Pol Network of Excellence.

Georgina Meakin is an Associate Professor at the Centre for the Forensic Sciences within the Department of Security and Crime Science at University College London. In addition to a PhD and employment background in molecular genetics, Georgina holds an MSc in Forensic and Analytical Science and went on to practice as a Forensic Scientist at The Forensic Institute in Glasgow. Georgina has consulted on over 120 criminal cases in the UK, USA, Australia and Canada, mostly centred on the interpretation and evaluation of DNA evidence. Building on this casework experience, Georgina conducts and supervises research focused on the transfer and persistence of DNA and other trace evidence, and lectures on UCL's Crime and Forensic Science MSc programme.

Sarah Meiklejohn is a Reader in Cryptography and Security at University College London. She has broad research interests in computer security and cryptography, and has worked on topics such as anonymity and criminal abuses in cryptocurrencies, privacy-enhancing technologies, and bringing transparency to shared systems.

Ruth M. Morgan is the Director of the UCL Centre for the Forensic Sciences and Professor of Crime and Forensic Science at UCL. The Centre facilitates a network of researchers from a wide range of different disciplines, to enable a strategic and multidisciplinary research programme in collaboration with external partners and forensic science stakeholders. Her research group is focused on developing the field of forensic science evidence interpretation. Professor Morgan has received the PW Allen Award from the Chartered Society of Forensic Sciences for best publication in the Chartered Society of Forensic Science journal *Science and Justice* in 2006 and 2017. She is the specialist advisor to the House of Lords Science and Technology Committee, and Vice Chair of the London Geological Society Forensic Geoscience Group. She is a regular speaker and advocate for addressing the challenges faced in forensic science with problem-based research that has an impact in the 'real world'.

Sherry Nakhaeizadeh is a Postdoctoral Researcher at the Department of Security and Crime Science, Centre for the Forensic Sciences, University College London. Her principle research interests include the effect of cognitive bias in forensic science and criminal investigations. She is particularly interested in judgement and decision-making in forensic evidence interpretations. Sherry's current research looks into the use of eye-tracking technology in forensic decision-making, and how such technology could aid in an empirical approach to advancing the understanding of complex visual tasks in forensic anthropology specifically, and forensic and crime science broadly. She has published and presented her scholarship internationally.

Ivan P. Parkin is a Professor of Materials and Inorganic Chemistry at UCL and currently Dean of the Mathematical and Physical Sciences Faculty. His group has published more than 700 research papers and 12 patents. Parkin has research interests in making and analysing materials. He has developed new detection methods to analyse toxic gases and methods to detect trace compounds (especially explosives). He has been awarded nine prizes and medals by learned societies. With Professor Ruth Morgan and others he was co-winner of the 2016 PW Allen award from the Chartered Society of Forensic Sciences.

William J. Peveler studied chemistry at the University of Oxford and University College London, where he completed his PhD in 2015 on the topic of 'Arrays for Explosives Detection'. Subsequently he undertook postdoctoral work with Professor William Rosenberg and Professor

Claire Carmalt at UCL, constructing chemical-nose sensors for biomedical applications and most recently he has been working at the University of British Columbia with Professor Russ Algar to construct smartphone-enabled sensors for use outside of the laboratory. Dr Peveler is now a Lord Kelvin Adam Smith Fellow at the University of Glasgow, where his research focuses on the design and application of synthetic materials, including nanomaterials, to analytical and sensing challenges. He has a particular interest in array-based sensors for both security and human health applications, and the translation of clinical tests into point-of-care diagnostics for use in resource-limited settings.

Jeremy Prichard is a Criminologist with a PhD in Law. He is an Associate Professor at the Law School, University of Tasmania. Before moving to the academic sector Jeremy worked at the Australian Institute of Criminology, the Crime and Misconduct Commission and the Department for the Premier and Cabinet (QLD). Jeremy's interests are in examining illicit markets with novel empirical methods. With the co–authors of this chapter, he conducts research on preventing the use of child exploitation material. He also collaborates with chemists, engineers and epidemiologists to study drug markets using wastewater analysis. He has over 50 publication outputs and has been involved in 11 funded research projects.

Carolyn Rando is Lecturer in Bioarchaeology and Forensic Anthropology at the UCL Institute of Archaeology, London. She obtained a BA in Physical Anthropology from the University of New Mexico, USA, an MSc in Skeletal and Dental Bioarchaeology from the UCL Institute of Archaeology, and a PhD in Bioarchaeology from UCL. Carolyn's research profile spans across the range of human remains research, including papers in areas such as: bioarchaeology, forensic anthropology, palaeopathology, digital methods for forensic archaeology, decision-making and cognitive bias, and forensic taphonomy.

Jason Roach is the Director of the Applied Criminology and Policing Centre at the University of Huddersfield, the Editor of the *Police Journal*, and a Chartered Psychologist. Jason has worked in an academic setting for the past 15 years and has previously worked for the UK Home office and for various mental health services in the north of England. He has published research on a wide range of topics including; investigative decision-making, terrorism, cold-case homicides, and evolutionary psychology and crime, and has also co-authored three books with Professor Ken Pease, the most recent being *Self-Selection Policing*, in 2016. His main area of research expertise is with police and offender decision-making, particularly with regard to the commission and investigation of violent crime, including preventing and investigating child homicide, and the self- selection policing approach to identifying active, serious criminals, from the minor crimes they commit.

Erwin Rosas Valdez is a doctoral student at the Department of Security and Crime Science, University College London. Erwin's research concerns modelling crime and the possible responses to it, drawing from computational and statistical techniques to test the effectiveness of a variety of interventions. Erwin has collaborated with the Dawes Centre for Future Crime and the Latin American and Caribbean Unit at UCL. He holds an MSc from Hild Bede College, Durham. Erwin's broader research interests include the application of data science and machine learning to solve crime and security problems.

Aaron Sell received his PhD in developmental and evolutionary psychology from the prestigious Center for Evolutionary Psychology at the University of California, Santa

Barbara. His dissertation introduced the 'recalibrational theory of anger', an evolutionary-computational model informed by models of animal conflict, game theory, criminology, and anthropological cross-cultural reports of human conflict. His research focuses on human conflict including anger, aggressive facial expressions, formidability assessment, anger-based arguments, and the importance of upper body strength as a psychological predictor in males. He uses multiple methodologies including classical psychological experiments, correlational studies, cross-cultural surveys, voice analyses, FACS coding, and vignette studies. Dr Sell is currently an Assistant Professor at Heidelberg University in the Department of Psychology and Criminal Justice.

Aiden Sidebottom is an Associate Professor in the UCL Jill Dando Institute of Security and Crime Science, University College London. His main research interests are situational crime prevention, problem-oriented policing and evaluation methods. Recent books include the *Handbook of Crime Prevention and Community Safety* (co-edited with Nick Tilley) and *Realist Evaluation for Crime Science: Essays in Honour of Nick Tilley* (co-edited with Graham Farrell).

Nissy Sombatruang is a PhD student at the Department of Security and Crime Science at UCL. Her research focuses on how we could apply behavioural economics principles and theories to influence users in making a better decision in cyber security. Specifically, she is interested in examining the risks of public Wi-Fi networks and why users keep using them, and identify workable interventions that could incentivise users to use these networks securely. Outside of her primary area of research, Nissy also work on projects related to usability of password, future crime, and the Internet of Things (IoTs) security.

Caroline Spiranovic has a PhD in Psychology and works predominantly in multidisciplinary teams on criminology, law and forensic psychology research projects focusing on crime prevention, public opinion and sex offending. Caroline is currently a Chief Investigator on two Australian Research Council grants: one focusing on demand reduction strategies for child exploitation material (DP160100601) and the other focusing on risk assessment of sex offenders in Australia (LP140100275). Caroline is a Senior Research Fellow at the Faculty of Law, College of Arts, Law and Education, University of Tasmania and an Honorary Senior Research Fellow, School of Population and Global Health, Faculty of Medicine and Medical Sciences, University of Western Australia.

Gianluca Stringhini is a Senior Lecturer (Associate Professor) in the Departments of Computer Science and Crime Science at University College London. He obtained a PhD in Computer Science from UCSB in 2014, where he worked under the supervision of Christopher Kruegel and Giovanni Vigna. Gianluca works in the area of data-driven security, analysing large datasets to better understand complex malicious online operations and developing mitigation techniques to fight them. He was awarded a Google Faculty Research Award in 2015, the Symantec Research Labs Fellowship in 2012, and multiple Best Paper Awards. He has published in top security conferences such as CCS, NDSS, and USENIX Security, as well as top measurement and Web conferences such as IMC, ICWSM, and WWW.

Nick Tilley is a member of the Jill Dando Institute of Crime Science at UCL, Emeritus Professor of Sociology at Nottingham Trent University and Adjunct Professor at the Griffith Criminology Institute in Brisbane. His long-term research interests lie in evaluation methodology, the international crime drop, problem-oriented policing and situational crime prevention. He was awarded an OBE for Services to Policing and Crime Reduction in 2005 and elected a Fellow of the Academy of Social Sciences (FAcSS) in 2009.

Michael Townsley is the Head of the School of Criminology and Criminal Justice, at Griffith University – the largest group of criminology researchers in Australia. He has previously held research positions at the UCL Jill Dando Institute of Crime Science, University College London and University of Liverpool. Townsley's research interests include crime analysis and prevention, with an emphasis on spatial patterns. Some of the problems he has worked on include burglary, maritime piracy, decision-making of insurgents in Iraq, clandestine meth labs, offender mobility and the journey to crime, alcohol-related violence, and drug operations to name a few.

Nilufer Tuptuk is working towards completion of her PhD in Security Science at the Department of Security and Crime Science, University College London (UCL). She also works as a research associate at UCL's Department of Computer Science, where she is studying the security of cyber physical systems. She holds an MRes degree in Security Science (UCL, 2014), an MSc in Advanced Computing (Imperial College London, 2003) and BSc (Hons) Computer Science (Queen Mary University of London, 2002). Her current research involves using AI and machine learning approaches to find security vulnerabilities in industrial control systems. She has been involved in European projects related to the various fields of information security, and she has developed CPD-type programmes in cybercrime aimed at training practitioners.

Paul Watters is Professor of Cybersecurity at La Trobe University in Melbourne, Australia. Professor Watters has research interests in malware, phishing, piracy, forensics and child exploitation. He has held academic positions at Macquarie University, the University of Ballarat and Massey University, with honorary roles at University College London and Unitec Institute of Technology in New Zealand. He is the academic director of La Trobe's cybersecurity programme.

Gabriel T. W. Wong is a Postdoctoral Fellow at the ANU Centre for Social Research and Methods. His research interests include adolescent drug involvement, policy decision-making, knowledge synthesis, economic analysis of crime prevention and efficiency in policing. Gabriel's recent research focuses on the use of multi-criteria frameworks to analyse the contributing factors of adolescent drug involvement and evaluate the drug policy preference in Hong Kong and Australia. These results are influential in informing the development of targeted institutional and criminal justice policies aimed at mitigating the adverse harms and consequences associated with illicit drug involvement.

Richard Wortley has been Director of the UCL Jill Dando Institute of Security & Crime Science since 2010, before which he worked in the Australian university system for 25 years. A psychologist by discipline, his research interests centre on the role that immediate environments play in criminal behaviour and the implications this has for situational crime prevention. He has a particular interest in the prevention of child sexual exploitation (CSE): both contact and online offending. He has been involved in around 20 funded research projects and has more than 100 scholarly publications, including nine books. In 2018 he was made a Member of the Order of Australia for the development of security and crime science education.

Kathryn Wuschke is an Assistant Professor in Criminology and Criminal Justice at Portland State University. With a background in geography, her primary research interests fall at the intersection of crime and place. Specialising in Geographic Information Systems, she studies the spatial patterns of crime with a focus on crime analysis and mapping. Her research considers the impact of crime maps on public perception and fear. In addition, Katie's research interests explore the connections between crime events and the built environment across spatial scales. Her work within this area aims to improve methods for analysing spatial crime patterns and to develop planning and resourcing tools that identify potential crime hotspots based on existing and planned urban structure.

1

What is crime science?

Richard Wortley, Aiden Sidebottom, Nick Tilley and Gloria Laycock

Introduction

Crime science is precisely what it says it is – it is the application of *science* to the phenomenon of *crime*. Put like this, it might seem that crime science simply describes what criminologists always do, but this is not the case.

First, many of the concerns of criminology are not about *crime* at all – they are about the characteristics of offenders and how they are formed, the structure of society and the operation of social institutions, the formulation and application of law, the roles and functions of the criminal justice system and the behaviour of actors within it, and so on. For crime scientists, crime is the central focus. They examine who commits crime and why, what crimes they commit and how they go about it, and where and when such crimes are carried out. The ultimate goal of studying crime is to learn how to reduce it.

Second, by no means is all criminological research *scientific*, nor does much of it aspire to be so. The scientific method is broadly defined as the systematic acquisition and testing of evidence, typically involving measurement, hypotheses and experimentation. There are branches of criminology (such as cultural criminology, see Hayward & Young, 2004) that eschew this empirical approach and instead rely on interpretive methods of enquiry that emphasise the subjective nature of knowledge. Moreover, when we examine the operation of the criminal justice system we encounter a great deal of policy and practice that is based on popular sentiment, ideology, political expediency, intuition, moralistic assumptions, 'good ideas' and 'what we have always done' rather than good science. Crime science is an evidence-based, problem-solving approach that embraces empirical research. Furthermore, the 'science' in crime science refers to more than the traditional fare of sociology, psychology and law that currently dominate criminology. The scientific theories, methods and findings needed to reduce crime may come from any discipline across the social, natural, formal and applied sciences.

Thus, crime science is at the same time more focused yet broader than criminology. It has the narrow mission of cutting crime but it is eclectic with respect to how this might be done and who might contribute to this mission. Putting the above elements together we arrive at the following definition:

> Crime science is the application of scientific methods and knowledge from many disciplines to the development of practical and ethical ways to reduce crime and increase security.

The term 'crime science' was created as a banner under which those interested in empirically based approaches to crime reduction might gather, be they within or beyond criminology. The theories and methods used in crime science are largely borrowed from existing approaches; what makes crime science distinctive is the deployment of these theories and methods around the unifying goal of crime reduction. While a growing band of researchers self-identify as crime scientists, there is much crime science also undertaken by researchers who are unfamiliar with the term. We trust that these researchers will not mind being badged fellow travellers.

This handbook is intended as a crime-science manifesto. In it we set out the case for crime science, define its key features, and showcase examples of crime science in action. This introductory chapter is divided into two main sections. In the first we trace the roots of crime science back to environmental criminology, describing some of the key philosophies and theoretical approaches that have helped shape the development of crime science and that remain important underpinnings. In the second section we discuss three defining characteristics of crime science, namely its determinedly outcome-focussed approach on crime reduction, its scientific orientation, and its embracing of diverse scientific disciplines.

Environmental criminology roots

During the 1970s, in both the USA and the UK, questions were raised about the extent to which the treatment of offenders could reduce crime. Offender treatment programmes were the dominant model for crime reduction at the time, and so concerns that 'nothing works' (Martinson, 1974) became something of a demotivating mantra for those working in the criminal justice system, particularly in prisons. It also left a policy vacuum on what to do about crime. From the early 1970s to mid- 1980s, a series of seminal publications appeared in the new field of environmental criminology that informed an alternative crime-reduction model (Table 1.1). From disparate disciplinary roots and with different foci, these approaches shared a common interest in crime events (rather than criminality) and the immediate circumstances in which crime occurs (rather than presumed distal causes) (Wortley & Townsley, 2017). In this section, we trace the development of environmental criminology, show how the various strands developed and came together to form a coherent perspective, and highlight the key assumptions and methods that influenced the conceptualisation of crime science.

Crime prevention through environmental design

Three years before Martinson's (1974) 'nothing works' report, C. Ray Jeffery (1971) published a book that anticipated the attack on rehabilitation and set out a radical prescription for crime prevention. Entitled *Crime Prevention through Environmental Design* – universally referred to as CPTED (and pronounced sep-ted) – the book presented a wide-ranging critique of the then dominant (and largely still current) criminal justice policies and practices. Jeffery argued that we lack the scientific knowledge to rehabilitate offenders and that we should instead focus on supressing their criminal behaviours. This required a shift in attention away from the presumed criminal dispositions of offenders and onto the immediate circumstances that facilitate or inhibit criminal acts. Jeffery was strongly influenced by arch behaviourist B. F. Skinner's (1953) model of operant conditioning. In essence, operant conditioning holds that our behaviour is contingent upon the consequences it produces – behaviour that is rewarded is reinforced and

Table 1.1 Chronology of seminal approaches in environmental criminology

Year	*Concept*	*Primarily associated with*	*Key idea*
1971	Crime prevention through environmental design	C. Ray Jeffrey	Crime is a function of its immediate consequences. Environments should be designed in ways to discourage the performance of criminal behaviour.
1972	Defensible space	Oscar Newman	Crime is a product of the anonymity associated with urban living. Urban design should facilitate citizens' ability to defend vulnerable spaces against intrusion by potential offenders.
1976	Situational crime prevention	Ronald V. Clarke	Crime can only occur where there is opportunity. The immediate environment should be altered to reduce opportunities on a crime-specific basis.
1979	Routine activities approach	Marcus Felson	Crime occurs when a likely offender and suitable target come together in the absence of a capable guardianship. The convergence of these three elements is by governed by socially determined routines.
1981	Geometry of crime/Crime pattern theory	Patricia & Paul Brantingham	Crime is not random. It is patterned in the urban environment by the distribution of criminal opportunities and the routine movements of offenders.
1985	Rational choice perspective	Derek Cornish & Ronald V. Clarke	Crime is purposive and always a choice. A particular crime occurs when the perceived benefits of committing the crime are judged to outweigh the perceived costs.

behaviour that is punished is discouraged. Applying this principle to crime, Jeffery asserted that 'there are no criminals, only environmental circumstances that result in criminal behaviour. Given the proper environmental structure, anyone will be a criminal or a non-criminal' (Jeffery, 1971, p. 177).

Jeffery proposed a new discipline of 'environmental criminology' to inform criminal justice policy and to promote crime prevention. In this new discipline, he wrote:

1 Scientific methodology is emphasized, in contrast with an ethical or clinical approach, limiting observations and conclusions to objective, observable behavior which can be verified
2 The approach is interdisciplinary, cutting across old academic boundaries and borrowing freely from each. The human being is regarded as a total system – biological, psychological and social
3 The human being is regarded as an input-output system, capable of receiving messages from and responding to the environment. Communications, cybernetics and feedback are critical concepts
4 Adaptation of the organism to the environment is the key process. Behavior is viewed as the means by which the organism adapts to an environmental system

5 A systems approach is used wherein emphasis is placed on the interrelatedness of parts, structural-functional analysis, and the consequences of action in one component of the system for the system in general
6 Future consequences of action, rather than past experiences or variables, is emphasized in behaviorism and in decision theory

(Jeffery, 1971, p. 167).

Crime Prevention through Environmental Design is a remarkable book. Written nearly 50 years ago, it was in many ways ahead of its time and it retains a currency few academic books of that age can claim. Elaborating on the nature of criminal behaviour, Jeffery took the deeply unfashionable view that it should be 'regarded as a biophysical phenomenon explainable in the same terms as other natural events' (p. 185). Even with the genomic revolution of recent years, many criminologists today remain resistant to according a meaningful role in crime to biological processes. More generally, Jeffery argued that 'science and technology can be applied to the prevention and control of crime' (p. 212). In response to the traditional dominance in criminology of 'law, sociology, and psychology' he called for radical 'interdisciplinarity' that embraced 'newer disciplines such as urban planning, public administration, statistics, systems analysis, computer engineering, and biopsychology' (p. 262). Few criminology departments today encompass the breadth of disciplines Jeffery advocated. As we will show later in this chapter, bridging the social and physical sciences as Jeffery proposed is even more important now as we seek to respond to the increasingly technologically-aided nature of crime of the 21st century. With just a little tweaking, Jeffery's six principles of environmental criminology could be turned into a modern-day blueprint for crime science.

Most crime researchers will know of CPTED but we suspect that few have actually read Jeffery's book. The biosocial model of behaviour and the environmental determinism that underpinned his approach to prevention proved unappealing to mainstream criminologists. Moreover, even for those researchers interested in environmental criminology, his book was quickly overshadowed by another book published the following year, Oscar Newman's (1972) *Defensible Space: Crime Prevention through Urban Design.*[1] Jeffery's term CPTED has endured but his approach has been supplanted: what most people think of as CPTED is in fact Newman's concept of defensible space.

Defensible space

Despite the similarity of the titles, Jeffery's and Newman's books are very different. As his title suggests, Newman was narrowly concerned with how the design of buildings, streets and open spaces influenced crime in urban settings. His central premise was that urban crime is a result of the anonymity and social fragmentation that characterises modern cities. People do not know their neighbours and they feel little personal investment in the surrounding environment. This in turn leads to a lack of vigilance and protective action by residents with respect to crime and antisocial behaviour. To Newman, what was needed to prevent crime was the stimulation of a sense of territoriality in residents. If residents could be encouraged to feel a greater sense of investment in their surroundings then they would be more likely to take actions that would defend those areas against intruders. So-called 'defensible space' could be created through a 'range of mechanisms – real and symbolic barriers, strongly defined areas of influence, and improved opportunities for surveillance – that combine to bring an environment under the control of its residents' (Newman, 1972, p. 3).

Narrowing the prevention task to the creation of defensible space has taken the Newman version of CPTED down a separate pathway to that taken by environmental criminology more generally. CPTED exists today as a more or less standalone model concerned principally with the design of the built environment (Armitage, 2017). Nevertheless, Newman's *Defensible Space* makes three important contributions to environmental criminology and ultimately to crime science.

First, Newman showed by example the value of expanding the disciplinary reach of criminology beyond the usual suspects. As an architect, Newman was one of the first non-social scientists to write about crime and its prevention. Environmental criminology is based on the premise that crime is the combined effect of the characteristics of the person and the situation in which the crime is performed. Because criminology largely comprises social scientists, there is an abundance of research addressing the nature of the person. Newman on the other hand could speak with authority on the situational side of the equation, providing informed advice on what architecture could offer to environmental criminology.

Second, Newman demonstrated the importance of operationalising prevention advice. Jeffery's *CPTED* was a polemic, long on theory but short on application; *Defensible Space* in contrast was essentially a how-to manual. Newman gave explicit instructions and offered many concrete examples of how to prevent crime: low-rise buildings have less crime than high-rise buildings; even low fences will deter many potential intruders; windows should look outwards onto the street so that passers-by can be observed; graffiti and rubbish invite disorder, and so on. Many of the principles of defensible space could be readily converted into policy statements and even codified into building and town-planning regulations.

Finally, Newman taught the value of understanding and altering the behaviour of those who were the potential victims and observers of crime. Where Jeffery presented a detailed psychological model of the offender, Newman barely mentioned offenders. His focus instead was on how urban design can change the behaviour of residents so that they might exercise greater levels of guardianship and thereby deter potential offenders. The focus on the role of residents as potential victims and guardians introduced additional elements to the crime dynamic, underscoring the point that crime prevention was not exclusively about dealing with offenders, nor was it the sole province of the criminal justice system.

Situational crime prevention

The next major contribution to environmental criminology came with Ron Clarke's situational crime prevention (SCP). In fact, Clarke's early writings on the role of situations in crime pre-date Jeffrey and Newman. Researching absconding from residential schools for juvenile offenders, Clarke found that the best predictors of absconding were institutional factors rather than any personal characteristics of the absconders. The best way to prevent absconding was not to try to identify potential absconders, but rather to change the way that institutions were built and run (Clarke, 1967). But it was in *Crime as Opportunity* published by Clarke and colleagues a decade later (Mayhew, Clarke, Sturman, & Hough, 1975) that the conceptual foundations of SCP were first set out in a comprehensive way, although the term itself was not used until Clarke's 1980 paper, '"Situational" Crime Prevention: Theory and Practice'.

SCP 'seeks to alter the situational determinants of crime so as to make crime less likely to happen' (Clarke, 2017, p. 286). The approach shows the influences of both Jeffery and Newman. The conceptual underpinnings of SCP, with its focus on the reduction of opportunity and the manipulation of the costs and benefits of crime as the bases for prevention, owe a clear debt to Jeffery. But like Newman, Clarke focused on providing concrete prevention techniques, with some of these borrowed directly from *Defensible Space*. At the same time, Clarke extended Newman in significant ways. He conceptualised the situation as being much broader than the built environment and so broke free of a narrow architectural approach to prevention.

He also emphasised the *re*design of existing situations that were known to be experiencing crime problems. He argued that the decision about how to intervene must be based on a thorough and systematic interrogation of the crime problem in question. An agenda focused on preventing 'crime' in the abstract is far too broad and cannot be operationalised. In contrast, SCP is much more sharply focused. Clarke argued that crime needs to be broken down into very specific types. In order to deal effectively with each crime type, a deep understanding is required of the specific features in the immediate environment that facilitate that behaviour. So, for example, in order to reduce violence, we need to distinguish between violence in the home involving intimate partners, violence associated with alcohol in pubs and clubs, violence between gangs of young people, and so on. Each of these sub-categories of violence is assumed to arise from different situational contingencies and therefore likely require different preventive action.

Clarke packaged his suggested interventions into a table, which has evolved and expanded over the years (Clarke, 1992, 1997; Cornish & Clarke, 2003). The latest iteration is shown in Table 1.2. Clarke identified five mechanisms through which situational measures might lead to reductions in crime – increasing the effort, increasing the risk, reducing rewards, reducing provocations and removing excuses, under each of which was listed five specific techniques, making 25 techniques in all. Examples are provided for each technique. Thus, for example, one way to increase the effort for potential car thieves is to target-harden cars by installing immobilisers. Clarke cautioned, however, that the table of 25 techniques should not be used as a cookbook of solutions. Each crime problem is assumed to have its own features and what works in one situation may not work in another. A problem-solving approach based on careful analysis of the specific crime problem is the key to effective SCP.

One fruitful application of SCP has been in the area of product design. Clarke realised that some products are inherently criminogenic because they are attractive and easy to steal. He described such 'hot products' as CRAVED, an acronym for concealable, removable, available, valuable, enjoyable and disposable (Clarke, 1999). For example, mobile phones meet all of the CRAVED criteria and have been a favoured target of street robbers in recent years (Farrell, 2015). However, many of the CRAVED attributes of hot products can be countered at the design stage. In the case of mobile phones, disposability is a particular problem – they are generally easy to re-programme and to sell on. Built-in biometric recognition technology is one technique for reducing the vulnerability of mobile phones by making them more difficult to hack and relaunch (Ohana, Phillips, & Chen, 2013; see Whitehead et al., 2008, for a comprehensive coverage of the prevention of mobile phone theft). This strand of SCP illustrates the crucial need for crime experts, designers and engineers to work together to devise solutions to crime problems (Ekblom, 2017).

Routine activities approach

Jeffery, Newman and Clarke were concerned with strategies for deterring offenders in the circumstances in which they were about to commit their crimes. The routine activities approach (RAA), advanced by Lawrence Cohen and Marcus Felson (1979), takes a step back from this point and seeks to describe how offenders and victims come together such that crime becomes a possibility. RAA draws on the observation that crime is the result of the routines of everyday life. Potential victims and potential offenders move around in the course of their lives and from time to time find themselves at the same place and time. There, in the absence of capable guardians, an offence may occur. Potential targets might be individuals, products or systems, all of which can be objects of crime. Potential offenders are those motivated to commit an offence at that time and place. Potential guardians are people – not necessarily formal security or law

Table 1.2 Twenty five techniques of situational prevention

Increase the effort	*Increase the risks*	*Reduce the rewards*	*Reduce provocations*	*Remove excuses*
1 *Target-harden* • Steering column locks and ignition immobilisers • Anti-robbery screens • Tamper-proof packaging	6 *Extend guardianship* • Go out in a group at night • Leave signs of occupancy • Carry cell phone	11 *Conceal targets* • Off-street parking • Gender-neutral phone directories • Unmarked armoured trucks	16 *Reduce frustrations and stress* • Efficient lines • Polite service • Expanded seating • Soothing music/muted lights	21 *Set rules* • Rental agreements • Harassment codes • Hotel registration
2 *Control access to facilities* • Entry phones • Electronic card access • Baggage screening	7 *Assist natural surveillance* • Improved street lighting • Defensible space design • Support whistleblowers	12 *Remove targets* • Removable car radio • Women's shelters • Pre-paid cards for pay phones	17 *Avoid disputes* • Separate seating for rival soccer fans • Reduce crowding in bars • Fixed cab fares	22 *Post instructions* • 'No Parking' • 'Private Property' • 'Extinguish camp fires'
3 *Screen exits* • Ticket needed for exit • Export documents • Electronic merchandise tags	8 *Reduce anonymity* • Taxi driver IDs • 'How's my driving?' decals • School uniforms	13 *Identify property* • Property marking • Vehicle licensing and parts marking • Cattle branding	18 *Reduce temptation and arousal* • Controls on violent pornography • Enforce good behaviour on soccer field • Prohibit racial slurs	23 *Alert conscience* • Roadside speed display boards • Signatures for customs declarations • 'Shoplifting is stealing'
4 *Deflect offenders* • Street closures • Separate bathrooms for women • Disperse pubs	9 *Use place managers* • CCTV for double-decker buses • Two clerks for convenience stores • Reward vigilance	14 *Disrupt markets* • Monitor pawn shops • Controls on classified ads • License street vendors	19 *Neutralise peer pressure* • 'Idiots drink and drive' • 'It's OK to say No' • Disperse troublemakers at school	24 *Assist compliance* • Easy library checkout • Public lavatories • Litter receptacles
5 *Control tools/weapons* • 'Smart' guns • Restrict spray-paint sales to juveniles • Toughened beer glasses	10 *Strengthen formal surveillance* • Red-light cameras • Burglar alarms • Security guards	15 *Deny benefits* • Ink merchandise tags • Graffiti cleaning • Disabling stolen cell phones	20 *Discourage imitation* • Rapid repair of vandalism • V-chips in TVs • Censor details of modus operandi	25 *Control drugs and alcohol* • Breathalysers in bars • Server intervention programmes • Alcohol-free events

Source: Clarke (2017)

enforcement personnel – whose very presence at that time and place can discourage crime from taking place. Depending on the opportunity presented, a large percentage of the general population might be tempted into offending, albeit that certain subsections of communities are more likely than others.

Cohen and Felson (1979) demonstrated the role of routine activities in crime through their analysis of crime rates in the US after WWII. Crime increased substantially in the post-war period. At the same time, economic conditions had generally improved. This pattern went against conventional criminological wisdom that poverty produced crime. Cohen and Felson (1979) argued that improved economic conditions and associated social changes had the effect of bringing potential victims, potential offenders, and unguarded potential crime locations together. For example, in the case of burglary, the increased participation of women in the workforce meant that there was an accompanying increase in the number of houses left unattended during the day. At the same time, domestic dwellings now contained more portable, high-value possessions worth stealing. Together these factors help explain a shift to daytime domestic burglary from night-time domestic burglary, within an overall shift to domestic burglary from commercial burglary.

RAA was originally formulated to explain the effect of macro-level social changes on broad crime patterns. However, further development of RAA by Felson (2002; 2017) showed that it could also be used at a micro-level to analyse the dynamics of individual crime events. RAA provides the basis for the familiar crime triangle (Figure 1.1; Clarke & Eck, 2005). The inner triangle of Figure 1.1 shows crime as requiring three necessary elements – an offender, a target or victim, and a place for the offence to occur. The outer triangle splits the concept of capable guardian into three types – guardians, who are in a position to protect potential victims or targets (e.g. parents, friends, security guards); handlers, who are able to exercise some control over potential offenders (e.g. parole officers, teachers, coaches); and place managers, who are responsible for looking after particular places where crime might occur (e.g. park rangers, bar owners, landlords). At this micro-level, RAA provides a useful companion to SCP. As the crime triangle neatly illustrates, just as there are three necessary elements to a crime, there are correspondingly three potential targets for crime prevention. Some crimes occur because of the easy accessibility

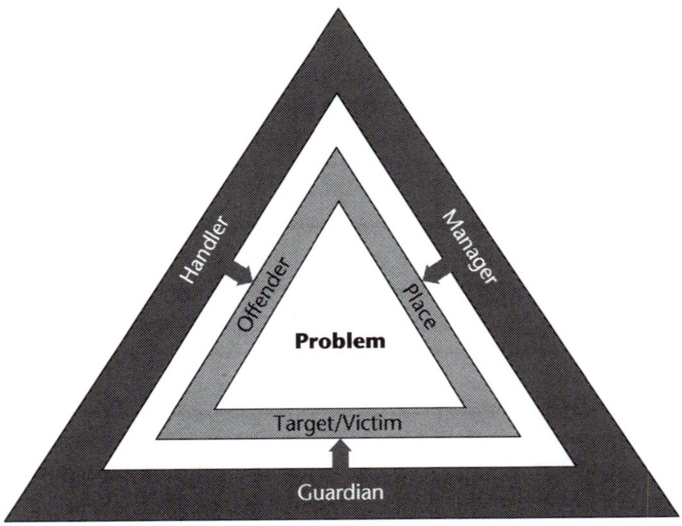

Figure 1.1 The crime triangle (Adapted from Clarke & Eck, 2005)

to targets and so intervention requires making those targets more difficult to reach; some crimes occur in locations that offer many crime opportunities and require interventions that address these environmental features; and some crimes are the result of the presence of a likely offender and strategies for deflecting or managing that individual are required. As with Newman, RAA emphasised that crime is about more than just criminals. Put differently, crime can be reduced by attending to the vulnerability of potential victims and actions of potential guardians.

Geometry of crime and crime pattern theory

A major lesson to be drawn from RAA is that crime is not random but is instead patterned in broadly predictable ways. However, RAA has little to say about the relationship between routine activities and the physical environment and, more particularly, the locations at which potential offenders and victims are most likely to converge. Brantingham and Brantingham (1981, 1993; Brantingham, Brantingham, & Andresen, 2017) provide an account of how urban form shapes the movement patterns of citizens and results in the clustering of crime in time and place. They refer to these movement patterns as the geometry of crime, which combined with other environmental criminology perspectives form a crime pattern meta-theory.

According to Brantingham and Brantingham, the routine activities of individuals are dominated by their need to travel regularly between various key locations, or 'nodes', such as home, work, school, shops, and entertainment areas. Typically, individuals will follow a preferred route, or 'path', to move from one node to another. Over time they will build up familiarity with the environment around these nodes and paths, while remaining relatively ignorant of the wider urban landscape that they seldom or never visit. These areas of familiarity are referred to as the individual's 'awareness space'. All things being equal, offenders prefer to commit crime within their awareness spaces, since it is in these areas that they feel the most comfortable and have greatest knowledge of crime opportunities and associated risks of detection.

But conditions conducive to crime are not uniformly distributed. Crime will concentrate where an offender's awareness space intersects with locations at which crime opportunities are relatively plentiful. Brantingham and Brantingham identified four kinds of location that facilitate crime. *Crime generators* are places that attract large numbers of people for legitimate purposes, including some liable to take advantage of crime opportunities. Sports stadia, shopping malls, bus stations and nightclubs are examples. These areas provide an abundance of potential crime targets for those who may be tempted to offend. *Crime attractors* are locations that draw potential offenders for the specific purpose of committing crime. They include seedy bars, drug markets, and red-light districts where offenders come to fence stolen goods, sell or obtain drugs, or pimp for prostitutes. *Crime enablers* are locations that lack capable guardianship at which crime can occur unobserved. Examples include unattended car parks and playgrounds. Finally, *edges* are the boundaries between neighbourhoods, between different land use zones (e.g. park land and residential housing) or between areas divided by some physical barrier (e.g. a main road). Edges are areas where strangers do not seem out of place and so they offer potential offenders a degree of anonymity without requiring them to stray too far from the safety of their own awareness space. Together, crime generators, crime attractors, crime enablers and edges help explain the development of crime hotspots.

While the Brantinghams were providing a theoretical account of the spatial and temporal distribution of crime, advances in computing and the widespread availability of geographic information system software (GIS) greatly facilitated the empirical analysis and visual representation of crime events. Mapping technology has allowed crime patterns to be readily modelled and for crime hotspots to be plotted. Hotspots are the obvious priority for the allocation of policing resources and crime prevention efforts. The geo-spatial analysis of crime has become a major strand within environmental criminology, and geography has become a core discipline within the field.

Rational choice perspective

The starting point for Jeffery was a psychological view of the offender that emphasised the situational dependence of behaviour. For Jeffery, environmental criminology only made sense if it could be established that human beings were fundamentally constructed to adapt their behaviour to immediate environmental conditions. Subsequently, Newman, Felson and the Brantinghams paid little attention to the psychology of the offender, simply taking for granted that behaviour was malleable. However, Clarke, with colleague Derek Cornish, returned to the issue of the offender in order to elaborate the theoretical underpinnings of SCP (Clarke & Cornish, 1985). After reviewing a wide range of theoretical perspectives from psychology, sociology, criminology, economics and human ecology that argued against pathological explanations of crime, they settled on rational choice as the model of offender decision-making which could accommodate environmental inputs being converted to situationally dependent action.

The rational choice perspective (RCP) shares Jeffery's assumption that behaviour is a function of its consequences. Through their actions, offenders, like everyone, invariably seek to benefit themselves in some way and to avoid unpleasant outcomes. Clarke and Cornish, however, disliked the deterministic, 'mindless' behaviourism that Jeffery advanced, fearing (rightly) that it would find little support among other criminologists. They argued that there was much to be learned by trying to understand the crime commission process from the subjective perspective of offenders. RCP portrays offenders as purposive, reasoning agents. It holds that crime always involves choice. Offenders are active decision makers who draw on environmental data in deciding whether or not to engage in a particular crime at a particular time and place. It is assumed that crime will occur when the perceived benefits outweigh the perceived costs. Benefits of crime are not limited to material rewards but include sexual gratification, peer esteem, excitement, revenge, and so on. The costs of crime are likewise not limited to the distant threats of criminal justice sanctions but also the immediate concerns about how difficult and risky it might be to commit the crime. As an underpinning for SCP, RCP suggests that crime can be prevented by implementing strategies at the potential crime scene that make crime a less attractive option from the perspective of potential offenders.

From the start, Clarke and Cornish presented the rationality of offenders in highly qualified terms. Following Simon (1957), they described offenders as exercising 'bounded' rationality to arrive at decisions that were merely 'satisficing' – satisfactory and sufficient. Clearly, on many occasions the decision to commit a crime turns out to be a poor one – the offence may not produce the anticipated payoff or the offender may be caught. An offender's capacity to make optimal decisions can be limited by a wide range of personal and environmental factors including intellectual capacity, cognitive biases, lack of information, emotional arousal, time pressure, and the effects of drugs or alcohol. Clarke and Cornish described RCP as a 'good enough' basis for SCP, and used the term 'perspective' – not 'theory' – advisedly. RCP was not intended as a rigorous psychological account of how offenders actually go about making decisions (see Wortley, 2013). Rather it is a rough-and-ready heuristic, primarily intended to provide a rationale for SCP that can be readily communicated to practitioners. It conveys in simple terms the basic message that all of us tend to act out of self-interest and all can be persuaded not to offend if the costs seem to be too high. RCP is akin to Popper's 'rationality principle': its flaws are acknowledged, but it is deemed sufficient to explain most criminal behaviour and to furnish a basis for designing strategies to change that behaviour (see Tilley, 2004). More generally, it assumes that the potential to commit crime is not a fixed attribute confined to a sub-section of the population, but is dynamic and depends upon the nature of the immediate environment. It follows that crime can be prevented by altering the immediate environment, via situational crime prevention.

Summary

Beginning as a series of largely independent insights into the relationship between crime and the immediate environment, environmental criminology has now developed into a complex set of inter-related ideas and approaches (Wortley & Townsley, 2017). With the benefit of hindsight we can identify three linked questions that the pioneers of environmental criminology sought to answer:

1 **Why do people commit crime?** Environmental criminology starts with the premise that whether or not an individual commits a criminal act is inextricably tied to the nature of the immediate environment. Insights into the situational nature of criminal behaviour were provided by Jeffery's (1971) CPTED and Clarke and Cornish's (1985) RCP.
2 **Where and when does crime occur?** Because the behaviour of offenders is situationally dependent, crime is distributed in time and space in non-random ways according to the location of criminogenic environments. Foundational concepts for understanding the patterned nature of crime were advanced in Cohen and Felson's (1979) RAA and Brantingham and Brantingham's (1981) geometry of crime.
3 **How do we prevent crime?** Understanding 1) how offenders are influenced by the immediate environment and 2) where and when crime concentrations occur provide the bases for preventative action. This aspect of environmental criminology was the primary focus of Newman's (1972) *Defensible Space* and Clarke's (1980) *SCP*.

Environmental criminology is now a firmly established branch of criminology. It is also a fertile source of inspiration for a vast number of effective crime-control initiatives (e.g., Clarke, 1992; 1997). Its strength lies in the systematic approach taken to the analysis of the crime problem and the rigorous application of different techniques or approaches to try to reduce the scale of the problem and to evaluate the effects. These are qualities that have been influential in the development of crime science, the topic to which we now turn.

Key characteristics of crime science

Crime science is a relatively recent term, coined by UK journalist and broadcaster Nick Ross in the late 1990s. With a background in psychology and as presenter of the UK television programme *Crimewatch*, Ross had a long-standing interest in crime (see Ross, 2013). He became highly critical of the prevailing crime prevention policies and of much of the criminological research that was meant to inform them. He believed that the reflexive focus on the assumed 'badness' of offenders was misplaced and that crime was largely a function of opportunity. He argued that crime research needed to draw on many disciplines and to be outcome focused, and he looked to evidence-based medicine as an exemplar of the approach required. Made aware of the overlaps in his thinking and environmental criminology, Ross made contact with leading environmental criminology researchers, including Ron Clarke, Ken Pease, Marcus Felson and Gloria Laycock, and from this dialogue the concept of crime science emerged. Then, in 1999,

Ross's co-presenter on *Crimewatch*, Jill Dando, was murdered. Ross, together with a group of friends and colleagues, set about raising money to establish an institute in Jill Dando's memory. This was used to found the Jill Dando Institute of Crime Science (the JDI) at University College London in 2001, where the ideas around crime science could be put into practice (Laycock, 2001, 2005; Ross, 2013).

While crime science draws on concepts and theories from environmental criminology, the two are not one and the same. As we shall see, crime science is a more broadly defined approach and has developed a distinctive set of features and identity. Breaking down the definition presented at the start of this chapter, in this section we unpack the three key features of crime science – reducing crime, thinking and acting scientifically, and bringing disciplines together.[2]

Reducing crime

The ultimate goal of crime science is the reduction of crime and associated harms. Pursuit of this goal is not unconditional – ethics, costs, public acceptability, politics, aesthetics, and unintended consequences are all crucial considerations in responding to crime and in any research agenda aiming to inform improvements in preventive performance. Situational approaches to crime reduction form a central part of the crime science armoury, primarily because there is strong evidence that such opportunity reduction measures are effective at reducing crime; however, other promising crime-reduction strategies are not excluded.

Defining crime

Crime is a legally defined action (or failure to act) that is liable to formal sanctions. What constitutes crime is to a certain degree chronically in flux; the definition of specific crimes varies from society to society and within any society over time. There are many examples of behaviours that were once crimes and are no longer so (e.g. homosexual acts) and new crimes are regularly created (e.g. the criminalisation of particular psychotropic substances). Take the example of child sexual abuse. The legal age of consent varies considerably across the world (from 12 to 21 years of age) and has steadily risen in most countries over the past 100 years or so (for example, in the UK it was 10 years old in 1800, but is at the time of writing 16 years) (Wortley & Smallbone, 2012). Thus, whether a person commits the crime of child sexual abuse may depend upon which country he/she lives in and into which era he/she was born.

Crime encompasses a wide spectrum of behaviour, from relatively minor antisocial acts, such as littering and disturbing the peace, to very serious offences, such as sexual assault and murder. Crime science approaches may be applied across this spectrum. Its focus includes crimes that have not often been addressed in criminological texts – acts of terrorism, human trafficking, theft of intellectual property, food adulteration, counterfeit products, maritime piracy, and so on. Moreover, the nature of crime is changing in response to social and technological changes. This will likely require corresponding changes in how we deal with crime. Crime science is uniquely placed to address the prevention challenges posed by digital and other technologies that are producing new crime threats such as Internet child exploitation, cyber bullying, identity theft, phishing, ransomware, and the criminal exploitation of the Internet of Things.

Person and situation

Most academic texts purporting to be about crime – often called 'the psychology of crime', 'the sociology of crime', and the like – are not about crime at all but are about criminals and criminality.

They are devoted to examining the psychological and sociological factors assumed to produce the *predisposition* to commit crime, but they rarely pay attention to the criminal act itself. The underlying assumption is that crime is the inevitable outcome of criminality (and that criminality is the primary cause of crime) and once criminality has been accounted for the explanatory job is done.

This person-centric view of crime is an example of a wider tendency – known as the 'fundamental attribution error' (Ross, 1977; Ross & Nisbett, 2011) – for human beings to interpret events in terms of the characteristics of actors and correspondingly to downplay the contribution of immediate environmental factors. When we see a person misbehaving we call them bad and possibly in need of punishment or correction. We are much better, however, at recognising the role of circumstances in our own behaviour; when we behave badly we attribute it to the situation in which we find ourselves (e.g. I was tired). This error pervades our view of crime control too and leads to the criminal justice system, which not only makes a statement about the limits of acceptable behaviour, and provides a means of delivering retribution and justice, but importantly is also seen as an effective vehicle for crime control.

Theoretically, if not in practice, there is wide acceptance in the social sciences that all behaviour, including criminal behaviour, is the result of a person–situation interaction, that is to say, the combined outcome of the characteristics of the person and the immediate circumstances in which the person finds him/herself at the time (Ross & Nisbett, 2011). While there is clearly a relationship between criminality and crime, the relationship is not one-to-one – many 'non-criminals' commit crime and 'criminals' do not commit crime all the time. Attempts to predict offending based on dispositional measures alone rarely produce correlations exceeding 0.4 (see Wortley, 2011).

As outlined above, the development of crime science has been strongly influenced by the theories and methods pioneered in environmental criminology. Accordingly, much of the research that we might label crime science has focused on the crime event as the prime source of data and on situational strategies as the preferred type of intervention. However, crime science is more inclusive than that. Any factor that is found to be a cause of crime, and any intervention that leads to a reduction in crime, is fair game for crime scientists.

Ross (2013, p. 1) explains the preference for working at the situational level as a case of directing one's resources to the 'low-hanging fruit'. It is a pragmatic decision rather than a matter of doctrine. Altering situations has proven to be effective at reducing crime and is relatively cheap and simple to do; there are lots of easy wins to be had for relatively little effort. This is not to deny that offender dispositions play a role in crime – common sense alone tells us that individuals with criminal propensities have a higher probability of offending in a given situation than those without. But changing dispositions is hard. As Clarke (2017, p. 289) puts it, 'we might all concede that lack of parental love is an important cause of delinquency, but . . . nobody knows how to make parents more loving'. Notwithstanding, scientific efforts to change the propensities of offenders in ways that result in a reduction in offending can legitimately be regarded as falling into the realm of crime science.

Proximal and distal causes

One way to think about the person–situation issue is in terms of a proximal–distal continuum (Ekblom, 1994). Working backwards from the crime event, we can identify a sequence of processes that have led up to that moment. Let's take the example of an assault in a pub. We start by examining what happened immediately prior to the first punch being thrown. Perhaps one patron spilled the drinks of another patron as they jostled to get through the crowd. Moving backwards in time, we find that the aggressor was already in a bad mood because door security staff were rude to him earlier in the night. Back further we find the aggressor has been unemployed for many months, as a result of which he has been depressed and has started drinking heavily. Continuing in this way, we eventually get to his childhood to discover he was raised in a chaotic household where his alcoholic father was frequently violent towards him and his mother. Finally, we discover that his mother smoked and drank heavily when she was pregnant with him, and he was born with some neurological impairment known to be associated with reduced levels of impulse control. Distal factors (prenatal and developmental experiences) are to do with the establishment of internalised criminal predispositions; proximal factors (situational aspects of the crime event) are about the expression of criminal behaviour at a given time and place.

We can apply the same process to the other two sides of the crime triangle – victims and locations. Did the victim of the pub assault do anything that might have unnecessarily provoked the aggressor? Had he had too much to drink that night? Does he possess long-standing dispositional factors that are associated with his victimisation? And so on. For location, the distance scale is micro–macro rather than temporal but the principle is the same. Is there something about the design and layout of the pub and the way it is run that facilitated the assault? Is it located in a seedy part of town? Is there a more general problem with violence in the local community? Is the assault reflective of national problem with respect to violence?

Distal causes are also called 'root causes' and as such are often accorded a privileged status as causal agents. 'Root' implies that the cause is fundamental to the outcome, and that any change effected without addressing the root cause can provide little more than a temporary Band-Aid solution. Root causes are the object of enquiry for much criminological theory and research. But do root causes deserve their elevated position? The problem with so-called root causes is that their role as behavioural determinants tends to emerge only in retrospect – a case of hindsight bias (Kahneman, 2011). It is easy to join the dots looking backwards but much more difficult to identify prospectively the long-term effects of behavioural inputs. The more distal the cause, the greater the potential for 'leakage' as we move towards the event, and the more tenuous the cause–effect link. For example, many people will grow up in abusive households without committing an assault in a pub (or indeed any crime). In comparison to distal factors, proximal circumstances can be more precisely identified and linked directly to a particular behaviour. Moreover, there is ample evidence that behaviour can be changed without addressing root causes. For example, random roadside breath testing has dramatically reduced the incidence of drink-driving (and associated road deaths) without attending to any distal causes of problem drinking (Homel, 1988). As a general rule, with an eye to the 'low-hanging fruit', crime scientists will try to operate on causes as close to the crime event as possible. However, there is no hard and fast dividing line between proximal and distal.

The scope of crime reduction

If we move beyond the crime event as the sole focus for the delivery of prevention strategies (as is the case for environmental criminology) then a wider range of potential intervention points open up. Crime reduction may be achieved through:

1 The **prevention** of crimes before they occur. This includes the usual environmental criminology approaches such as SCP and defensible space, but also allows for interventions further upstream and offender-focused, such as prenatal, developmental and social interventions.

2 The **disruption** of crimes that are underway. This is particularly applicable to organised crime and terrorism. Strategies include: disrupting criminal supply chains; cutting off illicit cash flows; seizing criminal assets; closing markets for illicit goods; and undermining crime networks.
3 The rapid **detection** of offenders after crimes have been committed. This involves the use of advanced police investigation methods (e.g. data-driven crime analytics, intelligence led policing), crime detection technologies (e.g. surveillance technologies, 'spyware'), and techniques from the forensic sciences (e.g. digital forensics, DNA identification, gunshot residue analysis).
4 The **management** of known offenders: This refers to criminal justice responses to crime that might reduce reoffending by delivering specific deterrence, incapacitating offenders for a period of time, providing rehabilitation and reintegration opportunities, and supervisory strategies that steer offenders from situations conducing to their involvement in crime.

Taking this wider view of crime reduction provides for a more inclusive and flexible approach but it is not without risks. A strength of environmental criminology is its clearly demarcated area of interest (the crime event) that has provided a sharp focus for prevention. Crime science must avoid the trap of becoming all things to all people. It is important that it retains a crime-control focus, if not a crime-event focus, if it is to retain its distinctive analytic bite.

Ethics and crime reduction

Crime scientists recognise that the physical and social conditions relevant to the production and prevention of crime are not morally neutral. Building bridges can literally and metaphorically connect just as building walls can metaphorically and literally divide. The Berlin Wall, Hadrian's Wall and the wall projected at the time of writing to keep Mexicans out of the United States all have political and moral purposes. In the distant past castle walls served similar ends. Gated communities are controversial because of their implications for social exclusion. CCTV is a technological device whose invasion of privacy has been stressed by critics. Alarms are also used in much crime prevention, but alarms can be alarming to those hearing them, and, when false, comprise a form of public nuisance. This is not to say that all walls and all CCTV are morally repugnant. It is only to say that crime scientists acknowledge that there is more to decisions about engineering improvements in security than technical issues of effectiveness and efficiency.

Tilley, Farrell and Clarke (2015; see also Farrell & Tilley, 2017) summarise what they deem to be desirable in design aiming to prevent crime, using the term 'DAPPER', as described below:

Default	The *default* condition is secure rather than insecure
Aesthetic	It is *aesthetically* neutral or pleasing
Powerful	It has a *powerful* preventive mechanism that is not easily circumvented
Principled	It is *principled* and acceptable to all, often increasing liberty and freedom
Effortless	It is *effortless*, taking little or no time and effort to engage
Rewarding	It brings preventive *rewards* greater than its cost.

These six characteristics include more than efficacy and convenience. They also refer to aesthetics and principles. The main example given in Tilley et al. (2015) relates to security devices fitted to cars, which have become increasingly DAPPER over time, for example in the following ways: automatically activated security, which makes the car secure in its default state (for example, door locks that engage when the car moves off or when it is left); inconspicuous security that does not affect the appearance of the car and hence its aesthetic qualities (for example, petrol caps that have to be opened from inside the vehicle); the operation of powerfully preventive mechanisms as shown by detailed analysis of car-crime patterns and their association with patterns of vehicle security (as with electronic immobilisers); measures that threaten no one's civil liberties, such as audio systems that are distributed across the vehicle); prevention requiring little or no effort to activate (for example, central locking that also engages the immobiliser and primes the alarm); and cheap-to-install features at the point of car manufacture (such as this suite of devices) with huge consequential savings in car crimes and their associated harms.

Crime science recognises that there is more to engineering improvements in response to crime than technical strength, albeit that this is important. The moral objections that can be raised in relation to some forms of technology when applied to crime may mean that there are what Ekblom (2017) refers to as 'troublesome tradeoffs' between developments that are most effective and those that least threaten moral principles. The balance between security and privacy, for example, often arises in connection with growing technological possibilities for collecting and interrogating emails with a view to identifying threats to public security. The application of such technologies turns on decisions about the risks and threats of possible terrorist attacks as against those jeopardising personal freedoms for citizens to communicate without the state interference.

Thinking and acting scientifically

Crime science embraces a scientific orientation to understanding and dealing with crime. To be clear, this does not entail dealing only with quantitative measurement, nor does it mean embracing positivism (understood as meaning the collection of observations and their summary in statements of 'laws'), and nor does it involve repudiation of any concerns with values, nor does it assume that everything is predetermined by inexorable physical laws that if only we were to understand them would allow us to predict everything and anything.

The scientific method

Crime science has an unequivocal commitment to science itself as a methodology for helping to find better ways of responding to crime, be the concern with prevention, disruption, detection or offender management. The position taken in crime science is broadly Popperian (Popper, 1957, 1959, 1972). This means the following:

1. Crime science devises testable hypotheses.
2. Crime science uses whatever methods are relevant to testing hypotheses.
3. Crime science aims at scientific progress by eliminating false theories and replacing them with those that are falsifiable but not yet falsified and are improvements on predecessor theories.
4. The theories of crime science can neither be proven, nor unequivocally disproven. Judgement is always needed and ultimately is in the hands of the informed scientific community. The fallibilism that Popper stresses is associated with his concerns for openness, diversity, and vigorous debate.

5 Human beings act intentionally, including in their commission of crimes, but not they do not act – including criminally – in conditions of their own choosing either in terms of social conditions or in terms of physical conditions. They act in terms of the 'logic of their situation' (i.e. intelligibly and attending to their interests in view of the conditions for their action).

6 Humans inhabit a world of ideas (for example, norms, laws, scientific theories) that they (or prior humans) have created. These ideas led, among other social phenomena, to the production of physical artefacts (for example knives, guns, safes, trains, TVs, computers, mobile phones, dishwashers) in relation to which human beings then act (sometimes stealing them or using them as weapons and sometimes mobilising them for crime prevention!). This is an interactionist, rather than reductionist, position. Popper refers to a World 1 of things, a World 2 of mind and a World 3 of ideas. Each exists *sui generis* and each interacts with the others, often producing unintended consequences. Understanding crime patterns involves understanding this interaction.

7 The future, including crime and crime controls, is indeterminate and open in the minimal sense that we cannot predict future ideas (or else we'd have them already) and those future ideas will help shape what then occurs (or is produced) through the interactive processes described in point 6.

8 Problem-solving is ubiquitous and follows an evolutionary path. Mutations comprise hypotheses that are tested by their survival or otherwise; those that survive embody hypotheses that are good enough fits with the problem situation (ecological niche) into which they are born. Theories follow a similar evolutionary path: they are tested by their adequacy to deal with the problem situation in science for which they have been developed. Everyday problem-solving (including that to deal with crime detection and prevention) again follows the same path: devise a tentative solution to the problem at hand, test it, eliminate failures, and then move on to a new attempted solutions or new problem situation. As problem-solvers humans differ from other biota in that we can formulate hypotheses without putting our individual survival at stake in testing them. We allow hypotheses to 'die in our stead'.

The commitment to scientific method, as described here, entails a repudiation of wishful thinking, emotion, ideology and prejudice as sufficient foundations for deciding what to do in dealing with crime, even though it is acknowledged that in practice these often play a part in shaping policy and practice. Crime science involves taking 'truth', at least as competent research finds it, as the regulative principle for what we say and a refusal to massage data at anyone's behest. Crime science can have no truck with 'post-truth' and 'post-facts' discourse on crime or in serving those embracing that discourse. Crime science's concern is with what is the case, and with real results of systematic research rather than simple rhetoric.

Identifying 'mechanisms'

In addition to these Popperian elements, our conception of crime science embraces 'realism'. By this we mean a concern with understanding the 'mechanisms' that lie behind observed patterns and changes in observed patterns (Sayer, 2000, Harré, 1972, Bhaskar, 1975, Koslowski, 1996). Mechanisms are involved in answering 'How?' or 'What is it about?' causal questions. Rather than being satisfied with constant conjunctions (the recurrent associations by succession between observed variables), realists are concerned with explaining what produces the association. We might, for example, observe the sun rise in the morning and set at night or that if we drop an item it always falls to the ground. The realist is concerned with what produces these regularities and what conditions are needed for them to be found. What are the underlying causal forces and what is needed for them to operate and what might stop them operating? In relation to patterns of repeat burglary of the same dwelling for example, we are interested in what produces the repeat patterns, and this typically leads us to routine behaviours of victims and offenders and minimum-effort offender-foraging patterns by burglars, maximising returns at minimum effort and risk (Johnson, 2014).

When it comes to testing the effectiveness of crime-preventive interventions the realist crime scientist is concerned with whether and how the mechanisms producing the problem crime patterns have been disrupted or replaced by alternative mechanisms producing different patterns. Moreover, the intervention is best framed as a theory specifying which particular crime-generating mechanisms will be undermined or replaced and therefore not only that a fall in crime will be expected but the details of how the fall will be manifested. The greater the detail in the expected outcome patterns that are specified, then the stronger the test of the theory, in Popperian terms, because it is more easily refuted. Farrell et al.'s (2011, 2016) test of the security hypothesis to explain the drop in car theft is a case in point. They specified conjectures concerning the causal mechanisms that would be activated by the installation of security devices to cars and the specific expected changes in pattern of car theft that would be expected as a consequence and sought data that could potentially falsify the hypothesis (see also Farrell, Tseloni, & Tilley, 2016; Tilley et al., 2019).

Action research

A distinction can be made between 'pure' academic research conducted to advance knowledge and research carried out in the field to support the implementation of interventions. The latter is often referred to as action research, a term coined by Kurt Lewin, and described as 'comparative research on the conditions and effects of various forms of social action and research leading to social action' (Lewin, 1946, p. 35). Action research is an interactive, iterative process involving 'a spiral of steps, each of which is composed of a circle of planning, action and fact-finding about the result of the action' (p. 38). The researcher/practitioner learns as he/she goes, and modifies the intervention in response to feedback at each stage of the implementation until success is achieved.

A well-known model of action research in the area of crime control is SARA (Eck & Spelman, 1987), an acronym for scanning, analysis, response and assessment (Figure 1.2). Originally developed as a framework for the implementation of problem-oriented policing (POP) (Goldstein, 1979), the SARA process is essentially the scientific method adapted for the field. SARA provides police – and practitioners more generally – with a step-by-step guide to implementing crime-control initiatives. The researcher/practitioner first identifies crime problems of concern and selects the most pressing and recurrent one (scan). Next, an in-depth analysis of the selected problem is conducted to look for patterns and to identify contributory causes (analysis). Possible responses are then generated and the most practical and cost-effective selected (response). Finally, the effectiveness of the response is evaluated (assessment). Throughout the process there are feedback loops such that failure at any stage results in a return to earlier stages.

The goal of action research is to develop a successful intervention rather than simply to test whether or not a particular intervention works. The SARA process can be applied in an informal way in the course of everyday practice without the need to mount a sophisticated research project. At the same time, there are lessons to be learned from successful case studies that can form an important part of the evidence base. For example, in the USA there is an annual Goldstein Award for the best example internationally of a crime-reduction initiative using SARA, and the database containing all submissions can be found on the POP website.[3]

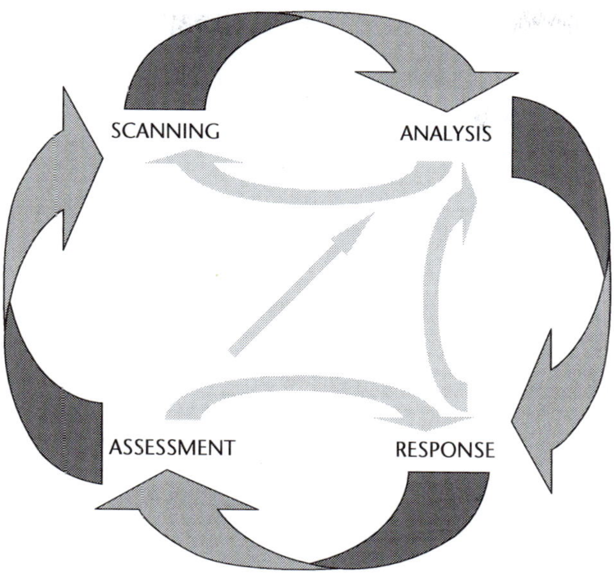

Figure 1.2 SARA (Source: Clarke & Eck, 2005)

Crime reduction as an engineering problem

There are parallels between the research challenges for crime science and the orientation and methods of engineering (Tilley & Laycock, 2016). Engineering is a) an applied, practical problem-solving endeavour which b) pragmatically draws on what is known, c) identifies pressing gaps in knowledge needed to improve effectiveness, d) tries to learn from systematically interrogated error, and e) tries to fill those gaps in knowledge and remedy identified errors with well-targeted programmes of research. Crime science adopts the same basic approach (Petroski, 1992, 1996, 2008; Syed, 2016).

Crime scientists begin with a specific problem and try to devise practical solutions whose effectiveness is checked in order to determine whether other measures are needed instead of, or as well as, those already tried. Crime scientists do not expect that precisely the same situation will recur from one problem to the next. Rather, the particularities of a given situation need to be taken into account and the relevance of tested theory and previous measures considered in light of the specific presenting conditions. In this respect, the crime scientist's approach is akin to that of the bridge builder. No two situations for a bridge are identical in terms of required span, expected traffic patterns, wind pressure, or characteristics of the ground on which the bridge's superstructure is to be built. Yet we can see clearly that each bridge builder draws on what has been achieved before as well as what has gone wrong. Moreover, engineers designing bridges make complex calculations about the pressures that a new structure will need to withstand and the responses of the new structure to these pressures. They create a margin for error. They often build virtual or physical models that replicate those that are envisaged, to work out how they will behave in differing conceivable conditions. Engineers try to anticipate future stresses to which a new structure is liable to be put in order to check that it will be capable of withstanding them. Of course, from time to time bridges do collapse and when they do so extensive efforts are made to work out what went wrong in order that lessons can be learned for the constriction of safer and more secure bridges in the future (see case study by Petroski, 1992).

This is emphatically not the way in which crime-related problems are ordinarily addressed! As we alluded to previously in this chapter, crime is more often treated as a matter of moral choice, defective personality, or pathological social conditions, calling respectively for moral improvement, treatment, or social reform as preventive strategies. Physical conditions may furnish the stage for criminal acts. They do not comprise the basic causes. Moreover, determining what to do (just as determining what comprises crime) involves moral discourse and moral choices. While crime scientists do take the view that physical conditions are causally important in producing crime patterns that can be modified by changing those physical conditions, they acknowledge that social arrangements are also causally important (for example, where cheque frauds were facilitated in the 1970s in parts of Sweden by policies that set a 300 Kronor threshold below which the bank did not require traders to make an independent check of the identity of the bearer for the cheques to be honoured) (Knutsson & Kuhlhorn, 1992).

Bringing disciplines together

Understanding crime and developing improved responses to it needs to draw on a wide range of disciplines. To date, law and the social sciences have been dominant. This situation reflects the aforementioned traditional focus in criminology on criminality as the prime driver of crime. With the problem of crime framed in this way, the prevention task requires disciplines that are person-focused. But if we expand our field of interest to take in the physical conditions that might facilitate or inhibit crime then a far wider range of disciplines comes into play. Crime science recognises that technology and engineering are crucial to understanding crime patterns and to developing effective responses to crime. The chapters that follow this introduction provide a range of examples showing what individual disciplines can bring to explaining and dealing with crime. Here we confine ourselves to discussion in more general terms of how and why crime science draws on the input of many disciplines.

Analogy with medical science

Crime science drew part of its inspiration from medical science (Ross, 2013). The inspiration comes from the fundamental concern of medical science for the improvement of health both by applying remedies for specific individuals as they need them and by the application of health measures preventing diseases and accidents, drawing on whatever disciplines have a contribution to make. Disciplines drawn on in health include physics, chemistry, biology, psychology, sociology, and mathematics. The counterparts in crime science are the twin concerns of improving the detection of specific crimes and support for specific victims as well as the prevention of future crimes, as indicated earlier in this chapter, drawing on any and all disciplines that might have a contribution (see also Laycock, 2001; Pease, 2005).

Medical science has been taken forward by blends of practitioners and researchers. Many medical researchers are also physicians who continue to practice part-time, to help ensure that their research endeavours speak to the realities of clinical work. Moreover, those who are mainly practitioners also engage with research by participating in projects, reading medical journals, reporting research findings, and by taking part in various continuing professional-development courses apprising them of research findings. Furthermore, practitioners' lengthy initial training ensures an appreciation of the science behind medicine. Indeed, certifying bodies require that medical practitioners are familiar with essential research findings.

So, crime science aims to undergird crime prevention and detection practices with robust scientific findings and routine attention to and participation in new research studies. And, as with medical science, the basic sciences to be drawn on are extensive.

Crime science is a long way short of medical science in terms of research findings, underlying theory, tested practices, professional training and practitioner orientation to continuous improvement through the accumulation of new knowledge. It is not even clear who, apart from the police and others working within the criminal justice system, comprise the relevant professional populations.

There are likely those whose main concern is not crime whose practices and policies nevertheless are crucial to crime and security. Such people would include, for example, architects, planners, Internet service providers, retailers, insurance companies, product manufactures, government officials, and licensees. The same, however, also goes for health where there is a similarly diverse population for whom health is not their major concern but whose practices and policies are crucial to physical wellbeing. In this case, relevant groups include cleaners, sanitation workers, restaurateurs, planners, architects, and manufacturers of a wide range of produce whose design and operations may have unintended health consequences. Here, a mix of education, training and regulation has routinised attention to the avoidance of inadvertent health harms, informed by research.

Part of crime science's future lies in developing the knowledge base for practitioners whose chief concern is crime, in educating them and in mobilising them as creators and users of emerging research findings. Another part of crime science's future lies in understanding how inadvertent crime consequences are produced and also avoided. Avoidance strategies might include education and training of those involved in relevant decision-making and maybe also the formulation of regulations that, as with public health, help prevent the production of harmful side effects.

What disciplines are relevant to crime science?

It is difficult to find whole areas of scientific work that could have no conceivable relevance to crime and crime control. The reader is invited to take any popular science journal and to think about which papers are and are not relevant to crime in one way or another. Here we take the 12 November 2016 issue of *New Scientist*. Material that explicitly refers to crime, crime detection and crime prevention can be distinguished from that which may be applicable, although its relevance is not discussed.

A Material that is explicitly relevant:

1 Forensic evidence related to infanticide. Patterns of head injury have been taken to indicate that a baby has been shaken to death; more specifically a combination of swelling of the brain, bleeding on the brain's surface and bleeding behind retinas. A review of 1,000 studies casts doubt on this assumption, which has been made by expert witnesses in the evidence they have given. Past convictions may be insecure (pp. 5, 8–9).

2 Skunk lock for bicycles. An innovative cycle lock is described. It sprays a thief with a pungent solution causing vomiting. The lock is given a distinctive appearance. The idea is that the lock with the smelly spray acts as a more effective deterrent than other similar locks (p. 56).

3 A machine that can listen out for crime and trigger an alarm. A computer model that has learned to discriminate sounds is described. One use that is mooted relates

to interpreting sounds signifying crime in the home, which can precipitate a call for help (p. 22).

4 Compromised face recognition. Face recognition is used in various security-related contexts. Printing particular patterns on the frames of spectacles compromises the ability of face recognition systems to identify individuals (p. 23).

5 Cultures and violent crime. Research distinguishing cultures based on 'honour' (valuing reputation) from those emphasising 'dignity' (valuing individuals) and their association with differing levels of and occasions for violence is described. 'Honour' cultures are associated with courtesy, but violence erupts when reputation is threatened. There is less violence in 'dignity' cultures, where personal affront and reputation are less significant (pp. 5, 32–35).

B Material that might be applicable to crime:

6 The manufacture of powerful but expensive new batteries (pp. 28–31). These are liable to become prime targets for crime as they become more widespread and hence of potential use to a growing number of users. This suggests a likely need for measures to make their theft too risky, unrewarding or difficult for many potential offenders. Also, better batteries are liable to make some criminal acts easier, for example to fly drones used for nefarious purposes over a growing distance.

7 Smoking and DNA mutation. There is evidently a predicable gene mutation pattern associate with smoking (p. 15). This might be drawn on from DNA stains, which could help identify the populations of those who might be eliminated as suspects or included as suspects in police investigations.

8 Uncoordinated cooperative predation by sailfish hunting sardines (p. 16). The sailfish's circling of a 'baitball' of sardines is analogous to collective uncoordinated attacks in riots or racial attacks.

9 Digital citizenship (pp. 18–19). Some countries are offering virtual citizenship (e-residency). This will evidently allow members to become subject to laws and other legal systems that are different from those where they reside physically (and perhaps avoid the inconvenience of those there). This may create novel problems for enforcement and opportunities for crime.

10 Artificial intelligence (pp. 42–43). If machines come to outsmart humans and have their own objectives, this may have profound implications for crime, enforcement and the prevention of predation.

These ten examples may not exhaust the range of material contained in the one issue of *New Scientist* examined, which could be relevant to crime science. What the examples should indicate, however, is how a broad swathe of science and scientific development can fruitfully be read with an eye to the main concerns of crime science. What this means is that crime science is marked by an orientation to crime and crime control that is open to and interested in what the full range of sciences might bring to effective and ethical means of dealing with crime.

Of course, different disciplines contribute in different ways and at different points of intervention. Figure 1.3 shows five broad intervention points, arranged chronologically with respect to the crime event, towards which crime-reduction efforts might be directed – biological risk factors, developmental experiences, the crime event, the investigation process, and the responses of the criminal justice system. Possible crime-reduction strategies and contributing disciplines are shown for each intervention point.

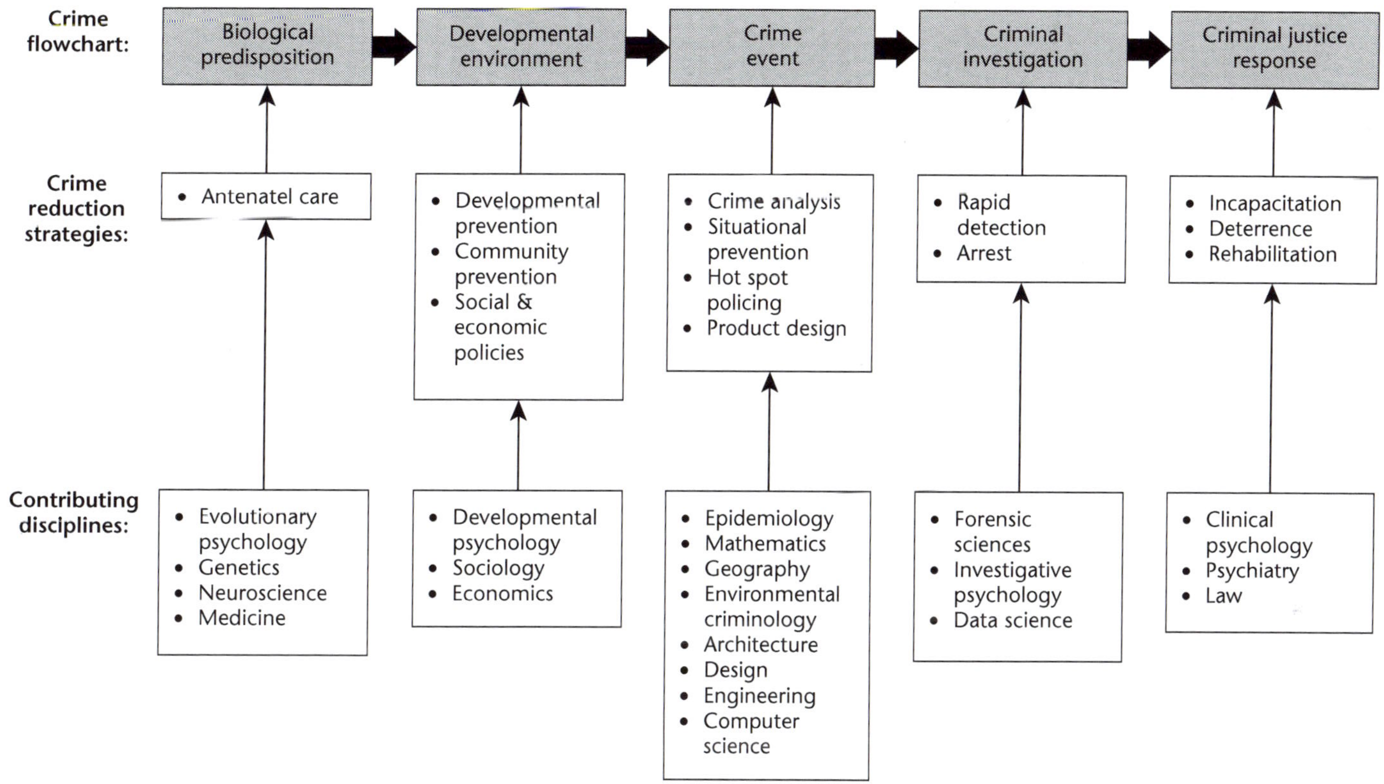

Figure 1.3 Possible contributions of different disciplines at different points of intervention for crime reduction. Suggested crime-reduction strategies and disciplines are illustrative and not intended to represent an exhaustive list

Ways of bringing disciplines together

Throughout this chapter we have argued that different disciplines might assist in better understanding and responding to crime. Yet we need to consider not just the range of disciplines that might contribute to crime science, but also on what basis might they come together. Presently, there seems to be almost universal agreement that mono-disciplinary silos are bad things and that most problems are best solved by bringing multiple perspectives to bear upon them. So far in this chapter we have avoided attaching any particular prefix to disciplinarity. Choices include multidisciplinarity, interdisciplinarity and transdisciplinarity (Austin, Park, & Goble, 2008; Choi & Pak, 2006; Henry, 2012; Klein, 2008). Each of these terms has a different meaning and denotes a different degree of integration. However, too often when people speak of bringing disciplines together they do not explain exactly how this is to be done, and terms to describe combined disciplinary approaches are used more or less interchangeably.

The various forms of disciplinarity are shown in Table 1.3. Crime science specifies no particular level of disciplinary integration. The type of disciplinarity that is undertaken is determined by the requirements of the problem at hand (Borrion & Koch, 2017; Huutoniemi, Klein, Bruun, & Hukkinen, 2010). At a minimum, bringing disciplines together requires the creation of a multidisciplinary team where researchers with different expertise collaborate on a problem. Each expert needs to know only enough about the other contributing disciplines for a meaningful exchange of ideas to occur within the team. Interdisciplinarity demands more of the researchers. While they may retain their primary disciplinary orientations, they need to understand, absorb and employ key concepts and methods from the other discipline(s). Fully integrated interdisciplinary fields are often indicated by their double-barrelled names (e.g., medical-physics). Finally, and most challengingly, transdisciplinarity aims to take us beyond the blending of disciplines. It requires researchers to break free of (transcend) disciplinary boundaries to create new ways of looking at and solving real world problems.

In practice, all types of disciplinary integration are difficult to achieve. 'Multidisciplinarity' and related terms often seem to be little more than buzzwords where the rhetoric around them is not matched by on-the-ground reality. At an individual level, researchers may resist moving beyond the comfort of their own disciplines. Moreover, there are many structural impediments to them doing so. Universities remain largely organised around disciplinary areas. Research councils and other funding bodies likewise often favour disciplinary-focused research – it is judged to be a less risky investment. Learned societies are typically disciplinary-based. And if researchers do manage to carry out multi-, inter- or trans-disciplinary research, they may encounter difficulty finding a journal willing to publish it. In spite of all this, bringing disciplines together is a cause worth pursuing. The crime problems we face today, and those that may arise in the future, are unlikely to be solved without the combined efforts of researchers from across the disciplinary spectrum.

Summary

Crime science focuses attention on concerns that, it was believed, were being neglected in mainstream criminology. In this respect, it builds on and extends environmental criminology, which itself began as a reaction to perceived gaps in criminological research. We have set out in this section the defining features of crime science – an uncompromising focus on crime control, the pursuit of this goal through scientific means, and an invitation to researchers from all disciplines to join in the endeavour.

Table 1.3 Types of disciplinarity

Type	*Features*	*Level of integration*	*Example*
Mono-disciplinary	Concentration on one field of study. Facilitates specialisation and the development of expertise but limits exchange of knowledge.	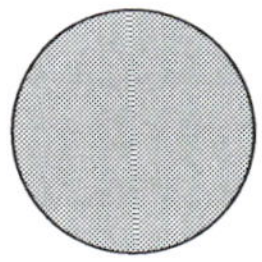	A geneticist isolates a gene associated with an increased risk of violence.
Multidisciplinary	Specialists from different disciplines come together, each contributing their own disciplinary expertise. Knowledge is distributed within the team.	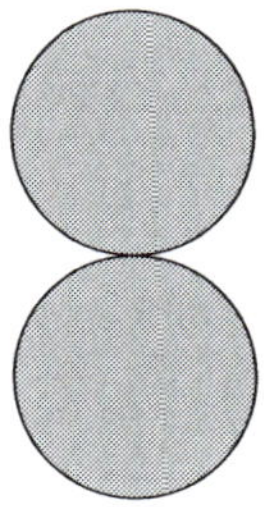	A psychologist and computer scientist work together to reduce child sexual abuse images on the Internet. The psychologist contributes knowledge on offender behaviour and the computer scientist contributes technical expertise on implementing strategies online.
Interdisciplinary	Experts come together to extend the disciplinary knowledge of individual members. Disciplinary borders begin to break down with the synthesis of ideas and techniques.	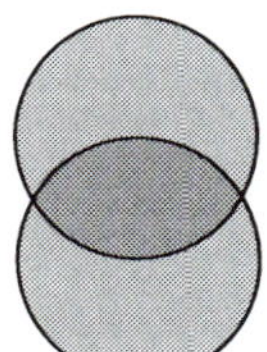	The field of computational criminology combines elements from computer science and criminology. Computational criminologists model crime and other complex criminological concepts and conduct simulated experiments to test hypotheses.
Trans-disciplinary	Disciplines combine in a holistic fashion to create new perspectives that go beyond the contributing disciplines.		The new field of data science integrates theories and techniques from many fields including mathematics, computer science, and statistics. Data science can be applied across diverse problem areas. In the case of crime, data scientists might mine big data sets to reveal underlying crime patterns.

At the same time, we understand that crime science is not a neatly circumscribed enterprise. Many of those who identify themselves as criminologists do crime science, as described in this book. Many of those who identify themselves as crime scientists work in criminology departments and contribute to criminological journals. Moreover, major crime scientists' work is widely cited by those who are not part of the community of crime scientists. In addition, crime scientists have much to learn from reading criminology, even when this is not centrally concerned with or framed as crime science. For example, issues concerning the ways in which crime is investigated, the role of the police, the operation of the criminal justice system and the courts, the characteristics of social groups most likely to be engaged in different types of crime, and the motives for crime all form important parts of the backcloth to the concerns of crime scientists.

There is nevertheless value, we believe, in establishing crime science as a distinct field of study in order to promote an agenda for radically changing the way that we think about crime and its control. Since the JDI was established in 2001 there are encouraging signs that the approach is gaining traction. The JDI itself has grown into a substantial entity with around 25 academic staff – from disciplines including psychology, sociology, geography, political science, economics, mathematics, forensic sciences, electronic engineering, and computer science. Crime science departments, research centres and/or degrees have been established in other universities in the UK, US, Australia, New Zealand and the Netherlands. There is now a journal of *Crime Science* and a *Crime Science* book series currently comprising some 16 volumes. There are crime-science entries in major criminology reference books. And finally, of course, there is now this handbook.

Conclusion

In this chapter we set out the case for crime science. We examined the roots of crime science in environmental criminology and described its key features. We argued that crime science provides a distinctive approach to understanding and dealing with crime, one that is outcome-oriented, evidence-based and fundamentally multi-/inter-/trans-disciplinary. The central mission of crime science is to find new ways to cut crime and increase security.

This *Handbook of Crime Science* provides the opportunity to showcase the scope of the crime-science field. The aim is to provide the reader with a good understanding of the assumptions, aspirations and methods of crime science, as well as the variety of topics that fall within its purview. The remainder of this book is divided into two sections. Section 1 comprises chapters by disciplinary specialists about the contributions their sciences can make or have already made to crime science. These are written to address both other specialists in that discipline and the reader who is interested in crime science as an approach. Hence they are designed to be accessible to the non-specialist. Section 2 comprises a series of exemplary case studies in crime science, showing a wide range of the kind of work that crime scientists do. The individual chapters are designed to again speak both to the specialist and the more general reader. We return in the final chapter of the volume to take stock and to consider future directions for crime science.

Notes

1 At the time of writing, Jeffery's book had just 227 citations on Google Scholar, compared with 3,524 for Newman's.
2 There are several earlier, less detailed definitions of crime science; see Clarke (2004), Cockbain & Laycock (2017), Laycock (2001; 2005).
3 www.popcenter.org.

References

Armitage, R. (2017). 'Crime prevention through environmental design'. In R. Wortley & M. Townsley (eds). *Environmental Criminology and Crime Analysis* (2nd ed.). London: Routledge.

Austin, W., Park, C., & Goble, E. (2008). 'From interdisciplinary to transdisciplinary research: a case study'. *Qualitative Health Research, 18*(4): 557–564.
Bhaskar, R. (1975). *A Realist Theory of Science.* Brighton: Harvester.
Borrion, H. & Koch, D. (2017). 'Integrating architecture and crime science: A transdisciplinary challenge'. In P. Gibbs (ed.). *Transdisciplinary Higher Education: A Theoretical Basis Revealed in Practice* (pp. 91–107). Cham, Switzerland: Springer.
Brantingham, P. J. & Brantingham, P. L. (1981). *Environmental Criminology.* Prospect Heights, IL: Waveland Press.
Brantingham, P. J. & Brantingham, P. L. (1993). 'Nodes, paths and edges: considerations on the complexity of crime and the physical environment'. *Journal of Environmental Psychology, 13*: 3–28.
Brantingham, P. J., Brantingham, P. L., & Andresen, M. A. (2017). 'Geometry of crime and crime pattern theory'. In R. Wortley & M. Townsley (eds). *Environmental Criminology and Crime Analysis* (2nd ed.). London: Routledge.
Choi, B. C. & Pak, A. W. (2006). 'Multidisciplinarity, interdisciplinarity and transdisciplinarity in health research, services, education and policy. Definitions, objectives, and evidence of effectiveness'. *Clinical and Investigative Medicine, 29*(6): 351.
Clarke, R. V. (1967). 'Seasonal and other environmental aspects of abscondings by approved school boys'. *British Journal of Criminology,* 7: 195–206.
Clarke, R. V. (1980). '"Situational" crime prevention: theory and practice'. *The British Journal of Criminology, 20*(2): 136–147.
Clarke, R. V. (1983). 'Situational crime prevention: its theoretical basis and practical scope.' In M. Tonry & N. Morris (eds). *Crime and Justice: A Review of Research* (Volume 4). Chicago and London: The University of Chicago Press.
Clarke, R. V. (1992). 'Introduction'. In R. V. Clarke (ed.). *Situational Crime Prevention: Successful Case Studies.* Albany, NY: Harrow and Heston.
Clarke, R. V. (1997). 'Introduction'. In R. V. Clarke (ed.). *Situational Crime Prevention: Successful Case Studies* (2nd ed.). Albany, NY: Harrow and Heston.
Clarke, R. V. (1999). *Hot Products: Understanding, Anticipating and Reducing Demand for Stolen Goods* (Volume *112*). Home Office, Policing and Reducing Crime Unit, Research, Development and Statistics Directorate.
Clarke, R. V. (2004). 'Technology, criminology and crime science'. *European Journal on Criminal Policy and Research, 10*(1): 55–63.
Clarke, R. V. (2017). 'Situational crime prevention'. In R. Wortley & M. Townsley (eds). *Environmental Criminology and Crime Analysis* (2nd ed.). London: Routledge.
Clarke, R. V. & Cornish, D. B. (1985). 'Modeling offenders' decisions: a framework for research and policy'. In M. Tonry & N. Morris (eds). *Crime and Justice: A Review of Research,* (Volume *6*). Chicago and London: The University of Chicago Press.
Clarke, R. V. & Eck, J. E. (2005). 'Crime analysis for problem solvers'. Washington, DC: Center for Problem Oriented Policing. www.popcenter.org/library/reading/PDFs/60Steps.pdf.
Cockbain, E. P. & Laycock, G. (2017). 'Crime science'. In H. Pontell and S. Lab, (eds). *The Oxford Research Encyclopedia of Criminology and Criminal Justice.* New York: Oxford University Press.
Cohen, L. & Felson, M. (1979). 'Social change and crime rate trends: a routine activity approach'. *American Sociological Review, 44*: 588–608.
Cornish, D. B. & Clarke, R. V. (2003). 'Opportunities, precipitators and criminal decisions: a reply to Wortley's critique of situational crime prevention'. In M. Smith and D. Cornish (eds). *Theory for Practice in Situational Crime Prevention, Crime Prevention Studies* (Volume 6). Monsey, NY: Criminal Justice Press.
Eck, J. E. & Spelman, W. (1987). *Problem-solving: Problem-oriented Policing in Newport News.* Washington, DC: Police Executive Research Forum.
Ekblom, P. (1994). 'Proximal circumstances: a mechanism-based classification of crime prevention'. In R. V. Clarke (ed.). *Crime Prevention Studies* (Volume *2*). Albany, NY: Harrow & Heston.
Ekblom, P. (2017). 'Designing products against crime'. In R. Wortley & M. Townsley (eds). *Environmental Criminology and Crime Analysis* (2nd ed.). London: Routledge.
Farrell, G. (2015). 'Preventing phone theft and robbery: the need for government action and international coordination'. *Crime Science, 4*(1): 4.
Farrell, G., Laycock, G., & Tilley, N. (2015). 'Debuts and legacies: the crime drop and the role of adolescence-limited and persistent offending'. *Crime Science, 4*(1): 16.
Farrell, G. & Tilley, N. (2017). 'Technology for crime and crime prevention: a supply side analysis'. In *Crime Prevention in the 21st Century* (pp. 377–388). Cham, Switzerland: Springer.

Farrell, G., Tseloni, A., & Tilley, N. (2016). 'Signature dish: triangulation from data signatures to examine the role of security in falling crime'. *Methodological Innovations, 9*: 1–11.

Farrell, G., Tseloni, A., Mailley, J., & Tilley, N. (2011). 'The crime drop and the security hypothesis'. *Journal of Research in Crime and Delinquency, 48*(2): 147–175.

Felson, M. (2002). *Crime and Everyday Life*. Thousand Oaks, CA: Sage.

Felson, M. (2017). 'Routine activity approach'. In R. Wortley & M. Townsley (eds). *Environmental Criminology and Crime Analysis* (2nd ed.). London: Routledge.

Goldstein, H. (1979). 'Improving policing: a problem oriented approach'. *Crime and Delinquency* (April): 234–258.

Harré, R. (1972). *The Philosophies of Science*. Oxford: Oxford University Press.

Hayward, K. J. & Young, J. (2004). 'Cultural criminology: some notes on the script'. *Theoretical Criminology, 8*(3): 259–273.

Henry, S. (2012). 'Expanding our thinking on theorizing criminology and criminal justice? The place of evolutionary perspectives in integrative criminological theory'. *Journal of Theoretical and Philosophical Criminology, 4*(1): 62–89.

Homel, R. (1988). *Policing and Punishing the Drinking Driver: A Study of General and Specific Deterrence*. New York: Springer-Verlag.

Huutoniemi, K., Klein, J. T., Bruun, H., & Hukkinen, J. (2010). 'Analyzing interdisciplinarity: typology and indicators'. *Research Policy, 39*(1): 79–88.

Jeffery, C. R. (1971). *Crime Prevention Through Environmental Design*. Beverly Hills, CA: Sage Publications.

Johnson, S. (2014). 'How do offenders choose where to offend? Perspectives from animal foraging'. *Legal and Criminological Psychology, 19*(2): 193–210.

Kahneman, D. (2011). *Thinking, Fast and Slow*. New York: Farrar, Straus and Giroux.

Klein, J. T. (2008). 'Evaluation of interdisciplinary and transdisciplinary research'. *American Journal of Preventive Medicine, 35*(2): S116–S123.

Knutsson, J. & Kuhlhorn, E. (1992). 'Macro-measures against crime: the example of check forgeries'. In R. Clarke (ed.). *Situational Crime Prevention: Successful Case Studies*. New York: Harrow and Heston.

Koslowski, B. (1996). *Theory and Evidence: The Development of Scientific Reasoning*. Cambridge, MA: MIT Press.

Lewin, K. (1946). 'Action research and minority problems'. *Journal of Social Issues, 2*(4): 34–46.

Laycock, G. (2001). 'Scientists or politicians – who has the answer to crime?' *Inaugural Professorial Lecture, UCL*, 26 April. London: Jill Dando Institute.

Laycock, G. (2005). 'Defining crime science'. In M. Smith and N. Tilley (eds). *Crime Science*. Cullompton, Devon: Willan.

Martinson, R. (1974). 'What works? Questions and answers about prison reform'. *The Public Interest, 35*: 22–54.

Mayhew, P., Clarke, R. V. G., Sturman, A., & Hough, J. M. (1975). *Crime as Opportunity*. London: Home Office Research and Planning Unit.

Newman, O. (1972). *Crime Prevention Through Urban Design: Defensible Space*. New York: Macmillan.

Ohana, D. J., Phillips, L., & Chen, L. (2013). 'Preventing cell phone intrusion and theft using biometrics'. In *Security and Privacy Workshops (2013)* (pp. 173–180). IEEE.

Pease, K. (2005). 'Science in the service of crime reduction'. In N. Tilley (ed.). *Handbook of Crime Prevention and Community Safety*. London: Routledge.

Petroski, H. (1992). *The Evolution of Useful Things*. New York: Random House.

Petroski, H. (1996). *Invention by Design*. Cambridge, MA: Harvard University Press.

Petroski, H. (2008). *Success through Failure: The Paradox of Design*. Princeton: Princeton University Press.

Popper, K. (1957). *The Poverty of Historicism*. London: Routledge.

Popper, K. (1959). *The Logic of Scientific Discovery*. London: Hutchinson.

Popper, K. (1972). *Objective Knowledge*. Oxford: Oxford University Press.

Ross, L. (1977). 'The intuitive psychologist and his shortcomings: distortions in the attribution process'. In L. Berkowitz (ed.). *Advances in Experimental Psychology* (Volume 10). New York: Academic Press.

Ross, L. & Nisbett, R. E. (2011). *The Person and the Situation: Perspectives of Social Psychology*. London: Pinter & Martin.

Ross, N. (2013). *Crime: How to Solve it – And Why So Much of What We're Told Is Wrong*. London: Biteback Publishing.

Sayer, A. (2000). *Realism and Social Science*. London: Sage.

Simon, H. A. (1957). *Models of Man*. New York: Wiley.

Skinner, B. F. (1953). *Science and Human Behavior*. New York: Macmillan.
Syed, M. (2016). *Black Box Thinking*. London: John Murray.
Tilley, N. (2004). 'Karl Popper: a philosopher for Ronald Clarke's situational crime prevention'. In S. Shoham and P. Knepper (eds). *Israel Studies in Criminology 8* (pp. 39–56). Willowdale, ONT: de Sitter.
Tilley, N., Farrell, G., & Clarke, R. V. (2015). 'Target suitability and the crime drop'. In M. A. Andresen & G. Farrell (eds). *The Criminal Act*. London: Palgrave Macmillan.
Tilley, N., Farrell, G., & Tseloni, A. (2019). 'Doing quantitative criminological research: the crime drop'. In P. Davies and P. Francis (eds). *Doing Criminological Research* (3rd ed.). London: Sage.
Tilley, N. & Laycock, G. (2016). 'Engineering a safer society'. *Public Safety Leadership Research Focus*, *4*(2): 1–6.
Whitehead, S., Mailley, J., Storer, I., McCardle, J., Torrens, G., & Farrell, G. (2008). 'In safe hands: a review of mobile phone anti-theft designs'. *European Journal on Criminal Policy and Research*, *14*(1): 39–60.
Wortley, R. (2011). *Psychological Criminology: An Integrative Approach*. London: Routledge.
Wortley, R. (2013). 'Rational choice and offender decision making: lessons from the cognitive sciences'. In B. Leclerc & R. Wortley (eds). *Cognition and Crime: Offender Decision-making and Script Analyses*. London: Routledge.
Wortley, R. & Smallbone, S. (2012). *Internet Child Pornography: Causes, Investigation and Prevention*. Santa Barbara, CA: Praeger.
Wortley, R. & Townsley, M. (2017). 'Environmental criminology and crime analysis: situating the theory, analytic approach and application'. In R. Wortley & M. Townsley (eds). *Environmental Criminology and Crime Analysis* (2nd ed.). London: Routledge.

Section 1
Disciplinary contributions to crime science

Overview

A defining feature of crime science is the breadth of disciplines on which it draws. For this section of the handbook, we have selected twelve disciplines, spanning the social, natural, formal, and applied sciences, to showcase this breadth. The twelve disciplines are:

- Evolutionary psychology
- Genetics
- Sociology
- Psychology
- Economics
- Epidemiology
- Mathematics
- Geography
- Architecture
- Engineering
- Computer science
- Forensic science

This is by no means an exhaustive list of those disciplines with something to offer the crime-science agenda. A conspicuous absence is environmental criminology, not included here because its seminal role in the development of crime science was outlined in detail in the introductory chapter of this volume. Aspects of environmental criminology are also picked up in several individual chapters (e.g. psychology, geography and architecture). Aside from this omission, we have generally stuck with broad fields of study and avoided drilling down to specific sub-disciplines. For example, subcategories of engineering include materials, nano, civil, chemical, electronic, mechanical, and systems engineering, all of which have contributions to make to crime science.

We asked authors to focus particularly on the ways in which their discipline contributes to crime science. A challenge for authors was to write in a style that was accessible to non-specialists while retaining the academic integrity of their discipline. We were looking for chapters pitched to the informed and interested reader at the level that might be found in a generalist science magazine. We believe that the authors have succeeded admirably in achieving this goal. This challenge – communicating across disciplinary boundaries – is of course a fundamental one for all multi-/inter-/trans-disciplinary enterprises such as crime science.

There are numerous rationales on which we might have ordered the chapters in this section. We have elected to follow the sequence shown in Figure 1.3 in the introductory chapter. This figure traces the progress of an offender from birth through to contact with the criminal justice system, identifying potential points of intervention along the way. It provides a template for suggesting where various disciplines might be most (but not necessarily exclusively) relevant. Accordingly we start with two chapters – Evolutionary psychology (Sell) and Genetics (Gajos, Boccio & Beaver) that, respectively, examine biological foundations of criminal conduct at a species and individual level. The next batch of chapters – Sociology (Tilley), Psychology (Wortley) and Economics (Manning) – comprises key social scientific perspectives on how criminal behaviour is acquired and expressed, and what might be done about it. There follows three methodologically focused chapters – Epidemiology (Fine & Edwards), Mathematics (Davies) and Geography (Andresen) – that are concerned with the task of analysing and modelling crime and its causes. The next three chapters – Architecture (Borrion & Koch), Engineering (Borrion) and Computer science (Hartel & Junger) – are relevant to designing out crime in both physical and virtual environments. Finally, the chapter on Forensic science (Morgan) examines the investigation of crime and the detection of offenders.

2
Evolutionary psychology

Aaron Sell

Life on Earth resulted from an evolutionary process that started with replicating entities of unknown substance. These replications were sometimes in error (i.e. a mutation occurred), and this mutation was then passed on to the descendent. Once these conditions were in place, a positive feedback loop resulted. Mutations that increased the rate of replication would spread. Those that failed to do so would be 'selected out'. The result was the accumulation in these 'organisms' of features that increase reproduction (Darwin 1872; Dawkins 1976; Williams 1966). Living organisms are – literally, not metaphorically – 'gene machines' (Dawkins 1976): constructs of dead matter (mostly carbon and water) that bring about otherwise unlikely functional outcomes, e.g. navigating home ranges, discovering and consuming fuel, disrupting the physical integrity of rivals, storing and computing information, developing senses, manipulating rivals, and everywhere reproducing their genes. The discovery of the origin and design of life is arguably the most important ever made (Dawkins 1976). And while viewing themselves as the soulless products of natural selection is generally anathema to humans, it is done routinely when studying literally any other life form, from primates to cockroaches, to plants, to fungi, to bacteria and viruses. The field of evolutionary biology uses the same models and theories to explain the maternal behaviour of chimpanzees as it does to explain the dynamic growth patterns of plants. Life is understood from a Darwinian point of view.

Evolutionary psychologists extend that view to the human brain. The result is a science that views human nature as the product of natural selection (Buss 2015; Tooby & Cosmides 1990). This chapter will give a necessarily brief introduction to the field of evolutionary psychology, and how it can be used to understand criminal behaviour. I will then highlight two criminological examples where an evolutionary perspective has been particularly successful: infanticide and domestic violence.

Human nature

Evolutionary psychologists argue that the mind/brain is composed of many information-processing mechanisms (called 'adaptations') that regulate behaviour and other bodily systems in ways that solved particular problems for human ancestors (Tooby & Cosmides 1992). For example, fear is an adaptation that evolved to regulate responses to ancestral dangers

(Tooby & Cosmides 1990). Rather than being 'basic' or 'simple' instincts, these adaptations are now understood (like their counterparts in non-humans) as complex machines composed of many subroutines, triggers, behavioural outputs, motivational states, specialised learning and memory systems, physiological regulators, and so on. These adaptations collectively make up 'human nature' and include evolved mental adaptations such as kinship-detection systems, sexual jealousy, anger, child identification and bonding, grief, our sense of territory, coalitional thinking, mate-quality assessment mechanisms, habitat-selection mechanisms, vision and other perceptual systems, mechanisms for detecting cheaters in social exchanges, voice production, grammatical learning systems, and hundreds of others (Barkow, Cosmides & Tooby 1992; Pinker 1997; Buss 2015).

Humans, by virtue of their evolved nature, have some insight into these adaptations already (Brüne & Brüne-Cohrs 2006), but without training in evolutionary biology this understanding will often be shallow and lacking in scientific rigour (just as our intuitive understanding of sight is no substitute for the science of optics). Unfortunately, few criminologists show a working knowledge of the principles of evolutionary psychology or biology. A full description of that science is beyond the scope of this chapter, but a brief sketch will be given below. Interested readers are encouraged to consult some of the classic introductions to this area, e.g. Davies, Krebs & West (2012), Daly & Wilson (1983), Tooby & Cosmides (1992), and to see previous work detailing evolutionary approaches in criminology more specifically (e.g. Daly & Wilson 1988; Durrant 2012; Duntley & Shackelford 2008).

The adaptationist programme: using evolutionary biology to understand living things

In the last 30 years, evolutionary biologists have pioneered a method for identifying the function of an adaptation, i.e. how it increased genetic replication in the past. This method is called the adaptationist programme and it involves matching the design in an organism, such as an infant's sucking reflex, with the problem it solved in our evolutionary past, such as a mammal getting nourishment from its mother. To demonstrate that a particular feature is an adaptation (i.e. that it was designed by natural selection for a specific reproductive function) one must demonstrate complex functional design in that feature for solving an ancestral problem of reproduction. The adaptationist programme is based on a kind of null-hypothesis testing logic, with the null hypothesis being that the features under study are by-products (e.g. accidental developments) and the alternative hypothesis being that the features enhanced reproduction ancestrally. To rule out the null hypothesis, one must show complex functional design, e.g. multiple features that seem improbably well designed to accomplish a function – and that function has to have improved reproduction in the past. For example, if the rooting reflex exhibited by child were a by-product of facial muscle development, then the functionality of the following features would have to have been coincidences: i) the reflex is triggered by friction on the cheek or mouth rather than any other part of the body, ii) the reflex moves the baby's face toward the nipple rather than away, iii) the reflex segues into the sucking reflex, iv) the reflex just happens to occur at the stage of development when the baby breastfeeds, v) the reflex extends the tongue to receive the nipple. All of those features enable successful suckling, and would have had to have been coincidences of development if the rooting reflex were a by-product. Given how unlikely this is, the null is rejected, and the alternative hypothesis is retained: the rooting reflex evolved via natural selection because babies who had each of those features fed more efficiently, were more likely to survive, and passed on the genes underlying each feature to the following generations.

Evolutionary psychologists use the adaptationist programme to discover the function of different parts of the human mind, including those parts that generate criminal behaviour. According to evolutionary psychologists, different parts of the mind have been designed by natural selection to solve different problems, just as different parts of our body have been designed for different problems, e.g. our heart circulates blood, our skull protects our brain, and so on. By identifying why a particular part of the human mind evolved, we can understand how it works and why it works that way; for example, by understanding that sexual jealousy is a part of the mind that evolved partly to prevent mates from leaving, we can explain why jealous individuals denigrate competitors, punish their mates, and sometimes even use violence against both (Buss 2011). Perhaps most importantly, by understanding why a part of the mind evolved we can discover what aspects of the environment the mind is designed to respond to. In this way, an evolutionary approach not only answers questions about the universal features of human beings, but also answers questions about why the environment has the effect that it does (e.g. why do girls with absent fathers mature faster (Ellis et al. 2003)? and why does our skin darken when we expose it to sunlight?).

Criminal behaviour can result from different aspects of human nature. Each type of crime needs to be studied and understood differently with an understanding of the evolutionary function of the part of the mind under study. I propose the following guide, based on the adaptationist program, as a way of using evolutionary theory to understand a given kind of crime.

Step 1: Identify the portion of human nature that resulted in the crime

To do this, it helps to consult with the evolutionary biological literature to see the kinds of adaptations natural selection designed in other animals. The evolved mechanisms that constitute animals are designed to overcome adaptive problems (i.e. problems of genetic reproduction). Thus animal adaptations commonly function to grant access to food and the territory that produces it, access mates and the resources that can attract them, protect offspring, avoid predators, sense, navigate, store relevant information, fight and avoid pathogens, combat rivals, and so on (Davies, Krebs & West 2012).

Keep in mind that the legal system will rarely categorise different behaviours in the same way as the human mind does. The killing of an infant by neglect is the result of different evolved systems than is the killing of a romantic rival and both likely differ from the mechanisms that cause the killing of an enemy in wartime (Daly & Wilson 1988). Ideally, one carves nature at the joints and attempts to isolate the portion of human nature that was primarily responsible for triggering the criminal behaviour. Finally, adaptations are often constructed to trigger an escalating range of behaviours, so that the adaptations underlying criminal acts will rarely be designed solely to commit the objectionable act; e.g. anger can lead to homicide, but most incidents of anger do not even involve the explicit threat of aggression, let alone lethal violence (Sell 2011).

Step 2: Map out the adaptations underlying this aspect of human nature

Adaptations are the parts of the organism that are designed by natural selection. They must be distinguished from by-products, which are features of organisms that result from adaptations but were not selected for their functionality. For example, fat and fat storage are adaptations in humans that evolved to buffer against starvation, and as a by-product humans are flammable. Fat storage is an adaptation. Human flammability is a by-product. To know if a feature is an adaptation, i.e. has a 'function', one should look for the following clues:

- Is the feature universal across cultures? Adaptations take a long time for evolution to design. As such, they should be universal across cultures and found in almost all human societies, e.g. maternal care of children is common to all known human societies (Brown 1991). This doesn't mean a tyrannical dictator couldn't confiscate all newborns and have them raised communally, only that it is part of evolved human nature for mothers to bond with their offspring.
- Is the feature universal across individuals in that age or sex range? Adaptations are universal but may only express themselves in one sex or at some stages of development, e.g. the rooting reflex in babies ends at about four months. Rare features, or features that only present in a small subset of the population, are unlikely to be adaptations, though there are exceptions from what is called frequency dependent selection (Figueredo et al. 2005).
- Does the feature develop without the need for explicit instruction? This does not mean that adaptations do not learn from their environment; many do, (e.g. imprinting in ducks, food choice mechanisms in humans). It means that the adaptations were not generated by the environment; rather, they evolved to interact with it in specific ways.
- Would there have been a clear selection pressure (i.e. adaptive problem) for the adaptation to solve? Adaptations result from selection pressures, i.e. circumstances that enabled an animal to increase their reproductive success. For example, the rooting reflex enabled reproduction by increasing infant feeding and decreasing the probability of starvation. This strict requirement is what sets evolutionary theories apart from social-science theories that posit functions with no known mechanism that can create such design, e.g. claims that anger functions to protect self-esteem. Evolutionary biologists make use of the fact that natural selection ultimately only creates complex adaptations for one function: increasing the frequency of the genes underlying that adaptation (Dawkins 1976; Williams 1966). If a posited function would not have increased the genetic replication of the genes underlying that adaptation in past environments, it cannot have evolved for that function.
- Does the feature show evidence of complex functional design? This is the decisive criterion (Williams 1966). Adaptations should show evidence of complex design toward the enhancement of reproduction in our past (Cosmides & Tooby 1994; Tooby & Cosmides 1992; Williams 1966). For example, the anger system appears primarily designed to bargain over current and future conflicts of interest. It is activated by indications that another does not value your interests highly (e.g. is willing to impose costs on you for trivial benefits), activates approach behaviour, harnesses the target's attention with vocalisations and a universal anger face (tailored to make the individual appear more formidable), and deploys demonstrations of bargaining power to the target in an attempt to recalibrate them (see Sell, Tooby & Cosmides 2009; Sell 2011; Sell, Tooby & Cosmides 2014; Tooby et al. 2008). Each functional feature of anger had to have increased reproduction by enabling the angry individual to win conflicts of interest.

Again, the evolutionary biological literature is of tremendous use here (see Table 2.1). While humans, like many species, have some unique adaptations, these too can be understood once one knows their evolved function (e.g. Pinker 1995). Regardless of whether there is an animal precedent, adaptations can be 'reverse engineered' to discover their function (Williams 1966). This means consulting their working parts to see what function they serve. For example, the eyebrows bear many features that suggest their function is to keep sweat or rain out of the eyes, e.g. there are two of them – one for each eye, they have a roof-shape that diverts water to the edges and away from the eyes, they have horizontally laid hairs that divert water to the sides, they are at the bottom of the forehead meaning that sweat glands on the forehead will not be able to leak into the eyes, and so forth.

Table 2.1 Crimes, biological precedents, and evolved adaptations underlying them

Crime	*Biological concepts*	*Human adaptations*	*Further reading*
Child abuse, neglect, infanticide	Parental investment, infanticide	Parental investment, infant quality assessment	Daly & Wilson 1984, 1988, 1998
Assault, male-male homicide	Dominance, animal conflict, intrasexual selection	Anger, mate competition, status competition	Daly & Wilson 1988; Sell 2011; Wrangham & Peterson 1996
Group aggression, war, gang violence	Coalitional killing	Coalitional psychology, possible war adaptations	Wrangham & Peterson 1996; Van Vugt 2011
Intimate partner violence	Male–female aggression, mate guarding, intersexual selection	Sexual jealousy	Buss 2011; Goetz et al. 2008; Wilson & Daly 1995
Rape, sexual coercion	Coercive sex, forced copulations, intersexual selection	Male mate-choice mechanisms, possible rape adaptations	McKibbin et al. 2008; Thornhill & Palmer 2001
Theft	Kleptoparasitism, parasitism, tolerated theft, animal-conflict theory	Resource-acquisition mechanisms, envy, entitlement	Kanazawa 2008
Drug use	N/A	By-product of mesocorticolimbic dopamine reward circuit. Possible 'substance-seeking' adaptation	Durrant et al. 2009; Sullivan & Hagen 2002

When identifying the function of adaptations, newer students of the science tend to make a common error and posit a function that does not relate to ancestral reproductive success. For example, anger-based aggression is almost certainly not designed to restore one's self-esteem. Merely thinking well of one's self is unlikely to lead to reproduction, and if it had, then humans would not have evolved to lower their own self-esteem in response to mistreatment by others. Most importantly, if the proper evolved function of anger were to recalibrate one's own estimate of one's own worth, it would have no need of an anger face, changes to the voice, approach orientation, or any of its other features of this complex adaptation. These features clearly indicate that anger is designed primarily to recalibrate the source of anger, not just one's self (see Sell 2011).

Discovering and mapping out the adaptations that underlie human nature has been the purview of evolutionary psychologists for the last 30 years (Buss 2015). Some headway has been made on adaptations underlying criminal behaviour (see Table 2.1) but much more is needed.

Step 3: Use those adaptations to understand the phenomena in modern contexts

Once the function of the adaptation is known, the researcher can derive features of the adaptation by understanding how it would efficiently have solved the adaptive problem in the species' past environments, e.g. what triggers the adaptation, what behavioural or cognitive variables does the adaptation regulate, what makes the adaptation increase or decrease in intensity, how does the adaptation differ between men and women or between children and adults?

For example, in the case of anger, if it is designed for bargaining in ancestral populations, then individuals with more bargaining power would have been better able to use anger. In particular, evolution would have designed anger so as to calibrate one's sense of entitlement to one's bargaining power. Powerful individuals should expect more, and become angry over a greater range of offences. One prediction from this is that physically stronger men, who were better fighters with ancestral weapons, would be more prone to anger in modern populations, a prediction confirmed across several populations (Sell, Tooby & Cosmides 2009; Sell, Eisner & Ribeaud 2016).

It is important to remember that adaptations – while usually universal are not universally or uniformly expressed. Many adaptations are triggered by specific circumstances that may never occur (e.g. pregnancy adaptations) or may occur differently as the system adapts itself to the local environment (e.g. food choice mechanisms will categorise some insects as edible or not depending on how one was fed as a child). Understanding both the design of the adaptation (including how it responds to developmental cues) and the history of learning the organism has undergone will be required to accurately predict how the mechanism is working in a given individual.

Example of the adaptationist programme in criminology: the case of infanticide

In the case of human infanticide, the offender is almost always the infant's caregiver, and the motive is usually to be rid of the responsibility to parent the child (Daly & Wilson 1984, 1988, 1998). This suggests that the system involved in infanticide is the parental bonding system that identifies and cares for one's kin (Bowlby 2008). In short, some parents are insufficiently bonded to their offspring and kill them as a result.

So are there adaptations for infanticide? Daly and Wilson considered the evidence from evolutionary biology, which showed that infanticide can be quite common in some species. Evolutionary biologists have found numerous cases where new males in a social group will kill the nursing children of the previous male in order to remove the lactational ovulatory suppression (i.e. lactating females often have suppressed ovulation such that they cannot conceive when lactating their young; killing the feeding offspring moves the female into oestrus again allowing the new male to impregnate her). Such behaviours have been seen in lions (Pusey & Packer 1990) and langur monkeys (Borries et al. 1999), and are believed to have occurred with such frequency that females (in some species) spontaneously abort their pregnancies when they smell a new male rather than waste energy gestating offspring that the male will kill anyway (Roberts et al. 2012).

Such infanticides are committed by non-relatives, but there are other categories where a parent kills their own young. In mammals, this is frequently the female and is done in response either to starvation pressure or because there are perceptible signs that the infant is unlikely to survive and reproduce (e.g. the runt of the litter is sometimes eaten by house cats). In such circumstances, the mother recoups some of the energetic cost of gestating an offspring by consuming it, and thus increases her lifetime reproduction.

Daly & Wilson (1984) looked at these adaptations and ruled out the possibility that they exist in humans. For example, while it is not unheard of for stepfathers to kill infants, the rate is massively lower than that which exists in lions and langar monkeys where such behaviour is downright routine. Human mothers also do not consume stillborn or sickly infants. Instead,

Daly & Wilson posited that infanticide in humans is a by-product of a different adaptation, specifically, an adaptation in parents that bonds them with children and leads them to sacrifice for their offspring. This category of adaptation is common in evolutionary biology and called 'parental investment' (Trivers 1972).

In essence, the parental investment theory says that parents have a finite amount of investment (e.g. food, protection) and that delivering it to one offspring prevents the parent from investment in other offspring (current and future). As a result, parents of many mammalian species evolved adaptations that respond to the long-term reproductive benefits of investing in an individual offspring. These adaptations typically withhold investment from offspring that are unlikely to survive or reproduce, or when investment places the parent's own survival in jeopardy. In short, the adaptation identifies one's offspring, regulates attention to and altruistic behaviour toward the offspring, and responds to variables like the health of the infant, distress from the infant, and so forth (Bowlby 2008).

This gave Daly & Wilson a theoretical start with which to derive predictors of infanticide in humans. If humans are designed to withhold investment from some infants under some evolutionary recurrent circumstances, and infanticide is a by-product of this withdrawal of self-sacrifice and care, then one can predict infanticide by knowing the circumstances that – ancestrally – made an infant a bad reproductive investment.

Being informed about the evolutionary biological literature drew Daly & Wilson to some of the same variables that led to infanticide in non-human animals: i) infants of poor health are less likely to survive and reproduce and so investing in them will often return less net reproduction, ii) when a parent is strained for resources or has too many offspring to invest in, then they may need to withdraw investment from some or all of their offspring to preserve their future reproduction or the health of the few, iii) when offspring are unrelated to the adult, then there would be substantially less (if any) selection pressure to care for the infants. Daly & Wilson (1988) reviewed the Human Relations Area Files, a searchable library of anthropological records that describe ethnographic research on the foraging peoples of the world. They found all the recorded cases of infanticide among these people and reviewed the circumstances of these deaths. Eighty-nine per cent were attributed to factors that fell into one of the three predicted categories. Nineteen per cent of the killed infants were killed because of an issue with their health, e.g. a deformity or being the product of an incestuous union. Fifty-two per cent were killed because the mother lacked enough resources to care for the infant, e.g. unexpected twins, loss of husband or father. And 18 per cent were the result of father doubting paternity of the child and either killing the infant himself or causing the mother to kill the infant. In sum, when humans living lifestyles most similar to our ancestors commit infanticide, they appear to be responding to situations that would have made the investment in offspring reproductively costly.

Additional research on western societies confirms predictions from the theory that infanticide is a by-product of parental investment adaptations that limit investment in offspring. For example, consistent with their first prediction, physical deformities in infants predict their abuse, neglect, and homicide in western societies as well (Van Horne 2014). Consistent with their second prediction, factors that lead a parent to feel that resources are limited also predict child mistreatment and infanticide (e.g., single parenthood, being young, being poor, Daly & Wilson 1988). Finally, in line with their third prediction, having a genetically unrelated adult living with an infant is arguably the most predictive demographic factor ever found for infanticide (Daly & Wilson 1998). This kind of analysis also allowed evolutionary theorists to predict more fine-grained features of parental investment, e.g. circumstances that moderate the choice to withdraw investment from a sickly child versus investing more to help it recover (Mann 1992).

The case of male-to-female spousal abuse and battery

Domestic violence is readily familiar to evolutionary biologists. Humans are far from the only species in which mates deploy aggression and threats in order to prevent their mate from engaging in sex with a rival (Davies, Krebs & West 2012; Wrangham & Peterson 1996). Biologists see this behaviour as part of a cluster of strategies called 'mate guarding' that evolved to lower the chance that a given mate will conceive with another individual. Given the fact that human males invest in their offspring, it would not be surprising if they had adaptations for guarding their mates, monitoring their sexual behaviour, and responding with threats, desertion, or actual aggression when interlopers were detected.

Evolutionary psychologists have claimed that the human emotion of sexual jealousy evolved for that function (Buss 2011). Sexual jealousy is almost certainly an adaptation. It is universal (Brown 1991), present in adults of reproductive age when in a relationship, and – at first glance – has evidence of complex design e.g. it is triggered by cues of infidelity, causes intense monitoring of the target of jealousy, and can activate aggression toward either the mate or the interloper (Buss 2011). There is no evidence that jealousy is explicitly taught to children, indeed it is frequently punished and explicitly taught against. Its evolved function is the same as mate guarding behaviour in other animals – to prevent interlopers from disrupting a beneficial mating relationship.

The evolutionary approach to sexual jealousy not only fits the data, but explains it in a principled way: e.g. each posited feature of sexual jealousy would have increased the reproduction of the individual possessing it in the past. The entire emotion – including the tendency toward certain criminal behaviour but not limited to it – can be conceptualised as a mechanism for monitoring and responding adaptively (i.e. in ways that increased reproduction ancestrally) to the possibility of partner infidelity or desertion. For example, the jealous individual will monitor their partner's behaviour, particularly behaviour with the opposite sex and even more particularly behaviour with a member of the opposite sex who is attractive and/or potentially interested in the partner. When a threat is detected, the jealous individual deploys strategies to denigrate the rival, to enhance themselves, and sometimes threaten or denigrate their partners in an attempt for coerce them to stay or minimise their chances of attracting another mate (Buss 2011; Goetz et al. 2008). These intuitive features of jealousy aside, such an understanding can also be used to derive predicted features of jealousy that are not commonly known. For example, sexual jealousy and the resultant behaviours are triggered particularly when an individual intends to have a longer term relationship with the victim (as opposed to a short-term relationship), tracks the actual probably of being abandoned by the partner, increases when there are cues that a partner is considering leaving or when the jealous individual believes they are likely to be left (e.g. men become less attractive to women when they lose their job, and therefore men elevate their jealousy after being fired) (Buss 2011; Goetz et al. 2008).

Furthermore, sex differences in the basic functioning of jealousy can be derived from its putative function. Males pay the largest cost when they are cuckolded and lose not only the opportunity to conceive a child with their mate but the investment that is reproductively 'wasted' on a child that is not their own. Females will almost never pay that cost because they can identify their children more easily than males. Rather, females pay a higher price when they lose investment from the male they are mated with. Predictably, experiments showed a sex difference in jealousy with men being more jealous than women when contemplating their partner's sexual infidelity, while women were more jealous than men when contemplating their partner's emotional divestment (Buss 2011; Goetz et al. 2008).

Conclusions: the promise of a better science

Evolution by natural selection is true. It doesn't just fit the data well, or provide a useful perspective, or offer new insights, or represent a theoretical advance. It is true. It is the actual explanation for the origin of life on Earth. It is the actual explanation for the organisation of human nature. It provides the actual explanation for why there is sexual reproduction (Tooby 1982), why there are males and females (Charlesworth & Charlesworth 2010), why people grow old (Williams 2001), and why all human societies are organised around the family (Brown 1991; Hamilton 1964). To ignore this theory when studying any life form is to ground one's field in 18th-century science. If our scientific understanding of crime and criminal behaviour is to advance, we must integrate with biology. Using the adaptationist programme to study human nature is an excellent way to start.

References

Barkow, J. H., Cosmides, L. & Tooby, J. (Eds). (1992). *The Adapted Mind: Evolutionary Psychology and the Generation of Culture*. Oxford: Oxford University Press.

Borries, C., Launhardt, K., Epplen, C., Epplen, J. T. & Winkler, P. (1999). DNA analyses support the hypothesis that infanticide is adaptive in langur monkeys. *Proceedings of the Royal Society of London B: Biological Sciences, 266*(1422), 901–904.

Bowlby, J. (2008). *Attachment*. New York: Basic Books.

Brown, D. E. (1991). *Human Universals*. New York: McGraw-Hill.

Brüne, M. & Brüne-Cohrs, U. (2006). Theory of mind – evolution, ontogeny, brain mechanisms and psychopathology. *Neuroscience & Biobehavioral Reviews, 30*(4), 437–455.

Buss, D. M. (2011). *The Dangerous Passion: Why Jealousy is as Necessary as Love and Sex*. New York: The Free Press.

Buss, D. (2015). *Evolutionary Psychology: The New Science of the Mind*. Needham Heights, MA: Allyn & Bacon.

Charlesworth, D. & Charlesworth, B. (2010). Evolutionary biology: the origins of two sexes. *Current Biology, 20*(12), R519–R521.

Cosmides, L. & Tooby, J. (1994). Beyond intuition and instinct blindness: toward an evolutionarily rigorous cognitive science. *Cognition, 50*(1), 41–77.

Daly, M. & Wilson, M. (1983). *Sex, Evolution & Behaviour*. Boston, MA: Willard Grant Press.

Daly, M. & Wilson, M. (1984). A sociobiological analysis of human infanticide. In Daly, M. & Wilson, M. (Eds). *Infanticide: Comparative and Evolutionary Perspectives* (pp. 487–502). London and New Brunswick: Aldine Transaction.

Daly, M. & Wilson, M. (1988). *Homicide*. Transaction Publishers.

Daly, M. & Wilson, M. (1998). *The Truth about Cinderella: A Darwinian View of Parental Love*. Yale University Press.

Darwin, C. (1872). *The Origin of Species*. New York: Books.

Davies, N. B., Krebs, J. R. & West, S. A. (2012). *An Introduction to Behavioural Ecology*. Oxford: John Wiley & Sons.

Dawkins, R. (1976). *The Selfish Gene*. Oxford: Oxford University Press.

Duntley, J. & Shackelford, T. K. (Eds). (2008). *Evolutionary Forensic Psychology*. Oxford: Oxford University Press.

Durrant, R., Adamson, S., Todd, F. & Sellman, D. (2009). Drug use and addiction: evolutionary perspective. *Australian and New Zealand Journal of Psychiatry, 43*(11), 1049–1056.

Durrant, R. (2012). The role of evolutionary explanations in criminology. *Journal of Theoretical and Philosophical Criminology, 4*(1), 1–37.

Ellis, B. J., Bates, J. E., Dodge, K. A., Fergusson, D. M., John Horwood, L., Pettit, G. S. & Woodward, L. (2003). Does father absence place daughters at special risk for early sexual activity and teenage pregnancy? *Child Development, 74*(3), 801–821.

Figueredo, A. J., Sefcek, J. A., Vasquez, G., Brumbach, B. H., King, J. E. & Jacobs, W. J. (2005). Evolutionary personality psychology. In Buss (Ed.). *The Handbook of Evolutionary Psychology* (pp. 851–877). Hoboken, NJ: John Wiley & Sons Inc.

Goetz, A. T., Shackelford, T. K., Starratt, V. G. & McKibbin, W. F. (2008). Intimate partner violence. In Duntley & Shackelford (Eds). *Evolutionary Forensic Psychology* (pp. 65–78). Oxford University Press.

Hamilton, W. D. (1964). The genetical evolution of social behaviour. *Journal of Theoretical Biology*, 7(1), 17–52.

Kanazawa, S. (2008). Theft. In Duntley & Shackelford (Eds). *Evolutionary Forensic Psychology* (pp. 160–175). Oxford: Oxford University Press.

Mann, J. (1992). Nurturance or negligence: Maternal psychology and behavioral preference among preterm twins. In Barkow, Cosmides & Tooby (Eds). *The Adapted Mind: Evolutionary Psychology and the Generation of Culture*. Oxford: Oxford University Press.

McKibbin, W. F., Shackelford, T. K., Goetz, A. T. & Starratt, V. G. (2008). Why do men rape? An evolutionary psychological perspective. *Review of General Psychology, 12*(1), 86–97.

Muller, M. N., Kahlenberg, S. M., Thompson, M. E. & Wrangham, R. W. (2007). Male coercion and the costs of promiscuous mating for female chimpanzees. *Proceedings of the Royal Society of London B: Biological Sciences, 274*(1612), 1009–1014.

Pusey, A. E. & Packer, C. (1994). Infanticide in lions: consequences and counterstrategies. In Parmigiani (Ed.). *Infanticide & Parental Care*. Chur, Switzerland: Harwood Academic Publishers.

Pinker, S. (1995). *The Language Instinct: The New Science of Language and Mind*. London: Penguin UK.

Pinker, S. (1997). *How the Mind Works*. New York: W. W. Norton & Co.

Roberts, E. K., Lu, A., Bergman, T. J. & Beehner, J. C. (2012). A Bruce effect in wild geladas. *Science, 335*(6073), 1222–1225.

Sell, A. N. (2011). The recalibrational theory and violent anger. *Aggression and Violent Behavior, 16*(5), 381–389.

Sell, A., Cosmides, L. & Tooby, J. (2014). The human anger face evolved to enhance cues of strength. *Evolution and Human Behavior, 35*(5), 425–429.

Sell, A., Eisner, M. & Ribeaud, D. (2016). Bargaining power and adolescent aggression: the role of fighting ability, coalitional strength, and mate value. *Evolution and Human Behavior, 37*(2), 105–116.

Sell, A., Tooby, J. & Cosmides, L. (2009). Formidability and the logic of human anger. *Proceedings of the National Academy of Science, 106*(35), 15073–15078.

Sullivan, R. J. & Hagen, E. H. (2002). Psychotropic substance-seeking: evolutionary pathology or adaptation? *Addiction, 97*(4), 389–400.

Thornhill, R. & Palmer, C. T. (2001). *A Natural History of Rape: Biological Bases of Sexual Coercion*. Cambridge, MA: MIT Press.

Tooby, J. (1982). Pathogens, polymorphism, and the evolution of sex. *Journal of Theoretical Biology, 97*(4), 557–576.

Tooby, J. & Cosmides, L. (1990). The past explains the present: Emotional adaptations and the structure of ancestral environments. *Ethology and Sociobiology, 11*(4–5), 375–424.

Tooby, J. & Cosmides, L. (1992). The psychological foundations of culture. In Barkow, Cosmides & Tooby (Eds). *The Adapted Mind: Evolutionary Psychology and the Generation of Culture* (pp. 19–136). Oxford: Oxford University Press.

Tooby, J., Cosmides, L., Sell, A., Lieberman, D. & Sznycer, D. (2008). Internal regulatory variables and the design of human motivation: a computational and evolutionary approach. In Elliot, A. J. (Ed.). *Handbook of Approach and Avoidance Motivation* (pp. 251–271). New York: Psychology Press.

Trivers, R. L. (1972). Parental investment and sexual selection. In B. Campbell (Ed.). *Sexual Selection and the Descent of Man, 1871–1971* (pp. 136–179). Chicago, IL: Aldine.

van Horne, B. (2014). Child maltreatment among children with specific birth defects: a population-based study, Texas 2002–2011. (Doctoral dissertation, The University of Texas School of Public Health).

van Vugt, M. (2011). The male warrior hypothesis. In Forgas & Kruglanski (Eds). *The Psychology of Social Conflict and Aggression* (pp. 233–248). New York and Hove: Taylor & Francis.

Williams, G. C. (1966). *Adaptation and Natural Selection: A Critique of Some Current Evolutionary Thought*. Princeton, NJ: Princeton University Press.

Williams, G. C. (2001). Pleiotropy, natural selection, and the evolution of senescence. *Science's SAGE KE*, (1)13.

Wilson, M. & Daly, M. (1995). The man who mistook his wife for a chattel. In Barkow, Cosmides & Tooby (Eds). *The Adapted Mind*, (pp. 289–322). Oxford: Oxford University Press.

Wrangham, R. W. & Peterson, D. (1996). *Demonic Males: Apes and the Origins of Human Violence*. New York: Houghton Mifflin Harcourt.

3
Genetics

Jamie M. Gajos, Cashen M. Boccio and Kevin M. Beaver

Society's interest in crime reduction strategies largely increased over the last few decades as incarceration rates and their associated costs skyrocketed. The expenses associated with law enforcement practices, legal fees, correctional facilities, and victim services have likely all contributed to this economic burden placed on society (Fass & Pi, 2002; Lovell & Jemelka, 1996; Miller, Cohen, & Rossman, 1993; Petersilia, 1992). Although a large proportion of government funding remains allocated towards supporting crime control and punitive practices, discussions of offender rehabilitation and crime prevention have resurfaced within the realm of the criminal justice system (Anestis & Carbonell, 2014; Davis, Sheidow, & McCart, 2015; Tripodi, 2014). This opportune shift in criminal justice practices is welcomed, given the failed crime preventive efforts and negative offender outcomes that are often associated with the punishment paradigm of the latter half of the twenty-first century.

Paralleling the movement towards reducing crime and its costs to society, but generally removed from such efforts, has been a body of research devoted to identifying the risk factors for criminality. Findings stemming from these studies indicate that biological and genetic factors are involved in the development and stability of antisocial and criminal behaviours (Barnes & Boutwell, 2012; Moffitt, 2005; Raine, 1993). Moreover, genetic factors have been shown to influence an assortment of maladaptive outcomes, including psychopathy, gang membership, weapon use, and illicit drug use (Beaver, Barnes, & Boutwell, 2014; Beaver, DeLisi, Vaughn, & Barnes, 2010; Deng et al., 2015; Fowler et al., 2009).

Despite the mounds of research revealing a strong link between biological and genetic factors and crime, limited attention has been given to the contribution that genetic research could make to preventing or reducing crime. Discussions of the potential use of genetic data in criminal trials have been faced with controversy, fear, and scepticism, in part, because of the concern that such information would be used to oppress offenders. Furthermore, fundamental misunderstandings regarding the ways in which genetic factors are involved in the aetiology of antisocial behaviours persists among scholars and the public. Findings derived from candidate-gene association studies, for instance, have likely encouraged the belief that genes work in a deterministic fashion, where the possession of one gene inevitably leads to antisocial behaviour. Despite these misunderstandings, mounting evidence reveals that human behaviour is far too complex to be attributed to a single gene, that nature *and* nurture are involved in the aetiology of antisocial behaviour, and that genetic factors interact with specific environments to produce criminal behaviours (Carey, 2003; Caspi et al., 2002; Pinker, 2002; Plomin, DeFries, Knopik, & Neiderhiser, 2013).

This chapter provides an overview of some of the key findings to emerge from behavioural genetic and molecular genetic research, as well as how these findings may be integrated into crime prevention and reduction strategies. To this end, the chapter is divided into three main sections. First, a brief overview of the empirical status on the genetics–crime association will be discussed. This section will begin by highlighting how behavioural genetic methodologies help to estimate both the genetic and environmental influences on antisocial behaviours. Additionally, we will review some of the findings derived from molecular genetic research, which has identified a number of genetic polymorphisms that are correlated with antisocial behaviours. Second, we will illustrate the ways in which environmental factors may be conditioned by one's genotype, a phenomenon known as gene–environment interactions. The discussion on gene–environment interactions will illuminate how genetic polymorphisms interact with certain environments to produce antisocial behaviours. Third, two distinct explanations for gene–environment interactions will be introduced, which are known as the diathesis-stress model and the differential-susceptibility model. This section will conclude with a discussion on how each of these theoretical models may be integrated into crime prevention and rehabilitative practices.

Genetic influences on antisocial behaviour

Behavioural genetic research designs estimate three separate components of the variance in antisocial behaviours. These three components are defined as heritability, shared environmental, and non-shared environmental estimates. Heritability estimates represent the proportion of variance in antisocial behaviours that is due to genetic factors. The variance not accounted for by genetic influences is partitioned to the environment. Behavioural geneticists make the distinction between two types of environments: the shared environment and the non-shared environment. Shared environmental influences work to make siblings similar to one another. An example of a shared environment would be exposure to the same parenting style during childhood. Shared environments are believed to make siblings more similar to one another on the assumption that if certain environments are salient for behaviours – and are experienced equally between siblings – they should exert a similar impact on each sibling's behaviour. In contrast, the non-shared environmental influences make siblings different from one another. One sibling may be differentially exposed to antisocial peers and become involved in delinquency during their teenage years, whereas another sibling may have prosocial friends and engage in no delinquency.

Although a variety of research designs are available to estimate both the genetic and environmental influences on antisocial behaviours, twin-based methodologies are commonly used by behavioural geneticists to obtain these estimates. Twin-based methods compare the similarity of monozygotic (MZ) and dizygotic (DZ) twin pairs on a particular measure of antisocial behaviour. This method is advantageous because it allows behavioural geneticists to estimate genetic influences more accurately. To illustrate, MZ twins share 100 per cent of their DNA, while DZ twins share approximately 50 per cent of their DNA. Because the environments experienced among MZ and DZ twins are assumed to be relatively similar, a greater similarity on a behavioural trait observed between MZ twins than between DZ twins would reveal that variance in that trait is under some level of genetic influence.

The evidence derived from behavioural genetic research designs in general, and from twin-based methodologies in particular, has revealed that genetic factors are responsible for about

50 per cent of the variance in antisocial behaviours. This overall conclusion regarding the heritability estimates for antisocial behaviours has been compiled from six meta-analyses to date (Burt, 2009a; Burt, 2009b; Ferguson, 2010; Mason & Frick, 1994; Miles & Carey, 1997; Rhee & Waldman, 2002). Additional support provided by a recent meta-analysis of more than 2,700 twin-based studies (and including more than 14,500,000 twin pairs), indicates that genetic factors account for approximately 49 per cent of the variance in human phenotypes, including antisocial traits (Polderman et al., 2015). The remaining variance in antisocial traits is due to the exposure to environmental factors. Estimations of environmental influences are further subdivided between the shared environment and the non-shared environment, which account for approximately 15–20 per cent and 30–35 per cent of the variance in antisocial behaviours, respectively (Moffitt, 2005). This body of research highlights the importance of both genetic risk factors and environmental exposure for fostering the development of antisocial behaviours.

Molecular genetics

Although behavioural genetic research designs provide researchers with an estimate of the genetic influences on an antisocial phenotype, they are unable to provide any information on the specific genes that are involved in fostering antisocial behaviour. Instead, molecular genetic research designs are needed to obtain this information. Findings stemming from molecular genetic research have identified several candidate genes that are involved in the development of criminality, aggression, and violence (DeLisi, Beaver, Vaughn, & Wright, 2009; Guo, Roettger, & Shih, 2007; Liao, Hong, Shih, & Tsai, 2004). It is important to note, however, that most of the genes that are implicated in the development of antisocial and criminal behaviour are associated with neurotransmission.

Briefly, neurotransmission is the process by which information is communicated throughout the body. Neurotransmitters are chemical messengers in the brain and are responsible for transmitting this communication from one brain cell, known as a neuron, to another. Neurotransmitters carry signals from one neuron to an adjacent neuron across a gap known as a synapse. After the neurotransmitters have delivered the signal to the post-synaptic neuron, they have to be cleared out of the synapse through one of two processes. First, neurotransmitters are cleared out of the synapse by transporter proteins that deliver the neurotransmitters back to the presynaptic neuron – referred to as re-uptake. Second, neurotransmitters that remain in the synapse are broken down by enzymes. If there are structural abnormalities to the transporter proteins or enzymes responsible for breaking down neurotransmitters, then neurotransmitter levels may be altered and the process of neurotransmission will no longer work effectively.

Genes that are involved in the transportation and breakdown of neurotransmitters, such as dopamine and serotonin, have been found to be associated with impulsivity, aggression, and criminal behaviour (Beaver, Wright, & Walsh, 2008; Retz, Retz-Junginger, Supprian, Thome, & Rösler, 2004; Faraone, Doyle, Mick, & Biederman, 2001; Raine, 1993). Some of the genes have different variants (i.e. alleles), meaning that different copies of the gene can be inherited. Genes with two or more alleles are called polymorphisms, and the alleles for some of these polymorphisms have been found to vary in their efficiency at removing or breaking down neurotransmitters in the synapse. Accordingly, certain alleles for genes involved in neurotransmission have been found to code for the production of proteins that differentially influence neurotransmitter levels, which may lead to unregulated behaviour and the risk for developing antisocial phenotypes.

Several dopaminergic polymorphisms, for instance, have been found to be related to involvement in antisocial and criminal behaviour. The 10-repeat allele of DAT1, a dopamine transporter gene, has been linked with aggression and criminal behaviour (Guo et al., 2007; Beaver, et al., 2008). Additionally, the A1 allele of DRD2, a dopamine receptor gene, has been found to be associated with violent delinquency (Guo et al., 2007) and an increased risk of violent victimisation (Beaver, Wright, DeLisi, Daigle, Swatt, & Gibson, 2007). Certain genes of the serotonergic system have also been found to be related to antisocial behaviour. For instance, the short allele of the serotonin transporter promoter gene (5-HTTLPR) has been found to account for variation in certain forms of antisocial behaviour (Retz et al., 2004; Liao et al., 2004).

Some of the genes that code for the production of enzymes, which are responsible for breaking down these neurotransmitters, have also been found to be associated with violence and criminal behaviour (Volavka, Bildern, & Nolan, 2004; Caspi et al., 2002). Monoamine oxidase A (MAOA), for instance, is a gene that codes for an enzyme involved in the breakdown of neurotransmitters such as dopamine and serotonin. The MAOA gene is polymorphic, and some MAOA alleles code for the production of high-activity MAOA while others code for the production low-activity MAOA. The low-functioning MAOA alleles are less efficient at metabolising neurotransmitters and have been linked to an assortment of antisocial outcomes (Beaver, Wright, Boutwell, Barnes, DeLisi, & Vaughn, 2013; Guo, Ou, Roettger, & Shih, 2008). All in all, the findings gleaned from molecular genetic research have provided some insight into systems of genes that might, in some capacity, be involved in the aetiology of antisocial behaviours.

Gene–environment interactions

Despite the supporting evidence found for the association between a number of genetic polymorphisms and antisocial behaviour, there is also evidence suggesting that the effects of some of these genes can be even stronger when paired with certain environmental conditions. This phenomenon is referred to as a gene–environment interaction (Rutter, 2006). The main premise of gene–environment interactions is that the effect of the environment depends on genotype, and the effects of genotype depend on the environment. To illustrate, an individual with a genetic predisposition towards antisocial behaviour is more likely to engage in criminal behaviour when exposed to a criminogenic environment. An individual without the genetic predisposition towards antisocial behaviour, in contrast, is significantly less likely to engage in criminal behaviour when exposed to the same criminogenic environment. Gene–environment interactions highlight the complex relationships that exist between genetic predispositions and environmental factors and can help to explain why different people respond to the same environment in different ways.

In one of the first studies to examine gene–environment interactions, the low-functioning MAOA genotype was found to interact with childhood maltreatment to predict the development of antisocial phenotypes in males (Caspi et al., 2002). According to the findings by Caspi and colleagues, even though only 12 per cent of the sample possessed both risk factors (i.e. the low-functioning MAOA genotype and exposure to maltreatment in childhood), this group accounted for 44 per cent of the violent convictions in the sample. Furthermore, 85 per cent of the subjects in the study who were exposed to both risk factors developed antisocial behaviour. This gene–environment interaction has been replicated in several other studies (Fergusson, Boden, Hornwood, Miller, & Kennedy, 2012; Kim-Cohen et al., 2006; Foley et al., 2004) and a recent meta-analysis examining this interaction reaffirms that the low-functioning MAOA genotype and childhood maltreatment interact to increase the likelihood of developing antisocial phenotypes (Byrd & Manuck, 2014).

More recent studies have uncovered gene–environment interactions between dopaminergic polymorphisms and environmental factors that affect the likelihood of developing antisocial phenotypes. For instance, DRD2 has been found to interact with having a criminal father to predict the development of serious delinquency, violent delinquency, and police contact (DeLisi, Beaver, Vaughn, & Wright, 2009). Additional research indicates that DRD2 and several other dopaminergic polymorphisms (DAT1, DRD4) interact with environmental factors to predict an array of behavioural outcomes including violent behaviour (Barnes & Jacobs, 2013; Beaver, Gibson, DeLisi, Vaughn, & Wright, 2012; Vaughn et al., 2009), early-onset offending (DeLisi, Beaver, Wright, & Vaughn, 2008), externalising behaviours (Bakermans-Kranenburg & van IJzendoorn, 2006), and number of police contacts (Vaughn et al., 2009).

Although gene–environment interactions have helped to shed light on some of the factors involved in the aetiology of antisocial behaviours, the underlying mechanisms which account for gene–environment interactions remain to be fully discovered. To date, scientists have advanced two models to account for gene–environment interactions: the diathesis-stress model and the differential-susceptibility model.

Until relatively recently, the diathesis-stress model provided the primary explanation for gene–environment interactions. The diathesis-stress model posits that genetic risk factors predict antisocial behaviours when coupled with the exposure to an adverse environment. Under this explanation, genetic polymorphisms partially determine how vulnerable a person is to a negative environment. A person with a genetic predisposition for antisocial behaviours, for example, will be more likely to engage in criminal behaviours when exposed to a criminogenic environment. In this light, adverse and criminogenic environments act to serve as triggers on genetic predispositions.

More recently, however, another explanation for gene–environment interactions has been developed by Belsky, which is known as the differential-susceptibility model (1997, 2005). Belsky's model suggests that rather than being viewed as an indicator of vulnerability to the negative environment, genetic predispositions should be viewed as an indication of plasticity to *both* a positive and a negative environment. Under the differential-susceptibility model, no longer are gene–environment interactions viewed as the result of negative environments interacting with genetic risk to predict negative outcomes. Instead, genetic risk is recast as genetic plasticity, thereby highlighting the potential for genetic polymorphisms to work with negative and positive environments in a 'for-better-or-for-worse' fashion. Individuals with genetic plasticity markers will respond the most positively when exposed to positive environments, just as they will respond the most negatively in the face of adversity.

The diathesis-stress and differential-susceptibility models can be used to help guide crime-prevention and reduction practices. Both frameworks posit that the influences of certain genetic polymorphisms can be moderated by the exposure to certain environments. In the following section, we will discuss how the differential-susceptibility model may be used to inform prevention programmes that seek to thwart antisocial outcomes from surfacing early in life. Following the discussion on crime-prevention efforts, we will illustrate how the diathesis-stress and differential-susceptibility models may be used to guide rehabilitative efforts among offender populations. Under this recommendation, both frameworks could be implemented in conjunction with the principles of effective intervention (PEI) to reduce recidivism rates.

Integrating genetic information into crime-prevention and reduction practices

Intervention attempts to reduce and/or prevent antisocial and other problem behaviours have been shown to exert modest effects at best. The long-term intervention benefits for reducing youthful antisocial behaviour, moreover, have been found to be less effective than anticipated

(Sawyer, Borduin, & Dopp, 2015). Most often, the lack of empirical support for some of these prevention and treatment programmes has been attributed to poor programme dissemination and implementation, as well as to variability in participant demographics and intervention features. A growing body of experimental-intervention research, guided by the differential-susceptibility framework, suggests that the reason for inconsistent programme efficacy could be due to ignoring participant variability in genetic susceptibilities to environmental influences (Belsky & van IJzendoorn, 2015). Thus, prevention efforts that fail to consider the importance of individual characteristics will not be as successful at identifying the individuals for whom the prevention programmes would be the most effective.

Genetically informed intervention research has already begun to examine whether genetic polymorphisms can moderate programme effectiveness among participants. Importantly, many of the genetic polymorphisms found to be associated with antisocial behaviours have also been identified as plasticity genes in randomised intervention trials. Research by Bakermans-Kranenburg and colleagues (2008), for instance, found that children with a history of externalising behaviour problems benefitted the most from family-based interventions if they also possessed the risk allele of the dopamine D4 receptor gene (DRD4). The moderating role of the DRD4 risk allele has also been revealed in substance use preventive interventions. Adolescents assigned to a family-oriented intervention programme displayed decreased substance use, especially if they were carriers of the 7 repeat allele of DRD4 (Brody et al., 2014).

The evidence gathered from genetically informed prevention science suggests that the moderating role of genotype has important implications for programme efficacy. If prevention interventions expanded their focus of participant characteristics to include genotype, then prevention scientists would be able to predict with more accuracy who would benefit the most from the intervention. Indeed, programme participants are commonly targeted for interventions based on a number of risk factors, which include sex, age, race, and a history of antisocial behaviours. With the implementation of a differential-susceptibility framework, no longer would participants be solely identified as belonging to the most at-risk population in need of intervention. Instead, participants would be targeted based on their susceptibility or plasticity for change. This 'change' would include change for the better. Many existing preventive interventions aimed at preventing or reducing antisocial behaviours could easily begin to include genetic data in their research designs. Again, the inclusion of data on participant genotype could explain more variation in programme effectiveness and increase the precision of programme implementation.

While the differential-susceptibility model has clear implications for increasing the effectiveness of prevention programmes, both the differential-susceptibility and diathesis-stress models have the potential to increase the effectiveness of rehabilitation/treatment programmes. The key way in which these models have application to these programmes is via their integration with the principles of effective intervention (PEI). The PEIs developed out of the need to increase rehabilitative success among offender populations (Andrews, Bonta, & Hoge, 1990; Bonta & Andrews, 2007). There are three principles of effective intervention, but only two that have direct application to genetic profiles: the risk principle and the responsivity principle. The risk principle suggests that high-risk offenders are the most amenable to change, and in turn, benefit the most from treatment programmes. The second PEI that is germane to genetic information is known as the responsivity principle and seeks to identify the most efficient modes of treatment for offender populations. The responsivity principle is further subdivided between general responsivity and specific responsivity. General responsivity posits that offenders will respond best to certain treatment models. In contrast, specific responsivity highlights the reality that offenders have individual needs and characteristics (e.g. learning styles, personalities, motivation, and abilities), which modify treatment success. Therefore, specific responsivity suggests that offenders will benefit the most from individualised treatment programmes.

The diathesis-stress and differential-susceptibility frameworks share similarities with the risk principle and the specific responsivity principle, respectively. First, recall that the diathesis-stress model suggests that individuals with genetic risk *and* exposure to environmental risk factors are the most likely to develop antisocial behaviours. The risk principle aligns with the theoretical framework of the diathesis-stress model, by virtue of the explicit focus on participant risk. Indeed, both theoretical models highlight the importance of individual-level risk factors for antisocial outcomes. Incorporating genetic data into risk assessments would allow the most at-risk offenders to be identified and treated in rehabilitative programmes. By default, the offenders with the lowest genetic risk would be diverted from such programmes. Utilising genetic data would allow practitioners to provide services to the offenders who are most in need of treatment.

Second, the specific responsivity principle aligns with the differential-susceptibility model because both theoretical models focus on how individual-level characteristics can moderate programme effectiveness. To illustrate, offenders could be assigned to various treatment programmes based on their level of genetic plasticity, personality traits, and learning styles. Once combining these theoretical models, practitioners might begin to recognise how genetic factors could work with other individual-level characteristics to help moderate the effectiveness of rehabilitative treatment programmes, and in turn, increase offenders' chances for success.

Conclusion

Incorporating genetic data into preventive and rehabilitative programmes has the potential to lead to positive outcomes for offenders. Instead of fearing the possibility that genetic data would be used to oppress offenders, practitioners and the public alike should begin to focus on the many ways genetic factors could increase crime-prevention efficacy and reduce recidivism. Incorporating the theoretical frameworks of gene–environment interactions into existing prevention practices and PEIs could ultimately lead to better programme implementation, more accurate risk assessments, and greater programme success rates.

References

Andrews, D. A., Bonta, J., & Hoge, R. D. (1990). Classification for effective rehabilitation: Rediscovering psychology. *Criminal Justice and Behavior, 17*, 19–52.

Anestis, J. C. & Carbonell, J. L. (2014). Stopping the revolving door: Effectiveness of mental health court in reducing recidivism by mentally ill offenders. *Psychiatric Services, 65*, 1105–1112.

Bakermans-Kranenburg, M. J. & van IJzendoorn, M. H. (2006). Gene-environment interaction of the dopamine D4 receptor (DRD4) and observed maternal insensitivity predicting externalizing behavior in preschoolers. *Developmental Psychobiology, 48*, 406–409.

Bakermans-Kranenburg, M. J., van IJzendoorn, M. H., Pijlman, F. T., Mesman, J., & Juffer, F. (2008). Experimental evidence for differential susceptibility: Dopamine D4 receptor polymorphism (DRD4 VNTR) moderates intervention effects on toddlers' externalizing behavior in a randomized controlled trial. *Developmental Psychology, 44*, 293–300.

Barnes, J. C. & Boutwell, B. B. (2012). On the relationship of past to future involvement in crime and delinquency: A behavior genetic analysis. *Journal of Criminal Justice, 40*, 94–102.

Barnes, J. C. & Jacobs, B. A. (2013). Genetic risk for violent behavior and environmental exposure to disadvantage and violent crime: The case for gene-environment interaction. *Journal of Interpersonal Violence, 18*, 92–120.

Beaver, K. M., Barnes, J. C., & Boutwell, B. B. (2014). The 2-repeat allele of the MAOA gene confers an increased risk for shooting and stabbing behaviors. *Psychiatric Quarterly, 85*, 257–265.

Beaver, K. M., DeLisi, M., Vaughn, M. G., & Barnes, J. C. (2010). Monoamine oxidase A genotype is associated with gang membership and weapon use. *Comprehensive Psychiatry*, *51*, 130–134.

Beaver, K. M., Gibson, C. L., DeLisi, M., Vaughn, M. G., & Wright, J. P. (2012). The interaction between neighborhood disadvantage and genetic factors in the prediction of antisocial outcomes. *Youth Violence and Juvenile Justice*, *10*, 25–40.

Beaver, K. M., Wright, J. P., Boutwell, B. B., Barnes, J. C., DeLisi, M., & Vaughn, M. G. (2013). Exploring the association between the 2-repeat allele of the MAOA gene promoter polymorphism and psychopathic personality traits, arrests, incarceration, and lifetime antisocial behavior. *Personality and Individual Differences*, *54*, 164–168.

Beaver, K. M., Wright, J. P., DeLisi, M., Daigle, L. E., Swatt, M. L., & Gibson, C. L. (2007). Evidence of a gene X environment interaction in the creation of victimization: Results from a longitudinal sample of adolescents. *International Journal of Offender Therapy and Comparative Criminology*, *51*, 620–645.

Beaver, K. M., Wright, J. P., & Walsh, A. (2008). A gene-based evolutionary explanation for the association between criminal involvement and number of sex partners. *Biodemography and Social Biology*, *54*, 47–55.

Belsky, J. (1997). Variation in susceptibility to rearing influence: An evolutionary argument. *Psychological Inquiry*, *8*, 182–186.

Belsky, J. (2005). Differential susceptibility to rearing influence: An evolutionary hypothesis and some evidence. In B. Ellis & D. Bjorklund (Eds). *Origins of the Social Mind: Evolutionary Psychology and Child Development* (pp. 139–163). New York: Guilford.

Belsky, J. & van IJzendoorn, M. H. (2015). What works for whom? Genetic moderation of intervention efficacy. *Development and Psychopathology*, *27*, 1–6.

Bonta, J. & Andrews, D. A. (2007). Risk-need-responsivity model for offender assessment and rehabilitation. *Rehabilitation*, *6*, 1–22.

Brody, G. H., Chen, Y. F., Beach, S. R., Kogan, S. M., Yu, T., DiClemente, R. J., . . . & Philibert, R. A. (2014). Differential sensitivity to prevention programming: A dopaminergic polymorphism-enhanced prevention effect on protective parenting and adolescent substance use. *Health Psychology*, *33*, 182–191.

Burt, A. S. (2009a). Are there meaningful etiological differences within antisocial behavior? Results from a meta-analysis. *Clinical Psychology Review*, *29*, 163–178.

Burt, A. S. (2009b). Rethinking environmental contributions to child and adolescent psychopathology: A meta-analysis of shared environmental influences. *Psychological Bulletin*, *135*, 608–637.

Byrd, A. L. & Manuck, S. B. (2014). MAOA, childhood maltreatment, and antisocial behavior: A meta-analysis of gene-environment interaction. *Biological Psychiatry*, *75*, 9–17.

Carey, G. (2003). *Human Genetics for the Social Sciences*. Thousand Oaks, CA: Sage.

Caspi, A., McClay, J., Moffitt, T. E., Mill, J., Martin, J., Craig, I. W., . . . Poulton, R. (2002). Role of genotype in the cycle of violence in maltreated children. *Science*, *297*, 851–854.

Davis, M., Sheidow, A. J., & McCart, M. R. (2015). Reducing recidivism and symptoms in emerging adults with serious mental health conditions and justice system involvement. *The Journal of Behavioral Health Services & Research*, *42*, 172–190.

DeLisi, M., Beaver, K. M., Wright, J. P., & Vaughn, M. G. (2008). The etiology of criminal onset: The enduring salience of nature and nurture. *Journal of Criminal Justice*, *36*, 217–223.

DeLisi, M., Beaver, K. M., Vaughn, M. G., & Wright, J. P. (2009). All in the family: Gene x environment interaction between DRD2 and criminal father is associated with five antisocial phenotypes. *Criminal Justice and Behavior*, *36*, 1187–1197.

Deng, X. D., Jiang, H., Ma, Y., Gao, Q., Zhang, B., Mu, B., . . . & Liu, Y. (2015). Association between DRD2/ANKK1 TaqIA polymorphism and common illicit drug dependence: Evidence from a meta-analysis. *Human Immunology*, *76*, 42–51.

Faraone, S. V., Doyle, A. E., Mick, E., & Biederman, J. (2001). Meta-analysis of the association between the 7-repeat allele of the dopamine D_4 receptor gene and attention deficit hyperactivity disorder. *American Journal of Psychiatry*, *158*, 1052–1057.

Fass, S. M. & Pi, C. R. (2002). Getting tough on juvenile crime: An analysis of costs and benefits. *Journal of Research in Crime and Delinquency*, *39*, 363–399.

Ferguson, C. J. (2010). Genetic contributions to antisocial personality and behavior: A meta-analytic review from an evolutionary perspective. *Journal of Social Psychology*, *150*, 160–180.

Fergusson, D. M., Boden, J. M., Hornwood, L. J., Miller, A., & Kennedy, M. A. (2012). Moderating role of the MAOA genotype in antisocial behavior. *The British Journal of Psychiatry*, *200*, 116–123.

Foley, D. L., Eaves, L. J., Wormley, B., Silberg, J. L., Maes, H. H., Kuhn, J., & Riley, B. (2004). Childhood adversity, monoamine oxidase A genotype, and risk for conduct disorder. *Archives of General Psychiatry, 61*, 738–744.

Fowler, T., Langley, K., Rice, F., van den Bree, M. B., Ross, K., Wilkinson, L. S., . . . & Thapar, A. (2009). Psychopathy trait scores in adolescents with childhood ADHD: The contribution of genotypes affecting MAOA, 5HTT and COMT activity. *Psychiatric Genetics, 19*, 312–319.

Guo, G., Ou, X.-M., Roettger, M., & Shih, J. C. (2008). The VNTR 2 repeat in MAOA and delinquent behavior in adolescence and young adulthood: Association and MAOA promoter activity. *European Journal of Human Genetics, 16*, 626–634.

Guo, G., Roettger, M. E., & Shih, J. C. (2007). Contributions of the DAT1 and DRD2 genes to serious and violent delinquency among adolescents and young adults. *Human Genetics, 121*, 125–136.

Kim-Cohen, J., Caspi, A., Taylor, A., Williams, B., Newcombe, R., Craig, I. W., & Moffitt, T. E. (2006). MAOA, maltreatment, and gene-environment interaction predicting children's mental health: New evidence and a meta-analysis. *Molecular Psychiatry, 11*, 903–913.

Liao, D. L., Hong, C. G., Shih, H. L., & Tsai, S. J. (2004). Possible association between serotonin transporter promoter region polymorphism and extremely violent crime in Chinese males. *Neuropsychobiology, 50*, 284–287.

Lovell, D. & Jemelka, R. (1996). When inmates misbehave: The costs of discipline. *The Prison Journal, 76*, 165–179.

Mason, D. A. & Frick, P. J. (1994). The heritability of antisocial behavior: A meta-analysis of twin and adoption studies. *Journal of Psychopathology and Behavioral Assessment, 16*, 301–323.

Miles, D. R. & Carey, G. (1997). Genetic and environmental architecture of human aggression. *Journal of Personality and Social Psychology, 72*, 207–217.

Miller, T. R., Cohen, M. A., & Rossman, S. B. (1993). Victim costs of violent crime and resulting injuries. *Health Affairs, 12*, 186–197.

Moffitt, T. E. (2005). The new look of behavioral genetics in developmental psychopathology: Gene-environment interplay in antisocial behaviors. *Psychological Bulletin, 131*, 533–554.

Petersilia, J. (1992). California's prison policy: Causes, costs, and consequences. *The Prison Journal, 72*, 8–36.

Pinker, S. (2002). *The Blank Slate: The Modern Denial of Human Nature.* New York: Penguin Books.

Plomin, R., DeFries, J. C., Knopik, V. S., & Neiderhiser, J. M. (2013). *Behavioral Genetics* (6th ed.). New York: Worth Publishers.

Polderman, T. J. C., Benyamin, B., de Leeuw, C. A., Sullivan, P. F., van Bochoven, A., Visscher, P. M., & Posthuma, D. (2015). Meta-analysis of the heritability of human traits based on fifty years of twin studies. *Nature Genetics, 47*, 702–709.

Raine, A. (1993). *The Psychopathology of Crime: Criminal Behavior as a Clinical Disorder.* San Diego, CA: Academic Press.

Retz, W., Retz-Junginger, P., Supprian, T., Thome, J., & Rösler, M. (2004). Association of serotonin transporter promoter gene polymorphism with violence: Relation with personality disorders, impulsivity, and childhood ADHD psychopathology. *Behavioral Sciences & the Law, 22*, 415–425.

Rhee, S. H. & Waldman, I. D. (2002). Genetic and environmental influences on antisocial behavior: A meta-analysis of twin and adoption studies. *Psychological Bulletin, 128*, 490–529.

Rutter, M. (2006). *Genes and Behavior: Nature-Nurture Interplay Explained.* Malden, MA: Blackwell.

Sawyer, A. M., Borduin, C. M., & Dopp, A. R. (2015). Long-term effects of prevention and treatment on youth antisocial behavior: A meta-analysis. *Clinical Psychology Review, 42*, 130–144.

Tripodi, S. J. (2014). Emphasis on rehabilitation: From inmates to employees. *International Journal of Offender Therapy and Comparative Criminology, 58*, 891–893.

Vaughn, M. G., DeLisi, M., Beaver, K. M., & Wright, J. P. (2009). DAT1 and 5HTT are associated with pathological criminal behavior in a nationally representative sample of youth. *Criminal Justice and Behavior, 36*, 1113–1124.

Volavka, J., Bilder, R., & Nolan, K. (2004). Catecholamines and aggression: The role of COMT and MAO polymorphisms. *Annals of the New York Academy of Sciences, 1036*, 393–398.

4
Sociology

Nick Tilley

Introduction

Much 'conventional' criminology is sociological in orientation. Sociology is marked by enormous diversity in method and theory. Much sociological criminology would be of little interest to crime science, but the general concerns of sociology and some specific threads within it are important.

Sociology

Sociology, as understood here, is the scientific study of social relationships, social institutions and social structures. Rather like crime science itself it draws on a wide range of other disciplines, whilst having its own distinctive concerns. Sociology, thus, draws in some psychology, biology, economics, geography, history, philosophy, politics and anthropology. Each of these helps us to understand conditions that affect social behaviour and social structure.

At the heart of sociology is the idea that 'social' comprises a reality *sui generis* with its own causal powers that are not reducible to the qualities of the individuals making up society. Social institutions such as the family and social divisions such as social class, for example, have their own attributes separate from their particular members and exert their own causal influences. As Emile Durkheim, one of the founding fathers of the discipline, pithily put it in his injunction to sociologists, 'Consider social facts as things' (Durkheim 1950). He went on to say that 'a social fact is every way of acting that is capable of exercising an external constraint upon the individual'. Durkheim emphasised the importance of science in understanding society. He dealt in statistical patterns. Perhaps his most famous study was *Suicide*, where he identified variations in recorded rates, which he associated with 'suicidogenic currents', brought about by the prevailing social conditions (Durkheim 1951). Hence individuals would kill themselves if required to do so by social norms – (altruistic suicide), or because they felt they had no way out but to kill themselves given their social conditions (fatalistic suicide), or because they lacked social obligations that would inhibit them from killing themselves (egoistic suicide), or because they lacked that normative regulation that would prevent suicidal behaviour (anomic suicide). The outcome might be the same, but different types of suicide need to be distinguished if we are to understand it. Moreover, these differences are not reducible to individual psychology or to genetic differences that are presumably more or less evenly distributed across the populations displaying different suicide rates.

Of course, Durkheim's work on suicide has not survived the critical scrutiny it has received since it first appeared, in terms of the data used, the types of suicide identified and the range of causes at work that help explain patterns (Douglas 1967; Atkinson 1971; Taylor 1982). It nevertheless serves to highlight sociology's claim to have some distinctive concerns and methods and to exemplify the discipline's emphasis on social causes that are at work even in what seem at first sight to be archetypally individual behaviours.

Notwithstanding Durkheim's recognition of social reality, contemporary sociology acknowledges a reciprocal relationship between the individual and the social, the individual side of which Durkheim ignored or denied. The individual and social are now widely seen to be 'mutually constitutive' (each involved in the formation of the other), with important implications both for theory (e.g. Elder-Vass 2010; Giddens 1984) and for statistical method (e.g. Goldthorpe 2016).

Goldthorpe's recent book, *Sociology as a Population Science* (2016), embraces 'methodological individualism' in contrast to Durkheim's 'holism' as foundational for a sociology whose focus, Goldthorpe contends, should be on identifying and understanding the generation of emergent patterns. Here social phenomena exist, but their consequences (and production) need to relate back to mechanisms that relate to human choices – people are not mechanical products of social arrangements but are intentional agents using bounded rationality (or 'rationality for mortals', as Gigerenzer put it in 2008). Although Goldthorpe has nothing significant to say about crime, his account of sociology sits well with crime science's concern to identify and explain patterns of crime event by reference to underlying causal mechanisms involving human choices.

There have also been and continue to be sociologies that are skeptical or even hostile to the mission of crime science. The purpose of this chapter is not to engage in a critical debate with them (but see Tilley and Selby 1976, where there is also an early pitch for a problem-solving 'applied sociology' that aligns well with the concerns of crime science). Rather, the aim of this chapter is to highlight the contribution of sociology to crime science to date and to emphasise its continuing relevance.

The social nature of crime

Crime is social in a variety of senses: crime is defined by social institutions; the criminal justice process is a social construction and operates through social processes; most crime is social in the sense of that is committed by one party against another, where each party is also often part of a social group; crime is experienced socially in that many of its harms are mediated by membership of social groups; crime patterns are enabled and inhibited at least in part through the social relationships between victims, offenders and relevant third parties; and the victims, offenders and third parties are themselves embedded in social relationships. Crime prevention turns on the workings of social institutions such as the police, family, government, business, and community. Ultimately, definitions of crime, decisions to offend, and responses to crime events, including efforts at detection, precautionary and protective actions, and preoccupations with crime are all shaped, at least in part, by the social.

None of this, of course, means that crime is the exclusive preserve of sociology. Just as sociology draws in other disciplines in understanding social processes in crime, it also leaves much to do with crime with other disciplines notwithstanding occasional expressions of that hubris that is apt to afflict those in many other disciplines also. Geneticists tend to see criminal activity through the lens of biological difference, psychology through intrapersonal and interactional processes, economics through utility-maximising choices, geographers through spatial configurations, materials scientists through the physical objects involved in the commission and response to crime, lawyers through statute and criminal justice systems, and so on. Crime science is a hybrid business with its own concerns and sociology is likewise a hybrid contributor to it.

This chapter draws from the broad sociological waterfront some elements that are especially important within crime science. The first relates to the real causal importance of the social in generating crimes and responses to crimes. The second relates specifically to the production of patterns of crime event. The third relates to the experience of crime.

The real causal importance of the social

Here is a baker's dozen of commonly held general sociological propositions that speak to the causes of crime and responses to it.

1. Social conditions are real in their consequences (Durkheim 1950, 1951)

The social groups to which individuals belong both create and limit their opportunities through the resources that they provide. Material, cultural, and interpersonal resources are amongst the real conditions giving rise to variations in the choices open to differing groups. A very general approach to crime prevention involves identifying resources available or needed for the prevention of crime and attempting to control their supply and distribution.

2. The definitions of situations are real in their consequences (Thomas and Thomas 1928; Berger and Luckmann 1967)

Individuals act in terms of their definitions of the situation. Definitions of the situation can emerge from any of a variety of sources, but primarily from the social groups to which individuals belong or with which they identify. Clearly offenders act in terms of the ways in which they define their situations. Interventions aiming to alter the definitions of situations that are favourable to crime (that it is easy, low risk, highly rewarding and permissible) are already part of the stock-in-trade of situational crime prevention.

3. Reference group membership activates and deactivates behavioural dispositions (Merton 1968)

Individuals define themselves and their aspirations by reference to significant others. Significant others are those with whom individuals identify as membership groups (for example family or friends) or comparison groups (for example celebrities). Collectively these are known as 'reference groups'. Criminal behaviour tends to be generated where a person's closest reference-group members behave criminally or express pro-crime sentiments. For crime scientists, reference groups comprise proximate causes of crime.

4. Formal labels attached to individuals shape the identities they adopt and the opportunities they encounter (Lemert 1951)

Individuals tend to adapt to the public labels bestowed on them. This is in part because those labels influence the options available to them and in part because individuals come to define themselves in the ways in which others treat them. Where criminal labels are attached it can become difficult to pursue some legitimate courses of action and to associate with some non-criminal peers. In both cases, further criminal behaviour becomes more likely. Responses to early criminal behaviours comprise proximate causes of later criminal behaviours.

5. Societies have major social divisions that give rise to variations in resources and reference groups available to their members (Dahrendorf 1959)

There are major social divisions in all societies. Advantaged groups tend to have the resources to maintain and reproduce their advantages. This is the case both with regard to resources and to prevailing ideas that legitimate the existing social order. With regard to resources, some are put to reducing crime risks. Because of their greater social capital the more advantaged are often well placed to take advantages of public benefits. Ethical crime scientists orientated to the allocation of effective preventive resources where they are most needed will need to attend to the ways in which their efforts may inadvertently contribute to the protection of the already safe and the neglect of those who are more vulnerable.

Social divisions also give rise to different reference groups as well as different crime opportunities. Corporate crime is therefore likely in companies where there are crime opportunities and there is tacit approval for it to occur. Expenses will be fiddled in those occupations where there are opportunities and within groups that tacitly approve it – as has apparently been the case amongst many British parliamentarians, who were able to make a wide range of unchallenged, dishonest claims for reimbursement including those for expenditure on 'moats, duck houses and bath plugs' as indicated in the title of one paper relating to the scandal (Allington and Peele 2010)!

6. Individuals and groups belong to networks that shape the resources available to pursue objectives (Simmel 1955)

All individuals are locked into networks of social relationships. The networks of social relationships in which people are enmeshed shape the resources available to them to act criminally (or otherwise) and influence their decisions as to whether or not to commit a crime. Networks enabling crime may inadvertently be facilitated by criminal justice policies, such as the congregation of likely offenders in the same prison where techniques of neutralisation may be learned, techniques passed on, mutually protective peer groups fostered, and collaborative criminal groups formed from those with complementary skills. At the same time membership of non-offending networks tends to atrophy.

7. Reasoning is involved in all social action and is influenced by the social situations of those engaged in that reasoning (Popper 1967)

The reasoning involved in all action is mediated by social context. The utilities at stake and their valuation by the individual is a function of the social group to which he or she belongs. Money, respect, admiration, power, food, reputation, and sexual titillation can all comprise utilities emphasised by differing social groups in different contexts. Such utilities may all be acquired using criminal means as well as legitimate ones.

8. Moral panics are associated with spirals amplifying crime and the severity of responses to it (Wilkins 1964)

Public concerns about crime can be heighted by specific cases and media treatment of them. These concerns create increased policy attention to the behaviours, which lead to the identification of more cases. This in turn leads to more severe criminal justice responses to the behaviours. The more severe criminal justice responses involve authoritative labelling of those deemed to have engaged in the behaviours. They then appropriate the identity and/or have reduced non-criminal options. The criminal behaviour spirals through a sequence of proximal causal mechanisms.

9. Much behaviour is produced and reproduced through habit (Weber 1978)

Much social behaviour is undertaken habitually and unreflectively. This will include the actions of victims, offenders and third parties. The routines of all will influence the supply of crime opportunities and hence criminal acts. Armed robbers, for example, were able to exploit regular collections of cash to pay workers and regular routes to transport it from a bank to a work place to identify suitable targets. Removing such routines comprised one measure to prevent such crimes. Making security-related activities matters of routine for potential victims comprises one method of improving their security, as occurred for example with the design of cars, all of whose security measures are activated automatically with the press of a button on the key as the driver leaves the vehicle. Facilitating such security routines comprises one important way of making crime prevention a default.

10. Actions have unacknowledged conditions and unintended consequences (Giddens 1984; Boudon 1982)

Social behaviour is produced and reproduced in ways only partially understood by those engaged in it. Practical knowledge describes the understanding individuals have of the actions they perform. But there are always limitations to this. Moreover, the consequences of actions undertaken by individuals are rarely fully grasped by them. Interventions aiming to alter behaviour, including that which is criminal, may focus on the unacknowledged conditions and hence operate behind the 'backs' of prospective offenders. Likewise interventions might increase consciousness of the consequences of criminal behaviour. In some cases identifying the unintended crime consequences of actions by the ostensibly law-abiding may be a precondition for them to change their behaviour in ways that will reduce the crime fall-out. Examples include manufacturers of products that can encourage and enable crime (such as cars and mobile phones), retailers creating increased criminal opportunities (such as self-service shops), and entertainment providers, whose management practices can enable and inadvertently encourage criminal behaviour (such as clubs and bars).

11. Impressions are managed through signals artfully or unintentionally emitted by and interpreted by involved individuals in pursuit of their ends (Goffman 1959)

In interactions, individuals act in relation to others in terms of their beliefs about the others' attributes. These beliefs can be misleading. Individuals will have interests in conveying impressions of their selves to pursue their own objectives. In regard to crime, for example, offenders have to manage self-presentation to differing constituencies including criminal rivals, potential criminal collaborators, possible underground police officers, potential informants, and potential customers for stolen goods. Misreading of others and failure in intended self-presentation will be risky for offenders, but can be exploited for the purpose of crime prevention and crime control.

12. Diverse mechanisms are at work in producing patterns of behaviour (Elster 2007)

Analytical sociology has identified a range of 'nuts' and 'bolts' producing behaviour that are often referred to as mechanisms. These include some more or less rational choices, emotions, and norms, all or which will be expected to be at work in criminal behaviour. In some cases, the direction of behaviour indicated by mechanisms lying behind it will be in conflict with one another producing uncertain outcomes. Murder-suicides illustrate the point. A strong desire to kill someone is accompanied by a strong moral injunction to kill no one. Capitulating to the impulse to kill is matched by insufferable shame at acting in the most morally reprehensible way.

13. Social organisations are marked by relationships of reciprocity and autonomy (Gouldner 1959, 1960)

There are almost ubiquitous relationships of reciprocity and autonomy, especially within and between organisations, where the 'centre' characteristically attempts to control the 'peripheral parts' and the peripheral parts attempt to maximise their autonomy. The centre, nevertheless, needs the peripheral parts to function and the peripheral parts likewise need the centre for their maintenance. The result is a characteristic tension, which would be expected in agencies and partnerships attempting to control crime as well as within more or less organised criminal groups.

Each of these 13 examples shows how core general propositions within sociology help understand crime patterns and methods for controlling them. Other, specific substantive areas of sociology, for example relating to urban structures and urban life, relationships within and across communities, and families, also speak to conditions that may favour or inhibit crime patterns.

Next we turn to specific ways in which sociology has fed into core ideas currently shaping the work of crime scientists.

The production and inhibition of patterns of crime event

The routine-activities approach comprises one cornerstone of crime science (Cohen and Felson 1979; Felson and Eckert 2015). This approach is profoundly sociological. It refers to the supply, distribution, and movement of the necessary and sufficient conditions for crime events to occur. These conditions refer to likely offenders, suitable targets and the kind of intermediary that would keep them apart should they meet. There are two types of intermediary: the capable guardian and the intimate handler. The capable guardian is someone (or the functional equivalent of a person, such as a CCTV camera) that has the power, inclination or credibility to protect the suitable target from the likely offender. The intimate handler is someone (or again a functional equivalent) whose views, perceived views, or actions are sufficient to inhibit the likely offender from committing a crime against the suitable target.

At any given point in time the distribution of likely offenders, suitable targets, capable guardians and intimate handlers will determine where the conditions for crime are present and hence the patterns of crime. The daily, weekly and monthly round of them shapes the seasonal and geographic patterns of crime. Over time, changes in the supply, distribution and movement shape crime trends. These simple ideas have enormous potential explanatory power. What they imply is the need to understand what produces the spatial and temporal supply, distribution, and movement of these key conditions for crime. Secular changes in society (for example technology, retail methods, educational facilities, transportation arrangements, employment patterns, and sports and entertainment provision) are all liable to impact the supply, distribution and movement of each of them and hence to help shape crime patterns.

The applied side of the routine-activities approach is fairly obvious. It implies many options that could be explored in relation to any given crime problem. What might be done to keep the likely offender and suitable target apart? What might reduce the likelihood of offending of those present? What might be done to make the target less suitable? What might be done to foster the supply and relevant distribution of, direct the movement of or build the capacity of potential guardians and intimate handlers? How might new convergences of conditions for crime be anticipated and forestalled before a crime harvest occurs and measures have to be retrofitted to contain it?

A second cornerstone of crime science, situational crime prevention, is also profoundly sociological in that its focus has not been on individual dispositions to commit crime but rather on the immediate situations that enable it or foster it or inhibit it or disable it (Mayhew et al. 1976; Clarke 1980: 162). Some of this foundational work drew explicitly on sociological theories relating to crime. For example, Clarke acknowledged that 'the scheme (situational crime prevention) owes something to the sociological model of crime suggested by the "new criminologists"' (1980) and Cornish and Smith note the influence of '[S]ociological accounts . . . [that] normalised rather than pathologised offending, and provided compelling explanations at the micro- and macro-levels' (Cornish and Smith 2010: 33–34).

One of the most influential studies underpinning situational crime prevention returns to the explanation of suicide rates, which Durkheim studied. Like Durkheim, Clarke and Mayhew (1988) focused on rates of suicide rather than individual incidents. Again like Durkheim, they were uninterested in the states of mind or particular circumstances that led people to want to take their lives. Instead, they were concerned with the circumstances for suicidal behaviour. Unlike Durkheim, however, the conditions they focused on were not the sets of social arrangements prevailing for those killing themselves. Instead, they highlighted the parallel trends in overall suicide rates and suicide rates involving the use of the domestic gas supply.

The reduced toxicity of the domestic gas supply in the UK reduced the availability of an on-tap painless means of committing suicide. The gradual removal of this method led to a reduction not only of suicide using this method but also of overall suicide rates, despite the fact that there are plentiful other methods of taking one's own life. The significance here is that that most personal and final decision is influenced by the apparently trivial local circumstance of the nature of the gas supply. None of this, of course, is to say that personal tragedies, individual circumstances and psychological attributes have nothing to do with suicidal behaviour – of course they do – it is only to note that at the level of rates and changes in rates (Durkheimian 'social facts') conditions matter enormously, and this has profound implications for policy and practice aiming to deal with problem behaviours. Moreover, although it will never be possible to determine who, exactly, has been saved from acting on suicidal impulses for want of the ready availability of a convenient method of acting on them, we can be confident that some of the unhappinesses – many short-lived – do not produce their potential tragic outcomes. Nor is it to say that there are none who are so determined to commit suicide that they will not find other methods. Some will clearly do so. Indeed, it is probably only those whose impulses are short-lived, and who hence otherwise have good reasons to stay alive, whose suicides are prevented by the removal of convenient means (Lester 2012).

Ronald Clarke, the founding father of situational crime prevention and a major source in inspiration for crime science, used the acceptance speech for his Stockholm Prize for criminology to remind us of the research on suicide and the domestic gas supply and of the way this speaks to the 'fundamental attribution error' (Clarke 2016). The error of the fundamental attribution error is to explain behaviour (especially that of others) in terms of their basic attributes or drives, rather than recognising the crucial role of immediate contingencies (Ross and Nisbett 2011). This error is manifest in everyday life, where we tend to explain others' wrongful behaviour in terms of their psychology, moral status, or social background, but our own in terms of the immediate situation (Pease and Laycock 2012): she hit him because she is a psychopath, a wicked person, or has not been well brought up; I hit him because he was unfaithful, was unkind, or hit me. Ironically, sociologists as well as psychologists (alongside many members of the public, including policymakers and practitioners) have fallen into the trap of the fundamental attribution error, over-emphasising dispositions and their sources and under-recognising the crucial role of the immediate conditions in producing behaviour patterns.

Part of sociology's contribution to crime science lies in its emphasis on the role of (modifiable) external conditions in producing patterns of criminal behaviour – not generally as sufficient causes of individual acts but as sources of recurrent patterns.

Sociologists have increasingly recognised that patterns of behaviour are not mechanically produced by external conditions, but that conditions influence behaviour through the way they are apprehended. This is recognised, for example, in propositions 2, 3, 4, 7, 8, 11, and 12 listed above. In the literature of situational crime prevention, this too is acknowledged in the ways in which perceived risks, perceived rewards, perceived effort, rules/excuses and provocations are mentioned. In each case, the importance of the prospective offender's understanding if the situation in which they are to act is highlighted. This is not to say they the situation is necessarily misapprehended (although it may be), only that the apprehension (whatever its source) is crucial to the action taken by the individual.

The modifiable experience of crime

For crime policy, the harm done by crime includes not only the direct loss experienced by the victim and those around them but also the sense of security and well-being that is undermined for many by the notion that one may be vulnerable to crime. Although 'fear' is rather poorly conceptualised and measured, it is the term often used in crime policy to capture some deleterious effects crime has on some citizens' sense of security.

Martin Innes (2004) has formulated a sociological theory of 'signal crimes' that explains how and why situations induce fear amongst some encountering them but not others, with implications for the focus of interventions that aim to reduce that fear of crime. Innes draws mainly on the work of Erving Goffman (1972) in developing his ideas, quoting him when he says,

> When an individual finds persons in his presence acting improperly or appearing out of place, he can read this as evidence that although the peculiarity itself may not be a threat to him, still, those who are peculiar in one regard may well be peculiar in other ways, too, some of which may be threatening. For the individual, then, impropriety on the part of others may function as an alarming signal.
>
> *(Goffman 1972: 285)*

Innes explored these ideas in fieldwork involving extended interviews with 30 subjects. Innes found that situations are construed as fearful in the circumstances Goffman describes.

Both physical environments and events are sometimes interpreted as markers for crime risks. The individuals seeing them as risky may then become fearful either for themselves and/or those near to them. They then adapt their behaviour accordingly. Ostensibly the same characteristics of the physical environment or the same behaviours will not elicit fear in all circumstances. It depends on the wider context. What is normal and hence what is abnormal, thereby fearful, varies from place to place. Moreover, fear of crime may not be created by crimes themselves. Rather, other indicators such as the presence of those who are drinking in the open may also sometimes produce fear of crime. In other circumstances, for instance where criminal behaviours are widespread, the emotional response provoked may be one of anger rather than fear, with rather different behavioural corollaries. Very often, Innes notes, signals function cumulatively, leading those in given situations to become fearful. Moreover the construction of situations as worrisome is often not undertaken by isolated individuals but by members of social networks which mediate their interpretation of potential signals as fearful or otherwise.

In practice, what this means is that policy concerns about fear of crime are not sensibly directed at specific behaviours or physical indicators that are intrinsically and universally fear-inducing. Rather, policy and practice needs to attend to local ways of construing crime risks, local emotional responses and local behavioural adaptation to put in place measures that are locally relevant to the groups affected.

Goffman himself was concerned with a range of sources of alarm and their capacity to elicit behaviours that would improve safety of self and near others. He suggests, in a Darwinian passage shortly after that quoted above by Innes, that eventually false impressions tend to self-correct:

> [C]learly something can seem to be up when, in fact, from the point of view of attention actually needed, nothing is up. Contrariwise, something indeed can be up that soon will sharply affect the welfare of the individual, and yet be so apparent that it escapes his immediate concern. Of course . . . over the longer run no person is likely to survive or pass his incapacity on to many descendants if he is constantly in error in monitoring the environment; even within a protective institution he will need to be right about apparent dangers and opportunities.
>
> *(Goffman 1972: 286)*

Innes is right, however, to highlight the important and avoidable harms caused by intelligible misconceptions, while Goffman is clearly also right to say that policymaking needs to be concerned with avoidable real risks (and the opportunities associated with them). It is not clear that self-correction, if it happens at all, happens quickly enough without attempts at corrective interventions where fears are unwarranted.

Signals and criminal behaviour

Offenders, like the rest of use, are embedded in social relationships. They face some distinctive problems. How do they collaborate? How do they decide on those they can trust in a criminal enterprise? How do they show that they can be trusted in a criminal enterprise? How do they disguise their criminality in dealings with non-offenders as well as with fellow offenders?

Carl Klockars (1974) wrote about this in talking about professional fences. In practice Klockars took only one fence, a 'Vincent Swaggi', as the focus of his ethnographic study. As Klockars shows, Swaggi's problem was to present his business as one that appeared at the same time to be a) a safe and welcoming place for thieves bringing and selling their stolen goods and b) an outlet where respectable citizens would not suspect that they were buying those stolen goods.

Diego Gambetta (2009) has written about the problems of offenders communicating with other criminals in the underworld, where there is a perpetual risk of betrayal and where the normal rules regulating interaction do not operate or are not enforced by third parties. Gambetta shows the logic behind apparently bizarre communicating behaviour patterns. For example, instead of discussing the conventional account of prisons as 'universities of crime', he refers to the credibility given to a potential new criminal collaborator's criminal record, the veracity of which can be checked through networks of other known offenders. He draws on works of behavioural ecology to make sense of 'costly signals', such as violent acts, self-harm and even killing others (with the multiple attendant risks of reprisal or criminal justice penalties) in establishing criminal bona fides with other offenders.

In prisons, displays of toughness are required to avoid exploitation, of which there is a high risk given a) that resources are restricted, b) that there is competition for those resources, and c) that companions cannot be chosen. Moreover, the contexts for the need for such displays are variable. The theory suggests that violence in stable prison settings where relative fighting ability is settled and known to all is less than in unstable (high turnover) settings where the pecking order has yet to be determined. The lower the level of uncertainty, the greater the risk of violence. Gambetta shows the communicative means used to try to establish one's toughness in a prison setting. The repertoire includes: deliberate self-harm, artfully chosen tattoos marking involvement in violent groups, looking mad, verbal abuse, and squaring up. Where inmates are inexperienced they will be less versed in reading and presenting signals of toughness or fighting ability and hence more likely to engage in actual violence. Violence in all-women prisons is higher than their all-male counterparts because of the reduced scope to establish pecking orders without the use of so much actual violence.

Using sociology in crime science

Crime science can draw on sociology both as background and as foreground. As background, sociology provides accounts of the social conditions for criminal action and for responses to crime that need to be taken into account in any effort to find and implement measures targeting pinch points in the complex causal processes producing crime patterns. As foreground, sociology's interests in the proximal external conditions for criminal behaviours provides one basis for identifying modifiable causes of criminality, crime events and crime harms that might furnish the focus for preventive or ameliorative interventions.

There may be some sociologists for whom crime science is anathema and there have certainly been schools of thought in sociology that have eschewed the middle-range, practical interests that lie at the heart of crime science (Tilley and Selby 1976). Nevertheless, as indicated in this chapter, sociology has much to contribute to crime science. Moreover, where universities are being encouraged to embrace 'impact' there may be an increased appetite and opportunity for sociologists to play a part in the fostering future developments in crime science.

References

Allington, N. and Peele, G. (2010) 'Moats, duck houses and bath plugs: members of parliament, the expenses scandal and the use of web sites'. *Parliamentary Affairs 63*(3): 385–406.

Atkinson, M. (1971) 'Societal reactions to suicide: the role of coroners' decisions'. In S. Cohen (ed.) *Images of Deviance* (pp. 83–92). Harmondsworth: Penguin.

Berger, P. and Luckmann, T. (1967) *The Social Construction of Reality*. Harmondsworth: Penguin.

Boudon, R. (1982) *The Unintended Consequences of Social Action*. London: Macmillan.

Clarke, R. (1980) 'Situational crime prevention: theory and practice'. *British Journal of Criminology 20*: 136–146.
Clarke, R. (2016) 'Criminology and the fundamental attribution error'. *The Criminologist 41*(3): 2–7.
Clarke, R. and Mayhew, P. (1988) 'The British gas suicide story and its criminological implications'. In M. Tonry and N. Morris (eds) *Crime and Justice: A Review of Research 10*: 79–116.
Cornish, D. and Smith, M. (2010) 'On being crime specific'. In N. Tilley and G. Farrell (eds) *The Reasoning Criminologist: Essays in Honour of Ronald V. Clarke* (pp. 30–45). London: Routledge.
Cohen, L. and Felson, M. (1979) 'Social change and crime rate trends: a routine activities approach'. *American Sociological Review 44*: 588–608.
Dahrendorf, R. (1959) *Class and Class Conflict in Industrial Society*. Stanford, CA: Stanford University Press.
Douglas, J. (1967) *The Social Meanings of Suicide*. Princeton, NJ: Princeton University Press.
Durkheim, E. (1950) *The Rules of Sociological Method*. New York: Free Press.
Durkheim, E. (1951) *Suicide*. New York: Free Press.
Elder-Vass, D. (2010) *The Causal Power of Social Structures: Emergence, Structure, Agency*. Cambridge: Cambridge University Press.
Elster, J. (2007) *Explaining Social Behavior: More Nuts and Bolts for the Social Sciences*. Cambridge: Cambridge University Press.
Felson, M. (1985) 'Linking criminal choices, routine activities, informal control and criminal outcomes'. In D. Cornish and R. Clarke (eds) *The Reasoning Criminal* (pp. 119–128). New York: Springer.
Felson, M. and Eckert, M. (2015) *Crime and Everyday Life*. London: Sage.
Gambetta, D. (2009) *Codes of the Underworld*. Princeton, NJ: Princeton University Press.
Giddens, A. (1984) *The Constitution of Society*. Cambridge: Polity Press.
Gigerenzer, G. (2008) *Rationality for Mortals*. Oxford: Oxford University Press.
Goffman, E. (1959) *The Presentation of Self in Everyday Life*. Harmondsworth: Penguin.
Goffman, E. (1972) *Relations in Public*. Harmondsworth: Penguin.
Goldthorpe, J. (2016) *Sociology as a Population Science*. Cambridge: Cambridge University Press.
Gouldner, A. (1959) 'Reciprocity and autonomy in functional theory'. In L. Gross (ed.) *Symposium on Sociological Theory*. Evanston, IL: Row, Peterson and Company.
Gouldner, A. (1960) 'The norm of reciprocity: a preliminary statement' *American Sociological Review 25*: 161–178.
Innes. M. (2004) 'Signal crimes and signal disorders: notes on deviance as communicative action'. *British Journal of Sociology 55*(3): 335–355.
Klockars, C. (1974) *The Professional Fence*. London: Tavistock.
Lemert, E. (1951) *Social Pathology*. New York: McGraw Hill.
Lester, D. (2012) 'Suicide and opportunity: implications for the rationality of suicide'. In N. Tilley and G. Farrell (eds) *The Reasoning Criminologist: Essays in Honour of Ronald V. Clarke* (pp. 160–171). London: Routledge.
Mayhew, P., Clarke, R., Sturman, A. and Hough, M. (1976) *Crime as Opportunity*. Home Office Research Study No. 34. London: HMSO.
Merton, R. (1968) *Social Theory and Social Structure*. New York: Free Press.
Pease, K. and Laycock, G. (2012) 'Ron and the Schipol fly'. In N. Tilley and G. Farrell (eds) *The Reasoning Criminologist: Essays in Honour of Ronald V. Clarke* (pp. 172–183). London: Routledge.
Popper, K. (1967) 'La rationalité et le statut du principle de rationalité'. In E. Claassen (ed) *Les Fondements philosophiques des systemes economiques* (pp. 142–150). Paris: Payot.
Ross, L. and Nisbett, R. (2011) *The Person and the Situation*. London: Pinter & Martin.
Simmel, G. (1955) *Conflict and the Web of Group Affiliations*. New York: Free Press.
Taylor, S. (1982) *Suicide*. London: Macmillan.
Thomas, W. I. and Thomas, D. S. (1928) *The Child in America: Behavior Problems and Programs*. New York: Knopf.
Tilley, N. and Selby, J. (1976) 'An apt sociology for polytechnics'. *Higher Education Review 8*(2): 38–56.
Weber, M. (1978) *Selections in Translation* (pp. 7–32). Cambridge: Cambridge University Press.
Wilkins, L. (1964) *Social Deviance*. London: Tavistock.

5
Psychology

Richard Wortley

Psychology is 'the scientific study of the human mind and its functions, especially those affecting behaviour in a given context' (Oxford English Dictionary, n.d.). Within this definition there is considerable variation in the assumptions, interests and activities of psychologists. Some psychologists are interested in the way individuals differ from one another; others examine the basic psychological similarities within the human species. Some see deviant behaviour as an expression of psychopathology; others stress the wide range of behaviour that can occur within the spectrum of normality. Some focus on the biological bases of behaviour; some emphasise the formative role of social and environmental forces; while others examine the interplay between these two influences. Some emphasise the role in behaviour of internal psychological constructs, such as attitudes, beliefs and personality; others focus on the power of immediate circumstances to initiate and shape behaviour. Across this diversity of approaches, the ultimate goal of all psychological endeavour is to learn how to predict and change behaviour (Fishbein & Ajzen, 2010; Wortley, 2011).

The purpose of this chapter is to outline the contribution psychology can make to the prevention of criminal behaviour. Psychology plays a pivotal role in the task of prevention. All crime is the ultimately result of behaviour and all crime prevention is directed at changing that behaviour. Irrespective of what model of prevention is adopted, a fundamental requirement is an understanding of the mechanics of how humans in general, and those who commit crime in particular, operate. Three different models of crime prevention are discussed in this chapter – developmental prevention, situational prevention, and offender treatment. These three approaches involve different assumptions about the psychological bases of criminal behaviour and are directed at different stages of the offending process – pre-offending, offending and post-offending. Respectively, they address three questions: How can we prevent individuals developing criminal propensities? If individuals are about to commit a crime, how can we stop them actually doing so? And, if they do commit crime, how can we prevent them from doing it again?

Developmental crime prevention

Developmental psychology

Psychologists who study human development are interested in the orderly changes and continuities over time in an individual's physical, cognitive and psychosocial functioning.

They examine the effects of developmental experiences – parenting and disciplinary strategies, childhood neglect and abuse, family dynamics, peer relations, educational experiences and the like – on how, for example, bonds form between children and their parents or primary caregivers, how children learn to behave as autonomous individuals, and how they learn the rules and expectations of society.

Most developmental psychologists understand human development as a biosocial process, the combined result of an individual's genetic endowment and his/her life experiences (Coll, Bearer & Lerner, 2014; Manuck & McCaffery, 2014; Plomin, DeFries, Knopik & Neiderheiser, 2013; Moffitt, 2005). A biosocial perspective means more than that both genes and the environment contribute to human development (G+E); rather, genes and the environment work in concert with one another in a complex interaction (GXE). As in statistics, an interaction means that the effect of one variable depends on the effect of another; when the two variables occur together their combined effect is greater than the sum of their individual effects (see Wortley, 2012). Thus, a gene–environment interaction occurs when the same environment affects genetically different individuals in different ways. For example, a child genetically predisposed to neuroticism (anxiety, depression, etc.) may experience the divorce of his/her parents more traumatically than will a child low on neuroticism. In this way, two individuals may have similar upbringings but develop in different ways depending upon their genetic make-up.

While a great deal of attention in developmental psychology is given to the critical early years of childhood, it is generally recognised that an individual's future is not set in concrete by their childhood experiences (Baltes, Staudinger & Lindenberger, 1999; Lerner, 2002; Shonkoff & Phillips, 2000). Development continues across the lifespan – from 'womb to tomb' – and is characterised by lifelong plasticity. Throughout each period of life there are critical transition points that may lead an individual down one pathway or another according to each individual's unique biological make-up and on-going environmental experiences.

Development and criminal behaviour

Developmental psychologists seek to identify risk and protective factors along the developmental pathway that increase or decrease the risk of criminality. Factors found to increase the probability of criminality include:

- Being raised in a single-parent home (Blazei, Iaconon & McGue, 2008; Kierkus & Hewitt, 2009). However, the deleterious effects of single-parent families disappear when levels of parental involvement and supervision are controlled for (Demuth & Brown, 2004), suggesting that effective parenting is more important than family structure.
- Being subject to physical abuse, neglect, sexual abuse, and psychological abuse (Mersky & Topitzes, 2009; Ryan & Testa, 2005; Stewart, Livingston & Dennison, 2008; Widom, 2003). The effects of maltreatment may be moderated by good social support systems – close ties with siblings, involvement in sporting teams, and so on (Kruttschnitt, Ward & Sheble, 1987) – and success at school (Zingraff et al., 1994).
- Being subject to parental disciplinary styles that are either too authoritarian (Farrington, Coid & Murray, 2009; Grogan-Kaylor, 2005; Verona & Sachs-Ericsson, 2005) or too permissive (Beck & Shaw, 2005; Frick, 2006; Schaffer, Clark & Jeglic, 2009; Warr, 2005). Parental corporal punishment, in particular, is associated with increased child delinquency, antisocial behaviour and aggression (Gershoff, 2002).
- Failing at school (Loeber, Farrington, Stouthamer-Loeber & Van Kammen, 1998). Conversely, delinquency is negatively correlated with the length of time spent at school

(Harlow, 2003; Lochner & Moretti, 2004). It is thought that poor education may decrease employment opportunities, damage the individual's self-image and create a generalised expectation of failure in other areas of life, and/or inhibit the development of the attachments to social institutions.

- Having delinquent peers (Akers, Krohn, Lanza-Kaduce & Radosevich, 1979; Alarid, Burton & Cullen, 2000; Haynie, 2002). Longitudinal research suggests that delinquents tend to gravitate towards each other and in the process exacerbate each other's delinquent tendencies (Matsueda & Anderson, 1998).

The factors above relate to the likelihood of whether or not an individual will begin committing crime. But what about factors that might encourage an individual to desist from engaging in crime once they have started? One of the most robust findings in criminology is the age–crime curve. It is routinely found that the rate of offending for individuals peaks at around 17 years of age, after which it rapidly declines (Hirschi & Gottfredson, 1983). Most individuals who engage in crime during adolescence 'age out' of it by their early 20s. This pattern suggests that a great deal of crime is associated with developmental changes and social experiences specific to adolescence. These so-called adolescent-limited offenders (Moffitt, 1993) do not have a fixed propensity to commit crime, and they desist from offending as they mature and/or their life circumstances change. It has been argued that the 'adolescent brain' is characterised by neurologically based impaired behavioural regulation (greater impulsivity, risk-taking, etc.), a feature that begins to rectify in early adulthood (Beaver et al., 2008; Blonigen, 2010). This is not to say that the decline in crime cannot be hastened through social and environmental changes that provide increased structure and responsibility in an offender's life. For example, desistence has been found to correlate with offenders entering into a stable loving relationship (Sampson, Laub & Wimer, 2006). However, many researchers argue that there is a relatively small core of career criminals who defy the age–crime curve. These individuals – referred to as life course persistent offenders (Moffitt, 1993) – commit frequent offences over an extended period and possess entrenched antisocial dispositions. These offenders may be particular targets for inclusion in rehabilitation programmes, as discussed in a later section of this chapter.

Developmental crime-prevention programmes

Developmental crime prevention 'involves the use of scientific research to guide the provision of resources for individuals, families, schools or communities to address the conditions that give rise to antisocial behaviour and crime before these problems arise, or before they become entrenched' (Homel & Thomsen, 2017, p. 57). While development is conceptualised as a lifelong process, most prevention programmes have focused on early intervention. Types of intervention include support for at-risk families, educational enrichment programmes for children, and skills training for children, parents and teachers. Notable examples of early intervention programmes are:

- The *Elmira Nurse Family Partnership programme*. The programme, operating in semi-rural New York state, involved the provision of family support via home visits for at-risk expectant mothers. Four hundred teenaged pregnant women, due to be first-time mothers and who were either single or of low socio-economic status, were recruited into the study. There were two treatment groups. In one group (n=100) the mother received regular visits from a nurse during pregnancy and in the other group (n=116) the visits continued until the child's second birthday. The remaining women (n=184) were assigned to the control group and received no visits. The nurse offered advice on child-care, nutrition and healthy behaviours. At 15-years follow-up, children in the pre- and post-natal visit treatment group had lower arrest rates than those in the comparison group (Olds et al., 1998). However, in the most recent follow-up (at 19 years) lower arrest rates for that group were accounted for mainly by girls (Eckenrode et al., 2010).

- The *Perry Preschool Project*. In addition to family support the programme provided enriched early education for at-risk children. Developed in Michigan, the project involved 123 children (3–4 years old) from impoverished backgrounds who were randomly allocated to control and experimental conditions. Those in the experimental group (58) attended a daily preschool programme and received weekly home visits for a two-year period; those in the control group (65) received no intervention. Participants were followed up on numerous occasions, most recently at age 40 (Schweinhart, 2013). At each point, those in the experimental group had fewer arrests, were more likely to have graduated from high school, have better employment records, have a higher income and were more likely to own their home.
- The *Seattle Social Development Project*. The programme involved school-based training for teachers, parents and children. Unlike the two previously described programmes, delivery was broadly based rather than targeted at at-risk groups. Around 500 first grade children (6 years) from eight schools were allocated to experimental and control groups. Children in the experimental group received training in problem solving while their parents and teachers received training in effective behavioural management. Follow-up at age 18 years revealed that those in the experimental group reported less involvement in delinquency, alcohol use and risky sexual behaviours than those in the control group (Hawkins et al., 1999) and these benefits were maintained at 21 years (Hawkins et al., 2005). However, follow-up at 27 years found that differences between the two groups in crime rates and substance abuse had disappeared, although there remained significant positive effects for educational and economic attainment, and mental and sexual health (Hawkins, Kosterman, Catalano, Hill & Abbott, 2008).

Developmental crime-prevention programmes have been subject to several meta-analyses. Farrington and Welsh (2003) analysed 40 family-focused programmes (home visiting, day care and preschool programmes, parent training, school-based programmes, home and community programmes, and multi-systemic therapy) and reported overall offending rates of 0.5 for controls and 0.34 for the treatment groups (effect size d=0.32). Behavioural parent training was found to be the most effective intervention and school-based programmes the least. Manning, Homel and Smith (2010) analysed 17 studies on early intervention (preschool programmes, home visitation, family support and parental education) with at-risk populations. The effect size (d) for lower criminal justice involvement was 0.24, with positive benefits also found for educational success (0.53), lower social deviance (0.48), greater social participation (0.37) and better cognitive development (0.34). Most recently, Piquero et al. (2016) analysed 78 studies examining the effectiveness of parental training programmes. They found an overall positive effect size of 0.37 for reduced delinquency and 0.32 for improved self-control. Overall, the three meta-analyses have produced positive effect sizes in the medium range, indicating that developmental crime prevention initiatives make a modest but worthwhile contribution to the prevention of crime as well as other worthwhile outcome measures.

Situational crime prevention

The situational perspective

Developmental psychology is concerned with the acquisition of internalised propensities – albeit not necessarily fixed ones – to behave in certain ways, but it has little to say about where and when those propensities are acted upon, if at all. Situational perspectives on behaviour take us to the point at which the individual is about to act. Psychologists interested in the situational perspective examine behaviour in ecological terms, as inextricably bound to the physical and social contexts in which it occurs.

With its roots in early 20th-century behaviourism – remember Pavlov's dogs salivating to the sound of a bell? – the situational perspective was most famously brought to prominence in a seminal book by Mischel (1968). Fanning what is known as the cross–situational consistency debate, Mischel challenged the primacy in psychology accorded to dispositions. He argued that internal traits – aggression, self-confidence, conscientiousness and so on – were poor predictors of behaviour, and instead, the same individual can behave very differently across different settings. Behaviour, he argued, is situationally specific, evoked by particularities of the immediate environment. We can recognise situational variability in our own behaviour; we might be extroverted in one situation – say with our friends at the pub – and reserved in another – such as when meeting someone famous. Given this variability, Mischel argued that the idea that behaviour is caused by generalised internal traits is untenable; the key to understanding and changing behaviour is to focus on the conditions under which the behaviour is performed.

As is often the case with debates, a compromise position on the respective roles of dispositions and situations has emerged (Kahle, 1984; Mischel, 2004; Mischel & Shoda, 1995: Ross & Nisbett, 2011). Psychometric research shows that the correlation between personality traits and their behavioural expression is typically of the order of 0.4. (e.g. Nisbett, 1980). This is a non-trivial level of association that suggests that traits do play a meaningful role in behaviour, while the unexplained variance supports a role for situational factors. While individuals do possess traits, those traits are expressed under certain prescribed conditions. It follows, too, that the effect of the situation on behaviour depends upon the traits a person possesses; that is, different individuals may react differently to the same situation. In short, behaviour occurs as the result of a person–situation interaction (see Wortley, 2012). This is a parallel process to the gene–environment interaction described earlier, but occurring at a later stage in the behavioural process. Gene–environment interactions determine the nature of one's internalised predispositions; person–situation interactions determine the behavioural expression (or not) of these predispositions. A particular behaviour is most likely to occur when an individual strongly predisposed to that behaviour enters a situation with strong activating properties for that behaviour.

Crime and the immediate environment

As should be clear from the above discussion, developmental and situational perspectives focus on different psychological phenomena. Developmental approaches – and indeed most traditional psychological (and criminological) accounts of offenders – are theories of criminality. They explain the acquisition of personal characteristics that purportedly distinguish offenders from non-offenders. In contrast, situational approaches are theories of criminal behaviour. While not denying that dispositions may play a role in crime, psychologists interested in the role of situations are concerned with the conditions that facilitate the carrying out of criminal acts.

Situational factors are an inescapable component of every crime. They determine why offenders commit their crimes when and where they do.

One implication of the situational perspective is that the population cannot be neatly divided into criminals and non-criminals. While those with entrenched criminal predispositions are likely to commit more crime than those without, given the right circumstances most people are capable of crime. A number of classic experiments support the idea that situations can induce otherwise good people to do bad things: a phenomenon Zimbardo (2007) has called the Lucifer Effect. In the famous Stanford prison experiment (Haney, Banks & Zimbardo, 1973; Zimbardo, 2007), college students randomly allocated to the role of guards in a mock prison quickly became brutal and authoritarian towards those allocated to prisoner roles. In the equally notorious obedience to authority studies (Milgram, 1974), the authority exuded by the experimenter induced nearly two-thirds of the participants to deliver what they believed to be life-threatening electric shocks to a confederate participant who was purportedly being punished for giving incorrect answers.

At the same time, even determined 'careers criminals' do not commit crimes indiscriminately but use situational data to select the most likely targets. For example, Bennett and Wright (1984) interviewed 316 persistent burglars and showed them videos and photographs of prospective targets. Burglars fell into three categories: opportunists (7 per cent), unskilled burglars who committed burglaries more-or-less on the spur of the moment; planners (10 per cent), highly skilled burglars who informed themselves in advance about the properties that they wanted to burgle; and searchers (76 per cent), burglars with mid-range skills who scanned houses sequentially until they encountered a suitable target. All groups, but 'searchers' in particular, looked for visual cues when selecting a target that indicated whether the house was likely to contain valuable goods, whether the house was occupied, whether they could burgle the house without being observed, whether there was easy accessibility, and whether there were security measures in place.

The usual account in criminology of the mechanisms by which situations affect the behaviour of offenders is the rational choice perspective (Clarke & Cornish, 1985), an adaptation of rational choice theory from economics and cognitive psychology (Becker, 1957; Kahneman & Tversky, 1973; Simon, 1983). According to the rational choice perspective, potential offenders are active decision-makers who weigh up the anticipated costs and benefits of contemplated crimes, as illustrated by our burglars described above. Potential offenders will desist from committing a particular crime if they judge the risks and effort too great and the rewards too little.

However, rational choice is just one of many ways that the relationship between behaviour and the immediate environment can be understood. Notwithstanding the dispositional bias in psychology, there is also a long history of situationalism, notably in learning theory, cognitive psychology and social psychology. Rational choice has been criticised as providing too narrow and crude an explanation of the person–situation interaction (Ekblom, 2007; Laycock & Pease, 2012; Nee & Ward, 2014; Sidebottom & Tilley, 2017; van Gelder, Elffers, Reynald & Nagin, 2014; Wortley, 1997, 2001, 2012, 2013, 2017; Wortley & Tilley, 2018). Taking in the broader sweep of psychology, the interaction between the individual and the immediate environment is shown to involve more than conscious cognitive processes. Situations also affect an individual's desires, beliefs, emotions and moral judgements. Further, the effects may be subtle, below the level of conscious awareness, automatic, and outside the individual's personal control. Individuals do not necessarily enter situations with a pre-formed intention to offend; situations can precipitate criminal behaviour by creating, triggering or intensifying the motivation to offend (Wortley, 1997, 2001, 2017).

Implementing situational crime prevention

Situational crime prevention (SCP) 'seeks to alter the situational determinants of crime so as to make crime less likely to happen' (Clarke, 2017, p. 286). Human beings have always practised SCP by building walls around their townships, fitting their homes with lockable doors, hiding their valuables, and so on. Clarke (1992, 1997; Cornish & Clarke, 2003) systematised these intuitive impulses to protect one's self, family, friends and valuables into a comprehensive taxonomy of 25 SCP techniques. In the latest version of the taxonomy (Cornish & Clarke, 2003), five broad prevention strategies are listed – increasing the effort, increasing the risk, reducing rewards, reducing provocations, and removing excuses – with five more specific techniques given for each.

There are many examples of successful interventions that might be cited to illustrate the application of SCP. Perhaps the most powerful demonstration from a psychological point of view – albeit one that was not primarily implemented on crime prevention grounds – is described in Clarke and Mayhew's (1988) British Gas Suicide Story. Clarke and Mayhew examined suicide rates in Britain over a 20-year period. In 1958 there were 5,298 suicides, around 40 per cent of which were achieved using domestic gas. By 1977 suicides had fallen to 3,944, only two of which involved gassing. Over the same period Britain had progressively switched from coal gas, which contains lethal carbon monoxide, to natural gas, which is non-toxic. The drop in suicides almost perfectly tracked the drop in the percentage of carbon monoxide in the domestic gas supply. Gassing is a relatively convenient and easy method of suicide, requiring little in the way of skill or planning. We can only imagine the desperation that might drive someone to contemplate suicide. And yet it seems that many potential suicide victims who might have selected gassing as their method of choice, abandoned their suicide attempt when that option was denied rather than seek out other less convenient methods.

SCP is being applied to an ever-increasing range of crimes, including organised crime (Bullock, Clarke & Tilley, 2010), cybercrime (Holt & Bossler, 2015; McNally & Newman, 2007; Newman & Clarke, 2003), child sexual abuse (Wortley & Smallbone, 2006, 2012), wildlife poaching (Lemieu, 2014; Moreto & Clarke, 2013), and terrorism and insurgency (Braithwaite & Johnson, 2012; Freilich & Newman, 2009; Newman & Clarke, 2006; Townsley, Johnson & Ratcliffe, 2008). Clarke (1992, 1997) has published two collections of successful case studies in SCP. There has also been a number of meta-analyses and systematic reviews of specific SCP techniques that attest to the efficacy of the approach. (See a comprehensive catalogue of technique-specific reviews – not all of them involving SCP – on the What Works in Crime Prevention website hosted by the College of Policing.) To take just one example, Welsh and Farrington (2009) examined the effectiveness of CCTV in reducing crime, finding a 51 per cent reduction in car parks, 23 per cent reduction on public transport, a 7 per cent reduction in town centres and public housing estates, and a 16 per cent reduction in crime overall. Finally, Guerette and Bowers (2009) examined the extent to which situational interventions led to crime displacement, that is, merely pushed crime to different times and places, or encouraged offenders to adopt different criminal strategies or behaviours, as would be expected if crime were simply the expression of criminal disposition unaffected by situational forces. They found that in 26 per cent of cases some displacement was reported, but that this was more than offset by diffusion of benefits – i.e. crime prevention gains in areas not included in the study area – in 27 per cent of cases. The accumulating empirical evidence for the effectiveness of SCP has led Clarke (2017, p. 301) to claim it as 'the fastest growing form of crime control worldwide'.

Offender treatment and rehabilitation

Psychotherapy

Situational and developmental approaches are examples of primary and secondary prevention – they involve measures applied to the general population or directed at at-risk groups designed to prevent problems occurring before they emerge. Psychotherapy on the other hand is about repairing damage once it becomes evident, and thus falls into the category of tertiary prevention. There are as many treatment approaches as there are psychological theories. The American Psychological Association (n.d.) lists five broad categories of psychotherapy – psychodynamic, behavioural, cognitive, humanistic, and integrative (or holistic) – within each of which there are numerous variations. While these approaches vary widely in their practices and underlying assumptions, they are all concerned – like developmental prevention and in contrast to situational prevention – with changing the individual in some fundamental way.

Perhaps the most widely practised and empirically supported model of psychological treatment today is cognitive behavioural therapy (CBT), and a description of it here will serve for illustrative purposes. As the name suggests, CBT sits at the intersection of behavioural and cognitive therapies (Butler, Chapman, Forman & Beck, 2006; Craske, 2010; Meichenbaum, Carlson & Kjos, 2001). The underpinning rationale of CBT is that problem behaviour occurs as a result of faulty thinking patterns. Put another way, it is not events per se that cause distress or maladaptive behaviour, but how the individual perceives, interprets and responds to those events. Therapists identify and challenge cognitive distortions and help the client replace them with more realistic and adaptive thought processes. For example, a client suffering depression may exhibit 'catastrophising' thought patterns, that is, the tendency to exaggerate the negative consequences of life's setbacks ('If this happens my life will be over'). With the aid of the therapist, the client learns to routinely self-question the veracity of such thoughts as they occur and to develop more effective thinking habits ('This is not what I wanted to happen but it is not a catastrophe').

With its behavioural heritage, CBT more so than most alternative therapies focuses on the immediate contexts of behaviour. In contrast to psychodynamic approaches in particular, little attention is paid to the historical causes of the client's problem. Cognitive behavioural therapists generally take the view that knowing the 'root causes' of a problem is unnecessary for the formulation of therapeutic responses while client 'insight' for its own sake is seen to be of little value. The focus of CBT is very much on coping in the here-and-now. In addition to cognitive restructuring described above, therapy may include behaviourally oriented activities, for example, where the client imitates and practises appropriate responses. One strategy – known as stimulus control - involves helping the client identify and avoid situations that might trigger maladaptive behaviour. For example, a client wanting to lose weight might be instructed to make sure all food is put away in cupboards and not left out on display where it might offer temptation. Stimulus control is, in effect, a personally tailored and self-monitored situational prevention strategy.

Treating offenders

The provision of psychotherapy to offenders is based on the rationale that criminal behaviour is the result of personal deficits that can be rectified such that offenders may be rehabilitated and so not reoffend. Offender rehabilitation has had a chequered history (see Cullen, 2012; Phelps, 2011). Arguably the heyday of the rehabilitation ideal was the 1960s and early 1970s. Then in

1974, Robert Martinson conducted a review of 231 prison rehabilitation programmes, covering 1945 to1967, from which he concluded that 'nothing works' (Martinson, 1974). This study proved to be very influential in setting correctional policy, and helped lay the ground work for the 'get tough' era in crime control that was to follow. However, it also caused researchers to take a more critical approach to what passed for rehabilitation. It was argued that the reason Martinson failed to find significant treatment effects was that most of the programmes he examined were poorly conceptualised and administered (e.g. Gendreau & Ross, 1979, 1987). His review spurred a more rigorous, theoretically informed and evidenced-based approach to rehabilitation.

Offender treatment programmes have benefited from the general developments in psychological theory and treatment technologies since Martinson's review. The emergence of CBT, for example, post-dates Martinson. Equally important has been the attention given to developing overarching principles to guide how treatment programmes, of whatever theoretical orientation, ought to be delivered in a correctional environment. The best-known offender service delivery framework is the Risk-Needs-Responsivity (RNR) model (Andrews & Bonta, 2000; Andrews, Bonta & Hoge, 1990; Day & Howells, 2002; Ogloff & Davis, 2004). The model emphasises matching intervention intensity to the level of risk, and targeting those risk factors that are dynamic (as opposed to static) and have been empirically found to increase (re) offending. According to the risk principle, those who are at highest risk are also those in highest need of intensive intervention. According to the needs principle, intervention must focus on those deficits that are demonstrably associated with criminal behaviour and that are amenable to change. According to the responsivity principle, the intervention must be matched to the offender's learning style, motivation and other personal circumstances that might enhance or get in the way of treatment.

Evaluation of offender rehabilitation

While the enthusiasm for rehabilitation has not returned to the pre-Martinson level, to varying extents most Western correctional systems do provide some access to treatment programmes, especially those targeted at high-risk sex and violent offenders (Cullen, 2012; Gendreau & Ross, 1979; Heseltine, Day & Sarre, 2009; Phelps, 2011). There is an extensive body of research on treatment effectiveness, with studies conveniently summarised in numerous systematic reviews and meta-analyses. Evidence for the effectiveness of offender treatment is mixed, with reductions in recidivism for those receiving treatment ranging from effectively zero (Schwalbe et al., 2012) to around 25 per cent (Landenberger & Lipsey, 2005). On balance, results suggest modest reductions in recidivism for participating offenders. As expanded upon below, the effectiveness of treatment can vary according to intervention type, offence type and offender characteristics.

With respect to intervention type, CBT has become the dominant (though by no means exclusive) therapeutic model for use with offenders. Meta-analyses indicate that CBT is moderately successful in reducing reoffending (Landenberger & Lipsey, 2005; Tong & Farrington, 2006; Wilson, Bouffard & MacKenzie, 2005). For example, Landenberger and Lipsey (2005) examined 58 studies involving CBT with both juvenile and adult offenders. They reported an overall reduction in reoffending of 25 per cent in comparison to controls (0.3 versus 0.4). Where studies have directly compared CBT with other treatment models, CBT is generally found to be superior (De Swart et al., 2012; Koehler, Lösel, Akoensi & Humphreys, 2013). For example, Koehler et al. (2013) examined 25 studies involving young offenders who received CBT, intensive supervision, or training programmes (e.g. education and vocational skills);

only CBT produced significant reductions in reoffending (13 per cent). That is not to say that reductions in reoffending have not been reported for other intervention types. Family treatment (Baldwin, Christian & Berkeljon, 2012; Schwalbe et al., 2012), multi-systemic therapy (Kim, Benekos & Merlo, 2016; van der Stouwe et al., 2014), aftercare (James et al., 2013) and adventure therapy (Bowen & Neill, 2013) have also produced small but significant reductions in reoffending.

Where studies specify offence type, sex offending is the most commonly examined (Hanson, Bourgon, Helmus & Hodgson, 2009; Kim, Benekos & Merlo, 2016; Långström et al., 2013). In the most recent study, Kim et al. (2016) synthesised findings from the five most recent meta-analyses and concluded that offender treatment resulted in a 22 per cent reduction in sexual reoffending. In studies of other specific offences, small positive effects have been reported for substance abusers (Baldwin, Christian, Berkeljon & Shadish, 2012) while no positive treatment effects were found for domestic assaulters (Arias, Arce & Vilariño, 2013).

Finally, studies examining the moderating effects of offender characteristics are generally characterised by inconsistent findings. Van der Stouwe et al. (2014) found treatment effects were greater for youths under 15 years; James et al. (2013) found greater effects for older youths; while De Swart et al. (2012) found no effect for age. Some studies have found that there are greater treatment gains with high-risk offenders (James et al., 2013; van der Stouwe et al., 2014) while others have reported better results for low-risk offenders (Tong & Farrington, 2016). De Swart et al. (2012) found no effect for gender.

Conclusion

The contribution that psychology makes to crime prevention is to provide agent-level models of behaviour and behaviour change. Psychology is not just a useful discipline for the crime prevention task; it is a necessary one. Irrespective of what crime prevention approach one adopts, it must be built on a sound, empirically based, theoretical understanding of how human beings function at an individual level. Ultimately, the interventions and strategies that comprise the crime prevention arsenal will only prove to be effective if they neutralise the drivers for individuals to commit crime.

This chapter has focused exclusively on offenders. But the scope of the chapter could have been much broader. Offenders are not the only individuals who are involved in crime events. Most crimes also involve a human victim and, in many cases, a potential guardian who might have intervened to deter the offender (Cohen & Felson, 1979). Thus, I might also have examined prevention programmes aimed at changing the behaviour of potential victims in ways that reduce their vulnerability (e.g. Walsh, Zwi, Woolfenden & Shlonsky, 2015), as well as efforts to encourage bystanders, home owners and facility managers to take crime-inhibiting actions (e.g. Reynald, 2011). Further, if one takes the view that a fair and efficient criminal justice system is an indispensable component of crime prevention, then the voluminous psychological literature on the behaviour and decision-making processes of police, crime witnesses, forensic scientists, judges, juries, prison officers and community corrections officers might also have been covered (e.g. Howitt, 2015). In the end, the decision to focus solely on offenders and potential offenders was made on pragmatic grounds to make the task manageable.

Three models of crime prevention were examined – developmental, situational, and therapeutic. Across the three models, a common theme was the interactive relationship between the forces that shape human behaviour. The age-old debate about whether behaviour is the result of nature or nurture – the person or the environment – is obsolete. It is abundantly clear that the person and the environment are inextricably bound in a complex interplay. We saw this operating for each of the three prevention models. The effects of developmental experiences on the acquisition of internalised dispositions will depend upon the genetic profile of the person. The impact of immediate environment on the performance of behaviour will depend upon the personal characteristics the individual brings into the situation. And the effectiveness of treatment interventions will depend upon the particular needs and responsivity of the individual offender. In short, what works to prevent crime for some people will not work for others.

Evidence was presented that each of these models could claim success in reducing offending. Of the three models, situational prevention is undoubtedly the dominant approach in crime science. The development of crime science has been strongly influenced by its environmental criminology heritage (see Wortley, Sidebottom, Tilley & Laycock, this volume). In environmental criminology the central unit of analysis is the crime event and the key to preventing crime is to analyse and change the situational determinants of criminal behaviour. Accordingly, crime science, too, tends to emphasise the proximal rather than distal causes of crime and to adopt situational crime prevention as the primary model for affecting change. But there is nothing in the definition of crime science that necessarily precludes developmental and therapeutic interventions (nor indeed other models of prevention not mentioned here). The only requirement from the crime science perspective is that the intervention demonstrably reduces crime. On that score, situational prevention is prioritised on empirical and logistical grounds, rather than as a matter of theory, as providing the 'biggest bang for the buck'. Of the three models, situational prevention offers the most direct, immediate and doable strategies for reducing crime, ones that do not depend upon knowing who the offender or potential offender is (an increasing issue as cybercrime increases). Moreover, situational prevention is scalable in a way that developmental and therapeutic interventions are not. The introduction of improved car security in the 1990s, for example, has led to a worldwide plunge in car theft (Farrell, Tilley, Tseloni & Mailley, 2011). Situational prevention targets the 'low-hanging fruit' and there remains plenty of low-hanging fruit to be had. That said, all successful approaches to reduce crime should be welcomed.

References

Akers, R. L., Krohn, M. D., Lanza-Kaduce, L. & Radosevich, M. (1979) 'Social learning and deviant behavior: a specific test of a general theory', *American Sociological Review, 44*: 636–655.

Alarid, L. F., Burton, V. S., Jr. & Cullen, F. T. (2000) 'Gender and crime among felony offenders: assessing the generality of social control and differential association theories', *Journal of Research in Crime and Delinquency, 37*: 171–199.

American Psychological Association (n.d.) 'Different approaches to psychotherapy'. www.apa.org/topics/therapy/psychotherapy-approaches.aspx.

Andrews, D. A., Bonta, J. & Hoge, R. D. (1990) 'Classification for effective rehabilitation: rediscovering psychology', *Criminal Justice and Behavior, 17*(1): 19–52.

Andrews, D. A., Bonta, J. & Wormith, S. J. (2000) *Level of Service/Case Management Inventory: LS/CMI.* Toronto, ONT: Multi-Health Systems.

Arias, E., Arce, R. & Vilariño, M. (2013) 'Batterer intervention programmes: a meta-analytic review of effectiveness', *Psychosocial Intervention, 22*(2): 153–160.

Baldwin, S. A., Christian, S., Berkeljon, A. & Shadish, W. R. (2012) 'The effects of family therapies for adolescent delinquency and substance abuse: a meta-analysis', *Journal of Marital and Family Therapy, 38*(1): 281–304.

Baltes, P. B., Staudinger, U. M. & Lindenberger, U. (1999) 'Lifespan psychology: theory and application to intellectual functioning', *Annual Review Psychology, 50*: 471–507.

Beaver, K. M., Wright, J. P., DeLisi, M. & Vaughan, M. G. (2008) 'Genetic influences on the stability of low self-control: results from a longitudinal sample of twins', *Journal of Criminal Justice, 36*: 478–485.

Beck, J. E. & Shaw, D. S. (2005) 'The influence of perinatal complications and environmental adversity on boys' antisocial behavior', *Journal of Child Psychology and Psychiatry, 46*: 35–46.

Becker, G. (1957) *The Economics of Discrimination*. Chicago, IL: University of Chicago Press.
Bennett, T. & Wright, R. (1984) *Burglars on Burglary: Prevention and the Offender*. Hampshire, UK: Gower.
Blazei, R. W., Iacono, W. G. & McGue, M. (2008) 'Father–child transmission of antisocial behavior: the moderating role of father's presence in the home', *American Academy of Child and Adolescent Psychiatry, 47*: 406–415.
Blonigen, D. M. (2010) 'Explaining the relationship between age and crime: contributions from the developmental literature on personality', *Clinical Psychology Review, 30*: 89–100.
Bowen, D. J. & Neill, J. T. (2013) 'A meta-analysis of adventure therapy outcomes and moderators', *The Open Psychology Journal, 6*(1): 28–53.
Braithwaite, A. & Johnson, S. D. (2012) 'Space–time modeling of insurgency and counterinsurgency in Iraq', *Journal of Quantitative Criminology, 28*(1): 31–48.
Bullock, K., Clarke, R. V. & Tilley, N. (eds) (2010) *Situational Crime Prevention of Organised Crimes*. Cullompton, UK: Willan.
Butler, A. C., Chapman, J. E., Forman, E. M. & Beck, A. T. (2006) 'The empirical status of cognitive-behavioral therapy: a review of meta-analyses', *Clinical Psychology Review, 26*(1): 17–31.
Clarke, R. V. (1992) 'Introduction'. In R. V. Clarke (ed.) *Situational Crime Prevention: Successful Case Studies*. Albany, NY: Harrow and Heston.
Clarke, R. V. (1997) 'Introduction'. In R. V. Clarke (ed.) *Situational Crime Prevention: Successful Case Studies* (2nd ed.). Albany, NY: Harrow and Heston.
Clarke, R. V. (2017) 'Situational crime prevention'. In R. Wortley & M. Townsley (eds). *Environmental Criminology and Crime Analysis* (2nd ed.). London: Routledge.
Clarke, R. V. & Cornish, D. B. (1985) 'Modeling offenders' decisions: a framework for research and policy'. In M. Tonry & N. Morris (eds) *Crime and Justice: An Annual Review of Research, Volume 6*. Chicago IL: University of Chicago Press.
Clarke, R. V. & Mayhew, P. (1988) 'The British gas suicide story and its criminological implications', in M. Tonry & N. Morris (eds) *Crime and Justice, Volume 10*. Chicago, IL: University of Chicago Press.
Cohen, L. E. & Felson, M. (1979) 'Social change and crime rate trends: a routine activity approach', *American Sociological Review, 44*: 588–608.
Coll, C. G., Bearer, E. L. & Lerner, R. M. (eds). (2014) *Nature and Nurture: The Complex Interplay of Genetic and Environmental Influences on Human Behavior and Development*. New York: Psychology Press.
College of Policing (n.d.) *What Works Crime Reduction: The Crime Reduction Toolkit*. http://whatworks.college.police.uk/toolkit/Pages/Toolkit.aspx.
Cornish, D. B. & Clarke, R. V. (2003) 'Opportunities, precipitators and criminal decisions: a reply to Wortley's critique of situational crime prevention'. In M. Smith & D. Cornish (eds) *Theory for Practice in Situational Crime Prevention, Crime Prevention Studies, Volume 6*. Monsey, NY: Criminal Justice Press.
Craske, M. G. (2010) *Cognitive-Behavioral Therapy*. Washington, DC: American Psychological Association.
Cullen, F. T. (2012) 'Taking rehabilitation seriously: creativity, science, and the challenge of offender change', *Punishment & Society, 14*(1): 94–114.
Day, A. & Howells, K. (2002) 'Psychological treatments for rehabilitating offenders: evidence-based practice comes of age', *Australian Psychologist, 37*(1): 39–47.
Demuth, S. & Brown, S. L. (2004) 'Family structure, family processes, and adolescent delinquency: the significance of parental absence versus parental gender', *Journal of Research in Crime and Delinquency, 41*: 58–81.
De Swart, J. J. W., van den Broek, H., Stams, G. J. J. M., Asscher, J. J., Van der Laan, P. H., Holsbrink-Engels, G. A. & Van der Helm, G. H. P. (2012) 'The effectiveness of institutional youth care over the past three decades: a meta-analysis', *Children and Youth Services Review, 34*(9): 1818–1824.
Eckenrode, J., Campa, M., Luckey, D. W., Henderson, C. R., Cole, R., Kitzman, H. & Olds, D. (2010) 'Long-term effects of prenatal and infancy nurse home visitation on the life course of youths: 19-year follow-up of a randomized trial'. *Archives of Pediatrics & Adolescent Medicine, 164*(1): 9–15.
Ekblom, P. (2007) 'Making offenders richer', in G. Farrell, K. Bowers, S. Johnson & M. Townsley (ed.) *Imagination for Crime Prevention: Essays in Honour of Ken Pease. Crime Prevention Studies 21*. Monsey, NY: Criminal Justice Press/ Devon, UK: Willan Publishing.
Farrell, G., Tseloni, A., Mailley, J. & Tilley, N. (2011) 'The crime drop and the security hypothesis', *Journal of Research in Crime and Delinquency, 48*(2): 147–175.
Farrington, D. P., Coid, J. W. & Murray, J. (2009) 'Family factors in the intergenerational transmission of offending', *Criminal Behaviour and Mental Health, 19*: 109–124.

Farrington, D. P. & Welsh, B. C. (2003) 'Family-based prevention of offending: a meta-analysis', *Australian & New Zealand Journal of Criminology, 36*(2): 127–151.

Fishbein, M. & Ajzen, I. (2010) *Predicting and Changing Behavior: The Reasoned Action Approach*. New York: Psychology Press.

Freilich, J. D. & Newman, G. R. (eds) (2009) *Reducing Terrorism through Situational Crime Prevention: Crime Prevention Studies, Volume 25*. Monsey, NY: Criminal Justice Press.

Frick, P. J. (2006) 'Developmental pathways to conduct disorder', *Child and Adolescent Psychiatric Clinics of North America, 15*: 311–331.

Gendreau, P. & Ross, B. (1979) 'Effective correctional treatment: bibliotherapy for cynics'. *Crime & Delinquency, 25*(4): 463–489.

Gendreau, P. & Ross, R. R. (1987) 'Revivification of rehabilitation: evidence from the 1980s', *Justice Quarterly, 4*(3): 349–407.

Gershoff, E. T. (2002) 'Corporal punishment by parents and associated child behaviors and experiences: a meta-analytic and theoretical review', *Psychological Bulletin, 128*: 539–579.

Grogan-Kaylor, A. (2005) 'Corporal punishment and the growth trajectory of children's anti-social behavior', *Child Maltreatment, 10*: 283–292.

Guerette, R. T. & Bowers, K. J. (2009) 'Assessing the extent of crime displacement and diffusion of benefits: A review of situational crime prevention evaluations', *Criminology*, 47(4): 1331–1368.

Haney, C., Banks, C. & Zimbardo, P. (1973) 'Interpersonal dynamics in a simulated prison', *International Journal of Criminology and Penology, 1*: 69–97.

Hanson, R. K., Bourgon, G., Helmus, L. & Hodgson, S. (2009) 'The principles of effective correctional treatment also apply to sexual offenders: a meta-analysis', *Criminal Justice and Behavior, 36*(9): 865–891.

Harlow, C. W. (2003) *Education and Correctional Populations. Bureau of Justice Statistics Special Report, NCJ 195670*. Washington, DC: US Department of Justice.

Hawkins, D. J., Catalano, R., Kosterman, R., Abbot, R. & Hill, K. (1999) 'Preventing adolescent health-risk behaviours by strengthening protection during childhood', *Archives of Pediatrics and Adolescent Medicine, 153*: 226–234.

Hawkins, J. D., Kosterman, R., Catalano, R. F., Hill, K. G. & Abbott, R. D. (2005) 'Promoting positive adult functioning through social development intervention in childhood: long-term effects from the Seattle Social Development Project', *Archives of Pediatrics & Adolescent Medicine, 159*(1): 25–31.

Hawkins, J. D., Kosterman, R., Catalano, R. F., Hill, K. G. & Abbott, R. D. (2008) 'Effects of social development intervention in childhood 15 years later', *Archives of Pediatrics & Adolescent Medicine, 162*(12): 1133–1141.

Haynie, D. L. (2002) 'Friendship networks and delinquency: the relative nature of peer delinquency', *Journal of Quantitative Criminology, 18*: 99–134.

Heseltine, K., Sarre, R. & Day, A. (2009). 2011. *Prison-based Correctional Offender Rehabilitation Programs: The 2009 National Picture in Australia*. Canberra: AIC

Hirschi, T. & Gottfredson, M.R. (1983) 'Age and the explanation of crime', *American Journal of Sociology, 89*: 552–584.

Holt, T. J. & Bossler, A. M. (2015) *Cybercrime in Progress: Theory and Prevention of Technology-Enabled Offenses*. Abingdon, UK: Routledge.

Homel, R. & Thomsen, L. (2017) 'Developmental crime prevention'. In N. Tilley & A. Sidebottom (eds) *Handbook of Crime Prevention and Community Safety*. London: Routledge.

Howitt, D. (2015) *Introduction to Forensic and Criminal Psychology* (5th ed.). Harlow, UK: Pearson.

James, C., Stams, G. J. J., Asscher, J. J., De Roo, A. K. & van der Laan, P. H. (2013) 'Aftercare programs for reducing recidivism among juvenile and young adult offenders: a meta-analytic review', *Clinical Psychology Review, 33*(2): 263–274.

Kahle, L. R. (1984) *Attitudes and Social Adaptation: A Person–Situation Interaction Approach*. New York: Pergamon Press.

Kahneman, D. & Tversky, A. (1973) 'On the psychology of prediction', *Psychological Review, 80*: 237–251.

Kierkus, C. A. & Hewitt, J. D. (2009) 'The contextual nature of the family structure/delinquency relationship', *Journal of Criminal Justice, 37*: 123–132.

Kim, B., Benekos, P. J. & Merlo, A. V. (2016) 'Sex offender recidivism revisited: review of recent meta-analyses on the effects of sex offender treatment', *Trauma, Violence, & Abuse, 17*(1): 105–117.

Koehler, J. A., Lösel, F., Akoensi, T. D. & Humphreys, D. K. (2013) 'A systematic review and meta-analysis on the effects of young offender treatment programs in Europe', *Journal of Experimental Criminology, 9*(1): 19–43.

Kruttschnitt, C., Ward, D. & Sheble, M. A. (1987) 'Abuse-resistant youth: some factors that may inhibit violent criminal behavior', *Social Forces*, *66*: 501–519.

Landenberger, N. A. & Lipsey, M. W. (2005) 'The positive effects of cognitive-behavioral programs for offenders: a meta-analysis of factors associated with effective treatment', *Journal of Experimental Criminology*, *1*(4): 451–476.

Långström, N., Enebrink, P., Laurén, E. M., Lindblom, J., Werkö, S. & Hanson, R. K. (2013) 'Preventing sexual abusers of children from reoffending: systematic review of medical and psychological interventions', *BMJ*, *347*, f4630.

Laycock, G. & Pease, K. (2012) 'Ron and the Schiphol fly'. In N. Tilley & G. Farrell (eds) *The Reasoning Criminologist: Essays in Honour of Ronald V. Clarke*, London: Routledge.

Lemieux, A. M. (ed.) (2014) *Situational Prevention of Poaching*. Abingdon, UK: Routledge.

Lerner, R. M. (2002) *Concepts and Theories of Human Development*. Mahwah, NJ: Lawrence Erlbaum Associates.

Lochner, L. & Moretti, E. (2004) 'The effect of education on crime: evidence from prison inmates, arrests, and self-report', *The American Economic Review*, *94*: 155–189.

Loeber, R., Farrington, D. P., Stouthamer-Loeber, M. & Van Kammen, W. B. (1998) *Antisocial Behavior and Mental Health Problems: Explanatory Factors in Childhood and Adolescence*. Mahwah, NJ: Lawrence Erlbaum Associates.

Manning, M., Homel, R. & Smith, C. (2010) 'A meta-analysis of the effects of early developmental prevention programs in at-risk populations on non-health outcomes in adolescence', *Children and Youth Services Review*, *32*(4): 506–519.

Manuck, S. B. & McCaffery, J. M. (2014) 'Gene-environment interaction', *Annual Review of Psychology*, *65*: 41–70.

Martinson, R. (1974) 'What works? Questions and answers about prison reform', *The Public Interest*, *35*: 22–54.

Matsueda, R. L. & Anderson, K. (1998) 'The dynamics of delinquent peers and delinquent behavior', *Criminology*, *36*: 269–308.

McNally, M. M. & Newman, G. R. (eds) (2007) *Perspectives on Identity Theft. Crime Prevention Studies*, Volume *23*. Monsey, NY: Criminal Justice Press.

Meichenbaum, D., Carlson, J. & Kjos, D. (2001) *Cognitive-Behavioral Therapy*. Mill Valley, CA: Psychotherapy.net.

Mersky, J. P. & Topitzes, J. (2009) 'Comparing early adult outcomes of maltreated and non-maltreated children: a prospective longitudinal investigation', *Children and Youth Services Review*, *32*: 1086–1096.

Milgram, S. (1974) *Obedience to Authority: An Experimental View*. New York: Harper and Row.

Mischel, W. (1968) *Personality and Assessment*. New York: Wiley.

Mischel, W. (2004) 'Toward an integrative science of the person', *Annual Review of Psychology*, *55*: 1–22.

Mischel, W. & Shoda, Y. (1995) 'A cognitive-affective system theory of personality: reconceptualizing situations, dispositions, dynamics, and invariance in personality structure', *Psychological Review*, *102*: 246.

Moffitt, T. E. (2005) 'The new look of behavioral genetics in developmental psychopathology: gene-environment interplay in antisocial behaviors', *Psychological Bulletin*, *131*: 533–554.

Moreto, W. D. & Clarke, R. V. (2013) 'Script analysis of the transnational illegal market in endangered species: dream and reality'. In B. Leclerc & R. Wortley (eds) *Cognition and Crime: Offender Decision-Making and Script Analyses*. London: Routledge.

Nee, C. & Ward, T. (2014) 'Review of expertise and its general implications for correctional psychology and criminology', *Aggression and Violent Behavior*, *20*: 1–9.

Newman, G. R. & Clarke, R. V. (2003) *Superhighway Robbery: Preventing E-commerce Crime*. Cullompton, UK: Willan Publishing.

Nisbett, R. E. (1980) 'The trait construct in lay and professional psychology', in L. Festinger (ed) *Retrospections on Social Psychology*. New York: Oxford University Press.

Ogloff, J. R. & Davis, M. R. (2004) 'Advances in offender assessment and rehabilitation: contributions of the risk–needs–responsivity approach', *Psychology, Crime & Law*, *10*(3): 229–242.

Olds, D., Henderson Jr, C. R., Cole, R., Eckenrode, J., Kitzman, H., Luckey, D. and Powers, J. (1998) 'Long-term effects of nurse home visitation on children's criminal and antisocial behavior: 15-year follow-up of a randomized controlled trial', *JAMA*, *280*(14): 1238–1244.

Oxford English Dictionary. Online version. https://en.oxforddictionaries.com/definition/psychology.

Phelps, M. S. (2011) 'Rehabilitation in the punitive era: the gap between rhetoric and reality in US prison programs', *Law & Society Review*, *45*(1): 33–68.

Piquero, A. R., Jennings, W. G., Diamond, B., Farrington, D. P., Tremblay, R. E., Welsh, B. C. & Gonzalez, J. M. R. (2016) 'A meta-analysis update on the effects of early family/parent training programs on antisocial behavior and delinquency', *Journal of Experimental Criminology, 12*(2): 229–248.

Plomin, R., DeFries, J. C., Knopik, V. S. & Neiderheiser, J. (2013) *Behavioral Genetics* (6th ed). New York: Worth Publishers.

Reynald, D. M. (2011) *Guarding Against Crime: Measuring Guardianship within Routine Activity Theory*. Farnham, UK: Ashgate Publishing, Ltd.

Ross, L. & Nisbett, R. E. (2011) *The Person and the Situation: Perspectives of Social Psychology*. London: Pinter & Martin Publishers.

Ryan, J. P. & Testa, M. F. (2005) 'Child maltreatment and juvenile delinquency: investigating the role of placement and placement instability', *Children and Youth Services Review, 27*: 227–249.

Sampson, R. J., Laub, J. H. & Wimer, C. (2006) 'Does marriage reduce crime? A counterfactual approach to within individual causal effects', *Criminology, 44*: 465–508.

Schaffer, M., Clark, S. & Jeglic, E. L. (2009) 'The role of empathy and parenting style in the development of antisocial behaviors', *Crime and Delinquency, 55*: 586–599.

Schwalbe, C. S., Gearing, R. E., MacKenzie, M. J., Brewer, K. B. & Ibrahim, R. (2012) 'A meta-analysis of experimental studies of diversion programs for juvenile offenders', *Clinical Psychology Review, 32*(1): 26–33.

Schweinhart, L. J. (2013) 'Long-term follow-up of a preschool experiment', *Journal of Experimental Criminology, 9*(4): 389–409.

Shonkoff, J. P. & Phillips, D. A. (eds). (2000) *From Neurons to Neighborhoods: The Science of Early Childhood Development*. Washington, DC: National Academy Press.

Sidebottom, A. & Tilley, N. (2017) Situational prevention and offender decision making. In W. Bernasco, H. Elffers & J.-L. Van Gelder (eds) *Oxford Handbook of Offender Decision Making*. Oxford: Oxford University Press.

Simon, H. A. (1983) *Reasoning in Human Affairs*. Oxford: Blackwell.

Stewart, A., Livingston, M. & Dennison, S. (2008) 'Transitions and turning points: examining the links between child maltreatment and juvenile offending', *Child Abuse and Neglect, 32*: 51–66.

Tong, L. S. J. & Farrington, D. P. (2006) 'How effective is the "Reasoning and Rehabilitation" programme in reducing reoffending? A meta-analysis of evaluations in four countries', *Psychology, Crime & Law, 12*(1): 3–24.

Townsley, M., Johnson, S. D. and Ratcliffe, J. H. (2008) 'Space–time dynamics of insurgent activity in Iraq', *Security Journal, 21*(3): 139–146.

van der Stouwe, T., Asscher, J. J., Stams, G. J. J., Deković, M. & van der Laan, P. H. (2014) 'The effectiveness of Multisystemic Therapy (MST): a meta-analysis', *Clinical Psychology Review, 34*(6): 468–481.

Van Gelder, J. L., Elffers, H., Reynald, D. & Nagin, D. S. (2014) Affect and cognition in criminal decision making: between rational choice and lapses of self control'. In J. L. Van Gelder, H. Elffers, D. Reynald, & D. S. Nagin (eds) *Affect and Cognition in Criminal Decision Making*. London: Routledge.

Verona, E. & Sachs-Ericsson, N. (2005) 'The intergenerational transmission of externalizing behaviors in adult participants: the mediating role of childhood abuse', *Journal of Consulting and Clinical Psychology, 73*: 1135–1145.

Walsh, K., Zwi, K., Woolfenden, S. & Shlonsky, A. (2015) 'School-based education programmes for the prevention of child sexual abuse. A Cochrane systematic review and meta-analysis', *Research on Social Work Practice, 28*(1), 1–23.

Warr, M. (2005) 'Making delinquent friends: adult supervision and children's affiliations', *Criminology, 43*: 77–105.

Welsh, B. C. & Farrington, D. P. (2009) 'Public area CCTV and crime prevention: an updated systematic review and meta-analysis', *Justice Quarterly, 26*(4): 716–745.

Widom, C. S. (2003) 'Understanding child maltreatment and juvenile delinquency: the research'. In J. Wiig, C. S. Widom & J. Tuell (eds) *Understanding Child Maltreatment and Juvenile Delinquency: From Research to Effective Program, Practice and Systematic Solutions*. Washington, DC: CWLA Press.

Wilson, D. B., Bouffard, L. A. & MacKenzie, D. L. (2005) 'A quantitative review of structured, group-oriented, cognitive-behavioral programs for offenders', *Criminal Justice and Behavior, 32*(2): 172–204.

Wortley, R. (1997) 'Reconsidering the role of opportunity in situational crime prevention'. In G. Newman, R. Clarke & S. Shoham (eds). *Rational Choice and Situational Crime Prevention* (pp. 65–82): Aldershot, UK: Ashgate.

Wortley, R. (2001) 'A classification of techniques for controlling situational precipitators of crime', *Security Journal, 14*(4): 63–82.
Wortley, R. (2011) *Psychological Criminology: An Integrative Approach*. London: Routledge.
Wortley, R. (2012) 'Exploring the person-situation interaction in situational crime prevention'. In N. Tilley & G. Farrell (eds) *The Reasoning Criminologist: Essays in Honour of Ronald V. Clarke*. London: Routledge.
Wortley, R. (2013) 'Rational choice and offender decision making: lessons from the cognitive sciences'. In B. Leclerc & R. Wortley (eds), *Cognition and Crime: Offender Decision-Making and Script Analyses*. London: Routledge.
Wortley, R. (2017) 'Situational precipitators of crime'. In R. Wortley & M. Townsley (eds) *Environmental Criminology and Crime Analysis* (2nd ed.). London: Routledge.
Wortley, R. & Smallbone, S. (2006) *Child Pornography on the Internet. Problem-Oriented Guides for Police Series*. Washington, DC: U.S. Department of Justice.
Wortley, R. & Smallbone, S. (2012) *Internet Child Pornography: Causes, Investigation and Prevention*. Santa Barbara, CA: Praeger.
Wortley, R. & Tilley, N. (2018) 'Does situational crime prevention require a rational offender?' In B. Leclerc & D. Reynald (eds) *The Future of Rational Choice for Crime Prevention: Criminology at the Edge*. London: Routledge.
Zimbardo, P. (2007) *The Lucifer Effect*. New York: Random House.
Zingraff, M., Leiter, J., Johnsen, M. & Myers K. (1994) 'The mediating effect of good school performance on the maltreatmen-delinquency relationship', *Journal of Research in Crime and Delinquency, 31*: 62–91.

6
Economics

Matthew Manning

Economics arose from the need to address scarcity. Since resources are limited, economics strives to make the best use of what is available. To achieve this end, economics proposes that: (1) societal wealth is derived from co-operation and specialisation. That is, more goods and services can be produced, for a given level of resource, if every person specialises in what they do best; (2) for specialisation to succeed, trade is required; and (3) if trade is to succeed, then law and order is necessary.

The Romans recognised the benefits of trade, but saw justice and economic welfare as enjoying a symbiotic relationship. Emperor Justinian (who reigned from 527–565 CE) sought to unify the empire's citizens and strengthen trade by extending citizenship outside of Rome, thus making its 'new citizens' subject to Roman civil law. He understood that for society to prosper through trade, the pursuit of self-interest must be constrained by ethical judgements. This notion is beyond economics, as it does not define a moral code. Economic argument, however, may be applied after the code has been agreed in order to apply efficiency. Short of providing a detailed history of economic thought, we can safely say that economics is not a standalone discipline – it never has been. Over its history (both ancient and modern) the discipline has, and is still, aligned closely with philosophy, justice, the study of society and national wealth. Thus, economics ranges from the old philosophy of 'balancing the books' to more modern notions that are associated with the creation of wealth, societal welfare, sustainability and law and order.

Unfortunately the role economics has played, or can play, in the prevention of crime is not particularly well understood among those outside the discipline. Economics does more than cost–benefit analysis! It possesses a range of tools that have the potential to assist in shaping modern crime prevention policy. Levitt & Dubner (2005) state:

> Since the science of economics is primarily a set of tools, as opposed to a subject matter, then no subject [including crime and its prevention], however offbeat, need be beyond its reach.
>
> *(p. 12)*

Most scholars would agree that responding to crime is a multidisciplinary endeavour. This sounds easy, but academic disciplines are renowned for their territoriality. This often makes for difficult and strained relationships. To overcome such difficulties transparency is necessary. Providing an understanding of what a discipline does and what it can offer goes some way to building efficacious relationships.

Economists and crime scientists alike attempt to identify pragmatic responses to what economists call 'market distortions'. Such distortions create market failures, which ultimately adversely affect individual and societal welfare. In criminology lingo, distortions may be thought of as crimes, and market failure as the subsequent negative externalities that affect both individuals and society at large. In terms of addressing market failure and minimising the negative externalities associated with that failure, economists envisage their purview in terms of the 'golden triangle' of research, policy and practice (Figure 6.1).

Research has always been an attribute of economics. The work has often shifted our understanding of an issue and advanced science through method, theory and application both across and within discipline. Levitt & Miles (2006) and Bushway & Reuter (2008) provide an extensive discussion of this contribution. In terms of shaping practice, economics plays instrumental (e.g. influencing the progress of practice or service delivery or modifying individual and collective behaviour), conceptual (e.g. shaping the understanding of policy issues and reframing debates) and capacity building roles through technical and personal skill provision. But less well understood is its role in influencing and shaping policy.

Economics is one of the few social sciences that controls a major branch of government policy (e.g. Federal Reserve in the US, Reserve Bank in Australia or the Bank of England in the UK) or for that matter has a dedicated office within government (e.g. the council of Economic

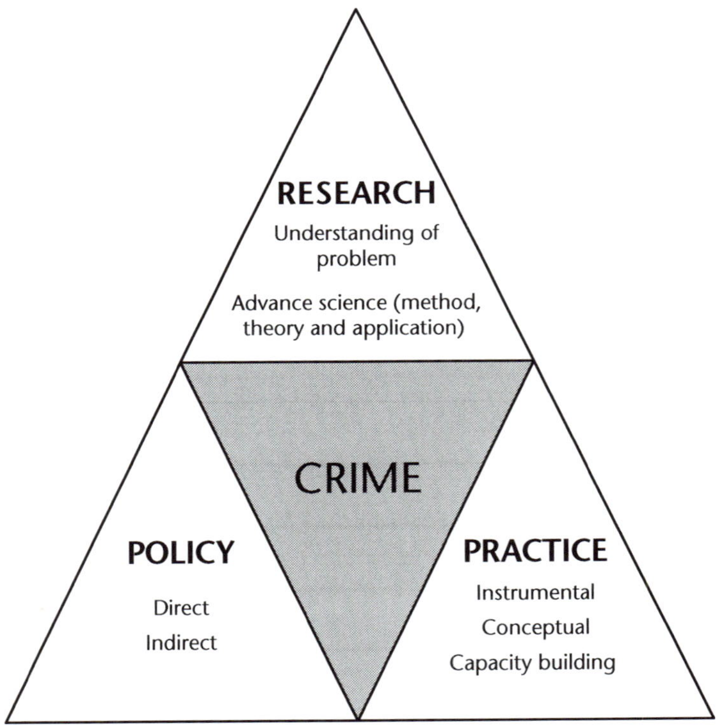

Figure 6.1 The golden triangle

Advisors in the White House). But economics is branching out with the establishment of more 'micro-focussed' policy departments or units. The UK government, for example, set up the Behavioural Insight Team (BIT), or 'Nudge Unit'[1] (Halpern, 2015). Their goal here is to apply economic theories (gained from behavioural economics and psychology) into public policy development and associated services. Described by Whitehead, Jones, Pykett, & Welsh (2012) as 'nudgeocracy' (p. 303), this form of economics has infiltrated mainland Europe with nudge theory gaining traction in France and Germany and also across the Atlantic in the USA, where President Obama initiated his own BIT – named the 'Nudge Squad' (Fox News, 2013).

But economists will tell you that this doesn't necessarily mean that politicians heed their advice. So if politicians don't necessarily take the advice of economists, what is their role in shaping public policy? To answer this question one needs to distinguish between direct and indirect influence. Direct influence is what we think of when we consider how experts might shape policy. This can be via: (1) a politician turning to a prominent academic to assist in crafting new legislation; (2) a party leader (e.g. Prime Minister) asking an economic advisor which of two policies is preferable; and (3) when the politician is an economist and draws from their background. This happens rarely and although politicians may ask for advice, their decision will often be dominated by political concerns. Often they heed advice that agrees with what they already want to do – hence the rise and popularity within government of think tanks! Direct effects are more likely to occur when a policy decision has already been defined as more technical than political or when possible solutions to a problem are yet to be defined – for example, policymakers seeking advice on how to deal with the global financial crisis.

Economists tend to have more influence on policy through indirect means. In short, prompting policymakers to think about the world in new ways. This can be through new forms of measurement and decision-making tools that shape public debate. A good example is gross domestic product (GDP). In the 19th century, politicians rarely spoke about the economy. In modern times this is a focal point of public debate. Less visible economic tools such as cost–benefit analysis also shape the political debate. Such indirect tools instigate conversations regarding key political issues as they make the issue or problem quantifiable. Economic ideas also have influence. Basic concepts such as incentives, efficiency, and opportunity cost have changed the way policymakers think. Although economists would like these concepts to be better understood and visible, particularly in areas such as criminal justice policy, these concepts more often than not underpin much policy deliberation. Government budgeting offices (e.g. the Congressional Budget Office), for example, are now formally responsible for quantifying policy trade-offs. The policy effects of economic styles of reasoning are difficult to pinpoint, but it can be argued that new policy areas have been reconceptualised in economic terms. A good criminological example would be the investment in human capital through early education and development. As well as responding to a social justice imperative and potentially reducing delinquency and crime by promoting positive pathways in individual development for those most at-risk, it also enhances productivity and increases technological innovations that lead to long-term economic growth and sustainability. In summary, economists do have influence when it comes to public policy.

In subsequent sections, I will dig a little deeper to showcase a few skills that economists possess. Underpinned by the vectors of the 'golden triangle', I reveal how economists build formalised models for the purposes of hypothesis testing and falsification and the use of specialised techniques for measuring the efficacy of prevention efforts. For those with such knowledge, I apologise. But I do hope my discussion will nonetheless further enrich your understanding of the discipline in the context of the prevention of crime.

Economic models of crime

Economists construct models, which in most cases are simplified descriptions of reality, to generate hypotheses about behaviour that can be tested. Although it is acknowledged that other disciplines also develop models, economists develop them in a rather special way. As such, it is worth exploring how this is done in some detail. To begin, there are two types of economic models: theoretical and empirical. Theoretical models attempt to develop verifiable implications about behaviour with the assumption that agents maximise their utility (or an outcome) subject to clearly defined constraints (e.g. one's budget). Here, qualitative answers to specific questions are provided – for example, problems associated with asymmetric information or, as discussed earlier in the chapter, solutions to market failure. In contrast, empirical models attempt to confirm the qualitative estimates of theoretical models and convert these estimates into accurate numerical outcomes.

Economic models can be derived mathematically or diagrammatically – both aim to describe a theory of behaviour. Economic modellers aim to include sufficient information (e.g. through equations) to provide clues about how rational agents behave. Models can be simple (e.g. demand for illicit drugs is inversely related to price *ceteris paribus*[2]), or complex, where economists use a large number of complex formulations (e.g. nonlinear, interconnected differential equations), for example to predict the output of an economy. Despite the diversity of models used in economics, they all share similarities in that they allow for inputs (or exogenous variables) and outputs (often called dependent variables) to explain when some or all of the exogenous variables become operative.

Economists, however, differ with regards to how an empirical model's equations should be derived. Some believe that the equations must assume maximising behaviour, an efficient market and progressive behaviour. There are others though who prefer a more nuanced approach. Their equations reflect, in part, their own experiences. Such economists are, essentially, questioning the realism of the behavioural constructs in the more formally derived models.

Market solution to crime

Clearly, similar to other disciplines, economists have differing opinions and positions regarding model specification. We do, however, collectively acknowledge Becker's (1968) seminal contribution to the market for 'crimes of commission'. Unfortunately, given the level of mathematical complexity used in Becker's paper, much is lost or not well understood by those outside the discipline. This is not to say that economists are smarter or better educated than other social scientists. Rather, the disciplines differ with regard to the language employed. Here, I intend to rectify this. In addition, Becker's model is a good example of where an economist has attempted to improve the efficiency of detection and punishment. To pave the way for this discussion it is necessary to introduce you to the market solution to crime.

Generally speaking, economists believe that the market cannot provide a complete solution to harmful behaviour, particularly when there is a state of lawlessness. Albertson & Fox (2012) state, 'as lawlessness increases it will choke off the very markets on which it feeds' (p. 33); and, according to Ratzinger (1986), 'the decline of such discipline [ethical behaviour] can actually cause the laws of the market to collapse' (p. 13). Similarly, Wilber (2004) proposed 'self-interest leads to the common good if there is sufficient competition and if most people in society have internalized a general moral law as a guide for their behavior' (p. 27).

It is important to note that a level of instability in the market can be instilled through market inefficiencies, for example rent-seeking behaviour. Rent-seeking behaviour occurs when there is a 'misuse of market or political power in such a way as to allow some agents to accumulate benefits from market inefficiencies' (Albertson & Fox, 2012, pp. 23–24). A good example of this is the exploitation of consumers in an oligopolistic market,[3] thus allowing the oligopoly to generate supernormal profits as a result of lack of competition. Although this is not illegal (but it is typically illegal where there is some form of collusive behaviour), rent seekers aim to create a market that allows them to accumulate wealth created by others. Society, as such, is made worse off as a result of this behaviour as the rent seekers produce less than they might as they devote resources to their schemes. This somewhat unethical behaviour means that freedom of the market is restricted and 'the return to those who engage in the market is reduced' (Albertson & Fox, 2012, p. 24). As such, economics suggests that society will be at its most productive (or least) where the pursuit of self-interest is controlled by ethical (or lack of ethical) judgement.

So how can market-based solutions address market failure, or in our case, unethical or harmful behaviour? Let's begin with two traditional responses – education and religion. To begin, neither is likely to be completely satisfactory. Education, for example, works at a level beyond rationality of the market in that: (1) it may be difficult to convince people that they should consider society's good as well as their own; and (2) such an approach requires universal coverage. Consider an education programme to enhance society's level of politeness. Some people may become more polite but many won't. Soon, polite individuals will question why they should be polite when they feel that those around them are not.

Religion, on the other hand, doesn't require universal coverage. Here, we appeal to individual self-interest with a promise of certain reward or punishment (often eternal and imposed by spiritual forces). Religion, like education, has its drawbacks; in this case the principal-agent problem. The principal-agent problem occurs when one person is able to make decisions on behalf of another person. In this case the decision of the agent impacts (in some way) on the principal. If we bring religion back into focus, the principal-agent problem suggests that religion benefits the good of those in charge rather than society as a whole, although many (particularly those of faith) would disagree with this statement. Marx stated:

> Religion is the sigh of the oppressed creature, the heart of a heartless world, and the soul of soulless conditions. It is the opium of the people. The abolition of religion as the illusory happiness of the people is the demand for their real happiness.
>
> *(Marx, 1884, p. 1)*

To be clear, Marx's main complaint was not against religion but against the market system promoted in capitalist economies. From this argument, economists would, on the whole, agree the role of the state should be curtailed to those areas where it is strictly necessary. Abraham Lincoln would agree. He stated,

> The legitimate object of government is to do for the people what needs to be done, but which they cannot, by individual effort, do at all, or do so well, for themselves.
>
> *(Cited in Shaw, 1950, p. 136)*

According to Albertson & Fox (2012) (ideally, from a societal perspective),

> government should reflect the moral and ethical stance of the community it serves. It should seek, through the most efficient means possible, to establish customs, laws and incentives which will allow both the flexibility of the market system, and the ethical and legal framework which will allow it to work to produce the best overall good.
>
> *(p. 35)*

However, this is not necessarily a straightforward balancing act. As Sayers (1945) states, 'What men need most is good government, with freedom and order. But order puts fetters on freedom and freedom rebels against order' (p. 58). In addition Plato proposed,

> If a city were composed entirely of good men, to avoid office would be as much an object of contention as to obtain office is at present . . . The true ruler is not meant . . . to regard his own interest, but that of his subjects.
>
> *(Plato cited in Ferrari & Griffith, 2000)*

So education and religion are not entirely the answer. In addition, government has a role, but this role is, and some respects should be, bound. There is, however, another possible solution – an incentive system so as to encourage selfless behaviour on the part of the agent and discourage behaviour which society finds costly. This is where Gary Becker enters, and one of the key roles economists can contribute to crime science is exhibited – building formalised models of efficiency based on theoretical insight.

The Becker model

Becker's contribution[4] was that crime, and the control of crime, are choices that can be modelled using the standard labour economic model of individual decision-making regarding the allocation of time. Simply, crime is another choice (in life) that can be made by an agent. Modelling choice, in this context, has a clear conceptual structure as agents are met with a series of options (e.g. activities) that are linked with outcomes. In a simple model, agents' choices are all known, as are the probabilities (i.e. perfect information). Such assumptions can be, and are, relaxed. An agent weighs outcomes through a statement of goals (i.e. objective function). Bushway & Reuter (2008) state that the objective function 'evaluates the various outcomes in terms of how well they help the individual achieve his or her goals' (p. 9). In a simple consumer choice model, an agent allocates a fixed amount of resources between two or more goods. The objective function describes the utility derived (i.e. happiest/most satisfied), given his/her available income. This leads to the concept of opportunity cost. Here the cost of choice X is not the monetary price of that choice. Rather, it is the cost of not choosing Y – in this case, the next best alternative.

With these concepts in mind, we can discuss the Becker model in detail. Becker considered the market for 'crimes of commission'. Here an agent chooses to undertake actions, which impose a cost on society[5]. The harm resulting from this choice or harmful activity (*O*) is something society wishes to discourage. Some agents will benefit from O otherwise this activity would be zero. Given that agents who undertake O are members of society, it holds that society is prepared to accept some level of O (e.g. pollution resulting from the use of fossil fuels). However, some activities will be so harmful that society strives to reduce these to a level of zero (e.g. murder). Figure 6.2 is a depiction of the relationship between the level of O and harm it does to society. We can see that for very low levels of O (less than O*) the harm to society is below the horizontal axis. Here, it is argued that society potentially benefits from very low levels of a given activity. For example, low levels of alcohol use produce a number of positive benefits (e.g. social networking, health) (Manning, Smith, & Mazerolle, 2013). Or in terms of crime, it may be worthwhile to tolerate low levels so as to maintain some degree of autonomy and freedom. However, as the level of activity increases (above O*) the level of harm increases as potentially does the level of activity – depending on the nature of the activity (Albertson & Fox, 2012).

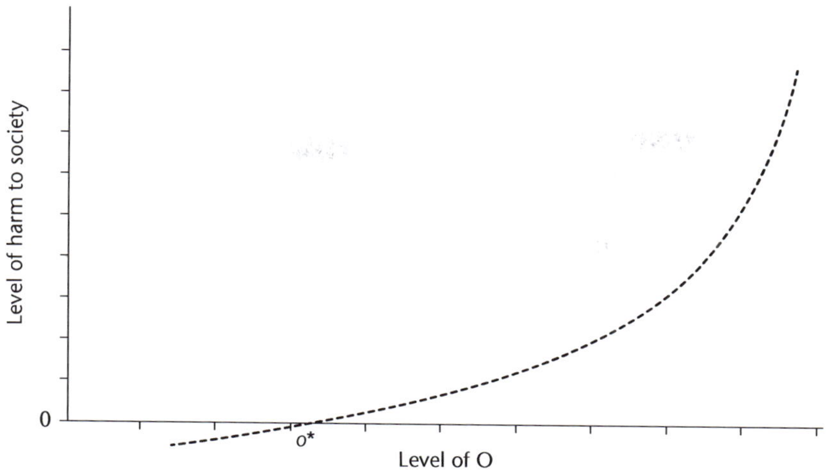

Figure 6.2 The harm resulting from activity *O*
Adapted from Albertson & Fox (2012)

Although society wishes to discourage agents from activity *O*, this comes at a cost. If there were no costs associated with creating a disincentive structure, society would get close to eliminating the activity altogether – but probably not completely. Becker envisaged two costs: (1) the cost of detection, apprehension and conviction (cost of CJ hereon); and (2) the cost of punishment. The cost of CJ arises because those agents who undertake *O* will most probably not voluntarily attend prison to 'repay their debt to society'. Thus society has to bear the harm of activity *O* and the cost of CJ. The cost of CJ and the cost of punishment will increase as more of the activity is undertaken. This raises an important question: what if theft was to double and society wished the clear-up rate[6] to remain the same? According to Becker: (1) the increase in theft would lead to a greater demand for conviction and punishment; (2) justice costs will increase as the level of theft increases; (3) justice system costs will increase as the clear-up rate increases because detection is expensive and more prisons will need to be built to deal with the increase in convictions; and (4) the cost of punishment will increase as the level of punishment increases.

An agent's response to justice

Now we consider the supply of offences. Because of different preference attributes among individuals, some agents will be discouraged from activity *O* fairly easily. However, others may take more persuasion. It is not unreasonable to assume some will become increasingly discouraged as the probability of being convicted and punished increases. Becker argued that the greater the level of justice (i.e. the greater the probability of conviction and punishment), the less effective is a further increase in the level of justice. This is depicted in Figure 6.3 where we see that the relationship becomes flatter as the probability of conviction increases. Importantly, Becker also noted a socially optimal level – this is at the level of punishment where (on average) crime does not pay. In short, those who continue to commit crime are clearly not risk-averse, rather, risk-seeking. Finally, Becker proposed that a 1 per cent increase in the probability of conviction would reduce *O* by more than a 1 per cent increase in punishment severity (Albertson & Fox, 2012).

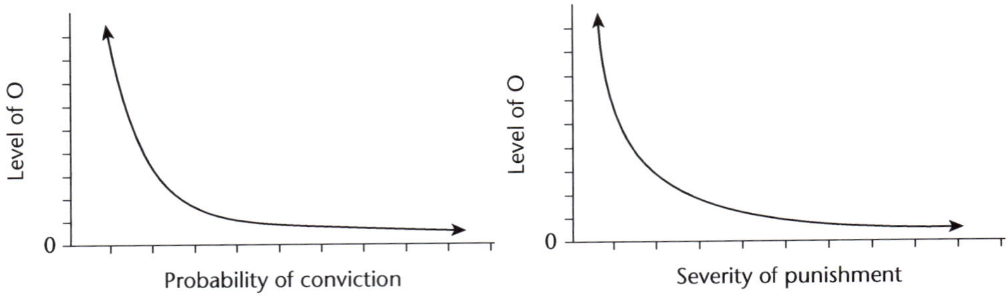

Figure 6.3 An agent's response to justice – probability of conviction and severity punishment
Adapted from Albertson & Fox (2012)

The most efficient level of justice

Becker believed that society could indeed influence the level of activity O by changing the probability of conviction and/or severity of punishment. However, increasing both of these factors increases criminal justice costs. Also noted was that the effectiveness of increases in conviction or severity of punishment will decline, the greater their level. So what is the most efficient combination of these policy tools? Becker takes the total cost of crime in society to be the sum of the damage done by O, the cost of CJ and the cost of punishment. So what is the effect of punishment severity on costs? Becker assumed that the more severe the sentence the less will be the supply of activity O. Further, as the level of O declines so will the harm it causes. So it follows that the fewer the agents who engage in O the less it will cost to convict them. Figure 6.4 (left) demonstrates that the sum of the harm of activity and the costs of CJ decline as the severity of punishment rises. In addition, the costs of punishment rise as the severity of punishment rises (right).

By combining the cost of punishment and the harm of O and cost of CJ we produce the total cost of activity O to society Labelled TCS in Figure 6.5.

What is important to note in Figure 6.5 is that TCS reaches a minimum point below which it cannot be reduced. Why is this? Because although increasing from zero, the severity of punishment will cause a significant reduction in the level of O, the severity of punishment becomes less a deterrent as it increases, while the cost of punishment continues to increase. According to Becker, the level of severity, which minimises total costs, is indicated by the vertical line in Figure 6.5.

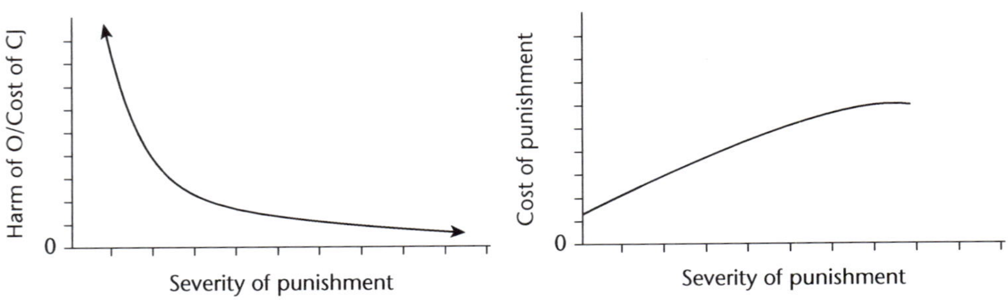

Figure 6.4 Relationship between harm of *O*/cost of apprehension and severity of punishment
Adapted from Albertson & Fox (2012)

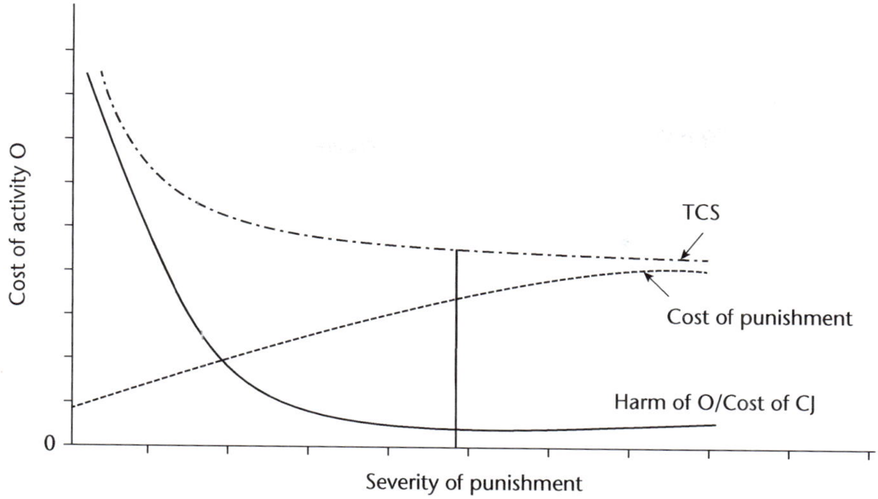

Figure 6.5 The effect of severity of punishment on cost of activity *O* to society
Adapted from Albertson & Fox (2012)

To the left of the line, not enough activity *O* is being deterred, to the right, the costs of punishment are too high.

If we focus on the most efficient clear-up rate (Figure 6.6), Becker proposed that the costs of conviction begin to rise as the clear-up rate increases. This phenomenon is represented by the bottom lowest curve in Figure 6.5. Although the level of activity *O* declines as the clear-up rate increases, the actual cost of conviction increases because more resources are required to detect and convict more occurrences of *O*. If the clear-up rate increases, the costs of punishment must also rise. The rationale is that more conviction means more punishment costs. Again, the vertical line indicates the socially efficient level of policy. If the clear-up rate is left of the line, society

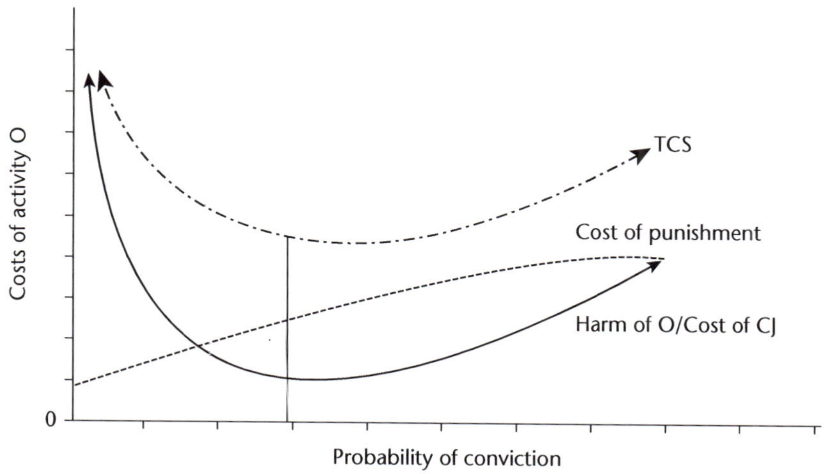

Figure 6.6 The effect of probability of conviction on cost of activity *O* to society
Adapted from Albertson & Fox (2012)

is not convicting enough agents of O. If the clear-up rate is to the right, society is allocating too many resources into CJ and punishment.

Other notable elements of the Becker model

Becker didn't stop there. He also considered the effect of an increase in the harm inflicted on society by an undesirable activity (O in our example). Here, he proposed that as the level of harm increases (or when we compare two activities – one with more harm than another) – so does the penalty and clear-up rate. A good example of this is the comparative cost of different types of O used for sentencing in the UK, where 'Parliament attaches to each criminal offence a maximum sentence that gives a broad indication of offence seriousness' (Sentencing Advisory Panel, 2010, p. 5). Similarly, in the US, sentence length is determined based on severity of O (or in our model TCS) and number of previous offences committed by the individual (United States Sentencing Commission, 2009).

Becker's model also considered changes in ease of detection. For example, the clear-up rate for crimes that are easier to detect is going to be higher than those where it is more difficult. Becker proposed that the optimal clear-up rate of Os that are easier to detect is greater than the optimal rate for Os of similar harm that are harder to detect. But as Os become easier to detect the optimal level of punishment falls. Given that agents typically respond more readily to detection than punishment the optimal level of O falls (Albertson & Fox, 2012). This is where society responds by 'making an example' of those agents who commit crimes that are more difficult to detect and being more tolerant of crimes that are more easily detected.

Finally, Becker concluded that the most efficient form of punishment to reduce or discourage O is through the use of fines. He defined a fine as any compensation payment made to a victim of crime as well as any further payments required of the agent (i.e. the offender) by way of deterrence and vengeance. In the case of fines, part of the cost of punishment is borne by the offender. As such, the cost to the whole of society is reduced. Becker believed that as the cost to society of punishment falls, the harshness of punishments will increase, the probability of conviction will weaken and the level of O will fall. Thus by setting the level of the fine equal to the harm done (which includes the cost of CJ and punishment) the optimal level of activity O can be achieved.

Now, one should be cautious in interpreting this part of the model as in reality not all crimes are met with a fine but some are. One of the finer details not always picked up is that Becker was trying to allude to the notion of equity. Former inmates may find it difficult to get employment but those who are fined are generally not discriminated against in this manner. This of course may be a function of the types of crimes that are met with a fine. However, Becker's point implies that there is no further sanction imposed on the individual by society once s/he has paid his/her debt (in this case the fine) and, as such, fines are preferred to custodial sentences. There are of course caveats. For example, there are some activities that cannot be fined (e.g. murder and armed robbery etc.). In addition, there is the case where the offender has no means to pay a fine and as such is met with a custodial sentence. Albertson & Fox (2012) state, 'even where the offender has no means to pay, the trade-off with the time spent in prison disadvantages the less well-off' (p. 46).

Although this is only a simplified, implicit, discussion of Becker's model, is it really so controversial? Well let's quickly summarise the main features. First, there is such a thing as society being too controlling for its own good – a society with excessive high levels of punishment. Second, it is not possible to completely reduce the level of an undesirable activity to zero – at least not by the criminal justice system alone. Many criminologists and sociologists have reached the same conclusion. Take Emile Durkheim for example, who argues that crime is a normal feature of society and the role of punishment is to act as a mechanism to reinforce the moral code (see discussion by Garland, 1991). Another example is Merton (1938) who saw crime as one form of innovation where agents use illegitimate means to obtain socially acceptable ends. In time, these innovations lead to the development of new socially acceptable 'moral' practices.

It is important to clarify that Becker did not attempt to explicitly model criminals' differing preferences and proclivities. Rather, his model focusses on the analysis of the socially optimal choice of detection and punishment. His supply of offences function recognises the cost to agents of punishment but not the opportunity cost of illegal activity. Such opportunity costs were formally modelled later by Ehrlich (1973). Here the model did not significantly deviate from what most criminologists and sociologists expect.

And the story goes on, where economists continue to develop formalised models of crime to assist in, among other things, identifying socially optimal levels of criminal justice intervention. One example is economists' work in the area of illicit drug markets. Economists who work in this area typically apply the basic concepts of demand and supply and also some elements of industrial organisation theory to examine the effects of different forms of drug prevention on outcomes such as price and availability. Models of price and availability are critical as they have important criminal justice consequences. If the price to buy a gram of methamphetamine were $20 per gram rather than $640 per gram, the model would predict that there would be many more users, but less crime (MacCoun & Reuter, 2001). The lower price would reduce the need for a dependent user to commit crime to fund their purchase of the product and also reduce the incentive for sellers of methamphetamine to compete violently to protect their individual market and any conflicts with competitors. As well as attempting to explain factors that affect the price of the illicit substance, a model could also examine the distribution of earnings of sellers. A model, for example, may predict that the illicit drug market would generate fewer problems if a methamphetamine dealer (manager level) earned less. The problem is that senior dealers earn as much as a medical specialist without the necessity of the degree. Hence, the question is how do you reduce their income?

Building formalised models, with regards to examining the determinants of prices or the distribution of profits provides further insights into how policy, through criminal justice agencies, responds to the problem in the most efficient and effective manner. There are also potential challenges to conventional market models that require a multidisciplinary effort to overcome. These include, for example, extreme price dispersion, the use of physical coercion in illicit markets, selection into an occupation by risk taking of a particular kind and links with other forms of crime (Bushway & Reuter, 2008). All these issues are where criminologists bring extensive expertise.

Economic tools used to measure efficacy

As highlighted earlier, economists possess a range of skills[7] that are of practical relevance (to crime science and criminology more broadly) with respect to assessing the efficacy of crime prevention initiatives. Importantly, to begin, economists formulate models based on theoretical insight. They then use the methods discussed below to: (1) test theories; and (2) model efficiencies or the marginal benefits and costs of different policy options or prevention alternatives. The first method involves measuring the impact of interventions or policies; the second assesses the desirability of an intervention or policy by weighing its costs and benefits, relative to other alternatives (Levitt & Miles, 2006). Used in conjunction with the techniques employed in crime science to reduce and control crime, the outcome is essentially a more efficient and effective response to crime.

Estimating causal impact

One notable skill that economists possess is identifying causal impact. Answering questions such as what is the impact of the size of the police force on crime have been extremely difficult, given that crime rates influence public policies that aim to combat crime. Take for example, the causal quandary – police reduce crime, but crime leads to the hiring of more police. This is a situation whereby the estimates we produce are potentially biased. Econometricians call this simultaneity bias. Here, 'standard correlational statistical approaches such as ordinary least squares estimation do not capture the [true] causal impact' (Levitt & Miles, 2006, p. 148).

To isolate the causal effect of a policy or intervention, one needs to exclude the influence of other factors. To achieve this, economists typically mimic the empirical designs of health studies. In short, they compare outcomes in different jurisdictions that adopt a particular policy, using a before-and-after design. Here, economists typically refer to persons who receive the intervention as the treatment group. They then draw these comparisons relative to a set of persons that did not receive the intervention (the control group). This design draws comparisons across two dimensions – before and after, and treatment. This is commonly termed a difference-in-differences approach.

The difference-in-differences approach, however, does not necessarily mean that there is causal impact. This is because the set of jurisdictions adopting a given policy is not randomly selected. Levitt & Miles (2006) proposed two reasons for this. First, 'the crime control policies that jurisdictions adopt are often themselves products of crime rates' (p. 150). That is, crime justice resources are a product of the crime rate. So when crime is higher, more resources are used. Therefore, the policies set the incentives to engage in crime while simultaneously responding to the incidence of crime. Second, 'the social and historical factors that influence the adoption of specific laws and enforcement policies may also affect the incidence of crime directly' (p. 150). Levitt & Miles use the example of capital punishment, where social norms in the Southern states of America shape capital punishment policy. Setting aside the impact of capital punishment, the norms in these states may directly affect crime. The simultaneous determination of policies and effects is a clear example of a simultaneity problem, where the 'problem bedevils measurements of the impact of crime-control policies on crime rates' (Levitt & Miles, 2006, p. 150).

To overcome potential simultaneity bias, economists primarily use Granger causality (Granger, 1969) and instrumental variables or natural experiments. Granger causality refers to a temporal relationship between variables, not genuine causation. As stated by Levitt & Miles (2006), 'one variable "Granger causes" another when changes in the first variable generally precede changes in the second' (p. 151). An example of the difference between Granger causality and actual causality is provided by Kennedy (1988). Because Christmas cards arrive in the post before December 25, Christmas cards 'Granger cause' Christmas. But true causation is in reverse. The pending arrival of Christmas causes people to send Christmas cards. As stated by Levitt & Miles (2006) 'forward-looking behavior produces a divergence between actual causation and Granger causation' (p. 151). Marvell & Moody (1996) were the first to apply Granger causality to the question of police and crime. Their results revealed that increases in police preceded declines in crime. In short, police 'Granger cause' crime drops, where a 10 per cent increase in urban police numbers produces a 3 per cent long-term decline in total crime. As argued by Levitt & Miles (2006), there are problems given the use of annual observations. Such observations may miss short-term anomalies and produce a biased estimate of the true relationship between police and crime. Here, the solution is to increase the frequency of data as done by Corman & Mocan (1996), in which they found governmental response to higher crime occurs quickly (within six months of the crime increase). Similarly, offending rates react quickly to more policing. Corman & Mocan (1996) employed the Granger causality method, estimating that a 10 per cent increase in police resulted in an equal drop in the crime rate.

Instrumental variables are also employed by economists to break the simultaneity of policies and outcomes. As described by Levitt & Miles (2006), 'a valid instrument is a variable correlated with the criminal justice policy of interest but otherwise uncorrelated with crime rates' (p. 152). Given the difficulty of assigning subjects randomly to experimental and control groups, economists look for naturally occurring phenomena that closely mimic random exposure to a particular policy. Here economists use naturally occurring phenomena as instrumental variables. Levitt (1997) suggested the timing of elections as a valid instrument given that police forces tended to grow during election years. Such growth, Levitt concluded, could be due to an electoral advantage in expanding the ranks of the police and thus being seen serious about dealing with crime. As stated by Levitt & Miles (2006): 'Thus, peculiar timing in the growth of police was plausibly exogenous to the incidence of crime because, after controlling for other factors, an election is not otherwise apt to influence the incentives for street crime' (p. 152). In short, elections are effectively a natural experiment that induce changes in the size of the police force but are otherwise exogenous to crime rates. Applying such a method, Levitt (1997) estimated that a 10 per cent increase in the police force led to a 3 per cent to 10 per cent reduction in the rate of crime.

Estimating economic benefits

Given the enormous investment by governments in trying to catch, prosecute, and punish offenders,[8] it is critical that each input (e.g. dollars spent by government) translates into good public policy, in terms of: (1) how and when to spend resources (i.e. are resources better allocated to dealing with crime or criminality or some combination?); and (2) the efficient allocation of resources (the economic effectiveness question). Economists address both these questions. For example, are additional increases in police resources (e.g. number of frontline officers) economically worthwhile? Levitt (1997) estimated that the marginal benefit associated with employing another police officer to reduce crime exceeded the cost. Marvell & Moody (1996) produced similar results indicating that the marginal benefit associated with hiring an additional police officer is likely equal to or exceeds the cost of doing so.

To reach such conclusions, economists need to undertake what is called economic analysis (EA). Cost–benefit analysis (CBA), for example, is a natural extension of the economist's normative framework, with a focus on maximising society's welfare. Bushway & Reuter (2008) state that CBA

> can help policymakers rationally choose between policies since it is an application of the rational choice model to the macro level of a policy maker choosing between different crime control strategies. Cost–benefit analysis starts with an assessment of whether any given program or treatment works to prevent crime, and then estimates the relative costs and benefits of such a policy.
>
> *(p. 41)*

Manning, Johnson, Tilley, Wong, & Vorsina (2016) state:

> Economic analysis (EA) aims to provide a rational basis for the allocation of scarce public resources. It provides results that promote economic efficiency and good fiscal management by assessing available options to identify those providing the greatest return on investment. EA also allows policymakers to gauge the economic implications of existing policies and/or programmes.
>
> *(p. 5)*

Table 6.1 Common EA techniques

Type of analysis	*Measure of cost/ inputs*	*Measure of outcomes*	*Strengths*	*Weaknesses*	*Analytical questions*	*Example/s*
Cost–feasibility	Monetary value of resources	N/A	Permits alternatives that are not feasible to be immediately ruled out before evaluating outcomes	Cannot judge overall worth of a project because it does not incorporate outcome measures	Can a single alternative be carried out within budget?	Manning, 2004; Manning, Homel, & Smith, 2006
Cost–effectiveness	Monetary value of resources used during implementation	Units of effectiveness (e.g. crimes prevented or treatments delivered)	Easy to incorporate standard evaluations of effectiveness Good for comparing the cost of delivery per unit of treatment across interventions Good for alternatives with a small number of objectives	Hard to interpret if there are multiple measures of effectiveness Only useful for comparing two or more alternatives	Which alternative yields a given level of effectiveness for the lowest cost (or highest level of effectiveness for a given cost)?	Cowell, Broner, & Dupont, 2004; McCollister, French, Prendergast, Hall, & Sacks, 2004
Cost–benefit	Monetary value of resources used during implementation	Monetary value of benefits	Can judge absolute worth of a project Can compare CB results across a variety of projects	Difficult to place monetary values on salient life benefits	Which alternative yields a given level of benefits for the lowest cost (or the highest level of benefits for a given cost)? Are the net benefits greater than the net costs?	Bowers, Johnson, & Hirschfield, 2004; Yeh, 2010

Cost–utility	Monetary value of resources used during implementation	Units of utility	Incorporates individual preferences for units of effectiveness Incorporates multiple measures of effectiveness onto a single measure of utility Promotes stakeholder participation in stakeholder decision-making	Difficult to derived consistent and accurate measure of individual preferences Cannot accurately judge overall worth of a single alternative Only useful for comparing two or more alternatives	Which alternative yields a given level of utility for the lowest cost (or the highest level of utility for a given cost)?	Dijkgraaf et al., 2005; Dolan & Peasgood, 2007
Frontier analysis (i.e. Data Envelopment Analysis (DEA))	Unit or monetary value of resources used during implementation	Units of effectiveness (e.g. crimes prevented or treatments delivered) and/or monetary value of benefits	DEA can handle multiple input and multiple output models DEA does not require an assumption of a functional form relating inputs to outputs Decision-Making Units (DMUs) are directly compared against a combination of peers Inputs and outputs can have different units. For example, X1 could be in units of lives saved and X2 units of dollars without requiring an a priori trade-off between the two	Since DEA is an extreme point technique, noise (even symmetrical noise with zero mean) such as measurement error can cause significant problems. DEA converges very slowly to 'absolute' efficiency. In other words, it can tell you how well you are doing compared to your peers but not compared to a 'theoretical maximum'	Which DMU is considered technical and allocative efficient? How can inputs be translated into more effective and efficient outputs?	Drake & Simper, 2005; Gorman & Ruggiero, 2008

Note: Adaption of table provided in Levin & McEwan (2001).

The most common forms of EA are cost–feasibility analysis (CFA), cost–benefit analysis (CBA), cost–effectiveness analysis (CEA), cost–savings analysis (CSA) and cost–utility analysis (CUA) For a full review of each EA technique and the conceptual foundations of EA see Manning et al. (2016).[9] Each technique answers different questions and requires different methods to answer the respective questions. Another recently employed economic method in the area of criminology is frontier analysis (for a full example see Chapter 24 by Manning & Wong). Table 6.1 provides a summary of the most common EA techniques.

A Normative framework and contribution to crime policy

Escalating rates of crime and drug abuse in America in the 1960s forced the hand of Congress to create a number of high-profile commissions to assess the underlying problem and recommend reforms that would turn it around. Initially turning to criminologists of the day, Congress found it had little to offer with regards to evidence. James Q. Wilson, a political scientist of the time, criticised criminology noting that its ability to provide evidence-based policy recommendations was limited given its sociological orientation. The notion that crime is a product of culture and social structure provided little guidance for policymakers, whose ability to change the structural aspects of society was limited. This was reinforced by sociology's lack of belief in deterrence.

Economics, could, however, provide guidance with respect to policy design and efficiency. This is primarily due to its presumption that 'behaviour is not the inevitable result of underlying social conditions, but rather results from individual choices influenced by perceived consequences' (Cook, Machin, Marie, & Mastrobuoni, 2013, p. 3). In short, by manipulating the consequences, behavioural changes will follow. As outlined in Becker's model, an economist's normative framework lends itself to policy prescription. Returning to Becker, he proposed that the social costs of crime are a sum of the direct (victimisation) and indirect (efforts to control crime) costs. If we wish to minimise total social costs then it is unlikely that the optimal level of *O* (harmful activity) will be zero as the marginal costs of additional prevention potentially exceed the marginal benefits of an additional reduction in *O*. But as Cook et al. (2013) stated: 'just because crime rates are declining does not mean that the "crime problem" is less overall – crime-control costs, such as large increases in the prison population in most countries . . . must be considered' (pp. 3–4). Finally, the normative framework not only provides answers to the question 'what works?', but also 'what is worthwhile?' (as discussed in Section 2).

Conclusion

This chapter has only provided a small insight into the role economists can play in developing practical solutions to crime and examining the efficiency or marginal costs and benefits of policy alternatives or prevention efforts. Given space restrictions, I purposely only selected a few areas which may be of interest and omitted the important contribution that economists can play with regards to the development and testing of both old and new or developing theories (e.g. rational choice and nudge theory, respectively). I also only discussed a few areas in which economists can contribute with respect to modern econometric and other applied analytical methods and their detailed knowledge of both licit and illicit markets (e.g. drug markets).

Notes

1 It should be noted that the UK government and BIT are now joint partners.
2 A Latin phrase meaning other things held constant.

3 An oligopolistic market is a market structure in which a small number of firms have a large majority of market share. An oligopoly is similar to a monopoly, except rather than one firm operating in the market, two or more firms dominate the market (Taylor & Weerapana, 2012).
4 Becker's contribution with respect to rational choice theory is widely acknowledged and understood by most criminologists. The goal here is to make explicit those contributions not necessarily understood because of differences in disciplinary terminology.
5 He did not, however, consider 'crimes of omission' (where an agent chooses not to undertake actions that benefit society). But, the basic analysis is generalisable.
6 The clear-up rate is the percentage of offenders caught by the police with respect to the total number of reported crimes.
7 It should be noted that a discussion of the full range of skills and methods economists possess is beyond the scope of this chapter. As such, I have selected what are essentially the two most prominent and widely applied.
8 Bauer and Owens (2004) estimate this to be approximately B$200 per year.
9 Other useful discussion of EA techniques can be found in Manning (2004) and Manning (2008).

References

Albertson, K. & Fox, C. (2012). *Crime and Economics: An Introduction*. Abingdon, UK: Routledge.

Bauer, L. & Owens, S. D. (2004). *Justice Expenditures and Employment in the United States, 2001*. Washington, DC: Bureau of Justice Statistics.

Becker, G. (1968). Crime and punishment: An economic approach. *Journal of Political Economy, 76*(2), 169–217.

Bowers, K., Johnson, S., & Hirschfield, A. (2004). Closing off opportunities for crime: An evaluation of alley-gating. *European Journal on Criminal Policy and Research, 10*, 285–308.

Bushway, S. & Reuter, P. (2008). Economists' contribution to the study of crime and the criminal justice system. *Crime and Justice, 37*(1), 389–451.

Cook, P., Machin, S., Marie, O., & Mastrobuoni, G. (2013). Lessons from the economics of crime. In P. Cook, S. Machin, O. Marie, & G. Mastrobuoni (Eds), *Lessons from the Economics of Crime: What Reduces Offending?* Cambridge, MA: MIT Press.

Corman, H. & Mocan, H. (1996). A time-series analysis of crime and drug use in New York city. *American Economic Review, 90*(2), 584–604.

Cowell, A., Broner, N., & Dupont, R. (2004). The cost-effectiveness of criminal justice diversion programs for people with serious mental illness co-occurring with substance abuse. *Journal of Contemporary Criminal Justice, 20*, 292–314.

Dijkgraaf, M., van der Zanden, B., de Borgie, C., Blanken, P., van Ree, J., & van den Brink, W. (2005). Cost utility analysis of co-prescribed heroin compared with methadone maintenance treatment in heroin addicts in two randomised trials. *British Medical Journal, 303*(7503), 1297.

Dolan, P. & Peasgood, T. (2007). Estimating the economic and social costs of fear of crime. *British Journal of Criminology, 47*(1), 121–132.

Drake, L. M. & Simper, R. (2005). Police efficiency in offences cleared: An analysis of English 'Basic Command Units'. *International Review of Law and Economics, 25*(2), 186–208.

Ehrlich, I. (1973). Participation in illegitimate activities: A theorectical and empirical investigation. *Journal of Political Economy, 81*(3), 521–565.

Ferrari, G. & Griffith, T. (2000). *Plato: 'The Republic'*. Cambridge: Cambridge University Press.

Fox News. (2013). Gov't Knows Best? White House creates 'nudge squad' to shape behavior. Retrieved from www.foxnews.com/politics/2013/07/30/govt-knows-best-white-house-creates-nudge-squad-to-shape-behavior.html.

Garland, D. (1991). Sociological perspectives on punishment. *Crime and Justice, 14*(1), 115–165.

Gorman, M. F. & Ruggiero, J. (2008). Evaluating US state police performance using data envelopment analysis. *International Journal of Production Economics, 113*(2), 1031–1037.

Granger, C. (1969). Investigating causal relations by econometric models and cross-spectral methods. *Econometrica: Journal of the Econometric Society, 37*(3), 424–438.

Halpern, D. (2015). *Inside the Nudge Unit: How Small Changes can Make a Big Difference*. London: Random House.

Kennedy, P. (1988). *A Guide to Econometrics*. Cambridge, MA: MIT Press.

Levin, H. M. & McEwan, P. J. (2001). *Cost-effectiveness Analysis* (2nd ed.). London: Sage Publications.

Levitt, S. (1997). Using electoral cycles in police hiring to estimate the effect of police on crime. *American Economic Review, 87*(3), 280–290.

Levitt, S. D., & Dubner, S. J. (2005). *Freaknomics*. New York: William Morrow.

Levitt, S., & Miles, T. (2006). Economic contributions to the understanding of crime. *Annual Review of Law and Social Science, 2*(1), 147–164.

MacCoun, R. & Reuter, P. (2001). *Drug War Heresies: Learning from Other Vices, Times and Places*. Cambridge: Cambridge University Press.

Manning, M. (2004). Measuring the costs of community-based developmental prevention programs in Australia. Masters (Hons), Griffith University, Brisbane.

Manning, M. (2008). Economic evaluation of the effects of early childhood intervention programs on adolescent outcomes. PhD, Griffith University, Brisbane.

Manning, M., Homel, R., & Smith, C. (2006). Economic evaluation of a community-based early intervention program implemented in a disadvantaged urban area of Queensland. *Economic Analysis and Policy, 36*(1 & 2), 99–120.

Manning, M., Johnson, S., Tilley, N., Wong, G., & Vorsina, M. (2016). *Economic Analysis and Efficiency in Policing, Criminal Justice and Crime Reduction: What Works?* London: Palgrave Macmillan.

Manning, M., Smith, C., & Mazerolle, P. (2013). *The Societal Costs of Alcohol Misuse in Australia. Trends and Issues in Crime and Criminal Jutice, 454*(1), 1–6.

Marvell, T. & Moody, C. (1996). Specification problems, police levels, and crime rates. *Criminology, 34*(4), 609–646.

Marx, K. (1884). Contribution to the critique of Hegel's Philosophy of Law. *Deutsch Franzosische Jahrbucher*, February.

McCollister, K., Frenca, M., Prendergast, M., Hall, E., & Sacks, S. (2004). Long-term cost effectiveness of addiction treatment for criminal offenders. *Justice Quarterly, 21*, 659–679.

Merton, R. (1938). Social structure and anomie. *American Sociological Review, 3*(5), 672–682.

Ratzinger, J. (1986). Market economy and ethics. Symposium in Rome: *Church and Economy in Dialogue*, 13–16.

Sayers, D. (1945). *The Man Born to be King*. London: Victor Gollancz.

Sentencing Advisory Panel. (2010). Overarching principles of sentencing. Retrieved from www.sentencingcouncil.org.uk/about-sentencing/about-guidelines.

Shaw, A. (1950). *The Lincoln Encyclopedia*. New York: Macmillan.

Taylor, J. & Weerapana, A. (2012). *Principles of Economics* (7th ed.). Mason, OH: Cengage Learning.

United States Sentencing Commission. (2009). 2009 Federal sentencing guidelines manual. Retrieved from www.ussc.gov/guidelines/archive/2009-federal-sentencing-guidelines-manual.

Whitehead, M., Jones, R., Pykett, J., & Welsh, M. (2012). Geography, libertarian paternalism and neuro-politics in the UK. *The Geographical Journal, 178*(4), 302–307.

Wilber, C. (2004). Ethics, human behavior and the methodology of social economics. *Forum for Social Economics, 33*(2), 19–50.

Yeh, S. (2010). Cost–benefit analysis of reducing crime through electronic monitoring of parolees and probationers. *Journal of Criminal Justice, 38*, 1090–1096.

7
Epidemiology

Paul Fine and Phil Edwards

Introduction

Epidemiology is a methodological discipline, providing a set of tools to describe patterns and to reveal causal mechanisms underlying characteristics and events in populations. For historical reasons the word 'epidemiology' has been most widely used with reference to studies of illness in human populations, but that represents only one of its many applications. Its language and practices are increasingly employed and familiar among all the population sciences, be they described as public health, or crime science, or sociology, or economics, or education (let alone those dealing with populations of non-human species).

In addition to introducing epidemiological language and ideas, the intent of this chapter is to provide an abbreviated overview of the subject, as presented in many textbooks and courses, and to encourage its research techniques becoming more widely appreciated and employed in crime science as in all realms of population science (Coggan et al. 2003; Freeman and Zeegers 2016; Gordis 2008; Rothman et al. 2008; Szklo and Nieto 2007; Webb and Bain 2011). By recognising common problems, language, and methods in related fields, each discipline can best improve its ability to investigate its own particular problems – for example those having to do with crime.

Evolution of epidemiology as a discipline

Though most contemporary epidemiology textbooks still emphasise studies of disease in (typically human) populations, this emphasis has shifted over time. The word itself has roots in ancient Greece and in particular the work of Hippocrates (*c.*460–375 BCE) who used the term *epidemic* to describe events which occurred in populations (epi = upon; demos = population), such as the infamous plague of Athens in 430 BCE. The term *epidemiology* owes its origin in the English language to the London Epidemiological Society in 1850, which brought together a group of distinguished individuals with interests in human but also animal and plant health (Fine et al. 2013). A key figure in this story is John Snow, a general practitioner who made important contributions to our understanding of cholera, and the transmission of its causative organism via water. He did this by relating patterns of the disease to particular water supplies, and famously identified the source of an outbreak in 1854 to a particular water pump on Broad Street in London, by carefully mapping the addresses of individuals who died of the disease (using data obtained from a government registry), recognising clustering, and then recommending removal of the pump's handle in order to stop the outbreak (Figure 7.1). Snow's approach, and this particular event, are widely cited as a model for solving population problems, and are revered in many disciplines, including crime science (Snow 1855; Weisburd and McEwen 2015). Interestingly, and ironically, some of the methods for geographic profiling and identification of 'hotspots', subsequently developed within the field of crime science, have now been recommended for infectious disease control (Le Comber et al. 2011)!

From an initial focus upon epidemics of infectious disease, the discipline which called itself 'epidemiology' expanded its territory to cover studies of all disease in populations, then to studies of 'health' in populations – and most recently to include 'health related events, states and processes . . .' (Porta 2014). Given that the World Health Organisation defines health as 'a state of complete physical, mental and social well-being', such a definition effectively covers much of the social and economic sciences (Fine 2015).

Along with this shift we find an increasing number of explicit links between health-related institutions and publications, and those devoted mainly to crime. Many crimes, and consequent incarceration, involve bodily and psychological harm – and hence directly affect morbidity and mortality – and so are of obvious concern to the health professions (Wilderman and Wang 2017). There is the tradition of applying disease terminology to describe anti-social behaviours (sociopath . . .), and the term 'epidemic' to describe any behaviour or trait which increases in frequency in a population (including 'epidemics' of various crimes [Slutkin et al. 2015]), and medical epidemiologists are often referred to as disease detectives. . . . Public health agencies such as the World Health Organisation and US Centers for Disease Control have divisions devoted to violence (WHO, CDC). And many public health and epidemiology journals publish articles on investigations of various crimes (Akers and Lanier 2009; Amber et al. 2014, Webster et al. 2002). Along with this we find frequent explicit reference to epidemiology in the legal and social science literatures devoted to crime (Freeman and Zeegers 2016; Philipson and Posner 1996; Vaughn et al. 2014).

All this is entirely appropriate given that academic epidemiology systematises methods which can be applied just as well to study various aspects of crime as to study the distribution and causes of schizophrenia or cancer, or the treatment of tuberculosis.

In this context it is worth pointing out that there has been much discussion in the crime science community of the relative value of emphasising either the traits of the perpetrators of crimes (individual risk factors for a 'criminal predisposition') or the circumstances in which crime takes place (situational analysis), as each approach has different implications for efforts to combat crime. There are parallels in work on health-related outcomes insofar as most work relates to characteristics of ill and healthy individuals, including genetic factors, but this often extends to consideration of environmental factors, to health services (e.g. hospital bed occupancy), to disease-causing agents (toxins, infectious organisms, genes) and reservoirs (e.g. non-human animals, water supplies), or vectors (e.g. mosquitoes). The 'populations' under study differ in each of these examples, but may include crimes, illness episodes, communities, hospitals, houses, bank accounts . . . or mosquitoes . . . as well as people. Studying any of them involves the application of epidemiological methods.

The strategies of epidemiology

The overall strategy of science is a sequence of steps from observational studies, which aim to describe natural phenomena, to analytic studies, which aim to understand underlying

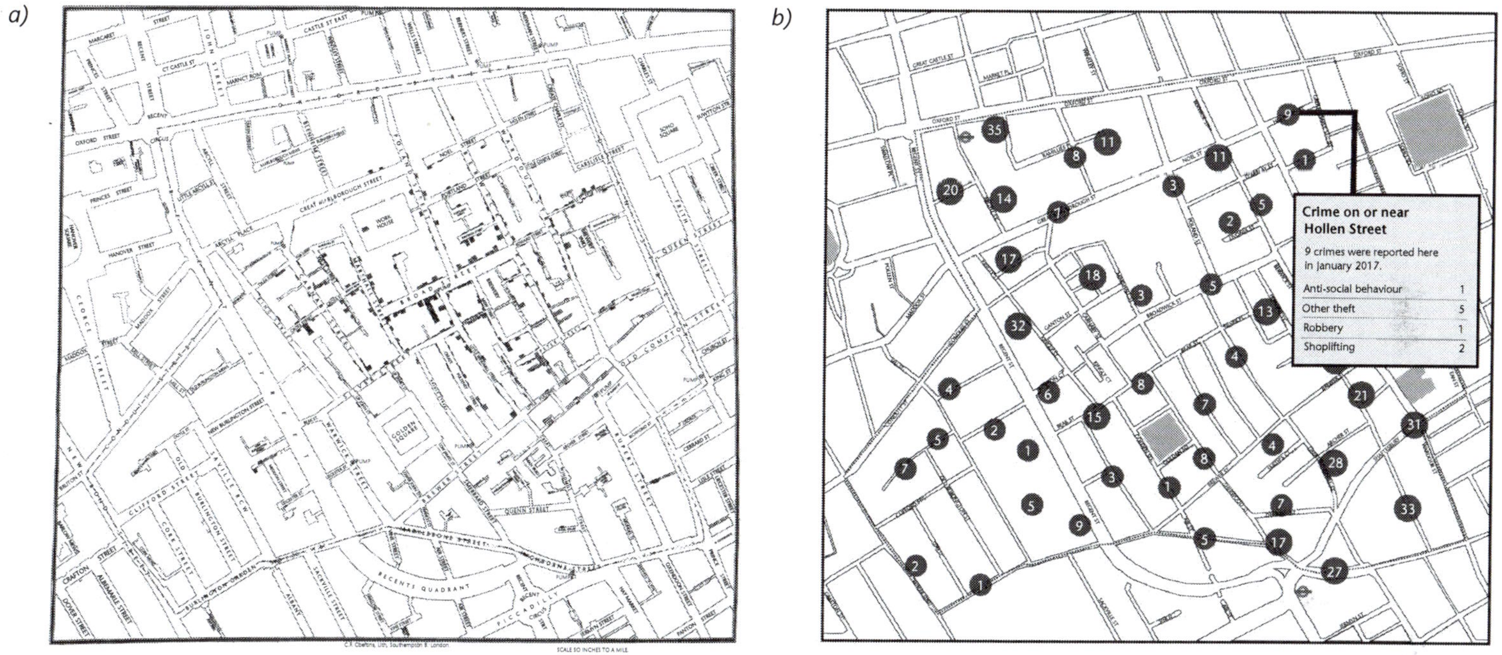

Figure 7.1 a and b A: John Snow's classic map showing locations of cholera deaths in London, August-September 1854 (Snow 1855). Positions of water pumps are also shown. Snow noted that the deaths clustered around the pump at the corner of Broad and Lexington Streets
B: Example of contemporary crime mapping in the same area of London: crimes reported in January 2017, as shown on the interactive website www.police.uk/metropolitan/00BK16N/crime. Clicking on any circle provides details by precise location. Note that Broad Street is now Broadwick

mechanisms, to (in many cases) intervention studies, which aim to manipulate circumstances – hopefully for the betterment of society. The outcomes are then monitored and evaluated, after an intervention, leading to new descriptions, new understanding of mechanisms and new opportunities for interventions. These steps are expanded in Figure 7.2, which sets out the various sorts of investigational approaches to any characteristic or experience in a population, for example relating to crimes, their perpetrators or their victims. Most of these methods are obvious, and many of the terms are now in common parlance – a familiarity which reflects the ubiquity of the epidemiological approach and language today. The fact that many of the formal methods may have been applied first to human disease problems reflects only the importance of human health and the attention and resources applied to these problems, and not to any restriction in their applicability. We describe them briefly here, italicising important terms as they first arise, and point out that in reality actual studies may not fit perfectly within any one category, but include aspects of two or more. The terms are still useful for description of research and as indicators of the sorts of logical inferences which can be drawn from the different types of studies. Examples from both the health and crime-related literatures are cited to illustrate various applications.

The first distinction is between *observational* and *intervention* studies. Observational work implies observation of nature as it is, with no effort to manipulate or to change it. Intervention research implies some active effort to rearrange or manipulate nature and an attempt to measure what happens as a result.

Studies of *routinely collected data* – be they related to automobile thefts or tuberculosis cases or anything else – represent a common and important form of basic observational research. The ongoing collection and analysis of routine data is called *surveillance*, and is a crucially important aspect of many disciplines including those relating to public health and to crime science (Logan et al. 2008). Practitioners emphasise that good surveillance implies not only the collection and analysis of data, but their appropriate interpretation, their distribution to all 'those who need to know' and the assurance that appropriate action is taken as a consequence (Teutsch and Churchill 2000).

Within observational studies there are two important categories: work that is merely *descriptive* in intent, and work that is *analytical*, in the sense that the intent is not just to describe

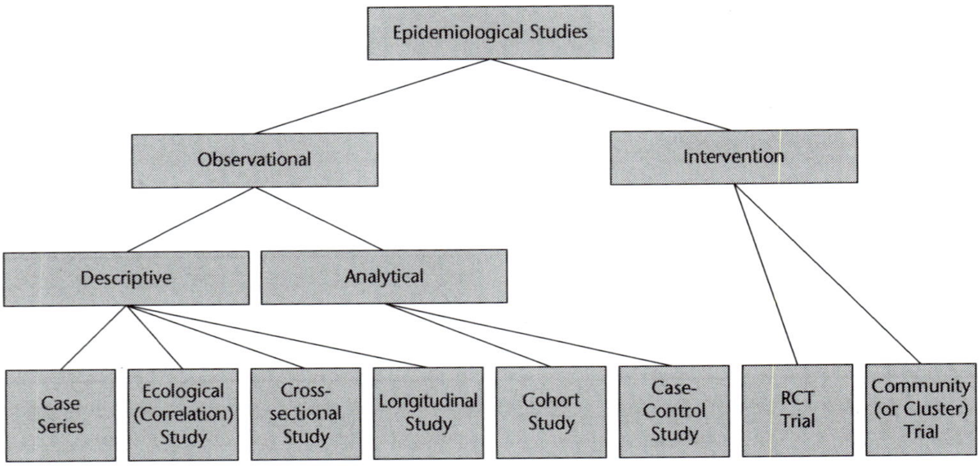

Figure 7.2 Flowchart showing relationships between the various sorts of approaches to studying things in populations. RCT = (individually) randomised controlled trial

superficially but to describe deeply, looking for underlying patterns and associations in order to infer underlying mechanisms. The distinction between these is often not clean, in that detailed descriptions (e.g. time and place of robberies) may well carry some implication of underlying causal processes (Figure 7.3). This overlap does not make the terms any less useful.

The simplest form of descriptive data consists of just a description of one or several events – called a *case series* in traditional epidemiological terminology. Depending upon how these data are collected they may or may not be representative of what actually occurs in society, and so they must be interpreted with caution. That said, they may give some indication of circumstances and may lead to more carefully designed studies or *surveys* of one sort or another.

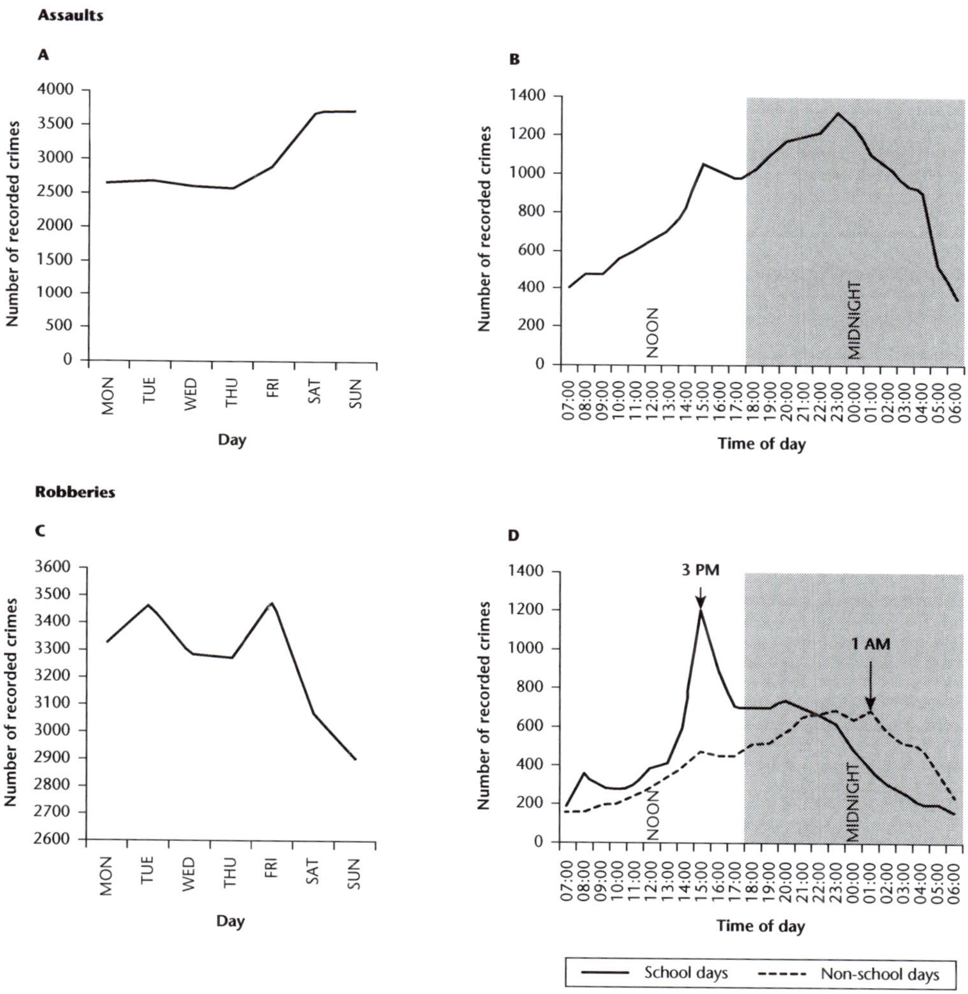

Figure 7.3 Temporal patterns of assaults and robberies in New York City. The frequency of assaults is highest on weekends (A) and late at night (B). The patterns for murder and shootings are similar to that of assaults. Robberies are at lower frequency on weekends (C) when they occur mainly at night, but on weekdays peak in mid-afternoon (D). The mid-afternoon peak is associated with robberies by and of school-age individuals, and cluster near subway stations (Adapted from Herrmann 2015)

An example of an important case series was the report of five cases of a rare form of pneumonia in Los Angeles in 1981 – which ultimately turned out to be the first recognised cases of AIDS (CDC 1981). The fact that all five patients were male homosexuals was an important early indicator of much which was to follow. Similarly, the first reported case of a car whose control was taken over by a computer hacker and driven into a ditch may signal the start of an 'Internet of Things' crime wave (whereby cars, security systems, pacemakers, etc. may be controlled remotely via the internet) (Wright 2011, Goodman 2015).

There is a particular sort of descriptive study, called a *correlation* or *ecological study* which is extremely common, simple to carry out, and often misinterpreted. These are studies which compare crude statistics between different populations. Given the large amount of detailed data now available, such studies are easily performed – for example comparisons between populations in terms of statistics on educational attainment or family size or diet or income and, for example, some disease or crime-related statistic such as the number of deaths from stroke, or the frequency of robberies, or homicides, or the number or proportion of individuals who have been convicted of one or another crime (Figure 7.4). It is important to recognise that such presentations can be – and often are – misleading in that they may show correlations which are not causal, but instead reflect a network of correlations between loosely or tightly linked socio-economic variables in the societies included in the study (for example the fact that poor living conditions and low income and low educational achievement and poor diets and various behaviours and illnesses often 'go together' as various manifestations of poverty – sometimes called the *poverty complex*). The common adage that *correlation need not imply causation* is a useful caution concerning such studies. Epidemiologists refer to the erroneous inference of cause in individuals, on the basis of correlations between populations, as the *ecological fallacy*. The fact that many socio-economic characteristics are likely to be correlated in various ways, with various sorts of crime, makes the analysis and interpretation of crime-related data, when presented in this manner, particularly challenging (Ogburn 1935). There has been much recent discussion of this methodological issue in the context of attempts to explain declines of crime in several high-income societies since the 1990s, as a consequence of changes in lead exposure, or abortion legislation, or policing, or security measures, or age distributions over time (Steffensmeier and Harer 1999; Donohue and Levitt 2001; Stretesky and Lynch 2004; Farrell et al. 2010).

It is helpful to break down *descriptive* research according to whether the data relate to a single 'point' or narrow period of time (often described as *cross-sectional* data or studies) or to changes over a longer period of time (often called *longitudinal* data or studies). This distinction is critically important, insofar as circumstances, the environment, and individual behaviours change with age and over time.

In simplest terms, cross-sectional data tell us only who, or what percentage, of 'individuals' of different sorts (e.g. by age or sex or socio-economic group) have some characteristic (e.g. a particular disease, or employment status, or a criminal record, or a history of having been abused). In epidemiological terms, we speak of cross-sectional data as providing *prevalence numbers* or *prevalence rates* of an illness or condition at some point in time. As prevalence statistics refer to a 'point' or narrow period of time, they are particularly appropriate for describing characteristics which are long lasting (the prevalence of short term conditions like influenza varies considerably over time). A prevalence statistic implies a numerator of the number of individuals with the condition, over a denominator of the total number *at risk* of the condition (i.e. who might or could have the condition). The denominator is crucially important, as the frequency of any sort of individual, or crime, or illness, is a function of the underlying population size, and a geographic or temporal cluster of events may just reflect that a large number of individuals

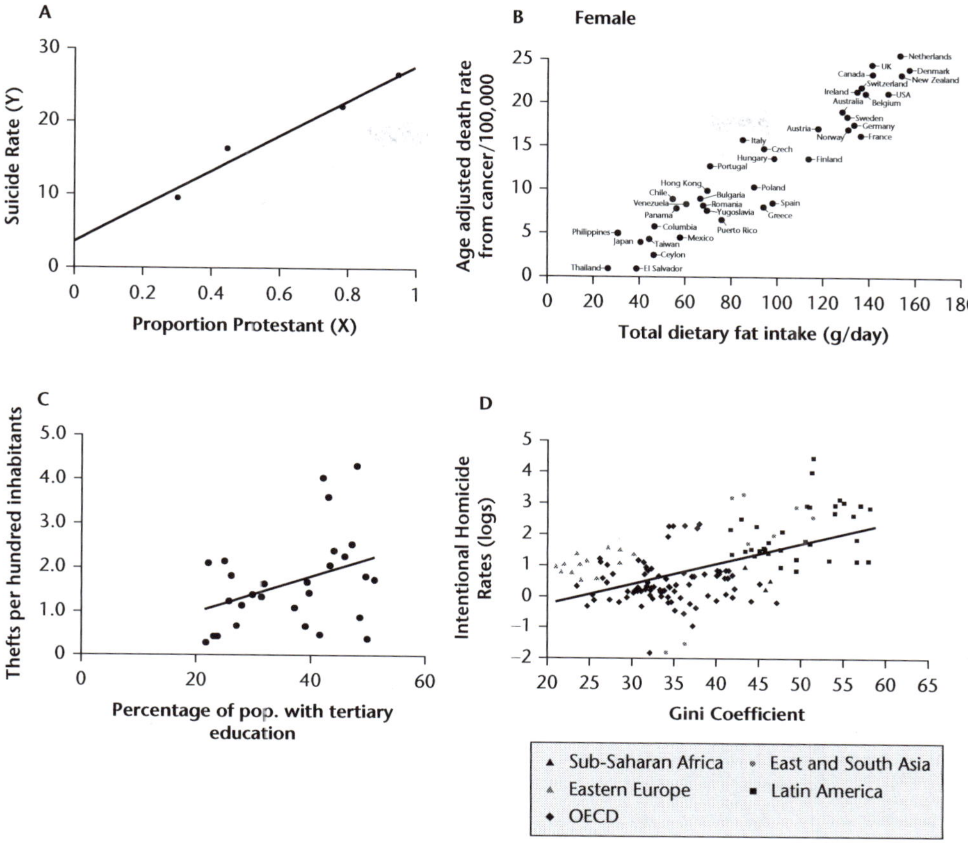

Figure 7.4 Examples of ecological studies and the ecological fallacy. A. Classic data on suicide rates in relation to proportion protestant in different provinces in Prussia 1883–1890. The provinces differed in many ways correlated to their religious composition, let alone that the relationship is uninterpretable as it is not clear whether the suicides were in Catholics or Protestants! (Durkheim 1897). B. Relationship between fat intake and breast cancer mortality in different countries (Carroll, 1975). The strong correlation is not because fat consumption causes breast cancer deaths – but because high fat consumption is a characteristic of wealthy populations which have relatively low fertility, and breast cancer rates are influenced by reproductive history (multiple pregnancies early in life reduces breast cancer risk). C. Relationship between thefts per 100 inhabitants and percent of population aged 30–34 with tertiary education among European nations, 2012. Positive correlation influenced by many differences between countries (Eurostat). D. Relationship between Gini coefficient for income inequality and homicide rate between countries (Fajnzylber et al. 2002). The authors explored whether the relationship was consistent within as well as between countries, or attributable to measurement error, or to factors such as GNP, unemployment, education or urbanisation, but concluded that it was real. Figures A, B, and D adapted from cited sources

happened to live or be present in a particular place at a certain time. Thus a prevalence rate of ovarian cancer should have only (adult) females in the denominator and a prevalence rate of motorists driving without insurance should have only adults in the denominator, though it may be further sub-divided by age or sex or ethnic or other social group. It is well recognised that criminal behaviour is more frequent among young adults, and males in particular – thus it is important to distinguish *crude prevalence* statistics, which have a total population denominator, from *age-specific*, or *age–sex specific* statistics, for which the denominator is restricted to particular population subsets (e.g. males aged 15–19, 20–24, 25–29, . . .) (Figure 7.5).

There is also a concept of *period prevalence*, relating to numbers and proportions of individuals who have some condition at any point over a period of time. This can be a complicated statistic as it combines prevalence at the start of a time period plus all new cases to arise during the period. For example, the 'period prevalence rate' of minors on probation in 2015 would be the number on probation on 1 January 2015 plus the number who were placed on probation during the course of the year 2015 (divided by the number of minors in the population, e.g. on 1 July 2015).

While prevalence is helpful, for example in measuring the magnitude or burden of some trait or problem, we often wish to understand and explain whatever pattern we observe. This means understanding mechanisms, which implies a time sequence (by definition: *causes precede outcomes*), as well as the contexts within which the mechanisms may (or may not) work. Thus an observation that, in a single-population survey, an unusually high proportion of youths are found to carry knives in a particular neighbourhood could be interpreted several ways: either something about the neighbourhood environment (e.g. a hangout which has become popular or for gangs) or some recent event (something in the news, even a popular song) has encouraged young people who live in the area to carry knives; or youths who are inclined to criminal behaviour but who live elsewhere tend to move to this particular neighbourhood; or there may be an even more complex relationship between time, location and behaviour. In order to understand this process one needs to study a population over a period of time, to see which comes first, for example the neighbourhood residence or media event or the criminal behaviour (Sariaslan et al. 2013).

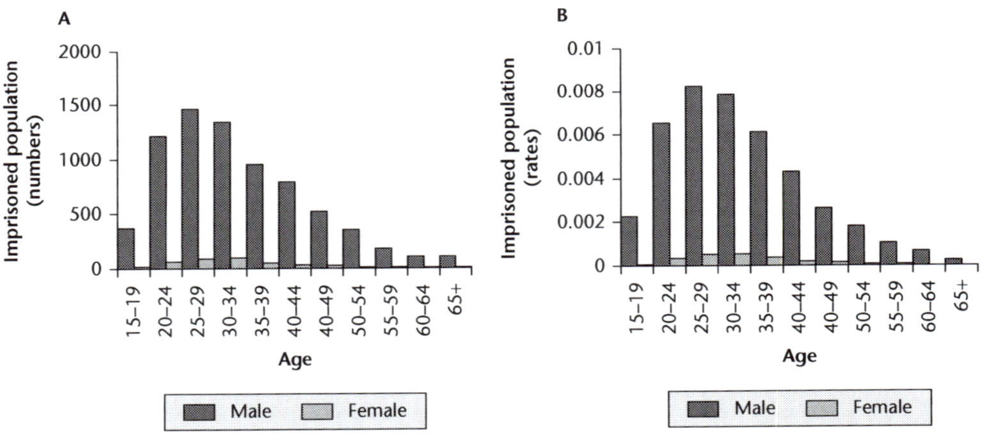

Figure 7.5 Prevalence and prevalence rates of the imprisoned population, Scotland, 2013, by age and sex. There were 7,883 individuals in prison, thus 1.5 per 1,000 of the total population of 5.3 million. Of these, 7,446 were males (2.9 per thousand males) and 437 females (0.1 per thousand females). Restricting the population to adults, 15 and over, these percentages are 3.5 per thousand males and 0.2 per thousand females. Numbers and rates by 5-year age groups are shown below, showing that almost 1 per cent (8.4 per thousand) of males aged 25 to 29 were in prison. Data from Scottish Government Prison statistics and population projections 2013/14

Studies which follow populations, or events in populations, over time are called *longitudinal*. In simplest form this may entail collection of data at two or more periods of time, for example descriptive data in successive years. This may show trends. More valuable are studies which trace or *follow-up* groups of individuals over time, for months or years. Such studies provide information on new instances of some illness or crime over time, giving measures of *incidence* (numbers of new events/outcomes over a specified period of time) or *incidence rates*[1] (numbers of new events/outcomes per 'persons at risk' over a specified period of time). Note that one may include either number of individuals with or responsible for at least one outcome, or the number of outcomes themselves (i.e. number of crimes) in the numerator. These statistics can be very different if a small number of individuals are responsible for large proportion of the outcomes (Figure 7.6).

As incidence rates are often low (many of the conditions of interest are relatively rare) incidence rates are often expressed per 1,000, per 10,000 or even per million individuals per year. Furthermore, depending upon circumstances, incidence may be expressed in terms of other sorts of denominators – for example burglaries per 1,000 dwellings per month, or accidents per 1,000 vehicle-miles travelled. It is particularly important to consider the implications of age in such studies, as many behaviours, like illnesses, are related to particular ages (thus incidence rates can be *stratified* for different age groups). Statistical techniques, known as *age standardisation* may be used to examine whether changes in crude (total population) rates over time are attributable to changes in age-specific rates or to changes in overall age composition. As an example, such techniques have been used to show that declines in crime in the late 20th century in the USA were in part, but not totally, attributable to changes in age structure (specifically a declining proportion of young adults in the population) (Figure 7.7) (Steffensmeier and Harer 1999).

If data are collected on individuals (or dwellings, or vehicle-miles), who are then followed over time, this provides an opportunity for *analytical* investigation of determinants, or *risk factors*.

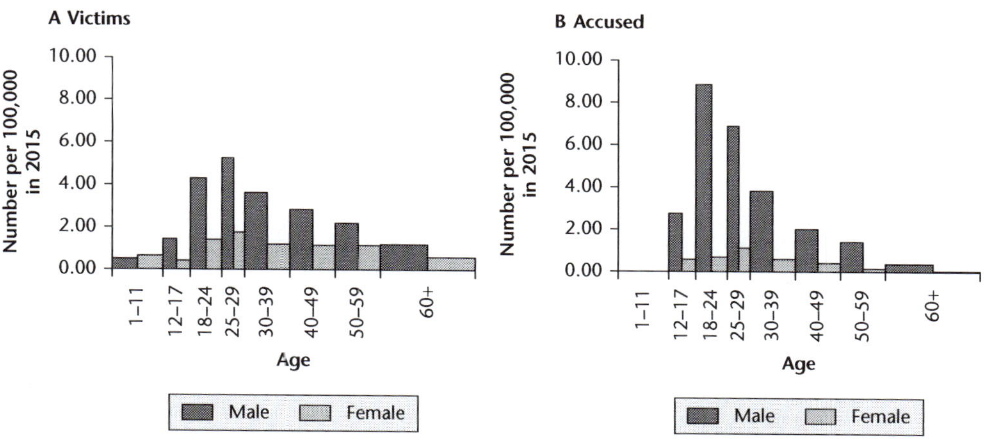

Figure 7.6 Incidence data on homicide in Canada. A: Annual incidence (risk) of being a victim of homicide, by age and sex, Canada, 2015. B: Annual incidence (risk) of being accused of homicide by age and sex, Canada, 2015. All risks per 100,000 population in that age and sex group. Note age categories, which reveal the peak incidence in young adults, and in particular in males, but do not show detailed age patterns in children and adolescents. Such figures do not reveal that some accused individuals may be responsible for multiple crimes, and/or that more than one person may be accused of an individual homicide. Data from Statistics Canada

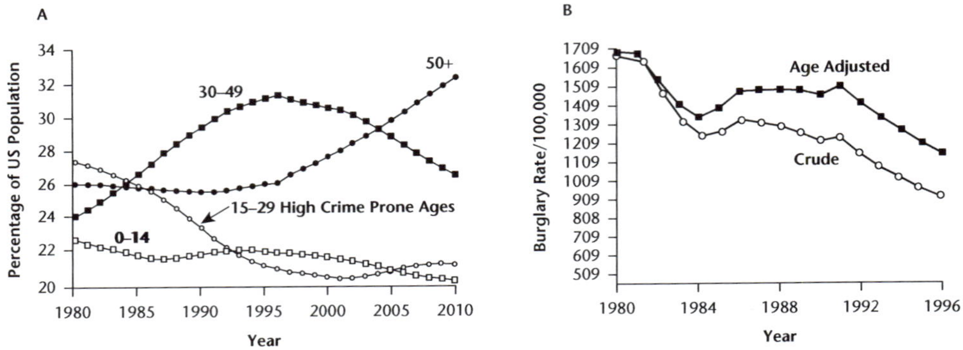

Figure 7.7 Implications of changing age distribution for uniform crime report statistics in the USA. A: changing age distribution over the years 1980–2010 (note dramatic decline in high-crime-prone age group 15–29). B: Crude and age-adjusted burglary rates in USA, 1980–1996, showing that decline in numbers of individuals in the peak crime age group (15–29) did not fully explain the overall decline in crime. Adapted from Steffensmeier and Harer, 1999.

underlying the development of some trait or outcome. The classic form of such studies, called a *cohort study*, follows up two (or more) groups of individuals (or *cohorts*, defined as groups of individuals, or things, who share some characteristic, which may be in terms of age or education or location or socio-economic background or . . .), in order to compare the *risk* or probability of some outcome between the groups. Thus a follow-up of smokers and non-smokers may (will) show that the smokers are more likely to develop lung disease and to die than are non-smokers (Doll et al. 2004). Similarly, records of road traffic accidents or of burglaries may be compared along roads whose street slighting has or has not been reduced (to save money and reduce greenhouse gas emissions), to evaluate whether the changed lighting has made any difference. In one such study, the cohorts being compared were roads where street lighting was or was not reduced, and the outcomes were incidence rates of accidents or burglaries (Steinbach et al. 2015). The key results of such investigations are the comparisons of incidence risks (or rates) between the cohorts followed up, either as a ratio or *relative risk* (one group is X *times* as likely to experience the outcome) or a *risk difference* (one group is Y percent *more* likely to experience the outcome). This is illustrated in Table 7.1.

Cohort studies are relatively simple in logic, but time consuming and expensive, as they typically require following up large numbers of individuals, sometimes for several years, in order to ensure that sufficient numbers of outcome-events are included. The need for *prospective* follow-up may be obviated if historical data exist on some risk factors in a population, in which case it may be possible to estimate incidence risks over past time, an approach known as an *historical*, or *retrospective cohort study*. Among many examples is a retrospective follow-up of 48,069 individuals registered for opioid substitution therapy between 1985 and 2010 in New South Wales, Australia for contact with the criminal justice system over subsequent years (1993–2011). This revealed detailed patterns over time and showed that 20 per cent of the individuals were responsible for two-thirds of all crimes committed by the cohort (Degenhardt et al. 2013).

Given the difficulty in organising cohort studies, it may be appropriate to approach a question differently, and to begin by selecting study subjects on the basis of their outcome experience (yes or no) and then collect historical information about previous experience with potential risk factors. This is the *case-control study* approach, whereby the investigator begins by identifying

Table 7.1 Logic of cohort and case-control studies. It is helpful to view the relationship between risk (e.g. potential causal) factors and outcomes as a *two-by-two table*, as here. In a cohort study one compares rows: i.e. the incidence of the outcome between individuals with and without the risk factor, thus a/(a+b) versus c/(c+d). The ratio of these proportions is the *relative risk* or *risk ratio*. It will be unity if the risk factor is irrelevant to the outcome, and greater than unity if the risk factor is associated with increased risk. In a case-control study one compares columns, i.e. the proportion with the risk factor between of those with and without the outcome, thus a/(a+c) versus b/(b+d). For statistical reasons, one typically compares the *odds* of having the risk factor between those with and without the outcome, thus a/c versus b/d, or (a × d)/(b × d), which is called the *odds ratio*. If the risk factor is irrelevant, thus not associated with the outcome, the odds ratio will approach unity; whereas if the risk factor is associated positively with the outcome the odds ratio will be greater than 1.

	Outcome *Yes*	*Outcome* *No*	
Risk factor Yes	a	b	a + b
Risk factor No	c	d	c + d
	a + c	b + d	Total a+b+c+d

Incidence (Risk) of outcome in those with the risk factor = R+ = a/(a+b)
Incidence (Risk) of outcome in those without the risk factor = R– = c/(c+d)
Relative risk (RR) = R+ / R– = [a/(a+b)] / [c/(c+d)]
Odds of having risk factor among those with the outcome = a / c
Odds of having risk factor among those without the outcome = b / d
Odds ratio = (a/c)/ b/d) = (a × d) / (b × d)

'cases' (which may be individual illness episodes or crimes [e.g. thefts] or individuals who have either suffered or committed a crime), and a group of 'control' institutions or individuals who are similar in general characteristics (age, sex, social group . . .) but did not experience the outcome of interest, and collects information by interview or other means as to their relevant background – for example family circumstances or education or other factors of potential relevance. The results of such an enquiry are in the form of a comparison of the proportion of those with or without the outcome, who had, or did not have, the risk factor experience. This is typically expressed in terms of an *odds ratio*, a statistic which is similar (but not identical) to the relative risk obtained in a cohort study. This is illustrated in Table 7.1. Among many examples: a study in Sweden compared characteristics of all 1,739 adult homicide victims over the years 1978–1994 with a sample selected from the general population, and found that a history of traumatic brain injury as well as physical abuse, alcohol dependence and criminal recidivism were all associated with being a homicide victim, with greater than ten-fold increases in risk (Allgulander and Nilssen 2000).

The goal of most research is the ultimate application of knowledge for the betterment of society, based upon the understanding derived from descriptive and analytical studies. It is this argument which justifies support for virtually all scientific work and institutions (even 'blue skies' research typically justifies itself as leading to future benefits). The betterment may be in terms of introducing a new vaccine to prevent a disease, or a new education curriculum to improve employment opportunities, a microfinance scheme to help poor families lift themselves out of poverty, or a sentencing policy to reduce recidivism. The performance of *intervention studies* to evaluate such efforts is a major enterprise in many fields today, and particularly interesting as the methods employed share many attributes, drawing from classical studies, mainly in the realm of health and agriculture, as well as the basic sciences (Fisher 1935). Most laboratory science disciplines use the word *experiment*, but population researchers often refer to *trials* to describe their intervention studies, to avoid negative ethical overtones of doing experiments on people. For a variety of reasons this approach has been applied less to date in the social sciences than in health, but there is now increasing application of such approaches in economics (Ranson et al. 2007), education (Torgerson 2011; Bannerjee et al. 2007) and also crime science (Bird et al. 2011; Farringdon and Jolliffe 2002; Garvin et al. 2013, Hayes et al. 2012; Olds et al. 1998).

There is a large amount of literature on issues which arise in such work, but one of the crucial initial distinctions is whether an intervention is directed at individuals (a vaccine or drug, or a counselling regimen, or custodial sentence) or at communities (an improved water supply, a school curriculum, or a piece of legislation) (Smith et al. 2015). The classic individual approach, called a *randomised controlled trial* (or RCT) provides a measure of *efficacy* of the intervention by comparing a randomised group who received versus those who did not receive the intervention (or who received some alternative – perhaps the previous standard – intervention). Randomisation provides a means to ensure that the compared groups are similar and comparable. This approach has been widely practised, and the *randomised, double-blind, placebo-controlled trial* is generally considered, at least in the health sciences, to be the strongest 'gold standard' study design for evaluating an intervention. The results are typically based on a comparison of the incidence rates of undesired outcome (e.g. disease, or death, or some crime) between those who did (R_i) and did not (R_n) receive the intervention. This is most simply done as a relative risk measure (R_i/R_n), which should be less than one if the intervention was beneficial. The efficacy (E) of the intervention may then be described as the per cent reduction in risk (of bad outcome) among those who received the intervention compared to those who did not, or

$$\begin{aligned} E &= (R_n - R_i)/R_n \\ &= 1 - R_i/R_n \end{aligned}$$

As an example, trials of measles vaccines in the 1960s showed them to have an efficacy of approximately 85 per cent in the prevention of clinical measles, leading to their widespread introduction in childhood vaccination programmes (MRC 1966).

A community intervention requires that the intervention be applied in several randomly selected communities (or *clusters*), in which the results are measured and compared to what happens in similar control communities or clusters which receive no – or a different – intervention. The randomisation of communities or clusters raises a variety of ethical and logistic as well as statistical problems, including the need to account for heterogeneity between the communities and the fact that some aspects of the intervention may diffuse, or leak, from intervention into control communities. Random allocation of a sample of neighbourhoods, villages, or schools to receive some sort of crime-prevention, economic or educational curriculum, or to be in a control group, is sometimes possible and has been achieved in a variety of examples (Garvin et al. 2013, Ranson et al. 2007; Bannerjee et al. 2007). A special type of *cluster randomised trial* design, called a *stepped wedge*, may be used when all communities are to receive an intervention, but it is logistically difficult to implement the change in all communities immediately. Implementation may then be allocated to one community selected at random, whilst the remaining communities serve as the control group. The next community to receive the intervention is selected at random, and the remaining communities remain in the control group. By the time the intervention has been rolled out to all communities, a stepped wedge will have been created of all communities before and after the intervention. Comparison between communities which had and had not received the intervention at successive periods of time forms the basis for the evaluation of effect of the intervention on measured outcomes (Smith et al. 2015).

Though the randomised controlled trial approach is widely accepted for evaluation of relatively simple interventions, there is some discussion over the most appropriate methods for the evaluation of complex social interventions, such as may be appropriate for crime prevention, given the complexity of the social factors which can influence effectiveness. Proponents of what is called, provocatively, 'realist evaluation' question the universal applicability of controlled trials, and emphasise the need to understand whether interventions work 'for whom and under what circumstances' (Pawson and Tilley 1997). The extent to which classical methods of random allocation of individuals or communities, the selection of appropriate control or comparison groups, and the examination of secondary outcomes can provide this information is debated (Bonell et al. 2013). Although there are considerable ethical and logistic problems, in addition to these more philosophical issues, involved in the evaluation of many sorts of social interventions, there is a general tendency in population research to move in the direction of various forms of controlled trials, including in education and economics, as well as crime science.

Data collection and quality

The implementation of any investigation raises many practical issues relating to the selection of an appropriate study population and the collection of required data. Cost is inevitably an issue as are concerns over access and geographic distribution and assurance of confidentiality, given the sensitive nature of much information. If a sample is to be studied, rather than an entire population, it is crucially important that the sample be representative of the population of interest, and of sufficient size to produce robust and convincing results. Virtually all research involving human subjects must pass review by institutional research ethics committees. The design of questionnaires and training and supervision of interviewers are more difficult to carry out well than is often appreciated. There is considerable accumulated experience on all of these issues (Smith et al. 2015). Collection of information relating to crimes and criminal behaviour can be especially difficult insofar as it relates to illegal acts and punishable behaviour and hence data may be hidden or denied. This may be a particular challenge for the field of crime science, but has interesting parallels in health, for example with reference to stigmatising diseases such as HIV or leprosy.

Related to this problem, the avoidance of *bias* (defined as *systematic error* – i.e. error which does not arise through chance sampling error but because the study subjects are not representative of the population, or they give deliberately wrong answers, or because the investigators were prejudiced and collected or recorded information selectively or wrongly) is a major issue in all population research and likely to be especially problematic in the study of crime. The potential for bias must be recognised, and requires detailed consideration of the representativeness and comparability of populations studied, as well as rigorous quality control of the instruments and staff involved in data collection.

Data quality is often described in terms of *validity* – defined as the extent to which they measure what they are supposed to measure. This is conventionally broken down into consideration of the ability of any measure or piece of information to correctly represent those with or without any particular characteristic. The terms *sensitivity* and *specificity* are used to describe these properties, respectively, as illustrated in Table 7.2. Separate studies are often set up in order to evaluate these parameters. It is important for investigators to critically assess the validity of their data if they are to arrive at correct conclusions.

Table 7.2 Validation. The validity of empirical data refers to whether they are correct or incorrect – i.e. whether they measure what they are meant to measure. This can be broken down into whether they correctly identify those with or without any characteristic, as set out below. The *sensitivity* of the test is the proportion of those who actually have the characteristic that the test correctly identifies, i.e. A/(A+C); the *specificity* of the test is the proportion of those who actually do not have the characteristic that the test correctly identifies, i.e. D/(B+D). Those individuals with the characteristic but not identified by the test (C) are the *false negatives*. Those individuals without the characteristic but wrongly identified by the test (B) are the *false positives*.

	Actually Yes	*Actually No*	
Test result Yes	A	B	A + B
Test result No	C	D	C + D
	A + C	B + D	Total A+B+C+D

The term *reliability* may also be used to describe data quality. This is defined less precisely than the term validity, but typically implies a measure of *repeatability* (defined as the consistency of a measurement or description between different observers or different measurement conditions).

Analysis And interpretation

A large number of statistical methods have been developed for the analysis and presentation of epidemiological research data of various sorts (Kirkwood and Sterne 2003; Rothman et al. 2008). We emphasise three major issues here.

Much research aims to find causal mechanisms underlying phenomena – factors which explain why something occurs. The *recognition and establishment of causal determinants* typically begins by demonstration of an *association* between some background factor and an outcome, be it smoking and lung cancer, or a history of sexual abuse as a child and prostitution. For an observed association to be credible it must first be of a magnitude which is unlikely to have arisen by chance – which means it much pass criteria of *statistical significance* (a commonly used criterion is that it would arise by chance less than one in 20 times, if there were no true relationship between the variables, i.e. '$p < 0.05$'). If one observes four crimes and three have some characteristic, that is far less informative than if one observes 100, of which 75 had the characteristic. Standard statistical methods allow one to calculate *confidence limits* for an observed proportion in a sample, and thus to be confident (in terms of probability) that the true proportion (i.e. of the total population) lies within specified bounds.

If an association looks to be real, and not explicable as a chance finding, a next question relates to the nature of the relationship, and in particular whether a risk factor can be considered *causal*. Epidemiologists have developed a set of criteria to assist in the argument whether a risk factor is causal, including such parameters as time sequence (which came first, as causes must precede effects), strength of association (measured by magnitude of relative risk or odds ratio), plausibility, coherence, specificity, gradient of effects and lack of alternative explanations (Hill 1965; see Table 7.3).

Table 7.3 Bradford Hill's (1965) guidelines for deciding whether an association (e.g. a statistically significant correlation) might indicate a causal relationship, with examples from health-related science and crime science

		Health-related	*Crime-related*
Strength (effect size)	The larger the relative risk, the more likely it is that an association is causal	The mortality from scrotal cancer in chimney sweeps was 200 times greater than that of persons not exposed to soot or tar or mineral oils	Strong association of homicide with narcotics trade
Consistency (reproducibility)	The repeated observation of an association in different circumstances increases the likelihood that it is causal	Many studies, in many populations, have shown an association between smoking and lung cancer	Alley gates are effective in reducing burglary in affluent and deprived areas, in different regions of the country
Specificity	An association between a risk factor and a specific effect or condition may be suggestive of causality*	HIV virus infection leads to a particular sort of immunosuppression (decline of CD4 lymphocytes)	Perpetrators of domestic violence are particularly likely to re-offend
Temporality	A cause must always happen before its effect	A dirty wound precedes onset of clinical tetanus	Drinking alcohol precedes dangerous driving
(Biological) gradient	A dose-response association between a risk factor and an effect increases the likelihood that it is causal	Risk of lung cancer increases with amount smoked (e.g. in terms of cigarettes per day); the greater the calorie intake, the greater the risk of obesity	Rates of anti-social behaviour in neighbourhoods increase as neighbourhood deprivation increases
Plausibility	A plausible mechanism between putative cause and effect increases the likelihood that an association is causal	The fact that obesity and heart disease both involve lipid metabolism supports the evidence for a causal relationship between them	Addicts commit crime to pay for drugs; treatments to recover from addiction could thus prevent crime
Coherence	If epidemiological findings agree with laboratory or other findings it is more likely to be causal	Measles vaccine induces antibodies to measles, similar to those found in individuals who are immune after natural infection	Association between crime and poor parental discipline on one hand and low self- control measures in offenders

(continued)

Table 7.3 (continued)

		Health-related	*Crime-related*
Experiment	Controlled experiment (trial) evidence for an association suggests causality	Randomised controlled trials showed that streptomycin was effective in curing tuberculosis	Randomised controlled trials show that hotspot policing reduces crime in that location
Analogy	Knowledge of a cause and effect relationship may be used to argue causality if a similar effect is associated with a new but similar risk factor	The fact that thalidomide in early pregnancy is known to lead to congenital malformations increases suspicion of causality if a new drug is associated with congenital malformation	The fact that tightening car security significantly reduced car theft suggests that mobile-phone thefts may be caused by poor phone security

Note: *Bradford Hill recognised specificity as a relatively weak criterion for causality arguments, given that some effects can have multiple causes (many things can lead to respiratory illness or religious conversion, or loss of a job, or a barroom brawl) and some causes can have multiple effects (a poor diet can lead to several different illnesses; a large inheritance may lead to wise investment and greater education or wealth, or to profligacy, laziness and abuse by con-men), contingent upon a variety of other factors

A major issue in such arguments is the distinction between associations which reflect causal mechanisms and those which reflect *confounding* – i.e. two factors may be associated not because one causes another but because both are related directly or indirectly to some other factor (see Figure 7.8). The clarification of such mechanisms can be a complicated problem, in particular when several variables are correlated – as for example are many factors associated with the poverty complex. The spurious correlations discussed above and in Figure 7.4 A–C are examples of associations having arisen because of confounding. There are several ways to detect whether an association is influenced by confounding and to make appropriate corrections, for example through ensuring that comparisons are made on data that have been stratified or matched for the potential confounding

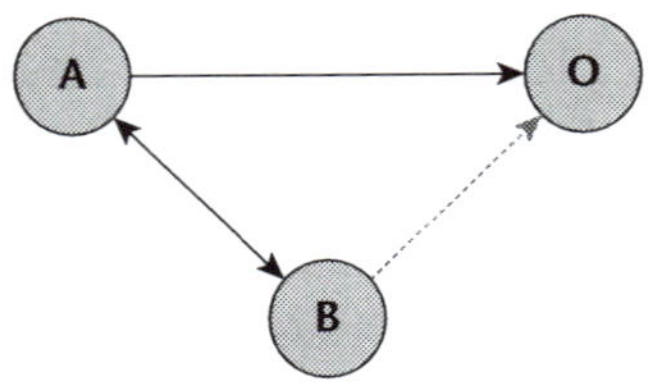

Figure 7.8 Confounding. Let us say that A is a causal factor for some outcome, O. Some other factor B is associated to A, but has no causal relation to O. If this is so, then B will appear to be associated (indirectly) with O (represented by a dotted line), and might be mistaken as a causal factor. For example, we know that smoking (A) is a cause of lung cancer (O). We also know that individuals who smoke are more likely to drink alcohol (B) than individuals who do not smoke. Because of this it will appear as though alcohol (B) is associated with lung cancer (O). On the other hand, we know that alcohol consumption (now A) is a causal factor in some violent crimes (O). Given that smoking (now B) is associated with alcohol consumption, we will observe that smoking is also associated with violent crime – an association which reflects confounding, not a direct causal relationship

factor. As an example, referring to Figure 7.4B, if one restricts comparisons between fat intake and breast cancer to women with similar reproductive histories, the correlation disappears.

While the concept of causality is important in understanding mechanisms, it is subtle, and a perennial favourite subject for philosophers. As an example of one sort of subtlety, there is overwhelming evidence, by all of the criteria mentioned above, that smoking can and does play a causal role in the aetiology of lung cancer. On the other hand, not everyone with lung cancer has been a smoker (i.e. smoking is not a *necessary cause* of lung cancer – as some people may contract lung cancer for other reasons – e.g. from occupational exposures to a variety of chemicals), and not everyone who smokes develops lung cancer (i.e. smoking is not a *sufficient cause* of lung cancer – for example some people may not be genetically disposed or may die before they develop lung cancer – or they may just be 'lucky'). It is likely that many factors associated with various crimes have similar incomplete causal relations. It is possible to measure the contribution of such causal factors in terms of the relative risk of the outcome (RR) associated with a particular risk factor, and the prevalence of the risk factor in the population (e.g. P). The basic measure, called the *population-attributable fraction* (*PAF*) gives the proportion of all outcomes (for example lung cancers) which can be attributed to smoking in a particular population, estimated as (Kirkwood and Sterne 2003):

PAF = (overall risk – risk among those without risk factor)/overall risk

PAF = P(RR-1)/[1+ P(RR-1)]

To extend the smoking and lung cancer example, it is known that in some populations smoking increases the risk of lung cancer in individual smokers by a factor of five (RR = 5) (Doll et al. 2004). If 60 per cent of individuals smoke in such a population this means that (0.6)(5-1)/[1+(0.6)(5-1)] = 0.71, thus 71 per cent of the lung cancer would be *attributable* to smoking. This is an important measure for policy discussions, insofar as the impact of any intervention on the overall frequency of any outcome is a function of the PAF associated with a particular risk factor, and the effectiveness of an intervention against that factor (e.g. the effectiveness of anti-smoking legislation in reducing smoking).

As another example: it has been estimated that people who keep guns in the home in the USA are at two times increased risk of dying from homicide in the home, compared to those who do not keep guns at home (relative risk RR=2, after adjusting for sex, age, race, education, marital status, residential status, alcohol consumption within four hours of death, illicit drug use) (Dahlberg et al. 2004). Given this result, and the fact that 40 per cent of adults in the USA keep a gun in the home, one might estimate a population-attributable fraction for the association between homicide at home and gun ownership as: PAF = (0.4)(2-1)/[1+(0.4)(2-1)] = 0.29. This implies that 29 per cent of all homicide deaths in homes were associated with keeping a gun in the home. Note however that caution is required in attributing the deaths directly to home ownership of guns, as this inference assumes that the relationship is causal. The fact that the study adjusted for many potential confounders gives some confidence in this inference, but the original paper discusses the complexity of such relationships.

Evaluation of efficacy, effectiveness and impact of interventions

We can now consider tying the various epidemiological threads together, to estimate the impact of an intervention to improve society. An intervention trial measures the *efficacy* of an intervention in individual recipients (i.e. the extent to which a preventive measure actually protects against some outcome under ideal controlled trial conditions). Being realistic, we recognise that it is likely that an intervention will not work as well when in routine practice as it does under research trial conditions. Thus we may speak of the *effectiveness* of the intervention under programme conditions. The ultimate *impact* of the intervention in improving health or well-being will then be a function of the effectiveness of the programme and the proportion of the outcome attributable to the target of the intervention (e.g. smoking and home gun ownership in the examples above).

While much research is devoted to measuring the parameters which should define the direct effect of an intervention, we also need to recognise that ultimate societal effects of policies may include additional *indirect effects*, sometimes called *externalities* by economists. The mechanisms underlying such indirect effects are many. A simple example is provided by vaccines, insofar as one can protect a total population from a disease by only vaccinating a proportion of them, by a process known as *herd immunity* (a susceptible individual may be protected just by being surrounded by individuals who have been protected by the vaccine) (Fine and Mulholland 2012). More complex examples are provided by interventions such as education, which can have many effects on individuals and societies. These indirect effects may be difficult to predict in advance, and some may even be detrimental – for example investment in education may bring benefits to certain sectors of society but the associated diversion of resources may lead to difficulties to other sectors. Recognition of such relationships illustrates the importance of the careful application of sound epidemiological methods in studying population characteristics, be they in terms of health, education, standard of living . . . or crime.

Conclusion

All of the descriptive and analytic concepts and methods described above are applicable in research on a very wide variety of attributes of populations, be they related to crime or to disease – or to educational attainment or fertility or economic circumstances or other individual or social circumstances or behaviours. The intervention methods are likewise applicable to efforts to change the frequency or pattern of any physical or social attributes within populations. It is and will be to the benefit of all the separate population sciences to learn from experiences of other – even apparently distantly related – disciplines to optimise the effectiveness of their research for the growth of knowledge and ultimate betterment of society. The crime science literature illustrates many examples of all these methods and is in the vanguard of the trend to establish the traditional social sciences on an increasingly firm and rigorous base.

Acknowledgements

The authors express their gratitude to Mark Fletcher for drawing the figures and to the editors for helpful comments on successive drafts of this chapter.

Note

1 Epidemiologists use the terms *risk* and *rate* with reference to incidence measures. Formally, according to some current usage, a *risk* is a probability of an *outcome* (an illness, or experience, e.g. being the perpetrator or a victim of a crime) over the given period of time. This is the proportion of individuals followed up who experience the 'outcome' over a specified time period, and thus is a number between 0 and 1. A *rate* is measured against a person time denominator (e.g. number of events per 100 person-years), and can in theory take any value from zero to infinity. For 'uncommon' outcomes, e.g. which occur to less than 10 per cent of individuals over the period of time, the risk and rate measures are numerically very similar, but they have particular properties appropriate for different statistical analyses (Kirkwood and Sterne 2003).

References

Akers, T. A., Lanier, M. M. Epidemiological criminology: coming full circle. *American Journal of Public Health* 2009; *99*(3): 397–402.

Allgulander, C., Nilssen, B. Victims of criminal homicide in Sweden: a matched case-control study of health and social risk factors among all 1,739 cases during 1978–1994. *American Journal of Psychiatry* 2000; *157*: 244–247.

Amber, L. Beckley, A. L., Kuja-Halkola, R., Lundholm, L., Långström, N., Frisell, T. Association of height and violent criminality: results from a Swedish total population study. *International Journal of Epidemiology* 2014; *43*(3): 835–842.

Banerjee, A., Cole, S., Duflo, E., Linden, L. Remedying Education: Evidence from Two Randomized Experiments in India. *Quarterly Journal of Economics* 2007; *122*: 1235–1264.

Bird, S. M., Goldacre, B., Strang, J. Give judges evidence on which to base sentencing. *BMJ* 2011; *342*: 335.

Bonell, C., Fletcher, A., Morton, M., Lorenc, T., Moore, L. Realist randomised trials: a new approach to evaluating complex public health interventions. *Social Science & Medicine* 2013; *75*: 2299–2306.

Carroll, K. K. Experimental evidence of dietary factors and hormone-dependent cancers. *Cancer Research* 1975; *35*: 3374–3383.

CDC Pneumocystis Pneumonia – Los Angeles. *MMWR*, 1981, *30*(21); 250–252. www.cdc.gov/violenceprevention.

Coggon, D., Barker, D., Rose, G. *Epidemiology for the Uninitiated.* 5th edition. London: Wiley-Blackwell, 2003.

Dahlberg, L., Ikeda, R. M., Kresnow, M.-J. Guns in the home and risk of a violent death in the home: findings from a National Study. *American Journal of Epidemiology* 2004; *160*: 929–936.

Degenhardt, L., Gisev, N., Travena, J., Larney, S., Kimber, J., Burns, L., Shanahan, M., Weatherburn, D. Engagement with the criminal justice system among opioid-dependent people: a retrospective cohort study. *Addiction* 2013; *108*: 2152–2165.

Doll, R., Peto, R., Boreham, J., Sutherland, I. Mortality in relation to smoking: 50 years observation on male British doctors. *BMJ* 2004; *328*: 1519–1533. doi:10.1136/bmj.38142.554479.AE.

Donohue, J. J., Levitt, S. D. The impact of legalised abortion on crime. *Quarterly Journal of Economics* 2001; *116*: 379–420.

Durkheim, E. *Le Suicide: Etude de Sociologie* (1897) (translated as *Suicide: A Study in Sociology* by J. A. Spaulding and G. Simpson. London: Routledge and Kegan Paul, 1952.

Fajnzylber, P., Lederman, D., Loayza, N. Inequality and violent crime. *Journal of Law and Economics* 2002; *45*: 1–40.

Farrell, G., Tseloni, A., Mailley, J., Tilley, N. The crime drop and the security hypothesis. *Journal of Research in Crime and Delinquency* 2010; *1*: 29.

Farringdon, D. P., Jolliffe, D. A feasibility study into using a randomised controlled trial to evaluate treatment pilots at HMP Whitemoor. Home Office Online Report 14/02, 2002.

Fine, P. E. M. Another defining moment for epidemiology. *Lancet* 2015; *385*: 319–320.

Fine, P. E. M., Goldacre, B. M., Haines, A. Epidemiology – a science for the people. *Lancet* 2013; *381*: 1249–1252.

Fine, P. E. M., Mulholland, K. Community immunity. Chapter 71 in *Vaccines*, 6th edition, edited by S. A. Plotkin, W.A. Orenstein and P.A. Offit. Philadelphia, PA: Elsevier Inc., pp. 1395–1412: 2012.

Fisher, R. A. *The Design of Experiments*, 5th edition. New York: Hafner Publishing Company, 1949.

Freeman, M., Zeegers, M. *Forensic Epidemiology: Principles and Practice.* Cambridge,MA: Academic Press, 2016.

Garvin, E. C., Cannuscio, C. C., Branas, C. C. Greening vacant lots to reduce violent crime: a randomised controlled trial. *Injury Prevention* 2013; *19*: 198–203.

Goodman, M. *Future Crimes: A Warning about the Internet of Things.* New York: Doubleday, 2015.

Gordis, L. *Epidemiology*, 4th edition. Philadelphia, PA: Elsevier Saunders, 2008.

Hayes, R., Downs, D. M., Blackwood, R. Anti-theft procedures and fixtures: a randomized controlled trial of two situational crime prevention measures. *Journal of Experimental Criminology* 2012; *8*: 1–15.

Herrmann, C. R. The dynamics of robbery and violence hot spots. *Crime Science* 2015; *4*: 33. doi10.1186/s40163-015-1142-5.

Hill, A. B. The environment and disease: association or causation? *Proceedings of the Royal Society of Medicine* 1965; *58*: 295–300.

Kirkwood, B. R., Sterne, J. A. C. *Essential Medical Statistics*, 2nd edition. Oxford: Blackwell Science, 2003.

Le Comber, S. C., Rossmo, D. K., Hassan, A. N., Fuller, D. O., Beier, J. C. Geographic profiling as a novel spatial tool for targeting infectious disease control. *International Journal of Health Geographics* 2011; *10*. Available at http://ij-healthgeographics.biomedcentral.com/articles/10.1186/1476-072X-10-3.

Logan, J., Hill, H. A., Black, M. L., Crosby, A. E., Karch, D. L., Barnes, J. D., Lubell, K. M. Characteristics of perpetrators in homicide-followed-by-suicide incidents: national violent death reporting system – 17 US States, 2003–2005. *American Journal of Epidemiology* 2008; *168*: 1056–1064.

MRC Measles Vaccine Committee. Vaccination against measles: a clinical trial of live measles vaccine given alone and live vaccine preceded by killed vaccine. *BMJ* 1966; I: 441–446.

Olds, D., Henderson, C. R., Cole, R., Eckenrode, J., Kitzman, H., Luckey, D., Pettitt, L., Sidora, K., Morris, P., Powers, J. Long term effects of nurse home visitation on children's criminal and antisocial behaviour: 15 year follow-up of a randomised controlled trial. *JAMA* 1998; *280*: 1238–1244.

Ogburn, W. F. Factors in variation of crime among cities. *Journal of the American Statistical Association* 1935; *30*: 12–34.

Pawson, R., Tilley, N. *Realistic Evaluation*. London: Sage, 1997.

Philipson, T. J., Posner, R. A. The economic epidemiology of crime. *Journal of Law Economics* 1996; *39*: 405–433.

Porta, M. (ed) *A Dictionary of Epidemiology*, 6th edition. Oxford: Oxford University Press, 2014.

Ranson, M. K., Sinha, T., Chatterjee, M., Gandhi, F., Jayswal, R., Patel, F., Morris, S. S., Mills, A. J. Equitable utilisation of Indian community based health insurance scheme among its rural membership: cluster randomised controlled trial. *BMJ* 2007; *334*: 1309.

Rothman, K. J., Greenland, S., Lash, T. L. *Modern Epidemiology*, 3rd edition. Philadelphia, PA: Lippincott Williams & Wilkins, 2008.

Sariaslan, A., Långström, N., D'Onofrio, B., Hallqvist, J., Franck, J., Lichtenstein, P. The impact of neighbourhood deprivation on adolescent violent criminality and substance misuse: A longitudinal, quasi-experimental study of the total Swedish population. *International Journal of Epidemiology* 2013; *42*(4): 1057–1066.

Slutkin, G., Ransford, C., Brent Decker, R. Cure violence: treating violence as a contagious disease. *Envisioning Criminology*. Dordrecht, Heidelberg, London, New York: Springer International Publishing, 2015; pp. 43–56.

Smith, P. G., Morrow, R. H., Ross, D. A. *Field Trials of Health Interventions: A Tool-box*, 3rd edition. Oxford: Oxford University Press, 2015.

Snow, J. *On the Mode of Communication of Cholera*, 2nd Edition. London: Churchill, 1855. Reproduced in *Snow on Cholera*, Commonwealth Fund, New York 1936. Reprinted by New York: Hafner, 1965.

Steffensmeier, D., Harer, M. D. Making sense of recent US crime trends, 1980 to 1996/1998: age composition effects and other explanations. *Journal of Research in Crime and Delinquency* 1999; *36*: 235–274.

Steinbach, R., Perkins, C., Thompson, L., Johnson, S., Armstrong, B., Green, J., Grundy, C., Wilkinson, P., Edwards, P. The effect of reduced street lighting on road casualties and crime in England and Wales: a controlled interrupted time series analysis. *Journal of Epidemiology and Community Health* 2015; *69*: 1118–1124. doi:10.1136/jech-2015-206012.

Stretesky, P. B., Lynch, M. J. The relationship between lead and crime. *Journal of Health and Social Behavior* 2004; *45*: 214–229.

Szklo, M., Nieto, F. J. *Epidemiology: Beyond the Basics*, 2nd edition. Burlington, MA: Jones and Bartlett Publishers, 2007.

Teutsch, S. M., Churchill, R. E. *Principles and Practice of Public Health Surveillance*, 2nd edition. Oxford: Oxford University Press, 2000.

Torgerson, C. Education research, call for controls. *Science 2011*, *333*: 1220.

Vaughn, M. G., Salas-Wright, C. P., Maynard, B. R., Qian, Z., Terzis, L., Kusow, A. M., DeLisi, M. Criminal epidemiology and the immigrant paradox: intergenerational discontinuity in violence and antisocial behaviour. *Journal of Criminal Justice* 2014; *42*: 483–490.

Webb, P., Bain, C. *Essential Epidemiology: An Introduction for Students and Health Professionals*, 2nd edition. Cambridge: Cambridge University Press, 2011.

Webster, D. W., Vernick, J. S., Hepburn, L. M. Effects of Maryland's law banning 'Saturday night special' handguns on homicides *American Journal of Epidemiology* 2002; *155*(5): 406–412.

Weisburd, D. L., McEwen, T. *Introduction: Crime mapping and Crime Prevention* 2015. Available at SSRN: http://ssrn.com/abstract=2629850 or http://dx.doi.org/10.2139/ssrn.2629850.

WHO: www.who.int/violence_injury_prevention/violence/en.

Wilderman, C., Wang, E. A. Mass incarceration, public health and widening inequality in the USA. *Lancet* 2017; *389*: 1464–1574.

Wright, A. Hacking cars. *Communications of the ACM* 2011; *54*: 18–19.

8
Mathematics

Toby Davies

Introduction

In 1940, towards the end of his career, the Cambridge mathematician G. H. Hardy wrote *A Mathematician's Apology*, which has come to be known as one of the most compelling accounts of what it is to study mathematics. One of the themes of the essay is the reverence afforded to pure mathematics – that which is not motivated by a real-world problem – to the extent that it has been characterised as a defence of mathematics as 'art for art's sake': that no truly worthy mathematics has any application in the real world. Although Hardy denies this, he does nevertheless state that 'nothing I have ever done is of the slightest practical use'; a statement somewhat at odds with the key principles of crime science. If this is indeed representative of the attitudes – and contributions of mathematicians, the fact that a chapter on this topic should appear in this handbook is perhaps, therefore, surprising.

The views of Hardy, however, belong to a different age, and the role of mathematics in modern science has evolved to such an extent that applied research is now far more common. Indeed, the distinction between the two forms has been shown to be illusory, nowhere more starkly than in Hardy's own field of number theory, which is concerned with the intrinsic properties of numbers and the relationships between them. What was once thought to be the most 'inapplicable' field of all now forms the basis for the encryption systems by which all online transactions are protected: in many respects the most significant security measure in the modern world.

While it is relatively intuitive that mathematics should play a role in technological development and the study of physical systems, however, its relevance to social phenomena such as crime is much less obvious. Indeed, social systems have traditionally been considered to be simply too complex to be suitable for mathematical treatment. The phenomena in question involve the actions of, and interactions between, human individuals, both of which are far more complex than the laws which govern physical systems. In recent years, however, a number of techniques and approaches have been developed in order to deal with the challenges posed by such complexity. These provide a foothold from which mathematical progress can be made, and have inspired a surge of interest in the application of mathematics to issues which were previously thought intractable. Among these is crime, the modelling and analysis of which has attracted substantial interest within the mathematical community in recent years.

Mathematics has a role to play across a number of aspects of crime science. By nature, it is a field that is concerned with formalisation and rigour, and it therefore provides a means by which concepts and relationships can be expressed in concrete terms. At its most basic, this may simply facilitate other work, for example by providing a framework for the analysis of social networks. The real power of the approach, however, lies in modelling: the encoding of behavioural mechanisms in simplified mathematical terms. By studying the properties and behaviour of such models, insight can be gained into the situations they represent: the range of possible outcomes, and the consequences of changes, for example. Given that many key concepts of crime science – intervention, evaluation and prediction – can be framed in such terms, the relevance of mathematical treatment begins to become much more apparent. Crucially, the approach also brings with it a uniquely logical and rigorous perspective, thereby complementing the strengths of other contributory disciplines.

The purpose of this chapter is to outline the aspects of mathematics which have greatest potential to be of value within a crime science approach. It will begin by giving an overview of the approaches and techniques which are likely to be of relevance, with particular emphasis on complexity science approaches. It will then give a number of examples of topics on which work has already been carried out, giving a brief review of past research and discussing its relevance to crime science. The chapter will conclude with a discussion of the prospects for the continued integration of mathematics within the crime science agenda.

What is mathematics?

So far in this chapter, the term 'mathematics' has been used in a general sense, and it seems sensible to begin by clarifying in what sense it will be used here. In truth, the term encompasses such a diverse range of approaches and techniques that it is difficult to define concisely, and attempts to do so – 'the study of quantity' or 'the study of patterns' – are so broad as to be uninformative. Maths is both a way of thinking and an array of techniques, many of which bear little relation to each other; the challenge here is to identify which of these can offer a meaningful contribution to crime science.

Some types of mathematics, of course, already arise frequently in the study of crime, and require no introduction: almost all research with a quantitative element will include some statistical analysis, for example. However, the role played by statistics in such work is primarily functional, in the sense that it provides tools which support other analytical approaches. Rarely are statistical methods the primary focus of criminological research, and their application to crime data is no different to that in many other fields. Although the techniques are undoubtedly sophisticated, the approach itself does not represent a singularly mathematical perspective.

Where mathematics does have the potential to make a distinctive contribution is through its ability to encode functional relationships. The crucial term here is 'functional': rather than simply expressing the numerical association between quantities, the purpose of such approaches is to describe the underlying mechanisms by which quantities are related. Rather than asserting that harsher sentences are associated with lower crime rates, for example, such a representation might describe the effect on the cost–benefit calculations of individual offenders, and express the result of this in the aggregated population. The duality between real-world processes and their representations means that analysis can be used to examine the true workings of the system, taking into account all instrumental relationships. This process can be summarised as mathematical modelling.

The basic premise of mathematical modelling is to produce a simplified representation of a system in quantitative terms. The process can be considered as a sequence of steps:

1 Observe some situation or phenomenon
2 Propose a hypothetical generative mechanism
3 Express this mechanism in mathematical terms
4 Verify that the behaviour of the model conforms to empirical observations
5 Investigate the properties of the model in order to gain more general insights.

It is relatively easy to see how this framework can be applied in crime science. Certainly there is no shortage of interesting phenomena (many of which are quantified statistically) and behavioural hypotheses which seek to explain them. The main challenges therefore lie in steps 3, 4 and 5, and concern the translation between these real-world concepts and their mathematical representation. Each of these steps, however, has the potential to be of value in understanding criminal phenomena.

Step 3 represents the key bridge between sociological and mathematical terminology. Because of the formality of mathematical language, model specification requires the researcher to express concepts (some of which may be qualitative in nature) in precise terms. This has a clarifying effect because it requires concepts to be concretely defined and relationships fully enumerated: any vagueness or inconsistency of theory must be eliminated. This is clearly well aligned with the need for transparency and precision in crime science, and it is also notable that this aspect comes as a by-product of the modelling process: no mathematical analysis is required, and it is simply an exercise in specification.

The model built in step 3 is a means of encoding a hypothesis so that its consequences can be explored quantitatively; in this sense, it represents a rigorous (and perhaps complex) thought experiment. The aim of step 4 is to examine how well these consequences match with reality, in order to assess the validity of the model. This represents a test of the underlying hypotheses: if the model fails to reproduce real-world behaviour, the proposed mechanism cannot be adequate. If, on the other hand, the model conforms to empirical observation, the assumed process can be considered to be a feasible candidate explanation. The notions of 'necessary' and 'sufficient' are important here (and, indeed, throughout mathematics). 'Sufficient' indicates that a model (or feature of one) produces the correct behaviour, but does not rule out other (perhaps simpler) explanations. 'Necessary', on the other hand, denotes a feature which must be present in order to generate a behaviour. Establishing which aspects of theory are essential, and which are superfluous, is clearly of value in the context of crime science.

Steps 3 and 4 are not necessarily unique to mathematical modelling, and similar principles are present in other approaches, such as agent-based modelling. Where a mathematical approach is truly distinctive, however, is in the level of analysis which can be performed on models. While the workings of other models can be opaque and difficult to unpick, the use of generalised mathematical methods means that sophisticated analytical methods can be applied. This means that deep insight can be drawn into the behaviour of such models: their response to changes in parameters, their evolution over time, the range of possible outputs and the circumstances under which they arise. Despite the mathematical language, in many cases these issues correspond to real-world questions. Examples of these include:

- How would behaviour differ in an alternative setting (e.g. a different country)?
- Are there adverse phenomena (e.g. crime outbreaks) which have not been observed but could arise?
- How will activity change over time?
- What would be the effect of an intervention (e.g. a design change or prevention strategy)?

In all cases, the crucial point is that the findings are quantitative and based on rigorous representation of the underlying system.

Mathematical modelling is not, of course, without shortcomings. The approach is based on simplification and, while much of its analytical power is derived from this, it also represents a weakness. Models of this type will, by definition, omit some effects and fail to capture the nuance of others, and this renders them an easy target for criticism. Questions of the form 'why is effect X not included?' will be familiar to any modeller, and are frequently cited when attempting to discredit any particular model.

Such criticisms, however, miss the point of the exercise; models are not intended to provide comprehensive descriptions. The key principle is that, by sacrificing exact correspondence with reality, other advantages can be gained, and these concern both the theoretical and practical objectives of modelling. The theoretical aspect is summarised well by the dictum 'the model is finished not when there is nothing left to add, but when there is nothing left to take away'. In crime science, the ability to reduce a phenomenon to its essential components is part of the problem-solving approach, and mathematics can prove valuable in that context. In practical terms, the argument is simply that the value of a model is determined exclusively by its utility: the proof is in the pudding, and if a model is of use in preventing crime, any omissions or simplifications are immaterial.

Mathematical approaches to crime

As stated previously, crime is not an issue which has traditionally been considered suitable for mathematical modelling. This view is largely due to the number and intricacy of behaviours involved: crime is simply too complex an issue to be captured in a few equations. In recent years, however, there has been a rapid growth in research concerned with precisely this kind of large real-world system. While these may never be as amenable to analysis as classical topics, the application of bespoke techniques does allow progress to be made.

There is no universal definition of a 'complex system', primarily because the scope of the field is so broad, and it is most often defined either by example of by specifying the general properties which characterise it. Exactly which of these is emphasised depends on context, but three properties are common to all working definitions (see Newman, 2011):

1 The system is composed of a large number of components
2 The behaviour and interaction of these components is non-trivial
3 The collective behaviour of the system does not follow straightforwardly from the micro-level mechanisms.

It is the third of these properties – the presence of so-called 'emergent' behaviour – which truly distinguishes complex systems. Such phenomena are typically non-linear, and span a wide range, from pattern formation to chaotic behaviour. The common attribute is that they are 'irreducible', in the sense that they are only observed at the macro-level.

That criminal phenomena can be considered in this way is relatively easy to see. Properties 1 and 2 above are almost immediate since crime occurs in large societies and involves human activities. With regard to property 3, a number of criminological phenomena can be considered to be emergent. An appealing example is the classic 'broken windows' hypothesis (Wilson & Kelling, 1982): this specifies an individual-level effect (the change in an offender's perception as a result of environmental cues) which ultimately is manifested as an area-level problem (the presence of endemic, and perhaps more egregious, criminality). For crime more generally, the presence of unexpected effects and the difficulty of exercising control are characteristic of the non-linearities and feedback loops associated with complex social systems (Castellano et al., 2009).

Complex systems arise in many domains, and examples can be found in ecology (Levin, 1998), finance (Mantegna & Stanley, 2000) and urban studies (Batty, 2007), to name only three. The focus here is on crime, however, and it therefore makes most sense to outline the various techniques that are most commonly applied. The field is inherently interdisciplinary and, whilst fundamentally mathematical, incorporates approaches from physics, economics and computer science. A selection of those which most readily apply to crime will now be described.

Dynamical systems

Dynamical systems theory is concerned with describing mathematically the evolution of quantities, or entities, over time. It is the aspect of complexity science which resembles classical applied mathematics most closely, and many of the models are closely related to those seen in other fields, such as fluid dynamics. The central objective is to describe the change over time of defined variables (f and g, say), which represent some properties of the system.

When the variables in question are continuous-valued (i.e. can take a smooth range of values) the description most often comes in the form of differential equations. Such equations specify the rate of change of a variable (denoted $\frac{df}{dt}$, for example) as a function of itself and other variables, the form of which reflects the hypothesised mechanism. It is these rates of change which determine the behaviour over time, and typically one equation will be defined for each variable of interest. Taken together, these constitute a system of equations, and these encode the model.

When the rate of change of one variable is a function of the value of another variable (e.g. when $\frac{df}{dt}$ is a function of g), this represents an interaction, and the differential equations are said to be 'coupled'. It is these couplings which generate interesting behaviours, and it is the intricate patterns of coupling which generate much of the distinctive behaviour of complex systems. Equation-based models, however, are some of the most mathematically tractable, as the field is well developed and includes a range of very powerful techniques (Arrowsmith & Place, 1992; Strogatz, 1994).

Mathematical analysis of dynamical systems can be used to characterise the evolution of a system over time and investigate issues such as pattern formation and stability. Stability refers to the effect on the system of small perturbations: a stable solution is one which is robust, whereas unstable solutions are liable to undergo dramatic qualitative changes. These are issues with important real-world interpretation: instability, in whatever form it takes, is generally an undesirable characteristic of a system, and is indicative of dramatic potential consequences.

Many criminal issues have a dynamic component – aggregate crime rates, levels of incarceration, spatial patterns, for example – and this type of modelling is a natural choice in such cases. The dynamic variables can be either macro-level (e.g. national crime rate) or micro- (e.g. the number of offenders at a certain location) and non-criminal quantities may also be included: a model for metal theft might incorporate commodity prices, for example. The challenge is to derive equations from hypothesised behaviours, but once this is done they can be used to investigate behaviour (or make forecasts) in great detail.

Networks

One of the topics which is most closely associated with complexity science is the study of networks. The term 'network' refers to a collection of discrete entities (called *nodes* or *vertices*) and connections between them (known as *edges* or *links*). Much of the terminology is derived from the mathematical field of 'graph theory', and networks can be thought of as graphs arising in the real world.

Social networks are one of the most well-known types of network, and provide a good illustrative example. In such networks, nodes represent actors (i.e. individuals) and links represent social relationships between them (such as friendship, communication or physical contact). Many other types of network are also studied, however: examples can be found in telecommunications (e.g. the internet), transport (e.g. air travel) and ecology (e.g. food webs). Network representations are versatile and can represent many different types of relationship: *directed* networks allow links to have directionality, and *weighted* networks are those in which some value can be associated with links (such as frequency of contact).

The study of networks involves both the analysis of real-world networks and their use in theoretical models. Research of the first type is concerned with characterising the structure of networks, in particular by measuring the 'centrality' of nodes. Many different notions of centrality exist – a simple one is the number of links a node has – and these emphasise different aspects of structure. Research has shown that many real-world networks exhibit common statistical properties (Albert & Barabási, 2002), and a wide variety of examples has been explored (Costa et al., 2011). This kind of analysis can be used to assess the importance of nodes, or the function they play in the network. A related topic is that of community detection, which seeks to identify meaningful groups of nodes.

Networks arise in a number of criminal contexts. Social relationships are a fundamental aspect of several criminological topics: while organised offending is perhaps the most common, network-based approaches can also be used to investigate relationships between victims, for example. As well as providing a convenient structure for data, analysis can offer insight into the roles played by various actors (e.g. command or brokerage) and reveal organisational signatures. Other criminal issues also involve networks. Transport networks are a key determinant of the built environment and may therefore exert a significant influence on spatial phenomena. In a more general security context, network concerns are also crucial in understanding the resilience of infrastructure (e.g. power networks) and must be considered in the profiling of risk.

Game theory

Game theory is a field which has primarily been developed within economics and which concerns decision-making. The term 'game' is slightly misleading: it simply refers to a scenario in which two or more actors (the *players*) must decide between a number of possible actions, after which they will receive a payoff. The crucial point is that the payoff to a given player is dependent upon the actions of the other player(s): Player A's payoff after taking action X depends on which action was taken by Player B. Game theory is therefore the study of decision-making and strategy in situations where it is necessary to account for the behaviour of others. The object of the analysis is typically concerned with finding *equilibria*: strategies for each player which are mutually optimal and therefore represent rational behaviour.

Games can vary in a number of respects – the number of players, the number of stages, whether actions are taken simultaneously – and can be very complex. A number of simple games (two players, two actions each), however, are very well known, such as the Prisoner's Dilemma. Although games such as these may seem abstract or whimsical, in fact they capture the essence of much more general concepts (e.g. co-operation and defection) and can be applied to a range of real-world situations.

Game theory can be used to study adaptation and evolution. In this context, games are played repeatedly between actors in a population, and actors are able to update their strategies in response to the outcome of each round. Over time, actors may gravitate towards certain strategies, thereby suggesting that they are dominant in some sense. This can be applied to the study of social norms, and a famous example concerns the emergence of co-operation in a repeated Prisoner's Dilemma (Axelrod, 1984).

Game theory applies naturally to criminal phenomena because rational behaviour is intrinsic to much criminological theory. Indeed the most fundamental decision of all – whether to commit a crime – can be framed in this way: crime offers a potential reward, but the actions of others determine whether it will instead result in capture and punishment. Many other issues could also be considered as games, such as willingness to intervene and severity of punishment. Resource allocation by law enforcement can also be framed as a game, and this can be used to explore preventative or defensive strategies.

Areas of application

The principles and techniques outlined in this chapter are versatile, in the sense that they can be applied to a wide range of topics; indeed, almost anything that can be quantified can, in principle, be modelled. Within crime science, a number of topics are particularly amenable to mathematical treatment, and research can be partitioned into a number of key areas. In this section, several of these topics will be reviewed: the motivation for, and value of, the mathematical approach will be described, and examples of research will be given.

Spatio-temporal patterns

The mathematical interest in spatio-temporal patterns of crime is an example of a field which has been motivated directly by empirical findings within geographical criminology. In particular, the observation of dynamic patterns within crime data – most notably the occurrence of hotspots and near-repeat victimisation – provides an ideal target for modelling: a stylised phenomenon for which analogies can be drawn with other physical processes. In this case, the apparent spreading of crime invites comparison with classical physical diffusion processes and related models of pattern formation.

In the case of urban crime, a number of behavioural hypotheses (including environmental theories) provide possible explanations for these patterns. The modelling task is therefore straightforward: to encode these hypotheses mathematically, and examine whether they are capable of generating patterns similar to those observed empirically. If a feasible model can be found, this is of potential value in a number of respects. At a basic level, it shows that the hypothesised behaviours do indeed provide a plausible explanation for real-world patterns. Furthermore, though, analysis of such a model can be used to investigate the conditions under which patterns form, and the way that they evolve. The latter of these is perhaps of greatest significance: if the dynamics of patterns can be understood, this raises the prospect that they can be extrapolated into the future. This amounts to spatial prediction, which is of clear potential value for prevention.

A prototypical example of this approach is the model of burglary introduced by Short et al. (2008). In its most basic form, this model is specified in terms of the behaviour of individual actors: burglars move between houses arranged on a grid, and are attracted towards properties of higher 'attractiveness'. When attractiveness is sufficient, they carry out offences, each of which triggers a temporary elevation in the attractiveness of the victimised property (representing a 'boost' effect; see Pease, 1998). Crucially, the authors are then able to express this model (essentially an agent-based one) in the form of differential equations. By analysing these mathematically, it is possible to establish the conditions under which hotspots form, and describe explicitly their morphology and evolution. This goes beyond what can be deduced form agent-based simulations, in which such phenomena can only be observed qualitatively.

The Short model has been adapted and extended in a number of ways, most notably through the inclusion of police activity (Pitcher, 2010; Jones et al., 2010). Motivated by the apparent role of street networks in crime patterning (see Davies & Johnson, 2014), a similar network-based model has also been proposed (Davies & Bishop, 2013). Other approaches have also been employed, with different theoretical emphasis: Nadal et al. (2010), for example, also include a notion of 'social tension' in their model, while the statistical approach of Mohler et al. (2011) models crimes by analogy with earthquakes. The real-world value of such modelling is exemplified by the fact that the latter of these forms the basis for a 'predictive policing' system in active use (Mohler et al., 2015).

Although the majority of published models are concerned with high-volume urban crime, several other phenomena have also been considered. Recent high-profile instances of rioting have stimulated interest in that area, with models proposed for the cases of London (Davies et al., 2013) and Paris (Berestycki et al., 2015). In both cases, the models seek to combine behavioural principles (target selection, contagious behaviour) with the effect of spatially varying demographic factors. Similar principles of target selection have also been employed in the context of maritime piracy (Marchione et al., 2014), with a view to informing defensive strategies.

Gang territoriality and interaction

An interesting modelling challenge is posed in situations in which crime results from the interactions between two criminal populations, most naturally exemplified by inter-gang rivalry and violence. The prominent role of territoriality means that this has a spatial component, and significant parallels can be drawn with spatial ecology: gangs are analogous to species, competing for resources and territory. The situation can also be cast as a 'predator–prey' system, in which predation may correspond to efforts by law enforcement to reduce gang size. Understanding the dynamics of these populations can be of value in anticipating territorial changes, predicting outbreaks of violence, and suggesting measures by which antagonistic activity can be minimised.

An early attempt to employ an ecological approach to examine gang dynamics was the work of Crane et al. (2000), which framed the growth of gangs as a competitive process between existing gangs and social control mechanisms. The model displays behaviour consistent with real-world observations, including abrupt shifts in gang size, and finds conditions under which social control is most effective. More recent approaches have used a similar framework, but instead applied to the hostile relationships between gangs. Brantingham et al. (2012) examined the formation of territorial boundaries between pairs of gangs, taking into account the location of their central 'set spaces', and this was extended to the case of more than two gangs by Smith et al. (2012).

The ecological approach is not, however, the only one to have been applied to gang dynamics. Using methods from statistical physics, for example, Barbaro et al. (2013) model the marking of territory using graffiti, and establish conditions under which distinct divisions form. Such work is of potential practical value because it is at these interfaces where flashpoints of violence are likely to occur. On a related theme, the point process formulation has also been applied, particularly as a model of retaliation (Egesdal et al., 2010; Short et al., 2014). This approach has shown potential as a means of predicting missing data, particularly with respect to the identification of unknown participants in violent crimes (Stomakhin et al., 2011).

Criminal networks

Many criminal phenomena involve interactions between actors, and networks provide a means by which these can be represented and studied. The interactions in question can take many forms antipathetic relationships such as gang rivalries have been studied in this way (van Gennip et al., 2013) – but most examples involve cooperative relationships, as in organised crime or terrorism. In such contexts, networks can be derived from various forms of data – communications, for example, or co-offending – and their structures examined. Various questions can then be addressed using social network analysis (Carrington, 2011): the extent to which a structure is hierarchical, the identification of roles and the measurement of influence. There are numerous examples of topics which have been investigated in this way, including organised crime (Ferrara et al., 2014), terrorism (Krebs, 2002; Medina, 2014; Gill et al., 2014) and trafficking (Mancuso, 2014).

The analysis of organised criminal networks is complicated significantly by their covert nature: by definition, such enterprises seek to conceal their association. How this can be addressed is a prominent theme of research in this area, with a number of approaches suggested for how probabilistic inferences about network structure can be made in clandestine settings (Gill & Freeman, 2013; Gerdes, 2014). The Dynamic Network Analysis approach introduced by (Carley, 2003) seeks to combine data from numerous sources with predictive network analysis techniques, and has been applied in the context of terrorism (Carley, 2006).

One of the most immediate motivations for studying criminal networks is the possibility of establishing how they might best be disrupted. The attack tolerance of networks has been well studied (Albert et al., 2000), and a number of general strategies exist, many of which focus on the elimination (via arrest, for example) of highly central or influential actors. However, recent research by Duijn et al. (2014) has suggests that such strategies are typically unsuccessful for criminal networks, which appear to display high resilience and the ability to re-organise after attack.

Resilience and inspection

While resilience of criminal networks is unwelcome, there are many other security contexts in which resilience is desirable. For potential targets of crime, for example, and especially those which are large inter-connected systems, the ability to withstand attack is something which a crime science approach would seek to foster. Since many such systems (e.g. infrastructure) can be represented as networks, mathematics can assist in this respect by examining their response to various types of attack. This can be used to identify weak points and to understand critical transitions: the points at which attacks are sufficient to cause catastrophic failure.

The resilience of networks to attack has been studied for some time (Latora & Marchiori, 2005), with critical phenomena investigated for energy networks in particular. More recent work has considered interdependencies between networks, such as those between the internet and energy distribution networks, which are believed to be responsible for previous blackouts (Buldyrev et al., 2010). The potential for catastrophic failure in such systems is striking (Gao et al., 2011), suggesting that such interdependencies should be taken into account when assessing the risks to such facilities. Unfortunately, little work has explicitly considered the security implications of such vulnerability; the work of Carvalho et al. (2014), considering the response of energy networks to real-world security risks, such as conflicts, is a notable exception.

One respect in which vulnerability and protection have been studied in depth is in the assignment of security resources to vulnerable locations. Such situations have been modelled as adversarial games between attackers (e.g. terrorists) and defenders (e.g. security forces). In these games, the attackers have a choice of targets, each of which has different reward and risk, and the task of the defender is to assign resources in a way which minimises this threat (Tambe, 2012). Crucially, however, both sides can take into account the decisions of the other (e.g. terrorists can observe how well defended each target is) when deciding on a course of action, and this makes the formulation as a game particularly apt. By solving these models, the optimal allocation of defensive assets can be calculated, which will typically involve a mixture of spatial assignments. Such strategies have been employed in real-world settings, including inspection at airports (Pita et al., 2008) and on transportation systems (Zhang et al., 2013).

Economic models

Inspection, in the wider sense of identifying wrongdoing, is one of the topics examined in the economic modelling of crime, which is typically concerned with studying the level of criminality – as a social phenomenon – in the population as a whole. Although this is perhaps not as well aligned with the crime science approach as the other topics discussed here, such is the volume of work that it would be remiss not to discuss it at all. A more comprehensive review, however, can be found in the article by Gordon (2010).

The general approach is well illustrated by the seminal work of Becker (1968) which initiated the field, and which is discussed at greater length in the chapter by Manning elsewhere in this handbook. Crime is postulated to be a rational choice, in which the economic outcomes of crime are captured in a 'social loss function'. This incorporates the volume of, and damage accruing from, offending, which is then balanced against the probability, severity and cost of punishment. Minimising this function suggests how many resources should be devoted to detection and punishment in order to achieve a situation which is economically optimal; in essence, how much crime should be 'tolerated' in society. This exemplifies the macro-level viewpoint of such models: effects are considered at a societal level. Various effects have been studied in this way: the propensity to offend (Nadal et al., 2010), the effect of punishment (Demougin & Schwager, 2003; Gordon et al., 2009a), and the role of inequality (Ehrlich, 1973; Deutsch et al., 1992; Bourguignon et al., 2003).

Later models have sought to account for the effect of social interactions on crime: Glaeser et al. (1996) suggested that this may explain variations in crime rates between US cities, and Gordon et al. (2009b) presented a general model for choices under social influence. The effect of punishment on criminal organisation has also been studied from an economic perspective (Garoupa, 2007). The role of interaction naturally leads to analogies with epidemiology, and in particular the notion that criminality is a contagious phenomenon (Crane, 1991). Compartmental models, in which the population can be partitioned into a number of states (e.g. 'susceptible' and 'criminal') and individuals transition between these, are common in the context and have also been proposed for crime (Campbell & Ormerod, 1997).

A more recent trend also considers compartmental models, but from a game-theoretic perspective. The model proposed by (Short et al., 2010), for example, includes four types of individual – 'informants', 'villains', 'paladins' and 'apathetics' – each of which have different propensities to commit crime and to serve as witnesses in criminal investigations. The game proceeds iteratively, with individual interactions (potential crimes) resulting in payoffs to each individual involved. After each round, individuals can transition between states, imitating the strategies of more successful counterparts, and ultimately the purpose of the model is to track the number of individuals in each state. The primary finding of the research is that informants are essential to the formation of a crime-free society, but the model is versatile: by manipulating the payoff structure, it is possible to investigate many strategies and interventions (Short et al., 2013). Indeed, this is indicative of the value of economic models: they facilitate the analysis of macro-scale policy changes on criminality as a whole.

Summary and outlook

One of the central objectives of crime science is to bring to the study of crime the kind of rigour and formalism that more traditionally characterises the physical sciences. It is natural, therefore, that mathematics, which provides much of the language and apparatus for these fields, should play a role in crime science. This chapter has sought to outline the particular ways in which mathematical approaches can contribute to crime science, by identifying those techniques which are most likely to be of use and by reviewing promising applications.

What is clear from the chapter as a whole is that the range of techniques relevant to crime science extends far beyond the classical disciplines of mathematics. It is no coincidence that interest in the modelling of crime has grown in line with a broadening of mathematics: several of the techniques described, such as network science, are relatively recent developments and are closely linked with increases in computational power and data availability. The prospect of further advances in these areas, and computational social science more generally, suggests that the field has a bright future: the scope and sophistication of mathematical approaches to crime science are both likely to increase.

Research to date has addressed a diverse array of criminal problems, ranging from the spatio-temporal patterning of crime to the size and structure of criminal groups. In each case, it is clear that mathematics offers a distinctive perspective: it is hard to imagine how predictive policing, for example, could properly be done without recourse to quantitative modelling. In most of the other examples cited, the absence of mathematics would not necessarily nullify the underlying principles, but would render them far more difficult to formalise and test.

Of course, offering formalisation is not an end in itself, and it makes sense to return now to the core issue of this chapter: the extent to which these approaches contribute to the crime science agenda. Although the examples cited here demonstrate the clear potential of the field, there is undoubtedly still work to be done to align it more fully with the aims of crime science.

Certainly mathematical modelling provides an ideal framework for the application of the scientific method to criminal phenomena: as outlined, it is the natural language for the encoding, analysis and possible falsification of hypotheses. Nevertheless, the extent to which this is realised in practice – particularly with respect to the comparison of models with real-world data – remains open to question. Modelling has shown great promise in replicating various general phenomena from criminology (e.g. hotspot formation), and it is tempting to view these as having strengthened the case for the underlying behavioural hypotheses that they encode. However, the fact that many of these approaches are formulated in extremely simplified settings – idealised two-dimensional domains, for example – limits the extent to which they can be believed to represent the real world.

Of perhaps even greater concern is the difficulty in differentiating between candidate models. In several contexts, a number of distinct approaches have been shown to successfully replicate a desired behaviour – hotspot formation is again a prominent example – and the question naturally arises of which is correct. This is, in many respects, an impossible judgement to make: when the target behaviour is as generic as 'areas of elevated crime risk', any model which produces such areas cannot be viewed as anything other than successful. In seeking to replicate such generic behaviours, therefore, the bar is perhaps being set too low, and models can too easily be viewed as viable.

This issue, however, is as much a challenge for crime science more generally as it is for mathematical modelling. To continue the previous analogy, the bar for such mathematical models can only be set higher if such a bar exists; in many cases, however, the extent to which phenomena have been characterised in empirical work remains relatively vague, to the extent that they are not sufficiently well-defined to discriminate between model outputs. Only when notions such as 'hotspot' can be defined at the level of precision that would be expected in the study of physical systems can techniques from those fields reasonably be expected to contribute to an equivalent extent. Stylised facts can only go so far in providing a target for modelling, and the increasing sophistication of empirical methods will, in time, address this issue.

Of course, a further concern for mathematical approaches relates to another fundamental pillar of crime science: their practical applicability. Success in replicating phenomena of interest will only be meaningful outside the academic context if it can be translated into real-world interventions – and in this respect there is much research still to do. The field of predictive policing is a clear example of the use of models to guide real-world activity, and has shown promising results with respect to crime prevention outcomes. Nevertheless, research concerning such real-world implementations is at a very early stage, and questions remain about the viability of such activity under many current policing models. For several of the other approaches outlined in this chapter, there is even more work to be done to explore the real-world applicability of mathematical approaches.

Looking to the immediate future, it seems clear that real-world applicability should be brought to the forefront of efforts to apply mathematics in the context of crime science. The approaches detailed in this brief overview are well suited to the field, and have shown clear promise, but will only be of value to crime science if the gap to real-world applicability can be bridged. Although this may require a shift in focus away from deeper mathematical analysis, it will ensure that the relevance of mathematics to the study of crime continues to grow.

References

Albert, R. & Barabási, A.-L. (2002). Statistical mechanics of complex networks. *Reviews of Modern Physics, 74*(1), 47–97.

Albert, R., Jeong, H., & Barabási, A.-L. (2000). Error and attack tolerance of complex networks. *Nature, 406*(6794), 378–382.

Arrowsmith, D. & Place, C. (1992). *Dynamical Systems: Differential Equations, Maps, and Chaotic Behaviour.* Boca Raton, FL: Chapman & Hall/CRC.

Axelrod, R. M. (1984). *The Evolution of Cooperation.* New York: Basic Books.

Barbaro, A. B. T., Chayes, L., & D'Orsogna, M. R. (2013). Territorial developments based on graffiti: A statistical mechanics approach. *Physica A: Statistical Mechanics and its Applications, 392*(1), 252–270.

Batty, M. (2007). *Cities and Complexity: Understanding Cities with Cellular Automata, Agent-Based Models, and Fractals.* Cambridge, MA: MIT Press.

Becker, G. S. (1968). Crime and punishment: An economic approach. *Journal of Political Economy, 76*(2), 169–217.

Berestycki, H., Nadal, J. P., & Rodríguez, N. (2015). A model of riots dynamics: Shocks, diffusion and thresholds. *Networks and Heterogeneous Media, 10*(3), 443–475.

Bourguignon, F., Nuñez, J., & Sanchez, F. (2003). A structural model of crime and inequality in Colombia. *Journal of the European Economic Association, 1*(2/3), 440–449.

Brantingham, P. J., Tita, G. E., Short, M. B., & Reid, S. E. (2012). The ecology of gang territorial boundaries. *Criminology, 50*(3), 851–885.

Buldyrev, S. V., Parshani, R., Paul, G., Stanley, H. E., & Havlin, S. (2010). Catastrophic cascade of failures in interdependent networks. *Nature, 464*(7291), 1025–1028.

Campbell, M. & Ormerod, P. (1997). Social interactions and the dynamics of crime. Technical report, available at www.paulormerod.com/wp-content/uploads/2012/06/social-interaction-crime.pdf.

Carley, K. M. (2003). Dynamic network analysis. In R. Breiger, K. Carley, & P. Pattison (eds). *Dynamic Social Network Modeling and Analysis: Workshop Summary and Papers*, pp. 133–145. Washington, DC: National Academies Press.

Carley, K. M. (2006). A dynamic network approach to the assessment of terrorist groups and the impact of alternative courses of action. In *Meeting Proceedings of Visualising Network Information – RTO-MP-IST-063*, pp. KN1-1 – KN1-10. Neuilly-sur-Seine, France.

Carrington, P. J. (2011). Crime and Social Network Analysis. In J. Scott & P. J. Carrington (eds). *Sage Handbook of Social Network Analysis*, pp. 236–255. London, UK: Sage.

Carvalho, R., Buzna, L., Bono, F., Masera, M., Arrowsmith, D. K., & Helbing, D. (2014). Resilience of natural gas networks during conflicts, crises and disruptions. *PLoS ONE*, *9*(3), e90265.

Castellano, C., Fortunato, S., & Loreto, V. (2009). Statistical physics of social dynamics. *Reviews of Modern Physics*, *81*(2), 591–646.

Costa, L. d. F., Oliveira, O. N., Travieso, G., Rodrigues, F. A., Villas Boas, P. R., Antiqueira, L., Viana, M. P., & Correa Rocha, L. E. (2011). Analyzing and modeling real-world phenomena with complex networks: a survey of applications. *Advances in Physics*, *60*(3), 329–412.

Crane, J. (1991). The epidemic theory of ghettos and neighborhood effects on dropping out and teenage childbearing. *American Journal of Sociology*, *96*(5), 1226–1259.

Crane, J., Boccara, N., & Higdon, K. (2000). The dynamics of street gang growth and policy response. *Journal of Policy Modeling*, *22*(1), 1–25.

Davies, T. P. & Bishop, S. R. (2013). Modelling patterns of burglary on street networks. *Crime Science*, *2*(1), 10.

Davies, T. P., Fry, H. M., Wilson, A. G., & Bishop, S. R. (2013). A mathematical model of the London riots and their policing. *Scientific Reports*, *3*, 1303.

Davies, T. & Johnson, S. D. (2014). Examining the relationship between road structure and burglary risk via quantitative network analysis. *Journal of Quantitative Criminology*, *31*(3), 481–507.

Demougin, D. & Schwager, R. (2003). Law enforcement and criminality: Europe vs. USA. *International Review of Law and Economics*, *23*(2), 217–225.

Deutsch, J., Spiegel, U., & Templeman, J. (1992). Crime and income inequality: An economic approach. *Atlantic Economic Journal*, *20*(4), 46–54.

Duijn, P. A. C., Kashirin, V., & Sloot, P. M. A. (2014). The relative ineffectiveness of criminal network disruption. *Scientific Reports*, *4*, 4238.

Egesdal, M., Fathauer, C., Louie, K., Neuman, J., Mohler, G., & Lewis, E. (2010). Statistical and stochastic modeling of gang rivalries in Los Angeles. *SIAM Undergraduate Research Online*, *3*, 72–94.

Ehrlich, I. (1973). Participation in illegitimate activities: A theoretical and empirical investigation. *Journal of Political Economy*, *81*(3), 521–565.

Ferrara, E., De Meo, P., Catanese, S., & Fiumara, G. (2014). Detecting criminal organizations in mobile phone networks. *Expert Systems with Applications*. ArXiv:1404.1295 [physics].

Gao, J., Buldyrev, S. V., Havlin, S., & Stanley, H. E. (2011). Robustness of a network of networks. *Physical Review Letters*, *107*(19), 195701.

Garoupa, N. (2007). Optimal law enforcement and criminal organization. *Journal of Economic Behavior & Organization*, *63*(3), 461–474.

Gerdes, L. M. (2014). MAPPing dark networks: A data transformation method to study clandestine organizations. *Network Science*, *2*(2), 213–253.

Gill, J. & Freeman, J. R. (2013). Dynamic elicited priors for updating covert networks. *Network Science*, *1*(1), 68–94.

Gill, P., Lee, J., Rethemeyer, K. R., Horgan, J., & Asal, V. (2014). Lethal connections: The Determinants of network connections in the Provisional Irish Republican Army, 1970–1998. *International Interactions*, *40*(1), 52–78.

Glaeser, E. L., Sacerdote, B., & Scheinkman, J. A. (1996). Crime and social interactions. *The Quarterly Journal of Economics*, *111*(2), 507–548.

Gordon, M. B. (2010). A random walk in the literature on criminality: A partial and critical view on some statistical analyses and modelling approaches. *European Journal of Applied Mathematics*, *21*(4–5), 283–306.

Gordon, M. B., Iglesias, J. R., Semeshenko, V., & Nadal, J.-P. (2009a). Crime and punishment: The economic burden of impunity. *The European Physical Journal B*, *68*(1), 133–144.

Gordon, M. B., Nadal, J.-P., Phan, D., & Semeshenko, V. (2009b). Discrete choices under social influence: Generic properties. *Mathematical Models and Methods in Applied Sciences*, *19*(Supp. 01), 1441–1481.

Jones, P. A., Brantingham, P. J., & Chayes, L. R. (2010). Statistical models of criminal behavior: The effects of law enforcement actions. *Mathematical Models and Methods in Applied Sciences*, *20*(Supplement), 1397–1423.

Krebs, V. E. (2002). Mapping networks of terrorist cells. *Connections*, *24*(3), 43–52.

Latora, V. & Marchiori, M. (2005). Vulnerability and protection of infrastructure networks. *Physical Review E*, *71*(1), 015103.

Levin, S. A. (1998). Ecosystems and the Biosphere as Complex Adaptive Systems. *Ecosystems*, *1*(5), 431–436.

Mancuso, M. (2014). Not all madams have a central role: Analysis of a Nigerian sex trafficking network. *Trends in Organized Crime*, *17*(1–2), 66–88.

Mantegna, R. N. & Stanley, H. E. (2000). *An Introduction to Econophysics: Correlations and Complexity in Finance*. Cambridge, UK: Cambridge University Press.

Marchione, E., Johnson, S. D., & Wilson, A. (2014). Modelling maritime piracy: A spatial approach. *Journal of Artificial Societies and Social Simulation*, *17*(2), 9.

Medina, R. M. (2014). Social Network Analysis: A case study of the Islamist terrorist network. *Security Journal*, *27*(1), 97–121.

Mohler, G. O., Short, M. B., Brantingham, P. J., Schoenberg, F. P., & Tita, G. E. (2011). Self-exciting point process modeling of crime. *Journal of the American Statistical Association*, *106*(493), 100–108.

Mohler, G. O., Short, M. B., Malinowski, S., Johnson, M., Tita, G. E., Bertozzi, A. L., & Brantingham, P. J. (2015). Randomized controlled field trials of predictive policing. *Journal of the American Statistical Association*, *110*(512), 1399–1411.

Nadal, J.-P., Gordon, M. B., Iglesias, J. R., & Semeshenko, V. (2010). Modelling the individual and collective dynamics of the propensity to offend. *European Journal of Applied Mathematics*, *21*(4–5), 421–440.

Newman, M. E. J. (2011). Complex Systems: A Survey. *American Journal of Physics*, *79*(8), 800–810.

Pease, K. (1998). Repeat victimisation: Taking stock. London: Home Office Police Research Group.

Pita, J., Jain, M., Marecki, J., Ordóñez, F., Portway, C., Tambe, M., Western, C., Paruchuri, P., & Kraus, S. (2008). Deployed ARMOR Protection: The Application of a Game Theoretic Model for Security at the Los Angeles International Airport. In *Proceedings of the 7th International Joint Conference on Autonomous Agents and Multiagent Systems: Industrial Track*, AAMAS '08, pp. 125–132. Richland, SC: International Foundation for Autonomous Agents and Multiagent Systems.

Pitcher, A. B. (2010). Adding Police to a Mathematical Model of Burglary. *European Journal of Applied Mathematics*, *21*(4–5), 401–419.

Short, M. B., Brantingham, P. J., & D'Orsogna, M. R. (2010). Cooperation and punishment in an adversarial game: How defectors pave the way to a peaceful society. *Physical Review E*, *82*(6), 066114.

Short, M. B., D'Orsogna, M. R., Pasour, V. B., Tita, G. E., Brantingham, P. J., Bertozzi, A. L., & Chayes, L. B. (2008). A statistical model of criminal behavior. *Mathematical Models and Methods in Applied Sciences*, *18*(S1), 1249–1267.

Short, M. B., Mohler, G. O., Brantingham, P. J., & Tita, G. E. (2014). Gang rivalry dynamics via coupled point process networks. *Discrete & Continuous Dynamical Systems-Series B*, *19*(5).

Short, M. B., Pitcher, A. B., & D'Orsogna, M. R. (2013). External conversions of player strategy in an evolutionary game: A cost–benefit analysis through optimal control. *European Journal of Applied Mathematics*, *24*(1), 131–159.

Smith, L. M., Bertozzi, A. L., Brantingham, P. J., Tita, G. E., & Valasik, M. (2012). Adaptation of an ecological territorial model to street gang spatial patterns in Los Angeles. *Discrete and Continuous Dynamical Systems*, *32*(9), 3223–3244.

Stomakhin, A., Short, M. B., & Bertozzi, A. L. (2011). Reconstruction of missing data in social networks based on temporal patterns of interactions. *Inverse Problems*, *27*(11), 115013.

Strogatz, S. H. (1994). *Nonlinear Dynamics and Chaos: With Applications to Physics, Biology, Chemistry, and Engineering*. Reading, MA: Perseus Books.

Tambe, M. (2012). *Security and Game Theory*. Cambridge, UK: Cambridge University Press.

van Gennip, Y., Hunter, B., Ahn, R., Elliott, P., Luh, K., Halvorson, M., Reid, S., Valasik, M., Wo, J., Tita, G., Bertozzi, A., & Brantingham, P. (2013). Community detection using spectral clustering on sparse geosocial data. *SIAM Journal on Applied Mathematics*, *73*(1), 67–83.

Wilson, J. Q. & Kelling, G. L. (1982). Broken windows. *Atlantic Monthly*, *249*(3), 29–38.

Zhang, C., Jiang, A. X., Short, M. B., Brantingham, P. J., & Tambe, M. (2013). Modeling Crime diffusion and crime suppression on transportation networks: An initial report. AAAI Symposium on Social Networks and Social Contagion, 2013.

9
Geography

Martin A. Andresen and Kathryn Wuschke

Introduction

Crime science is the study of crime, and quite often its events, in an effort to reduce and/or prevent criminal activity. This method of crime prevention is not focused on any particular theory, but is multidisciplinary in nature, guided by the scientific method. As such, rather than being self-fulfilling, at least in its essence, crime science has the purpose of developing new knowledge with the goal of reducing crime. This is accomplished through the identification of empirically supported evidence for crime prevention, the integration of that empirically supported evidence across disciplines, and the further development of that empirically supported evidence.

One of the disciplines contributing to crime science is geography. At its essence, (human) geography is the study of people and their communities and how those people interact within and through their environment. Critical to this discipline are the concepts of space and place, which bring together an understanding of how spatial relationships and local-level investigations help us to comprehend human activities in particular places. One of those activities is crime.

Geography, or at least the knowledge of spatial variations, has been a part of criminology for nearly 200 years. It should then come as no surprise that geography is a part of contemporary crime science. In short, criminal opportunities vary across space, as do motivated offenders; as such, crime exhibits predictable spatial patterns. In this chapter we will cover some of the contributions of geography to crime science: spatial analysis, the importance of scale and place, and policy mobilities.[1] Though we cover topics that crime scientists may approach through the use of computer software, such as geographic information systems, we try to emphasise how thinking geographically, even within numerical calculations, can help to understand spatial crime patterns. This, in turn, will help inform the development of policies and practices to reduce and/or prevent criminal activity.

Spatial analysis

The most obvious contribution of geography to crime science is the development and use of spatial analysis. In fact, the use of maps to show geographical crime patterns goes back at least as far as the work of Guerry (1832, 1833) and Quetelet (1831, 1842) in early eighteenth-century

France. Quite simply, spatial analysis is the examination of spatially referenced data that considers the geographical relationships between spatial units of analysis. It is critical to consider the importance of such relationships because spatially referenced data can be analysed without considering spatial relationships. For example, a researcher may have criminal event and census data, all at the level of the census tract. The researcher *could* use a spatial analysis method because census tracts have spatial information available, but the researcher could also simply undertake classical statistical analysis using the census tracts as observations. Such approaches have been commonplace, at least up until the last couple of decades when spatial analysis methods have become more available. However, ignoring spatial relationships can lead to statistical problems, and may also prevent the discovery of important theoretical and practical insights for the study of criminal activity.

There are three fundamental spatial units of analysis: points, lines, and areas. In crime science, points (criminal events, for example) and areas (neighbourhoods, for example) are the most common, but some research does consider line segments (street networks, for example). Though spatial-linear analyses were not undertaken, some research in the crime and place literature that uses line segments as the unit of analysis very clearly shows evidence for 'linear clustering' of criminal events (Curman et al., 2012; Weisburd et al., 2012). When one considers that the activity patterns of individuals tend to follow major arterial roadways (Brantingham & Brantingham, 1981, 1993), it should come as no surprise that criminal activity tends to cluster along these roadways. Because of the dominance of points and areas in criminological research, we will focus on those two spatial units of analysis here.

The geographic element that is used most frequently within crime science is the hotspot map. Hotspot maps are generated using (criminal event) point data to create a surface over the entire study area representing the density of those points. Broadly speaking, the methods that can be used to create these hotspots are surface-generating techniques or spatial interpolation. The most common of these is called kernel density estimation.

The kernel density process is illustrated in Figure 9.1, considering theft from vehicle in Vancouver, Canada. Figure 9.1a is a dot map showing the locations of all the thefts from vehicle in a year. Because of the relatively low volume of this criminal event, approximately 10,000 events, a spatial pattern emerges over the city – a more common crime type may cover the entire city with dots, such that there is no discernable concentration of criminal events. The greatest density of theft from vehicle occurs in the northern peninsula of the city (within Vancouver's central business district) and on the east side of the city; these areas represent a high density of targets, and relatively lower socio-economic status, respectively. Despite these densities, it should be clear that theft from vehicle occurs all over the city.

Figure 9.1b is a hotspot map created using the same data from Figure 9.1a through kernel density estimation. Figure 9.1b definitely shows a high density of theft from vehicle in the central business district area, but a relatively low density everywhere else. Though such a representation does show the overall pattern – almost the entire central business district is covered with dots – it gives the idea that theft from vehicle is not a problem for most of the city. In fact, this just means that the rest of the city has a relatively low density of theft from vehicle (when compared to the central business district) but it may still have a high volume of theft from vehicle. Such a potential problem in inference emerges because kernel density estimation provides a picture of crime based on comparative levels of concentration.

Figure 9.2 clarifies why this generalisation takes place. When making a kernel density map, the entire study area is covered in a grid; the size of the grid cells can be defined by the user, but tend to be rather small. Each one of these grid cells is represented by a location (point) s, which is the centroid of the cell. And at each one of these locations in the study area, a circle is drawn with a radius, or bandwidth, that is also defined by the user – most GIS software programs have default settings determined by the size of the study area. The number of events within the circle are counted and then used to calculate the 'height' of the location, called the kernel. These values can also be used to create 3D maps. Two aspects of this estimation should be emphasised. First, as the bandwidth increases in size, more events will be captured within the circle to calculate the kernel. This creates a smoothing effect for the hotspot map. Consequently, hotspots will often appear to be bigger than they really are. Second, it is quite likely (perhaps even common) that no events occur close to the location (point) *s*, but the location is given a positive value due to a large default bandwidth setting. As a result, a location that is crime free will have a positive value because criminal events occurred 'nearby'. One could argue that this must still be representing the reality of crime in the neighbourhood. However, we recently created a kernel density map with a default bandwidth of just under 600 metres. Though this could be classified as 'close' it would be far enough away to have very different characteristics – this will be further discussed in the spatial scale and the crime at places section, below. These two characteristics of kernel density estimation emphasise the importance of careful consideration of both the default settings within GIS software programs, and of the generalised results of such mapping techniques.

Another issue that is often overlooked relates to the data used to calculate hotspot maps. Figure 9.3a is another kernel density hotspot map created using only criminal event data. This is the most common type of hotspot map. However, it is well accepted that there will be more criminal events where there are more targets, and people are an excellent representation of those

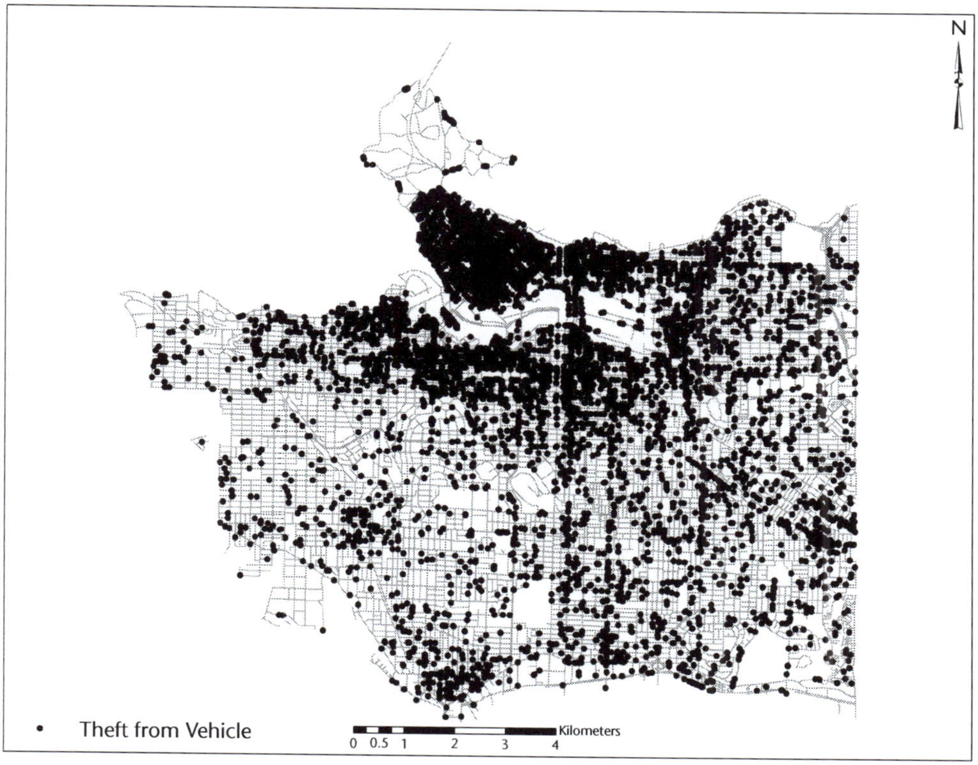

a) Dot map

Figure 9.1a Theft from vehicle, dot map (Vancouver, 2001)

(continued)

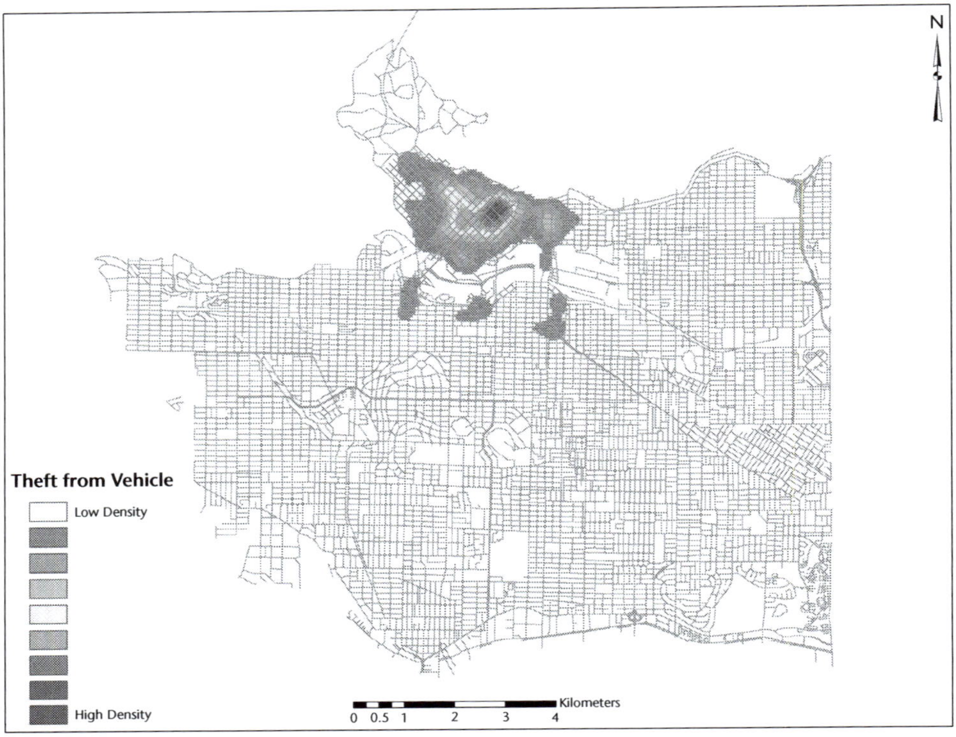

b) Hotspot map

Figure 9.1b Theft from vehicle, hotspot map (Vancouver, 2001)

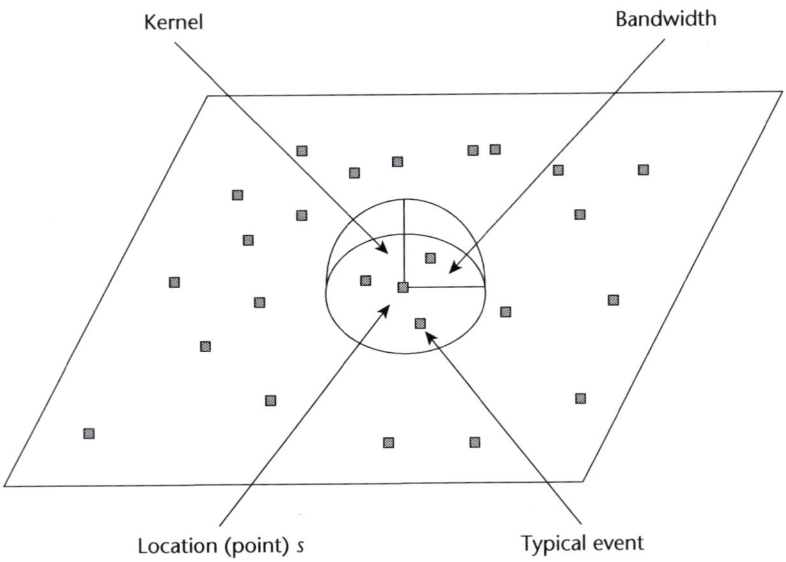

Figure 9.2 Kernel density estimation

Source: Andresen (2014).

targets. More people means more direct targets for violent crime and more indirect targets for property crime because people bring property with them wherever they go.

Because only one variable was used to calculate the hotspot map displayed in Figure 9.3a, it is called a single kernel. Figure 9.3b, on the other hand, is called a dual kernel hotspot map because it considers two variables: criminal event data, and residential population count data from the census. The latter variable represents the population at risk of criminal victimisation and should be considered as part of the calculation. Why? Because we know, and we have known for a long time, that more crime occurs where there are more targets, particularly in central business districts such as the dark area in Figure 9.3a (Andresen & Jenion, 2010; Boggs, 1965; Schmid 1960a, 1960b). One can think of Figure 9.3b as being the result of subtracting a kernel density map of the population at risk from the original criminal event kernel density map. With a dual kernel that considers the population at risk, Figure 9.3b shows that the hotspot is actually not as 'bad' as it looked in Figure 9.3a. As such, Figure 9.3a is best thought of as a map showing the *volume* of criminal events whereas Figure 9.3b is best thought of as a map showing the *risk* of being a victim of a criminal event: similar to comparing criminal event counts to crime rates. This discussion should emphasise how geography can contribute to crime science not only through the application of geographical methods to criminal event data, but also through its underlying understanding of the spatial representations used in crime science.

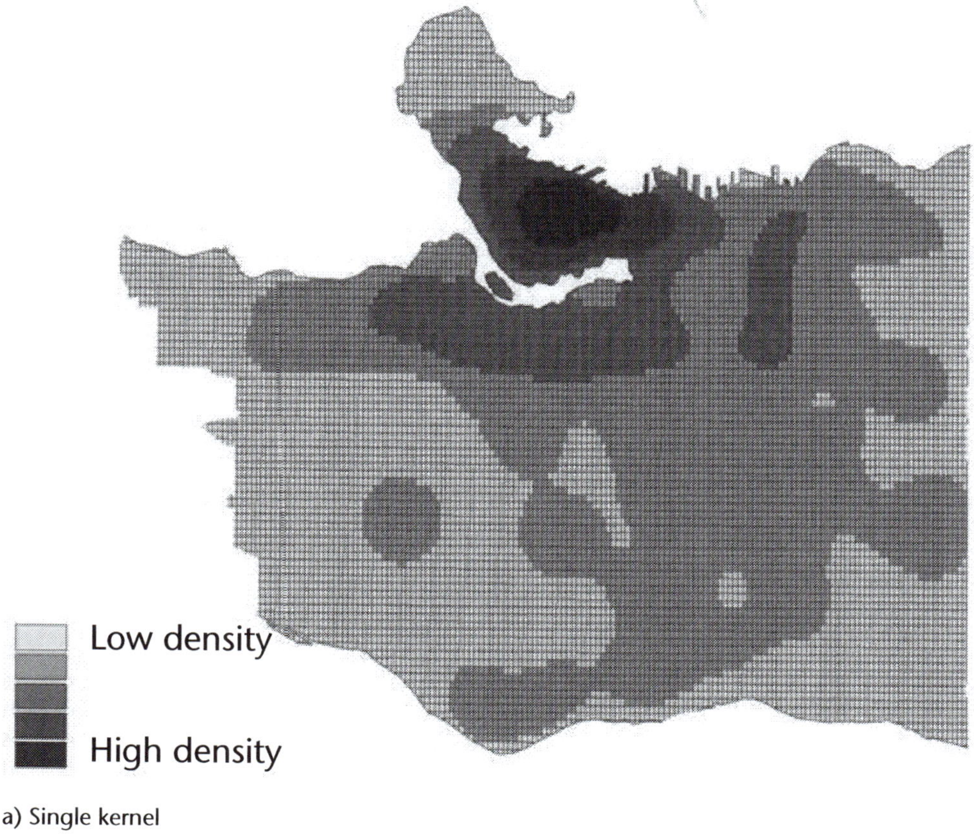

a) Single kernel

Figures 9.3a Theft from auto, single versus dual kernel density estimation (Vancouver, 2001)

Source: Andresen (2014).

(continued)

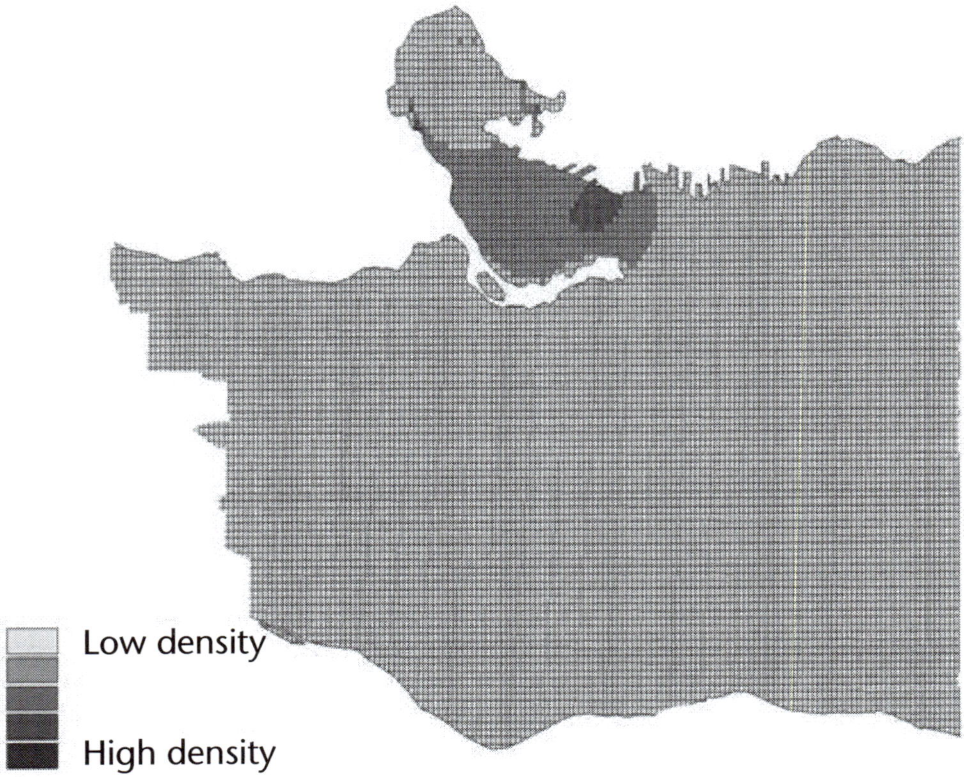

b) Dual kernel

Figures 9.3b Theft from auto, single versus dual kernel density estimation (Vancouver, 2001)

Source: Andresen (2014).

In Figures 9.1 and 9.3 it is clear that locations that are close to one another have similar values. This is often referred to as spatial autocorrelation – a numerical representation is shown in Figure 9.4. Figures 9.1, 9.3, and 9.4 are examples of positive spatial autocorrelation: areas are surrounded by other areas with *similar* values; there is also the case of negative spatial autocorrelation: areas are surrounded by other areas with *dissimilar* values.

4	6	5	4	6
6	8	8	9	5
5	7	10	7	6
4	9	7	8	6
5	6	4	6	5

Figure 9.4 An example of positive spatial autocorrelation

Source: Andresen (2014).

Though negative spatial autocorrelation does emerge in the social sciences and, consequently, crime science, positive spatial autocorrelation is the most common. Interesting in its own right, (positive) spatial autocorrelation is problematic for statistical analysis. Many statistical techniques require the independence of observations, so if you can predict the value for one spatial unit of analysis when you know its neighbour's value, independence is violated.

This issue is most manifest in the context of regression analysis. In the presence of positive spatial autocorrelation, ordinary least-squares regression underestimates the standard errors for coefficients. Consequently, some explanatory variables may appear to be more significant than they really are. In purely academic circles, the consequences of retaining theoretically informed variables in a regression model are not particularly severe: theoreticians may think something matters more than it really does, if it matters at all. However, in the context of crime science, this could lead to the belief that a relationship exists when it does not and may lead to inappropriate crime prevention interventions. This undermines the credibility of crime science and wastes crime prevention resources. Spatial statistical methods that address this spatial autocorrelation are instructive here because they can filter out the problematic spatial autocorrelation and provide more reliable statistical results for the application of crime science. Two such methods include spatial lag models and spatial error models.

Though extremely useful and appropriate for the analysis of spatial data, techniques such as spatial lag and spatial error regression are 'global' statistics, representing the entire study area. Fundamental to geography is the recognition that relationships are specific to places and vary across space. This does not mean that geographers do not believe in global processes, just that they must be interpreted with caution. It should therefore not come as a surprise that the *local* has become particularly important in the field of geography in recent decades (Fotheringham, 1997). There are many forms of local statistical analysis that could be utilised in crime science, but the statistics that are most commonly used in geography of crime studies relate to forms of spatial clustering (the recognition of positive and negative spatial autocorrelation occurring within the same study area) and geographically varying regression coefficients (also being positive in some places and negative in others).

The most commonly used spatial statistic for local spatial clustering is local Moran's *I*, developed by Anselin (1995). Local Moran's *I* is part of a subset of local spatial statistics called local indicators of spatial association (LISA) because it is related to a global statistic. Moran's *I*, the global statistic, measures the presence of spatial autocorrelation (positive, negative, or neither) across an entire study area. Though instructive, and important for residuals in the context of a regression using spatial data, global patterns most often hide local patterns. Local spatial statistics produce a statistic for each spatial unit under analysis; as such, local Moran's *I* generates a statistic that measures the degree of spatial autocorrelation for each unit as it relates to every other spatial unit of analysis. With a set of local statistics this information can be mapped to search for local patterns, such as clustering.

A map of local Moran's *I* is presented in Figure 9.5, showing clusters of crime in the central business district of Vancouver: High–High refers to places with high crime surrounded by other areas with high crime, Low–High refers to places with low crime surrounded by areas with high crime, and so on. Recalling from above (Figures 9.1 and 9.3), this is an area of high crime. However, this map shows that within this area of high crime there are pockets of low crime that do not emerge when using more conventional spatial analysis techniques, particularly kernel density estimation hotspot maps. The largest of these low-crime areas, located close to the centre of the map, is a relatively recent expensive and trendy development that has been able to repel crime within while being surrounded by older areas that historically have high levels of crime. It has been found that the areas exhibiting positive spatial autocorrelation (High–High and Low–Low)

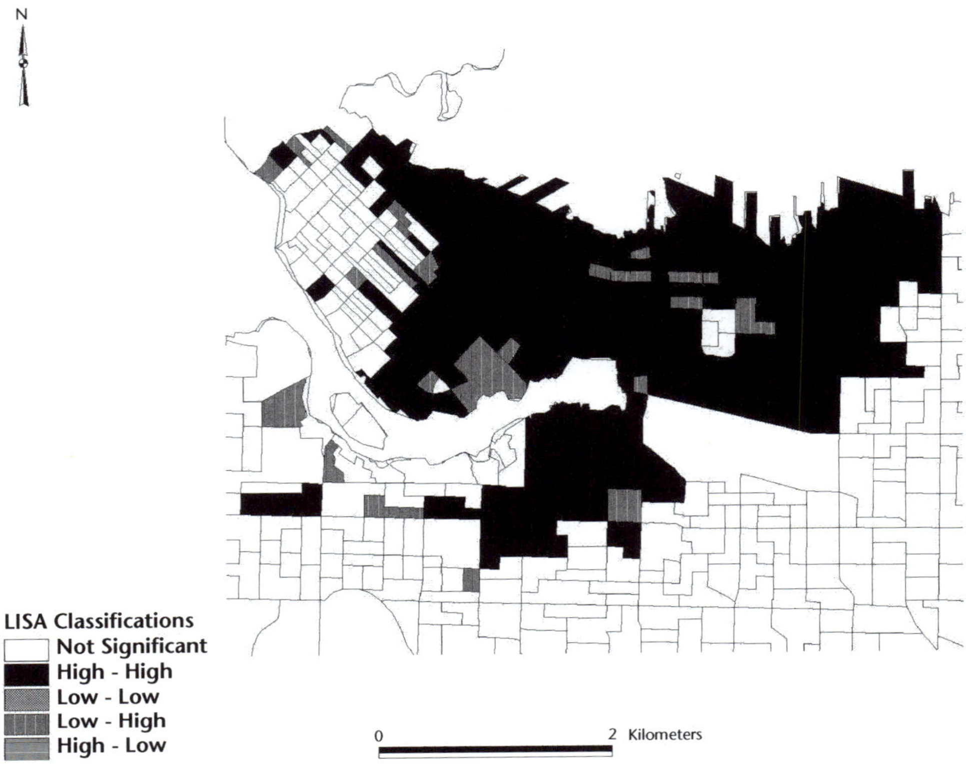

Figure 9.5 Theft from Auto, Local Moran's (Vancouver central business district, 2001)

Source: Andresen (2011, 2014).

can be predicted from social disorganisation theory (Sampson & Roves, 1989) and routine activity theory (Cohen & Felson, 1979), whereas the areas exhibiting negative spatial autocorrelation (Low–High and High–Low) tend to not follow these expectations (Andresen, 2011).

The last spatial analysis method to be discussed here, though there are many more, is a locally based regression technique called geographically weighted regression. As with local Moran's *I*, geographically weighted regression recognises that regression parameter estimates may vary across space. As such, with geographically weighted regression a map of parameter estimates is generated with each spatial unit of analysis having its own value (see Brunsdon et al., 1996 and Fotheringham et al., 2002). This local spatial analytic technique is particularly interesting because regression analysis is a common statistical method in crime science. However, geography tells us that while there may be global tendencies, there are almost always local variations that may prove to be instructive.

In an analysis of violent crime in Portland, Oregon, Cahill and Mulligan (2007) compared ordinary least-squares results with geographically weighted regression results, arriving at some interesting findings. In short, these authors found that regression parameters do vary across space, in some cases rather extremely. Moreover, the use of geographically weighted regression was able to explain one counter-intuitive finding within the ordinary least-squares results: affluent areas have higher levels of violence. When considering the geographically weighted regression results, these authors found that most of the city had either statistically non-significant relationships or negative relationships, as expected, but a small number (10 per cent) of affluent areas had greater than expected levels of violent crime. These areas dominated the ordinary least-squares regression, making the estimated parameter positive at a global level. Consequently, not only did the use of geographically weighted regression show that local parameter estimates can be statistically insignificant, negative, and positive within the same study space, it was also able to explain why counter-intuitive results emerged in a global statistical technique. This underscores why such a geographical (local) perspective should be considered important within crime science when aiming to understand spatial patterns and prevent criminal activity.

The importance of scale, its complications, and the understanding of place

It is almost tautological to state that one of the contributions of geography to crime science is the importance of scale. Scale, when considered as defining the nature of the data: points, lines, and areas, has implications for the method of (spatial) analysis and any subsequent interpretations. Though arguments can be made for which is the most ideal form of (spatial) data, usually micro-level data are better because they can be aggregated: address level data can be aggregated to neighbourhoods that can be aggregated into cities, depending on research needs. However, we are often circumscribed by the data provided to us by various agencies. As such, we need to be cognizant of the challenges that go along with spatial data, and of the corresponding limitations in any interpretations. These are, primarily, the ecological/atomistic fallacy and the modifiable areal-unit problem (MAUP) – both of which are related to spatial heterogeneity.

The ecological fallacy can occur when research is undertaken that uses aggregate data such as neighbourhoods, municipalities, states/provinces, or countries. The fallacy actually occurs when the researcher (or someone interpreting the research) makes assumptions about individual units (persons living within an area, for example) based on the statistical characteristics of their aggregated areas. In essence, the fallacy occurs when someone assumes that what is true of the whole is also true of its parts – the atomistic fallacy operates in the opposite direction. Technically, what is true of the whole is true, on average, for its parts, but to say that any one individual is the average can be quite a leap. The ecological fallacy is a fallacy, of course, because such a relationship cannot be assumed.

The ecological fallacy was first formally discussed by Robinson (1950) in the context of the census and the individuals on whom it was conducted. More than three decades later, Openshaw (1984a) investigated the relationships, if any, between individual-level correlations and area-level correlations. Generally speaking, Openshaw (1984a) found that the severity of any problems with interpretation that would emerge depended on the particular method of analysis. Further, he found that the differences in the individual-level and area-level correlations cannot be known before the analysis, and any subsequent comparisons are undertaken. In a study of two census units of analysis in each of Vancouver, Canada and Leeds, England, Andresen and Malleson (2013) most often found that there was a small set of geographically smaller units driving the change for the geographically larger units. This confirmed that what is true of the whole is not necessarily true of *all* of its parts. However, they found in a number of cases that (statistically speaking) none of the geographically smaller units of analysis exhibited the same change as the geographically larger units of analysis.

Though the ecological fallacy is easy to avoid, in theory (never make inferences at a level different from your unit of analysis), it is a very easy fallacy to commit when interpreting data. This highlights the importance of understanding scale when undertaking (spatial) analysis.

The modifiable areal-unit problem (MAUP), though formally defined and discussed by Openshaw (1984b), was first identified by Gehlke and Biehl (1934). The MAUP is an issue that emerges in the analysis of spatial data because of the arbitrary nature in which micro-level (individuals or individual households) data are often aggregated into areas. This is most common in the analysis of census data in census tracts, block groups, and output areas. The MAUP has two common forms: the scale problem and the zoning problem. The scale problem manifests itself when the same analysis is undertaken at two different scales: census tracts and neighbourhoods, for example. The zoning problem manifests itself when the size and shape of the spatial units of analysis are the same, but they are placed differently on the study area.

Though there is no intrinsic problem with changing the scale or zoning in a spatial analysis, research has consistently shown that when the spatial units of analysis are changed in some manner, the statistical relationships between the variables under analysis change. Typically, as found by Gehlke and Biehl (1934), as the geographical size of the units of analysis increases so does the strength of the correlation between those variables. However, more troubling is the research of Fotheringham and Wong (1991) who found in a regression context almost any result could be generated using different aggregations of data. This is highly problematic because most research only considers one spatial unit of analysis. Is any given piece of research using the 'correct' geographical aggregation, by chance, or it is using one of the many others producing spurious results? Basic probabilities do not bode well here.

However, in the context of geographical criminology research, Wooldredge (2002) has found that the geographic size of the spatial units of analysis matters very little, generating very similar results considering multiple scales of analysis. The limitation with Wooldredge (2002), however, is that his analyses were only a comparison of a few aggregations in one location. Perhaps all census-based and neighbourhood-based statistical results are similar, but all incorrect. Geography has a lot to add to crime science with regard to the unit of analysis when investigating crime patterns.

Recognising the importance of scale in understanding spatial crime patterns, it is no surprise that concern over the appropriate spatial unit of analysis goes back almost 200 years to the work of Adolphe Quetelet and André-Michel Guerry. This concern is rooted in the finding that when geographically smaller units are analysed, researchers find spatial heterogeneity: a province or state may have a high crime rate relative to the rest of the country, but the municipalities within that province or state vary significantly. This phenomenon has been illustrated indirectly through a series of different research studies analysing different spatial units of analysis, and directly within one research study conducted by Brantingham and colleagues (1976). In their study, the authors analysed crime patterns at the national, state, municipality, census tract, and block group levels, each time finding significant variations in crime rates within the geographically smaller units of analysis. Because of this spatial heterogeneity, the trajectory over the past 200 or so years has been toward increasingly smaller spatial units of analysis (Weisburd et al., 2009a).

The more recent crime and place literature emphasises the importance of spatial scale and the understanding of place. Crime and place research considers the micro-spatial unit of analysis, often street segments, intersections, and specific addresses. Weisburd and colleagues (2012) have argued that the street segment – both sides of the street between two intersections– is optimal for understanding geographical crime patterns because it is small enough to avoid significant concerns regarding spatial heterogeneity and large enough to gather data about for subsequent analysis. The first citywide crime and place study, conducted by Sherman and colleagues (1989), found that approximately 5 per cent of street segments account for approximately 50 per cent of crime, or calls for police service. This statistic has been replicated in a number of other contexts in different countries around the world (Andresen & Linning, 2012; Andresen & Malleson, 2011; Curman et al., 2015; Groff et al., 2010; Melo et al., 2015; Weisburd, 2015; Weisburd et al., 2004, 2009b, 2012).

One criticism of this statistic is that when one investigates crime patterns at the street-segment level for an entire municipality, one will almost certainly find concentrations. This is because there will be thousands (even tens of thousands) of street segments and likely fewer criminal events. If a researcher is analysing 1,000 criminal events on 10,000 street segments, at the very least (assuming no clustering of crime) 90 per cent of the municipality will be free from these criminal events. Though this must be kept in mind when interpreting any such statistics, it is still meaningful because the researcher can know that very few places actually have crime. However, research that has considered only those street segments that experience crime still finds high degrees of concentration within that subset of street segments (Andresen & Linning, 2012; Andresen & Malleson, 2011; Melo et al., 2015).

Perhaps most interesting is that some of this research has found 'place' to be critical for understanding crime patterns. For example, Groff and colleagues (2010) found that the trajectories of street segments[2] can vary considerably from street segment to street segment. Moreover, from a place perspective, the street segment may even be considered too large to really understand the underlying crime patterns. Why would two contiguous street segments have completely different trajectories when one of the long-standing facts within the geography of crime research is that crime clusters in space? The short answer is that it depends what is on each of those street segments. One street segment with nothing but residential housing and another that has a convenience store or a drinking establishment will have very different crime patterns, whether they're geographically close or not. In fact, most of the street segment containing the convenience store or drinking establishment will likely be 'crime free' – barring any spillover effects – and, therefore, similar to its neighbouring street segment. As such, understanding the geography of crime makes understanding the importance of place and local context critical.

Policy mobilities and crime prevention

The reduction and/or prevention of crime is the fundamental goal of crime science, and much of what we know regarding practical crime prevention today is rooted explicitly or implicitly in situational crime prevention (Clarke, 1980, 1983, 2012). Situational crime prevention recognises the importance of the situation at hand when designing a specific crime prevention application. In geography, the equivalent terminology would be understanding the 'local', emphasising the importance of local spatial analysis, as discussed above.

Situational crime prevention applies to the crime types that one is trying to prevent or reduce, the location(s) where crime is occurring, when those crimes are occurring, and so on. Situational crime prevention is not without its critiques (Wortley, 2010), but is an integral component of crime science due to its focus on prevention (see Clarke, 1997, 2012) and its recognition of the importance of the local when implementing initiatives. What works in one place may not work in another, and what works at one time may not work at another. Quite simply, different crime types, locations, and times have different opportunities and will attract different offenders. Consequently, without a focus on the local/situational factors, crime prevention initiatives are unlikely to be successful. But is this focus on the local restricted to the crime prevention initiatives themselves? We would argue no.

Over the past decade in human geography, a new branch of literature has developed that recognises the importance of the local when developing policy. This literature, 'urban policy mobility', has shown that (urban) policy has a number of factors that affect its successful implementation: spatial scales, communities, and institutions (McCann, 2008, 2011; Peck, 2011; Temenos & McCann, 2012, 2013). In other words, urban policy is highly situational. This means that any policy aimed at the reduction of crime is a geographical process because of the varying social, political, and crime cultures in a place (McCann, 2013; McCann & Temenos, 2015; Robinson, 2011; Ward, 2006); (crime prevention) policy itself, therefore, moves through and is shaped by the local. From a geographical perspective, understanding urban local policy mobility becomes critical for knowing if and when any global crime prevention policy can be applied in a local context.

The urban policy mobility literature shows that the situational component of situational crime prevention not only operates for crime prevention initiatives, but at the level where the crime prevention policies are developed. We need to conduct investigations into local conditions to not only design successful crime prevention initiatives, but also to design the crime prevention policies considering local conditions so that they may be applied in their respective locations with success. Though such a statement may appear trite, its importance and relevance becomes clear when we recognise that crime prevention policies are often set at the national, state/provincial, and municipal levels. However, recall from the discussion of scale and place above that crime can vary from street block to street block. When success is measured against nationally defined performance measures and crime patterns change on the next block, sustained support for crime prevention activities in the context of crime science, despite its empirical support, may lose traction. As such, crime prevention policy is empty without considering the local and the ability of the policy to be mobile to particular places.

Conclusion

Geography has informed criminological research for nearly two centuries, emphasising the importance of considering space when investigating crime. This spatial perspective is particularly relevant within crime science. Geography has offered a number of concepts and approaches to the field of crime science; within this chapter we have focused on three such contributions.

Crime science has adopted a variety of spatial analytical approaches for representing and understanding crime events. From hotspot mapping to spatial statistics, geography has emphasised the need for special consideration of space and place, particularly when studying human behaviour. One must pay careful attention to the spatial units of analysis (points, lines and areas) as well as to scale, in order to limit the likelihood of spurious analytical results. Such attention is particularly important when considering the policy implications, where results translate to actionable crime reduction approaches. In this vein, policy mobilities literature guides the successful implementation of crime reduction policy by re-emphasising the importance of adopting a local focus at all stages of investigation – from the spatial crime analysis, to the policy implementation, and into the development of crime prevention initiatives.

Notes

1 Policy mobilities refers to the transferability of policies developed in other locations and how they are altered and applied in different contexts.
2 Trajectories are often defined as increasing, decreasing, or stable over time and with high, moderate, and low levels of crime.

References

Andresen, M. A. (2011). Estimating the probability of local crime clusters: The impact of immediate spatial neighbors. *Journal of Criminal Justice, 39*(5), 394–404.

Andresen, M. A. (2014). *Environmental Criminology: Evolution, Theory, and Practice.* New York: Routledge.

Andresen, M. A. & Jenion, G. W. (2010). Ambient populations and the calculation of crime rates and risk. *Security Journal, 23*(2), 114–133.
Andresen, M. A. & Linning, S. J. (2012). The (in)appropriateness of aggregating across crime types. *Applied Geography, 35*(1–2), 275–282.
Andresen, M. A. & Malleson, N. (2011). Testing the stability of crime patterns: Implications for theory and policy. *Journal of Research in Crime and Delinquency, 48*(1), 58–82.
Andresen, M. A. & Malleson, N. (2013). Spatial heterogeneity in crime analysis. In M. Leitner (ed.), *Crime Modeling and Mapping Using Geospatial Technologies* (pp. 3–23). New York: Springer.
Anselin, L. (1995). Local indicators of spatial association – LISA. *Geographical Analysis, 27*(2), 93–115.
Boggs, S. L. (1965). Urban crime patterns. *American Sociological Review, 30*(6), 899–908.
Brantingham, P. L. & Brantingham, P. J. (1981). Notes on the geometry of crime. In P. J. Brantingham & P. L. Brantingham (eds), *Environmental Criminology* (pp. 27–54). Prospect Heights IL, Waveland Press.
Brantingham, P. L. & Brantingham, P. J. (1993). Nodes, paths and edges: Considerations on the complexity of crime and the physical environment. *Journal of Environmental Psychology, 13*(1), 3–28.
Brantingham, P. J., Dyreson, D. A., & Brantingham, P. L. (1976). Crime seen through a cone of resolution. *American Behavioral Scientist, 20*(2), 261–273.
Brunsdon, C. F., Fotheringham, A. S., & Charlton, M. E. (1996). Geographically weighted regression: A method for exploring spatial non-stationarity. *Geographical Analysis, 28*(4), 281–298.
Cahill, M. & Mulligan, G. (2007). Using geographically weighted regression to explore local crime patterns. *Social Science Computer Review, 25*(2), 174–193.
Clarke, R. V. G. (1980). Situational crime prevention: Theory and practice. *British Journal of Criminology, 20*(2), 136–147.
Clarke, R. V. (1983). Situational crime prevention: Its theoretical basis and practical scope. *Crime and Justice: An Annual Review of Research, 4*, 225–256.
Clarke, R. V. (1997). *Situational Crime Prevention: Successful Case Studies* (2nd ed.). Monsey, NY: Criminal Justice Press.
Clarke, R. V. (2012). Opportunity makes the thief. Really? And so what? *Crime Science, 1*, Article 3.
Cohen, L. E. & Felson, M. (1979). Social change and crime rate trends: A routine activity approach. *American Sociological Review, 44*, 588–608.
Curman, A. S. N., Andresen, M. A., & Brantingham, P. J. (2015). Crime and place: A longitudinal examination of street segment patterns in Vancouver, BC. *Journal of Quantitative Criminology, 31*(1), 127–147.
Fotheringham, A. S. (1997). Trends in quantitative methods I: Stressing the local. *Progress in Human Geography, 21*(1), 88–96.
Fotheringham, A. S., Brundson, C., & Charlton, M. (2002). *Geographically Weighted Regression: The Analysis of Spatially Varying Relationships*. Chichester, UK: John Wiley & Sons.
Fotheringham, A. S. & Wong, D. W. S. (1991). The modifiable areal unit problem in multivariate statistical analysis. *Environment and Planning A, 23*(7), 1025–1044.
Gehlke, C. E. & Biehl, H. (1934). Certain effects of grouping upon the size of the correlation coefficient in census tract material. *Journal of the American Statistical Association, Supplement, 29*(185), 169–170.
Groff, E. R., Weisburd, D., & Yang, S-M. (2010). Is it important to examine crime trends at a local 'micro' level? A longitudinal analysis of street to street variability in crime trajectories. *Journal of Quantitative Criminology, 26*(1), 7–32.
Guerry, A.-M. (1832). La statistique compare de l'état de l'instruction et du nombre des crimes. *Revue Encyclopédique, 55*, 414–424.
Guerry, A.-M. (1833). *Essai sur la statistique morale de la France*. Paris: Crochard.
McCann, E. (2008). Expertise, truth, and urban policy mobilities: Global circuits of knowledge in the development of Vancouver, Canada's 'four pillar' drug strategy. *Environment and Planning A, 40*(4), 885–904.
McCann, E. (2011). Urban policy mobilities and global circuits of knowledge: Toward a research agenda. *Annals of the Association of American Geographers, 101*(1), 107–130.
McCann, E. (2013). Policy boosterism, policy mobilities, and the extrospective city. *Urban Geography, 34*(1), 5–29.
McCann, E. & Temenos, C. (2015). Mobilizing drug consumption rooms: Inter-place connections and the politics of harm reduction drug policy. *Health & Place, 31*(1), 216–223.
Melo, S. N., Matias, L. F., & Andresen, M. A. (2015). Crime concentrations and similarities in spatial crime patterns in a Brazilian context. *Applied Geography, 62*, 314–324.
Openshaw, S. (1984a). Ecological fallacies and the analysis of areal census data. *Environment and Planning A, 16*(1), 17–31.

Openshaw, S. (1984b). *The Modifiable Areal Unit Problem. CATMOG (Concepts and Techniques in Modern Geography) 38*. Norwich, UK: Geo Books.
Peck, J. (2011). Geographies of policy: From transfer-diffusion to mobility-mutation. *Progress in Human Geography, 35*(6), 773–797.
Quetelet, L. A. J. ([1831] 1984). *Research on the Propensity for Crime at Different Ages* (translated by S. F. Sylvester). Cincinnati, OH: Anderson Publishing.
Quetelet, L. A. J. (1842). *A Treatise on Man and the Development of his Faculties*. Edinburgh: W. and R. Chambers.
Robinson, J. (2011). 2010 Urban Geography Plenary Lecture – The travels of urban neoliberalism: Taking stock of the internationalization of urban theory. *Urban Geography, 32*(8), 1087–1109.
Robinson, W. S. (1950). Ecological correlations and the behavior of individuals. *American Sociological Review, 15*(3), 351–357.
Sampson, R. J. & Groves, W. B. (1989). Community structure and crime: Testing social-disorganization theory. *American Journal of Sociology, 94*(4), 774–802.
Schmid, C. F. (1960a). Urban crime areas: Part I. *American Sociological Review, 25*(4), 527–542.
Schmid, C. F. (1960b). Urban crime areas: Part II. *American Sociological Review, 25*(5), 655–678.
Sherman, L. W., Gartin, P., & Buerger, M. E. (1989). Hot spots of predatory crime: Routine activities and the criminology of place. *Criminology, 27*(1), 27–55.
Temenos, C. & McCann, E. (2012). The local politics of policy mobility: The education of attention in developing a municipal sustainability fix. *Environment and Planning A, 44*(6), 1389–1406.
Temenos, C. & McCann, E. (2013). Geographies of policy mobilities. *Geography Compass*, 7(5), 344–357.
Ward, K. (2006). Policies in motion, urban management and state restructuring: The trans-local expansion of business improvement districts. *International Journal of Urban and Regional Research, 30*(1), 54–75.
Weisburd, D. (2015). The law of crime concentration and the criminology of place. *Criminology, 53*(2), 133–157.
Weisburd, D., Bushway, S., Lum, C., & Yang, S-M. (2004). Trajectories of crime at places: A longitudinal study of street segments in the City of Seattle. *Criminology, 42*(2), 283–321.
Weisburd, D., Bruinsma, G. J. N., & Bernasco, W. (2009a). Units of analysis in geographic criminology: Historical development, critical issues, and open questions. In D. Weisburd, W. Bernasco and G. J. N. Bruinsma (eds), *Putting Crime in its Place: Units of Analysis in Geographic Criminology* (pp. 3–31). New York: Springer.
Weisburd, D., Morris, N. A., & Groff, E. R. (2009b). Hot spots of juvenile crime: A longitudinal study of arrest incidents at street segments in Seattle, Washington. *Journal of Quantitative Criminology, 25*(4), 443–467.
Weisburd, D., Groff, E. R., & Yang, S-M. (2012). *The Criminology of Place: Street Segments and our Understanding of the Crime Problem*. New York: Oxford University Press.
Wooldredge, J. (2002). Examining the (ir)relevance of aggregation bias for multilevel studies of neighborhoods and crime with an example of comparing census tracts to official neighborhoods in Cincinnati. *Criminology, 40*(3), 681–709.
Wortley, R. (2010). Critiques of situational crime prevention. In B. Fisher & S. Lab (eds), *Encyclopedia of Victimology and Crime Prevention* (pp. 885–888). Thousand Oaks, CA: Sage Publications.

10

Architecture

Hervé Borrion and Daniel Koch

Introduction

An important aspect of environmental criminology, and therefore crime science, concerns the built environment. Specifically, researchers have examined how the built environment can contribute to the emergence of crime generators, crime attractors, crime detractors, crime facilitators or crime precipitators; in other words, how urban design structures possibilities and restrictions that might enable, facilitate, restrict or hamper a range of criminogenic behaviours.

Here, we consider architecture – that, in a wider sense, can be understood as that which pertains to built forms, their culture and their becoming – to be concerned primarily with the design and making of the built environment. The term 'wider sense' is important to keep in mind as it engenders architecture (both as physical form and discipline) with a certain role in embedding and transmitting culture and values through society through how it structures social relations, erects borders and boundaries, enables or creates connections – but also how it represents society through who and what is given (visual, physical and symbolic) presence, representation, and a place to be – and, conversely, who and what is excluded in either sense. As a theoretical discipline, architecture therefore encompasses the design of (i.e. giving shape and form to) buildings, cities and other built environments. In addition, it also studies discursive fields regarding architecture and cities as well as the discipline of architecture and its boundaries, built environments broadly defined, and the effects of society on both discipline and built form – and, conversely, the ways that the discipline and built form affect society. This makes it perhaps even more important to insist on the term 'architecture' instead of an ostensibly more neutral 'built environment' as these historical, social, aesthetical and cultural values and negotiations need to be, at least to an extent, integrated into crime prevention discussions as it concerns 'the built environment'. With this in mind, when we say architecture in the coming text, we primarily mean built form, or the practice of designing the same.

This chapter begins with an overview of the main principles and theoretical developments in the field of Crime Prevention through Environmental Design (CPTED). This is followed by a section illustrating important contributions that architects have made to the instantiation of criminological principles. The last section of the chapter presents computational tools that have been developed to support architects in designing more secure and more resilient buildings.

Crime and the built environment

Early defensive architecture

The environment appears to have always had a critical influence on the safety and security of people against external threats. Certainly, the construction of protective walls predates modern history; and several centuries after the largest and most renowned example of a protective wall was erected in China, structures built for similar purposes (including the Maginot Line, the West Bank barrier and the wall proposed by Trump at the US–Mexican border) continue to instil feelings of security, fear, fascination and tension within communities. Besides these physical barriers, remains of fortified homesteads, bastions and bunkers can also be found that offer a glimpse of historical battles fought by locals. On another level, these ruins evidence the thirst for security that exists across continents and civilisations, and illustrate people's capacity to shape their environment to feel safe.

Major progress was made in defensive architecture between the 15th century and the 17th century. Successful military engineers and urbanists of that era have become household names in many European nations; they include Francesco di Giorgio Martini in Italy, Luís Serrão Pimentel in Portugal or Sébastien Vauban in France. Advocates of a mathematical approach to conducting and resisting sieges, these experts in poliorcetics not only transformed urban landscapes but they were also the first to put scientific thinking at the heart of security practice (Conde and Massa-Esteve, 2018; Duffy, 2015, di Giorgio Martini and Saluzzo, 1841). Since then, many studies have been conducted that have contributed to our understanding of vulnerabilities within man-made structures, and how to make these structures less susceptible to victimisation, more defensible, or more resilient (see Eck et al., 2007; Rayment-McHugh, 2015).

Wood, Jacobs, Newman and Jeffery

Whilst architecture and planning have been recognised as core components of military strategies for some time, their contribution to reducing crime and fear of crime was not studied to the same extent. Modern examples of crime-proof architecture whilst around us (e.g. Fussey et al., 2016) do not come to mind as easily. Whilst the use of architectural and engineering features to reduce crime is not new – theft prevention is a renowned architectural feature of pyramids in Ancient Egypt – it is only in the 20th century that their contribution to reducing crime and fear of crime was formally considered. Elizabeth Wood, the first executive director of the Chicago Housing Authority, is hailed for conceiving projects of urban renewal as a means to support social welfare and address the problems of the city. An advocate of residential diversity by race and income, she promoted the creation of public housing projects scattered throughout the city, adequate indoor and outdoor recreation gathering spaces to encourage socialisation, and selection policies to achieve racial balance within buildings (Ware, 2004:699). Radically opposed to the mentality of the time, she often urged planners to move away from gridiron streets and to develop integrated and workable neighbourhoods fit for mixed use. Her obituary makes mention of her preference for the development low-rise buildings such that 'a mother in a window could be heard when calling to a child in a playground' (Lambert, 1993; Wood, 1961, 1964). She is also remembered as a catalyst in thinking about how the built environment can reduce crime, and she made specific other recommendations to enhance natural surveillance within public housing developments. Whilst those ideas were never implemented, they are considered to have been influential in shaping some of the later thinking around CPTED.

Another proponent of urban diversity was American-Canadian author and journalist Jane Jacobs, who is credited for much of the theoretical foundation underpinning CPTED. Focusing on what makes for a successful neighbourhood, Jacobs was resolutely against the designation of urban zones for particular land uses (residential, commercial or industrial), advocating instead greater diversification within the city.[1] Regarding public safety as an indicator of success in urban planning, Jacobs (1961) devoted a whole chapter of her then controversial book, *The Death and Life of Great American Cities*, to the hypothesised mechanisms connecting diversity of land use to reduction in crime and delinquency. Much of her legacy revolves around three recommendations to planners:

> There must be a clear demarcation between what public space is and what private space is. There must be eyes upon the street; eyes belonging to those we might call the natural proprietors of the street. [. . .] The sidewalk must have users on it fairly continuously, both to add to the number of effective eyes on the street and to induce the people in buildings along the street to watch the sidewalks in sufficient numbers.
>
> *(Jacobs, 1961:35)*

Influenced by Jacobs's work, American architect Oscar Newman (1973:50) introduced the concept of defensible space, which he defined as 'a residential environment whose physical characteristics – building layout and site plan – function to allow inhabitants themselves to become key agents in ensuring their security'. As a means to prevent the crimes resulting from increasing social disorganisation, the theory of defensible space points to factors of the environment influencing crime, namely the perception of zones of territorial influence; surveillance opportunities for potential guardians (residents and guests); perception of adequate management and maintenance of an area; and geographical juxtaposition with 'safe-zones' on the security of adjacent areas (and vice versa) (see Figure 10.1). Newman's framework was refreshing but it also highlighted fundamental conflicts with Jacobs's recommendation for urban forms with greater spatial permeability. His practical ideas quickly propagated within government administrations, where planning practices had been recently shaken by the introduction of the National

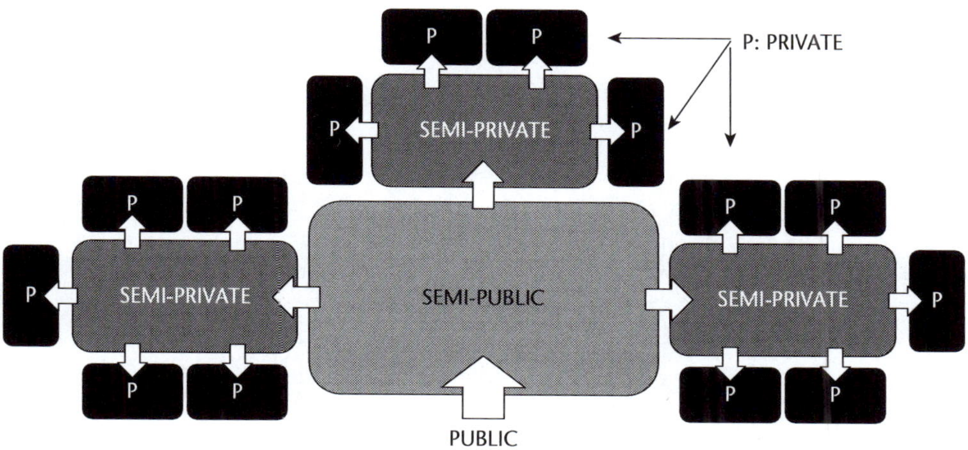

Figure 10.1 Hierarchy of defensible space with white arrows representing connections between different zones (Newman 1973: 9)

Environmental Policy Act (US Congress, 1970). The US Department of Housing and Urban Development and the Law Enforcement Assistance Administration (LEAA) provided funding to implement and test defensible space principles in a range of residential, transportation, commercial and educational settings. The LEAA project was known under the name Crime Prevention through Environment Design (CPTED pronounced sep-ted); a term coined by criminologist C. Ray Jeffery.

Like others mentioned in this chapter, Jeffery's (1971) work explored the influence of the environment on human behaviour. He saw in the social and physical environment a source of reinforcement conducive to the conduct of criminal acts. In opposition to traditional criminology, he believed that environmental circumstances, and notably opportunities, were the main sources of crime, writing that 'given the proper environmental structure, anyone will be a criminal' (Jeffery, 1977:177). In his view, altering the environment could therefore be an effective means to disrupt those reinforcements, remove the effect of the conditioning history of people, change the opportunity structure to commit the act, increase the risk of being apprehended during the crime commission process, and in turn reduce crime. Conducted in parallel to Newman's work,[2] Jeffery's research was grounded in a broader theoretical framework including not only the physical environment but also the biological organisms within. He wrote, for example, that the 'environment never influences behaviour directly, but only through the brain. Any model of crime prevention must include both the brain and the physical environment' (Jeffery and Zahm, 1993:330). Despite pioneering many principles at the heart of situational crime prevention, Jeffery did not, however, become so much a household name as Jacobs or Newman; and many architects and planners who follow his crime prevention principles are oblivious of his role in the emergence of CPTED (see Wortley et al., Chapter 1).

First-generation CPTED

Framework and principles

As explained by Crowe (2000:46), the philosophy underpinning CPTED is that 'the proper design and effective use of the built environment can lead to a reduction in the fear and incidence of crime, and an improvement in the quality of life'. Building on the work of Wood, Jacobs, Newman, Jeffery and others (see Angel, 1968 for instance), frameworks have been proposed to organise concepts of CPTED, and explain how to implement them in urban projects. In their review of CPTED frameworks, Cozens et al. (2005) (see also Cozens and Love, 2015) adapted a diagram originally developed by Moffat (1983) to categorise the various strategies. They identified seven areas – territorial reinforcement; surveillance; access control; target hardening; image management; activity support; and geographical juxtaposition – that pertain to what is now known as first-generation CPTED. According to Crowe (2000), *territorial reinforcement* constitutes an overarching strategy in CPTED. A concept perhaps less straightforward than the others, it involves fostering a sense of ownership in legitimate users and conveying that ownership to potential intruders in order to dissuade them from engaging in illegitimate actions. Represented in Figure 10.1, Newman's delineation of private, semi-private and public areas is a classic example of a design principle in this category. Although it constitutes a CPTED concept in its own right, territoriality can also be supported by other measures primarily aimed at enhancing the level of social control through, for example, visibly enforcing *access control* in certain zones, and increasing *surveillance* opportunities for residents. Additional strategies were subsequently added that include image management; legitimate activity support; and target hardening. *Image management* is closely related to broken-window theory and the idea that crime can be reduced by creating a sense of social cohesion and informal social control through appropriate maintenance of the environment (Wilson and Kelling, 1982). *Activity support* relates to the properties of the environment that attract vulnerable actors and activities – e.g. handling of money and high value items vulnerable to theft – to safer locations; and encourage people to engage in legitimate activities in certain places where their presence might make crime less likely. Target hardening, described by Clarke (1997:17) as 'obstruct[ion] by physical barriers through the use of locks, safes, screens or reinforced materials' is another approach that can be used to prevent crime through environmental design. The last strategy of first-generation CPTED, *geographic juxtaposition*, is directly extracted from Newman's (1973) defensible space framework and concerns the influence of 'safe-zones' on the security of adjacent areas, and vice versa.

Critiques

The aforementioned description of the CPTED framework is not without contention though. To start with, different competing frameworks exist, all of which claim to describe the structure of modern CPTED. Of the seven strategies listed by Cozens and Love (2015), Severin et al. (2013:88) explicitly recognised five, discarding target hardening and geographical juxtaposition. The inclusion of *target hardening* in the CPTED toolbox is particularly controversial for many reasons.

First, there are often misconceptions about the meaning of this term. Target hardening is sometimes understood as synonymous with situational crime prevention (SCP) and any overt security measure (such as a CCTV camera) often associated with this category, even though the SCP literature clearly describes *target hardening* as just one of 25 possible techniques to remove crime opportunities (Smith and Clarke, 2012). Another element in the list of SCP techniques is *access control*, which is noteworthy as it implies that target hardening is not a sub-principle of access control as was suggested by Fennelly and Perry (2018) and Gibson (2016:190). Our interpretation is that target hardening goes beyond the mere control of access/entry. It could be said that target hardening aims to confer an ecosystem with suitable properties to physically *resist* the occurrence of specific criminogenic actions/events within it. In this definition, we borrow the concept of *resistance* from Ekblom (2011): 'hardening refers to the (usually) preparatory preventive task intended to give targets and enclosures alike the property of *resistance to manipulation* by offenders in an attempt to achieve a whole range of criminal means and ends'. Depending on the physical, emotional, cognitive and financial resources available to offenders, target hardening may indeed assist in controlling people's access and entry, but it can control other criminogenic activities as well, with misuse being another obvious one. Examples of target-hardening measures include locks to immobilise vehicles, metal sheets on walls to obstruct mobile phone signals, and filters in Heating, Ventilation, and Air-Conditioning (HVAC) systems to stop the propagation of hazardous agents within a building.

Second, the effects of target hardening on crime are often debated (Tseloni et al., 2017). It is often perceived that this crime prevention approach works by removing (perceived) opportunities, i.e. making it less likely that potential offenders find themselves (or see themselves) in a suitable situation to commit crime. Focusing only on the situational effects that target hardening has on people at/near the time of offending (i.e. reducing the temptation to commit crime and the successful commission of crime) can give the impression that this approach only displaces crime to other locations without actually reducing it. After all, a motivated burglar finding it too difficult to break into a given house would only need to walk a few more metres to make another attempt at the neighbouring house. However, this is a very simplistic view because it assumes that offenders are all highly professional criminals, that their motivation to conduct criminal acts does not vary much over time, and that they have ready access to the required resources throughout the day. These three assumptions are far from reflecting actual behaviour. In another domain, it is well known that people play less sport on rainy days, even if, technically, they could have rescheduled all their training sessions to sunnier times or indoor places. By analogy, it is not reasonable to expect that all crimes that were not attempted, were disrupted, or were unsuccessful, are systematically displaced to more suitable times and/or places. Moreover, these assumptions assume that the environment has no influence on the emergence of people's intent. By analogy again, we might question why children suddenly crave ice cream when they see an ice-cream van. Furthermore, the idea that all target hardening can do is displace crime assumes that this strategy has no positive cumulative and long-lasting effects, such as increasing disengagement from crime by offenders who might find it an overly inefficient and stressful business. Despite evidence that situational crime prevention measures, and in particular target hardening ones, can reduce crime without necessarily causing displacement (Guerette and Bowers, 2009), the displacement fallacy remains widely accepted amongst the public, practitioners and criminologists.

Third, target hardening is often perceived negatively on a socio-cultural level and even on ethical grounds (see von Hirsch et al., 2000). Rather than designing regular (i.e. non-security) elements with security in mind, this approach generally involves adding elements in the environment whose function is exclusively a protective one. Many architects are trained in an architectural tradition where 'good design' is often associated with criteria of aesthetics, functionality, a pleasant atmosphere, inclusivity, openness, or characteristics more directly related to the particular project and its intents (or the identity of its intended inhabitants). As a result, they regard target-hardening measures as intrinsically conflicting with the values they would like their projects to embody. This can prove an even greater challenge if such security measures are added late in the process, or if their design conflicts with the aesthetics or atmosphere of the project. Fennelly and Perry (2018), for instance, recommend applying target hardening as 'the last resort'. The negative perception of target hardening is not restricted to architects. The visual, emotional and ethical impact of security measures implemented in the 'everyday' urban landscape are common concerns for the public too (Borrion et al., 2012; Fussey, 2008). Reflecting on the post-9/11 investment in protective security by municipalities, Coaffee et al. (2009) examined the symbolic messages that are conveyed by counter-terrorism measures, and noted that 'while security regimes may attempt to "transmit" feelings of safety and security through the built environment and to reassure the public, the "reception" of these very same messages may be "lost in translation"'. Paradoxically, features designed to improve security may simultaneously create feelings of fear and anxiety amongst citizens (Boddy, 2007:279).

Developments in CPTED

Second-generation CPTED

As explained in the previous section, CPTED has been the object of criticisms since the 1970s, on both theoretical and practical grounds. In turn, many of those criticisms have contributed to the evolution of the framework and of its original principles. In perhaps the most notable critique of CPTED, Saville and Cleveland (1997, 2013) argued that the holistic approach proposed by Jacobs and Newman 'has, in many instances, been lost in the service of hardening targets'. Specifically, they claimed that first-generation CPTED neglected social factors, and that the needs of communities should be taken more into account to shape safe environments. Saville and Cleveland (1997) explained that a sense of 'shared belonging' and 'neighborliness' is required for residents to develop territorial feelings. This argument, which forms the basis of second-generation CPTED, is grounded in traditional criminology, in particular strain theory, according to which crime can be reduced by increasing social cohesion and collective efficacy (Sampson, Raudenbush, and Earls 1997). Better considering social factors in the development of interventions may also support target hardening in the longer term, as measures that conflict with people's interests or values are unlikely to be sustained within communities (Nissen, 2014).

The complementary perspective proposed by Saville and Cleveland (1997) was instantiated through four new principles – social cohesion, connectivity, community culture, and threshold capacity:

Social cohesion is described as the core of second-generation CPTED. It comprises the social glue that brings members of the community together and enhances positive self-esteem, and is described as a necessary quality that individuals must have for cohesion to occur. By enhancing the relationships between residents, social cohesion interventions can help foster effective networks of engaged citizens that are not only able to provide guardianship in neighbourhoods but also resolve conflicts within them. *Connectivity* relates to the communities' relationships and influence with external agencies (e.g. media, local councils, etc.) that could empower them to deal with minor issues. Initiating and sustaining relationships may require interpersonal skills, cyber connectivity (emails) and physical connectivity (roads, paths). The next component, *community culture* is implemented by bringing residents together. Events, programmes, policies and attributes of the environment foster community culture and give residents a sense of place and stimulate greater willingness to exert territorial control (Adams and Goldbard, 2001). The last component, *threshold capacity* (also referred to as ecological threshold) is arguably more difficult to delineate. It relates to the 'capacity of any given activity or space to properly support the intended use' (Saville and Cleveland, 1997). This involves establishing balanced, or more diverse, land uses and social activities, introducing social stabilisers (e.g. community gardens, street entertainments) or keeping crime generators low.

With second-generation CPTED, the contribution of architects to crime reduction lies less in removing crime opportunities through design than in fostering a sense of belonging within community, empowering residents to find ways to address conflicts, and reducing the opportunities for conflicts and criminogenic tipping points. In line with Jacobs's principle of eyes upon the street, it is also about attracting people to various areas of neighbourhoods to increase guardianship. In this second layer, the 'environmental design' dimension is not evident, at least not in the material sense, and the role of architects less clearly articulated. Gibson (2016) argues that the principles of second-generation CPTED 'are just a reflection of modern day community safety efforts in Canada and the USA but bear little relevance to First Generation CPTED or even environmental design'. Many have even questioned whether they should be part of CPTED at all. Ekblom et al. (2013:94), for example, argue that this approach dilutes the unique 'environmental design' aspects of CPTED. In response to the growing ambiguity surrounding CPTED, they called for a refinement of the CPTED framework and the terminology that is employed (see also Crowe, 2000; Ekblom 2011, 2013; Gibson and Johnson, 2016).

Third-generation CPTED

With the growing backcloth of frameworks in this area, the very essence and terminology of CPTED have been questioned by Ekblom who subsequently provided a more detailed definition:

> CPTED is reducing the possibility, probability and harm from criminal and related events, and enhancing the quality of life through community safety, by the process of planning and design of the environment . . . on a range of scales and places, to produce designs fit for purpose and contextually appropriate, whilst achieving a balance between the efficacy of avoiding crime problems before construction, and the adaptability of tackling them through subsequent management and maintenance.
>
> *(Ekblom, 2013:13)*

The search for third-generation CPTED is ongoing and, although it is still too early to really speculate what this will look like, recent developments in this area are worth highlighting.

For her doctoral thesis, titled Third Generation CPTED? Rethinking the Basis for Crime Prevention Strategies, Gibson (2016) conducted a review of the CPTED knowledge base. Like Ekblom, she came to the conclusion that there is 'substantial inconsistency in definitions; confusion over the position of territoriality within the CPTED framework; and the absence of a formally integrated social component within each of the CPTED concepts'. She saw no clear theoretical basis in second-generation CPTED, not enough information about the different strategies, or enough evidence of its effectiveness in reducing crime. She therefore decided to restructure and relabel the CPTED framework to give it more clarity and consistency and to unpick the operational and preparatory division within the various strategies (see also Gibson and Johnson, 2016). Her framework comprises three concepts, each of them further divided into two sub-concepts: surveillance (formal surveillance and informal surveillance); positive reinforcement (image management/maintenance and activity support); and access control (target hardening and boundary definition).

At the other end of the spectrum, there have been attempts to integrate new technological developments and global concerns, in particular sustainability, into CPTED. Saville (2013) has drawn attention to a report published by United Nations InterRegional Crime and Justice Research Institute in collaboration with the Massachusetts Institute of Technology Senseable City Lab titled 'New Energy for Urban Security: Improving Urban Security through Green Environmental Design'). In the report, the authors propose 'a third generation of CPTED framework that focuses on sustainable green environmental design strategies and insists on practical measures, physically or cybernetically enhanced, that foster the perception of urban space as safe beyond mere concerns about crime' (UNICRI, 2011). The framework borrows from first- and second-generation CPTED principles but adds to those in suggesting how some of the proposed measures can be implemented in a green fashion (e.g. the use of harvested energy as a power source for street lighting). It also considerably extends the scope of CPTED in suggesting non-situational strategies such as poverty reduction.

In the next section we move away from the conceptual aspects discussed above to focus on the practical difficulty of preventing crime through environmental design. Whilst the theoretical tenets of CPTED are not exactly rocket science, implementing them is not that simple in practice. The main reason is that, for them to work, interventions must be both crime- and context-specific; and practitioners must ensure that security measures do not conflict with each other or with other (commercial or ethical) priorities that people and organisations might have. Depending on the physical and operational constraints to satisfy, those trying to embed security in the built environment can therefore face intractable problems. Over the years, many such issues have been identified empirically and experienced practitioners have developed and learned heuristics rules to resolve them. For those designing against the growing wave of terrorist attacks, however, the challenge is different and arguably much greater. This is partly because they cannot draw upon a similarly rich experience of designs implemented in our everyday environments but also because the implications of getting it wrong can be substantial. In response, innovative analytical approaches have been adopted such as those discussed in the remainder of the chapter.

Computational tools for CPTED

Designing-out terrorism

Architecture has often worked in conjunction with engineering to address the most serious risks to public security (Borrion, 2018; Borrion and Koch, 2017). Following the terrorist attacks on US soil in September 2001, a major security programme was initiated by the Bush administration to protect large cities against explosive attacks (Willis, 2007). Bollards and barriers were deployed near government buildings; Closed-Circuit Television (CCTV) and Automated Number Plate Recognition (ANPR) systems were either introduced or afforded greater coverage across towns; security requirements were given higher priority in the design of new public transport hubs such as train stations and airports (Borrion et al., 2014; Coaffee, 2004; Enoma et al., 2009). With the rise in the number of terrorist attacks against soft targets in Europe, counter-terrorism interventions are being extended to more cities and more places within them.

Already, several of the concepts associated with first-generation CPTED have played a decisive role in preventing attacks or reducing their consequences. In the 2007 terrorist attack at Glasgow Airport, a car loaded with propane canisters was stopped at the entrance of the terminal by security bollards (Brocklehurst, 2017). The capacity of the terrorists involved in the 2017 attacks in Westminster and London Bridge were similarly disrupted by physical structures into which their cars crashed. Two years earlier, a security guard controlling people's access to the Stade de France in Paris prevented one of the terrorists from detonating their explosives inside the stadium (Robinson and Landauro, 2015). Natural surveillance was also found to be effective on many occasions, such as when members of the public identified weapons concealed in cars and train carriages (MPS, 2017). To encourage such behaviours, many buildings and public transport systems are now fitted with furniture and elements that make it difficult for planted weapons to go unnoticed (Borrion et al., 2014), as illustrated by Figure 10.2.

For architects, not only is the counter-terrorism challenge to successfully instantiate security principles in public spaces but also to accommodate interventions from other domains. On the security-management side, for example, more thorough screening procedures (such as manual search and use of X-ray scanners) at airports can yield improvement in weapon detection; however, it also increases queue lengths and therefore places greater demand on space. To address those challenges, more advanced technology (e.g. sensors and tracking systems) and computational tools (e.g. algorithms and software packages) are being developed that can assist architects in better understanding the relationships between design choices and security risks.

Case study: Resilient Infrastructure and Building Security (RIBS)

To illustrate how CPTED principles can be supported by computational tools, we draw on a case study developed in the EU FP7 project on Resilient Infrastructure and Building Security (RIBS). The purpose of the research was to support the design of effective and viable security measures by creating a design process that integrates a broader understanding of the built environment and the human elements within which these measures are meant to be implemented. The work was carried out by a multi-disciplinary team and examined a range of security threats including intruders, explosives, chemical agents and biological agents. Architecture, especially

Figure 10.2 Lockers at Seoul station. The top panel was retrofitted to prevent the planting of explosive devices (Credit: Borrion)

spatial analysis, has pervaded every aspect of the research because of the imperative to understand the spatial characteristics of terrorist attacks, and the effects of interventions on those.

The research began with the creation of an infrastructure model representing a building that, at the time, was used as a retail bank branch (as an example of a commercial building comprising areas with public, semi-public and private functions), its services, occupants and assets. The method then involved the elicitation of the stakeholder requirements (i.e. objectives and constraints) from a range of individuals including members of various departments within the organisation. A number of scenarios were then developed and simulated (using computer modelling tools) that represented both ordinary and extraordinary situations. Considering the attack scenarios as misuse cases of the ecosystem of interest, the high-level requirements concerning the overall ecosystem were then derived by a team of experts in biological, chemical and explosive protection. Different strategies, security principles and intervention mechanisms were selected and later used to specify the precise functions of future protection measures, and some of their qualities. Functional requirements (i.e. the effect to be caused by the intervention on the ecosystem) and non-functional requirements (i.e. any additional goals and constraints that have to be met) were then prioritised and verified.

The contribution of the spatial analysis team was found in many areas of the research. In the following sections, we present some of the techniques that have been developed and implemented for this project, as a means to illustrate how the CPTED principles proposed by Jeffery and others are applicable to this problem.

Characterising routine micro-behaviour in space and time

The ability to observe, forecast or even control how space is used in 'normal' conditions can offer very concrete benefits to crime reduction practitioners (Cohen and Felson, 1979). Knowing what routine micro-behaviours (e.g. people's trajectory within a room) take place in a given building is often a prerequisite to estimating the consequences of hypothetical attacks. In RIBS, a technology was developed to automatically record routine micro-activities conducted in the studied building as seen in Figure 10.3.

The data were then used to estimate the number of fatalities each attack scenarios might cause. Occupancy patterns of staff and visitors were used to estimate the likely effects of explosive devices triggered in different areas of the building. Similarly, modelling the movement of occupants on normal days enabled us to determine what would happen if a biological or chemical agent was released in the building, considering various times, locations and concentrations (Figure 10.4).

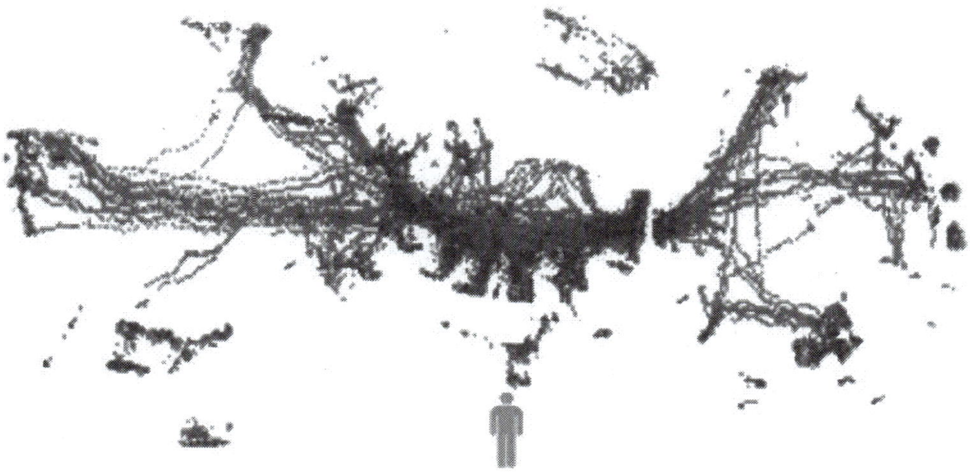

Figure 10.3 Trajectory of visitors on the ground floor, captured by the RIBS technology. (Credit: Ingwar and Jensen)

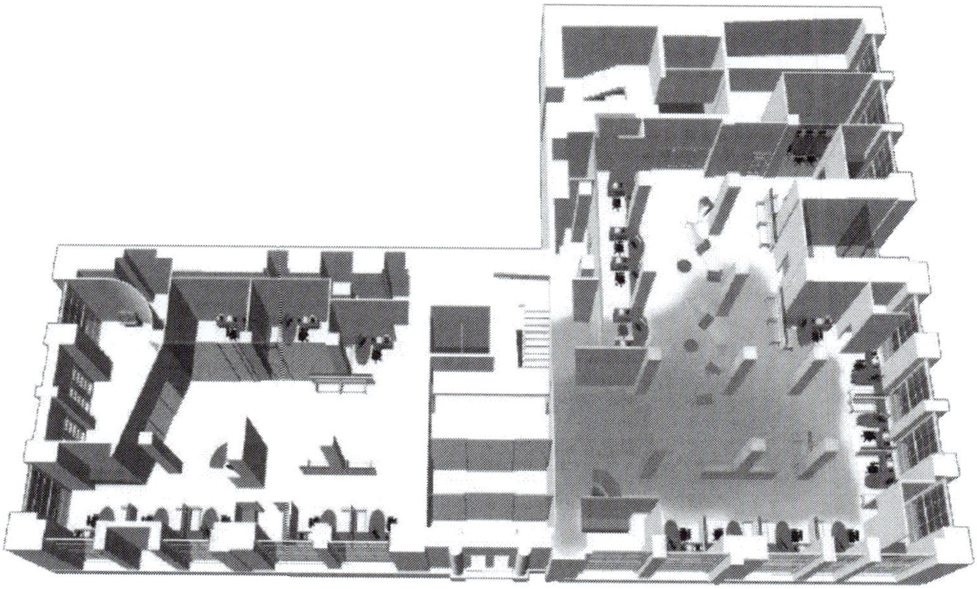

Figure 10.4 Dispersal of a hazardous agent simulated in the bank branch (Credit: Technion – Israel Institute of Technology)

Characterising normal behaviours has proved particularly useful to identify security vulnerabilities inherent to the use of the building. From the results, we have identified that a very large proportion of visitors were systematically coming in contact with the same object in the lobby of the branch, making it a potentially very effective contamination point for terrorists, if they had access to the right kind of materials. Another useful insight related to access control and use of space was gained from observing people's movements. Related to Newman's hierarchy of space, space–time analysis of traces allowed us to identify routine micro-activities that were not strictly justified by the intended functions of the space. This included that most visitors, even if ending up using one specific function of the branch, followed something akin to a multi-purpose routine. For instance, while the ground floor was divided into a main hall with staffed counters and a waiting room (to the right from the entry), with some additional sub-spaces personal banking advice, another hall with personal advisors and Automated Teller Machines (ATMs) (left of the entry) and a second floor with additional services, a fair portion of visitors went into at least both entry floor halls before ending up performing their actual task. In addition, a notable share of visitors simply went through one or both of the halls in the entry floor and left again. When employees were confronted with this observation, they were first surprised by how common it was, but after consideration insisted that this was important to maintain – they are perhaps potential customers, or existing customers stepping in to see how long the queue is or whether their particular contact is free, etc. As an opportunity for relation-building and customer-recruitment, this unintended activity was then shifted to an intended one. As a result, RIBS identified and emphasised the need for projects aimed to increase security to include phases where the routine activities of occupants are elicited so as to ensure security measures support not only *programmed* but de facto routines too.

Characterising abnormal behaviour

To some extent, identification of routine activities can also allow analysts to define and recognise abnormal behaviours. Here, it was evident from analysing the movement traces collected by the spatial analysis team (Figures 10.3 and 10.5) that customers entering the bank were following various *scripts*. Defined by Schank and Abelson (1977:41) as 'a predetermined, stereotyped sequence of actions that define a well-known situation in a particular context', the script-theoretic approach is particularly useful to label, classify and analyse customer behaviour. In RIBS, we were able to identify more than 45 scripts clustered into 11 overall types in the bank branch such as a visitor using the ATM, a customer attending an appointment, etc.

Those behaviours that do not conform to any of the scripts identified on normal days can be classified as abnormal scripts (from a functional perspective) and potentially as outliers (from a statistical one). At the bank, the aforementioned behaviours (whereby people enter and leave the premises without engaging with any of the banking services) are certainly at odd with the intended functions of the place. However, they were not considered as outliers because such behaviours turned out to be common practice at the branch. Other patterns of activities, whilst closer to certain behaviours aligned with the intended function of the bank, might actually be regarded as anomalous by those familiar with this particular environment.

Modelling offender behaviour in space and time

The concept of script is a particularly useful one in crime science as it allows us to represent the successive situations, decisions and actions that are involved in the commission of crime (see Borrion, 2013; Borrion et al., 2017; Cornish, 1994). To model those scripts, a spatial graph was created that represents the possible discrete locations of the offender in the branch. Indeed, multiple options are usually available to the offender at every step of their scripts, and it is impossible to represent all the possible strings of actions that form the entire pool of possible scenarios. To reduce the complexity of the modelling problem, methods must be adopted that enable analysts to focus on high-enough-risk scenarios (Toubaline et al., 2012). A common strategy involves discarding scenarios that are extremely unlikely, unless they can have extremely severe consequences. Using an agent-based modelling approach, value judgement can be simulated based on situational information about the environmental elements that can be sensed by agents. For this, a computational tool was developed to automatically determine what lies within the field of view of the offender as they move in space. This functionality can be used not only to simulate offender decision-making (to some extent) but also to model hostile reconnaissance scripts. Alternatively, it can be used in an inverse fashion to determine the areas of the room that benefit from the highest and lowest levels of visibility, as represented in Figure 10.5. Adapting Jacobs's concept of 'eyes on the streets', it is also possible to estimate the levels of natural surveillance across a large room by additionally considering occupancy and attentiveness patterns.

Distribution of assets and structure of the architectural interface

From a use point of view, a building can be regarded as an ecosystem of spaces through which the routines of, and relations between its inhabitants and visitors are enacted (e.g. Hillier and Hanson, 1984). As such, a building can be understood to consist of a number of interfaces that facilitate and communicate its intended and possible uses (Koch, 2013; Markus, 1993; Peponis, 2012). On an overall scale, the building is an interface between inhabitants and visitors, but it is

Figure 10.5 Trajectories of the visitors and visibility levels in the modelled building (Credit: Koch and Miranda)

also an interface between different inhabitants, such as between management and staff, or one group of staff and another – or between different functions such as meetings and working desk areas. An inhabiting social organisation – such as a bank organisation – then arranges its various functions, staff, and amenities to facilitate its many different needs and routines, which can be technical, social, organisational, or of any other kind. Here, we can consider mainly three general types of interfaces: the building as an interface within the organisation, the building as an interface between the organisation and visitors, and the building as a generic interface, i.e. the affordance of the building's spatial structure and how it allows or prevents possible and plausible ranges of specific interfaces and routines.

In RIBS, these interfaces could be abstracted as shown in Figure 10.6, describing first the 'whole' bank, and second the way the subset which concerns the main staff areas. Focusing on organisational and security logic, these could potentially be rearranged as in the bottom two diagrams in the figure, where first, internal communications are separated from public space, and second, the spatial arrangement of personnel is arranged to follow the hierarchy of the organisation. This, potentially, allows for an easier set of access controls and focuses interactions and/or overlaps of routines to more clearly conform to functional intent.

However, in addition to what we refer to as organisational logic and functional intent, organisations are social entities that have routines, identities and social intents (Amin and Cohendet,

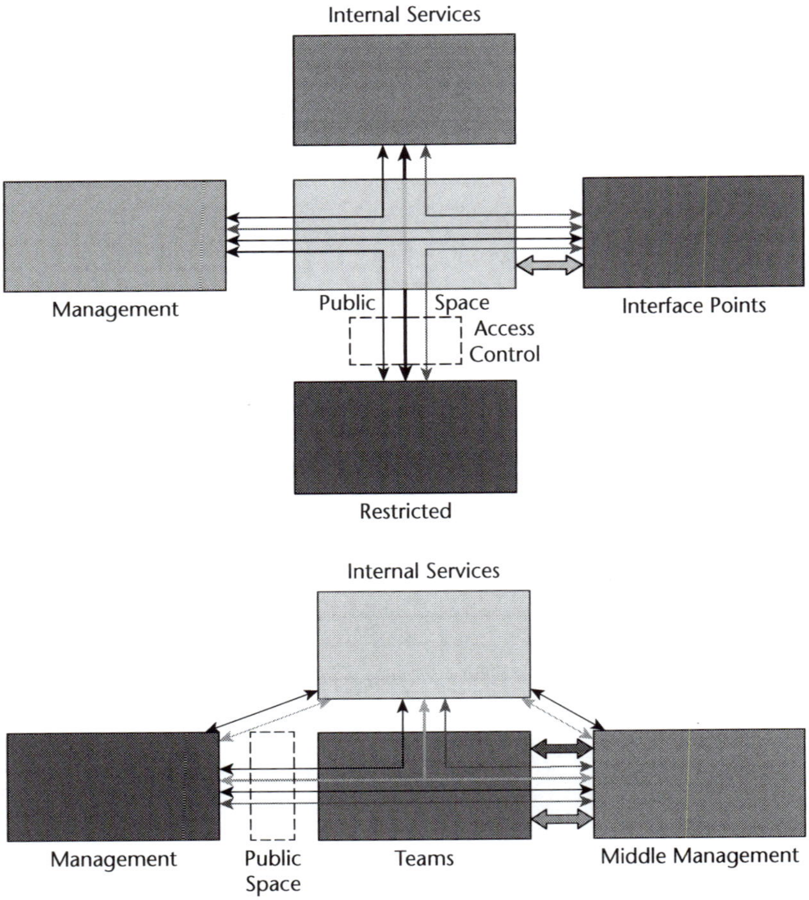

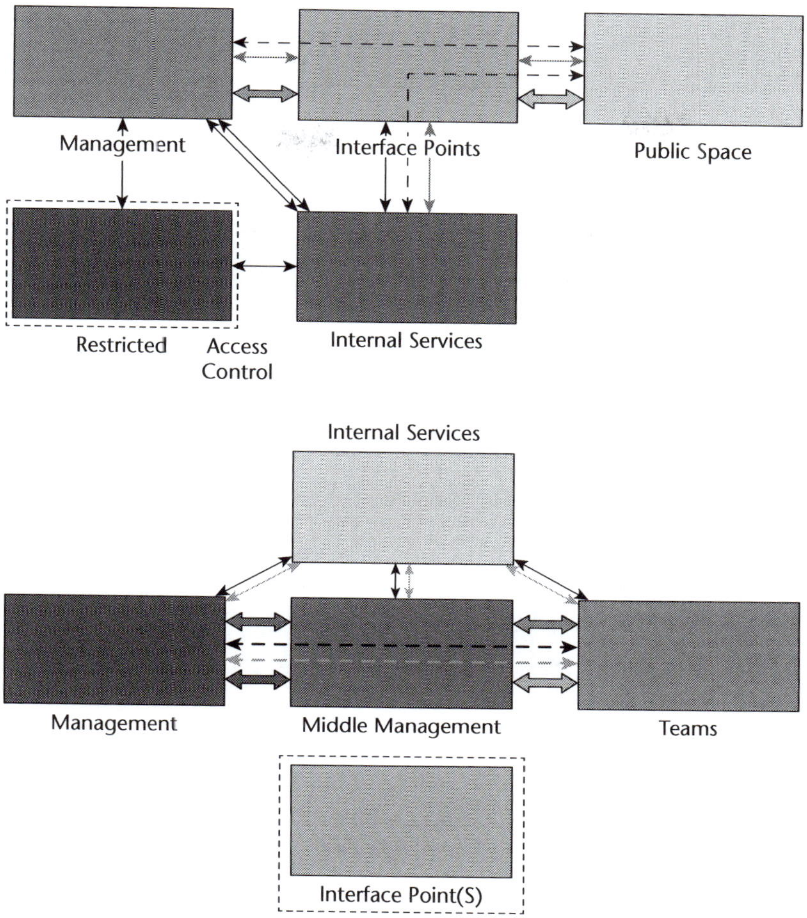

Figure 10.6 Space-programme conceptual maps for the public (left) and private (right) portions of the building. The upper is the then-current organisation whereas the lower demonstrates a potential altered situation

2004; Peponis, 1985; Sailer and McCulloh, 2011; Sailer and Penn, 2010). That management and middle management needed to pass through general staff areas, for instance, was considered a means to reduce hierarchies and make management more accessible to staff – and also to contribute significantly to an identity of the bank, considered as a workplace, where all parts worked together and was part of the same community. Similar arguments were made regarding some of the communication going through the public sections.

Our argument here is not that this is either a good or bad practice, but that security measures need to take such into consideration as well as challenge and rearrange when needed. If one lets go of specific spaces for these arrangements and instead understands the building as an ecosystem of spaces and activities (as was the case in this project), it is possible to (re)distribute functions and activities with security in mind. This includes how different forms of value assets are distributed in relation to one another and to the public, set in relation to necessary or practical proximities. As a simple example, 'high-risk assets' (such as top management, bank vault and critical data) can be separated both to reduce risk of collateral and to reduce concentration of high-risk targets (threat attraction), and additionally reduce generation of 'secondary' risks – while arguments can be made for the symbolic positive of managers visiting public space, this is different from it being a *necessary* route, or even the most convenient route, to large ranges of management activity. Similarly, the way the public is allowed to browse, in which portions of the building, and through which paths becomes part of this ecosystem, which can be structured to facilitate and make easy the ranges of activity that is wished and restrict and prohibit those which are not. This includes how the overall architectural spatial structure of the publicly available parts tend to significantly affect browsing behaviour (visitors wandering around with a more or less defined purpose; Hillier, 1996; Koch, 2013), whereas distribution of specific functions tends to more directly affect visitors with a more specific functional purpose of their visit where, as noted above, most visits form a composite of the two.

Similar points can be made on an urban level, even though relations between specific and generic, and their specific characters, alter. In RIBS, it was confirmed that architectural configuration of visibility and accessibility into integration (a specific form of centrality; see Hillier and Hanson, 1984), as measured through the use of Visibility Graph Analysis (Turner, 2001; Turner and Penn, 1999), was strongly correlated to movement flow rates, collective patterns of movement traces, and consequently a share of the overall presence of visitors in the public bank. In addition, the reasoning above considering interfaces and how co-location, clustering and separation of assets in relation to accessibility (i.e. how they can be reached from the entry or from one another) and proximity (if they are physical close or far apart) was further developed into digital tools to measure this more precisely in buildings (see Helme et al., 2014), and recent developments of spatial analysis tools such as Place Syntax Tool (PST) (Ståhle et al., 2005; Marcus et al., 2017), or specific uses of GIS software, allows similar analyses to be performed on an urban level.

Spatial and configurational resilience

Another aspect that can be studied is how the building is able to respond to disruptions, and specifically disruptions affecting its spatial organisation. In principle, this concerns how disruption in connectivity affects the internal organisation of buildings. In Figure 10.7, we illustrate how a building with the same amount of rooms (top) but with different connectivity is affected by the same disruption (middle and bottom). This demonstrates that not only are the effects different, but they are differently different – that is, for one type of disruption, the effect on the two hypothetical buildings is noticeably very different (second row in the figure), and for the other, the difference is arguably marginal (third row). Studying more complex cases including the building modelled in RIBS, these principal observations became validated and nuanced (Koch and Miranda, 2013). It turned out that rather large disruptions in terms of number of connections or physical impact on the building could have rather small effects, whereas rather small disruptions could have system-changing effects. The effects could also be differentiated between those that affected the whole building, and those that had a local effect.

Several tools were developed in the project to work with the question of configurational resilience in a more precise way. One key technology was the automated development of what is known as a 'convex space graph' (Miranda and Koch, 2013), which identifies the type of structural properties of space that enable a reading of resilience as pertains to connectivity. Subsequently, Abshirini and Koch (2017) (see also Esposito and Di Pinto, 2014) have explained how these developments can be brought to a city scale to understand spatial resilience of cities as social interfaces. Combined with already existing tools (or those developed in parallel) these developments offer rich and precise opportunities to understand how a given spatial organisation is resilient to specific types of threats and from specific points of view.

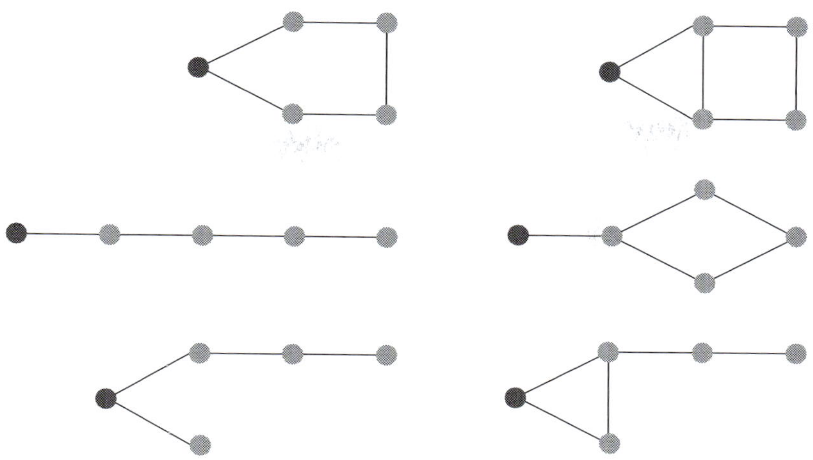

Figure 10.7 Effects on configurational depth by cutting the first or second link from the entrance (dark node) on the middle and lower series respectively. Adding a second vertical (right) makes the effects of the same cuts as on the left quite different for syntactic depth as well as cycles

Synthesis

The work described above was conducted to contribute to the CPTED scholarship but also to broaden its philosophy by considering the roles of scripts and the impact of crime in terms of disruption, losses and harm. To an extent, the interface investigation expands and develops on the division of spaces into public, semi-public and private spaces, enabling a more precise and deliberate treatment of architectural variables (such as building design and programmatic distribution) in relation to security and use. The configurational resilience allows one to further refine structuring of access restrictions as well as a further refinement of how to consider risks and not only local but contextualised risk mitigation by considering system effects of spatial disruptions.

The scripts here provide a method whereby the ethical, economic and programmatic aspects of scenario can be analysed to support CPTED efforts. As we have noted, architects have to balance concerns of security and safety against other values and expectations. For this, the creation of scripts allows micro-routines, both intended and wished for, to be analysed carefully. Embedded in spatial analysis work, the script-theoretic approach allows one to assess how CPTED measures might alter an environment, and whether they would do so in unintended or unwanted ways. In addition, it can help understand whether an ostensibly large change has large, small, or even marginal effects on activities that are intended. At the same time, it is a useful methodological approach to understand where and how to work with CPTED measures to address a range of malicious threats (including the most serious ones, as seen here) and, in turn, enables architecture work to consider wider and more differentiated ranges of possible design options. In RIBS, multiple protective measures were re-evaluated as a result of this combination to provide an overall stronger protection that simultaneously would have a limited impact on the day-to-day use of the bank.

The interface and asset distribution discussion was also found very useful in that it makes it easier for security concerns to be considered in the structure of space and arrangement of programmes: two key elements in architecture projects. Specifically, it can assist in understanding where other CPTED measures should be used and offer opportunities to increase security at reduced cost if, for example, by identifying that a rearrangement of programmes would be a more suitable solution. As it extends the notion of access and accessibility into a systemic question including spatial configuration, it also allows for the assessment and implementation of security needs and measures that can operate either over several steps, or 'remotely'. For example, depending on configuration and programmatic arrangement, CPTED measures intended to protect a given asset could be deployed at a very specific location (one particular door) or alternatively they could be distributed to several places, each with different economic, symbolic and social connotations. Furthermore, while CPTED has identified the need for diversification between private and public and the potential of in-between zones, the applicability of the generic CPTED zoning varies over time, space, and culture (see e.g. Steadman, 2014; Peponis, 1989; Madge, 2007; Koch, 2014; Giuliani, 1987). From a CPTED perspective, the concept of interface therefore offers a more precise and adaptable understanding of the various transitions between 'private' and 'public' space, and allows architects work more sensitively and more precisely. Scripts and interfaces can here be closely linked and integrated as studying from the different sides of the built form and people's activity.

In this chapter, syntactic resilience was concerned with extending the notion of security and disruption into a systemic spatial perspective. Understanding the vulnerabilities of an environment seen as a system of accessibilities also provided useful information to decide where to employ CPTED measures. The methods developed in RIBS extends this by considering the spatial properties of the place that could affect and relate to cognitive and social routines (Marcus, 2018; Peponis, 2012; Hillier and Iida, 2005; Legeby, 2018). It further allowed threats to be evaluated in terms of the amount and character of disruption within a building and its wider environment. We also noted that disruption can come from illicit actions, but also from security systems being activated, highlighting the need for architects to understand the systemic dependencies that might exist between CPTED measures and the environment within which they are implemented.

Conclusions

Over the last decades, research has shown that properly designed features of the built environment can encourage legitimate behaviours, whilst preventing illegitimate or even criminal ones. The literature has focused on security-sensitive planning of cities and neighbourhood on the one hand, and on the choice of material and characteristics of architectural elements (windows, doors, gates) on the other. In global cities, entire districts have been transformed to satisfy the demand for more (and often visible) security. In response to the terrorist threat, train stations, streets and bridges have been fitted with rails, fences and bollards to prevent vehicle-ramming attacks. Iconic places such as the Eiffel Tower in Paris or the House of Commons chamber in London have been shielded with transparent panels. Benches, public art and trees have been installed near stadiums and other crowded public spaces. Traditional windows in public buildings have been replaced in favour of laminated window glazing, etc.

One of the great challenges for crime prevention through environmental design is to look at micro-environments, and design of buildings, corridors and rooms that reduce crime whilst satisfying all other legitimate concerns of people and organisations. For this, knowledge of architecture, urban planning and behavioural science will need to be integrated together to better understand the many different relationships between built forms and behaviour on a micro scale. More advanced tools, possibly relying on artificial intelligence, will have to be developed for the collection and analysis of high quality – high-resolution data, and assist architects in better designing-out crime and terrorism.

With such tools, new generations of architects could soon be able to more easily identify the criminogenic properties of their designs, and improve them by simulating the likely effects of architectural modifications on public safety and security. With the advent of digital transformation in the construction industry and the growing need to retrofit our urban environments (to accommodate for a range of technological innovations including new energy systems, smart infrastructures and autonomous vehicles), there has perhaps never been a better opportunity for architects to join the crime science community, start addressing urban challenges holistically and ultimately make their mark against crime.

Acknowledgements

The research described in this chapter was carried out as part of the RIBS project on Resilient Infrastructure and Building Security. The RIBS consortium was funded by the European Commission under the European Framework Programme 7 (ID: 242497) and included AEDAS, DTU, KTH, Technion – Israel Institute of Technology, UCL and 2E. The spatial analysis team included, in alphabetical order, H. Borrion, C. Derix, L. Helme, P. M. Ingwar, Å. Izaki, P. Jagannath, C. Jensen, D. Koch and P. Miranda.

Notes

1 Land-use diversity is a concept also found in second-generation CPTED.
2 Jeffery's seminal publication predates Newman's one by a year.

References

Abshirini, A. and Koch, D. 2017. Resilience, space syntax and spatial interfaces: the case of river cities. *A | Z ITU Journal of the Faculty of Architecture*, 14(1), 25–41.

Adams, D. and Goldbard, A. 2001. *Creative Community: The Art of Community Development*. New York: Rockefeller Foundation.

Amin, A. and Cohendet, P. 2004. *Architectures of Knowledge: Firms, Capabilities, and Communities*. Oxford: Oxford University Press.

Angel, S. 1968. *Discouraging Crime through City Planning*. University of California Institute of Urban & Regional Development.

Boddy, T. 2007. Architecture emblematic: hardened sites and softened symbols. In M. Sorkin (ed.) *Indefensible Space* (pp. 277–304). London: Routledge.

Borrion, H. 2013. Quality assurance in crime scripting. *Crime Science*, 2(1), 6.

Borrion, H., Bordeanu, O. and Toubaline S. Forthcoming. Simulation of dependencies between armed response vehicles and CPTED measures in counter-terrorism resource allocation. In R. Armitage and P. Ekblom (eds) *Re-Building Crime Prevention through Environmental Design: Strengthening the Links with Crime Science*. Abingdon, UK: Routledge.

Borrion, H., Dehghanniri, H. and Li, Y. 2017. Comparative analysis of crime scripts: one cctv footage – twenty-one scripts. In *Intelligence and Security Informatics Conference (EISIC), 2017 European* (pp. 115–122). Piscataway, NJ: IEEE.

Borrion, H. and Koch, D. 2017. Integrating architecture and crime science: a transdisciplinary challenge. In P. Gibbs (ed.) *Transdisciplinary Higher Education* (pp. 91–107). Cham, Switzerland: Springer.

Borrion, H., Mitchener-Nissen, T., Taylor, J. and Lai, K. M. 2012. Countering bioterrorism: why smart buildings should have a code of ethics. In *Intelligence and Security Informatics Conference (EISIC), 2012 European* (pp. 68–75). Piscataway, NJ: IEEE.

Borrion, H., Tripathi, K., Chen, P. and Moon, S. 2014. Threat detection: a framework for security architects and designers of metropolitan rail systems. *Urban, Planning and Transport Research*, 2(1), 173–194.

Brocklehurst, S. 2017. The day terror came to Glasgow Airport. *BBC Scotland News website*. Available at: www.bbc.co.uk/news/uk-scotland-40416026# [Accessed 30 Jun. 2018].

Clarke, R. V. G. (ed.) 1997. *Situational Crime Prevention* (pp. 53–70). Monsey, NY: Criminal Justice Press.

Coaffee, J. 2004. Rings of steel, rings of concrete and rings of confidence: designing out terrorism in central London pre- and post-September 11th. *International Journal of Urban and Regional Research*, 28(1), 201–211.

Coaffee, J., O'Hare, P. and Hawkesworth, M. 2009. The visibility of (in)security: the aesthetics of planning urban defences against terrorism. *Security Dialogue*, 40(4–5), 489–511.

Cohen, L. E. and Felson, M. 1979. Social change and crime rate trends: a routine activity approach (1979). In M. A. Andresen, P. J. Brantingham and J. B. Kineey (eds) *Classics in Environmental Criminology* (pp. 203–232). Boca Raton, FL: CRC Press.

Conde, A.F. and Massa-Esteve, M. R. 2018. Teaching Engineers in the Seventeenth Century: European Influences in Portugal. *Engineering Studies*, pp. 1–18.

Cornish, D. B. 1994. The procedural analysis of offending and its relevance for situational prevention. *Crime Prevention Studies*, 3, 151–196.

Cozens, P. and Love, T. 2015. A review and current status of crime prevention through environmental design (CPTED). *Journal of Planning Literature*, 30(4), 393–412.

Cozens, P. M., Saville, G. and Hillier, D. 2005. Crime prevention through environmental design (CPTED): a review and modern bibliography. *Property Management*, 23(5), 328–356.

Crowe, T. D. 2000. *Crime Prevention through Environmental Design: Applications of Architectural Design and Space Management Concepts*. Oxford: Butterworth-Heinemann.

di Giorgio Martini, F. and Saluzzo, C. 1841. *Trattato di architettura civile e militare* (Vol. 3). Turin: Tipographia Chirio e Mina.

Duffy, C. 2015. *The Fortress in the Age of Vauban and Frederick the Great 1660–1789* (Vol. 8). Abingdon, UK: Routledge.

Eck, J. E., Clarke, R. V. and Guerette, R. T. 2007. Risky facilities: Crime concentration in homogeneous sets of establishments and facilities. *Crime Prevention Studies*, 21, 225.

Ekblom, P. 2011. Deconstructing CPTED . . . and reconstructing it for practice, knowledge management and research. *European Journal on Criminal Policy and Research*, 17(1), 7–28.

Ekblom, P. 2013. Redesigning the language and concepts of crime prevention through environmental design. Reconstructing CPTED. Paper presented at the *6th Ajman International Urban Planning Conference: City and Security*, March, Ajman, United Arab Emirates.

Ekblom, P., Armitage, R., Monchuk, L. and Castell, B. 2013. Crime prevention through environmental design in the United Arab Emirates: a suitable case for reorientation? *Built Environment*, 39(1), 92–113.

Enoma, A., Allen, S. and Enoma, A. 2009. Airport redesign for safety and security: case studies of three Scottish airports. *International Journal of Strategic Property Management*, 13(2), 103–116.

Esposito, A. and di Pinto, V. 2014. Urban resilience and risk assessment: how urban layout affects flood risk in the city. *14th International Conference on Computational Science and Its Applications, Guimaraes, 2014* (pp. 204–207).

Fennelly, L. J. and Perry, M. A. 2018. Target Hardening. In *CPTED and Traditional Security Countermeasures* (pp. 10–11). Boca Raton, FL: CRC Press.

Fussey, P. 2008. Beyond liberty, beyond security: the politics of public surveillance. *British Politics*, 3(1), 120–135.

Fussey, P., Coaffee, J. and Hobbs, D. 2016. *Securing and Sustaining the Olympic City: Reconfiguring London for 2012 and Beyond*. Abingdon, UK: Routledge.

Gibson, V. 2016. Third generation CPTED? Rethinking the basis for crime prevention strategies. Doctoral dissertation, Northumbria University.

Gibson, V. and Johnson, D. 2016. CPTED, but not as we know it: investigating the conflict of frameworks and terminology in crime prevention through environmental design. *Security Journal*, 29(2), 256–275.

Giuliani, M. V. 1987. Naming the rooms: implications of a change in the home model. *Environment and Behavior*, 19(2), 180–203.

Guerette, R. T. and Bowers, K. J. 2009. Assessing the extent of crime displacement and diffusion of benefits: A review of situational crime prevention evaluations. *Criminology*, 47(4), 1331–1368.

Helme, L., Derix, C. and Izaki, Å. 2014. Spatial configuration: semi-automatic methods for layout generation in practice. *The Journal of Space Syntax*, 5(1), 35–49.

Hillier, B. 1996. *Space is the Machine*. Cambridge, MA: Cambridge University Press.

Hillier, B. and Hanson, J. 1984. *The Social Logic of Space*. Cambridge, UK: Cambridge University Press.

Hillier, B. and Iida, S. 2005. Network and psychological effects in urban movement. In A. G. Cohn, D. M. Mark (eds), *Spatial Information Theory* (pp. 475–490). Berlin: Springer.

Jacobs, J. 1961. *The Death and Life of Great American Cities*. New York: Vintage.

Jeffery, C. R. 1971. *Crime Prevention through Environmental Design*. Beverly Hills, CA: Sage Publications.

Jeffery, C. R. 1977. *Crime Prevention through Environmental Design*. Beverly Hills, CA: Sage.

Jeffery, C. R. and Zahm, D. L. 1993. Crime prevention through environmental design, opportunity theory, and rational choice models. *Routine Activity and Rational Choice*, 5, 323–350.

Koch, D. 2013. The architectural interface inside-out: interior-exterior relations, spatial models, and configurational mirroring. In Y. O. Kim, H. T. Park, and K. W. Seo (eds), *Proceedings of the Ninth International Space Syntax Symposium* (pp. 67: 1–16). Seoul: Sejong University Press.

Koch, D. 2014. Changing building typologies: the typological question and the formal basis of architecture. *The Journal of Space Syntax*, 5(2), 168–189.

Koch, D. and Miranda, P. 2013. Syntactic resilience. In Y. O. Kim, H. T. Park, K. W. Seo (eds), Proceedings of Ninth International Space Syntax Symposium (pp. 54: 1–54: 16). Seoul: Sejong University Press.

Lambert, B. 1993. Elizabeth Wood, 93, innovator in early days of public housing. *The New York Times*. Available at: www.nytimes.com/1993/01/17/us/elizabeth-wood-93-innovator-in-early-days-of-public-housing.html [Accessed 17 Jun. 2018].

Legeby, A. 2018. Everyday Urban Life at Neighbourhood Centres: Urban Design and Co-Presence. In A. E. Toft and M. Rönn (eds), *The Production of Knowledge in Architecture by PhD Research in the Nordic Countries* (pp. 73–100). Hisings Backa: Nordic Academic Press of Architectural Research.

Madge, J. 2007. Type at the origin of architectural form. *The Journal of Architecture*, 12(1), 1–34.

Marcus, L. 2018. Overcoming the subject-object dichotomy in urban modeling: axial maps as geometric representations of affordances in the built environment. *Frontiers in Psychology*, 9(449), 1–10.

Marcus, L., Berghauser Pont, M. and Bobkova, E. 2017. Cities as accessible densities: adding attraction variables to configurational analysis. In T. Heitor, M. Serra, J. P. Silva, M. Bacharel, and L. C. Da Silva (eds), *Proceedings of the 11th International Space Syntax Symposium* (pp. 167.1–167.12). Lisbon: Instituto Superior Técnico.

Markus, T. A. 1993. *Buildings & Power: Freedom & Control in the Origin of Modern Building Types*. London: Routledge.

Miranda, P. and Koch. D. 2013. A computational method for generating convex maps using the medial axis transform. In Y. O. Kim, H. T. Park, and K. W. Seo (eds), *Proceedings of Ninth International Space Syntax Symposium* (pp. 64: 1–64: 11). Seoul: Sejong University Press.

Moffat, R. 1983. Crime prevention through environmental design–a management perspective. *Canadian Journal of Criminology*, 25(4), 19–31.

MPS. 26 May 2017. Student jailed for 15 years for leaving homemade bomb on tube train. Available at: http://news.met.police.uk/news/student-jailed-for-15-years-for-leaving-homemade-bomb-on-tube-train-243652 [Accessed 30 Jun. 2018].

Newman, O. and National Institute of Law Enforcement and Criminal Justice. 1973. *Architectural Design for Crime Prevention* (pp. 2700–00161). Washington, DC: National Institute of Law Enforcement and Criminal Justice.

Nissen, T. G. 2014. Designing for socially acceptable security technologies. Doctoral dissertation, University College London.

Peponis, J. 1985. The spatial culture of factories. *Human Relations*, 38(4), 357–390.

Peponis, J. 1989. Space, culture and urban design in late modernism and after. *Ekistics*, 56(334/335), 93–108.

Peponis, J. 2012. Building layouts as cognitive data: purview and purview interface. *Cognitive Critique*, 6, 11–50.

Rayment-McHugh, S., Adams, D., Wortley, R. and Tilley, N. 2015. 'Think Global Act Local': a place-based approach to sexual abuse prevention. *Crime Science*, 4(1), 22.

Robinson, J. and Landauro, I. 15 November 2015. Paris attacks: suicide bomber was blocked from entering Stade de France. *The Wall Street Journal*. Available at: www.wsj.com/articles/attacker-tried-to-enter-paris-stadium-but-was-turned-away-1447520571 [Accessed 28 Jun. 2018].

Sailer, K. and Penn, A. 2010. Towards an architectural theory of space and organisations: cognitive, affective and conative relations in workplaces. *2nd Workshop on Architecture and Social Architecture* (pp. 1–16). EIASM, Brussels, May 2010.

Sailer, K. and McCulloh, I. 2011. Social networks and spatial configuration – how office layouts drive social interaction. *Social Networks*, 34(1), 47–58.

Sampson, R. J., Raudenbush, S. W. and Earls, F. 1997. Neighborhoods and violent crime: a multilevel study of collective efficacy. *Science*, 277(5328), 918–924.

Saville, G. 2013. 3rd generation CPTED and the eco-friendly city. [Blog] SafeGrowth Blog. Available at: http://safe-growth.blogspot.com/2013/06/3rd-generation-cptd-and-eco-friendly.html [Accessed 28 Jun. 2018].

Saville, G. and Cleveland, G. 1997. December. 2nd generation CPTED: an antidote to the social Y2K virus of urban design. In *2nd Annual International CPTED Conference, Orlando, FL* (Vol. 3, No. 5).
Schank, R. C. and Abelson, R. P. 1977. *Scripts, Plans, Goals, and Understanding: An Inquiry into Human Knowledge Structures*. Hillsdale, NJ: Erlbaum.
Schank, R. C. and Abelson, R. P. 2013. *Scripts, Plans, Goals, and Understanding: An Inquiry into Human Knowledge Structures*. Hove, UK: Psychology Press.
Severin, L., Sorensen, S., Hayes, J. and Atlas, R. 2013. Understanding CPTED and situational crime prevention. In R. I. Atlas (ed.), *21st Century Security and CPTED: Designing for Critical Infrastructure Protection and Crime Prevention* (pp. 50–90). Boca Raton, FL: CRC Press.
Smith, M. J. and Clarke, R. V. 2012. Situational crime prevention: classifying techniques using 'good enough' theory. In B. C. Welsh (ed.) *The Oxford Handbook of Crime Prevention* (pp. 291–315). Oxford: Oxford University Press.
Ståhle, A., Marcus, L. and Karlström, A. 2005. Place syntax: geographic accessibility with axial lines in GIS. In A. van Nes (ed.), *Proceedings, Fifth International Space Syntax Symposium* (pp. 131–144). Delft: Techne Press.
Steadman, P. 2014. *Building Types and Built Forms*. Leicestershire: Matador.
Turner, A. 2001. Depthmap: a program to perform visibility graph analysis. In J. Peponis, J. Wineman, and S. Bafna (eds), *Proceedings, Space Syntax 3rd International Symposium* (pp. 31.1–31.9). Michigan: A. Alfred Taubman College of Architecture and Urban Planning.
Turner, A. and Penn, A. 1999. Making isovists syntactic: isovist integration analysis. *2nd International Symposium on Space Syntax*. Universidad de Brasilia, Brazil, April.
Toubaline, S., Borrion, H. and Le Sage, T. 2012. Dynamic generation of event trees for risk modelling of terrorist attacks. In *Homeland Security (HST), 2012 IEEE Conference on Technologies for Homeland Security* (pp. 111–116). Piscataway, NJ: IEEE.
Tseloni, A., Thompson, R., Grove, L., Tilley, N. and Farrell, G. 2017. The effectiveness of burglary security devices. *Security Journal*, 30(2), 646–664.
UNICRI. 2011. New Energy for Urban Security: Improving Urban Security Through Green Environmental Design. Available at: www.unicri.it/news/files/2011-04-01_110414_CRA_Urban_Security_sm.pdf [Accessed 24 Jun. 2018].
US Congress. 1970. National Environmental Policy Act, pp. P.L. 91–190, S. 1075.
von Hirsch, A., Garland, D. and Wakefield, A. (eds). 2000. *Ethical and Social Perspectives on Situational Crime Prevention* (Vol. 1). Portland, OR: Hart Publishing.
Ware, S. 2004. *Notable American Women: A Biographical Dictionary Completing the Twentieth Century* (Vol. 5). Cambridge, MA: Harvard University Press.
Willis, H. H. 2007. Guiding resource allocations based on terrorism risk. *Risk Analysis*, 27(3), 597–606.
Wilson, J. Q. and Kelling, G. L. 1982. Broken windows. *Atlantic Monthly*, 249(3), 29–38.
Wood, E. 1961. Housing design: A social theory. *Ekistics*, 12(74), 383–392.
Wood, E. 1964. Social-welfare planning. *The ANNALS of the American Academy of Political and Social Science*, 352(1), 119–128.

11
Engineering

Hervé Borrion

Introduction

Technology can support security. This argument is neither novel nor the object of intense debates. It is well known that advances in military warfare, for example, were often decisive in conflicts between nations. The link between crime analysis and engineering, however, seems a lot more tenuous, and collaboration between criminologists and engineers is relatively seldom. That is not to say that engineering has little to offer to crime prevention and counter-terrorism, nor that it does not intersect with the scholarship of social scientists. This chapter will argue quite the opposite. The absence of a clearly delineated academic agenda shared by both communities is therefore somewhat perplexing.

The connection between crime science and engineering has only been sporadically discussed, and often reduced to the development of security technology (Davis & Pease, 2001; Kemp et al., 2003; Metke & Ekl, 2010; Qadri & Asif, 2009; Savona, 2004). It can be argued though that engineering has a broader influence on crime (Junger, Laycock, Hartel, & Ratcliffe, 2012) and perhaps that crime science might have influenced engineering. Focusing on the first point, this article examines and discusses the impact the engineering community has (or could have) on crime-related harm in society.

For our purpose, it is important to appreciate that those effects can come from at least two different sources: the contribution of research engineers to knowledge and the work of practising engineers in society. In addition, to err is human. Crime-related harm is therefore not limited to the harm caused by criminal activities but also includes the unintended harm caused by inadequate crime-reduction activities (Borrion et al., 2012; Grabosky, 1996; Norrie, 2002). With this in mind, we can refine the scope of this inquiry to the following question: how can the knowledge developed in engineering and the work of practising engineers influence the harm caused by criminal offences and crime-reduction interventions?

Engineering in the 21st century

Before getting to the heart of the matter, this section touches upon the fundamental issue of what engineering is. The intent is to show that oil-smeared mechanics and Victorian pioneers are as good as illustrations of 21st-century engineering as Miss Marple is of predictive policing.

The field of engineering (eng.) contains many different areas including aerospace eng., chemical eng., civil eng., electrical eng. environmental eng., medical eng., mechanical eng., and systems eng., which makes it notoriously difficult to define. The Merriam-Webster dictionary for students, for example, refers to it as 'the application of science to the goal of creating useful machines (such as automobiles) or structures (such as roads and dams)'. In the regular edition, the definition is broadened to encompass the management (not just creation) of any useful systems (beyond just physical ones): 'the application of science and mathematics by which the properties of matter and the sources of energy in nature are made useful to people'. This more inclusive definition is interesting for it includes scientific areas that do not revolve around machines or structures, such as bio-engineering – 'the application of biological techniques (such as genetic recombination) to create modified versions of organisms' (ibid.). Even more inclusive is the following definition which focuses solely on the intended outcome, with no restriction about the type of systems concerned or the disciplines from which the techniques involved in their development originate: 'the control or direction of something (such as behaviour)' (ibid.).

In the absence of an official definition, the term engineering continues to be construed in different ways by different communities, including the engineering community itself. For our benefit, we shall avoid any dogmatic discussion and concentrate on the most distinctive and consensual characteristics:

Lifecycle management of systems to meet specific needs

Engineering is not just – or no longer just – about building physical things. Its purpose is the lifecycle management of systems to meet specific needs (INCOSE, 2015). In this context these terms refer to the different stages (from cradle to grave) of artificial products ranging from genetically modified bacteria to the International Space Station or the internet.

The engineering philosophy is that every decision in a product's life should be strictly based on one driver: the fulfilment of specific requirements that represent the needs of the relevant parties. This relation to problem-solving – defined as 'any goal-directed sequence of cognitive operations' (Anderson, 1980, p. 257) – is also what distinguishes engineering design from artistic design.

Greater capability under greater constraints

In most people's minds, it seems that technological innovation equates to greater capability in the service (or disservice) of the population. In the media, technology headlines tend to be about the impressive features of a new smartphone or a new world record (e.g. fastest communication link, tallest building, longest bridge, largest plane, etc.). Less glamourous but more representative of everyday engineering practice is the ability to meet ever more stringent demands. For example, changing commercial and regulatory pressures created the need for engineers to design cars that are more affordable and have a reduced carbon footprint, without sacrificing performance or comfort.

Research and practice in engineering

As with other applied fields, novel engineering knowledge is generated through research activities and subsequently applied by practitioners to achieve specific outcomes in society. For various reasons, the engineering community is not neatly divided between research engineers and practising ones but instead is distributed across a wide spectrum, with many jobbing engineers carrying out research and development activities in industry and university researchers also developing close-to-market innovations.

Scholarship

A significant part of engineering scholarship concerns the ways in which requirements can be elicited and then how the resources available around us can be harnessed to ensure that man-made systems satisfy those requirements. Contributing to this overall aim, engineering activity typically draws on the more fundamental sciences to create application-focused knowledge:

- On the theoretical side of the spectrum is the scientific research conducted to characterise existing phenomena and understand 'how they work'. There, the inquiry process is generally conceptualised around specific explanatory hypotheses of cause-and-effect relationships. As an example, knowledge is continuously gained to better model and analyse electromagnetic fields because of their application to wireless communication technology in general.
- On the more applied side of the spectrum are actual engineering projects. In those, the knowledge available in various disciplines is combined to satisfy the needs of specific stakeholders (such as contractors, regulators and users). The development of a fully operational wireless detection system for an indoor environment would require knowledge of physics and electronics but also other disciplines to ensure that the final product satisfies the operational, legal, ethical, environmental and commercial constraints that exist in the real world.
- Engineering research tends to lie somewhere between the two. It aims to identify how scientific knowledge can be exploited to support a range of applications. In a typical project, researchers would propose a technical innovation (e.g. a method to detect and localise moving targets by analysing ambient Wi-Fi signals) and demonstrate that it has certain properties likely to be sought after in industry. That a given element in its design confers on it those properties is the so-called research hypothesis – though it is rare for engineers to present it as such.

The distinction between research and practice can perhaps explain the lack of collaboration between criminologists and engineers at university. Like other scholars, research engineers focus on producing original knowledge in their field. To this aim, the development of a complete and operational system that can directly or indirectly help reduce crime (e.g. a system to detect illegal logging) would often prove too time- and resource-intensive. Development and evaluation of a communication protocol or a prototype sub-system (e.g. a component in the electronic circuit of such a system) is generally sufficient to demonstrate progress beyond the current state of the art. A lot more work would usually need to take place before an operational system can be manufactured that could be used in the field, and while the overall system (and the environment) might be outlined, research engineers (as opposed to practising engineers) would normally put as little effort as possible into this since this is not the focus of the work.

In crime science, however, evaluating an intervention often requires working on complete systems in their actual contexts of implementation as people's behaviour can be very sensitive to situational conditions (Lewin, 1936). A scientific criminological evaluation of alley gating such as that conducted by Bowers, Johnson, and Hirschfield (2004) requires data about the occurrence of burglary in real (gated and ungated) alleys, as many ecological factors would be impossible to replicate with high fidelity in a laboratory setting.

In spite of this, there are many reasons why anyone embracing the outcome-focused approach promoted in crime science ought to take an interest in engineering scholarship:

1 Systems engineering – 'an interdisciplinary approach and means to enable the realization of successful systems' (INCOSE, 2015) – can offer valuable processes, techniques and principles to manage the lifecycle of crime-reduction measures including new policies and procedures.
2 Analysts and designers may need to call upon engineering knowledge whenever human-made systems are relevant to the stages of those processes. In particular, they may need it:
    - To analyse the products and services created by engineers in order to assess how they might affect crime and reduce their criminogenic characteristics
    - To create security systems for the purpose of detecting crime, preventing it or reducing the harm it causes.

System: an interdisciplinary concept

Origins

The terms 'system' and 'systems thinking' are both so fundamental to engineering sciences that appreciating the relevance of engineering to crime science requires some understanding of them. For this reason, we shall start with an overview of those concepts. For a more comprehensive introduction, the reader is encouraged to read the system engineering handbook by INCOSE (2015):

- A system is an integrated set of elements including products, processes, people, techniques, facilities, services and other support elements.
- The surroundings in which the system of interest is developed, produced, used and retired is called the environment.
- A system is often characterised through the description of its boundary, structure, behaviour and function, adopting both internal and external views.

Systems thinking can be traced back to Aristotle's time, when he described a hierarchic order in nature. In more recent times, it has been linked to the concept of holism, introduced by Smuts (1926) as an alternative to the reductionist approach. Holism promotes the idea that systems cannot be fully understood by considering them as collections of parts. In the same vein, the most emblematic tenet of systems theory – 'the whole is greater than the sum of the parts' – was articulated by Wertheimer (1938), a contributor to Gestalt psychology.

An application of systems theory referred to as the systems approach considers that all aspects of human problems should be addressed together in a rational manner. In essence, this approach advocates that attempts to meet a specific need should be done in a top-down manner, considering the impact of interventions on other needs too. For example, first-generation biofuel was initially proposed as a solution to reduce the ecological and health impacts of motor vehicles. According to the systems approach, this is not a proper solution because its production would stimulate major changes to land use that would affect food security in different parts of the world (Rulli et al., 2016).

Clayton & Radcliffe (1996, p. 18) write that the 'systems approach involves placing as much emphasis on identifying and describing the connection between objects and events as on identifying and describing the objects and events themselves'. This is particularly important with so-called open systems (i.e. systems that both affect and are affected by their environment). Summarising the work of scholars such as Ludvig von Bertalanffy (1950) and Joseph Litterer (1969), Skyttner (2005, p. 53) explains that 'there is near total agreement on which properties together comprise a general theory of open systems: Interrelationship and interdependence of objects and their attributes, Holism, Goal seeking, Transformation process, Inputs and outputs, Entropy, Regulation, Hierarchy, Differentiation, Equifinality and multifinality'.

Drawing on those elements, the first systems engineering methods were developed by NASA to help engineers deal with the complexity of space projects in the 1960s (ibid., p. 472). Forty years later, those methods and their terminology continue to unify the various domains of engineering.

Systems thinking

Within engineering, adoption of a systems-thinking approach is recommended to design, retrofit or reverse-engineer products and infrastructures. Taking a wind-energy system as an example, an engineer would aim to reach the point where they understand how the design parameters of the system influence the supply of electricity in people's homes. Based on their knowledge of the system and its environment, engineers would then try to model its behaviour under different conditions, assess the various risks of failure over time, and ultimately validate or improve it.

It is by identifying, understanding and controlling the interactions that are involved in the process supported by the system that the sought output is eventually secured. This task typically involves creating an inventory of all contributing elements; defining the boundaries of the different subsystems; and developing a range of physical, operational and logical models for every element within those subsystems (such as the turbine's rotor blades, shaft, nacelle, gearbox, generator, cables, and power substation) and for the interactions between them (e.g. the wind applies a force on the blades which makes the drive shaft spins, etc.).

Because their development, deployment and operation phases are not conducted in a vacuum, systems must be analysed in relation to other systems in their environment. In the above example, a systems-thinking approach would lead engineers to understand what influence external events can have on the constituents of the system and the system as a whole. They might use agent-based models to simulate wind power integration with a smart grid, and understand how demand response might mitigate the impact of wind power variability (Brooer et al., 2014). In principle, they would also assess the negative effects of, say, wind turbines on other human activities such as air traffic control (Nicholls & Racey, 2007) and on wildlife (Lemmon, Carroll, Sanders, & Turner, 2008).

Systems thinking is routinely applied to manage systems across industrial sectors (e.g. defence, energy and transport) in order to build enhanced capability or tackle problematic phenomena. It is, for example, used to create physical and cyber-security systems (e.g. Evans et al., 2004; Lee, 2008) and reduce the environmental impact of industrial activities and citizens' actions in society (e.g. Seiffert & Loch, 2005). Although generic systems engineering frameworks exist, their contextualisation to crime has been mostly limited to the area of information security and cyber-security.

Systems and crime

There are noticeable differences between engineering and crime science (see Table 11.1). To date, crime-science research has been mainly focused on crime reduction (with only a few articles evaluating the wider effects of interventions), the analysis of crime phenomena (rather than the development of interventions to prevent them), and the factors influencing offenders' decisions to commit crime (rather than the impact of offenders' actions on people, infrastructures and electronic systems). Despite this, engineers and crime scientists share the core objective of solving problems in an effective and ethical way, and the differences summarised in Table 11.1 are perhaps more due to the fact that crime science is still in its infancy and crime-science research remains dominated by the work of researchers trained in criminology, psychology and geography.

Pragmatically and intellectually, the proposition that crime science is a field analogous to medicine (Laycock, 2005) is very attractive. To support this interdisciplinary vision, the crime-science community will need to acknowledge that the field goes beyond environmental criminology. It will also need to identify how other research areas (in architecture, biology, chemistry, computer science, economics, physics, etc.) relate to criminological theories and where they fit in the 'big picture' of crime reduction (Borrion & Koch, 2017). Owing to its broad scope, systems engineering can offer a unifying framework for this task.

Integrating crime science with engineering is challenging in practice. If it does happen in the future, it is likely to be around the concept of systems. The main reason is that many of the principles and techniques found in crime science are related to problem-solving and systems theory:

- Problem-Oriented Policing (POP) is a goal-based approach inspired from Operations Research and similar to that followed in engineering (Goldstein, 1979; Wilkins, 1997).
- Problem-solving models such as Scanning-Analysis-Response-Assessment were derived from systems theory (Eck & Spelman, 1987).
- Environmental criminology is based on the fundamental distinction between individuals and their environment, and the recognition that, as open systems, both exert causal influences on the other (Clarke & Eck, 2005; Wortley & Mazerolle, 2013).
- The components of systems analysis are also found in Routine Activity Theory where occurrence of crime events is said to be influenced by people's routine activities (Cohen & Felson, 1979), and can thus be regarded as an emerging property of the ecosystem.
- Realistic evaluation is also closely linked to systems thinking theory in that it argues that evaluators should seek to understand the causal mechanisms (i.e. cause-and-effect interactions) that are responsible for the occurrence of outcome patterns (including crime events), as well as those that prevent them (Pawson & Tilley, 1997).

Table 11.1 Characteristics of engineering and crime science

	Engineering	*Crime science**
• Aim	• Satisfaction of the stakeholders' needs	• Reduction of crime, increases in security
• Unit of analysis	• Multiple units (including high-level ones) based on the stakeholders' requirements	• The crime event
• Type of work process	• Multi-criteria systems engineering frameworks	• Crime-centric problem-solving models (e.g. SARA)
• Main stages	• Eliciting stakeholder requirements • Specifying every aspect of a system's lifecycle and managing it to satisfy stakeholder needs	• Identifying crime patterns • Analysing their causes • Identifying and implementing interventions to disrupt causes • Evaluating effectiveness of interventions
• Researchers' bias	• Toward system development	• Toward problem analysis

Note: *These are dominant characteristics observed in the literature

When engineering matters

The concept of causal chains of events

In crime science, systems thinking is perhaps most evident in the implementation of agent-based models. With those, offenders' behaviour is represented as a function of their inherent disposition to commit certain actions and the influence of the environment on their motivation (Malleson et al., 2013). For this reason, those developing agent-based models of crime must make a conscious effort to identify the main situational elements that impact on offenders' intent, motivation and capability (c.f. Hill et al., 2014; Le Sage et al., 2013; Thornton, 2015).

Analogous to the previous example about wind energy, controlling crime requires understanding how exposure to and interactions with other systems affect human behaviour. With this information, it is then possible to hypothesise specific chains of events that could modify the conditions that give rise to crime, and identify the properties a system should have so as to effectively trigger or enable such properties to happen. This point is illustrated in Example 1.

Example 1: CCTV security process

In many countries, Closed-Circuit TeleVision (CCTV) is deployed in public and private spaces to address crime problems. In many people's minds the security measure is the camera; in practice though, it is only a part in a larger system, and would have a limited impact on its own. Tilley (1993) identified several ways in which CCTV systems might plausibly affect crime. To deter offenders, it must make offenders 'perceive an elevated risk of apprehension'. This presupposes that offenders notice the camera and that they have developed certain schemas about CCTV and the risk of being caught. Depending on the way it is implemented, a camera may or may not deter an offender. Similarly, the deterrent effect of a camera probably depends on the experience an offender previously had with CCTV cameras.

To interdict offenders, a camera is used as part of a security process. As represented in Figure 11.1, an Individual's image is first captured by a Camera, transmitted over the Network, rendered on a Screen and analysed by an Operator. Based on the information provided by the latter, the security Manager will then use their Radio and task a security Guard to physically intervene against the Individual. Each component of the chain is identified by its initial in the figure (I for Individual, C for CCTV, etc.). To understand the requirements that CCTV-based security systems must meet, it is critical to be able to model the various stages of the process, and identify the factors that may affect those.

Wider impacts of crime-reduction measures

Introducing crime-control measures presents many challenges. In the case of Situational Crime Prevention in particular, modifying an environment often causes changes in the behaviour of people and physical systems, which means the impacts of security technologies should be

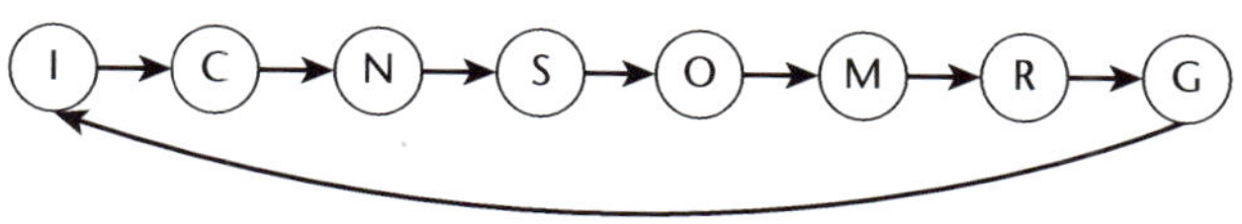

Figure 11.1 Interactions between the various elements of the CCTV security process

monitored very closely. Designers must therefore consider a very large number of potential chains of events to ensure that they meet the stakeholders' wider needs (in terms of their implementation cost but also ethical and environmental impacts).

In socio-technical systems, many of the interactions that contribute to those events involve people. This is why contemporary engineering cannot be limited to the physical sciences but also draws upon expertise from the cognitive and behavioural sciences for the lifecycle management of systems (e.g. Tripathi & Borrion, 2015). Evidence of this can be found in the existence of academic communities specialising in the areas of human-machine interface, systems ergonomics, human errors and safety issues. The importance of human factors in security engineering is further discussed through the case of airport security scanners in Example 2.

Example 2: airport security

Since 9/11, significant changes have been made to airport security checkpoints across the world (Blalock et al., 2007). In this example, we examine some of the dependencies that exist between a luggage scanner and the entities that surround it. The manifestation of the properties of the scanner (e.g. what is displayed on the screen), for instance, depends upon the supply of electricity from another system (e.g. the power distribution network), the way the scanner is operated, and the inputs it receives (e.g. the bags to be scanned). It also depends upon the occurrence of external events that would affect its performance (e.g. high temperature). The scanner may be affected by sabotage attempts too.

The relevance of human factors is most obvious when examining the effect of the scanner on its environment. As soon as it is deployed, the device impresses upon passengers that security is a serious business. It changes the spatial properties of the security checkpoint, influences the speed, trajectory, actions and mood of individual passengers, and affects the security guards' field of view and movements. Depending on the situation, the scanner can also cause different responses from the guards (such as questioning passengers or searching their bags), including unethical ones. Deterrence is only one of many different impacts that a scanner can have on people, and focusing exclusively on it would be regarded as very poor engineering practice.

From behavioural requirements to system requirements

Overlooking some of the stakeholders' needs is very common in engineering projects. This may happen when those needs are not (or not properly) articulated in the first instance or when designers focus too much on the functional aspects of those systems. However, too narrow an approach could result in the creation of interventions with unacceptable side effects. To ensure that they produce the sought-after outcomes and foster the expected behaviours, designers of crime-reduction interventions must likewise understand what constraints prevention measures should meet. They must also develop a thorough understanding of the interactions that are relevant to those needs, both within and between systems (Blanchard & Fabrycky, 1990). In practice, however, it can be difficult for experts to translate requirements about human behaviour into technological requirements, as shown in Example 3.

Example 3: CCTV failures

Many of the failures associated with control measures are not due to technological defects but poor specifications (van Lamsweerde, 2009). As an example, I was made privy to an anecdote

Table 11.2 List of CCTV systems failures

Type of issue	*Example*
Implementation	Introducing a camera as a deterrent but not making it sufficiently visible
Implementation	Orienting a camera toward a wall or setting it up in a location where it is regularly obstructed by lorries
Quality	Having an image resolution so low that the retrieved information is not actionable; performing poor or no maintenance
Capacity/ usability	Deploying more camera feeds than can be monitored by CCTV operators
Capacity	Lacking CCTV personnel who could detect threats or act upon them
Integrity	Lacking a suitable process to manage the chain of evidence for forensic use
Interoperability	Recording video data in a format that cannot be retrieved by police investigators
Acceptability	Misusing CCTV equipment resulting in loss of public confidence or distrust (e.g. making CCTV feeds accessible to unauthorised parties; using it for an illegitimate purpose)
Security	Deploying CCTV equipment in locations where offenders can easily destroy them

concerning an electric gate that was repeatedly damaged in a private residence. To deal with the problem, one of the residents had suggested that, on future occasions, the management company should use the CCTV camera monitoring the gate to identify the culprits. The answer he received was that this was logistically impossible because, by the time the company processed the request, the standard 30-day data retention period would have expired and the CCTV footage would have been erased!

A list of similar issues that can influence the effectiveness of CCTV-based security processes are presented as an example below (Table 11.2). It is noticeable that many of them would typically occur if technologists were to overlook behavioural requirements or if behavioural analysts were unable to translate them into technological requirements

Interactions with/within engineered systems

So far we have highlighted that designers must consider the interactions between systems that could affect crime reduction and other stakeholder needs. Because crime events take place in real-world environments, those interactions may happen not just between people, but also between people and human-made systems; or even between human-made systems only. It seems that the main reason for taking an interdisciplinary approach in crime science lies in this diversity.

Understanding what influences people's motivation and behaviour is the bread and butter of scholars in the cognitive and behavioural disciplines. However, this expertise alone is not sufficient to tackle the numerous research challenges that exist in crime science:

- Not every aspect of the causal chains of interest is about people's motivation or self-control. For instance, a different type of expertise is needed to propose a method that can determine whether the cause of, say, a child's bone fracture is really accidental (osteology and mechanical engineering); to propose and assess tactics against drone-borne explosive devices (mechanical and electronic engineering); or to assess how many computers are likely to be infected by a given type of malware (computer science).

- Where interactions are concerned with human behaviour, they may also be influenced by a number of factors that are best understood with some knowledge of engineering. For example, people's intent and motivation to carry out an action depend on their awareness of the opportunity (i.e. that the action is an option and that it would support their goals), and their perceived capability to carry it out successfully. When those actions directly concern a technological system (e.g. computer or weapon), in-depth analysis cannot always be done without a minimum understanding of the technology.

For years, crime scientists have been studying crimes such as theft and physical violence. Their choice can be explained by the prevalence of those types of crime in society and their desire to achieve impact. We can also note that most social scientists would be familiar with the type of environments in which those crimes occur, and could rapidly come to terms with the rather unsophisticated modus operandi used by criminals.

In contrast, contextualising crime-science principles to problems involving more complex targets, advanced weapons, sophisticated modus operandi, high-tech control measures or unusual environments is not as straightforward. For instance, not every crime scientist has the domain knowledge needed to carry out research on money laundering involving Asian arts and antiques in the 19th century.

For the same reason, engineering knowledge may be required whenever the emerging properties of an ecosystem are based on human-made systems. In many cases, adopting a black-box approach whereby systems are only described in terms of inputs, outputs and the relation between those, without looking at what happens 'inside' them, is an option. However, this presupposes that sufficient information is available about the behaviour of the studied systems under a wide range of external conditions. In practice, this is rarely possible for socio-technical systems and a more interdisciplinary approach must be adopted.

Without some overlap in their knowledge base, it would be difficult for a crime expert and an engineer to collaborate effectively. Crime experts cannot be expected to ask pertinent questions about a system if they do not know anything about it; and engineers cannot guess what information crime experts might need to know about a system if they have no understanding of behavioural and crime-prevention principles. This is also why greater integration between these domains is needed.

Conclusion

University researchers can usually select the problems they wish to study. Most criminologists and crime scientists are free to cast their eyes only on problems that can be analysed without understanding a great deal about technology. They can restrict their creativity to propose only interventions that can be identified without engineering knowledge. They can also decide to evaluate only crime-reduction measures that do not interact with engineered systems. Academic journals are home to millions of articles written by experts who have found a niche where they can enjoy the reassurance of a monodisciplinary life. Nevertheless, the increasing presence of technology (such as autonomous systems, crypto-currency, internet-enabled services or smart cities) in society calls for a new breed of experts capable of engineering crime out while minimising the negative consequences of interventions. If, like an intrepid hobbit, you think you might be ready for an adventure, this article will have hopefully helped you see untapped opportunities in crime science.

References

Alexander, I. F. & Maiden, N. (2005). *Scenarios, Stories, Use Cases: Through the Systems Development Life-Cycle.* Chichester, UK: John Wiley & Sons.

Anderson, J. R. (1980). *Cognitive Psychology and Its Implications.* San Francisco, CA: Freman, *119*, 257.

Blalock, G., Kadiyali, V., & Simon, D. H. (2007). The impact of post-9/11 airport security measures on the demand for air Travel. *Journal of Law and Economics*, *50*(4), 731–755.

Blanchard, B. S. & Fabrycky, W. J. (1990). *Systems Engineering and Analysis* (Vol. 4). Englewood Cliffs, NJ: Prentice Hall.

Borrion, H. & Koch, D. (2017). Integrating architecture and crime science: a transdisciplinary challenge. In P. Gibbs (ed.) *Transdisciplinary Higher Education* (pp. 91–107). Cham, Switzerland: Springer.

Borrion, H., Mitchener-Nissen, T., Taylor, J., & Lai, K. M. (2012, August). Countering bioterrorism: why smart buildings should have a code of ethics. In Intelligence and Security Informatics Conference (EISIC), 2012 European (pp. 68–75). Piscataway, NJ: IEEE.

Bowers, K. J., Johnson, S. D., & Hirschfield, A. F. (2004). Closing off opportunities for crime: an evaluation of alley-gating. *European Journal on Criminal Policy and Research*, *10*(4), 285–308.

Broeer, T., Fuller, J., Tuffner, F., Chassin, D., & Djilali, N. (2014). Modeling framework and validation of a smart grid and demand response system for wind power integration. *Applied Energy*, *113*, 199–207.

Clarke, R. V. & Eck, J. E. (2005). *Crime Analysis for Problem Solvers.* Washington, DC: Center for Problem Oriented Policing.

Clayton, A. M. & Radcliffe, N. J. (1996). *Sustainability: A Systems Approach.* London: Earthscan.

Cohen, L. E. & Felson, M. (1979). Social change and crime rate trends: A routine activity approach. *American Sociological Review*, 588–608.

Davis, R. & Pease, K. (2001). Crime, technology and the future. *Security Journal*, *13*(2), 59–64.

Eck, J. E. & Spelman, W. (1987). *Problem-solving: Problem-oriented Policing in Newport News.* Washington DC: Police Executive Research Forum.

Ekblom, P. (2003). Organised crime and the conjunction of criminal opportunity framework. Transnational organised crime: perspectives on global security In A. Edwards & P. Gill (eds) *Transnational Organised Crime: Perspectives on Global Security* (pp. 241–263). London: Routledge.

Evans, S., Heinbuch, D., Kyle, E., Piorkowski, J., & Wallner, J. (2004). Risk-based systems security engineering: stopping attacks with intention. *Security & Privacy, IEEE*, *2*(6), 59–62.

Goldstein, H. (1979). Improving policing: A problem-oriented approach. *Crime & Delinquency*, *25*(2), 236–258.

Grabosky, P. N. (1996). Unintended consequences of crime prevention. *Crime Prevention Studies*, *5*, 25–56.

Hill, J. F., Johnson, S. D., & Borrion, H. (2014). Potential uses of computer agent-based simulation modelling in the evaluation of wildlife poaching. *Situational Prevention of Poaching.* In A. Lemieux (ed.) *Situational Prevention of Poaching* (pp. 144–177). New York: Routledge.

Lee, E. A. (2008). Cyber physical systems: design challenges. In *Object Oriented Real-Time Distributed Computing* (ISORC), May 2008, 11th IEEE International Symposium on (pp. 363–369). Piscataway, NJ: IEEE.

INCOSE (2015). *Systems Engineering Handbook: A Guide for System Life Cycle Processes and Activities.* Hoboken, NJ: John Wiley & Sons.

Jacobson, I., Booch, G. & Rumbaugh, J., 1999. *The Unified Software Development Process* (Vol 1). Reading: Addison Wesley.

Junger, M., Laycock, G., Hartel, P., & Ratcliffe, J. (2012). Crime science: editorial statement. *Crime Science*, *1*(1), 1–3.

Kemp, M. C., Taday, P., Cole, B. E., Cluff, J., Fitzgerald, A. J., & Tribe, W. R. (2003). Security applications of terahertz technology. Paper presented at the AeroSense 2003.

Laycock, G. (2005). Defining Crime Science. In M. J. Smith & N. Tilley (eds) *Crime Science: New Approaches to Preventing and Detecting Crime* (pp. 3–24). Collumpton, UK: Willan Publishing.

Le Sage, T., Toubaline, S., & Borrion, H. (2013). An object-oriented approach for modelling security scenarios. In *Computer Modelling and Simulation* (UKSim), 2013 UKSim 15th International Conference, May (pp. 396–400). Piscataway, NJ: IEEE.

Lemmon, J. J., Carroll, J. E., Sanders, F. H., & Turner, D. (2008). Assessment of the effects of wind turbines on air traffic control radars. Washington, DC: National Telecommunications & Information Administration, US Department of Commerce.

Litterer, J. A. (ed.). (1969). *Organizations: Systems, Control and Adaptations*. Chichester, UK: John Wiley & Sons.

Kurt, L. (1936). *Principles of Topological Psychology*. New York, London: McGraw-Hill.

Malleson, N., Heppenstall, A., See, L., & Evans, A. (2013). Using an agent-based crime simulation to predict the effects of urban regeneration on individual household burglary risk. *Environment and Planning B: Planning and Design*, *40*(3), 405–426.

Metke, A. R. & Ekl, R. L. (2010). Security technology for smart grid networks. *IEEE Transactions on Smart Grid*, *1*(1), 99–107.

Nicholls, B. & Racey, P. A. (2007). Bats avoid radar installations: could electromagnetic fields deter bats from colliding with wind turbines? *PloS One*, *2*(3), e297.

Norrie, A. (2002). Ethical and Social Perspectives in Situational Crime Prevention, edited by A. Von Hirsch, D. Garland and A. Wakefield/The Judicial Role in Criminal Proceedings, edited by S. Doran and J. Jackson. *King's Law Journal*, *13*(1), 128–131.

Pawson, R. & Tilley, N. (1997). *Realistic Evaluation*: Thousand Oaks, CA: Sage.

Qadri, M. T. & Asif, M. (2009). Automatic number plate recognition system for vehicle identification using optical character recognition. Paper presented at the Education Technology and Computer, 2009. ICETC 2009. International Conference on Education Technology and Computer.

Read, T. & Tilley, N. (2000). *Not Rocket Science. Problem-solving and Crime*. Crime Reduction Research Series. London: Home Office.

Rullli, M.C., Bellomi, D., Cazzoli, A., De Carolis, G., & D'Odorico, P. (2016). The water-land-food nexus of firstgeneration biofuels. *Nature Scientific Reports*, *6*. DOI: 10.1038/srep22521.

Savona, E. U. (2004). *Crime and Technology: New Frontiers for Regulation, Law Enforcement and Research*. Dordrecht: Springer Science + Business Media.

Seiffert, M.E.B. & Loch, C. (2005). Systemic thinking in environmental management: support for sustainable development. *Journal of Cleaner Production*, *13*(12), 1197–1202.

Smuts, J. C. (1926). *Holism and Evolution*. London: Macmillan.

Skyttner, L. (2005). *General Systems Theory: Problems, Perspectives, Practice*. Singapore: World Scientific Publishing.

Thornton, A. (2015). *Understanding Radicalisation*. London: University College London.

Tilley, N. (1993). *Understanding Car Parks, Crime, and CCTV: Evaluation Lessons from Safer Cities*. London: Home Office Police Department.

van Lamsweerde, A. (2009). *Requirements Engineering: From System Goals to Uml Models to Software Specifications*. Chichester, UK: John Wiley & Sons.

von Bertalanffy, L. (1950). An outline of general system theory. *British Journal for the Philosophy of Science*, *2*(1), 134–165.

Wertheimer, M. (1938/1924). *Gestalt Theory*. In W. D. Ellis (ed.) *A Source Book of Gestalt Psychology* (pp. 1–11). London: Routledge & Kegan Paul.

Wilkins, L. T. (1997). *Wartime Operational Research in Britain and Situational Crime Prevention*. In G. Newman, R. V. Clarke, & S. Shoham (eds) *Rational Choice and Situational Crime Prevention*. Aldershot, UK: Avebury.

Wortley, R. & Mazerolle, L. (2013). *Environmental Criminology and Crime Analysis*. London: Willan Publishing.

12

Computer science

Pieter Hartel and Marianne Junger

Introduction

Marcus Felson and Mary Eckert, in their recent book *Crime and Everyday Life* (Felson and Eckert, 2016) describe how technology has influenced crime. When most people lived in 'the village' without the technology to venture far from home, villagers suffered crime from marauding bandits. The domestication of horses increased people's reach and created 'the town'. Horses and wagons became new tools and targets of crime. Then nautical technology created 'the convergent city', with ships providing new tools and the cargo the target. Then 'the divergent metropolis', arrived, thanks to modern transportation technology. Cars are not only an important target of crime but a powerful tool too.

We now live in 'the connected world', where computers and networks are both a target of crime as well as a powerful tool. A recent report from the UK National Crime Agency states that for the first time in history there is more recorded cyber-crime than traditional crime (NCA, 2016). Therefore students of crime need at least a basic understanding of the role that computers and networks play in the commission of crime, in the prevention of crime, and also in the study of crime. This chapter gives an introduction to these topics from the crime-science perspective, but we begin by giving three examples to illustrate the main point.

- Phishing is one of the most popular ways of using computers and networks in the commission of crime because the technology scales well. It is almost as easy to send one phishing email as to send millions. Even with a success rate as low as 10^{-5} phishing can be profitable (Milletary, 2013).
- Security cameras are ubiquitous in the UK and in many other countries. In a modern city with a good networking infrastructure, security cameras are a scalable technology. Therefore, it is possible to keep a watchful eye on many places of interest and indeed studies have shown that the technology can contribute to crime prevention (Welsh and Farrington, 2008).
- Computational social science is a field of study where the power of computers and networks is used to study social sciences. For example, a computer program can simulate behaviour predicted by a theory. If the results are not realistic, the theory is probably wrong.

This is usually a much cheaper way of refuting a theory than conducting an experiment (von der Heyde, Miebach, and Kluge, 2014; Rosoff, Cui, and John, 2014). Again the technology scales well.

In this chapter we will explore the relationship between crime and computers and networks by answering the following questions:

- Which techniques from computer science can be used to prevent crime?
- Which techniques from computer science can be used to study crime?

To address the first question we use the 25 techniques of situational crime prevention to provide a systematic assessment of how computer and network technology can be used to prevent crime. The second question will be addressed by discussing computer simulation methods in cases where real experiments with crime prevention would be too costly or impractical.

Crime prevention

Borrowing from situational crime prevention, crime science offers five principles to prevent crime or to deter the offender.

1. Increase the effort needed for crime, for example better locks require more effort to pick, or better passwords require more effort to guess.
2. Increase the risks of crime, for example well-lit windows increase the risk of being caught during burglary, or an operator monitoring the network increases the risk of being caught during a hacking attempt.
3. Reduce the rewards of crime, for example marked parts of a stolen vehicle are harder to fence, or encrypted data is harder to sell.
4. Reduce provocations that invite criminal behaviour, for example rapid cleaning of graffiti discourages the application of more graffiti, or rapid restoration of defaced websites discourages repetition.
5. Remove excuses for criminal behaviour, for example many systems specify an acceptable use policy that informs users of what behaviour is acceptable.

For each of the five principles, five generic techniques of situational crime prevention have been developed. Together, they are known as the '25 techniques of situational crime prevention'.

We have found seven reviews in the literature that suggest how computers and networks can be used as a specific instance of the 25 generic techniques (Beebe and Rao, 2005; Brookson et al., 2007; Coles-Kemp and Theoharidou, 2010; Morris, 2004b; Newman and Clarke, 2003; Willison and Siponen, 2009; Reyns, 2010).

Table 12.1 compares the way in which the reviews suggest how computer science techniques can be used to prevent crime. We list 12 techniques that have been mentioned at least three times in the reviews and then describe them in some detail below. For the remaining techniques we refer the reader to the references provided.

1. A password or PIN code used to authenticate a user.
2. Encryption of data files to ensure that once encrypted, they can be read only when the correct decryption key is known.
3. A firewall that is used to stop potentially malicious connections to a computer or network.

Table 12.1 The 25 generic techniques used to structure popular information security techniques (some definitions of acronyms follow)

Increase effort	*Increase risks*	*Reduce rewards*	*Reduce provocation*	*Remove excuses*
1 Harden target • Firewalls • Vulnerability patches • Encryption • Antivirus • ISP as a first line of defence • IDS	**6 Extend guardianship** • RFID	**11 Conceal targets** • DMZ	**16 Reduce frustrations**	**21 Set rules** • Educate end-users • Provide a clear code of conduct
2 Control access • Authentication using passwords, pins • Caller-ID like technology for internet • Logical: IDS • Logical: Firewalls	**7 Natural surveillance** • Report suspect email and information request to ISP	**12 Remove targets**	**17 Avoid disputes**	**22 Post instructions**
3 Screen exits • IDS • Antivirus • Audit trail • Audit trail • Logical: Firewalls	**8 Reduce anonymity** • RFID • Caller-ID • Audit trails	**13 Identify property** • RFID	**18 Reduce arousal**	**23 Alert conscience** • Public awareness on the consequences of crime • Educate: 'copying software is stealing'
4 Deflect offenders	**9 Place Managers** • IDS	**14 Disrupt markets** • ISP should be keen to assist investigations	**19 Neutralise peer pressure**	**24 Assist compliance** • Security education of staff
5 Control facilitators • Caller-ID • Make the ISP accountable for the traffic	**10 Formal surveillance** • Auditing and trail reviews • RFID • Early warning systems of viruses and hacking attacks • IDS	**15 Deny benefits** • Encrypt valuable data	**20 Discourage imitation** • Prompt software patching	**25 Control disinhibitors** • Cyber-ethics education • Campaign against hacker culture

4 A de-militarised zone (DMZ) used to isolate the public web server of an organisation from the internal network.
5 An intrusion detection system (IDS) used to stop potentially malicious information being sent to a computer or network.
6 A virus scanner used to detect malicious code in the information being sent to a computer or network.
7 Prompt software patching to remove vulnerabilities as soon as a correction has been published.
8 A radio-frequency identification (RFID) tag used to provide information about the product to which it is attached.
9 The caller-ID feature of the telephone system used to inform the recipient of a telephone call who is calling.
10 An audit log used to collect relevant operational data that can be analysed when there is an incident.
11 An internet service provider (ISP) can assist its clients in using the information super highway responsibly.
12 User education, which is included in the list to emphasise that humans play an important role in crime prevention.

We will now discuss the 12 techniques in more detail.

Passwords and PIN codes are mentioned in all reviews, as these are standard tools. Unfortunately, a good password or PIN code is hard to remember so that as a result passwords and PIN codes that are currently in use are often weak (Anderson, 2008).

Encryption is seen by two reviews (Brookson et al., 2007; Morris, 2004b) as a means to harden targets and by the others (Beebe and Rao, 2005; Coles-Kemp and Theoharidou, 2010; Willison and Siponen, 2009; Newman and Clarke, 2003) as a means to deny benefits. The apparent ambiguity can be resolved if we take a crime specific example, such as stealing a laptop with full disk encryption. Disk encryption increases the efforts on the part of the offender because s/he will now have to break the disk encryption. If the offender is unable to break the disk encryption, the laptop will be worth less; hence encryption will also reduce rewards.

Spatial fragmentation is a target-hardening technique that can be used to prevent products from being lost or stolen. For example, an in-car entertainment system that consists of separate components built into various places into a car is harder to steal than a single component (Ekblom, 2008). Spatial fragmentation is more easily applied to a networked system, for example peer to peer systems usually apply spatial fragmentation to improve resilience, but the spatial fragmentation could be leveraged to prevent illegal downloading too. In a sense threshold cryptography is an instance of spatial fragmentation too. In (n,t) threshold cryptography the decryption key is split into n shares in such a way that decryption can only take place when the number of shares present during decryption equals or exceeds a previously determined threshold t.

Firewalls are mentioned in four reviews (Beebe and Rao, 2005; Brookson et al., 2007; Morris, 2004b; Newman and Clarke, 2003) as a specific technique for target hardening. One review (Coles-Kemp and Theoharidou, 2010) proposes firewalls as a technique for access control and screening exits. Screening exits is an interesting application, as it is as relevant to prevent offenders from getting information out of an organisation as it is to prevent offenders from getting into the organisation in the first place.

A *DMZ* is mentioned by three reviews (Brookson et al., 2007; Beebe and Rao, 2005; Coles-Kemp and Theoharidou, 2010) as a method for target concealment, typically the internal network of an organisation.

An *IDS* is mentioned in five reviews (Morris, 2004b; Brookson et al., 2007; Willison and Siponen, 2009), but in two different ways: as a form of formal surveillance (Coles-Kemp and Theoharidou, 2010; Willison and Siponen, 2009), and as an example of utilising place managers (Brookson et al., 2007). The difference between the two generic techniques is best explained in the physical world: formal surveillance is carried out by specially appointed personnel, whereas place managers could be colleagues watching each other. An IDS can also be used for access control (Coles-Kemp and Theoharidou, 2010), target hardening (Morris, 2004b), and screening exits (Beebe and Rao, 2005).

A *virus scanner* is mentioned as a measure for target hardening (Brookson et al., 2007), and formal surveillance (Morris, 2004b).

Prompt software patching is mentioned in four reviews. Software patching is a standard method for target hardening (Beebe and Rao, 2005; Morris, 2004b), but it can be used to discourage imitation (Willison and Siponen, 2009; Coles-Kemp and Theoharidou, 2010), since hackers, who often use each other's exploits, cannot do so if a vulnerability is patched.

RFID tags are mentioned in one review (Brookson et al., 2007), but in three different capacities: (1) to extend guardianship to reflect the idea that the tag can be used to raise the alarm in the case of shoplifting; (2) to reduce anonymity since tagged goods can be used to trace the person carrying the goods; (3) to enable formal surveillance, since tagged goods make it easier to recognise shoplifters. RFID tags can be thought of as a technique to identify property. RFID tags can be used for all of the 25 generic techniques.

Caller-ID is mentioned in two reviews (Brookson et al., 2007; Morris, 2004b) as an effective technique to control access, reduce anonymity, and to control facilitators. In the real world, caller-ID has reduced the number of nuisance calls in the telephone network (Clarke, 1990). This suggests that a fruitful line of research would be to look for similar, effective techniques for the internet. We have found two relevant papers. The first approach, called IPclip (Widiger et al., 2008), requires hardware support and changes to the way that an ISP operates. The second approach, called Clue (Afanasyev et al., 2011), adds identification information in software. As long as offenders use their own PCs to approach their victim, both IPclip and Clue could be effective. However, since offenders prefer to use hijacked computers rather than their own, the trace from the victim to the offending PC will end at the hijacked PC and not at the offenders PC, thus defeating the objective of the two techniques that have been published thus far.

An *audit trail* is mentioned by several reviews (Beebe and Rao, 2005; Brookson et al., 2007; Coles-Kemp and Theoharidou, 2010; Morris, 2004b; Newman and Clarke, 2003) as a tool to investigate the sequence of events leading up to an incident. An audit trail does not prevent crime per se, but the fact that all actions are logged can be used as a deterrent (Newman and Clarke, 2003).

The *ISP* should be more active in the prevention of crime. This conclusion is shared by all reviews. We have also found suggestions in the related work to empower the ISP. For example some years ago only 5 per cent of all downloads were paid for (Kennedy, 2009), which caused a serious problem for the music industry. Kennedy describes two approaches where the ISP can play a key role. For example, using bandwidth for illegal downloads reduces bandwidth for legal use of the network. A typical ISP would block or throttle bit-torrent traffic, when it is responsible for illegal downloads. This would be an instance of the generic technique of control facilitators. Reducing the potential for illegal downloads automatically increases the available bandwidth for legal use. Whether this is an appropriate solution is open to debate, as bit torrent also has legal uses. There is also a fundamental issue here in the sense that an ISP blockade goes against the principle of net neutrality (van Schewick and Farber, 2009). ISP blocking can even help the offender rather than preventing crime: Clayton (2005) describes how a major

ISP implemented a system for blocking content (child pornography), which leaked the list of blocked sites. The blocking system could then be used by the offenders as an 'oracle' to discover which sites were on the black list, so that they could take evasive action. The main conclusion of Clayton's paper is that a 'fit and forget' approach to designing internet-based crime prevention is doomed to failure; instead the potential targets are engaged in a perpetual arms race with the offenders.

The Morris reports (Morris, 2004a, 2004b) contain suggestions for empowering the ISP. The Morris panels (2004b) would like to see the ISP as a first line of defence (i.e. target hardening) to assist consumers in keeping their computers clean and healthy. The services provided by the ISP can also be seen as a tool for the offender to reach his or her targets. In this sense, making the ISP more accountable for what goes on in its network can be seen as an instance of the control facilitator's generic technique. Finally, the ISP could advertise that it is proactive in preventing crime, and that the ISP will cooperate closely with the police wherever possible. This falls into the generic technique of alert conscience.

Education of offenders, targets, and guardians is considered useful by all reviews to remove excuses. Brookson et al. (2007) believe that if we alert their consciences potential offenders might be discouraged from engaging in software and content piracy. In the context of their work on insiders, Willison and Siponen (2009) suggest that the education of staff might assist compliance with company policies. The Morris (2004b) report asserts that customer security education for e-banking, for example using the five 'golden rules' of e-banking, is a specific case of set rules. Finally, using education to control disinhibitors merits a little digression. Before the internet went commercial in the early 1990s some users adhered to the 'hacker's ethic' which held that information should be free (Furnell et al., 1999). When the internet opened for business, new information was made available that is clearly not free. However the hackers' ethic is still with us today, which is a disinhibitor for good behaviour (Newman and Clarke, 2003). Education would be appropriate to explain the difference between information that is free and information that is not.

Having established how useful it is to adopt the systematic approach of crime science to information security, we now turn our attention to the converse, discussing the use of computer science techniques for the study of crime.

Crime simulation

Science uses computers to collect and analyse experimental and simulated data, using networks to collaborate. For example the high-energy physics community was the first non-military user of the internet and thanks to the computers and networks e-science is flourishing today (Craddock et al., 2008). The development of computational social science follows the lead of natural science. For example Lazer et al. (2009) observe that what we all do in our everyday life leaves traces on the internet, thus providing a source of information that can be mined and analysed. Privacy concerns limit the data available to researchers, but there is hope that these problems can be resolved (Kenneally and Claffy, 2010).

Crime science is a member of the computational social-science family because the analysis of crime data is an important aspect of crime science. However, this is not all. Crime science emphasises that each new idea for the prevention of crime must be properly evaluated, preferably in a well-designed experiment or else in a quasi-experiment or a well-designed time-series analysis. Unfortunately, there are practical limitations to what can be achieved in a real-life experiment.

Firstly, some experiments are just too costly. For example if we believe that changing the street pattern of a city might reduce crime, then it will be hard to convince the authorities to change the street pattern just for a scientific experiment (Brantingham and Brantingham, 1993).

Secondly, crime data contains systematic errors. Sometimes, neither the offender, nor the target, or the police, have an interest in providing correct data (Gove et al., 1985; Langworthy, 1999; Thornberry and Krohn, 2000). For example, a repeat offender has a vested interest in keeping silent about his crimes, and the police might be interested in inflating the crime rate to ensure that the police force will receive more funding (Eck and Liu, 2008a). It is well known that police recording policies and practices have a strong impact on the officially registered volume of crime, particularly violent crime (Shepherd and Sivarajasingam, 2005; Wittebrood and Junger, 2002).

Computer-based simulated experiments can help to circumvent these problems (Groff and Mazerolle, 2008). For example, in a computer-based experiment we can change the map of a street pattern. We can also use a simulation-based experiment to fill the gaps in available crime data. However, in a computer-based experiment we do not have access to the actors involved, such as the offender, the target, or the capable guardian. Therefore, the behaviour of these actors must be modelled too. Modelling humans is hard, but in the study of crime we are primarily interested in behaviour that is believed to be represented by a number of relatively manageable perspectives, such as rational choice, routine activity, and crime pattern theory. These perspectives can be codified to a certain extent (Bosse et al., 2009b), thus endowing the actors in a simulation with behaviour relevant for a human actor. With a model of the actors and the relevant environment we can use a computer to simulate crime events.

We consider computer-based modelling and analysis of crime as part of crime science. However, the term 'computational criminology' is also being used; it seems to have been employed first by Patricia and Paul Brantingham (2005). We will now discuss the research of the main groups working on crime simulation.

The main idea of crime simulations is to compute the steps leading to a crime event so that predictions about real crime and its prevention can be made. Agent-based simulations are commonly used (Eck and Liu, 2008a), since the behaviour of human actors can be codified by way of rules that determine the behaviour of the agents. The aim of a simulation is then to infer aggregate behaviour from the individual behaviour of crime agents. Epstein (1999) argues that the main reason why this works is that the principle of 'bounded rationality' (which is an aspect of RCP) is also the essence of generative simulation. Quoting Epstein (1999, p. 42): 'Situate an initial population of autonomous heterogeneous agents in a relevant spatial environment; allow them to interact according to simple local rules, and thereby generate – or grow– the macroscopic regularity from the bottom up'. The agents of crime include the offender, the target, and the capable guardian. The simple local rules are provided by the relevant perspective, for example bounded rationality restricts the decision of the offender agent to local knowledge, and ensures that the decision is a rational one taking account of risk. The rules for the offender steer the latter towards a state where the crime has been committed, whereas the target and the guardian try to avoid the crime. The fact that the offender and the target have opposing goals naturally leads to the suggestion that game theory could be a useful meta-theory. The spatial environment could be a geographical environment modelled by a geographical information system (GIS), or it could be a social network. The macroscopic regularity could be a statement such as: 'burglary is communicable', which means that the spreading of burglaries follows the same pattern as a communicable disease (Bowers et al., 2004).

The strength of generative simulation is that it can be used to discount inappropriate theories, since a simulation that does not generate the sought-after macroscopic regularity is probably based on a theory that does not apply (Birks et al., 2012). The limitation of generative simulation is that there could be more than one theory that can grow the regularity, so generative simulation should not be interpreted as a proof that the theory is the best or only explanation of a certain macroscopic regularity.

Our primary interest is in the ability of generative crime simulation to answer what-if questions. For example, 'what would happen to crime rates if we change the layout of the street pattern?' If the simulation indicates that this would not be useful, then a costly empirical experiment can be avoided. To answer what-if questions we could vary the initial configuration or the rules of the agents. For example, the effect of increasing the number of capable guardians can be studied simply by increasing the number of agents playing the role of a capable guardian. However, in practice, the number of configurations that one can choose from is often huge, so skill and intuition are required to drive the simulations. As yet there is insufficient progress in the field to make simulated what-if experiments routine (Glässer and Vajihollahi, 2008).

Any simulation must ultimately be validated with real data (Berk, 2008). We have not found reports of such validations, presumably for reasons of cost, ethics, and privacy (Lazer et al., 2009).

We have found several strands of work in the literature on the generative simulation of crime. We differentiate related work on the way in which the macroscopic regularity is specified.

- Researchers at the Vrije Universiteit in Amsterdam use a logical approach to the specification of the macroscopic regularity, where a kind of model checking separates simulated behavioural traces that lead to crime from those that do not lead to crime (Bosse et al., 2007a, 2007b; Bosse and Gerritsen, 2008, 2009; Bosse et al., 2009b, 2009a; Bosse et al., 2009b).
- Researchers at Simon Fraser University in Vancouver use an interactive approach towards the detection of the macroscopic regularity, in the sense that successful simulations exhibit for example crime hotspots (Glässer et al., 2006; Glässer and Vajihollahi, 2008; Glässer et al., 2008; Brantingham et al., 2004, 2005). Crime Pattern Theory (Brantingham and Brantingham, 1993, 1995) forms the basis of the simulations; hence the focus is on the spatial and temporal behaviour of the offenders and their targets (Short et al., 2010).
- Researchers at the University of Cincinnati (Eck, 1998; Eck and Liu, 2008b, 2008a; Liu et al., 2005; Wang et al., 2008) and the University of Virginia in Charlottesville (Brown, 1998; Brown et al., 2000; Brown and Gunderson, 2001; Brown and Oxford, 2001; Gunderson and Brown, 2000; Gunderson, 2002; Lin and Brown, 2003, 2006; Porter and Brown, 2007; Xue and Brown, 2003, 2006) use statistical approaches towards the specification of the macroscopic regularity, such as clustering (Brown and Gunderson, 2001), and data association (Brown et al., 2000).

We found one proposal on agent-based simulation of cyber-crime. Gunderson and Brown (2000), from the University of Virginia propose using the same methods and tools that are used successfully to predict traditional crime, without elaborating what the notion of space in the cyber-world might be.

Computational social science is relatively young but has a lot to offer to social science in general and to crime science in particular.

Conclusions

In conclusion, we found a considerable amount of work in the literature that suggests how crime-science methods can be used by computer scientists and vice versa. We have provided references to relevant related work, but space limitations preclude us from citing more than the tip of the proverbial iceberg.

Acknowledgements

We are grateful to Ron Clarke, Hans Hendrickx, Ken Pease, Roel Wieringa, and the reviewers for their feedback on drafts of this chapter.

References

Afanasyev, M., Kohno, T., Ma, J., Murphy, N., Savage, S., Snoeren, A. C., and Voelker, G. M. (2011). Privacy-preserving network forensics. *Communications of the ACM, 54*(5): 78–87.

Anderson, R. J. (2008). *Security Engineering: A Guide to Building Dependable Distributed Systems*. New York: John Wiley & Sons.

Beebe, N. L. and Rao, V. S. (2005). Using situational crime prevention theory to explain the effectiveness of information systems security. In *Conference on Protecting the Intangible Organizational Assets (SoftWars)*. Las Vegas, NV: The Information Institute.

Berk, R. (2008). How you can tell if the simulations in computational criminology are any good. *Journal of Experimental Criminology, 4*(3): 289–308.

Birks, D., Townsley, M., and Stewart, A. (2012). Generative explanations of crime: using simulation to test criminological theory. *Criminology, 50*(1): 221–254.

Bosse, T. and Gerritsen, C. (2008). Agent-based simulation of the spatial dynamics of crime: on the interplay between criminal hot spots and reputation. In *7th International Joint Conference on Autonomous Agents and Multiagent Systems (AAMAS)*, pp. 1129–1136. Estoril, Portugal: International Foundation for Autonomous Agents and Multiagent Systems.

Bosse, T. and Gerritsen, C. (2009). Comparing crime prevention strategies by agent-based simulation. In *IEEE/WIC/ACM International Joint Conference on Web Intelligence and Intelligent Agent Technologies (WI-IAT)*, volume 2, pp. 491–496. Milan, Italy: IEEE.

Bosse, T., Gerritsen, C., and Treur, J. (2007a). Case analysis of criminal behaviour. In *20th International Conference on Industrial, Engineering and Other Applications of Applied Intelligent Systems (IEA/AIE) – New Trends in Applied Artificial Intelligence*, volume 4570 of *LNCS*, pp. 621–632. Kyoto, Japan: Springer.

Bosse, T., Gerritsen, C., and Treur, J. (2007b). Cognitive and social simulation of criminal behaviour: the intermittent explosive disorder case. In *6th International Joint Conference on Autonomous Agents and Multiagent Systems (AAMAS)*, pp. 1–8. Honolulu, HI: ACM.

Bosse, T., Gerritsen, C., Klein, M. C. A., and Weerman, F. M. (2009a). Development and validation of an agent-based simulation model of juvenile delinquency. In *International Conference on Computational Science and Engineering (CSE)*, pp. 200–207. Vancouver, BC: IEEE.

Bosse, T., Gerritsen, C., and Treur, J. (2009b). Towards integration of biological, psychological and social aspects in agent-based simulation of violent offenders. *Simulation, 85*(10): 635–660.

Bowers, K. J., Johnson, S. D., and Pease, K. (2004). Prospective hot-spotting – the future of crime mapping? *British Journal of Criminology, 44*(5): 641–658.

Brantingham, P. L. and Brantingham, P. J. (1993). Environment, routine and situation: towards a pattern theory of crime. In Clarke, R. V. and Felson, M. (eds) *Routine Activity and Rational Choice*, volume Advances in Criminological Theory 5, pp. 259–294. Piscataway, NJ: Transaction Publishers.

Brantingham, P. L. and Brantingham, P. J. (1995). Criminality of place: crime generators and crime attractors. *European Journal on Criminal Policy and Research, 3*(3): 5–26.

Brantingham, P. L., Brantingham, P. J., and Glässer, U. (2004). Computer simulation in criminal justice research. *Criminal Justice Matters, 58*(1): 18–19.

Brantingham, P. L., Glässer, U., Kinney, B., Singh, K., and Vajihollahi, M. (2005). A computational model for simulating spatial aspects of crime in urban environments. In *International Conference on Systems, Man and Cybernetics*, volume 4, pp. 3667–3674. Waikoloa, HI: IEEE.

Brookson, C., Farrell, G., Mailley, J., Whitehead, S., and Zumerle, D. (2007). ICT product proofing against crime. *ETSI White Paper 5*. Sophia Antipolis, France: European Telecommunications Standards Institute

Brown, D. E. (1998). The regional crime analysis program (ReCAP): a framework for mining data to catch criminals. In *3rd IEEE International Conference on Systems, Man, and Cybernetics (ICSMC)*, pp. 2848–2853. San Diego, CA: IEEE.

Brown, D. E. and Gunderson, L. F. (2001). Using clustering to discover the preferences of computer criminals. *IEEE Transactions on Systems, Man and Cybernetics, Part A: Systems and Humans, 31*(4): 311–318.

Brown, D. E. and Oxford, R. B. (2001). Data mining time series with applications to crime analysis. In *International Conference on Systems, Man and Cybernetics*, volume 3, pp. 1453–1458. Tucson, AZ: IEEE.

Brown, D. E., Gunderson, L. F., and Evans, M. H. (2000). Interactive analysis of computer crimes. *IEEE Computer*, *33*(8): 69–77.

Clarke, R. V. (1990). Deterring obscene phone callers: preliminary results of the New Jersey experience. *Security Journal*, *1*(3): 143–148.

Clayton, R. (2005). Failures in a hybrid content blocking system. In *5th International Workshop on Privacy Enhancing Technologies (PET)*, volume 3856 of LNCS, pp. 78–92. Cavtat, Croatia: Springer.

Coles-Kemp, L. and Theoharidou, M. (2010). Insider threat and information security management. In Probst, C. W., Hunker, J., Gollmann, D., and Bishop, M. (eds) *Insider Threats in Cyber Security*, volume Advances in Information Security 49, pp. 45–71. New York, Dordrecht, Heidelberg, London: Springer.

Craddock, T., Harwood, C. R., Hallinan, J., and Wipat, A. (2008). Opinion: e-science: relieving bottlenecks in large-scale genome analyses. *Nature Reviews Microbiology*, *6*: 948–954.

Eck, J. E. (1998). What do those dots mean? Mapping theories with data. In Weisburd, D. and McEwen, T. (eds) *Crime Mapping and Crime Prevention*, volume Crime Prevention Studies 8, pp. 379–406. Monsey, NY: Criminal Justice Press.

Eck, J. E. and Liu, L. (2008a). Contrasting simulated and empirical experiments in crime prevention. *Journal of Experimental Criminology*, *4*(3): 195–213.

Eck, J. E. and Liu, L. (2008b). Varieties of artificial crime analysis: purpose, structure, and evidence in crime simulations. In Liu, L. and Eck, J. E. (eds) *Artificial Crime Analysis Systems: Using Computer Simulations and Geographic Information Systems*, pp. 413–432. Hershey, PA: Information Science Reference.

Ekblom, P. (2008). Designing products against crime. In Wortley, R. and Mazerolle, L. (eds) *Environmental Criminology and Crime Analysis*, pp. 195–220. Uffculme, UK: Willan Publishing.

Epstein, J. M. (1999). Agent-based computational models and generative social science. *Complexity*, *4*(5): 4160.

Felson, M. and Eckert, M. (2016). *Crime and Everyday Life*, Fifth Edition. London: Sage publishing.

Furnell, S. M., Dowland, P. S., and Sanders, P. W. (1999). Dissecting the hacker manifesto information. *Management & Computer Security*, 7(2): 69–75.

Glässer, U. and Vajihollahi, M. (2008). Computational modeling of criminal activity. In *1st European Conference on Intelligence and Security Informatics (EuroISI)*, volume 5376 of *LNCS*, pp. 39–50. Esbjerg, Denmark: Springer.

Glässer, U., Rastkar, S., and Vajihollahi, M. (2006). Computational modeling and experimental validation of aviation security procedures. In *International Conference on Intelligence and Security Informatics (ISI)*, volume 3975 of *LNCS*, pp. 420–431. San Diego, CA: IEEE.

Glässer, U., Rastkar, S., and Vajihollahi, M. (2008). Modeling and validation of aviation security. In *Intelligence and Security Informatics*, volume 135 of Studies in Computational Intelligence, pp. 337–355. Berlin: Springer.

Gove, W. R., Hughes, M., and Geerken, M. (1985). Are uniform crime reports a valid indicator of the index crimes – an affirmative answer with minor qualifications. *Criminology*, *23*(3): 451–502.

Groff, E. and Mazerolle, L. (2008). Simulated experiments and their potential role in criminology and criminal justice. *Journal of Experimental Criminology*, *4*(3): 187–193.

Gunderson, L. F. (2002). Using data mining and judgment analysis to construct a predictive model of crime. In *7th International Conference on Systems, Man and Cybernetics*, pp. 246–250. Yasmine Hammamet, Tunisia: IEEE.

Gunderson, L. F. and Brown, D. E. (2000). Using a multi-agent model to predict both physical and cyber criminal activity. In *International Conference on Systems, Man, and Cybernetics*, volume 4, pp. 2338–2343. Nashville, TN: IEEE.

Kenneally, E. E. and Claffy, K. (2010). Dialing privacy and utility: a proposed data-sharing framework to advance internet research. *IEEE Security & Privacy*, *8*(4): 31–39.

Kennedy, J. (2009). Digital music report 2009: new business models for a changing environment. IFPI. www.ifpi.org/content/library/DMR2009.pdf.

Langworthy, R. H. (1999). Measuring what matters: proceedings from the Policing Research Institute meetings. Washington, DC: National Institute of Justice, Office of Community Oriented Policing Services (COPS).

Lazer, D., Pentland, A., Adamic, L., Aral, S., Barabási, A.-L., Brewer, D., Christakis, N., Contractor, N., Fowler, J., Gutmann, M., Jebara, T., King, G., Macy, M., Roy, D., and Alstyne, M. V. (2009). Computational social science. *Science*, *323*(5915): 721–723.

Lin, S. and Brown, D. E. (2003). Criminal incident data association using the OLAP technology. In *First NSF/NIJ Symposium on Intelligence and Security Informatics (ISI)*, volume 2665 of *LNCS*, pp. 13–26. Tucson, AZ: Springer.

Lin, S. and Brown, D. E. (2006). An outlier-based data association method for linking criminal incidents. *Decision Support Systems*, *41*(3): 604–615.

Liu, L., Wang, X., Eck, J. E., and Liang, J. (2005). Simulating crime events and crime patterns in RA/CA model. In Wang, F. (ed.) *Geographic Information Systems and Crime Analysis*, pp. 197–231. London: Idea Group.

Milletary, J. (2013). Technical trends in phishing attacks. Technical publications, United States Computer Emergency Readiness Team (US-CERT). www.us-cert.gov/security-publications/technical-trends-phishing-attacks.

Morris, S. (2004a). The future of netcrime now: Part 1 threats and challenges. Online report 62/04. UK Home Office.

Morris, S. (2004b). The future of netcrime now: Part 2 responses. Online report 63/04. UK Home Office.

NCA (2016). Cyber Crime Assessment 2016. UK National Crime Agency. www.nationalcrimeagency.gov.uk/publications/709-cyber-crime-assessment-2016.

Newman, G. R. and Clarke, R. V. (2003). *Superhighway Robbery: Preventing E-Commerce Crime* (Crime Science). Uffculme, UK: Willan Publishing.

Porter, M. D. and Brown, D. E. (2007). Detecting local regions of change in high-dimensional criminal or terrorist point processes. *Computational Statistics and Data Analysis*, *51*(5): 2753–2768.

Reyns, B. W. (2010). A situational crime prevention approach to cyberstalking victimization: Preventive tactics for internet users and online place managers. *Crime Prevention and Community Safety*, *12*(2): 99–118.

Rosoff, H., Cui, J., and John, R. (2014). Behavioral experiments exploring victims' response to cyber-based financial fraud and identity theft scenario simulations. In *10th Symposium On Usable Privacy and Security (SOUPS)*, pp. 175–186. Menlo Park, CA: USENIX Association.

Shepherd, J. and Sivarajasingam, V. (2005). Injury research explains conflicting violence trends. *Injury Prevention*, *11*(6): 324–325.

Short, M. B., Brantingham, P. J., Bertozzi, A. L., and Tita, G. E. (2010). Dissipation and displacement of hotspots in reaction-diffusion models of crime. *Proceedings of the National Academy of Sciences (PNAS)*, *107*(9): 3961–3965.

Thornberry, T. P. and Krohn, M. D. (2000). The self-report method for measuring delinquency and crime. In Duffee, D. (ed.) *Measurement and Analysis of Crime and Justice*, volume 4, pp. 33–84. Washington, DC: National Institute of Justice.

van Schewick, B. and Farber, D. (2009). Point/counterpoint network neutrality nuances. *Communications of the ACM*, *52*(2): 31–37.

von der Heyde, A., Miebach, J., and Kluge, A. (2014). Counterproductive work behaviour in a simulated production context: an exploratory study with personality traits as predictors of safety-related rule violations. *Journal of Ergonomics*, *4*(2): 1000130.

Wang, X., Liu, L., and Eck, J. E. (2008). Crime simulation using GIS and artificial intelligent agents. In Liu, L. and Eck, J. E. (eds) *Artificial Crime Analysis Systems: Using Computer Simulations and Geographic Information Systems*, pp. 209–225. Hershey, PA: Information Science Reference.

Welsh, B. and Farrington, D. (2008). Effects of improved street lighting on crime. *Campbell Systematic Reviews 13*, The Campbell Collaboration. https://campbellcollaboration.org/library/effects-of-improved-street-lighting-on-crime.

Widiger, H., Kubisch, S., Danielis, P., Schulz, J., Timmermann, D., Bahls, T., and Duchow, D. (2008). IPclip: an architecture to restore trust-by-wire in packet-switched networks. In *33rd IEEE Conference on Local Computer Networks (LCN)*, pp. 312–319. Montréal, QC: IEEE.

Willison, R. and Siponen, M. (2009). Overcoming the insider: reducing employee computer crime through situational crime prevention. *Communications of the ACM*, *52*(9): 133–137.

Wittebrood, K. and Junger, M. (2002). Trends in violent crime: a comparison between police statistics and victimization surveys. *Journal of Social Indicators Research*, *59*(2): 153–173.

Xue, Y. and Brown, D. E. (2003). Decision based spatial analysis of crime. In *First NSF/NIJ Symposium on Intelligence and Security Informatics (ISI)*, volume 2665 of *LNCS*, pp. 153–167. Tucson, AZ: Springer.

Xue, Y. and Brown, D. E. (2006). Spatial analysis with preference specification of latent decision makers for criminal event prediction. *Decision Support Systems*, *41*(3): 560–573.

13
Forensic science

Ruth M. Morgan

Introduction: a conceptual overview of forensic reconstruction, detection and disruption

There are many well-established disciplines that are applied to the questions addressed by crime science (Cockbain and Laycock 2017; Wortley et al. 2019 (Section 1, this volume)). Forensic science is one such discipline that traditionally offers a retrospective approach for the reconstruction of crime events, yet increasingly contributes predictive intelligence that can be applied to areas of crime disruption and prevention (Ribaux and Talbot-Wright 2014; Ribaux et al. 2010). This chapter provides an overview of the conceptual constructs and foundation of forensic science, and explores the challenges for the detection and disruption of crime in a manner that works in synergy with the key actors of the criminal justice system. The synergy that exists between forensic science and crime science is drawn out with a focus on the common aim of seeking evidence-based practice to achieve implementable solutions to critical questions.

What is forensic science?

Forensic science is the application of science to criminal and civil investigations and court proceedings, and is situated at the nexus between the domains of law, policy, science, policing and practice (Fraser and Williams 2009). It is therefore widely acknowledged that forensic science is highly complex, particularly because it necessarily operates within a matrix of cultural, economic and political factors that interact with each of these domains in multifaceted ways, at different times and in different places (Morgan 2017a).

Forensic science can be considered as a process that encompasses a number of stages from the crime scene to the court room (Inman and Rudin 2002; Morgan and Bull 2007). Each stage is connected and linked to the outcomes of the previous stage, often in an iterative manner (Figure 13.1), and there is, therefore, significant value in understanding forensic science as a holistic process. By incorporating an understanding of the generation of trace materials, the effective management and processing of a crime scene, the collection of specimens, their analysis, the interpretation of that analysis to produce intelligence (for an investigation) or evidence (for court), it is possible to identify where evidence bases underpin practice, where there may

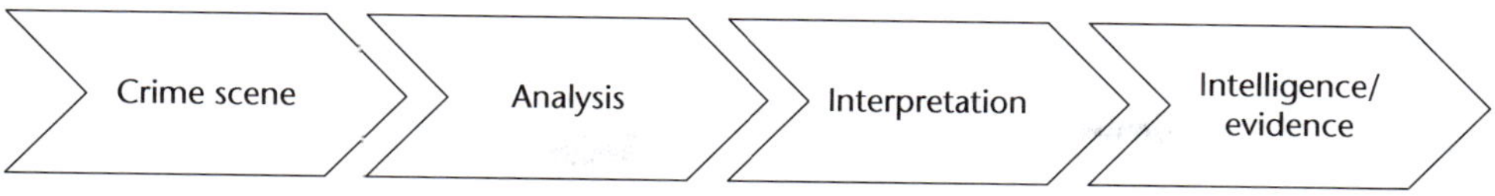

Figure 13.1 The forensic science process

be gaps in our understanding, and ultimately indicate the basis of a forensic reconstruction that is developed.

Traditionally within forensic science there has been a strong focus upon the analysis stage (Figure 13.1). This has been characterised by developing new techniques and applications to enhance our ability to accurately detect and classify materials that have been recovered from a crime scene or a victim, or that may have been transferred to a relevant exhibit such as footwear, clothing and vehicles (for example van Oorschot and Jones (1997) (DNA); Jamieson and Moenssens (2009) (trace); Cadd et al. (2016) (fingerprints)). It is therefore not surprising that the scrutiny levied on forensic science has focussed upon the validation of techniques, standards and quality assurance (National Academy of Sciences 2009, PCAST 2016). However, increasingly it is being recognised that achieving the goal of robust forensic reconstruction (Roux et al. 2012; Morgan 2017a), calls for a focus on the interpretation stage (The Forensic Science Regulator 2015, 2016; The Government Chief Scientific Advisor 2015). Furthermore, the value of incorporating both the physical and social sciences, and tacit and explicit forms of knowledge in each stage of the process has been articulated (Morgan 2017b), alongside the importance of establishing an evidence base that underpins each stage of the process (Morgan et al. 2009; Mnookin et al. 2011).

Within this framework, it is also important to acknowledge that a fundamental premise of forensic science is to take an exclusionary approach (Walls 1968; Morgan and Bull 2007) rather than seeking to establish a 'match' as is often seen in practice and in the published literature (Saks and Koehler 2008). The integrity of the analytical approaches and decision-making that underpins the comparison of specimens is reliant on acknowledging the probabilistic nature of forensic materials in forensic reconstructions. To seek unequivocal 'matches' or to assign the provenance of a material to a particular source to the 'exclusion of all other sources' is highly problematic (Dror 2015; Saks and Koehler 2008). It is of course recognised that different types of forensic material operate within different paradigms when it comes to the interpretation of comparative analyses (Broeders 2006). Perhaps most notably, there is necessarily a different approach to the interpretation and presentation of DNA analysis in comparison to other forms of forensic material as the comparison of profiles can be interpreted in the context of population databases of allele frequencies (Steele and Balding 2014). However, it still holds that across all forms of forensic evidence, an exclusionary approach is a foundational principle for robust and transparent forensic reconstructions. This is particularly the case given the sometimes competing requirements of the intersecting domains of science, law, policy and policing that must be considered in forensic science.

How is a holistic forensic science approach distinctive and necessary?

It is well understood that forensic science takes a multidisciplinary approach drawing on well-established methods and theory from other disciplines. However, it is also increasingly recognised that forensic science is a developing discipline that is now emerging as a truly interdisciplinary field in its own right. Forensic science has distinctive and bespoke research methods, concepts, theory, and a growing body of primary (as opposed to applied) literature (Margot 2011a, 2011b; Roux et al. 2015; Morgan 2017b). Therefore, forensic science is an important discipline that can provide an additional perspective to addressing significant questions in crime science that concern the detection of crime.

Taking a holistic approach that incorporates an appreciation of the different domains and their actors, and the whole process from crime scene to court is important (Morgan 2017b). This approach has significant value in enabling context sensitive forensic reconstructions to be developed, whilst maintaining scientific robustness, and adhering to generalisable theoretical underpinnings. For example, interpreting the significance of trace particles on a suspect requires both the ability to accurately classify and establish how distinctive those particles are, but also to understand under what conditions they may have been transferred to the suspect in the specific case in question. Reconstructions that are based on robust and reliable evidence bases yet are sensitive to the individual context of each case is a lofty goal, but one that forensic science can contribute to when approached in a holistic manner.

In addition, by incorporating an understanding of the environment and society as well as the situational aspects of crime, the scope of forensic science is growing in ways that can also contribute to the prediction, disruption and ultimately the prevention of crimes. For example, the ability to detect certain chemicals in the wastewater system (in combination with an understanding of water flow rates and pipe matrices) can lead to the identification of the source of those chemicals (Rapp-Wright et al. 2017), which may assist in directing surveillance to particular dwellings and thereby the disruption of homemade bomb making activities.

The forensic science process and conceptual approach

The forensic science process: crime scene to court

As set out in Figure 13.1, the forensic process addresses each stage from crime scene to court. This is a connected approach, recognising that the questions asked and the activities that take place at the crime scene will influence what materials are collected, how those specimens are analysed in the laboratory, what methods are used to infer the meaning of the results of that analysis, and the approach to presenting those findings as intelligence and/or evidence. This process, however, does not occur in isolation and needs to be considered in the context of the different types of knowledge that are embedded in that process. These different forms of knowledge include the experience and expertise of the different actors at each stage; the type of forensic material that is present and its interaction with other trace materials pertinent to the case; and the extent to which that material can be used to infer source and/or activities that are relevant to the forensic reconstruction. It is important to recognise that being aware of the holistic nature of this process impacts upon the articulation of the most relevant questions that need to be answered at the outset (usually the crime scene). This in turn will influence the types of questions asked of forensic materials at the analysis and interpretation stages, which will impact the methods used to analyse, classify and interpret forensic samples. Account also needs to be taken of the likely eventual use of that analysis and interpretation, whether it be intelligence and/or evidence. Thus, considering each of the stages of the forensic process in a holistic and interconnected manner will assist in the formulation of the most effective questions to be addressed and approaches to take at each stage to achieve a robust and accurate reconstruction.

The forensic science conceptual approach

The FoRTE model (Morgan 2017a) seeks to capture this process and set it in the context of a forensic reconstruction as presented in Figure 13.2.

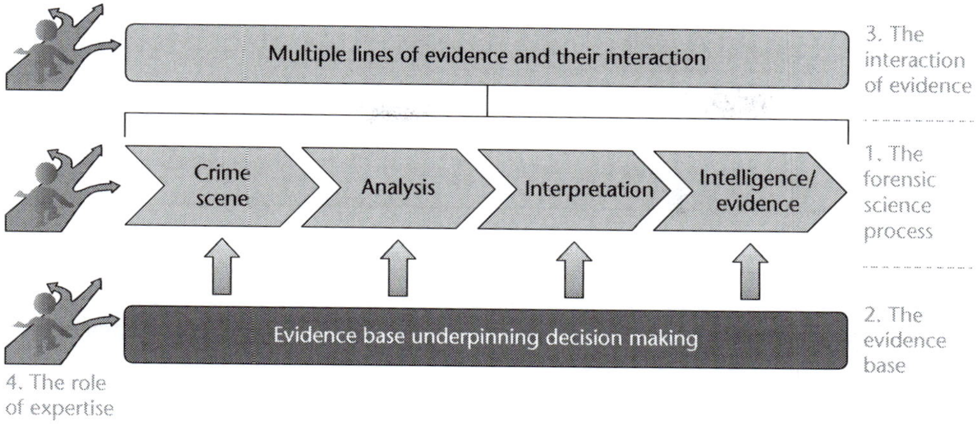

Figure 13.2 A conceptual model of forensic reconstruction and the role of trace evidence (FoRTE) (Morgan 2017a)

The forensic-science process is at the heart of the model (component 1) with three further integral components that are required for accurate reconstructions. An evidence base (component 2) is required to underpin each stage of the forensic-science process. The form that this evidence base takes will be broad, incorporating both the established knowledge bases from so-called 'parent' disciplines (such as fluid mechanics (blood pattern analysis) or genetics (DNA)), and from specifically 'forensic' evidence bases that can address pertinent factors to the forensic case in question (such as the approach outlined in Farmer et al. 2015). In addition, the evidence base needs to incorporate more generalisable factors that include trace evidence dynamics (Morgan et al. 2018a), and human decision-making (Morgan et al. 2018b). After the collection, analysis and interpretation of the intelligence and/or evidence, it is important to address the multiple lines of intelligence and/or evidence that have been identified. Understanding the degree to which these different lines of intelligence and/or evidence interact with each other will enable a more robust, evidence-based understanding of what has happened prior to, during and after a crime event (component 3). A crucial consideration is then the role of expertise (knowledge and skill) in each of these three component parts to ensure that both empirical evidence bases and expertise are incorporated within each component (Morgan 2017a) and to be able to achieve the scientific 'endeavour' of a forensic reconstruction (Roux et al. 2012) that is required. This is a contentious premise (see R. v. Weller; Dror 2015; Casey et al. 2016; and Meakin and Jamieson 2016). However, it has been argued that only with this form of nuanced approach, one that is underpinned by both empirical evidence bases and expertise (necessarily incorporating experience), that transparent, robust and reproducible forensic reconstructions can be delivered that are sensitive to the context of each individual case (Smit et al. 2016, Morgan 2017a).

For forensic science to be able to achieve these goals, it is recognised that the growing body of published literature is essential. The forensic science literature is broadly divided into research papers that address four main themes. First there are the studies that seek to develop new technologies, or harness existing analytical technologies for forensic applications (such as Bailey et al. 2012; Newell et al. 2012; NicDaeid et al. 2011; Fairley et al. 2012; Cadd et al. 2016; van Dam et al. 2016) reflecting the traditional focus on the 'analysis' stage of the forensic process. Second, there are the papers that document particular case examples where a particular form of trace material was utilised to provide intelligence or evidence for an investigation (such as Ruffell and Murphy 2011; Lepot et al. 2017). These studies predominantly draw significantly on the expertise that was learnt during the specific case in question, and seek to build a body of knowledge that is based on experience to inform future practice. These two themes arguably represent the majority of published findings within forensic science at the turn of the 21st century. Third, and generally since 2005, there has been increasing engagement with interpreting trace materials and assessing the weight of that evidence in a given context (e.g. Saks and Koehler 2008; Charlton et al. 2010; Nakhaeizadeh et al. 2014; Smit et al. 2016; Dror 2017). However, it is only latterly that there has been a growing body of research of experimental work designed to complement and develop existing practice and develop a body of knowledge that builds theory within the discipline (e.g. Morgan et al. 2009; French and Morgan 2015; Palmer et al. 2017). All these four themes of research are necessary for the establishment of evidence bases to underpin forensic science and ensure that both evidence dynamics and the human factors in interpreting findings, are appropriately understood and incorporated into the inferences and conclusions that are drawn (components 2, 3 and 4 in Figure 13.2).

There are three important characteristics of research within the forensic-science discipline that are integral to developing the holistic approach to forensic science as outlined in Figure 13.2; research that is empirical, casework-informed and mindful of implementation (Morgan 2017a). First, whilst case studies are important and can offer helpful insights, empirical studies have significant value in acting as a foundation for underpinning 'evidence-based' robust processing, management and analysis practices, as well as establishing clear justifications for the approaches taken in the interpretation and presentation stages (Figure 13.1). Second, the value of research being informed by casework is critical to ensure that challenges faced in the practice of forensic science are being addressed at the outset. Third, it is important that the research design is tailored around the context of forensic science in practice, in a manner that looks forward to the implementation of the findings in casework. It is important to take into consideration the key challenges in the practice of forensic, such as the cost of and time for analysis and interpretation activities when crafting the aims and objectives of a piece of research. For example, research that addresses the development of a new approach to distinguish between two forensic samples is important and valid research. If that research also seeks to reduce sample preparation and analysis time and use equipment that is readily available in forensic laboratories, it clearly has significant added value for the discipline (see McCulloch et al. 2017).

Where are the challenges?

Forensic science faces clear challenges. These challenges are a result of the discipline seeking to address the questions posed by multiple domains (including science, law, policy and policing) each of which has different aims and methods of knowledge creation and acquisition (Morgan 2017a).

Science and the law

The National Academy of Sciences report (2009) highlighted significant issues concerning the scientific validity of forensic-science methods and techniques. There have been a number of reports published since (such as the Law Commission report on the admissibility of expert witness testimony (Law Commission 2011)), many of which have focussed on the issue concerning the 'dearth of peer reviewed published studies, establishing the scientific bases and validity of many forensic methods' (National Academy of Sciences 2009: 8). A particular concern that has been highlighted is the lack of empirical evidence to underpin the interpretation of forensic evidence, which has been highlighted in the UK Government Chief Scientific Advisor annual report (2015), The Forensic Science Regulator reports (2015 and 2016) and the publication by the USA President's Council of Advisors on Science and Technology (2016). A common theme throughout these reports concerns the ways in which forensic-science evidence can and should be interpreted and the basis on which different forensic-science fields are considered to be 'valid'. This is a complicated issue particularly due to the different requirements of the sciences and the law. In a court of law, science enters a world that has different requirements (Jasonoff 2006). There is an interplay between the scientific and law communities who are involved in forming the science that is being presented to assist a court for the purpose of legal-decision-making (Jasonoff 1998; Lynch 2004; Lawless 2016). As such, the different epistemological foundations of science and the law are brought together in forensic science to shape forensic knowledge when it enters the courtroom (Edmond 2001) in a manner that is necessarily adjusted for different cases (Lawless 2016).

Therefore, a transition occurs when scientific observations become legal evidence. This stems from the value science puts on findings contributing to general validity in comparison to the legal domain, where facts need to be legally relevant to a specific case. The issue of timescale is also critical, with the courts requiring relatively quick answers from scientists that are relevant to the case in question, in comparison to the world of science where there is time for iteration, validation, replication and development of theory. The court requires 'certainty' in a manner that is juxtaposed with the capacity for speculation and testing within the sciences. Indeed, the value and significance of science in the court is usually ultimately judged by non-scientists in the form of a jury or members of the judiciary, which stands in contrast to the peer-review process within the sciences (Lynch and Jasanoff 1998, Jasanoff 2005).

Forensic science, therefore, sits at the interface between two contrasting domains, which leads to forensic-science knowledge being produced and applied in contexts that have different requirements, motivations and goals (Cole 2013, Morgan 2017b). This certainly leads to challenges for both scientists and those involved in the court processes (Edmond et al. 2016). However, acknowledging this context opens up huge opportunities for gaps in our understanding to be identified, research to be undertaken to address those gaps, and ultimately for the science to be formed and developed in a manner that enables the findings to be more able to assist a court and play a part in the justice system.

Knowledge and evidence bases

A key challenge faced by forensic science is establishing the validity of the 'science' in this criminal justice context as outlined in the section 'Science and the law'. It has been asserted that for trial purposes it is not possible to separate science evidence that is presented and the testimony of forensic experts (Kiely 2006). This raises a significant challenge for forensic science in two ways. First in terms of the foundation upon which expert testimony is based (introduced in the section 'The forensic science conceptual approach') and, second, the degree to which that science is demonstrably based upon a knowledge base that is widely accepted (such as foundational principles and theory from the disciplines of, for example, genetics, geoscience, or physics), and an evidence base that provides an empirical foundation that informs practice, methods and interpretation of findings in a specifically forensic context (Morgan et al. 2009). It is important to appreciate the differences between the general theories that have been tested, validated and established in the contributing disciplines, and the specifically forensic evidence base that is needed to underpin crime-scene management, and forensic sample identification, collection, analysis, interpretation and presentation. Whilst there is little disagreement around the validity of such knowledge bases, there has been considerable discussion around the importance and need for specifically forensic evidence bases (Mnookin 2011; Margot 2011b; Roux et al. 2012; Morgan 2017a, b). This issue of established empirical data that can act as an evidence base for the whole forensic-science process (Figure 13.2) has been highlighted by the UK Forensic Science Regulator (2015, 2016) as one of the 'highest priorities' to increase the quality of forensic science to ensure that forensic reconstructions are accurate, robust, transparent and reliable. There is a growing body of literature that seeks to address these issues as set out in Morgan et al. (2018a, 2018b) by producing data that can underpin the interpretation of forensic samples. This is not however, the entire issue. A further challenge lies in the fact that every case is different. What is a clear and testable principle in a laboratory setting where variables are controlled and extraneous variables limited, can face complications when it is applied to a case in the 'real' world where the number of unknowns can be large and a priori knowledge is often not available. Therefore, effective forensic reconstructions require an approach that can be sensitive to the context of each case. There is thus a need to consider the best way of developing problem-solving reconstruction approaches that incorporate both empirical evidence bases and expertise to account for this.

A consideration of the different forms of knowledge that are required for forensic reconstructions is helpful in this endeavour, as outlined in Morgan (2017b). It is argued that there is a need to generate new knowledge that is context sensitive (applicable to a particular case), at the same time as being sufficiently generalisable (building general scientific theory). To achieve this, evidence bases are needed that can act as a foundation upon which inferences can be drawn, and that interact with the different empirical evidence bases underpinning each stage of the forensic process (which offer the knowns or clear unknowns) and the evidence bases created from expertise (which will be made up of both explicit (often taught) and tacit (developed over time) attributes that include technical knowledge, skills, experience and routines). Thus, both empirical evidence and expertise must be considered to be integral attributes of the scientific endeavour of forensic reconstruction (Morgan 2017b). It is important to be clear about the balance between empirical evidence and expertise in a given situation. This will enable a careful and transparent approach to be taken with regard to the way inferences can be made and presented to both investigators (as intelligence) or the courts (as evidence). This form of clarity is also clearly valuable when assigning significance and/or weight to specific findings.

An additional challenge lies in the intersecting domains that contribute to forensic science. These different domains, science, law/policy, policing/forensic services are made up of different types of institutions. Each of these institutions has contrasting infrastructures, dominant knowledge bases, types of expertise, and approaches to generating, acquiring and retaining knowledge. It is therefore important to incorporate an understanding of these different approaches to knowledge production and how different institutions seek to interact with one another in the collective endeavour of providing robust forensic reconstructions required by forensic science (Morgan 2017b). For example, within the policing/forensic services domain there is a requirement to develop standard operating procedures for a chain of custody procedures of exhibits that are collected from a crime scene, and for any analytical test used to classify the components of a forensic specimen. This can be achieved through the codification of explicit knowledge that can be consistently applied and learnt through formal study. In contrast within the science domain, the approach taken to collect a trace sample from an item of footwear or examine a fingermark has been observed to vary from examiner to examiner based on the context of the case, and the experience and training of the scientist (Doak and Assimakopoulos 2007; Earwaker et al. 2015). This is arguably due to the need to draw on expertise in order to be sensitive to a specific case context so that it is possible to respond to the unique interplay of factors in a specific case to enable a 'problem-solving' approach (Roux et al. 2012).

Therefore, any consideration of the validity of forensic science must take into account the requirements and infrastructures of the intersecting domains of science, law/policy, policing/forensic services, and also the need for evidence bases that incorporate different forms of knowledge and can incorporate both empirical data and expertise. Such considerations have the potential to go a long way towards addressing what has been considered the 'false dichotomy' between experience and empirical evidence bases (Morgan 2017b). Both forms of knowledge are required in forensic science. However, how this synergy is achieved is still a challenging issue.

Implementation

Effectively incorporating both empirical data and expertise in the evidence bases used to inform practice at each stage of the forensic-science process (Figure 13.2) is a further challenge to forensic science. This will be contingent on the degree to which there is an appreciation of the different knowledge institutions (as outlined in the section 'Knowledge and evidence bases'), and their complementary approaches to knowledge creation. In order to produce these evidence bases, the antecedent research needs to be informed by casework so that the research questions are addressing 'real world' problems. This requires collaboration between actors in the science and practice domains so that the nuances of these 'problems' can be fully explored and research questions can be formed that are 'fit for purpose'. This is a critical step. It is common for 'solutions' to be identified before a full consideration of the 'problem' has been undertaken. For example, it could be suggested that mobile analysis technology is needed to address the issue of generating quicker 'real-time' intelligence from a crime scene. Exploring the issue further, however, opens up alternative avenues that may reveal that the issue in a particular case or type of cases is more about triaging and identifying the most profitable samples that will ultimately provide the strongest intelligence that can form the basis of building an admissible case.

It is then important that research questions are framed and methods developed that address the problem that has been identified. This needs to be carried out in a way that is mindful of the constraints that exist within the practice and delivery of forensic science. These will be primarily issues of cost and time. For example, it can be argued that developing a new technique to discriminate between comparator forensic samples has significant value in adding to the toolkit of the forensic scientist and in assisting the inferences made about the provenance of a trace recovered from a vehicle. It is however, important to do this while mindful of the analytical techniques available in most forensic service laboratories and how long it takes to prepare and analyse the sample. It is clear that an approach that can be developed that uses existing machinery, and that reduces current preparation and/or analysis time will have significant value (for example McCulloch et al. 2016). An approach that requires a new (expensive) machine or that requires long preparation or analysis time is unlikely to have impact in the 'real world'. However, in seeking to address 'real world' problems it is important to acknowledge that research is an iterative process and the development of new capabilities is rarely achieved in one step. Research that addresses each stage of development must be valued. There will be some research projects that can produce findings that can be utilised to address 'real world' problems within months. There will be others that lay the foundation for critical breakthroughs, but their impact is unlikely to be realised for a number of years. Both types of research are critical and need to be valued.

Finally, the outputs of research need to be 'fit for purpose' and be developed in a way that enables implementation in the 'real world'. For example, the development of approaches to identify explosive materials and their provenance has significant value in assisting surveillance and potentially the disruption of activities that may lead to criminal acts. However, such an approach must be deployable in a way that adheres to privacy laws; for example, developing approaches where sampling can occur on public property as outlined by Rapp-Wright et al. (2017).

Context

Challenges also arise as a result of the context within which forensic science is situated in terms of the cultural, economic and political factors that influence each domain that intersects with forensic science (as outlined in the section 'What is forensic science?'). The influence of these factors in the UK on the practice of forensic science, as outlined by Lawless (2010) and Ludwig (2016), has been a source of much contention, particularly in terms of the 'marketization' of forensic science (Lawless 2010) and the focus on demonstrating the 'value' of forensic service to the police and criminal justice system (Ludwig 2016) that has occurred in the UK in recent years. While there have been different sides presented in these debates (Silverman 2011; Maguire et al. 2012; Roux et al. 2012) it is clear that forensic science is inextricably linked to the operational context. Whilst there have been calls for research to underpin the practice of forensic science through the creation and development of appropriate evidence bases (Mnookin et al. 2011; Morgan 2009), there remains a chronic lack of funding available for such research. There are understandable reasons why a commoditised industry struggles to carry out and publish its research so that it is publicly available, but there are warning signs that this situation needs to be addressed (Smit et al. 2017). It is one thing to espouse the importance of industry and academic partnerships to address this need for research, it is quite another to ensure that it is enabled. There have been a number of excellent initiatives in the UK, including the Knowledge Transfer Network Special Interest Group that was set up to foster collaboration between industry and academia, but the impact and value of such endeavours are limited without sufficient funding to support and nurture collaborations to maturity. Whilst there have been a few isolated cases of funding for forensic science-related research these calls have predominantly been focussed on bringing to market technological solutions to support the crime scene and analysis phases of the forensic-science process. The effective loss of dedicated funding for forensic science within the UK Research Councils has also increased the challenge for researchers to carry out the research that is needed that addresses the full spectrum of forensic science. Market forces may be powerful, but it is clear that forensic science research needs to be prioritised and enabled. This will require a funding stream at the national level to ensure that research is undertaken that addresses the holistic remit of forensic science to ensure that it is equipped to innovate and develop implementable, robust and truly valuable methods and approaches in a manner that ensures that this discipline can continue to assist the criminal justice system.

What do we need going forward?

This chapter has outlined the value of considering forensic science as a holistic process, the importance of evidence bases to underpin each part of that process, and the significance of incorporating both empirical data and expertise (encompassing explicit and tacit forms of knowledge) into both those evidence bases and the decision-making that is integral to the production of forensic reconstructions. It has been acknowledged that the different institutions within the domains of science, law/policy, policing/forensic services generate and accumulate knowledge in different ways and that this diversity impacts the way that the different actors within those domains interact with one another with a concomitant impact on forensic science (Morgan 2017b). In order to harness the value of forensic science as a multifaceted discipline in crime detection and prevention applications, the creation of channels that enable the ultimate aim of transparent, reproducible and accurate forensic reconstructions are necessary. These channels should enable the interaction between actors and domains, ensure the impact of research in practice, assure access to research, and safeguard quality (Morgan 2017b).

Interaction

For effective interaction between the different actors who are integral to the delivery and development of forensic science, opportunities need to be created and a common language established (Howes 2015). Solutions need to be worked out in a healthy environment of discussion, debate, and even disagreement, to arrive at a clear articulation of the problem to be addressed and of the characteristics of a successful solution that needs to be produced (Morgan 2017b). Such an approach has been highly successful in crime science where the development of crime prevention approaches has been realised in collaboration with a wide range of actors from the police, policy, local authority, industry and research domains (for example Laycock 2004; Wortley and Smallbone 2006; Bullock et al. 2010; Clarke 2012; Johnson et al. 2012; Farrell et al. 2014). There is significant potential for forensic science to increasingly operate within such a multidisciplinary setting, particularly where there is a collective commitment to address the most pressing issues of establishing validity, addressing evidence bases in a holistic manner, and ensuring research is crafted for implementation.

Impact

To achieve effective impact of the innovation created in forensic science, the most salient questions need to be agreed and research designed with implementation in mind at both institutional and individual levels. At the institutional level we need to foster infrastructures that reward innovation and facilitate the development of both explicit knowledge-based standards and tacit knowledge expertise. At the individual level, researchers, professionals (investigators, forensic scientists, lawyers and the judiciary), and policymakers need to have open lines of communication and opportunities to interact in meaningful and ongoing ways so that research addresses the most germane questions in creative and ultimately impactful ways (Morgan 2017b). This will require an investment in establishing a culture that is sensitive to the drivers and requirements of the different actors. Crime science has developed in a manner that has promoted and enabled this kind of approach in the field of crime prevention by fostering collaboration between key actors (Wortley and Townsley 2016). There is therefore significant promise that the early steps in forensic science on this path have the potential to develop and provide significant value and innovation in crime detection and disruption.

Access

An area where crime science has invested is that of enabling access to research for all stakeholders. Access to research findings is an issue on the basis of cost and format. It is appropriate for research findings to be published in internationally peer-reviewed journals; indeed that level of scrutiny and academic rigour is essential for a discipline to establish foundational bodies of theory and build and contribute to the sum of knowledge. However, this format can limit access for stakeholders not within the research community. Access is restricted to those with a subscription (institutional or personal) or those willing to pay the financial fee for access. Access is also restricted by the format and language used in the presentation of research findings for the academic audience that can make it less easy to see how a finding may be relevant in practice or for future policymaking. Creating platforms that can secure intellectual property and commercial sensitivity but also ensure that new knowledge is shared in a truly accessible way that will a) foster multi-domain engagement that will inform future research and b) ultimately increase the impact forensic science can have in the criminal justice system (Morgan 2017b).

Quality

Quality needs to be a primary concern of forensic science, especially in the light of the critical scrutiny given to quality and validity of forensic science (National Academy of Sciences 2009, PCAST 2016). As such, quality assessment and validation approaches are crucial to setting standards for processes and procedures integral to the delivery of forensic science. It is, however, important that different forms of knowledge that are integral to successful forensic science are acknowledged. The approach to establish the quality standard of a laboratory procedure or the accuracy of a particular analytical technique must necessarily be different to any approach taken to establish the quality of problem-solving approaches that are required in parts of the forensic science process. This is in part due to the different types of knowledge that are used in, for example, a standard procedure in a laboratory setting (such as a method for analysing a substance with a specific analytical technique) in comparison to the knowledge required in the problem-solving approaches that require sensitivity to the specific and variable context of a case (such as the best approach in a given situation to recover particulate material from an item of clothing). In the assessment of the high quality that is required within forensic science, an approach that recognises the importance and role within holistic forensic reconstruction of explicit and tacit forms of knowledge is essential (Morgan 2017b). There are significant drives towards the development of accreditation structures in forensic science and it is no surprise that this is a highly contentious issue and one where an 'easy fix' is not apparent. However, given the holistic approach outlined in this chapter for forensic reconstruction, there appears to be value and promise in seeking to develop accreditation approaches that can acknowledge the importance and synergy of both tacit and explicit forms of knowledge within high-quality forensic science (Morgan 2017b).

Conclusion

Taking a holistic approach to forensic science that incorporates all parts of the forensic-science process in a collaborative manner between different actors will enable forensic science to provide good science that answers the most pressing questions to achieve implementable solutions. The interpretation of evidence in forensic science is a critical and integral, but often overlooked, stage. It is important that the value of robust, transparent and reproducible interpretation as a core part of forensic science is recognised and supported by all the key stakeholders.

This chapter has set out core concepts of forensic science and explored a number of the challenges that the discipline faces to achieve forensic reconstructions that can assist in the detection and potentially the disruption of crime events. The contribution that forensic science makes to crime science lies in the common commitment to evidence-based practice, and the aims of addressing crime in a multidisciplinary manner that incorporates the key actors and stakeholders to ensure the identification and creation of implementable and effective solutions.

References

Bailey, M. J., Morgan, R. M., Comini, P., Calusi, S., and Bull, P. A. (2012) An evaluation of particle induced X-ray emission and particle induced gamma ray emission of quartz grains for forensic trace sediment analysis. *Analytical Chemistry, 84*: 2260–2267.

Broeders, A. P. A. (2006) Of earprints, fingerprints, scent dogs, cot deaths and cognitive contamination – a brief look at the present state of play in the forensic arena. *Forensic Science International, 159*: 148–157.

Bullock, K., Clarke, R.V., and Tilley, N. (2010) *Situational Prevention of Organized Crimes*. Cullompton, UK: Willan Publishing.

Cadd, S., Li, B., Beveridge, P., O'Hare, W. T., Campbell, A., and Islam, M. (2016) A comparison of visible wavelength reflectance hyperspectral imaging and Acid Black 1 for the detection and identification of blood stained fingerprints. *Science & Justice; 55*(4): 247–255.

Casey, D. Clayson, N. Jones, S. Lewis, J. Boyce, M. Fraser, I. Kennedy, F., and Alexander, K. (2016) Response to Meakin and Jamieson DNA transfer: review and implications for casework. *Forensic Science International, 21*: 117–118.

Charlton, D., Fraser-Mackenzie, P., and Dror, I. E. (2010) Emotional experiences and motivating factors associated with fingerprint analysis. *Journal of Forensic Sciences, 55*(2): 385–393.

Clarke, R. V. (2012) Opportunity makes the thief. Really? And so what? *Crime Science, 1*(1): 1–9.

Cockbain, E. and Laycock, G. (2017) Crime Science. *Oxford Research Encyclopedia of Criminology*. Retrieved 21 Aug. 2017, from http://criminology.oxfordre.com/view/10.1093/acrefore/9780190264079.001.0001/acrefore-9780190264079-e-4.

Cole, S. A. (2013) Forensic culture as epistemic culture: the sociology of forensic science. *Studies in the History and Philosophy of Science C: Biological and Biomedical Sciences, 44*(1): 36–46.

Doak, S. W. and Assimakopoulos, D. (2007) How do forensic scientists learn to become competent in casework reporting in practice: a theoretical and empirical approach. *Forensic Science International, 167*(2–3): 201–206.

Dror, I. E. (2015) Cognitive neuroscience in forensic science: understanding and utilizing the human element. *Philosophical Transactions of the Royal Society B, 370*: 20140255.

Dror, I. E. (2017) Human expert performance in forensic decision making: seven different sources of bias. *Australian Journal of Forensic Sciences, 49*(5): 541–547.

Earwaker, E., Morgan, R. M., Harris, A. J. L., and Hall, L. (2015) Fingermark submission decision making within a UK fingerprint laboratory: do experts get the marks they need? *Sci & Justice, 55*(4): 239–247.

Edmond, G. (2001) The law-set: the legal-scientific production of medical propriety. *Science, Technology and Human Values, 26*(2): 191–226.

Edmond, G., Found, B., Martire, K., Ballantyne, K., Hamer, D., Searston, R., Thompson, M., Cunliffe, E., Kemp, R., San Roque, M., Tangen, J., Dioso-Villa, R., Ligertwood, A., Hibbert, D., White, D., Ribeiro, G., Porter, G., Towler A., and Roberts A. (2016) Model forensic science. *Australian Journal of Forensic Sciences, 4*(5): 496–537.

Fairley, C., Bleay, S. M., Sears, V. G., and NicDaeid, N. (2012) A comparison of multi-metal deposition processes utilising gold nanoparticles and an evaluation of their application to 'low yield' surfaces for fingermark development *Forensic Science International, 217*(1–3): 5–18.

Farmer, N., Ruffell, A., Meier-Augenstein, W., Meneely, J., and Kalin, R.M. (2015) Forensic analysis of wooden safety matches - a case study, *Science and Justice, 47*: 88–98.

Farrell, G., Tilley, N., and Tseloni, A. (2014) Why the crime drop? Why crime rates fall and why they don't. *Crime and Justice: A Review of Research 43*: 421–490.

Forensic Science Regulator (2015) Annual report. Available at www.gov.uk/government/uploads/system/uploads/attachment_data/file/482248/2015_FSR_Annual_Report_v1_0_final.pdf.

Forensic Science Regulator (2016) Annual report. Available at www.gov.uk/government/uploads/system/uploads/attachment_data/file/581653/FSR_Annual_Report_v1.0.pdf.

Fraser, J. and Williams, R. (2009) *Handbook of Forensic Science*. Cullompton, UK: Willan Publishing.

French, J. and Morgan, R. M. (2015) An experimental investigation of the indirect transfer and deposition of gunshot residue: further studies carried out with SEM-EDX analysis. *Forensic Science International, 247*: 14–17.

Government Chief Scientific Advisor (2015) Forensic science and beyond: authenticity, provenance and assurance, evidence and case studies. Available at: www.gov.uk/government/publications/forensic-science-and-beyond.

Howes, L. M. (2015) The communication of forensic science in the criminal justice system: A review of theory and proposed directions for research. *Science & Justice, 55*(2): 145–154.

Inman, K. and Rudin, N. (2002) The origin of evidence. *Forensic Science International, 126*(1): 11–16.
Jamieson, A. and Moenssens, A. A. (2009) (eds) *Encyclopedia of Forensic Science*. Hoboken, NJ: Wiley-Blackwell
Jasanoff, S. (1998) The eye of everyman: witnessing DNA in the Simpson trial. *Social Studies of Science, 28*(5–6): 713–740.
Jasanoff, S. (2005) Law's knowledge: science for justice in legal settings. *American Journal of Public Health, 95*(Supplement 1): S49–S58.
Jasanoff, S. (2006) Just evidence: the limits of science in the legal process. *Journal of Law, Medicine and Ethics, 34*(2): 328–341.
Johnson, S. D., Guerette, R. T., and Bowers, K. J. (2012) Crime displacement and diffusion of benefits. *The Oxford Handbook of Crime Prevention* (p. 337). Oxford: Oxford University Press.
Kiely, T. F. (2006) *Forensic Evidence: Science and the Criminal Law* (Second Edition). Boca Raton, FL: CRC Press.
Law Commission (2011) The forty-fifth annual report of the Law Commission. London: Law Commission.
Lawless, C. (2010) *A Curious Reconstruction? The Shaping of 'Marketized' Forensic Science*. London: Centre for Analysis of Risk and Regulation, London School of Economics and Political Science.
Lawless, C. (2016) *Forensic Science: A Sociological Introduction*. Abingdon, UK: Routledge.
Laycock, G. K. (2004) The UK car theft index: an example of government leverage. In M. G. Maxfield, and R. V. G. Clarke (2004) *Understanding and Preventing Car Theft* (Vol. 17). Monsey, NJ: Criminal Justice Press.
Lepot, L., Vanden Driessche, T., Lunstroot, K., Barret, A., Gason, F., and De Wael K (2017) Extraneous fibre traces brought by river water – a case study. *Science and Justice, 57*: 53–57.
Ludwig, A. (2016) E 'value' ating Forensic Science. *Forensic Science Policy & Management: An International Journal*, 7(3–4).
Lynch, M. (2004) Circumscribing expertise: membership categories in courtroom testimony. In S. Jasanoff (ed.) *States of Knowledge: The Co-Production of Science and Social Order* (pp. 161–180). London and New York: Routledge.
Lynch, M. and Jasanoff, S. (1998) Contested identities: science, law and forensic practice. *Social Studies of Science, 28*(5/6): 675–686.
Maguire, C., Houck, M. M., Williams, R., and Speaker, P. J. (2012) Efficiency and the cost-effective delivery of forensic science services: insourcing, outsourcing, and privatization. *Forensic Science Policy and Management: An International Journal, 3*(2): 62–69.
Margot, P. (2011a) Forensic science on trial – what is the law of the land? *Australian Journal of Forensic Sciences, 43*(2–3): 89–103.
Margot, P. (2011b) Commentary on the need for a research culture in the forensic sciences. *UCLA Law Review, 795*.
McCulloch, G., Bull, P. A., and Morgan, R. M. (2016) High performance liquid chromatography as a valuable tool for geoforensic soil analysis. *Australian Journal of Forensic Science*. DOI: 10.1080/00450618.2016.1194474.
Meakin, G. E. and Jamieson, A. (2016) A response to a response to Meakin and Jamieson DNA transfer: review and implications for casework. *Forensic Science International Genetics, 22*: e5–e6.
Mnookin, J. L., Cole, S. A., Dror, I. E., Fisher, B., Houck, M. M., Inman, K., Kaye, D. H., Koehler, J. J., Langenburg, G., Risenger, D. M., Rudin, N., Siegel, J., and Stoney, D. A. (2011) The need for a research culture in the forensic science. *UCLA Law Review, 725*: 725–779.
Morgan, R. M. (2017a) Conceptualising forensic science and forensic reconstruction; Part I: a conceptual model. *Science and Justice, 57*(6): 455–459.
Morgan, R. M. (2017b) Conceptualising forensic science and forensic reconstruction; Part II: the critical interaction between research, policy/law and practice. *Science and Justice, 57*(6): 460–467.
Morgan, R. M. and Bull, P. A. (2007) The philosophy, nature and practice of forensic sediment analysis. *Progress in Physical Geography, 31*(1): 43–58.
Morgan, R. M., French, J. C., and Meakin, G. E. (2019) Understanding forensic trace evidence. In R. Wortley, A. Sidebottom, G. Laycock, and N. Tilley (eds), *Handbook of Crime Science*. Abingdon, UK: Routledge.
Morgan, R. M., Nakhaeizadeh, S., Earwaker, H., Rando, C., Harris, A. J. L., and Dror, I. (2019) Interpretation of evidence (cognitive decision making under uncertainty at every step of the forensic science process). In R. Wortley, A. Sidebottom, G. Laycock, and N. Tilley (eds), *Handbook of Crime Science*. Abingdon, UK: Routledge.
Morgan, R. M., Cohen, J., McGookin, I., Murly-Gotto, J., O Connor, R., Muress, S., Freudiger-Bonzon, J., and Bull, P. A. (2009) The relevance of the evolution of experimental studies for the interpretation and evaluation of some trace physical evidence. *Science and Justice, 49*: 277–285.

Nakhaeizadeh, S., Dror, I. E., and Morgan, R. M. (2014) Cognitive bias in forensic anthropology: visual assessments of skeletal remains is susceptible to confirmation bias. *Science and Justice*, *54*(3): 208–214.
National Academy of Sciences (NAS) (2009) Strengthening forensic science in the United States: a path forward. Washington, DC: National Academy of Sciences.
Newell, A. J., Morgan, R.M., Bull, P. A., Griffin, L. D., and Graham, G. (2012) Automated texture recognition of quartz sand grains for forensic analysis for forensic applications. *Journal of Forensic Sciences*, *57*(5): 1285–1289.
NicDaéid, N., Meier-Augenstein, W., and Kemp, H. F. (2011) Investigating the provenance of un-dyed spun cotton fibre using multi-isotope profiles and chemometric analysis. *Rapid Communications in Mass Spectrometry*, *25*(13): 1812–1816.
Palmer, R., Sheridan, K., Puckett, J., Richardson, N., and Lo,W. (2017) An investigation into secondary transfer – the transfer of textile fibres to seats. *Forensic Science International*, *278*: 334–337.
President's Council of Advisors on Science and Technology (PCAST) (2016) Report to the President. Forensic science and the criminal courts: ensuring scientific validity of feature comparison methods. Available at: https://obamawhitehouse.archives.gov/sites/default/files/microsites/ostp/PCAST/pcast_forensic_science_report_final.pdf.
R. v. Weller. EWCA Crim (2010) 1085.
Rapp-Wright, H., McEneff, G., Murphy, B., Gamble, S., Morgan, R. M., Beardah, M., and Barron, L. (2017) Suspect screening and quantification of trace organic explosives in wastewater using solid phase extraction and liquid chromatography-high resolution mass spectrometry. *Journal of Hazardous Materials*, *329*: 11–21.
Ribaux, O., Baylon, A., Roux, C., Delemont, O., Lock, E., Zingg, C., and Margot, P. (2010) Intelligence led crime scene processing. Part I: forensic intelligence. *Forensic Science International*, *195*(1–3): 10–16.
Ribaux, O. and Talbot-Wright, B. (2014) Expanding forensic science through forensic intelligence. *Science and Justice*, *54*(6): 494–501.
Roux, C., Crispino, F., and Ribaux, O. (2012) From forensics to forensic science. *Current Issues in Criminal Justice*, *24*(1): 7–24.
Roux, C., Talbot-Wright, B., Robertson, J., Crispino F., and Ribeaux, O. (2015) The end of the (forensic science) world as we know it? The example of trace evidence. *Philosophical Transactions of the Royal Society B: Biological Sciences*, *370*(1674): 20140260.
Ruffell, A. and Murphy, E. (2011) An apparently jawless cadaver: a case of post-mortem slippage. *Science and Justice*, *51*(4): 150–153.
Saks, M. J. and Koehler, J. J. (2008) The individualization fallacy in forensic science evidence. *Vanderbilt Law Review*, *61*(1): 199–220.
Silverman, B. 2011 Research and development in forensic science: a review. Accessed 1 September, 2017. www.gov.uk/government/uploads/system/uploads/attachment_data/file/118916/forensic-science-review-report.pdf.
Smit, N. M., Lagnado, D. A., Morgan, R. M., and Fenton, N. E. (2016) Using Bayesian networks to guide the assessment of new evidence in an appeal: a real case study. *Crime Science*, *5*: 9–21.
Smit, N. M., Morgan, R. M., and Lagnado, D. A. (2017) A systematic analysis of the misleading evidence in unsafe rulings in England and Wales. *Science & Justice*, *58*(2): 128–137.
Steele, C. D. and Balding, D. J. (2014) Choice of population database for forensic DNA profile analysis. *Science and Justice*, *54*(6): 487–493.
Tilley, N. and Laycock, G. (2002) Working out what to do: evidence based crime reduction. *Crime Reduction Research Series Paper 11*. London: Home Office.
van Dam, A., Aalders, M. C. G., Todorovski, T., van Leeuwen, T. G., and Lambrechts, S. A. G. (2016) On the autofluorescence of aged fingermarks. *Forensic Science International*, *258*, 19–25.
van Oorschot, R. A. H. and Jones, M. (1997) DNA fingerprints from fingerprints Nature, *387*: 767.
Walls, H. J. (1968) *Forensic Science*. London: Sweet and Maxwell.
Wortley, R. K. and Smallbone, S. (2006) Applying Situational Principles to Sexual Offending Against Children. *Crime Prevention Studies* (Volume 19). Monsey, NY: Criminal Justice Press.
Wortley, R. and Townsley, M. (2016) Environmental Criminology and Crime Analysis (Second Edition). Abingdon, UK: Routledge.
Wortley, R., Sidebottom, A., Tilley, N., and Laycock, G. (eds) (2019) *Handbook of Crime Science*. Abingdon, UK: Routledge.

Section 2
Crime science in action

Overview

In this section we present a range of chapters that showcase the application of crime science. Given the scope of crime science, with arguably every scientific discipline having something to offer, the choice of what to include was difficult. Our aim, therefore, has been to show its diversity with no pretence of completeness. While we did not set out with a rigid taxonomy of pre-determined issues or themes we were seeking to cover, the 17 chapters include empirical and conceptual contributions; are underpinned by disciplines from the social and physical sciences; demonstrate a range of analytic techniques; and variously address the concerns of crime analysis, prevention and detection.

As with the previous section, there are numerous ways we might have organised the chapters. We have resisted the temptation to divide them on disciplinary grounds, for example, social sciences versus physical sciences – this, we believed, would be counter to the multi-/inter-/trans-disciplinary ethos we are trying to promote. Rather, while this section is not formally divided in to sub-sections, chapters can be broadly categorised in terms of the general purpose they serve.

The first eight chapters (Chapters 14–21) are largely to do with the analysis and prevention of specific types of crime – social networks and gang violence (Bichler & Malm), organised crime (Lavorgna), terrorism (Marchment & Gill; Ekblom & Gill), cyber-assisted crimes (Stringhini; Meiklejohn; Tuptuk & Hailes; Prichard, Krone, Spiranovic & Watters).

The next seven chapters (Chapters 22–28) examine various aspects of investigation and detection – the allocation of policing resources (Birks & Townsley; Manning & Wong), security technologies (Chetty; Peveler & Parkin), and the use of forensic evidence (Morgan, French & Meakin; Morgan, Earwaker, Nakhaeizadeh, Harris, Rando & Dror).

Finally, the last three chapters (Chapters 29–31) look to the future – the role of horizon scanning to identify crime risks (Lacey), the changing nature of crime in the 21st century (Johnson, Ekblom, Laycock, Frith, Sombatruang & Valdez) and future directions for crime science (Wortley, Sidebottom, Tilley & Laycock).

14

Social network analysis

Gisela Bichler and Aili Malm

Introduction

To be part of society means that you have at least one social relation. While relations may run the gamut from fleeting associations (e.g. an interaction with the mail carrier) to relatively permanent social bonds (e.g. parent–child relation), relations entangle individuals in a social network. The network presents the context or framework through which individuals navigate life. Your social network provides access to opportunities and information. It also provides social support and helps reaffirm values and attitudes, and in doing so, the network can constrain behaviour, censure ideas, and limit opportunity. The network is a web of connections that shapes behaviour.

Thinking about crime from a network perspective is useful to crime scientists in many ways. In particular, we find the network perspective aids in: (1) tracking the transmission of crime risk (***contagion models*** applied to gang violence), (2) identifying suitable co-offenders (***hubs*** and ***homophily***), and (3) dissecting the structure of crime groups (indicators of ***efficiency*** and ***security*** applied to terrorism and drug trafficking).

This chapter begins with a brief primer about social network analysis, to familiarise the reader with key concepts and basic terminology. Then, we summarise what the current network-oriented research has discovered about gang violence, co-offending, and the structure of crime groups. Within each section we emphasise emerging research areas and analytic developments that may be useful for crime prevention and disruption.

Social network analysis

A social network is simply a set of actors and the relations among them. 'Actors is a general term that can refer to individuals, groups, organisations, websites, nation-states, or any social unit of interest. Similarly, relations can refer to any sort of connection that may exist among units – e.g. co-membership in a gang, money transfers between companies, co-offending activity, commodity flow in a drug distribution operation, or friendship and trust among co-conspirators. Underpinning social network analytics is mathematical graph theory; hence, we often see social units referred to as a set of vertices representing a group of actors, and a set of edges (or arcs) defining the relations among them (Wasserman & Faust, 1994). Graphs (a network) are illustrated, or mapped, by depicting vertices as a nodal symbol, often a circle, and edges as lines connecting the nodes.

Social network analysis (SNA) is an interdisciplinary field of study concerned with exploring the regularities and patterns of social relations and their effects on behaviour, perceptions, beliefs, and decisions (Knoke & Yang, 2008; Wasserman & Faust, 1994). Several assumptions underlie research in this area.

(1) Interdependencies among actors are more important for understanding observed behaviour than actor attributes, i.e. age and sex. While studies often include actor attributes as covariates, social network structure is the primary focus of inquiry.
(2) Relations among actors causally influence behaviour, perceptions, and beliefs. This causal influence can occur through complex pathways, both direct (x comes into contact with y) and indirect (through intermediaries). Because relations can be directed – meaning the channels among actors may not be bi-directional, e.g. Tom sells methamphetamine to Chris, but Chris does not sell methamphetamine to Tom – the indirect connections linking actors can be very complex. For example, the local neighbourhood influencing behaviour is often set at three steps, meaning that a friend of a friend of a friend may exert some influence.
(3) Social networks are dynamic, continually evolving as actors interact. Actors transform relational structures, intentionally or unintentionally, by forming or discontinuing relations, sharing information and materials, or changing perceptions, beliefs, or feelings.
(4) Macro-level social structures and transformations emerge from the combined behaviour and preferences of individual actors navigating their social worlds with bounded knowledge of the larger social network within which they are enmeshed. Thus, studies will investigate network influences at different scales – an individual's position (egocentric approach) within their local social context examining the focal actor of interest (ego) and their direct connections (alters) and the associations among alters; cohesive subgroups within the larger network; or, the network as a whole.

Theoretical congruence

Theoretically, SNA principles are congruent with major principles and practices in environmental criminology and crime analysis. For instance, from the rational choice perspective (Cornish & Clarke, 2017) and related arguments about the situational precipitators of crime (Wortley, 2017), we know that decision-making is based on bounded knowledge, in part gained through routine interactions with others and constrained by the situational context within which offenders act, including changes in peer-group associations and life circumstances, such as marriage. In addition, several key situational precipitators of crime – such as pressures to conform, obey, and comply with social demands to behave inappropriately, or provocations such as crowding or territoriality – develop from social processes that can be modelled with SNA. Moreover, social networks are a critical element of crime pattern theory: arguing that 'most people do not function as individuals, but have a network of family, friends and acquaintances' who influence their behaviour, Brantingham and Brantingham (2008, p. 81) call attention to the roles that social networks play in shaping behavioural patterns, exposing offenders to opportunities, and placing potential victims at risk. Likewise, the routine activity approach to crime events also highlights the critical role that social relations play in generating and preventing crime (e.g. intimate handlers' ability to constrain the behaviour of would-be offenders) and sustaining co-offending relations (Felson, 2006).

The network perspective is useful in preventing an array of different crime problems (Bichler & Malm, 2015), in part because network concepts and social processes are often embedded in formalised prevention strategies. For instance, crime prevention through environmental design aims to reduce crime by increasing collective efficacy through environmental modifications that enhance surveillance and foster pro-social interactions (Armitage, 2017); some personal crime repeat victimisation can be explained by the social context that makes certain targets more available to offenders, leading to crime prevention strategies to reduce social interactions; and, reviewing the eight core ideas of broken windows theory, Wagers, Sousa and Kelling (2008) remind us that reversing social disorder (disrupting anti-social networks) requires efforts to strengthen information social controls and facilitate pro-social interactions by community members in concert with local law enforcement. Thus, from the perspective of environmental criminology and crime analysis, social networks are instrumental to explaining and reducing crime.

Analytics

Most SNA metrics and analytic procedures examine social interactions using dyads (two actors and the ties among them) or triads (associations among sets of three actors) as the base unit. For example, Figure 14.1 depicts a hypothetical methamphetamine drug production and distribution network involving a bounded group of actors. This network includes 33 people connected to each other through 84 relations. Each circle represents a person involved in the drug supply chain, including a high-level cook (person 1) and mid-level retail distributors (persons 2 and 3). This fictitious network was developed to reflect the structures found by ethnographic investigation of methamphetamine markets (see for example, *Methamphetamine: A Love Story*, by Rashi Shukla, 2016).

Symbol size in Panel A varies to reflect the degree centrality score for each person in the network. Degree centrality is a dyad level metric that counts the number of direct connections or ties a person has in the network. It is often interpreted as a level of influence or popularity, and individuals with high scores, relative to all others in the network, are described as ***hubs*** (Wasserman & Faust, 1994). High-degree actors are also associated with greater exposure to different sources of information, as they draw from many others. These individuals are often of interest to crime scientists as their high connectivity serves to shorten the social distance between others in the network, particularly when hubs link to other hubs. We will pick up on this idea again later in this chapter.

Another dyadic measure that calibrates an individual's position within the network is 'betweenness centrality'. Betweenness centrality measures the extent to which an actor can control or mediate the relations between dyads not directly connected, meaning that the actor of interest sits *between* pairs of others along the shortest path that could join them. Panel B illustrates that actor 4, for example, occupies an important position in the drug distribution network, as drugs must pass from the cook through him/her to reach distributor number 3. Person 4 is positioned to be a broker or gatekeeper, and they may have protected this position by maintaining several contacts, such as persons 6 and 7, who can access the drug supply. Redundant relations, such as the link between persons 4 and 5, help to ensure that if the relation between 4 and 3 fails, 4 will still be able to supply this part of the network with drugs. The implications of this pattern for drug-trade disruption are self-evident, but identifying actors positioned as brokers is equally important when understanding resource flow in support of terrorism, tracking weapons trafficking, mapping the organisational structure in emerging crime syndicates, and the like, as we will discuss later in this chapter.

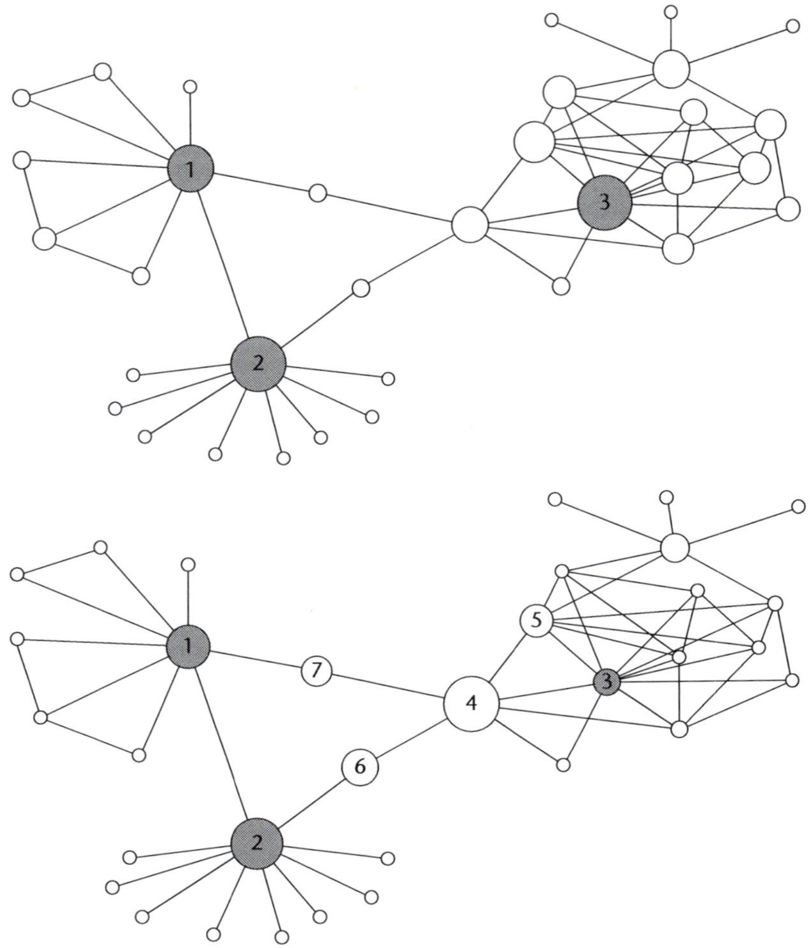

Figure 14.1a and b **Illustration of a hypothetical methamphetamine drug supply network: a. degree centrality (hubs) b. betweenness centrality (brokers)**

It is also important to identify cohesion among actors in sub-regions of a network. Measures of cohesion often look for triadic structures that identify relational patterns among sets of three actors. Figure 14.1 depicts distinct groupings. Comparing the local neighbourhood of retail distributor 2 (bottom) to distributor 3 (top right-hand section of the network), we find distributor 3 is more entangled with others. Because distributor 3 is enmeshed within a highly interconnected subgroup, targeted law enforcement action will not disrupt the flow of drugs to or among actors in this portion of the network. The drug supply is ***efficient*** in the sense that methamphetamine need only pass among a couple of people in order to reach everyone in the subgroup. On the other hand, if distributor 2 were removed from the network, drug supply would cease to reach nine people (directly), and may indirectly affect drug accessibility to other parts of the network.

Sparse networks, defined as those exhibiting low interconnectivity among actors are considered to be ***secure*** (from an offender's perspective) in the sense that the arrest or removal of any one person will not reveal much of the illicit network. Each person has limited contact with others. Now that we have reviewed some basic terminology, we turn to a discussion of recent applications of SNA to investigate the contagious nature of gang violence.[1]

Crime-risk contagion

> Gangs, as groups, and gang members, as individuals, are not partitioned off from their communities, socially or criminally. The lives of gang members are woven into the larger social fabric of their neighborhoods, social networks, families, and friends.
>
> *(Papachristos, Braga, Piza, & Grossman, 2015, p. 627)*

Investigating the contagious properties of violence with logistic regression models, Papachristos and colleagues (Papachristos 2009, 2013; Papachristos, Hureau, & Braga, 2013) put forth convincing evidence in support of the argument that the risk of being involved in gun violence is significantly related to one's position within a social network of risky behaviour. Moreover, while being a gang member significantly increases the odds of being shot, risk is also transmitted to those who are socially proximate to gunshot victims (see Table 14.1). Measuring involvement in risky behaviour through police data (e.g. co-arrest or evidence of hanging out together as determined by field interrogation reports), the five studies undertaken by Papachristos and colleagues show that gun violence within high-crime, gang-entrenched communities in the US is not randomly distributed across the social network. Rather, violence is concentrated within small sectors, and diffuses through the network via social contagion. For example, Papachristos and Wildeman (2014) discovered that 41 per cent of homicides happening in Chicago, IL, over a five-year period occurred in a network containing less than 4 per cent of the population, and each additional social tie removed from the victim decreased the odds of being a victim by 57 per cent.

Social contagion

Violence is not unlike other social phenomena. Just as information, disease, and resources flow through networks, so too does violence, moving from person to person like an infection. This means that the causal influence of a network extends beyond the simple dyadic relation between the offender and the shooting victim to include their associates, as well as others beyond but not directly involved in the crime event. Coined as *hyperdyadic contagion* by Christakis and Fowler (2009), understanding the structure of the local social neighbourhood is key to tracking pathogens through a social system. The local social neighbourhood within which individuals are ensnared influences how information reaches them, whom their reactions will affect, and so on. Studies show that social influences extend to about four steps, lessening with each association – a friend will have more influence than a friend of a friend, or the friend of a friend of a friend and so on (see Christakis & Fowler, 2009 for a general review of this research). Returning to gun violence, Green, Horel, and Papachristos (2017) find that social influence is strongest within three steps of a gunshot victim, and that on average, victimisation occurred about 125 days after exposure. Of note, while gang membership increases the odds of victimisation, social proximity is a significant predictor (e.g. Papachristos, Braga, & Hureau, 2012).

The reason why violence spills over to socially proximate individuals is that social networks position individuals in such a way that they are liable to respond to acts of violence. As Papachristos observes:

> Gang members do not kill because they are poor, black, or young or live in a socially disadvantaged neighbourhood. They kill because they live in a structured set of social relations in which violence works its way through a series of connected individuals.
>
> *(Papachristos, 2009, p. 75)*

Table 14.1 Selected gang violence research documenting contagion effects

Study	*Scope*	*Location*	*Focus*	*Generator: source*	*Network size*	*Findings*
Papachristos et al., 2015	City	Newark, NJ	1 year: fatal and non-fatal gunshot injuries	Co-offending: 1 year of arrests, field interrogation reports, and quality-of-life summons	10,731 individuals, 12,736 ties	– 33% of shootings occurred in network components with <4% of the entire population of Newark (city) – Two factors, being a gang member and closer social proximity to a gang member, significantly increased the odds of being a victim
Papachristos and Wildeman, 2014	High-crime community	Chicago, IL	5 years of gun homicides	Co-offending: 5 years of arrest records	8,222 individuals, ties not reported	– 41% of homicides occurred in a network containing <4% of the community's population – Each additional social tie away from the homicide victim decreased odds of being a victim by 57%
Papachristos, Braga, and Hureau, 2012	High-crime community	Boston, MA	Fatal and non-fatal gunshot injuries	Co-activity: snowball sample from 238 gang members including associates named in 1 year of field interrogation intelligence cards	763 individuals	– 85% of gunshot victims were in one network containing <2% of the community's population – About 1/3 of this network were gang members – Each association removed (a step away from a victim) decreased the odds of victimisation by 25%
Papachristos, Wildeman, and Roberto, 2015	City	Chicago, IL	>6 years non-fatal gunshot injuries	Co-offending: >6 years of arrest data	169,725 individuals	– 70% of non-fatal shootings occurred in networks containing <6% of the city's population – All victims in the network had been arrested (at least once) within 5 years of their shooting – Odds of being shot increase at least 3-fold if the individual is a gang member – Odds of being shot increase significantly with each additional percent of associates who are victims – Being positioned up to a social distance of 3 (handshakes removed from a victim) increases the odds of victimisation
Green, Horel, and Papachristos, 2017	City	Chicago, IL	8 years fatal and non-fatal gunshot injuries	Co-offending: >8-years of arrest data	Largest component included 138,163 individuals	– Social contagion (being within a social distance of 3 steps from a victim) accounted for 63.1% of the 11,123 gunshot violence episodes observed in the network – On average, victimisation occurred 125 days after being exposed (associate was shot)

At the macro-level, patterns of networked violence emerge from the aggregation of individual-level disputes associated with historic rivalries, retaliation for perceived harms, and efforts to retain or elevate social status (Papachristos, 2009). As individuals and groups jostle for social position or respond to real or imagined harm/threats, conflict can emerge among individuals or groups thought to be in alliance with the (alleged) traducer (Descormiers & Morselli, 2011; Decker & Curry, 2002). Because network clusters of violence are found in high-crime areas, where spatial proximity is consistent across the sample, social connectivity often offers more insight into conflict patterns than models looking exclusively at spatial proximity or contiguity (e.g. Papachristos & Wildeman, 2014; Tita & Radil, 2011).

The implications raised by this research for the prevention of violence, particularly violence associated with gang activity, are twofold. First, deterrence strategies must consider the social structure within which individuals are embedded, as well as their group's cohesion, and linkage to other groups (Papachristos, 2013). Second, since networks are dynamic, effort is needed to routinely update information about the contours of the social landscape, including current alliances and conflict (Sierra-Arevalo & Papachristos, 2015), as well as the web of non-gang affiliations, friends, family, and other relations associated with behavioural and association networks – criminal or otherwise (Papachristos et al., 2017; Malm, Bichler, & Van de Walle, 2010). A case study illustrates these points.

Illustrative case study

Mapping the violent crime occurring in the City of Los Angeles between January 1, 2002 to December 31, 2010 among 158 gangs, Randle and Bichler (2017) discovered that much of the prosecuted violence involving members of Bloods and Crips gangs targeted non-gang community members (67.4 per cent of 625 victimisations). Investigating a subset of violence, the 205 gang-on-gang victimisations, the authors discovered that most of the attacks occurred within the gang consortium (e.g. Bloods attacking Bloods) – 52 per cent of the victimisations were between different factions of the consortium and 10 per cent of attacks were within the same faction. Only 38 per cent of victimisations involved a conflict *between* Bloods and Crips gangs. While the analysis was not dynamic, visualising conflict revealed two dominant structures: star formations, where a group was attacked by several other groups or a group attacked many different groups, and chain structures, where one group was in conflict with another, who attacked a third gang in a domino fashion. Thinking about the implications of these patterns, the authors note that many of the gangs examined were under civil gang injunctions. Civil gang injunctions are court orders prohibiting gang members from associating with each other in public space within a designated safety zone, typically set by the boundaries of their claimed turf. These mechansims aim to remove the opportunity for conflict by prohibiting public congregation. And yet, when under the microscope of law enforcement it is feasible that gang members avoid safety zones and continue gang activity elsewhere. Displaced gangs may become embroiled more conflict when their new behaviour patterns take them into rival territory.

In a subsequent study, Bichler and colleagues explored whether gang-on-gang violence changed when groups were enjoined (Bichler, Norris, Dmello, & Randle, 2017). Using the 23 Bloods and Crips gangs under injunction as seeds, the authors generated networks of gang violence by linking defendants and victims named in 272 court cases prosecuted in the greater Los Angeles area (1997–2015) involving at least one conviction for a violent crime and a defendant tried as an adult. Three findings are noteworthy.

First, the most violent groups attack (out-degree centrality) and are attacked the most (in-degree centrality), though not in a reciprocal fashion.[2] Instead, the triadic census[3] indicates that local hierarchies exist and that these structures are highly dynamic. Star-shapes and chains are evident.

Second, using the Jaccard coefficient of similarity[4] to compare the overall structure of pre- and post-injunction violence for nine gangs (three Bloods and six Crips gangs) highly involved in violent behaviour, the study authors found that all but one gang had less than 30 per cent consistency across observation periods. Looked at another way, this means that at least 70 per cent of the conflict patterns were different post-injunction for most of the gangs. Figure 14.2 illustrates the structural changes observed for the Black P. Stone Bloods. Arrowheads indicate

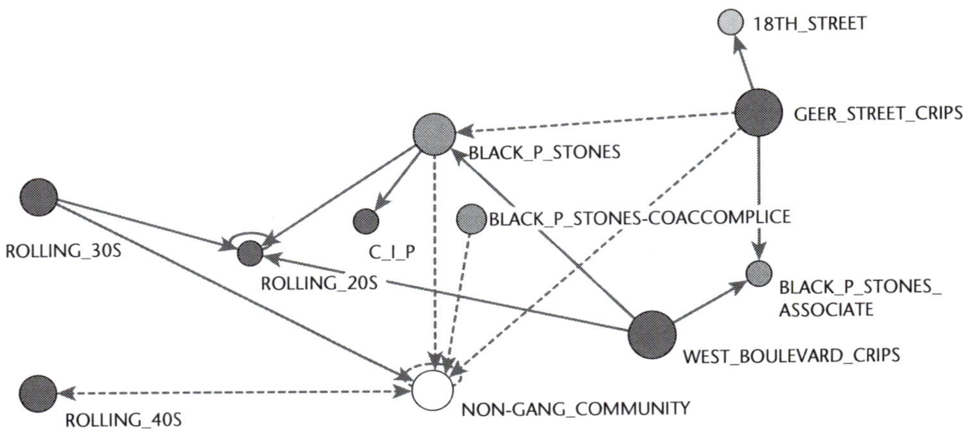

a) Pre-injunction conflict involving the Black P. Stones

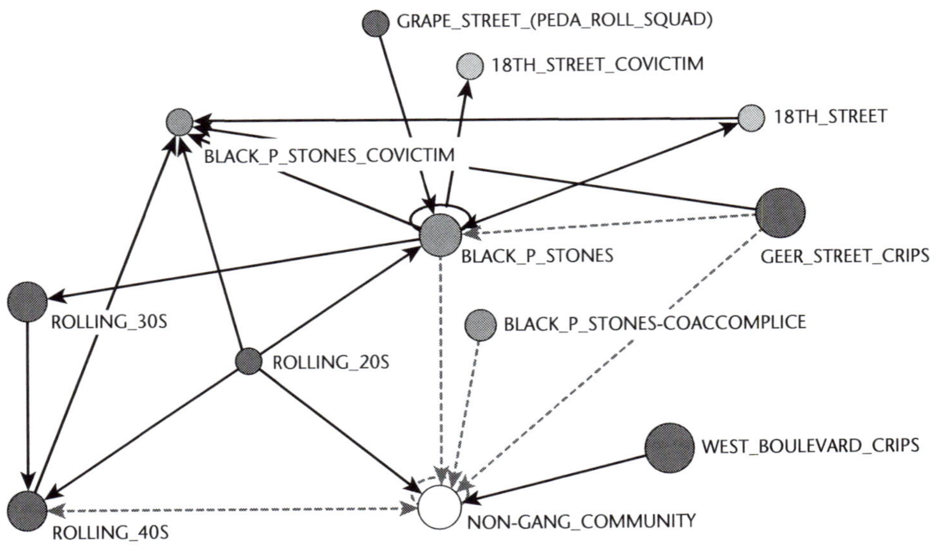

b) Post-injunction violence involving the Black P. Stones

Figure 14.2 Case study of violence involving the Black P. Stone Bloods pre- and post-injunction the direction of the attack, dotted lines indicate conflict patterns that are observed in both networks, and colours denote gang consortium (blue indicates a Crips gang and red indicates a Bloods gang). Non-gang associates and co-victims are indicated. Notice that only five lines are dotted: these conflicts continued after the injunction was implemented; all other conflict in Panel B is new.

Third, examining the nature of the change post-injunction, gangs exhibited more complex triadic patterns with embedded chain-like and star formations suggestive of shifts in local hierarchies among the gangs. Returning to Figure 14.2, Panel B illustrates a greater level of conflict among alters (other groups attacking or being attacked by the Black P. Stones). Post-injunction the web of conflict thickened (became more cohesive). Note the 'halo' for the Black P. Stones that indicates violent internal conflict began post-injunction. Among the implications of this research is that efforts to suppress gang violence must be based on current assessments of inter and intra-group hostilities.

Co-offending

It is well established that much crime, particularly that which is committed by juveniles, is undertaken in the presence of others. SNA has contributed to the co-offending literature by furthering theory describing the processes leading to co-offending (Nguyen & McGloin, 2013). The field started with researchers theorising about the connection between networks and co-offending (Sarnecki, 1990, 2001; Waring & Weisburd, 2002) and evolved to research examining both networks and co-offending simultaneously (Grund & Densley, 2015; Nguyen & McGloin, 2013; McGloin & Piquero, 2010; Malm, Nash & Vickovic, 2011; Papachristos, 2011; Warr, 1996). In this section we examine two network concepts of interest to crime scientists – hubs and homophily.

Hubs (instigating offenders)

Network methods can further our understanding of co-offending by identifying instigating offenders. SNA research has helped this effort through the identification of hubs. As previously mentioned, hubs are people with more direct connections relative to others in the network. Theoretically, hubs have a larger degree of influence on the network as they have the opportunity to directly share information with more people. Perhaps the most influential of all instigating co-offenders is the mentor.

Mentors are co-offenders who provide instruction and/or support. Kleemans and de Poot (2008) investigated the co-offending careers of roughly 1,000 offenders involved in organised crime. They concluded that mentors are both central in the overall co-offending network and instrumental in its formation. Morselli et al. (2006) showed that mentor hubs also increase criminal achievement through financial earnings. Utilising data collected from a survey of incarcerated adult males in Quebec, Canada, they conclude that mentorship leads to greater achievements and lowers the costs of crime. Bouchard, Alain and Nguyen (2009) extend this research and show that, in the context of cannabis cultivation, individuals with a mentor co-offending connection were less likely to be apprehended by law enforcement. Another study by Bouchard and Nguyen (2011) found that mentors also facilitate criminal escalation among cannabis growers, helping their mentees develop as professional growers.

The identification of hubs in co-offending networks can also aid crime control efforts through the possibility of network disruption. Malm and Bichler (2011) illustrate this process by showing how hub identification and removal fragments drug trafficking networks. By selecting hubs in the middle of the market (trafficking and supply), the drug market is fragmented in an efficient manner. Duijn, Kashirin and Sloot (2014) furthered this effort by using simulation models calibrated with intelligence data from the Dutch police. They showed that hub identification and disruption at an early stage, before the network reorganises and becomes resilient, is an optimal law enforcement strategy for combatting cannabis cultivation.

Homophily and selection of co-offenders

Another area where network methods can further our understanding of co-offending is at the selection stage, where decisions are made about who will take part in a crime. SNA research has shown the concept of homophily to be paramount in both initial co-offender selection and continuation of the relationship. Simply put, homophily is the tendency for people to associate with similar others. Tremblay's (1993) study using routine activity theory to explain the search for suitable co-offenders explicitly connects co-offending selection and SNA. If there is indeed a 'search' for co-offenders, after all, this search will exclude a number of potential accomplices that could most easily be identified if the social network around an offender is mapped. In this sense, co-offending decisions are inherently networked decisions.

To illustrate, Malm, Bichler and Nash (2011) examined co-offending networks of organised crime groups and show that co-offenders are drawn from both within and outside the group based on the purpose of the criminal venture. As such, the use of SNA allowed the authors to show that the ethnic classification strategies of organised crime often used by police are flawed and may consequently undermine investigations. Mapping the co-offender networks of groups has allowed us to realise that not only do members co-offend with non-group members, but also that these co-offending relationships are particularly important.

While choosing co-offenders from within the group increases the criminal productivity of the group and enhances trust (Bouchard & Spindler, 2010), group contacts are unlikely to elicit new opportunities. A concrete example of this is provided in Morselli`s (2009) analysis of a well-known street gang in Montreal. Using wiretap data of telephone conversations between group members and their criminal contacts, Morselli shows that non-group members appeared to act as brokers around which the supply depended. Contextualising these results with Granovetter`s (1973) original formulation of a job search, connecting with co-offenders outside of one's group requires offenders to take some risks, but produces some of the most lucrative opportunities (Tremblay, 1993). Charette and Papachristos (2017) recently extended this research by showing how co-offending relationships with similar age, race, gender, demographic proximity, and group membership are more likely to continue through multiple criminal events. In other words, homophilous co-offenders are more likely to be repeat co-offenders.

In addition to understanding homophilous co-offending decisions, network studies also examine specialisation. For example, in their study of youth co-offending networks, McGloin and Piquero (2010) used SNA to show that repeated use of co-offenders increases with offender specialisation. While most youth co-offending is isolated to a single crime (Sarnecki, 2001; Reiss & Farrington, 1991; Warr, 1996), the more criminally specialised are likely to choose familiar co-offenders (Morselli, Tremblay, & McCarthy, 2006). Malm, Nash, and Vickovic (2011) found that offenders specialising in cannabis cultivation often re-used co-offenders. They concluded this was due to the profit-oriented nature of the crime and the need for trust inherent in working within a drug market. Malm et al. (2017) extended this research and found that cannabis cultivators whose co-offenders knew one another were more likely to perceive lower risk of police apprehension. These results can be contextualised with theory stating that re-using a co-offender with a shared network increases trust (Coleman, 1988; Granovetter, 1985).

Group structure

Efforts to map the structure of crime groups examine both the associations among group members, as well as the linkages among individuals that connect the group to the larger social network of criminal activity. Exposing connectivity at different scales (inter-group and system-wide) informs efforts to target specific, localised crime problems, as well as disrupt the larger crime infrastructure. In this section of the chapter we discuss two streams of research investigating group structure; specifically, terror groups and drug trafficking. As explained below, while the objectives of studies vary, a focal interest of researchers is the cohesiveness of crime groups and whether they have efficient or secure structures. Studies also seek to identify individuals with greater positional importance than others.

Terrorism

Network-oriented studies of terror group structures typically adopt one of two approaches: studies examine associations among individuals involved in planned or realised attacks as revealed by court transcripts supplemented with open source information (e.g. Ouellet & Bouchard, 2016); or researchers investigate the general organisational framework with information derived from communications (e.g. Bush & Bichler, 2015) or a mix of public and intelligence sources (e.g. Belli, Freilich, Chermak, & Boyd, 2015; Carley, Lee, & Krackhardt, 2002; Sageman 2004). Generally, this body of work investigates two structural characteristics: (1) the cohesion of the larger network compared to subgroups, and (2) the central positioning of specific actors. Often, the objective of this research is to explore theoretical concepts, e.g. whether connectivity to unique sets of actors improves operational success, such as criminal social capital (Bichler & Bush, 2016) or to assess disruption tactics (e.g. Everton & Cunningham, 2014; Xu, Hu, & Chen, 2009).

Cohesion and Network Security. Research shows that terror networks tend to be sparse, exhibiting low density (Krebs, 2002) and chain-like structures. Comparatively, terror groups are not as dense as other criminal networks (Morselli et al. 2007). Arguably, network sparsity permits greater control over how information passes through the network while reducing the visibility/exposure of actors to law enforcement – if a member is captured or compromised, only a few people would be exposed (Krebs 2002). This structure is associated with greater security. The drawback is that sparsity increases the number of people information must pass through, potentially extending the time needed to pass from the originator to the intended recipient, as well as the time-to-task function (e.g. Krebs, 2002; Jones et al., 2003; Morselli et al., 2007; van der Hulst, 2011). Situated within these globally sparse networks, are socially-isolated operational cells comprised of a dense cluster of actors bound by trusted relations (e.g. Sageman, 2004; Xu & Chen, 2005). At least one person in the cell will exhibit a positional advantage over the others, due to access to resources or links to leaders in the larger network.

Positional Importance. Centrally positioned figures exist with leadership roles (e.g. Brams et al., 2006; Bush & Bichler, 2015; Ouellet & Bouchard, 2016), although their true connectivity may not be visible until prior to an attack (e.g. Koschade, 2006). For example, Brams and colleagues (2006) found various 'mutual influence sets' where important people had more ties and influenced less 'important people': Centrality metrics can identify leaders at multiple organisational levels, such that targeted counter-insurgent action could fragment lines of communication. In other research, key figures emerged as an attack is launched (Magouirk et al., 2008); often these are individuals that have critical roles or skills material to the success of the initiative. For example, Krebs (2002) found that pilots were most central to the 9/11 attacks.

When central actors (hubs) connect with other centrally positioned individuals, the distance across the network reduces, meaning that fewer intermediaries are needed to spread information to any individual – the network will have higher efficiency. Efficiency also improves when the activation of previously hidden ties shortens path lengths: communications more directly reach their intended recipients (Krebs, 2002; Koschade, 2006; Morselli et al., 2007).

Studies also find that functional leaders might not appear to be the most 'central' actors in the network, until one considers their role within the flow of information (Farley, 2003) or their access to resources (Crossley et al., 2012). It follows that attention must be paid to the supporting staff, particularly those positioned as 'emergent leaders', who may be able to step in to leadership roles when called upon (Carley, Lee, & Krackhardt, 2002; Wu, Carleton, & Davies, 2014). Removing prominent hubs can trigger the disintegration of a network (Everton & Cunningham, 2014); however, the key is to remove *all* prominent hubs at the same time, or else others will emerge to fulfil central roles (Helfstein & Wright, 2011; Sageman, 2004).

Three related issues complicate efforts to map the structure of terror groups – missing information, fuzzy group boundaries, and latent or dormant ties. Since many of the relationships are old, based on shared experiences or kinship, they may appear to be invisible until activated to support a pending attack. Group boundaries are difficult to set. Individuals connected to known terrorists through familial ties, co-membership in legitimate organisations, professional relations, and the like, may or may not be associated with insurgent activity. Moreover, connectivity is often established through surveillance of behaviour, communications, or other visible exchanges. Latent or dormant relations would not be visible if the period of observation were short. Thus, the true shape of the network is only visible over time and with the integration of various information sources (Everton & Cunningham, 2014; Sageman, 2004).

Drug trafficking

For decades, organised crime researchers faced difficulty trying to describe the structure of illicit market 'organisations', while simultaneously arguing that such groups are too flexible and dynamic to be considered organisations at all. Approaching this issue using SNA shows us that organisations can be flexible and dynamic, and that these characteristics are the driving force behind illicit markets (Bruinsma & Bernasco, 2004). Four studies illustrate the utility of applying SNA to drug trafficking.

Carlo Morselli's (2001) analysis of the drug trafficking career of Howard Marks, who evaded detection for 30 years, represented an important milestone in the application of social network analysis to drug trafficking. Drawing from multiple sources, including the autobiography *Mr Nice*, Morselli systematically mapped his trafficking network over time, and concluded that Marks's success was due in large part to his ability to act as a broker upon which others depended. Marks was able to fill gaps in the international cannabis trade, thereby providing lasting resilience.

Malm and Bichler (2011) mapped a network of individuals involved in drug trafficking in British Columbia with information extracted from criminal intelligence records. Malm and Bichler reproduced the full drug distribution chain, including production, transport, financial, courier, parasite, supply, and retail roles. Some individuals occupied more than one role, increasing the efficiency of the market. These individuals turned out to be the key players and removing them fragmented the commodity chain it into unconnected components.

Network data and methods also allow us to measure the effect of law enforcement interventions on criminal networks. Morselli and Petit (2007) studied how traffickers react and re-organise after the seizure of a drug shipment. The police delayed arrests in this case for a period of two years. This allowed the network structure to change. The police saw new routes and new contacts being made through potentially safer sources. This provides a unique case study of network adaptation only visible through a network lens.

A recent systematic review of scholarship on drug trafficking networks provides an illustration of just how far networked criminology has come, but also how far we have to go. Examining 34 studies, describing 54 illicit drug supply networks, Bichler, Malm, and Cooper (2017) found drug trafficking networks tended to be sparse with central individuals connecting the group and linking between different groups, suggesting a preference for security. They suggest directing crime prevention efforts at targeting central individuals who may fragment the network, while cautioning police that increased law enforcement attention will cause the organisation to adapt in ways that may lead to more resilient and efficient operation.

Future/conclusions

We designed this chapter specifically for an audience interested in crime prevention. Understanding how victims and offenders interact through networks is essential to preventing crime, and network methods are the best tools to understand a networked criminology. We urge crime prevention scholars to think about how crime is embedded in a social structure. It is the *interaction* between a victim and offender, or between offenders, that creates the crime. We advise researchers and practitioners alike to familiarise themselves with the research reviewed in this chapter and a few particularly good edited books (see Bichler & Malm, 2015; Morselli, 2009).

While the application of network analysis to crime prevention has seen dramatic advances over the past two decades, we are sure to see progress in the following areas: (1) the evolution of criminal networks; (2) the integration of spatial and social networks; (3) network simulation studies; and, (4) policy evaluation using network analysis. Aspiring network scholars need to pay particular attention to systematically documenting data collection and reporting techniques. We also urge interested individuals to attend the annual Illicit Networks Workshop, which is held in locations around the world to support the continued advancement of the field (Malm & Bichler, 2015).

Notes

1 Readers interested in conducting social network research should consider starting with relatively inexpensive software, like UCInet and its partner visualization software, NetDraw. A free 60-day trial version is available from www.analytictech.com/archive/ucinet.htm. A free methods textbook with software instruction is available at http://faculty.ucr.edu/~hanneman/nettext.

2 As described previously, degree centrality counts the number of direct ties an actor has in the network. When networks are directed, meaning the formation of a tie extends from one to another, i.e. drugs pass from an origin to a recipient, we can calculate two different measures of degree. Out-degree measures the number of ties extended by an actor and in-degree centrality calculates the number of ties received.

3 A triadic census is a count of the different patterns of connectivity among sets of three actors. When an undirected network is examined, sets of three actors are intransitive (empty sets with no connections, or sets with only one edge), potentially transitive (two out of three ties are present), or transitive (all three actors connect to each other). When directed networks are examined, the triadic census tallies for 16 different structures. Bichler et al. (2017) examined seven types of transitive structures indicative of complex structural patterns: (1) $i \rightarrow j \leftarrow h, i \rightarrow h$; (2) $i \leftarrow j \leftarrow h, i \rightarrow h$; (3) $i \leftarrow j \rightarrow h, i \leftrightarrow h$; (4) $i \rightarrow j \leftarrow h, i \leftrightarrow h$; (5) $i \rightarrow j \rightarrow h, i \leftrightarrow h$; (6) $i \rightarrow j \leftrightarrow h, i \leftrightarrow h$; and (7) $i \leftrightarrow j \leftrightarrow h, i \leftrightarrow h$.

4 The Jaccard coefficient of similarity measures the extent to which two networks exhibit the same pattern of ties. Generally, when scores fall below 0.2 the two networks are not the same – only 20 per cent of the two networks are the same; values above 0.6 (or 60 per cent) are indicative of a high level of similarity (or stability); scores falling in between this range suggest that the network is the same, but it exhibits substantive evolution (Snijders, van de Bunt, and Steglich, 2010).

References

Armitage, R. (2017). Crime Prevention through Environmental Design. In *Environmental Criminology and Crime Analysis*. R. Wortley & M. Townsley (Eds). London: Routledge, pp. 259–285.

Bichler, G. & Bush, S. (2016). Staying Alive in the Business of Terror. In *Disaster Forensics: Understanding Root Cause and Complex Causality*. A. J. Masys (Ed.). Cham, Switzerland: Springer, pp. 271–294.

Bichler, G. & Malm, A. (2015). *Disrupting Criminal Networks: Network Analysis in Crime Prevention*. Boulder, CO: FirstForum Press.

Bichler, G., Malm, A., & Cooper, T. (2017). Drug Supply Networks: A Systematic Review of the Organizational Structure of Illicit Drug Trade. *Crime Science*, *6*(1), 2.

Bichler, G., Norris, A., Dmello, J. & Randle, J. (2017). The Impact of Civil Gang Injunctions on Networked Violence between Bloods and Crips. *Crime & Delinquency*. DOI: 10.1177/0011128717739607.

Bouchard, M., Alain, M., & Nguyen, H. (2009). Convenient Labour: The Prevalence and Nature of Youth Involvement in the Cannabis Cultivation Industry. *International Journal of Drug Policy*, *20*(6), 467–474.

Bouchard, M. & Nguyen, H. (2011). Professionals or Amateurs? Revisiting the Notion of Professional Crime in the Context of Cannabis Cultivation. In *World Wide Weed: Global Trends in Cannabis Cultivation and its Control*. T. Decorte, G. Potter, & M. Bouchard (Eds). Farnham, UK: Ashgate, pp. 109–126.

Bouchard, M. & Spindler, A. (2010). Groups, Gangs, and Delinquency: Does Organization Matter? *Journal of Criminal Justice*, *38*(5), 921–933.

Brams, S. J., Mutlu, H., & Ramirez, S. L. (2006). Influence in Terrorist Networks: From Undirected to Directed Graphs. *Studies in Conflict & Terrorism*, *29*(7), 703–718.

Brantingham, P. & Brantingham, P. (2008). Crime Pattern Theory. In *Environmental Criminology and Crime Analysis*. R. Wortley & L. Mazerolle (Eds). Milton, UK: Willan, pp. 78–93.

Bruinsma, G. & Bernasco, W. (2004). Criminal Groups and Transnational Illegal Markets. *Crime, Law and Social Change*, *41*(1), 79–94.

Burt, R. S. (2000). The Network Structure of Social Capital. *Research in Organizational Behavior*, *22*, 345–423.

Bush, S. & Bichler, G. (2015). Measuring Disruption in Terrorist Communications. In *Disrupting Criminal Networks: Network Analysis in Crime Prevention*. *Crime Prevention Studies*, Vol. *28*. G. Bichler & A. Malm (Eds). Boulder, CO: First Forum Press, pp. 177–208.

Carley, K. M., Lee, J. S., & Krackhardt, D. (2002). Destabilizing Networks. *Connections*, *24*(3), 79–92.

Charette, Y. & Papachristos, A. V. (2017). The network dynamics of co-offending careers. *Social Networks* *51*, 3–13.

Christakis, N. A. & Fowler, J. H. (2009). *Connected: The Surprising Power of Our Social Networks and how they Shape Our Lives*. Boston, MA: Little, Brown.

Coleman, J. S. (1988). Social Capital in the Creation of Human Capital. *American Journal of Sociology*, *94*, 95–120.

Cornish, D. B., & Clarke, R.V. (2017). The Rational Choice Perspective. In *Environmental Criminology and Crime Analysis*. R. Wortley & M. Townsley (Eds). London: Routledge, pp. 29–61.

Crossley, N., Edwards, G., Harries, E., & Stevenson, R. (2012). Covert Social Movement Networks and the Secrecy-Efficiency Trade Off: The Case of the UK Suffragettes (1906–1914). *Social Networks*, *34*(4), 634–644.

Decker, S.H. & Curry, D.G. (2002). Gangs, Gang Homicides, and Gang Loyalty: Organized Crimes or Disorganized Criminals. *Journal of Criminal Justice*, *30*, 343–352.

Descormiers, K. & Morselli, C. (2011). Alliances, Conflicts, and Contradictions in Montreal's Street Gang Landscape. *International Criminal Justice Review*, *21*(3), 297–314.

Duijn, P. A., Kashirin, V., & Sloot, P. M. (2014). The Relative Ineffectiveness of Criminal Network Disruption. *Scientific Reports*, *4*, 4238.

Everton, S. F. & Cunningham, D. (2014). Terrorist Network Adaptation to a Changing Environment. In *Crime and Networks*. C. Morselli (Ed.). New York: Routledge, pp. 287–308.

Farley, J. D. (2003). Breaking Al Qaeda Cells: A Mathematical Analysis of Counterterrorism Operations (A Guide for Risk Assessment and Decision Making). *Studies in Conflict & Terrorism*, *26*(6), 399–411.

Felson, M. (2006). *Crime and Nature*. Thousand Oaks, CA: Sage.

Granovetter, M. S. (1973). The Strength of Weak Ties. *American Journal of Sociology*, *78*(6), 1360–1380.

Granovetter, M. (1985). Economic Action and Social Structure: The Problem of Embeddedness. *American Journal of Sociology*, *91*(3), 481–510.
Green, B., Horel, T., & Papachristos, A. V. (2017). Modeling Contagion through Social Networks to Explain and Predict Gunshot Violence in Chicago, 2006 to 2014. *JAMA Internal Medicine*, *177*(3): 326–333. DOI:10.1001/jamainternmed.2016.8245.
Grund, T. U. & Densley, J. A. (2015). Ethnic Homophily and Triad Closure: Mapping Internal Gang Structure Using Exponential Random Graph Models. *Journal of Contemporary Criminal Justice*, *31*(3), 354–370.
Helfstein, S. & Wright, D. (2011). Covert or Convenient? Evolution of Terror Attack Networks. *Journal of Conflict Resolution*, *55*(5), 785–813.
Kleemans, E. R. & de Poot, C. J. (2008). Criminal Careers in Organized Crime And Social Opportunity Structure. *European Journal of Criminology*, *5*(1), 69–98.
Knoke, D. & Yang, S. (2008). *Social Network Analysis* (2nd edition). Thousand Oaks, CA: SAGE.
Koschade, S. (2006). A Social Network Analysis of Jemaah Islamiyah: The Applications to Counterterrorism and Intelligence. *Studies in Conflict & Terrorism*, *29*(6), 559–575.
Krebs, V. E. (2002). Mapping Networks of Terrorist Cells. *Connections*, *24*, 43–52.
McGloin, J. M. & Piquero, A. R. (2010). On the Relationship between Co-offending Network Redundancy and Offending Versatility. *Journal of Research in Crime and Delinquency*, *47*(1), 63–90.
Magouirk, J., Atran, S., & Sageman, M. (2008). Connecting Terrorist Networks. *Studies in Conflict & Terrorism*, *31*(1), 1–16.
Malm, A. & Bichler, G. (2011). Networks of Collaborating Criminals: Assessing the Structural Vulnerability of Drug Markets. *Journal of Research in Crime and Delinquency*, *48*(2), 271–297.
Malm, A., Bichler, G., & Nash, R. (2011). Co-offending Between Criminal Enterprise Groups. *Global Crime*, *12*(2), 112–128.
Malm, A., Bichler, G. & van de Walle, S. (2010). Comparing Ties that Bind Criminal Networks: Is Blood Thicker than Water? *Security Journal*, *23*, 52–74.
Malm, A., Bouchard, M., Decorte, T., Vlaemynck, M., & Wouters, M. (2017). More Structural Holes, More Risk? Network Structure and Risk Perception among Marijuana Growers. *Social Networks*, *51*, 127–134.
Malm, A., Nash, R., & Vickovic, S. (2011). Co-offending Networks in Cannabis Cultivation. *World Wide Weed: Global Trends in Cannabis Cultivation And Its Control*. T. Decorte, G. Potter, & M. Bouchard (Eds). Farnham, UK: Ashgate Publishing, pp. 127–132.
Morselli, C. (2009). *Inside Criminal Networks*. New York: Springer.
Morselli, C. & Petit, K. (2007). Law-enforcement Disruption of a Drug Importation Network. *Global Crime*, *8*(2), 109–130.
Morselli, C., Giguère, C., & Petit, K. (2007). The Efficiency/Security Trade-off in Criminal Networks. *Social Networks*, *29*(1), 143–153.
Morselli, C., Tremblay, P., & McCarthy, B. (2006). Mentors and Criminal Achievement. *Criminology*, *44*(1), 17–43.
Nguyen, H. & McGloin, J. M. (2013). Does Economic Adversity Breed Criminal Cooperation? Considering the Motivation Behind Group Crime. *Criminology*, *51*(4), 833–870.
Ouellet, M. and Bouchard, M. (2016). Terror on Repeat: Criminal Social Capital and Participation in Multiple Attacks. *International Criminal Justice Review*, *26*(4), 316–336.
Papachristos, A. V. (2009). Murder by Structure: Dominance Relations and the Social Structure of Gang Homicide. *American Journal of Sociology*, *115*(1), 74–128.
Papachristos, A. V. (2011). The Coming of a Networked Criminology. *Advances in Criminological Theory*, *17*, 101–140.
Papachristos, A. V. (2013). The Importance of Cohesion for Gang Research, Policy, and Practice. *Criminology & Public Policy*, *12*(1), 49–58.
Papachristos, A. V., Braga, A. A., & Hureau, D. (2012). Social Networks and the Risk of Gunshot Injury. *Journal of Urban Health*, *89*, 922–1003. DOI:10.1007/s11524-012-9703-9.
Papachristos, A. V., Braga, A. A., Piza, E., & Grossman, L.S. (2015). The Company You Keep? The Spillover Effects of Gang Membership on Individual Gunshot Victimization in a Co-Offending Network. *Criminology*, *53*(4), 624–649.
Papachristos, A. V. & Wildeman, C. (2014). Network Exposure and Homicide Victimization in an African American Community. *American Journal of Public Health*, *104*(1), 143–150.

Papachristos, A. V., Wildeman, C., & Roberto, E. (2015). Tragic, but not Random: The Social Contagion of Nonfatal Gunshot Injuries. *Social Science & Medicine, 125*, 139–150.

Randle, J. & Bichler, G. (2017). Uncovering the Social Pecking Order in Gang Violence. In *Crime Prevention in the 21st Century: Insightful Approaches for Crime Prevention Initiatives*. B. Leclerc & E. U. Savona (Eds). Cham, Switzerland: Springer, pp. 165–186.

Reiss, A. J. & Farrington, D. P. (1991). Advancing Knowledge about Co-offending: Results from a Prospective Longitudinal Survey of London Males. *The Journal of Criminal Law and Criminology, 82*(2), 360–395.

Sageman, M. (2004). *Understanding Terror Networks*. Philadelphia, PA: University of Pennsylvania Press.

Sarnecki, J. (1990). Delinquent networks in Sweden. *Journal of Quantitative Criminology, 6*(1), 31–50.

Sarnecki, J. (2001). *Delinquent Networks: Youth Co-offending in Stockholm*. London: Cambridge University Press.

Shukla, R. (2016). *Methamphetamine: A Love Story*, Oakland, CA: University of California Press.

Sierra-Arevalo, M. & Papachristos, A. V. (2015). Applying Group Audits to Problem-Oriented Policing. In *Disrupting Criminal Networks: Network Analysis in Crime Prevention*, Crime Prevention Studies, Vol. *28*. G. Bichler and A. Malm (Eds). Boulder, CO: First Forum Press, pp. 27–46.

Snijders, T., van de Bunt, G., & Steglich, G. (2010). Introduction to Stochastic Actor-Based Models for Network Dynamics, *Social Networks, 32*, 44–60.

Tita, G. & Radil, S. (2011). Spatializing the Social Networks of Gangs to Explore Patterns of Violence. *Journal of Quantitative Criminology, 27*(4), 521–545.

Tremblay, P. (1993). Searching for Suitable Co-offenders. *Routine Activity and Rational Choice, 5*, 17–36.

van der Hulst, R. C. (2011). Terrorist Networks: The Threat of Connectivity. In *The SAGE Handbook of Social Network Analysis*. J. Scott & P. Carrington (Eds). Thousand Oaks, CA: SAGE Publications.

Wagers, M., Sousa, W., & Kelling, G. (2008). Broken Windows. In *Environmental Criminology and Crime Analysis*. R. Wortley and L. Mazerolle (Eds). Uffculme,UK: Willan, pp. 247–262.

Waring, E. J. & Weisburd, D. (Eds). (2002). *Crime and Social Organization*, Vol. *10*. Piscataway, NJ: Transaction Publishers.

Warr, M. (1996). Organization and Instigation in Delinquent Groups. *Criminology, 34*(1), 11–37.

Wasserman, S. and Faust, K. (1994). *Social Network Analysis: Methods and Applications*. Cambridge, UK: Cambridge University Press.

Wortley, R. (2017). Situational Precipitators of Crime. In *Environmental Criminology and Crime Analysis*, 2nd edition. R. Wortley & M. Townsley (Eds). London: Routledge, pp. 62–86.

Wu, E., Carleton, R., & Davies, G. (2014). Discovering bin-Laden's Replacement in al-Qaeda, using Social Network Analysis: A Methodological Investigation, *Perspectives on Terrorism, 8*(1), 57–73.

Xu, J. & Chen, H. (2005). Criminal Network Analysis and Visualization. *Communications of the ACM, 48*(6), 100–107.

Xu, J., Hu, D., & Chen, H. (2009). The Dynamics of Terrorist Networks: Understanding the Survival Mechanisms of Global Salafi Jihad. *Journal of Homeland Security and Emergency Management, 6*(1), 27. DOI: 10.2202/1547-7355.1477.

15

Analysis and prevention of organised crime

Anita Lavorgna

Organised crime, crime science, and situational crime prevention

In the long history of organised crime research, crime science is an emerging approach. Traditionally, organised crime (hereafter, OC) has been interpreted variously as: 1) the result of an alien conspiracy of outsiders threatening democratic societies ('alien conspiracy model'), 2) having a specific organisational form ('bureaucracy model'), or 3) a legal enterprise ('illegal enterprise model') (Kleemans, 2014). In all these cases, the focus is on the groups of offenders, the *who*. Likewise, from a practical perspective, dealing with OC attention has generally focused on the detection and conviction of offenders rather than on situational measures. Despite the political appeal of these responses, however, OC continues to prosper. OC, in its various manifestations, has shown itself to be 'tenacious in its ability to change' as it responds to new criminal opportunities (Albanese et al., 2003: 438). It is therefore surprising that 'situational crime prevention' (hereafter, SCP), an approach to crime control grounded in the idea that opportunity is a major driver for crime, has been applied to OC only in recent years. Such an approach promises to alter criminals' perceptions of the risks and benefits of committing crime and therefore could serve to prevent and disrupt criminal activities rather than curb them through the application of the criminal justice system.

SCP generally seeks to alter the 'near' or immediate causes of crime by modifying the decisions that precede its commission (Clarke, 2008). The reduction of crime is achieved through 25 techniques that can be grouped according to five mechanisms: increase the offender's perceived effort, increase the risk, reduce the rewards, reduce provocations, and remove excuses (Clarke, 1992/1997; Cornish and Clarke, 2003).[1] In practice, some techniques of SCP are already used to counter OC, even if they are not explicitly recognised as such. As Bouloukos et al. (2003: 188) report, passports are a way of increasing the risk of crossing international borders illegally. Another example is the Italian *certificazione antimafia* (certificate of non-involvement in mafia-type OC), attesting that a person or a firm is not subject to security measures applied in mafia cases. According to this approach, that made inroads since the mid-1990s, a different type of certification (*autocertificazione, comunicazione*, or *informazione*, depending on the object and the value of the contract) is required to carry out works or provide goods to the Public Administration. This measure increases the offender's perceptions of both effort and risk.

From an analytical perspective, SCP has been applied mainly to conventional high-volumes crimes. However, over the years this approach has been constantly under refinement and its scope increasingly extended (Newman and Freilich, 2012). SCP, for instance, has been used to inform the research agenda on, among other things, child sexual abuse (Wortley and Smallbone, 2006), corruption (Gorta, 1998), cyber-security (Hinduja and Kooi, 2013), and even terrorism (Clarke and Newman, 2006). Traditionally, OC researchers have been reluctant to adopt situational approaches. Especially over the last decade, however, academia has explicitly recognised that there are potential benefits in combining the experiences from research in OC and SCP. The need to develop more analytical, systematic, and problem-solving approaches in respect of OC has been emphasised as necessary to reduce this criminal phenomenon (Levi and Maguire, 2004). Among the studies dedicated to this topic are two edited volumes (Bullock et al., 2010; van De Bunt and van der Schoot, 2003) and a thematic special issue in *Trends in Organised Crime* (Felson and Clarke, 2012; Kleemans et al., 2012).

This chapter provides an overview of SCP-inspired knowledge of OC. Before moving to the core of the chapter, given that OC has come to mean different things to many different people, the notion of OC will be defined.

What is 'organised crime'?

A problem of definition

The term OC has come to be widely used by social scientists, policymakers, and law enforcement officials to refer to a variety of phenomena and has attracted and maintained media attention. OC, however, covers a whole range of different types of crime and crime group. To give but a few examples, in the US, OC refers both to mafia-style local organisations and to international criminal groups involved in illegal trade. The presence of a 'political coalition' dimension is stressed in countries such as Australia and Japan, while in north-western Europe the element of cross-border trade is emphasised (Kleemans et al., 2010; Levi, 1998; Van Duyne, 1995). A certain section of Italian scholarship seems to reduce OC to the mafia, which is a specific type of OC (Lavorgna and Sergi, 2014). The EU is mainly concerned with cross-border aspects of OC and the consequent need for consistent European-level actions to tackle it. To borrow the words of Siegel and van De Bunt (2012: vii), 'there is no doubt that organised crime has many faces, but it is also holding up a mirror to every society in which it is able to manifest itself'.

One could argue that commonality in understanding is more important than precise definition, but in the case of OC this is not so, with the OC narrative being employed in ambiguous and inconsistent ways. This inconsistency threatens not only to impede our understanding of OC but also, as stressed by Edwards and Levi (2008) among others, to diminish political enthusiasm for producing increased resources, domestic powers, and international cooperation. In fact, views on what OC is and what it is not differentially influence the practical work of the relevant agencies since defining illegal activities as OC suggests the existence of a specific mechanism or set of mechanisms appropriate to tackling it (Ashby, 2016; Lavorgna 2016, 2018). What is deemed OC can trigger greater investigative powers and tougher sentences in many countries (Levi, 1998). Overall, OC has often been used as 'a catchphrase to express the growing anxieties' on the expansion of illegal markets and the perceived growing subversion of the legal economy and political institutions (Paoli, 2002: 51).

In an attempt to better capture conceptual complexities, some efforts have been made to modify the lexicon (for instance by introducing the terms 'transit crimes' or 'the organisation of serious crimes for gain', see respectively Kleemans, 2007 and Levi, 2014). Besides the OC narrative, the expressions 'serious crime' and 'serious and organised crime' have started to be used, marking a shift of focus from the structure of criminal groups to the activities and the harm they cause. However, this new narrative is not consolidated yet and it is muddled with the resilient and still predominant OC terminology, causing confusion without solving the definitional problems with the OC vocabulary (Felson and Eckert, 2016; Lavorgna and Sergi, 2015).

Unpacking organised crime

As summarised by von Lampe (2008), when we boil down the notion of OC we find three basic dimensions: OC as activities, as associational structures, and as systemic conditions.

First, organised criminal *activities* are characterised by a certain level of sophistication and continuity (hence the focus is on organised *crimes*). In this perspective OC is generally associated with the provision of illegal goods and services (Paoli, 2002), but evidence shows that OC is involved also in other activities and particularly in predatory crimes such as fraud and robbery, and that its reach often extends to legal businesses.

Second, OC can encompass *associational structures* indicating the presence of (more or less stable and structured) links among offenders. A criminal organisation is generally understood 'as a large-scale collective primarily engaged in illegal activities with a well-defined collective identity and subdivision of work among its members' (Paoli, 2002: 52). Here, the focus is on *organised*. OC groups are supposed to be functionally different from other types of offender group, as organisation within a criminal group creates economies of scale by reducing the time needed to search for co-offenders, integrating the functional elements in crimes, and offering reputation benefits (Levi, 2014).

Finally, OC – and specifically mafia-type OC (Lavorga and Sergi, 2014) – denotes a *systemic condition* where the focus is on the concentration of power in the form of an underworld government or an alliance between criminals and political and economic elites. Therefore, OC evokes the idea of an interpersonal and social threat.

This chapter will maintain this distinction among different dimensions of OC because, as we will see, different crime-prevention approaches target them differently.

Analysis and prevention of organised crimes

Focusing on the activities

Given the nature of SCP, it is not surprising that most analyses have focused on (organised) criminal activities, and thus on the *how* (these are committed and the *crime opportunities* they exploit) rather than on the *who*. Often ambiguities surrounding the notion of OC are avoided by situational advocates by focusing on specific crimes, without entering the debate on whether or not these are carried out by OC groups in a specific case. A broad range of criminal activities are often associated with OC: drug trafficking, human trafficking and smuggling, the illegal cigarette trade, trafficking in stolen motor vehicles, trafficking in stolen arts and antiquities, and many others (von Lampe, 2012).

There are several difficulties in applying SCP to complex criminal phenomena such as organised crimes. As underlined by Laycock (2010), it might be difficult to identify a common modus operandi. Moreover, some of these activities can be so complex that even a tangible target might be absent or difficult to identify, and the offenders involved seem to be very resourceful and do not depend on any specific set of crime opportunities (von Lampe, 2010, 2011). Also, the outcomes of preventive measures applied might be extremely difficult to measure, for instance in terms of displacement (Nelen, 2010).

Nonetheless, some potential or actual uses of SCP in relation to OC have already been discussed for – among other things – sex trafficking (Finckenauer and Chin, 2010), the cigarette black market (von Lampe, 2010), timber theft (Graycar and Felson, 2010), and the drug trade (Kleemans et al., 2010). What emerges from these studies is that most potential points for intervention have been identified in reducing the rewards – in particular by disrupting markets and denying benefits – as well as in increasing the risk by strengthening formal surveillance, utilising place managers, and reducing anonymity. Moreover, the idea of extending guardianship and assisting natural surveillance has been stressed in cases where complex illegal trade is at issue (Kleemans et al., 2010; von Lampe, 2010): for instance, to counter trafficking in chemical precursors for the production of ecstasy, Kleemans et al. (2010: 23) suggest to raise awareness among glassblowers, whose glassworks are used in the production of synthetic drugs.

From an SCP perspective, organised crimes can be seen as 'a chain of criminogenic events' relying on an environment that provides opportunities to make profit (Kirby and Penna, 2010: 209). In order to identify potential points of intervention, SCP teaches us to deconstruct the complexity of crimes to comprehend how they operate or need to operate, breaking them up into the sequential phases of its commission. In a way, SCP can be considered a version of the 'action research model' in which individuals work together in a diagnostic and problem-solving way (Clarke 1995). Cornish (1994) used the concept of 'crime scripts' to describe the essential stages of this criminal activity, making the decision points explicit. Script analysis proved to have an important role in identifying, step-by-step, crime opportunities exploited in organised crimes and therefore provided potential for analysis and prevention. This approach demonstrated increasing interest in investigating when, where, and how criminal opportunities are exploited, rather than relying only on macro level analysis that addresses OC as one single entity.

For instance, von Lampe (2010), in his analysis of the cigarette black market, broke the crime down into scripts of illicit activities according to their setting. Chiu et al. (2011) used a seven-stage crime script as a tool to better understand the criminal process of clandestine drug laboratories and identify potential points for preventive measures. Savona (2010) analysed the chain of events in the infiltration of OC in the public construction sector by considering five main script scenes, from the agreement among offenders to commit the criminal activity to subsequent behaviours resulting from the crime under investigation. Similarly, Rowe et al. (2012) and Zanella (2014) utilised a crime script to investigate respectively OC and corruption in public sector corruption; Hiropoulos et al. (2013) to apply SCP mechanisms to a complex scheme of cigarette smuggling committed by Hezbollah supporters in the United States; and Savona et al. (2014) to guide the analysis of sex trafficking cases.

Hancock and Laycock (2010: 185–186) proposed 'the integrated organised crime script' for cases concerning drug or people trafficking, operating at an even more thorough level of empirical specificity by distinguishing functions, script categories, and actions in the script scenes and by stressing the pinch points for interventions. They suggested that crime scripts can improve our understanding of OC also by distinguishing and addressing its components parts – namely the 'primary criminal act' in the trafficking activity, the 'criminal lifestyle' (series of activities that are independent from any active offending process), and the 'participation in/ the access to criminal networks, groups or individuals' – rather than considering these elements together. Indeed, they represent 'three separate but interrelated streams of opportunity for preventive/disruptive effort' (Hancock and Laycock, 2010: 188). More recently, Lavorgna used Hancock and Laycock's script approach to pinpoint the criminal opportunities made available by the specificities of cyberspace, and to investigate how such opportunities are exploited for a series of internet-facilitated criminal activities including drug trafficking, the trade in counterfeit pharmaceuticals, and wildlife trafficking (Lavorgna 2014a, b, 2015).

In all these cases, the SCP approach was slightly modified, and in particular the level of analysis was often broadened toward more general contexts. As Kleemans (2014) underlines, since SCP is crime-specific it cannot address OC in general, but it should concentrate 'on cocaine smuggling or even more specific activities or events, such as passengers smuggling swallowed "balloons" of cocaine on transnational flights'. Indeed, being crime-specific allows for the identification of the particular opportunity structure exploited by criminals. However, the existing studies mentioned above focused on specific criminal activities but not as specific as the example of the airplane passengers smuggling cocaine. Even if it is true that studies not looking at specific points in space and time of the criminal act lose some explanatory and predictive power, they nonetheless show how opportunities and constraints arising from the external environment delineate patterns and trends with regard to complex criminal activities.

Focusing on the products

A second, less explored research area has focused on the products typically trafficked by OC groups. This research draws heavily on the CRAVED model, an acronym (concealable, removable, available, valuable, enjoyable, and disposable) used to explain offender decision-making by describing the type of goods more likely to be theft targets (Clarke, 1999). While CRAVED was originally intended to spell out the characteristics of attractive items sought by thieves, it has been subject to numerous refinements and its scope expanded. Indeed, CRAVED-derived approaches have been used to explain target choices for parrot poaching in Mexico (Pires and Clarke, 2012), illegal commercial fishing (Petrossian and Clarke, 2014), and trafficking activities in general (Natarajan, 2012). Consequently, CRAVED has found a new application in the analysis of market-based activities.

Natarajan (2012) applied CRAVED to selected trafficked goods (heroin, small arms, stolen cars, elephant ivory, and endangered parrots) and scored each according to CRAVED components. This approach was reportedly not easy because CRAVED elements might be rated differently depending on the different stages of the trafficking process. To overcome this problem, Natarajan suggests focusing on 'the *choice structuring properties* of each form of trafficking at each trafficking stage' (2012: 200, emphasis added),[2] which is consistent with the general SCP approach of being specific. Therefore, the stages of the trafficking activity should be considered separately in order to apply the CRAVED model to trafficked goods more effectively: the initial procurement of the goods to be trafficked, smuggling them into the destination country, and, finally, their distribution. Moreover, according to Natarajan, the CRAVED model covers only partially the attributes of the trafficked goods. Indeed, it fails to capture certain elements that could affect criminal choices, such as potential dangers in the criminal activity, the fact that trafficking a certain good might be more or less morally reprehensible, the profitability of the trade, or the fact that different penalties might be envisaged. Despite these limitations, Natarajan's analysis concludes that the CRAVED model can nonetheless lead to important insights for trafficking activities and particularly its systematic application might help in determining the type of criminal organisations involved in the illegal trade of specific products. Lavorgna (2014c) applied this framework in an exploratory analysis looking at the extent to which CRAVED maintains its explanatory and predictive power in cyberspace as concerns physical goods that are illegally sold online, and underlined its potential in informing the research agenda on Internet-mediated trafficking activities.

To sum up, the CRAVED model has usefully contributed to shifting attention to the *targets* of certain criminal activities. It forces us to recognise that certain products are 'hotter' from the point of view of (potential) offenders, and thus they should receive more attention from a crime-prevention perspective. Even if this model demonstrates its value mostly as concerns predatory crimes and particularly in understanding theft choices, emerging research suggests that CRAVED might also inform the analysis of certain marked-based (organised) crimes. It can be particularly useful as a reasoning tool to identify the characteristics of trafficked goods, to help explain patterns of traffickers' choices and consumers' demand and to shed light on the organisation of trafficking in different stages of the criminal activity. For instance, if the criminal business depends on a continuous flow of lower-value goods, this might suggest the presence of a criminal network professionally involved in large-scale criminal trades.

Analysis and prevention of associational structures and systemic conditions

Associational structures and systemic conditions of OC are generally not explicitly considered by SCP. However, some of the principles of SCP can help us to identify and interpret attitudes of OC groups and the characteristics of their concentrations of power. By examining OC groups from an SCP perspective, it is possible to analyse their decision-making processes, interfere with the decisions they make, and find effective interventions. These interventions may be directed not only at their criminal activities, but also at their networks and their influence over a certain territory (especially in the case of mafia-type OC).

As noted by Felson (2006), when it comes to 'criminal cooperation and organization' (p. 7) it is important not only to consider the opportunity structure of criminal activities but also the underlying processes of offender networking. In particular, there are some places – so-called 'offender convergence settings' – where offenders cluster, and such places 'are important for understanding crime cooperation, and how to interfere with it' (p. 9). While groups may vary, convergence settings remain relatively stable (and therefore easier to target); moreover, 'society can protect public places' in a way that is 'far less dangerous to freedom than focusing on human suspects' (p. 10). As von Lampe (2011) pointed out, beyond the typical offender convergence settings giving rise to short-term endeavours and described by Felson (for instance, a street corner or a bar), OC relies on more complex settings, allowing for longer planning horizons (for instance, a prison). Also, these places are increasingly targeted by focused and intelligence-led interventions to prevent OC from prospering, leading, for example to the use of separate detention units for OC members. Once again, this approach stretches the usual level of analysis of SCP, bending it toward more general contexts. Furthermore, while SCP implies the idea that motivated offenders will refrain from committing a crime in the presence of other persons (or 'guardians' as Cohen and Felson (1979) would describe them), we have to keep in mind that OC often relies on social bonds, corruption, intimidation, or on a pervasive atmosphere of fear of retaliation (Edwards and Levi, 2008), so that the presence of other persons does not necessarily discourage the commission of a crime (Huisman and Jansen, 2012; von Lampe, 2011). Nonetheless, the teaching of SCP would be extremely beneficial to direct efforts and resources in an efficient and efficacious way in risky areas.

Last but not least, SCP-informed approaches can prove useful in developing crime-proofing legislation (Morgan and Clarke, 2006; Vander Beken, 2005). The basic idea is that legislation may produce unintended criminal opportunities, which can be identified (*ex ante* or *ex post*) and reduced or removed. This should minimise possible risks arising from the laws' weakness, hence disrupting systemic crime opportunities that might facilitate OC.

Conclusion

This chapter provided an overview of the current and potential use of SCP approaches in dealing with OC. We have seen that SCP might be very useful not only to inform the development of policies and practices to prevent and reduce OC activities, but it can also remind OC researchers of the importance of precision and of being context-specific in analysing crime trends and patterns. Furthermore, an SCP approach can also be used to design and refine regulatory frameworks, policies, and social environments to avoid unintended crime opportunities beyond the commission of a specific criminal act. It could be suggested that these interventions might also produce diffusion of benefits – that is, the unexpected reduction of crimes not directly targeted by the preventive action of an SCP measure (Clarke and Weisburd, 1994) – to the wider society.

Some of the limits and challenges of current applications of SCP to OC were also stressed. Particularly, we have seen how many scholars, in applying SCP approaches to analyse OC, have broadened the level of analysis in order to cover the complexity of the contexts in which OC thrives rather than focusing on the (very) specific circumstances creating opportunities for crime. In outlining future directions for research, it would be interesting to see the SCP approach applied to more specific contexts and circumstances giving rise to OC in order to use SCP at its full potential. It would also be useful to further develop the potential of opportunity-based approaches in preventing OC in its manifestations as associational structures and systemic conditions (hence overcoming the limited understanding of OC as serious or sophisticated criminal activities).

Also, SCP in this domain could be successfully complemented by community crime-prevention approaches (Hope, 1995). By targeting the social opportunities, conditions, and institutions that influence offending in residential communities in risky areas (for instance, where the presence of OC groups and their concentration of power is particularly problematic), OC capacity to establish and reinforce criminal networks and influence over a certain territory might be better tackled. After all, broadening opportunity-reduction approaches (and, consequently, SCP) is not something new. In conclusion of their seminal work, Cohen and Felson themselves (1979: 605) foresaw that routine activity theory could be applied not only to criminal activities but also to criminal offenders and their inclinations, to the point that they have suggested the integration of their work with approaches focusing on different criminogenic factors that might affect the likelihood of a crime, such as social control. Indeed, as already underlined by Mayhew et al., the notion of 'opportunity' had been introduced into criminological discourse with Merton's theory of anomie and his idea that restricted socioeconomic opportunities encourage the working class to commit crime as a way to ameliorate its status (1976: 3 ff.). This notion, then, is not irrelevant to different criminological approaches. The broadening of opportunity approaches (via the broadening of their working definition of 'opportunity') could be particularly useful when it comes to OC, which is a phenomenon that often transcends sets of given criminal activities and organisational features and manifests itself through its ability to manipulate social networks and relationships by being entrenched in given social structures – the very characteristic that makes OC so difficult to eradicate.

Notes

1 Freilich and Newman (2014) recently expanded the SCP framework by suggesting mechanisms to provide opportunities to manipulate behaviours, such as assisting compliance, offering alternatives, and legalising.

2 The concept of 'choice-structuring properties' as developed by Cornish and Clarke (1987) refers to the constellation of opportunities, costs, and benefits for particular types of crime.

References

Albanese, J. S., Das, D. K. and Verma, A. (eds) (2003) *Organized Crime: World Perspectives*. Upper Saddle River, NJ: Pearson Education.

Ashby, M. P. J. (2016) Is metal theft committed by organized crime groups, and why does it matter? *Criminology & Criminal Justice 16*(2): 141–157.

Bouloukos, A., Farrell, G. and Laycock, G. (2003) Transnational organised crime in Europe and North America: towards a framework of prevention. HEUNI Report N. *40*. Helsinki: Heuni.

Bullock, K., Clarke, R. V. and Tilley, N. (eds) (2010) *Situational Prevention of Organised Crimes*. Cullompton, UK: Willan Publishing.

Chiu, Y. N., Leclerc, B. and Townsley, M. (2011) Crime script analysis of drug manufacturing in clandestine laboratories. *British Journal of Criminology 51*(2): 355–374.

Clarke, R. V. (ed.) (1992/1997) *Situational Crime Prevention: Successful Case Studies*. New York: Harrow and Heston.

Clarke, R. V. (1995) Situational Crime Prevention. *Crime & Justice 19*: 91–150.

Clarke, R. V. (1999) Hot products: understanding, anticipating and reducing demand for stolen goods. Paper 112. *Police Research Series*. London: Home Office.

Clarke, R. V. (2008) Situational Crime Prevention. In Wortley R. and Mazerolle L. (eds) *Environmental Criminology and Crime Analysis*. Cullompton, UK: Willan Publishing.

Clarke, R. V. and Newman, G. R. (2006) *Outsmarting the Terrorists*. Westport, CT: Praeger Security International.

Clarke, R. V. and Weisburd, D. (1994) Diffusion of crime control benefits: observation on the reverse of displacement. In Clarke, R. V. (ed.) *Crime Prevention Studies 2*. Monsey, NY: Criminal Justice Press.

Cohen, L. E. and Felson, M. (1979) Social change and crime rate trends: a routine activity approach. *American Sociological Review 44*: 588–608.

Cornish, D. B. (1994) The Procedural Analysis of Offending and Its Relevance for Situational Prevention. In Clarke, R. V. (ed.) *Crime Prevention Studies 3*. Monsey, NY: Criminal Justice Press.

Cornish, D. B. and Clarke, R. V. (1987) Understanding crime displacement: an application of rational choice theory. *Criminology 25*: 901–916.

Edwards, A. and Levi, M (2008) Researching the organization of serious crimes. *Criminology and Criminal Justice 8*(4): 363–388.

Felson, M. (2006) The ecosystem for organized crime. HEUNI Paper no. *26*. Helsinki: Heuni.

Felson, M. and Clarke, R. V. (2012) Comments on the special issue. *Trends in Organized Crime 15*(2–3): 215–222.

Felson, M. and Eckert, M. (2016) *Crime and Everyday Life* (5th ed). London: Sage.

Finckenauer, J. O. and Chin, K. L. (2010) Sex trafficking: a target for situational crime prevention? In Bullock, K., Clarke, R. V. and Tilley, N. (eds) *Situational Prevention of Organised Crimes*. Cullompton, UK: Willan Publishing.

Freilich, J. D. and Newman, G. R. (2014) Providing opportunities: a sixth column for the techniques of situational crime prevention. In Caneppele, S. and Calderoni, F. (eds) *Organised Crime, Corruption and Crime Prevention*. London: Springer.

Gorta, A. (1998) Minimizing corruption: Applying lessons from the crime prevention literature. *Crime, Law and Social Change 30*(1): 65–87.

Graycar, A. and Felson, M. (2010) Situational prevention of organised timber theft and related corruption. In Bullock, K., Clarke, R. V. and Tilley, N. (eds) *Situational Prevention of Organised Crimes*. Cullompton, UK: Willan Publishing.

Hancock, G. and Laycock, G. (2010) Organised crime and crime scripts: prospects for disruption. In Bullock, K., Clarke, R. V. and Tilley, N. (eds) *Situational Prevention of Organised Crimes*. Cullompton, UK: Willan Publishing.

Hinduja, S. and Kooi, B. (2013) Curtailing cyber and information security vulnerabilities through situational crime prevention. *Security Journal 26*: 383–402.

Hiropoulos, A., Freilich, J. D., Chermak, S. and Newman, G. R. (2013) Cigarette smuggling and terrorism financing. In Leclerc, B. and Wortley, R. (eds) *Cognition and Crime: Offender Decision Making and Script Analyses*. London: Routledge, pp.186–208.

Hope, T. (1995) Community Crime Prevention. In Tonry, M. and Farrington, D. P. (eds) *Building a Safe Society: Strategic Approaches to Crime Prevention*. Chicago, IL: University of Chicago Press.

Huisman, S. and Jansen, F. (2012) Willing offenders outwitting capable guardians. *Trends in Organised Crime 15*(2): 93–110.

Kirby, S. and Penna, S. (2010) Policing mobile criminality: towards a situational crime prevention approach to organised crime. In Bullock, K., Clarke, R. V. and Tilley, N. (eds) *Situational Prevention of Organised Crimes*. Cullompton, UK: Willan Publishing.

Kleemans, E. R. (2007) Organized crime, transit crime, and racketeering. *Crime & Justice 35*: 163–215.

Kleemans, E. R. (2014). Theoretical perspectives on organized crime. In Paoli, L. (ed.) *Oxford Handbook of Organized Crime*. Oxford: Oxford University Press.

Kleemans, E. R., Soudjin, M. R. J. and Weenink, A. W. (2010) Situational crime prevention and cross-border crime. In Bullock, K., Clarke, R. V. and Tilley, N. (eds) *Situational Prevention of Organised Crimes*. Cullompton, UK: Willan Publishing.

Kleemans, E. R., Soudijn, M. R. J. and Weenink, A. W. (2012) Organized crime, situational crime prevention and routine activity theory. *Trends in Organized Crime 15*(2–3): 87–92.

Lavorgna, A. (2014a) Internet-mediated drug trafficking: towards a better understanding of new criminal dynamics. *Trends in Organized Crime 17*(4): 250–270.

Lavorgna, A. (2014b) Wildlife trafficking in the Internet age: the changing structure of criminal opportunities. *Crime Science 3*(5): 1–12.

Lavorgna, A. (2014c) Hot products in Internet-mediated trafficking activities and the limits of CRAVED. The International Symposium on Environmental Criminology and Crime Analysis (ECCA), NSCR, Kerkrade (Netherlands), 16–19 June 2014.

Lavorgna, A. (2015) The online trade in counterfeit pharmaceuticals: new criminal opportunities, trends, and challenges. *The European Journal of Criminology 12*(2): 226–241.

Lavorgna, A. (2016) Exploring the cyber-organised crime narrative: The hunt for a new bogeyman? In van Duyne, P. C., Scheinost, M., Antonopoulos, G. A., Harvey, J. and von Lampe, K. (eds), *Narratives on Organised Crime in Europe: Criminals, Corrupters and Policy*. Den Haag: Wolf Legal Publishers.

Lavorgna, A. (2018) Cyber-organised crime. A case of moral panic? *Trends in Organized Crime* (online first).

Lavorgna, A. and Sergi, A. (2014) Types of organized crime in Italy. The multifaceted spectrum of Italian criminal associations and their different attitudes in the financial crisis an in the use of Internet technologies. *International Journal of Law, Crime and Justice 42*(1): 16–32.

Lavorgna, A. and Sergi, A. (2015) Serious, therefore organised? A critique of the 'serious and organised crime' and 'cyber-organised crime' rhetoric in the United Kingdom. *International Journal of Cyber Criminology 10*(2): 170–187.

Laycock, G. (2010) Foreword. In Bullock, K., Clarke, R. V. and Tilley, N. (eds) *Situational Prevention of Organised Crimes*. Cullompton, UK: Willan Publishing.

Levi, M. (1998) Perspectives on 'organized crime': an overview. *Howard Journal of Criminal Justice 37*: 335–345.

Levi, M. (2014) Thinking about Organised Crime. Structure and Threat. *The RUSI Journal 159*(1): 6–14.

Levi, M. and Maguire, M. (2004) Reducing and preventing organised crime: An evidence-based critique. *Crime, Law and Social Change 41*(5): 397–469.

Morgan, R. and Clarke, R. V. (2006) Legislation and Unintended Consequences for Crime. *European Journal on Criminal Policy and Research 12*(3–4): 189–211.

Natarajan, M. (2012) A rational choice analysis of organized crime and trafficked goods. In Tilley, N. and Farrell, G. (eds) *The Reasoning Criminologist: Essays in Honour of Ronald V. Clarke*. Abingdon, UK: Routledge.

Nelen, H. (2010) Situational organised crime prevention in Amsterdam. The administrative approach. In Bullock, K., Clarke, R. V. and Tilley, N. (eds) *Situational Prevention of Organised Crimes*. Cullompton, UK: Willan Publishing.

Newman, G. R. and Freilich, J. D. (2012) Extending the reach of situational crime prevention. In Tilley, N. and Farrell, G. (eds) *The Reasoning Criminologist: Essays in Honour of Ronald V. Clarke*. Abingdon, UK: Routledge, pp. 212–225.

Paoli, L. (2002) The Paradoxes of Organized Crime. *Crime, Law and Social Change 37*(1): 51–97.

Petrossian, G. A. and Clarke, R. V. (2014) Explaining and controlling illegal commercial fishing. An application of the CRAVED theft model. *British Journal of Criminology 54*: 73–90.

Pires, S. and Clarke, R. V. (2012) Are parrots CRAVED? An analysis of parrot poaching in Mexico. *Journal of Research in Crime and Delinquency 49*(1): 129–146.

Rowe, E., Akman, T., Smith, R. G., and Tomison, A. M. (2012) Organised crime and public sector corruption: A crime scripts analysis of tactical displacement risks. *Trends and Issues in Crime and Criminal Justice*, issue 444.

Savona, E. U. (2010) Infiltration of the public construction industry by Italian organised crime. In Bullock, K., Clarke, R. V. and Tilley, N. (eds) *Situational Prevention of Organised Crimes*. Cullompton, UK: Willan Publishing.
Savona, E. U., Giommoni, L. and Mancuso, M. (2014) Human trafficking for sexual exploitation in Italy. In Leclerc, B. and Wortley, R. (eds) *Cognition and Crime: Offender Decision Making and Script Analyses*. London: Routledge, pp.140–163.
Siegel, D. and van de Bunt, H. (eds) (2012) *Traditional Organized Crime in the Modern World: Responses to Socioeconomic Change*. New York: Springer.
van De Bunt, H. G. and van der Schoot, C. (eds) (2003) *Prevention of Organised Crime. A Situational Approach*. Den Haag: Wetenschappelijk Onderzoek – en Documentatiecentrum (WODC).
van Duyne, P. C. (1995) The phantom and threat of organized crime. *Crime, Law and Social Change 24*(4): 341–377.
Vander Beken, T. (ed.) (2005) *Organised Crime and Vulnerability of Economics Sectors: The European Transport and Music Sector*. Antwerp: Maklu Publishers.
von Lampe, K. (2008) Organized crime in europe: conceptions and realities. *Policing 1*(2): 7–17.
von Lampe, K. (2010) Preventing organized crime: the case of contraband cigarettes. In Bullock, K., Clarke, R. V. and Tilley, N. (eds) *Situational Prevention of Organised Crimes*. Cullompton, UK: Willan Publishing.
von Lampe, K. (2011) The application of the framework of situational crime prevention to 'organized crime'. *Criminology and Criminal Justice 11*(2): 145–163.
von Lampe, K. (2012) Transnational organized crime and challenges for future research. *Crime Law and Social Change 58*(2): 179–194.
Wortley, R. and Smallbone, S. (eds) (2006) Situational Crime Prevention for child sexual abuse. *Crime Prevention Studies* 19. Monsey, NY: Criminal Justice Press.
Zanella, M. (2014) Script analysis of corruption in public procurement. In Leclerc, B. and Wortley, R. (eds) *Cognition and Crime: Offender Decision Making and Script Analyses*. London: Routledge, pp.164–185.

16

Terrorists are just another type of criminal

Zoe Marchment and Paul Gill

Introduction

Terrorism studies began as a niche area of enquiry in the early 1970s within history, political science and sociology. Such approaches explain the emergence of, and motivation for, politically violent campaigns within their socio-political context. From the outset, terrorism studies was not so interested in the terrorist event itself. Instead, studies focused upon two almost incompatible approaches, each with varying, and often dubious levels, of scientific rigour. First, analyses sought to discover the dispositional traits of terrorist group members (Cooper, 1978). Such approaches initially offered anecdotal glimpses into the supposed 'irrationality' of the individual perpetrator by emphasising psychopathy and other particular personality traits. Second, analyses focused on the 'root causes' of terrorist grievances (Alexander, 1976), offering empirical descriptions of the 'rationality' of terrorist groups turning toward violence. The emphasis was on individual and group 'agency' in strategic decision-making. For example, various studies examine how terrorism can be an effective political strategy that is more optimal than other forms of military engagement, can produce effective gains, and can undermine confidence in the functioning and authority of the state.

The initial dominance of history and political science had a major path-dependent effect upon the study of terrorism. Instead of viewing a terrorist attack as a single crime, the tendency within the literature has been to explain the attack in terms of a group's ideological position (Drake, 1988) or strategic orientation (Abrahms, 2008). Such depictions emphasise terrorism as a political, rather than a criminal, problem. Correspondingly, whereas these studies traditionally focused upon the rational adoption of terrorism as a strategy or a tactic, they typically do not look at the 'rationality' underpinning the actual commission of a terrorist offence – a key component of crime science.

In the past few years however, there has been a major shift within terrorism studies. A greater variety of disciplines now bring their methodological expertise to the domain. Insight from the humanities now extends beyond the discipline of history and includes linguistics, the visual arts and theology (Maher, 2016). The social sciences have increased their problem-oriented approaches, bringing in a diverse range of disciplines, including geography (Bahgat & Medina, 2013) and psychology (Horgan, 2015). The natural sciences have also applied their methodological tools and paradigms to understand terrorist behaviour (Johnson et al., 2013; Manrique et al., 2016). The growth of importance in the internet for radicalisation and terrorist engagement (Gill et al., 2017) has also witnessed more input from computer science (Brynielsson et al., 2013). Terrorism studies, as a whole, is becoming increasingly more empirically and quantitatively oriented after years of questionable data and science (Schuurman, 2018).

Perhaps the greatest increase in research activity has been in criminology, particularly environmental criminological perspectives that have been so influential in the development of crime science. Although it still may be true that the 'criminological study of terrorism [lags] far behind many other specialized branches of criminology' (LaFree, 2009:434), there have been major advances recently in a variety of areas. Research increasingly covers issues such as target choice, weapon choice, the spatio-temporal clustering of offences, the distances travelled to commit a terrorist attack, victimology, and the displacement of incidents. Findings show great promise, and reinforce the argument that when we focus on terrorism from a preventative angle, we should focus on terrorist behaviours – *what they do* – rather than remain preoccupied with concerns about *who they are* or *why they have become terrorists.*

Taking Wortley et al. (this volume) as an inspiration, this chapter is structured around the 'three linked questions that the pioneers of environmental criminology sought to answer'. We adapt these three questions for a terrorism-specific context: Namely 'why do people commit terrorist acts'; 'where, when and how does terrorism occur' and 'how do we prevent terrorism'. In attempting to answer these questions, we draw upon literature from outside of environmental criminology thus reflecting the broader approach utilised within crime science.

Why do people commit terrorist acts?

Insights from crime science into why people engage in terrorist acts have been limited, to date, for a number of reasons. First, the overwhelming emphasis within the field has been to explain the 'terrorist' as opposed to explaining the 'terrorist act'. Second, existing studies have tended to focus on entirely different units of analysis than is traditionally the case within crime science. For example, Desmarais et al. (2017) conducted a systematic review of the scientific knowledge regarding risk factors for terrorist involvement. The review demonstrates the existing literature has tended toward 'distal' explanations rooted in factors associated with socio-demographic characteristics, criminal history, religiosity, attitudes and beliefs, employment status, education, poverty, relationship status and mental health. On the other hand, studies looking at the association between personal experiences (e.g. proximal factors) and terrorist engagement were depicted as 'rare' and 'infrequently examined' (p. 190). Second, there has also been a lack of rigorous attention to causal *mechanisms* behind radicalisation and engagement in terrorism. Gøtzsche-Astrup (2018) evaluated several common approaches to understanding such mechanisms. These approaches leant on aspects of social-identity theory, ideology and values, and various motivational frameworks. The study concluded that research designs insufficiently demonstrated causality and could only offer simple correlations.

Finally, perhaps the biggest problem has been the field's lack of specificity in terms of the dependent variable being considered. To date, academic approaches to understanding who becomes a 'terrorist' have largely tended toward generalist explanations. Such explanations, be they psychopathological, psychoanalytical, theoretical models or descriptive analyses of large-N datasets, tend to treat each individual group member equally. That is, they fail to effectively distinguish different member types, not just across terrorist groups, but also within them. Analyses of 'the terrorist' frequently treat actors as monolithic in nature, differing merely in presumed personality traits and little else. Terrorist organisations, however, tend to possess some form of command and functional structure, be it hierarchical or linear. Within this structure, a wide variety of roles, responsibilities and behaviours are delegated to individual members and sub-units. Such responsibilities may range from storing weapons to engaging in shooting attacks; from procuring vehicles for car-bombing attacks to being a bomb-maker; from being a suicide bomber to being a recruiter of suicide bombers; from being a foot soldier to being an executive leader. Because of this differentiation of focus and task, there are some important differences in both the nature and level of involvement by different members of terrorist groups. An individual may hold one or several distinct roles over time in their 'terrorist career'. These roles may be distinctive in the nature of the social, psychological and organisational demands required of the person in that role. The differences range from the level of violence the individual either directly engages in or merely facilitates; in expertise levels; individual risk to personal liberty and harm; and responsibility for overall strategy (Taylor and Horgan, 2006:595).

Anecdotal evidence further suggests that when individuals join terrorist organisations, either (a) recruiters assign roles and tasks based on an assessment of organisational needs and the individuals' ability or (b) the new recruit has a sense of what roles they are willing or eager to adopt. For example, when US troops raided an al-Qaeda safe house in the Iraqi town of Sinjar in October 2007, they found a wealth of data on the biographies of individuals who had signed up for the insurgency. Of those who joined, most requested assignment as a fighter, combatant or martyr. However, others asked to be doctors, journalists and to occupy other media roles. Furthermore, in an interview with Horgan (2009:80), a former member of the Provisional Irish Republican Army stated:

> There have always been very astute people involved in recruiting to the IRA . . . There is a sense in which people were evaluated and put into certain roles . . . Every large organization is going to have that challenge – how do you fit people into things?

This suggests that (at least in the case of the Provisional IRA) there is often a purposeful relationship between individuals and the roles into which they are initially guided. In addition, there may be a natural logic to how actual and subsequent involvement unfolds and diversifies for the individual. Taylor and Horgan (2006:595) argue that some roles and activities might 'tend to cluster together more naturally than others' (they give the example of financing, political and community activism), but to date there is no empirical evidence to support this claim.

Understanding the nature and function of terrorist roles is important for many reasons. From a disruption perspective, policies need to be tailored for role-specific interventions. Because their behaviours, routines and proximity to violent plots differ substantially, what works in the effective disruption of tasks conducted by a bomb-maker may not necessarily be applicable to those of a financier of a terrorist organisation. From a justice perspective, a greater understanding of roles may help with targeted treatment policies and risk assessments (Tracy & Kempf-Leonard, 1996). From a research perspective, it will ultimately help with our understanding of who joins terrorist organisations, the nature of their involvement with the terrorist organisation, how individuals migrate from one kind of role to another over time, and ultimately how they desist or disengage from terrorist activities (Horgan, 2009; Taylor & Horgan, 2006). Investigating whether particular variables more closely correlate with particular terrorist roles also concerns the very nature of how we theorise about terrorist involvement and whether general models of 'radicalisation' or 'pathways' into terrorism are appropriate or whether they should be tailored for particular manifestations of terrorist activity.

As Monahan (2012) notes, *lumping* all forms of terrorism into one outcome variable is at odds with criminological studies where the norm is to typically *split* the outcome variable. Rather than assessing general risk, studies that split the outcome variable tend to assess the risk for specific types of violence. Examples include domestic violence, sexual violence, workplace violence, and so on. With the exception of the suicide bomber, rarely does the study of individual terrorist roles figure in the existing literature (see Merari, 2010 for the best example). Existing approaches, therefore, may miss the subtle psychological, behavioural, socio-demographic or organisational factors that may explain how and why some individuals are more likely to take part in particular terrorist roles than others. Plentiful evidence suggests that disaggregating our understanding of the terrorist is of value. Studies have compared male and female terrorists, lone and group actors, foreign and domestic fighters, violent and non-violent group members, and mentally ill and non-mentally ill lone actors (Corner & Gill, 2014; Gill, Horgan & Deckert, 2014; Gruenewald, Chermak & Freilich, 2013; Hegghammer, 2013; Jacques & Taylor, 2008; Perliger, Koehler-Derrick & Pedahzur, 2016) Few, if any, studies have done this systematically with regards to terrorist roles and such an endeavour is important in order to help develop our understanding of individual risk assessment (Monahan, 2012).

Where and when does terrorism occur?

Terrorists make cost–benefit decisions in much the same way as ordinary criminals. The field of crime prevention is testament to the vast potential for situationally focused crime-prevention approaches. Situational prevention means focusing on the settings in which offences take place, rather than the underlying motivation or criminal disposition of the individual. Reducing the opportunities for terrorism via environmental design broadly construed is, therefore, a valid and worthwhile pursuit. Each type of terrorist attack, be it a vehicular assault or a bombing, depends on a crystallisation of multiple opportunities. In turn, each specific attack type offers its own set of environmental opportunities that can be manipulated with the intention of impacting the terrorist cost–benefit calculus. Such endeavours increase the effort via target hardening, controlling access to facilities, deflecting offenders, and controlling access to the necessary weapons. They also increase the risks by extending guardianship, assisting with natural surveillance, increasing surveillance. They may also reduce the rewards of an attack by concealing or removing potential targets. Such approaches focus on the situational qualities of terrorist behaviour (e.g., what terrorists do and how they do it) and are largely informed by developments in the area of environmental criminology and situational crime prevention.

Much like 'ordinary' criminals, terrorists make a series of cost–benefit analyses to judge whether an act is worth committing (Gill et al., 2018). They make carefully calculated decisions that are utility-maximising (Asal et al., 2009) and likely to increase their probability of success (Clarke & Newman, 2006; Hoffman, 2006). A terrorist's rationality is bounded by a number of individual factors such as risk sensitivity, group guidance, prior experience, and personality. Rationality, in this sense, is bounded by time, effort, experience, and knowledge, which in turn feed into the weighting of rewards, costs, and alternative action plans. Such rational calculations may include having to choose between terrorism and opting for the strategically most advantageous tactics. Pape's (2005) work on suicide terrorism is probably the most oft-cited example of such an approach. Rational calculations are also framed by the group's ideological content and therefore targeting practices may differ across the ideological spectrum. For example, Drake (1998) notes that a terrorist organisation's ideology relates to targeting practices because 'it sets out the moral framework within which they operate.' Considerations of issues like security, avoiding detection, clean getaways, and an awareness of how vulnerable targets are stratified are regularly engaged upon. In this section, we particularly focus upon (a) spatial, temporal and spatio-temporal patters of terrorist attacks, (b) distance decay, (c) risk-terrain modelling, and (d) attack planning.

Spatial, temporal and spatio-temporal patterns of terrorist attacks

If terrorists are selecting targets in a rational manner, then the spatial distribution of attacks should be non-random. When examining terrorist acts, it is evident that, just like more traditional crimes, attacks non-randomly occur across time and place. Factors such as the location of the attack and the time passed since the previous incident have been shown to help determine the location of future attacks (Behlendorf et al., 2012; Berrebi & Lakdawalla, 2007; Johnson & Braithwaite, 2009; LaFree et al., 2012; Medina et al., 2011; Mohler, 2013; Siebeneck et al., 2009; Tench et al., 2016; Townsley et al., 2008). Townsley et al. (2008) examined IED attacks in Iraq and found that they were spatially and temporally clustered. Johnson and Braithwaite's (2009) study of insurgent attacks had a similar finding, with an increased period of risk for a further attack in the immediate vicinity of an initial attack of four to five weeks. In an analysis of group attacks in Israel, Berrebi and Lakdawalla (2007) found four key determinants of risk variation according to space, the most useful being that of proximity of terrorist operational bases. Areas near to international borders were twice as likely to be attacked. Similarly, Rossmo and Harries (2011) found that terrorist cell sites were clustered and found evidence for distance decay in a study of organisations in Turkey.

Other studies have identified temporal variations in spatial patterns, such as changes in incidents and intensity of attacks per the changes in strategy of the organisation, or increases in attacks due to symbolic dates or special events. Siebeneck et al. (2009) identified variations in patterns of attack frequency and intensity (number of victims) in Iraq during the period 2004–2006. As the number of attacks per month increased, the intensity of the attacks decreased. They also found a statistically significant decrease in frequency and intensity on or around Islamic holidays, and an increase on or around American holidays. Medina et al (2011) expanded on this to examine the spatial, temporal and spatio-temporal patterns of incidents from 2004–2009. They found variations in attack patterns over time and that while frequency of attacks correlated with population variables, the intensities of the attacks did not. Behlendorf et al. (2012) examined attacks by Euskadi ta Askatasuna (ETA) in Spain, as well as the Farabundo Marti National Liberation Front (FMLN) in El Salvador. Using a dataset of 4,000 attacks, they identified spatio-temporal clustering, and found the two groups exhibit substantial similarities. They call these clusters 'violent microcycles' (2012:50), and found that bombings and non-lethal attacks were more likely to be part of these microcycles than other types of attacks.

For urban crimes, this elevation in risk extends beyond the location of the original offence (Farrell et al., 1995; Pease, 1998). Townsley et al. (2003), and Johnson and Bowers (2004), found that after a residence has experienced an initial burglary there is a temporary elevation in risk of a further burglary at the same premise or a neighbour's house. This is likely due to the number of potential opportunities identified by the offender when committing the initial offence. Similar patterns have been observed within and across different countries (Johnson et al., 2007). This pattern has also been demonstrated across different crimes, for example assaults and robberies (Grubesic & Mack, 2008), shootings (Ratcliffe & Rengert, 2008), vehicle theft (Lockwood, 2012) and maritime piracy (Marchione & Johnson, 2013). Hotspots of violence during violent campaigns have been identified and spatio-temporal trends of terrorism have been found to decay in similar manner to traditional crimes. For example, Berrebi and Lakdawalla (2007) found that the risk of a subsequent related incident rose after an initial attack in Israel before returning to the baseline after approximately eight weeks. LaFree et al. (2012) used logistic regression analyses to examine attacks by Euskadi ta Askatasuna (ETA) using data on previous incidents to aid in the prediction of the location of future attacks. They found differences in spatial patterns according to variations in the group's strategy. The locations of previous incidents and the time elapsed since these incidents were significant predictors of subsequent attacks. Townsley et al. (2008) used the Knox (1964) test to analyse IED attacks by insurgents in Iraq. Attacks were non-random and were clustered in space and time. After an initial attack, a further attack was likely within 1 km and within 2 days. Braithwaite and Johnson (2012) found similar results in their analysis of insurgent attacks alongside counter-insurgency operations. Insurgent attacks clustered, and there was an immediate increase in risk in close proximity to the attack, which sharply decreased after. They conclude that risk heterogeneity is an especially important factor when understanding spatial-temporal patterns of IED attacks.

Distance decay

One of the most fundamental relationships in environmental criminology is that of spatial interaction and distance. As demonstrated above, terrorists, just like ordinary criminals, are limited by geographical constraints, and numerous patterns of spatial clustering that are evident for traditional crimes are reflected in terrorism (Clarke & Newman, 2006). Collectively, rational choice perspectives, routine activity approach and crime-pattern theory suggest offenders will actively select areas and targets in a way that minimises effort and risks and maximises rewards (Johnson & Bowers, 2004; Felson, 2006).

The least effort principle (Zipf, 1965) assumes that when considering a 'number of identical alternatives for action, an offender selects the one closest to him in order to minimize the effort involved' (Lundrigan & Czarnomski, 2006:220). An urban crime offender's journey to crime typically demonstrates the distance-decay function, whereby chances of offending and frequency of offences decrease as distance from their home increases (Bernasco & Block, 2009; Wiles & Costello, 2000). Likewise, to increase the utility of their attack the terrorist offender would aim to keep the distance travelled minimal, and proximity to the target has been considered a key feature of terrorist target selection (Clarke & Newman, 2006). As well as considering effort, the risk of interception before an attack will also be taken into consideration (Townsley et al., 2008). Racial or ethnic barriers may also further restrict an individual's willingness or capability to travel further from their home to commit an offence. Bernasco and Block discuss how travelling to unknown areas may increase risk:

> for individuals who plan illegal activities, it may be outright dangerous. Strangers 'stand out' more easily in unknown territory, that is, in places where they do not know the customs and rules of the street and possibly dress and behave in ways that attract the attention of the local residents. . . . In segregated cities, those who cross racial or ethnic boundaries cannot blend in easily are likely to be recognized as strangers in the community and be subjected to the 'social eyes' of the local population.
>
> *(2009:99)*

Such concerns were apparent for organisational decision-making within the Palestinian conflict. Bloom (2005) argues that groups were more likely to choose educated or female individuals to conduct suicide terrorism operations within Israel because their language skills and looks would fit in more easily within Israeli society and not draw as much attention.

Proximity to a terrorist's home location has shown potential as a useful predictor of where an attack may take place. The distance-decay effect that is consistently found for urban crimes is also evident in terrorism. It has been demonstrated for group and lone actors in the US, lone actors in Western Europe, Palestinian suicide bombers, and for members of the Provisional Irish Republican Army (PIRA) (Cothren et al., 2008; Gill, 2012; Gill & Horgan, 2012; Gill,

Horgan & Corner, 2017, Marchment, Gill & Bouhana, 2018). Rossmo and Harries (2011) found that there is a 'buffer zone' around terrorist cells, with a limited amount of activity within their immediate vicinity. Higher levels of activity occur beyond this zone, which gradually decrease as distance increases. At a much larger level, the number of terrorist incidents decline as the distance between the home country and the target country increases (Neumayer & Plümper, 2010).

LaFree, Yang and Crenshaw (2009) concluded that 96 per cent of domestic anti-US attacks between 1970 and 2004 involved local targets close to terrorists' homes. Cothren et al. (2008) found that 46 per cent of group attacks in the US took place within 30 miles of the home location. Eby's (2012) analysis of 53 lone actors in the US found a large range of distances between home and target locations. It was shown that many of the actors remained in their hometowns in their attack attempts, although six of his sample travelled extremely long distances, which may have skewed the results. Becker (2014) examined 84 lone actors in the US between 1940 and 2012. Most actors in this study appeared to select targets in a logical manner. Although the notion of the 'awareness space' of an individual was considered, the methods used were mainly qualitative and there was no attempt to empirically examine spatial patterns. Sixty per cent of the sample studied had an identifiable geographical connection to the target. Klein et al. (2017) found extreme right-wing terrorists preferred to attack unsecured targets that were near to their residence.

The function of distance decay has been empirically supported when examining the activities of PIRA (Gill et al., 2016). Nearly two-thirds of a sample of core active members travelled less than 4 miles to commit their attacks, with 40 per cent of all attacks occurring within 1 mile of the offender's home location (Gill et al., 2017). Complex attacks typically involved greater distances. Younger offenders (those aged 20 or under) travelled significantly shorter distances. This suggests that there may be predictable behaviours amongst subsamples of terrorist offenders.

Geographical constraints may be amplified for lone actors, who may lack the resources and support of a larger network. When considering the rational choice perspective, on a basic level an offender should choose a shorter distance over a longer one, to minimise time and effort. As lone actors lack the resources and support of a wider network it is likely that they will keep distances travelled minimal, to increase the utility of their attack (Clarke & Newman, 2006). As well as limiting the actor's capability (Boyns & Ballard, 2004), a lack of resources may also restrict the sophistication of the attack, which is dependent on the individual's level of expertise, skills and knowledge (Gill & Corner, 2016). Lone actors are more likely to attack 'soft' targets such as civilians and most attacks occur in public locations (Gill et al., 2014). Complex attacks, such as those on iconic targets with high levels of security are likely to be beyond most lone actors' individual capability. The level of protection and difficulty in accessing these types of targets increases the complexity of the attack, which is amplified for lone actors as they lack human capital. Sixty per cent of Becker's (2014) sample chose civilian targets; hard targets, such as governmental or military targets, tend to be avoided (Spaaij, 2012; Borum, 2013; Becker, 2014; Gill & Corner, 2016).

The distance-decay effect has recently been replicated for lone actors in Western Europe and the US (Marchment et al., 2018). The mean distance of attacks from the actor's home was 90 miles (144 km), however more than half of all the attacks (56.5 per cent) occurred within 10 miles (6 km) of the individual's home location, and 36 percent of all attacks occurred within 2 miles (3 km). In Western Europe, a high concentration of attacks occurred around the actor's home, with more than half (56 per cent) of all the attacks occurring within 2 miles of the home location. However, only 18.5 per cent of attacks occurred within this vicinity for the US. 75.5 per cent of attacks occurred within 10 miles in Europe, whereas just 40 per cent of attacks occurred within this range in the US.

Variations in distances for different target types reflected previous literature on traditional crimes (Hesseling, 1992; Fritzon, 2001; Santilla et al., 2007). The mean trip length for iconic targets was much longer than for symbolic or arbitrary targets. Those attacking arbitrary targets travelled the shortest distance of the three target types. This suggests that a consideration of costs vs. benefits may take place in decision-making regarding target selection, and that there is a trade-off between distance to the target and the representative value of the target, as lone actors are willing to travel further for targets that are more in line with their grievance. This is consistent with findings of traditional crimes that longer distances are travelled if the expected value of the outcome is higher (Pyle, 1974; Repetto, 1974; Baldwin & Bottoms, 1976; Hesseling, 1992; Rhodes & Conly, 1981; Tita & Griffiths, 2005), and further implies that some cost–benefit consideration is taken.

Communication with others was associated with longer distances. Those who had face-to-face interactions were over four times more likely to travel further than 10 miles. However, no significant difference was found for individuals who had virtual interactions with members of a wider network.

Environmental backcloth

As discussed above, a common finding in analyses demonstrating spatial and temporal variation in risk of terrorist attacks is that they are spatially clustered (Berrebi & Lakdawalla, 2007; Townsley et al., 2008; Johnson & Braithwaite, 2009; Siebeneck et al., 2009; Medina et al., 2011; Behlendorf et al., 2012; Mohler, 2013; Tench et al., 2016). However, the spatial analyses that have been completed thus far have been unable to identify the *causes* of these hotspots – just the fact that they exist.

Local infrastructure is an important element to consider as variations offer different opportunities, risks and rewards. However, a consideration of how the environmental backcloth (Brantingham & Brantingham, 1993, 2008) of a city shapes the behaviour of terrorists has largely been neglected. Zhukov (2012) demonstrated the importance of road networks in a study of insurgent activity in North Caucasus and concluded that they were the most important determining factor for the location of attacks. Johnson and Braithwaite (2009) postulate that attacks by violent actors such as insurgents are concentrated in certain areas for tactical reasons, in an attempt to exhaust the resources of the opposition.

Risk-terrain modelling (RTM) was developed in the study of volume crime to quantitatively assess the spatial influence of features of the urban landscape to identify areas where criminal activity is likely to occur or emerge. RTM has been applied to many different urban crimes including burglaries (Gale & Hollernan, 2013; Moreto et al., 2014), robberies (Kennedy & Gaziarifoglu, 2011; Dugato, 2013), shootings (Caplan et al, 2011; Drawve et al., 2016; Xu & Griffiths, 2017), aggravated assaults (Kennedy et al., 2011; Kennedy et al., 2016; Anyinam, 2015; Kocher & Leitner, 2015), and assaults on police (Drawve & Barnum, 2018).

Because RTM includes contextual information relevant to the social and spatial environment it should be an appropriate approach to assessing terrorism risk. Whilst retrospective hotspot mapping attempts to predict the likelihood of the locations of future attacks based solely on where attacks have previously occurred (Johnson et al., 2007), RTM can be used to estimate future risks of all areas. To the author's knowledge, at present there have only been two applications of RTM to terrorist attacks at the micro level. Onat (2016) identified areas that were at risk of attack from terrorist groups in Istanbul. He found the riskiest factor in the urban environment to be the presence of bakeries. Although this type of building has no symbolic value, bakeries have a social meaning in Turkish culture and are visited frequently by most residents.

Thus, bakeries have a role in an individual's daily routine. Because they attract large numbers of people daily, they can be considered an attractor for many available targets. This again highlights the importance of considering an individual's everyday behaviour, and their awareness space, in the selection of targets. Other significant correlates included religious facilities, bars and clubs, and grocery stores.

Onat and Gul (2018) identified differences in terrorist targeting according to two ideologies: separatist and leftist groups. Grocery stores, bakeries, bars/clubs, and educational facilities were identified as risk factors for both types. They also found differences in risk factors for attacks by each group. Religious facilities and office blocks were significant correlates of separatist attacks but not for leftist attacks. Government buildings were found to be a risk factor for leftist attacks only. This paper also built on Onat (2016) by testing the predictive accuracy of the RTM. They found that a model based on the preceding 36-month period was accurate in predicting the locations of almost half the attacks in the top 10 per cent highest-risk cells, and nearly 80 per cent in the top 20 per cent highest-risk cells in the 20-month period that followed.

Attack planning

Gill et al. (2018) examined over 90 terrorist autobiographies for evidence of what the terrorist decision-making process looked like. They came to eight broad conclusions. First, there is wide variance in the attack planning process. On one end of the spectrum are accounts of attacks being 'more or less spontaneous' (Baumann, 1979:31) and involving 'no great pre-planning . . . done in minutes' (Bradley, 2009:82). On the other end of the spectrum is attack planning occurring for six months (Stone, 2008:84).

Second, terrorists conduct cost–benefit analyses. In March 1988, Loyalist Michael Stone single-handedly attacked an Irish Republican funeral in Belfast with grenades and firearms. Stone hoped to 'take out the Sinn Fein and IRA leadership at the graveside'. Faced with thousands of mourners as well as policing and army units nearby, this was undoubtedly a highly risky attack. 'Most of the time it was 50:50. I figured [this attack] would be at least 60:40 against me, but could even be less.' Stone, however, felt the benefits were too great to pass up. 'I believed it was worth a risk if it meant the leadership of the Republican movement was wiped out' (Stone, 2008:125).

Third, where planning is involved, several targets are often considered. Take for example Wilkerson's (2007:341) account:

> When the proposal was floating about [targeting] Fort Dix, no one argued against it, but the tension in the air seemed to crystallize into a fine mist . . . As yet, however, we knew nothing concrete about the base, or exactly what we were talking about or whether it would be possible. We agreed to investigate other targets as well . . . One team went to each of the possible sites to do reconnaissance . . . [once completed] . . . The conversation focused on which of the targets we had investigated were feasible. Then we discussed the logistical details required for each action.

Fourth, subjective factors play a large role in terrorist cost–benefit analyses. Many of the autobiographical accounts of the planning phase noted internal feelings of 'tension', 'stress', 'frayed nerves', 'doubt', 'frustration', 'paranoia', 'fear', 'inborn sense of danger', 'premonition of disaster', 'highly sensitised', 'hyper-aware', 'anxious', and 'scared'. Such feelings were also common during the commission of an attack. They also noted physiological reactions like 'hand shaking', 'heart thumped like a drum', and an inability to sleep (see Gill et al., 2018).

Fifth, objective security features play a large role in terrorist cost–benefit analyses. For example, Michael Stone's first assassination target was the Sinn Fein politician Owen Carron. Initially Stone surveilled Carron's home address:

> I knew he had two dogs . . . I knew that all over the house and garden he had the best security and surveillance equipment money could buy. He had cameras and sensors. He even had tin cans tied to a tripwire strung across the field at the back of his house to alert him to the security forces that watched his every move . . . I ruled out attacking him at his home because he had too much security and I could not get close enough to kill him without being spotted or killed myself. My best option was his constituency advice clinic . . . [it] was the weakest link in his daily routine.
>
> *(Stone, 2003:64)*

Sixth, terrorists expect security features. They actively search for poor deployment of security. Eric Rudolph's reconnaissance of the Atlanta Olympics Park noted:

> Hundreds of security guards and cops patrolled the park. They eyeballed me going through the entrances. But there were no metal detectors, and bags were searched selectively. After sundown the crowds grew enormous . . . Security at the park became overwhelmed. They stopped searching bags altogether, and the entrances flew wide open. I knew then that I could smuggle in a bomb.
>
> *(Rudolph, 2013:10)*

Seventh, perceptions of the security effectiveness matter more than their simple deployment. For example, this was evident in Gerry Bradley's account of his PIRA activities. In particular, the use of helicopters and sangers in surveillance: 'The chopper destroyed us. If the chopper was up, you weren't allowed to move out of a house . . . Ops were cancelled regularly because of it. They could read newspaper over your shoulder from the chopper' (2009:254).

Finally, perceptions of risk shift with experience. The criminological literature highlights that experience of not being caught for previous crimes downplays immediate situational risks. The same is true for terrorists: 'A steady diet of small illegal activities had boosted my confidence in our abilities to get away with things. I no longer imagined a cop hiding behind every obstacle and actually found myself feeling quite relaxed out on a mission' (Hansen, 1981:70).

How do we prevent terrorism?

Clarke identified five basic prevention mechanisms: increase the effort, increase the risk, reduce rewards, reduce provocations, and remove excuses. Situational factors that increase the risks associated with a criminal opportunity can strongly influence criminal decision-making. A sub-section on each prevention mechanism now follows.

Increase the effort

One obvious SCP measure that comes to mind when thinking about ways to counter terrorism is the use of metal detectors at airports. This measure has been widely recognised as an effective measure in reducing airline hijackings or other types of incident (Cauley & Im, 1988; Enders, Sandler & Cauley, 1990). Enders and Sandler (1993) found a statistically significant reduction after the introduction of metal detectors to airports in the 1970s. Hsu and Apel (2015) found significant reductions in likelihood of terrorist attacks at airport locations where metal detectors had been installed, and concluded that this type of intervention did not displace terror attacks.

High-level security measures were introduced in Belfast in 1970s in response to the threat from the Provisional Irish Republican Army (PIRA). High steel gates were erected at all entrances into Belfast city centre (Coaffee, 2009; Brown 1985; Jarman, 1993). This became known as the 'ring of steel', a highly visible terrorism-prevention measure. A more extreme version was the West Bank Barrier built in response to the threat of suicide bombings by Palestinian terrorist groups. It was built in different sections over different periods of time, between 1999 and 2011. Gibbs (2010) found that attacks decreased from an average of 17 per month in 2001, to two attacks per month in 2004. Attempts by individuals to attack the barrier also decreased. Perry et al. (2017) also examined its effectiveness using a time series of terrorist attacks and fatalities and their location in respect to the barrier. They found it was effective in preventing suicide bombings and other attacks, with very little apparent displacement. Fatalities and attacks were also reduced on the Palestinian side of the barrier. In some locations, terrorists adapted to changed circumstances by committing more opportunistic attacks that required less planning, such as vehicular assaults and stabbing sprees. However, the ethics and proportionality of erecting the barrier as a response to terrorism has been rightfully called into question in both policy and academic circles.

The City of London was also attacked by PIRA multiple times during the 1990s. The initial response to these attacks was to implement traffic management. Vehicle checkpoints were set up and CCTV was used. In 1993, a 'ring of steel' – often referred to as the 'ring of plastic' as it was initially constructed of plastic cones – was set up which secured all entrances. Most routes into the City were closed or made exit-only. Seven routes were left where it was possible to enter the City, which were manned by armed police conducting vehicle checks. This has now been replaced by more permanent structures. Roads entering the City have been narrowed and small chicanes constructed of plastic-coated concrete force drivers to slow down, meaning it is hard to avoid being recorded by one of the many CCTV cameras in place.

Whereas the West Bank Barrier and rings of steel-type SCP measures are highly visible, there are several measures that can be implemented in a subtler fashion. Anti-ramming landscape features are now prevalent in the architectural design of London and other major cities. Reinforced concrete planters, bollards, benches that can withstand vehicle-borne impact are placed in-between roads and important buildings, acting as a 'standoff' buffer zone. At London's Whitehall (the centre for the UK government), steel sandwich bollards are used. Also in London, the Emirates Stadium, which is home to Arsenal football club, has several SCP measures in place. Large concrete letters spelling out the word 'Arsenal' at the stadium's main entrance act as a barrier to vehicles. There are also concrete benches on the forecourt, designed to prevent a vehicle from weaving across, and giant ornate cannons form an obstacle for vehicles driving towards the stadium building.

Increase the risk

The opportunity to commit crime depends on finding a suitable target that is insufficiently guarded (Cohen & Felson, 1979; Tewkesbury & Mustaine, 2000; Roach et al., 2005). The presence of situational factors providing guardianship increases the risk of apprehension. Hollis et al. (2013:66) are strong advocates for the effects of guardianship: 'the most important mechanism involved is the feeling that someone is watching and could observe inappropriate behaviours thus increasing the risk'. The offender's perception of a situation and how this relates to their decision to commit the attack is essential. Therefore, it logically makes sense that proxy measures such as CCTV (whether manned or otherwise) or factors that make it more likely that a guardian will observe the crime should be incorporated within the concept of 'guardianship'. These levels of guardianship indicate an increased amount of risk alluding to risk of apprehension, increasing fear in the offender.

Terrorists often keep several potential targets in mind and choose the one with the relatively fewest risks. In their study of terrorist autobiographies, Gill et al. (2018) found that, no matter the length of the planning process, terrorists weigh up various risks and benefits during the planning phase. The factors considered are both subjective and objective and, in many ways, mirror criminological findings related to criminal cost–benefit decision-making. There were many depictions of how fear and nerves negatively impacted the decision-making processes in planning and carrying out an attack. These appeared to be most intense during the commission of an attack. The weighing of security features necessitates hostile reconnaissance which itself offers risk to the terrorist in terms of detection. The conscious awareness of these objective security factors often leads to doubts, irregular behaviour, and an almost paranoid state where the terrorists often over-exaggerate the degree to which they are being watched, and the number of security measures.

Reduce the rewards

Although there is the need to communicate threat to relevant audiences, caution must be taken to prevent the glorification of terrorist actors (Bakker & de Graaf, 2011). In cases where they commit more than one act, the release of the profile(s) of the suspect(s) to the media can be a useful tool in the interdiction of terrorism. For example, in the case of David Copeland, a neo-Nazi militant who became known as the 'London Nail Bomber', several CCTV images taken during his first bomb attack were released to the press. This release resulted in hundreds of reports of information relating to the suspect and led to his arrest (Spaaij, 2012). However, Freedman (2005) cautions that any communication given to the public prior to an anticipated attack to aid in its interdiction may provide information to the terrorist actors, who may alter their behaviour and actions accordingly. Copeland altered his final attack in response to the release of his image to the public, bringing it forward by one day, and as such was able to successfully complete it before detection (Spaaij, 2012). Similarly, in the 2008 Mumbai attacks, the terrorists involved made attack-related decisions through the monitoring of situational information from live media and the internet (Oh et al., 2011).

In the mitigation of a terrorist event, efforts must be made to counter the narratives put forward by the offenders to deter copycat behaviour and avoid contagion-like effects, as well asking the public to increase vigilance and look out for similar offenders (Bakker & de Graaf, 2011; Gill, 2015). Counter-narratives can be used to undermine the actions of recent events and address and counter underlying grievances to prevent copycat attacks (Gill, 2015). Copycat elements in attacks are a specific issue for lone actors, with one study finding evidence for such behaviour in 33 per cent of cases (Hamm & Spaaij, 2015).

Reduce the provocations

The tendency within some counter-terrorism circles has been to choose knee-jerk policy options that fail to reduce provocations and instead exacerbate them. For example, countering terrorism with punitive enforcement measures like targeted assassinations has a long history. In the aftermath of 9/11, the merits of 'war' approaches to countering terrorist groups became highly salient within public discourse. Proponents claimed that such measures promise to reduce subsequent terrorism by degrading terrorist group capacity in several ways. First, they reduce the pool of cadres and recruits. Second, they impose costs on those who provide financial and other forms of support for terrorists. Third, they have the potential to remove terrorist group leaders and other skilled members. Fourth, they serve as a deterrent for would-be terrorists and supporters. Fifth, they impose costs on terrorist group members who have to spend more time and finances in changing locations and avoiding detection. This lessens their ability to commit terrorist attacks. Sixth, they reduce the flow of internal communications within the terrorist groups. Finally these policies are often popular within a country's domestic constituency.

Critics suggested otherwise and made a number of compelling arguments. Cumulatively, these arguments suggested that the above arguments would only serve to increase provocations. First, this approach violates basic democratic and human rights. Second, other initiatives such as arresting terrorists may prove more effective. Third, it may in fact prompt a backlash from the terrorist group. Fourth, it may erode public support for state counter-terrorism officials. Fifth, it may kill non-combatants. Sixth, it may enhance sympathy for terrorists. Finally, it provides the targeted terrorist movement with propaganda (Byman, 2006).

Empirically, the results only point in one direction. Provocative counter-terrorism approaches increase provocations and increase the volume of terrorist attacks. Amongst the handful of studies Lum et al. (2006) could find in their systematic review, there was a suggestion that 'retaliatory attacks (for example, the US attack on Libya in 1986 or attacks by Israel on the PLO) have significantly increased the number of terrorist attacks in the short run' (2006:1). In the 12 years that have passed since the systematic review, empirical approaches to understanding this question have flourished. In particular, these studies have tested whether punitive counter-terrorism measures downgrade or foster future terrorist attacks. Aided by parallel major data collection, efforts have allowed analyses to be carried out on conflicts such as Northern Ireland, Palestine, Chechnya, Afghanistan, Iraq, Spain and Pakistan (Asal et al., 2015; Gill et al., 2016). In a relatively short period of time, we have gone from very few analyses to many analyses, of which there have been very quick improvements in terms of the methodological rigour and theoretical nuance. The American political scientist Joseph K. Young succinctly expresses the aggregate impression that one generates from this wealth of studies:

> In social science, there aren't really laws like gravity. There are always exceptions. Most theories are probabilistic. We expect something *on average* to go up whenever another thing goes down (or up). We look at trends and note the exceptions and hope to get it right more than we get it wrong. One process, from my observation, seems nearly law-like. Violence begets violence . . . Sometimes violence is necessary, sometimes it is unavoidable, sometimes it may be the moral decision, but I think whatever the justification for its use, it will (almost) always generate more of itself

Of course, terrorism can sometimes be a response to extreme state provocation and reducing provocation may involve acquiescing to some of the group's demands; for example, the Good Friday Agreement in Northern Ireland.

Remove the excuses

Terrorist groups utilise a range of neutralisation techniques to downplay their culpability, guilt or shame for their violence. One prominent recurring justification posits suicide bombing as a response to state provocation. By doing so, terrorist organisations seek the image of the repressed underdog and the image of an organisation that reluctantly turned to a tactic that guarantees the death of one of its own constituency. Hamas labelled one set of bombings 'the natural retaliation by a people slaughtered day and night, whose dignity is humiliated by the Zionist enemy's war machine' (cited in Human Rights Watch, 2002: 27–28). Another recurring narrative frames suicide bombing as a tactic that balances power in an otherwise asymmetric war. In turn, militant organisations regularly use the argument that suicide bombings lessen power asymmetry. For example, Sheikh Fadlallah of Hezbollah noted that his organisation is 'obliged to use all the ways and possibilities to face the enemy. Due to . . . weak military possibilities, we were forced to use the weapon of human bodies to make advances on the front. It was . . . [either this option or] . . . giving up' (cited in Termos, 1995). There is an onus therefore on combatting these neutralisation techniques via counter-narrative campaigns.

Other potential avenues seek to assist compliance from statutory bodies (e.g. mandating the reporting of radicalisation concerns) and members of the public (e.g. the 'See It, Say It, Sorted' campaign, implemented throughout the UK's rail network) that seek to increase informal surveillance by reporting concerns of suspicious or threatening behaviours. The UK's experience of rolling out such measures has been met with criticism and debate from within a number of these statutory bodies (Hurlow et al., 2016; O'Donnell, 2016; Taylor & Soni, 2017).

Conclusion

In order for terrorism studies to develop as a serious field of study, it would do well to follow several basic crime-science principles. It has already made significant improvements in terms of data generation and collation and the input of several previously overlooked scientific disciplines. However, there is still a significant gap in three areas compared to other crime problems that crime science has consistently studied. First, evaluation in the terrorism and countering-radicalisation space is sorely lacking in many key areas. This is perhaps most significantly the case in the current 'countering violent extremism' space where so-called 'vulnerable' individuals are offered diversion routes out of extremism. The lack of evaluation is compounded by two additional factors: (a) policy in several European countries has pushed this to the forefront of the counter-terrorism agenda, meaning there has been little to no time for adequate piloting and (b) this problem is being treated as something entirely new and there is very little learning from analogous crime problems (e.g. domestic violence) where offender-oriented treatments have been common. The lack of validation testing on existing terrorism risk-assessment tools is also a significant concern given their potential to exacerbate problems, and stigmatise communities. More and more tools are being developed, commercially sold and potentially applied in contexts for which they were not designed.

Second, as mentioned in the core part of the text, there is a lack of specificity in the terminology utilised within the research literature. Terrorism studies, as a whole, largely treat each individual the same despite their offences, criminogenic motivations and other characteristics being different. This is where criminology was 40 years ago. Crime science tells us that to understand a crime event or a criminal, specificity matters.

Third, there needs to be less attention paid to who the offender is, what their personal characteristics are, and their ideological belief system. This has unduly narrowed the ways in which social science has tried to feed into counter-terrorism practice. Much more focus needs to be placed on the ecology in which the individual became exposed to rule-breaking norms, the interaction of this insight with the individual's cognition and criminogenic needs, and the development of finer-grained understandings of the repertoire, and sequencing, of behaviours that underpin violent outcomes.

References

Abrahms, M. (2008). What terrorists really want: terrorist motives and counterterrorism strategy. *International Security, 32*(4), 78–105.
Alexander, Y. (Ed.). (1976). *International Terrorism: National, Regional, and Global Perspectives*. New York: Praeger.
Anyinam, C. (2015). Using risk terrain modeling technique to identify places with the greatest risk for violent crimes in New Haven. *Crime Mapping & Analysis News* (online journal).
Asal, V. H., Rethemeyer, K., Anderson, I., Stein, A. Rizzo, J., & Rozea, M. (2009). The softest of targets: a study on terrorist target selection. *Journal of Applied Security Research, 4*(3), 258–278.
Asal, V., Gill, P., Rethemeyer, R. K., & Horgan, J. (2015). Killing range: explaining lethality variance within a terrorist organization. *Journal of Conflict Resolution, 59*(3), 401–427.
Bahgat, K. & Medina, R. M. (2013). An overview of geographical perspectives and approaches in terrorism research. *Perspectives on Terrorism*, 7(1).
Bakker, E. & De Graaf, B. (2011). Lone wolves: how to prevent this phenomenon? *Expert Meeting Paper, 1–8*. The Hague: International Centre for Counter-Terrorism.
Baldwin, J. & Bottoms, A. E. (1976). *The Urban Criminal: A Study in Sheffield*. London, UK: Tavistock.
Baumann, M. (1979). *Terror or Love?* New York: Grove.
Becker, M. (2014). Explaining lone wolf target selection in the United States. *Studies in Conflict and Terrorism, 37*(11), 959–978.
Behlendorf, B., LaFree, G., & Legault, R. (2012). Microcycles of violence: evidence from terrorist attacks by ETA and the FMLN. *Journal of Quantitative Criminology, 28*(1), 49–75.
Bernasco, W. (2010). A sentimental journey to crime: effects of residential history on crime location choice. *Criminology, 48*, 389–416.
Bernasco, W. & Block, R. (2009). Where offenders choose to attack: a discrete choice model of robberies in Chicago. *Criminology, 47*(1), 93–130.
Bernasco, W. & Kooistra, T. (2010). Effects of residential history on commercial robbers' crime location choices. *European Journal of Criminology*, 7(4), 251–265.
Berrebi, C. & Lakdawalla, D. (2007). How does terrorism risk vary across space and time? An analysis based on the Israeli experience. *Defence and Peace Economics, 18*(2), 113–131.
Bloom, M. (2005). *Dying to Kill: The Allure of Suicide Terror*. New York: Columbia University Press.
Borum, R. (2013). Informing lone-offender investigations. *Criminology & Public Policy, 12*(1), 103–112.
Boyns, D. & Ballard, J. D. (2004). Developing a sociological theory for the empirical understanding of terrorism. *The American Sociologist, 35*(2), 5–25.
Bradley, G. (2009). *Insider: Gerry Bradley's Life in the IRA*. Dublin: The O'Brien Press.
Braithwaite, A. & Johnson, S. D. (2012). Space–time modeling of insurgency and counterinsurgency in Iraq. *Journal of Quantitative Criminology, 28*(1), 31–48.
Braithwaite, A. & Johnson, S. D. (2015). The battle for Baghdad: testing hypotheses about insurgency from risk heterogeneity, repeat victimization, and denial policing approaches. *Terrorism and Political Violence, 27*(1), 112–132.
Brantingham, P. J. & Brantingham, P. L. (2008). Crime pattern theory. In R. Wortley & L. Mazerolle (Eds), *Environmental Criminology and Crime Analysis* (pp. 78–93). Portland, OR: Willan Publishing.
Brown, S. (1985) Central Belfast's security segment – an urban phenomenon. *Area, 17*(1), 1–8.
Brynielsson, J., Horndahl, A., Johansson, F., Kaati, L., Mårtenson, C., & Svenson, P. (2013). Harvesting and analysis of weak signals for detecting lone wolf terrorists. *Security Informatics, 2*(1), 11.
Byman, D. (2006). Do targeted killings work? *Foreign Affairs, 85*, 95–111.
Canter, D. (2004). Offender profiling and investigative psychology. *Journal of Investigative Psychology and Offender Profiling, 1*(1), 1–15.
Canter, D. & Larkin, P. (1993). The environmental range of serial rapists. *Journal of Environmental Psychology, 13*(1), 63–69.
Caplan, J. M., Kennedy, L. W., & Miller, J. (2010) Risk terrain modeling: Criminological theory and GIS methods for crime forecasting. *Justice Quarterly, 28*(2), 360–381.
Caplan, J. M., Kennedy, L. W., & Miller, J. (2011). Risk terrain modeling: brokering criminological theory and GIS methods for crime forecasting. *Justice Quarterly, 28*, 360–381.
Cauley, J. & Im, E. I. (1988). Intervention policy analysis of skyjackings and other terrorist incidents. *The American Economic Review, 78*(2), 27–31.

Clark, W. (2009). Bioterrorism: A situational crime prevention approach. Reducing terrorism through situational crime prevention. *Crime Prevention Studies, 2*, 93–109.

Clarke, R. V. & Newman, G. R. (2006). *Outsmarting the Terrorists*. New York: Praeger.

Coaffee, J. (2009). *Terrorism, risk and the global city: Towards urban resilience*. Abingdon, UK: Routledge.

Cohen, L. E. & Felson, M. (1979). Social change and crime rate trends: a routine activity approach. *American Sociological Review, 44*, 588–608.

Cooper, H. H. A. (1977). What is a terrorist: A psychological perspective. *Legal Medical Quarterly, 1*, 16.

Corner, E. & Gill, P. (2015). A false dichotomy? Mental illness and lone-actor terrorism. *Law and Human Behavior, 39*(1), 23.

Cothren, J., Smith, B. L., Roberts, P., & Damphousse, K. R. (2008). Geospatial and temporal patterns of preparatory conduct among American terrorists. *International Journal of Comparative and Applied Criminal Justice, 32*(1), 23–41.

Desmarais, S. L., Simons-Rudolph, J., Brugh, C. S., Schilling, E., & Hoggan, C. (2017). The state of scientific knowledge regarding factors associated with terrorism. *Journal of Threat Assessment and Management, 4*(4), 180.

Drake, C. J. (1998). The role of ideology in terrorists' target selection. *Terrorism and Political Violence, 10*(2), 53–85.

Drawve, G. & Barnum, J. D. (2018). Place-based risk factors for aggravated assault across police divisions in Little Rock, Arkansas. *Journal of Crime and Justice, 41*(2), 173–192.

Drawve, G., Moak, S. C., & Berthelot, E. R. (2016). Predictability of gun crimes: a comparison of hot spot and risk terrain modelling techniques. *Policing and Society, 26*(3), 312–331.

Dugato, M. (2013). Assessing the validity of risk terrain modeling in a European city: Preventing robberies in the city of Milan. *Crime Mapping, 5*(1), 63–89.

Eby, C. A. (2012). The nation that cried lone wolf: a data-driven analysis of individual terrorists in the United States since 9/11. Monterey, CA: Naval Postgraduate School. Department of National Security Affairs.

Enders, W. & Sandler, T. (1993). The effectiveness of antiterrorism policies: A vector-autoregression-intervention analysis. *American Political Science Review, 87*(4), 829–844.

Enders, W., Sandler, T. & Cauley, J. (1990). Assessing the impact of terrorist-thwarting policies: an intervention time series approach. *Defence Economics, 2*(1), 1–18.

Farrell, G., Phillips, C & Pease. K. (1995) Like taking candy: why does repeat victimization occur? *British Journal of Criminology, 35*(3), 384–399.

Felson, M. (2006). *Crime and Nature*. Thousand Oaks, CA: Sage.

Freedman, L. (2005). The politics of warning: terrorism and risk communication. *Intelligence and National Security, 20*(3), 379–418.

Fritzon, K. (2001). An examination of the relationship between distance travelled and motivational aspects of firesetting behavior. *Journal of Environmental Psychology, 21*(1), 45–60.

Gale, R. & Hollernan, D. (2013). An application of risk terrain modeling to residential burglary. *TCNJ Journal of Student Scholarship, 15*, 1–9.

Gibbs, S. (2010). Applying the theory and techniques of situational criminology to counterinsurgency operations: reducing insurgency through situational prevention. Doctoral dissertation. Monterey, CA: Naval Postgraduate School.

Gill, P. (2012). Assessing contemporary trends and future prospects in the study of the suicide bomber. *Negotiation and Conflict Management Research, 5*(3), 239–252.

Gill, P. (2015). *Lone-actor Terrorists: A Behavioural Analysis*. London: Routledge.

Gill, P. & Corner, E. (2016). Lone-actor terrorist target choice. *Behavioral Sciences and the Law, 34*(5), 693–705.

Gill, P., Corner, E., Conway, M., Thornton, A., Bloom, M., & Horgan, J. (2017). Terrorist use of the internet by the numbers. *Criminology & Public Policy, 16*(1), 99–117.

Gill, P., Horgan, J. & Corner, E. (2017). The rational foraging terrorist: analysing the distances travelled to commit terrorist violence. *Terrorism and Political Violence*. DOI: 10.1080/09546553.2017.1297707.

Gill, P., Horgan, J., & Deckert, P. (2014). Bombing alone: tracing the motivations and antecedent behaviors of lone-actor terrorists. *Journal of Forensic Sciences, 59*(2), 425–435.

Gill, P., Marchment, Z., Corner, E., & Bouhana, N. (2018). Terrorist Decision-Making in the Context of Risk, Attack Planning and Attack Commission. *Studies in Conflict & Terrorism*. DOI: 10.1080/1057610X.2018.1445501.

Gill, P., Piazza, J. A., & Horgan, J. (2016). Counterterrorism killings and provisional IRA bombings, 1970–1998. *Terrorism and Political Violence, 28*(3), 473–496.

Gøtzsche-Astrup, O. (2018). The time for causal designs: review and evaluation of empirical support for mechanisms of political radicalisation. *Aggression and Violent Behavior, 39*, 90–99.
Grubesic, T. H. & Mack, E. A. (2008). Spatio-temporal interaction of urban crime. *Journal of Quantitative Criminology, 24*(3), 285–306.
Gruenewald, J., Allison-Gruenewald, K., & Klein, B. R. (2015). Assessing the attractiveness and vulnerability of eco-terrorism targets: A situational crime prevention approach. *Studies in Conflict & Terrorism, 38*(6), 433–455.
Gruenewald, J., Chermak, S., & Freilich, J. D. (2013). Distinguishing 'loner' attacks from other domestic extremist violence. *Criminology & Public Policy, 12*(1), 65–91.
Hamm, M. & Spaaij, R. (2015). Lone wolf terrorism in America: using knowledge of radicalization pathways to forge prevention strategies. Washington, DC: US Department of Justice Report.
Hegghammer, T. (2013). Should I stay or should I go? Explaining variation in Western jihadists' choice between domestic and foreign fighting. *American Political Science Review, 107*(1), 1–15.
Hesseling, R. B. (1992). Using data on offender mobility in ecological research. *Journal of Quantitative Criminology, 8*(1), 95–112.
Hoffman, B. (2006). *Inside Terrorism*. New York: Columbia University Press.
Hollis, M. E., Felson, M., & Welsh, B. C. (2013). The capable guardian in routine activities theory: A theoretical and conceptual reappraisal. *Crime Prevention and Community Safety, 15*(1), 65–79.
Horgan, J. G. (2009). *Walking Away from Terrorism: Accounts of Disengagement from Radical and Extremist Movements*. New York: Routledge.
Horgan, J. G. (2015). *The Psychology of Terrorism* (2nd edition). London: Routledge.
Hsu, H. Y. & Apel, R. (2015). A situational model of displacement and diffusion following the introduction of airport metal detectors. *Terrorism and Political Violence, 27*(1), 29–52.
Human Rights Watch (2002). *Erased in a Moment: Suicide Bombing Attacks Against Israeli Civilians*. New York: Human Rights Watch.
Hurlow, J., Wilson, S., & James, D. V. (2016). Protesting loudly about Prevent is popular but is it informed and sensible? *BJPsych Bulletin, 40*(3), 162–163.
Jacques, K. & Taylor, P. J. (2008). Male and female suicide bombers: different sexes, different reasons? *Studies in Conflict & Terrorism, 31*(4), 304–326.
Jarman, N. (1993). *Intersecting Belfast*. Oxford: Berg Publications.
Johnson, N. F., Medina, P., Zhao, G., Messinger, D. S., Horgan, J., Gill, P., . . . & Manrique, P. (2013). Simple mathematical law benchmarks human confrontations. *Scientific Reports, 3*, 3463.
Johnson, S. D. & Bowers, K. (2004). The stability of space–time clusters of burglary. *British Journal of Criminology, 44*, 55–65.
Johnson, S. D. & Braithwaite, A. (2009). *Spatio-temporal Modelling of Insurgency in Iraq. Criminal Justice Press* (pp. 9–32). Monsey, NY: Criminal Justice Press.
Johnson, S. D., Bernasco, W., Bowers, K., Elffers, H., Ratcliffe, J., Rengert, G. & Townsley, M. (2007). Space-time patterns of risk: A cross national assessment of residential burglary victimization. *Journal of Quantitative Criminology, 23*, 201–219.
Kennedy, L. W. & Gaziarifoglu, Y. (2011). Applying RTM to street robberies. In *Risk Terrain Modeling Compendium* (pp. 73–78). Newark, NJ: Rutgers Centre on Public Security.
Kennedy, L. W., Caplan, J. M., & Piza, E. (2011). Risk clusters, hotspots, and spatial intelligence: risk terrain modeling as an algorithm for police resource allocation strategies. *Journal of Quantitative Criminology, 27*(3): 339–362.
Kennedy, L. W., Caplan, J. M., Piza, E. L., & Buccine-Schraeder, H. (2016). Vulnerability and exposure to crime: Applying risk terrain modeling to the study of assault in Chicago. *Applied Spatial Analysis and Policy, 9*(4): 529–548.
Klein, B. R., Gruenewald, J., & Smith, B. L. (2017). Opportunity, group structure, temporal patterns, and successful outcomes of far-right terrorism incidents in the United States. *Crime & Delinquency, 63*(10), 1224–1249.
Kocher, M. & Leitner, M. (2015). Forecasting of crime events applying risk terrain modeling. *GI_Forum, 2015*, 30–40.
LaFree, G. (2009). Criminology's third war. *Criminology & Public Policy, 8*(3), 431–444.
LaFree, G., Dugan, L., Xie, M. & Singh, P. (2012). Spatial and Temporal Patterns of Terrorist Attacks by ETA 1970 to 1007. *Journal of Quantitative Criminology, 28*, 7–29.
LaFree, G., Yang, S. M., & Crenshaw, M. (2009). Trajectories of terrorism. *Criminology & Public Policy, 8*(3), 445–473.

Lum, C., Kennedy, L. W., & Sherley, A. (2006). Are counter-terrorism strategies effective? The results of the Campbell systematic review on counter-terrorism evaluation research. *Journal of Experimental Criminology*, *2*(4), 489–516.

Lundrigan, S. & Czarnomski, S. (2006). Spatial characteristics of serial sexual assault in New Zealand. *Australian & New Zealand Journal of Criminology*, *39*(2), 218–231.

Maher, S. (2016). *Salafi-Jihadism: The History of an Idea*. Oxford: Oxford University Press.

Manrique, P., Cao, Z., Gabriel, A., Horgan, J., Gill, P., Qi, H., . . . & Johnson, N. (2016). Women's connectivity in extreme networks. *Science Advances*, *2*(6), e1501742.

Marchione, E. & Johnson, S. D. (2013). Spatial, temporal and spatio-temporal patterns of maritime piracy. *Journal of Research in Crime and Delinquency*, *50*(4), 504–524.

Marchment, Z., Bouhana, N. & Gill, P. (2018) Lone-actor terrorists: a residence-to-crime approach. *Terrorism and Political Violence*. DOI: 10.1080/09546553.2018.1481050.

Medina, R. M., Siebeneck, L. K., & Hepner, G. F. (2011). A geographic information systems (GIS) analysis of spatiotemporal patterns of terrorist incidents in Iraq 2004–2009. *Studies in Conflict & Terrorism*, *34*(11), 862–882.

Mohler, G. (2013). Modeling and estimation of multi-source clustering in crime and security data. *The Annals of Applied Statistics*, 7(3): 1525–1539.

Monahan, J. (2012). The individual risk assessment of terrorism. *Psychology, Public Policy, and Law*, *18*(2), 167.

Moreto, W. D., Piza, E. L., & Caplan, J. M. (2014). 'A plague on both your houses?': risks, repeats and reconsiderations of urban residential burglary. *Justice Quarterly*, *31*(6): 1102–1126.

Neumayer, E. & Plümper, T. (2010). Galton's problem and contagion in international terrorism along civilizational lines. *Conflict Management and Peace Science*, *27*(4), 308–325.

O'Donnell, A. (2016). Securitisation, counterterrorism and the silencing of dissent: The educational implications of prevent. *British Journal of Educational Studies*, *64*(1), 53–76.

Oh, O., Agrawal, M. & Rao, H. R. (2011). Information control and terrorism: tracking the Mumbai terrorist attack through twitter. *Information Systems Frontiers*, *13*(1), 33–43.

Onat, I. (2016). An analysis of spatial correlates of terrorism using risk terrain modeling. *Terrorism and Political Violence*. DOI:10.1080/09546553.2016.1215309.

Onat, I. & Gul, Z. (2018). Terrorism Risk Forecasting by Ideology. *European Journal on Criminal Policy and Research*. DOI: 10.1007/s10610-017-9368-8.

Pape, R. (2005). *Dying to Win: The Strategic Logic of Suicide Terrorism*. New York: Random House

Pease, K. (1998). Repeat victimisation: taking stock (Vol. *90*). London: Home Office Police Research Group.

Perliger, A., Koehler-Derrick, G., & Pedahzur, A. (2016). The gap between participation and violence: Why we need to disaggregate terrorist 'profiles'. *International Studies Quarterly*, *60*(2), 220–229.

Perry, S., Apel, R., Newman, G. R., & Clarke, R. V. (2017). The situational prevention of terrorism: an evaluation of the Israeli West Bank barrier. *Journal of Quantitative Criminology*, *33*(4), 727–751.

Pyle, (1974). *The Spatial Dynamics of Crime. Department of Geography Research Monograph No. 159*. Chicago, IL: The University of Chicago.

Ratcliffe, J. H. & Rengert, G. F. (2008). Near-repeat patterns in Philadelphia shootings. *Security Journal*, *21*(1–2), 58–76.

Repetto, T. (1974). *Residential Crime*. Cambridge, MA: Ballinger.

Rhodes, W. M. & Conly, C. C. (1981). Crime and mobility: an empirical study. In P.J. Brantingham & P.L. Brantingham (Eds.) *Environmental Criminology* (pp. 167–188). Prospect Heights, IL: Waveland Press.

Roach, J., Ekblom, P. & Flynn, R. (2005). The conjunction of terrorist opportunity: A framework for diagnosing and preventing acts of terrorism. *Security Journal*, *18*(3), 7–25.

Rossmo, D. K. & Harries, K. (2011). The geospatial structure of terrorist cells. *Justice Quarterly*, *28*(2), 221–248.

Santtila, P., Laukkanen, M., & Zappalà, A. (2007). Crime behaviours and distance travelled in homicides and rapes. *Journal of Investigative Psychology and Offender Profiling*, *4*(1), 1–15.

Schuurman, B. (2018). Research on terrorism, 2007–2016: a review of data, methods, and authorship. *Terrorism and Political Violence*. DOI: 10.1080/09546553.2018.1439023.

Siebeneck, L. K., Medina, R. M., Yamada, I., & Hepner, G.F. (2009). Spatial and temporal analyses of terrorist incidents in Iraq, 2004–2006. *Studies in Conflict and Terrorism*, *32*(7), 591–610.

Spaaij, R. (2012). *Understanding Lone Wolf Terrorism*. Springer Briefs in Criminology.Berlin: Springer Science + Business Media.
Stone, M. (2003). *None Shall Divide Us*. London: John Blake Publishing.
Taylor, L. & Soni, A. (2017). Preventing radicalisation: a systematic review of literature considering the lived experiences of the UK's Prevent strategy in educational settings. *Pastoral Care in Education*, *35*(4), 241–252.
Taylor, M. & Horgan, J. (2006). A conceptual framework for addressing psychological process in the development of the terrorist. *Terrorism and Political Violence*, *18*(4), 585–601.
Tench, S., Fry, H., & Gill, P. (2016). Spatio-temporal patterns of IED usage by the Provisional Irish Republican Army. *European Journal of Applied Mathematics*, *27*(03), 377–402.
Tita, G. & Griffiths, E. (2005). Traveling to violence: the case for a mobility-based spatial typology of homicide. *Journal of Research in Crime and Delinquency*, *42*(3), 275–308.
Townsley, M., Homel, R., & Chaseling, J. (2003). Infectious burglaries: a test of the near repeat hypothesis. *The British Journal of Criminology*, *37*(3), 615–633.
Townsley, M., Johnson, S. D., & Ratcliffe, J. H. (2008). Space–time dynamics of insurgent activity in Iraq. *Security Journal*, *21*(3), 139–146.
Tracy, P. E. & Kempf-Leonard, K. (1996). *Continuity and Discontinuity in Criminal Careers*. Berlin: Springer Science + Business Media.
von Lampe, K. (2011). The application of the framework of situational crime prevention to 'organized crime'. *Criminology & Criminal Justice*, *11*(2), 145–163.
Warren, J., Reboussin, R., Hazelwood, R.R., Cummings, A., Gibbs, N., & Trumbetta, S. (1998). Crime scene and distance correlates of serial rape. *Journal of Quantitative Criminology*, *14*, 35–59.
Weisburd, D. (2015). The law of crime concentration and the criminology of place. *Criminology*, *53*(2), 133–157.
Wiles, P. & Costello, A. (2000). *The'Road To Nowhere': The Evidence for Travelling Criminals* (Vol. *207*). London: Research, Development and Statistics Directorate, Home Office.
Wilkerson, C. (2011). *Flying Close to the Sun: My Life and Times as a Weatherman*. New York: Seven Stories Press.
Xu, J. & Griffiths, E. (2017). Shooting on the street: measuring the spatial influence of physical features on gun violence in a bounded street network. *Journal of Quantitative Criminology*, *33*(2): 237–253.
Yun, M. (2009). Application of situational crime prevention to terrorist hostage taking and kidnapping: a case study of 23 Korean hostages in Afghanistan. In Joshua D. Freilich & Graeme R. Newman (Eds), *Reducing Terrorism Through Situational Crime Prevention*. NCJ-229596.
Zhukov, Y. M. (2012). Roads and the diffusion of insurgent violence: The logistics of conflict in Russia's North Caucasus. *Political Geography*, *31*(3), 144–156.
Zipf, G. K. (1965). *Human Behavior and the Principle of Least Effort: An Introduction to Human Ecology*. New York: Hafner.

17

Evolution, crime science and terrorism

The case of Provisional IRA weaponry

Paul Ekblom and Paul Gill

Introduction

Crime and terrorism are not static problems. They change on timescales from days to decades. In part, this flux stems from offenders adapting to exploit opportunities afforded by exogenous social and technological developments in society, and to cope with threats from other offenders. But significantly too it derives from *arms races* between offenders and those on the security side. On the security side, however, the consensus among change-minded commentators has been that 'contemporary crime control policies are hopelessly static' (Cohen et al., 1995:216; see also Dietl, 2008). Ekblom (1997, 2016a) argues that to win campaigns rather than merely individual battles against criminals and terrorists, we must routinely *out-innovate* adaptive offenders against a background of technological and social change that may first favour one side, and then the other. The classic example is Shover's (1996) study of safes and safe-breakers, where new, emerging technologies including combination locks, cutting tools, new hardened alloy casings and so forth flipped the advantage back and forth between the opponents.

Accounts of longer-term change and innovation processes have often drawn on *evolutionary* themes, as does the present chapter. Such themes extend beyond conventional, biological evolution to include cultural, and specifically technological, counterparts. Evolution covers processes highly relevant to the strategic view on crime prevention and counter-terrorism – adaptation, innovation and improvisation. As we shift focus from casual opportunistic offending and its short-term decision/action cycles to that which is persistent, motivated and perhaps well-resourced, these factors become salient.

Crime science has only recently begun to incorporate evolution – see Cohen et al. (1995), on theft; Ekblom (1997, 1999) and Brown (2016) on arms races; Felson (2006) on crime and nature. Roach and Pease (2013) supply an excellent introduction to the field which argues the case for linking evolution with situational prevention in particular and with social science in general. Sell (this volume) presents a guide for using evolutionary theory to understand a given kind of crime. A useful attempt to link more traditional criminological topics with evolutionary thinking is by Durrant and Ward (2012). If studies connecting evolution and crime are rare, those combining evolution, terrorism and crime science are scarcer than a fossilised Denisovan finger bone. Ekblom et al. (2016) apply explicit evolutionary psychology perspectives to illuminate and enhance situational prevention of terrorism. Ekblom (2016) addresses terrorist/security arms races from the perspective of cultural and technological evolution, innovation, and design; the evolution of offender rationality (2017a); and the evolution of technology (2017b).

This chapter blends a crime-science approach to prevention, with ideas from cultural and biological evolution, covering both the entities that are evolving, and the environment or ecosystem to which they are adapting. We show how, together, they can provide a fresh perspective and a richer understanding, supporting attempts to control terrorist attacks that are more strategic and change-oriented than before.

We discuss in detail how evolutionary processes operating at the technological and tactical level played out in a specific, prolonged period of conflict between the Provisional Irish Republican Army (PIRA) and the UK security services including the police and the military from 1970–1998. This conflict saw not just a steady evolution of terrorist attack techniques and weapons technologies including improvised explosive devices (IEDs), but a *co*-evolutionary arms race with the security side.

From 2010 to 2012, a team of researchers at Pennsylvania State University and elsewhere sought to understand the behavioural underpinnings of PIRA's improvised explosive device creation and implementation (Gill, Horgan and Lovelace, 2011). It led to a series of publications regarding creativity and innovation (Gill, 2017; Gill et al., 2013; Johnson et al., 2013), red-team blue-team interactions (Asal et al., 2015; Gill, Piazza and Horgan, 2016) and the social networks that created the IEDs (Gill et al., 2014, Gill and Horgan, 2013). The papers built upon the then relatively underdeveloped research ideas behind creativity and innovation and terrorist behaviour. Collectively the papers utilised insights from diverse disciplines including organisational and industrial psychology and political science and they helped identify the individual, network, organisational and environmental traits that combined to make the ground for PIRA's innovation so fertile.

This chapter re-purposes the findings from these research papers to help illustrate the evolutionary dynamics behind these processes. The aims are first, to illustrate evolutionary thinking and second, to demonstrate how it can organise practically and theoretically relevant empirical knowledge, identify significant gaps and aid the adoption of more strategic responses to such arms races. Our emphasis is thus on cultural/technological evolution rather than, say, the evolutionary psychology of offending, which Ekblom et al. (2016) and Sell (this volume) cover elsewhere. The evolving entities or units of interest here comprise individual weapon designs and techniques.

The next two sections cover the basic mechanisms of evolution, and how evolving entities relate to their environment by a combination of adaptation and niche construction. After that there are sections on: higher-level processes of change, centring on accelerants of evolution; the 'flying leaps' of advancement feasible in cultural/technological evolution; and co-evolutionary arms races. The concluding section identifies lessons for policy and practice in terms of the importance of anticipation, running arms races and the employment of design, not only in solving complex security problems but in reframing them.

Before proceeding further, we should note that some of the links to evolution we draw on are by analogy, helping just to broaden thinking in crime science; but others can be deemed formal equivalents between biological evolution and technological/cultural counterparts. The latter of course differs by including purposive and anticipatory processes rather than being mindless, goalless and confined to local maximisation of survival/reproductive benefit. This chapter has for reasons of space and audience tended to slide between the two but proper research and application across the disciplines needs to be done carefully and with precision. Good guides to the relationship between biological and cultural evolution are in Laland (2017) and Mesoudi (2017).

Evolution: basic mechanisms

The fundamental process of biological evolution comprises:

1) *Variation* of physiological, anatomical and behavioural traits among the population of a species
2) *Selection* through differential survival and reproductive success of organisms possessing those trait variants best adapted to the relevant habitat – living conditions which may challenge individuals through competition and conflict over territory, resources or mates, and predation
3) *Transmission or inheritance* of those advantageous traits through replication across successive generations, so they become more prevalent in the population, perhaps eliminating less fit alternatives and leading to divergent species adapted to different habitats.

This model has been extended from what is nowadays understood as gene-based evolution to cover evolution based on behavioural and symbolic processes (Jablonka and Lamb, 2014) including linguistic and cultural processes. While these follow the same 'evolutionary algorithm' (Dennett, 1995) of variation, selection and transmission, they are mediated by very different underlying mechanisms of increasing, and nested, complexity (Vinicius 2010). Cultural evolution (including the more specific evolution of technology and the explicit use of design) can be viewed as the variation, selection and replication of 'memes' (Dawkins, 1976; Blackmore, 1999; Aunger et al., 2000) or more generally the operation of social learning processes in cultural evolution (Laland, 2017; Mesoudi, 2017). In some ways analogous to DNA-based genes, memes are ideas, designs for tools and weapons, tunes, behaviours, and wider complexes like religions or moral causes. They are seen as competing for space in the minds of individual humans and for opportunity to be replicated by us and our machines.[1]

We now cover these three basic mechanisms in turn, while acknowledging the interactions between them.

Variation, creativity and innovation

Variation provides the raw material of evolution. In biological evolution variation derives mainly from mutations in DNA copying, and recombination/mixing of parental genes during sexual reproduction. In multicellular organisms, such variation is expressed during the development process from fertilised egg to adult. This is where the information in the genotype (the 'replicator' or blueprint) becomes expressed in a phenotype, the real-world 'vehicle' through which the genes are tested against the environment. Cultural evolution generates variety through several mechanisms operating on different scales (Godfrey-Smith, 2012) from localised imitation to major shifts such as the Neolithic farming revolution.

Imitation is widespread – indeed, the PIRA's pioneering use of car bombs was imitated worldwide. Cultural variety can come from 'blind' copying errors in imitation (which may not always be advantageous, e.g. in recipes for explosives), or from generative processes of creativity and innovation. Creativity generates novel ideas; depending on one's viewpoint it can, of course, be malevolent (Cropley et al., 2010 cover its 'dark side'). PIRA showed both imitation and malevolent creativity in operation (Gill, 2017; Gill et al., 2013). But in practice imitation and creativity overlap more than we think. According to Jablonka and Lamb (2014) the former involves a significant element of *reconstruction*. Thus imitators must translate the target behaviour from perceived movements into their own hierarchy of movement control commands at one end of the scale, or reverse-engineer some tool or weapon at the other.

Innovation at the cultural level is a more complex process which takes creatively-generated ideas through to practical applicability (cf. Dolnik, 2011; Ekblom and Pease, 2014; HM Treasury, 2005). Innovation may also involve selection (e.g. through iterative development trials where unworkable designs are weeded out) and replication (manufacture and perhaps deployment). Incidentally, this deliberate, self-aware process of design improvement more closely resembles *artificial* selection of the kind used to improve breeds of cattle, or wheat. And, more broadly speaking, there are interesting resonances between replication and innovation in crime-prevention practice: Ekblom (2002, 2011), building on Tilley (1993), notes that every replication involves some innovation in adjusting the action to new contexts.

Given the circumstances PIRA faced (relatively limited resources, constant threat from the security services and Loyalist opponents), *improvisation* was the norm. Gill (2016) provides an extensive discussion of this concept. Here, we can view it as highly constrained innovation: rather than bottom-up creation, it involves using 'off-the-shelf' products or materials with little modification, only the production of novel combinations and/or some repurposing; likewise, trialling and improvement may be limited. In fact, this is rather like what happens in the early stages of emergence of a novel trait in biological evolution. An example is where a bird's feathers, probably originally acquired for insulation, became repurposed to enable flight. This is known as 'exaptation'. In more advanced species like proto-birds, *exploratory* behaviour, e.g. trying out lift from feathers, often serves to 'pilot' more systematic evolution. If the feathers work sufficiently well to soften falls or prolong a glide towards prey or away from predators, natural selection can take more systematic improvements in hand, eventually permanently embedding feather-growing and feather-using tendencies in the genes in a process called 'facilitated variation' (Laland et al., 2015).

Evolutionary progression occurs in steps of varying size. Large leaps forward are rare in biology (e.g. from single-celled to multicellular organisms) but commoner culturally. Arthur (2009), analysing technological evolution, distinguishes degrees of 'saltation' – advances can range from minor tweaks (e.g. from single to compound steam engines) to major changes (e.g. the shift from steam to electric power). PIRA's development of mortar bombs is a perfect example of incremental innovation (Gill, 2017). Radical innovation was also evidenced, including the use of secondary devices (e.g. booby traps); bomb content (e.g. nails); and methods of delivery, initiation and detonation. One contact-initiation system, incorporated in an improvised anti-armour grenade, appears particularly creative. It debuted in 1987 and was an 'underarm-thrown grenade which deployed a small parachute to enable the charge to detonate at the desired angle and penetrate tank armour' (Oppenheimer, 2009:239). As another example, in 1981, PIRA debuted a bomb that incorporated remote-control initiation mechanisms, allowing PIRA to plan detonations well in advance. The peak of this innovation came several years later. In October 1984, PIRA targeted the British Executive, including Prime Minister Margaret Thatcher, during a Conservative Party conference in Brighton. Using a home-video recorder, a bomb was concealed within the hotel 24 days before detonation (Oppenheimer, 2009:239).

One particular kind of radical advance is based on the discovery/exploitation of *new physical phenomena* – whether using light in the development of vision among predators and prey, or radio waves in technological evolution. Although not in the same league, PIRA improved a radio-controlled device with the discovery of the 'white band' – an 'unimpeachable' radio signal immune from jamming (Oppenheimer, 2009:209). A contrasting instance of *recombination of existing phenomena and materials* relied on sheer technical ingenuity: an initiation system devised in 1983 'consisted of two copper plates insulated by greaseproof paper and was intended to be initiated by a sniper firing a shot through the plates' (Ryder, 2005:210).

Selection

When an animal is foraging for food, establishing a territory or seeking a mate, it experiences various 'selection pressures' coming from the physical environment and the other organisms within it. These pressures together help determine the 'fitness landscape' to which the animal must *adapt* as an individual (through learning and/or development) or as a species (through genetic evolution) to flourish, not perish. On the human/cultural level, the fitness landscape itself comprises a succession of immediate opportunities and wider opportunity structures (Clarke and Newman, 2006) generating those opportunities; also various hazards to be avoided or coped with. A related concept is the niche – a career-level counterpart of opportunity – where adaptation is to a particular way of life, in a particular environment (applied to crime by Brantingham and Brantingham, 1991). Biologically, an animal must, for example, have good-enough hearing, armour or mobility to avoid or withstand its predators sufficiently often to survive for sufficiently long in order to breed; or it must catch and subdue its prey. Culturally, individuals and organisations must be able to make a living and/or achieve their strategic goals over sustained periods.

Selection in the technological/cultural domain of terrorism is about weapon designs and attack techniques working sufficiently well to be chosen for re-use and wider dissemination, versus failing and being abandoned.

The sheer *scarcity of resources* may be an important selection pressure. PIRA's dwindling stock of commercial explosives due to effective counter-terrorism efforts forced experimentation with homemade explosives, whose consequences are discussed below.

Products and techniques *compete* for adoption by the terrorist organisation and individual operatives. At an elementary level, the pressure for some innovation simply to work, i.e. having basic *functionality*, is considerable, whether it concerns a knee joint operating smoothly or a bomb initiator mechanism avoiding premature triggering. Working *better* is also important. Petroski (1992) noted that shortcomings of existing inventions may drive evolution of designs, citing everyday examples like zips. PIRA's early attack method of hijacking cars and planting bombs within them caused problems for synchronised warnings: using radio to initiate detonation conferred more control.

To generate fully functional phenotypes, and then to go on to confer advantage, both biological and cultural evolution must address *multiple fitness requirements* (Ekblom, 2012a, 2014). This necessitates the evolutionary 'learning' process (Watson and Szatmary, 2016), handling design contradictions, and trade-offs. Bomb-delivery systems were required, say, to be easy to control, destroying intended targets at the flick of a switch while simultaneously minimising civilian casualties or 'own goals'. But sometimes the trade-offs were too complex to resolve and the technique was abandoned. PIRA also introduced a method utilising infrared sensors like those used for remote operation of garage doors (Oppenheimer, 2009). While they allowed devices to be detonated from afar, they were temperamental and could be triggered by innocent passers-by.

Besides pressures of competition, devices and technique feature in *conflict* with the security services. An equivalent major selection pressure in the natural world is *predation*. Predators often track prey. The infrared sensors just described had the advantage in this respect of leaving no chemical forensic evidence behind for the police.

But who is the predator, and who is the prey, can vary. Felson (2006) describes possible interactions in three-party criminal relationships – victims, offenders, police – and notes that the latter's actions as top-predator may sometimes *benefit* the offenders' position as middle-predator, by preventing their runaway over-exploitation of the prey. How far this applies to the terrorist situation is unclear; techniques such as agent-based modelling, already used in crime (Birks, this volume) and often deriving from biological ecology, could help explore the possibilities and contexts where it might occur. We do know, however, that indiscriminate and fatal operations by British security services on the Catholic community led to spikes in PIRA activities, presumably due to increased popular support and the need to be seen to strike back (Gill, Horgan and Piazza, 2016; Asal et al., 2015).

There is a basic asymmetry of selection pressures between predators and prey, known (Dawkins and Krebs, 1979) as 'life versus dinner': if the predator succeeds, the prey dies; if the prey escapes, the predator only loses a meal. There are uncomfortable parallels here with PIRA's announcement immediately after the 1984 Brighton bombing: 'We only have to be lucky once, but you have to be lucky always . . .' (Gill et al., 2013).

Fitness landscapes and their exploration

The 'fitness landscape' is a notional surface whose height reflects an organism's reproductive fitness relative to its customary habitat, and whose other spatial dimensions represent variation in any number of inherited traits.[2] The landscape is often rugged, with peaks and valleys representing respectively fitter and less fit combinations of traits – for example, a particular length of legs plus a particular musculature and particular acuity of vision may be fitter for the habitat than alternative variants. The cultural counterpart could be a combination of a particular weapon with a particular attack technique and particular communications technology when pitted against the customary enemy in the customary (say urban) habitat. In nature, evolutionary processes explore this landscape blindly, crawling over it nose-to-the-ground as variations are tried out, but wherever there is an upwards gradient, inexorably ascending.

Selection pressures thus tend to lead evolving generations of organisms up to the nearest, local, fitness peak they stumble upon. But here they often remain stuck, despite the existence of higher peaks across the valley floor. They are trapped by the fact that any change from local fitness is downhill in terms of performance, so moving out across the valley requires sustaining significant temporary disadvantage (perhaps relative to competitors) before previous fitness is regained and then exceeded. However, a route to higher performance may materialise when changes in the wider environment cause the local peak to collapse, evicting the organism from its formerly advantageous position.[3]

One illustration of this process in terrorism is where the security services reduced PIRA's access to explosives. Here, the effect was actually counterproductive for security, leading PIRA to adopt car bombs.

Car bombs possessed several advantages (Ryder, 2005): they could carry far more explosives; a car provided ample room for the firing mechanism; both car and device could be booby-trapped; planting a car bomb and keeping it undetected proved easier than with a bomb in a bag; and less manpower was needed for delivery. But this higher peak of fitness remained unexplored despite the clear tactical advantages – the leap in organisational and practical terms was too great.

The decision to innovate with these devices actually stemmed from the already mentioned diminution of PIRA's stock of commercial explosives due to British counter-terrorism action. PIRA was forced to experiment with heavier, bulkier fuel-based explosives, which necessitated a new delivery system. But that system, although arrived at by disruption of previously successful techniques, actually proved advantageous: it displaced PIRA from the previous peak and caused them to seek another one – which happened to be higher in fitness. Moreover, the above-mentioned benefits were amplified further by the fuel within the exploding vehicle; together these accidentally-encountered advantages helped account for the car bomb's significant proliferation in the 1970s (Ryder, 2005).

A subsequent instance of security service actions engendering a 'jump from the frying pan into the fire' centred on firebombs. The novel components of a new device included metal piping filled with commercial explosive attached to a container of petrol and a timer-power unit. Once detonated, the petrol boosted the incendiary effect. Intelligence experts believed that petrol was originally adopted in these devices, again purely to conserve commercial explosive stocks; but when PIRA realised the destructive effect of this IED, its use increased (Ryder, 2005:190).

Both fertiliser and incendiary changes, introduced initially as a means of coping with a new constraint but then leading to wider benefit, are reminiscent of what may have happened with the emergence of photosynthesis and its waste product, oxygen. Margulies and Sagan (1986) argue that aerobic respiration may have evolved initially as a way of blotting up this highly reactive poisonous pollutant, but it also happened to yield a major power boost. This may in turn have paved the way for active animal life, enabling predation and necessitating intelligence.

Replication/transmission

Replication in nature is determined by three factors: *fidelity* (how accurately the previous generation of genes is copied), *fecundity* (how many offspring can be produced) and *longevity* (how long the replicating generation lives and remains fertile). In nature, replication is predominantly via vertical transmission, i.e. from one generation to another; horizontal transfer is rare (e.g. gene transfer in bacteria and imitation in higher animals).

In human culture, the reproducing entities are not genes, but, say, designs of weapon or attack technique, where the replication machinery is not DNA transcription and protein-synthesis mechanisms, but mental and social processes like perception, memory, imitation, recall and communication[4]; and perhaps generic manufacturing tools like soldering irons, lathes, chemistry labs and control software, plus the accompanying procedures of use. Besides the vertical transfer from experienced practitioners to novices, our imitative and linguistic abilities support an ever-increasing capacity for horizontal transmission, whether via face-to-face networks or, nowadays, the internet. And unlike in biological evolution, knowledge acquired in an individual's lifetime is inheritable by others.

With PIRA attack techniques, for obvious reasons fidelity in deployment of explosives was ensured by thorough training. This typically occurred within small groups, whose leader tended to have the requisite experience to convey to newer recruits. But the limited supply of expert teachers constrained the fecundity of such vertical replication mechanisms; horizontal mechanisms were also constrained, by considerations of security in face-to-face situations, where the cell structure of the organisation limited who knew whom.

In cultural replication, copying the *instructions* for making some artefact or undertaking some activity offers higher fidelity than copying the *end product* itself (Blackmore, 1999). Hence manuals, e.g. for bomb-making and deployment, can boost longevity, fidelity and fecundity combined.

Jurassic Park apart, once a species is extinct, nature is stumped. But printed documents are durable and can even help to resuscitate any prior practice or product fallen into disuse. In cultural replication *reverse engineering* can revive defunct weapons and enable their reproduction. Here, the fitness function depends on having the capacity to develop an understanding (usually drawing on theory, if only of the elementary operation of gears and levers) of how some found product works, and is constructed.

The benefit of textual instructions may be constrained if *tacit* knowledge is also needed to replicate the weapon and/or its use – e.g. 'stir the mixture this way, till it starts to feel lumpy, thus'. But fidelity in this respect can nowadays be significantly boosted by YouTube-type video instructions, as with online guides to bomb-making (see Gill's, 2015, discussion of Ian Copeland's 1999 bombing campaign and Anders Breivik's 2011 bombing).

The internet further amplifies the benefits of textual and visual material alike: digital documents or video clips are less prone to copying error, and can last indefinitely; helpful forums offer advice from experienced practitioners. Fecundity, too, is amplified by the virtually zero cost of dissemination. Here, we seem to have switched from the cultural equivalent of what biologists call 'K strategy' – dedicating many resources to a few well-guarded and well-nourished offspring – to 'r strategy' – where, as with codfish, millions of eggs are churned out with very little cost per egg, very little prospect of any individual egg surviving, but a high chance that enough will do so to populate the next generation.

Besides the methods of replication such as the blueprints or procedural manuals just discussed, fidelity and fecundity can depend on what is replicated. The improvised nature of the weapons used by PIRA and other terrorists is relevant here.

In some circumstances, however, this logistical advantage was outweighed by unreliability. During the early 1970s, PIRA regularly used beer-can nail bombs because of their simplicity and cost-effectiveness (O'Doherty, 2008:59). However, their use proved dangerous to operators because they were manually-ignited and contained a short fuse. Upon detonation, the nails would explode in each direction. The fuse was also awkward to light because of nerves or strong winds. It was not always obvious that it *had* been lit, leaving the bomber seconds to decide whether to throw it or try lighting it again (and risk it detonating). Investment in greater sophistication and complexity of weapons – equivalent to the K strategy of replication above – was thus necessary in some circumstances.

The *persistence* of terrorist organisations like PIRA supports longevity in several ways. It allows experience to be accumulated and then transmitted to new generations of recruits over an extended period. Weaponry and techniques can be developed through sufficient iterations to remove snags and increase efficiency and effectiveness, promoting durability in the field. And these designs attain sufficient quality that other organisations choose to copy them. According to Asal et al. (2015), it was perhaps PIRA's expertise in IED technology that has had the longest impact upon terrorist activity globally. Arguably PIRA was responsible for the greatest innovations and the deepest expertise in the construction and deployment of IEDs by any non-state militant group. PIRA IED technology re-emerged in conflicts within Colombia, Spain (especially with mortar technology), Israel, Lebanon, Iraq, and Afghanistan.

Finally, there is *failure* to replicate. At one level, there may be just too few opportunities to use the techniques. One bombing in 1989 used a railway track to carry the pulse to initiate the concealed IED, based on a rare 'lucky' configuration. Or an entirely practical technique can fail for human-factor reasons (see Ekblom, 2012b for a wider discussion of 'involvement failure' in crime prevention). For example, condom-based timer devices (slowly eaten through by acid) worked well enough, but proved culturally unacceptable to Catholic terrorists, who would not want their parents to find the packets in their homes (O'Doherty, 2008:59). Conducive environments apart, broader reproductive factors are also important. However creative and technically successful they may be, particular attack techniques may fail in practice if the organisational/logistical ability for execution is lacking. In PIRA, an ingredient of their high level of performance was the successful combining of multiple levels of interacting actors as teams, leaders and organisations.

But at whatever level replication failure operates, it can be instructive. Knowledge of why particular weapons and techniques were tried but abandoned could shape preventive interventions, and turn incidental inhibitors into systematic blockers.

Entities and their environments

Adaptation

We have seen how variation, selection and replication of entities ranging from life forms, product designs, behaviours, and techniques, to wider social practices, together mediate the fundamental evolutionary algorithm, whether this is done genetically, psychologically or culturally. The outcome is that successive generations of these entities become better adapted to the existing fitness landscape and the hazards, opportunities and niches that shape it. Thus, they become better able to survive and replicate – or in the case of terrorist weapons and techniques, to be replicated by their human producers/users.

All three components of the algorithm are necessary for creativity to move from mere novelty generation towards innovation. If the innovation process is persistent, it moves the entity in a consistent direction, significant evolution occurs, and the entity becomes an ever-better match for its habitat. But tension between contradictory requirements (e.g. strength versus weight) means the solutions developed are usually optimal compromises rather than maximisations. Human culture can explore the fitness landscape in subtler and more systematic ways – for example, the invention of the internal combustion engine enabled the tank to simultaneously combine armour and mobility, whereas previously it had been one or the other. But the time and resources available to terrorists may be limited in the case of a clandestine organisation harried by the security services. Thus, in the absence of secure home territory and/or backing by states or large companies, what terrorists can do is limited by the need to *improvise* rather than thoroughly research, develop, produce and deploy entirely new weapons and tactics of substantial complexity and sophistication. But these hindrances may not always apply.

Construction and affordance

Adaptation is not the whole story. Recent takes on evolution (e.g. Laland et al., 2015) have flagged the importance of the process of 'niche construction' – for example, where grazing-adapted mammals keep the landscape free of bushes, to their own benefit. Cultural-level examples of this process include places modified as concealed arms dumps, lookout posts, ambush sites or loopholes for shooting. All of these niche construction efforts facilitate the use of evolved weapons and attack techniques, and of course they evolve themselves. Wider *social* niche construction processes could include 'climate setting' (Ekblom, 2011) where terrorists exploit, and actively manage, acceptance of the use of particular weapons and techniques among a supportive population. A related evolutionary perspective – the affordance landscape – has recently been developed by Walsh (e.g. 2015) as a contrast to the conventional fitness-landscape point of view. Here, the evolving organism, seen as an active agent, seeks out what is useful and useable in its environment. The resonance with weapon improvisation is clear, and Walsh's thinking can be applied to build further on the (non-evolutionary) treatments of terrorism and affordance in the volume by Taylor and Currie (2012).

In the face of change

The abstraction that is the fitness landscape is no more static than its geological counterpart. It undergoes the equivalent of mountain building, valley formation and occasional landslips due to changes in the environmental, economic, technological, political and social background, operating over various temporal and geographical scales. Some of the changes experienced by adaptive entities are entirely exogenous, such as when an earthquake diverts a river, the market suddenly raises the price of copper or a new religious movement emerges. In terms of crime, see reviews of the wider effects of technological change by Ekblom (2017b) and Felson and Eckert (2015). Other changes result from the actions of third parties, e.g. when a rival gang seizes territory, or police priorities change; and still others from an entity's own actions, e.g. overgrazing, whether of pastureland or of houses to burgle. Whatever the case, as the Provisionals and their opponents discovered, over some appropriate timescale, fitness is therefore always precarious, and . . . provisional.

How do biological or cultural entities cope with these changes? Before adaptability comes *resilience*. Resilience at its most elementary is about simply tolerating the change (e.g. a terrorist organisation accepting more arrests by the security services while continuing as before). In more advanced instances, resilience includes deploying alternative responses from one's existing repertoire. An example is where the growth of British Army intelligence in Northern Ireland raised the difficulty for PIRA to plant big car bombs. Road checks and security cordons limited opportunities, so PIRA strategists turned to smaller, easily concealed incendiary devices (Ryder, 2006).

True dynamic adaptability comes with innovation in, say, anatomy, behaviour or technology, which tracks the changes in the fitness landscape. Genetic evolution is the slowest adaptive process, taking generations; learning can pick up changes during the lifetime of individuals or groups; deliberate design-based problem-solving can be rapid; and cultural-level change is variable – adoption of mobile phones being lightning-fast but gender-equality rather slower.

In the rest of this section on change we first address factors that accelerate adaptation, and then cover the issue of co-evolution, which often serves as an accelerant in its own right.

Accelerants of adaptation

Various *accelerants* facilitate adaptation and reduce the waste and hazards of failure.

A feature of more advanced biological organisms is the capacity to generate *plausible variety* – novel body forms that have a fair a priori chance of conferring advantage (or at least of being neutral) rather than being a totally blind guess (Kirschner and Gerhart, 2005). A mutation for longer leg bones, say, is accompanied by matching developmental growth of muscles, nerves and blood vessels rather than these being entirely out of step (which would not get the animal very far). This coordination is mediated by complex systems for control of anatomical development through regulatory genes, and leads, for example, to the astonishing range of plausible, workable body-shapes expressed by vertebrates all based on variants of the same underlying plan. This is an instance of the wider concept of the 'evolution of evolvability' (Dawkins, 2003), i.e. the invention of means to make evolution faster, more efficient and of wider scope. In cultural evolution terms, Ekblom (2014) flags its significance in the design of crime-prevention measures which are theoretically and practically plausible rather than a complete shot in the dark. The body of theory and practice knowledge, and the skill in applying this in generating, testing and improving new weapons and techniques, amounts to *innovative capacity* (Ekblom and Pease, 2013). This is to be distinguished from *operational capacity*, which depends merely on deployment of existing weapons/techniques.

The same holds for design by terrorists, but here the underlying knowledge covers the physics and chemistry of weapons, camouflage, how to mislead opponents, etc. (variation); development and testing procedures (selection); and, as seen, how to supply apprenticeship experience, handbooks and YouTube instructional videos (replication).

One of the hallmarks of PIRA's ability to survive and adapt was its substantial technical and innovative acumen in IED development. Arguably PIRA produced the greatest innovations and the deepest expertise in construction and deployment of IEDs by any non-state militant group. Underlying this was the propensity of the PIRA engineers to come from professions whose skills directly applied to the craft of bomb-making; and the Engineering Department's coordination of research and development in armaments. Often the seniors in the Engineering Department included many skilled technicians (see Gill, 2017).

Flying leaps

As said, fitness peaks can trap evolving organisms when there is no way to change which does not involve first going downhill. But humans can sometimes leap from one fitness peak to a higher one *without* traversing the valley of degraded operational performance. This releases significant constraints on evolution, which moves from purely local maximising of benefit, to a more global reach (i.e. from the best of all local possibilities to, in the extreme, the best ever, anywhere). The variation and selection process in human technology can involve taking evolving tools and weapons *out* of the real-world fitness landscape and harsh, immediate selection pressures, and *into* protected and even imaginary landscapes of backs-of-envelopes, workshops and field trials. Here, exploration and invention can be undertaken with significantly reduced risk from failure, where psychological pressures of, say, risk of arrest or accident are lower too, and where what is good about some innovation can be salvaged even though the product as a whole did not succeed. Popper's (1972) maxim is particularly apt here: while in the real world, almost every exploratory action puts animals' survival on the line, in the course of imagination and trials we humans allow ideas to die in our stead. Dennett's (1995) concept of the 'tower of generate and test' extends this idea by documenting a range of progressively smarter ways of adapting and learning – Pavlovian, Skinnerian, Popperian and Gregorian – where we invent tools which themselves make us smarter. This was very much the case with the PIRA Engineering Department. Many of its senior members were skilled technicians, who undertook much co-ordinated 'backroom' research and development in armaments, a factor fostering operational success (Horgan and Taylor, 1997).

Co-evolutionary arms races

When entities are evolving side-by-side, pursuing a mix of competing, conflicting and collaborative goals, and each comprises a significant part of the other's environment, we enter the domain of *complex adaptive systems* (e.g. see www.cas-group.net). These are particularly tricky for policymakers to influence (Chapman, 2004; Kurtz and Snowden, 2003): any perturbation they attempt to introduce usually has unpredictable and complex effects as one entity adjusts to exogenous changes or to those brought about by the others, like the clampdown on commercial explosives described above. When complex adaptive systems generate a progression of changes leading in a consistent direction we can talk about co-evolutionary arms races.

Arms races arise in the gene-level world mainly between predators and prey (e.g. ever-harder shells vs. ever-stronger teeth), and pathogens and hosts (e.g. fungal infection vs. inherited resistance genes). They also emerge between humans and nature (e.g. pesticides vs. pests) and between different groups of humans (e.g. in military domains such as radar vs. stealth). Ekblom reviews criminal (Ekblom, 1997, 1999) and terrorist arms races (Ekblom, 2016), as do many of the chapters in Sagarin and Taylor (2008). Move, counter-move and counter-counter-move can unfold. In the everyday crime world, the aforementioned co-evolution of the safe and safe breaking techniques (Shover, 1996) is a good example.

In our case study of terrorism, the security services jammed PIRA's radio-controlled IEDs, leading PIRA to refine the radio-control mechanism to incorporate encoding and decoding (Oppenheimer, 2009). And PIRA turned from car bombs to van bombs to restrict the line-of-sight of explosive ordnance disposal (EOD) teams (Ryder, 2005).

In a longer sequence, standard PIRA IEDs were incrementally accompanied by secondary, anti-handling devices. The 'Castlerobin' was a wooden box containing both anti-opening and anti-lifting micro-switches, introduced in 1971. If it was moved, tilted, or opened, it would detonate. It killed the first EOD operative to attempt to defuse it. A second EOD death through this IED illustrated more malevolent creativity in which the designers anticipated, and manipulated, the perceptions and scripts of the EOD team. By burning the fuse on the IED, PIRA made it look inoperable. However, anti-handling mechanisms detonated the IED as the EOD officers moved the device by wire. The natural world is replete with examples of different kinds of *deceit* on the part of predators and prey alike (Stevens, 2016), the glowing lure of the angler fish being just one instance. Research by behavioural ecologists into when and how these techniques work, and how countermeasures can evolve, may not yield many specific ideas we can copy (Ekblom, 1999), although animal camouflage tricks were consciously adopted during both world wars (Stevens, 2016). But the principles of advantage, disadvantage and contextual fitness factors can be abstracted and applied by security services.

A noteworthy arms-race process exclusive to human culture involves, again, *reverse engineering*. Either side can use this, whether in copying a captured weapon, or in understanding how it works in order to overcome it. After five of PIRA's 'Castlerobins' were captured, unexploded, at a bomb-making factory, EOD operatives quickly learned how to disarm them.

The military concern with 'capture-proofing' advanced weapons illustrates yet another strategy – *controlling information about offensive/defensive tactics* – which does have counterparts in biological evolution (Vermeij, 2008). Such information can be used against opponents, much as HIV exploits what it has 'learned' about the response of the immune system to gain a foothold in the human host. Equivalently, PIRA scouts started noticing British soldiers collecting unlit nail bombs. Consequently, PIRA members began leaving seemingly unlit ones in locations where the soldiers would likely find them. The 'safe' nail bombs were accompanied by mercury tilt switches, however, so that moving the device detonated them (Gurney, 1993).

Humans have evolved to be *unpredictable* predators par excellence. Tooby and DeVore (1987) argue that the evolution of human intelligence allows us to mount *evolutionary 'surprise attacks'* which escalate the arms race against prey, such that the latter cannot keep up through their own biologically evolving counter-adaptations which are more limited in scope and slower to emerge. When we try this against our human enemies, of course, the tactical advantage of surprise is still a potent one, but the enemy may be on the alert, may have anticipated some such move, and may have surprises of their own in store.

Central to surprise is radical innovation, demonstrated by the PIRA despite their reliance on improvisation. We have already seen the novel use of the video recorder timer in the

Brighton bombing of 1984, enabling its planting weeks in advance. Another example was in 1971, when PIRA placed an IED in a sewer, to float downstream under an Army post. The effort failed as it detonated beneath an empty bar (Ryder, 2005); but today's GPS capability in smartphones could overcome navigational inaccuracy; and various autonomous robot crawlers could remove the dependence on water currents and subterranean channels. Indeed, aerial drones are now a risk.

A related arms-race issue is that of *silver bullets*. Although they can only be used once before rapidly deployed protective measures obliterate the opportunity, single-shot attacks can be game-changing, as 9/11 showed. A PIRA example was a delivery system used once only, in 1992, involving a stolen excavator and laundry van. PIRA volunteers removed the van's tyres to enable it to run along a railway track on its rims. The excavator lifted the van onto the tracks. The van was loaded with 1,000lb of explosives. The van was put into gear and sent along the track, driverless. Its open backdoors allowed for the command wire to unreel alongside the railway tracks. As it got close to an Army Barracks, it was detonated (Gill, 2017). Here, the strategic issue for the terrorists and security services alike is to ensure their innovative capacity can continue to generate a stream of surprises, with both tactical advantage and strategic shock value. But one drawback of continual surprise is the limited scope for consistent improvement, and in some cases the risk of failure – of either the device/technique not working, or blowing up one's own personnel, including valuable experts.

Ecological circumstances may influence whether ad-hoc exploration and limited clashes of offensive and defensive technologies and techniques become prolonged evolution in a consistent direction. In some cases, PIRA did move into more systematic research and development (see Oppenheimer, 2009).

So what?

This chapter has focused on the technological innovation of weaponry and attack techniques in PIRA, but the processes abstracted with the aid of evolutionary thinking apply to other terrorism-waged conflicts and to the struggle with organised crime (Kenney, 2007).

We argue that adopting an evolutionary perspective on terrorism and counter-terrorism helps us understand and exploit past history, beneficially influence present risks, and prepare for future challenges. The *co*-evolutionary perspective confers additional benefits in highlighting the simultaneous consideration of attack and defence, move and counter-move, and the symmetries and asymmetries between the opposing parties in a complex adaptive system. More generally, it enables us to detach ourselves from immediate battles and view the conflict strategically.

Evolutionary thinking does not just bring in genetic or cultural processes, significant though these are: it facilitates interdisciplinary links to other fields where the evolutionary algorithm is considered to apply. These include the immune system, learning, and thinking mechanisms (e.g. Plotkin, 1997; Watson and Szatmary, 2016). And divining the *differences* between the different evolutionary domains (cf. Jablonka and Lamb, 2014) helps to clarify concepts, surface assumptions, and see what is distinctive about cultural/technological evolution. In turn, this shows us how to hinder adaptation in terrorists while boosting it for the security side, without jeopardising wider societal values. In crime science in particular, the evolutionary perspective helps set opportunity-based approaches (Gill et al., 2018) in a context of longer-term processes of adaptation, and wider ecological structures such as niches.

We focus next on three aspects of counter-terrorism policy and practice which seem particularly informed by the evolutionary perspective – the need for an anticipatory stance, how to handle co-evolution, and the importance of design.

The guessing game

The substantial lag in time to detect a potential threat, decide what to do and implement it in the field means that careful *anticipation* is better than reaction alone.

It is virtually impossible to predict the precise onset of specific innovations within terrorist organisations (the same is true with technological innovations in general). But it may be possible to predict *evolutionary trends* in various technological fields. The TRIZ approach, described in Ekblom (2012a) and https://triz-journal.com/triz-what-is-triz, identifies such trends. An example is evolution from fixed mechanical links between components, to hinged links, to infinitely variable links, like bicycle chains, to electromagnetic fields. Knowing such trends can help us anticipate where the next development in some product, process or system might be expected to come from, whether introduced by legitimate engineers or terrorist ones. We can also undertake more specific *technology road-mapping* (identifying the sequence of innovations needed for a particular new technology to become feasible). On the last, we can understand what upcoming innovations could be misused by terrorists (Ekblom 2005) and take advance action to make this difficult. This equates to the way disease control experts now assess how many mutations some disease might need to undergo to gain the capacity for human-to-human transmission (e.g. www.sciencedaily.com/releases/2016/04/160404090554.htm).

Undertaking *future-proofing* is also worthwhile. For example, we can make security measures easily upgradeable rather than locked into a system that gets left behind by malevolent or incidental changes in technology or tactics (what use was the Maginot Line in the face of new, highly mobile, Wehrmacht armour that simply drove round the end?).

The adaptive stance also requires us to *build and maintain our repertoire of knowledge* in terms of generic principles, theories and practices of counter-terrorism that together with on-the-ground intelligence, enable us to design, develop, test and deploy our own plausible innovative variety of offensive and defensive measures. Conceptual frameworks of the kind cited in this chapter can help here, much as the rich web of regulatory genes generates plausible variety in nature.

The arms race

The adoption of a co-evolutionary perspective on terrorism suggests that we should both view and do things differently. In viewing, we get to see the conflict from a standpoint that rises above the month-to-month slog and counter-slog of the arms race, which could enable us to think more widely about responses. In so doing, if we want to avoid losing whole campaigns despite winning individual battles, we must continually out-innovate adaptive/innovative offenders against a background of changing technology and other contextual factors that favour first one, then the other, side. We must deliberately accelerate our adaptation. Ekblom (1997, 2016, 2017b) lists approaches which could be adopted to '*gear up against crime*'. Strategic examples include encouraging plausible variety as already discussed; and abstracting generic *principles of inventiveness* (e.g. the 40 inventive principles and 39 contradiction principles of the TRIZ approach – Ekblom, 2012a) which could specifically be applied to crime, terrorism, and perhaps the military.

We should also hinder the adaptation of the terrorist side. Understanding of biological counterparts may suggest how to disrupt research and development processes by confining terrorists to exploration/simple improvisation rather than allowing them to progress to R&D proper.

It may also be possible, given the correct information, to predict a terrorist organisation's *capacity for innovation* and attempt to downgrade that accordingly. For example, organisational-level innovation such as changing from a strictly hierarchical structure with a clear command

and control to a more linear one has the potential to increase the levels of tactical innovation that may follow (Gill et al., 2013). If certain conditions are known to favour the persistence or re-emergence of hierarchy, other things being equal it may be possible for the security services (and/or civil society more generally) to act in ways that support this trend. For example, this could involve deliberate (albeit ethically sound) efforts to sow distrust within terrorist networks.

To finish on a more generic point, constantly changing ecological conditions have tended to favour generalists and prevent specialists from evolving (think rats versus highly desert-adapted rodents). However, this risks the entities evolving higher-level adaptive capabilities: arguably this happened with human ancestors who gained intelligence under the very changeable climate of the African Rift Valley (Shultz and Maslin, 2013). A terrorist organisation that is always being challenged in new ways may either succumb or – on the principle of that which doesn't kill you makes you stronger – become more agile and adaptive. More tactically speaking, too, it is debatable which is better for the security services (and the society they serve) – facing a whole series of diverse improvisations or a steadily more advanced, but knowable, technological progression.

Design

Design is needed when we face challenging, competing or conflicting requirements. With terrorism, these are obvious: balancing security against the need for economy and efficiency (tactically combating terrorism, and maintaining an adaptive stance, are costly); the need to protect the full range of wider societal values such as democratic principles, privacy and inclusivity; the need to boost enterprise and economic growth; and the requirement to reduce our carbon footprint. Governments are constrained by these considerations; terrorists are often free to set many of them aside although they have constraints of their own (relating to resources, the risk of capture/defeat, the need to maintain a supportive constituency or to out-compete rivals). Design enables us to live with this asymmetry – for example, by finding ways that degrade terrorist innovation *without* similarly degrading that of legitimate businesses; or at a more tactical level, of scanning passengers' bodies at airport security gates *without* intrusion on privacy (millimetre-wave scanners are designed to display schematic body images rather than intimate details of individual passengers).

But design goes beyond ingenuity in addressing known problems, to *reframing* the problems themselves. Dorst (2015) gives many examples of this process, including turning a yearly drunken riot in Sydney's Kings Cross area into a civilised festival; and reframing the requirement to design an anti-terrorist litter bin for a railway operator, into one that also reduces false alarms – thankfully a much more common, but very disruptive, problem (see also Lulham et al., 2012). Jumping out of the direct ding-dong of arms races is a major such reframe, perhaps the biggest, but which may not always be possible, is to arrive at some mutually beneficial political settlement between the conflicting parties.

Conclusion

Terrorist attacks will never go away, and no adaptations to them can be perfect, nor predictions reliable. The 'War on Terror' can never be won – protective action and pursuit of perpetrators can only keep the problem under control until political resolutions become possible. It is an instance of the 'Red Queen's Game' (van Valen, 1973, from Lewis Carroll's *Alice Through the Looking Glass*). In that game you must keep running merely to remain in the same place.

(Schneier, 2012 offers a detailed exploration of its security implications.) This is true both as a general principle and for the technological examples we have presented in the case of PIRA weaponry and techniques.

But we cease to run the arms race at our peril. Studying evolution, and more specifically co-evolution, gives us knowledge of generic solutions that have been tried and tested in the very long run, over a wide range of 'universal' ecological problems faced by natural organisms of all kinds; and recapitulated over a far shorter timescale by humans in conflict with 'nature' and each other.

An evolutionary approach that draws in crime science, engineering science and design together with evaluation of effectiveness and systematic accumulation of process knowledge (know-how), can provide a fresh perspective and a richer understanding of terrorist attacks, supporting attempts to control them that are more strategic and change-oriented than have customarily been the case. This is especially so when we add in sophisticated knowledge management. In this manner, we can hopefully out-innovate adaptive terrorists while preserving our cherished values and serving the widest range of societal priorities in a proportionate way.

Notes

1 A useful critique of the original meme concept is in Jablonka and Lamb, 2014. This accords less weight to the copying element and more to the social and ecological context in which the copying occurs.
2 A good account of the fitness-landscape concept, with some interesting graphics, is at https://en.wikipedia.org/wiki/Fitness_landscape.
3 For a schematic representation of this process, see https://en.wikipedia.org/wiki/Fitness_landscape and scroll down to the gif diagrams of static and dynamic fitness landscapes.
4 Although the biological replication layers are still necessary to support the cultural ones.

References

[Weblinks are current at 25 June 2018.]

Arthur, W. B. (2009). *The Nature of Technology: What it is and How it Evolves*. London: Allen Lane.

Asal, V., Gill, P., Rethemeyer, K. and Horgan, J. (2015). Killing range: explaining lethality variance within a terrorist organization. *Journal of Conflict Resolution, 59*(3): 401–427.

Aunger, R. (ed.) (2000). *Darwinizing Culture: The Status of Memetics as a Science*. Oxford: Oxford University Press.

Blackmore, S. (1999). *The Meme Machine*. Oxford: Oxford University Press.

Brantingham, P. and Brantingham, J. (1991). Niches and predators: theoretical departures in the ecology of crime. Handout presented at Western Society of Criminology, Berkeley, CA.

Brown, R. (2016). Vehicle crime prevention and the co-evolutionary arms race: recent offender countermoves using immobiliser bypass technology. *Security Journal, 30*(1): 60–73. DOI:10.1057/s41284-016-0001-1.

Chapman, J. (2004). *System Failure: Why Governments Must Learn to Think Differently*. London: Demos.

Clarke, R. and Newman, G. (2006). *Outsmarting the Terrorists*. London: Praeger Security International.

Cohen, L., Vila, B. and Machalek, R. (1995). Expropriative crime and crime policy: An evolutionary ecological analysis. *Studies on Crime and Crime Prevention, 4*: 197–219.

Cropley, D., Cropley, A., Kaufman, J. and Runco, M. (2010). *The Dark Side of Creativity*. Cambridge: Cambridge University Press.

Dawkins, R. (1976). *The Selfish Gene*. Oxford: Oxford University Press.

Dawkins, R. (2003). The evolution of evolvability. In S. Kumar and P. Bentley (eds), *On Growth, Form and Computers*. London: Academic Press.

Dawkins, R. and Krebs, J. (1979). Arms races between and within species. *Proceedings of the Royal Society of London. Series B, Biological Sciences, 205*(1161): 489–511.

Dennett, D. (1995). *Darwin's Dangerous Idea*. London: Penguin.

Dietl, G. (2008). Selection, security and evolutionary international relations. In R. Sagarin and T. Taylor (eds), *Natural Security: A Darwinian Approach to a Dangerous World*. Berkeley, CA: University of California Press.

Dolnik, A. (2011). *Understanding Terrorist Innovation*. London: Routledge.

Dorst, K. (2015). *Frame Innovation: Create New Thinking by Design*. Cambridge, MA: MIT Press.

Durrant, R. and Ward, T. (2012). The role of evolutionary explanations in criminology. *Journal of Theoretical and Philosophical Criminology*, *4*(1): 1–37.

Ekblom, P. (1997). Gearing up against crime: a dynamic framework to help designers keep up with the adaptive criminal in a changing world. *International Journal of Risk, Security and Crime Prevention*, *214*: 249–265. www.veilig-ontwerp-beheer.nl/publicaties/gearing-up-against-crime/at_download/file.

Ekblom, P. (1999). Can we make crime prevention adaptive by learning from other evolutionary struggles? *Studies on Crime and Crime Prevention*, *8*(1): 27–51. www.veilig-ontwerp-beheer.nl/publicaties/can-we-make-crime-prevention-adaptive-by-learning-from-other-evolutionary-struggles/at_download/file.

Ekblom, P. (2002). From the source to the mainstream is uphill: the challenge of transferring knowledge of crime prevention through replication, innovation and anticipation. In N. Tilley (ed.), *Analysis for Crime Prevention*, Crime Prevention Studies 13, pp. 131–203. Monsey, NY: Criminal Justice Press; Devon, UK: Willan Publishing.

Ekblom, P. (2005). How to police the future: scanning for scientific and technological innovations which generate potential threats and opportunities in crime, policing and crime reduction. In M. Smith and N. Tilley (eds), *Crime Science: New Approaches to Preventing and Detecting Crime*. Cullompton, UK: Willan Publishing.

Ekblom, P. (2011). *Crime Prevention, Security and Community Safety Using the 5Is Framework*. Basingstoke: Palgrave Macmillan.

Ekblom, P. (2012a). Happy returns: ideas brought back from situational crime prevention's exploration of design against crime. In G. Farrell and N. Tilley (eds), *The Reasoning Criminologist: Essays in Honour of Ronald V. Clarke*, pp. 163–198. Cullompton, UK: Willan Publishing.

Ekblom, P. (2012b) Citizen participation in crime prevention – capturing practice knowledge through the 5Is framework. In M. Coester and E. Marks (eds), *International Perspectives of Crime Prevention 4. Contributions from the 4th and the 5th Annual International Forum 2010 and 2011 within the German Congress on Crime Prevention*. Mönchengladbach: Forum Verlag Godesberg GmbH. www.erich-marks.de/Biografie/InternationalPerspectivesofCrimePrevention42012.pdf.

Ekblom, P. (2014). Design and security. In M. Gill (ed.), *The Handbook of Security* (2nd edition), pp. 133–156. Basingstoke: Palgrave MacMillan.

Ekblom, P. (2016). Terrorism – lessons from natural and human co-evolutionary arms races. In M. Taylor, J. Roach and K. Pease (eds), *Evolutionary Psychology and Terrorism*. London: Routledge.

Ekblom, P. (2017a). Evolutionary approaches to rational choice. In W. Bernasco, H. Elffers and J-L. van Gelder, *The Oxford Handbook on Offender Decision-Making*. Oxford: Oxford University Press.

Ekblom, P. (2017b). Technology, opportunity, crime and crime prevention – current and evolutionary perspectives. In B. Leclerc and E. Savona (eds), *Crime Prevention in the 21st Century*. New York: Springer.

Ekblom, P. and Pease, K. (2014). Innovation and crime prevention. In G. Bruinsma, and D. Weisburd (eds), *Encyclopedia of Criminology and Criminal Justice*. New York: Springer Science + Business Media.

Ekblom, P., Sidebottom, A. and Wortley, R. (2016). Evolutionary psychological influences on the contemporary causes of terrorist events. In M. Taylor, J. Roach and K. Pease (eds), *Evolutionary Psychology and Terrorism*. London: Routledge.

Felson, M. (2006). *Crime and Nature*. Thousand Oaks, CA: Sage.

Felson, M. and Eckert, M. (2015). *Crime and Everyday Life* (5th edition). London: Sage.

Gill, P. (2015). *Lone-Actor Terrorists: A Behavioural Analysis*. London: Routledge.

Gill, P. (2017). Tactical innovation and the Provisional Irish Republican Army. *Studies in Conflict and Terrorism*, *40*(7), 573–585.

Gill, P. and Horgan, J. (2013). Who were the volunteers? The shifting sociological and operational profile of 1240 Provisional Irish Republican Army members. *Terrorism and Political Violence*, *25*(3): 435–456.

Gill, P., Horgan, J. and Lovelace, J. (2011). Improvised explosive devices – the problem of definition. *Studies in Conflict and Terrorism*, *34*(9): 732–748.

Gill, P., Horgan, J., Hunter, S. and Cushenbery, L. (2013). Malevolent creativity in terrorist organizations. *Journal of Creative Behavior*, 47(2): 125–151.

Gill, P., Horgan, J. and Piazza, J. (2016). Counterterrorism killings and Provisional IRA bombings, 1970–1998. *Terrorism and Political Violence, 28*(3): 473–496.

Gill, P., Lee, J., Rethemeyer, K., Horgan, J. and Asal, V. (2014). Lethal connections: the determinants of network connections in the Provisional Irish Republican Army, 1970–1998. *International Interactions, 40*(1): 52–78.

Gill, P., Marchment, Z., Corner, E. and Bouhana, N. (2018). terrorist decision-making in the context of risk, attack planning and attack commission. *Studies in Conflict and Terrorism.* DOI: 10.1080/1057610X.2018.1445501.

Gurney, P. (1993). *Braver Men Walk Away.* London: HarperCollins.

HM Treasury (2005). *The Cox Review of Creativity in Business.* London: HM Treasury.

Horgan, J. and Taylor, M. (1997). The provisional Irish Republican army: command and functional structure. *Terrorism and Political Violence, 9*(3): 1–32.

Jablonka, E. and Lamb, M. (2014). *Evolution in Four Dimensions. Genetic, Epigenetic, Behavioral, and Symbolic Variation in the History of Life* (Revised edition). Cambridge, MA: MIT Press.

Johnson, N., Zhao, G., Qi, H. and Gill, P. et al. (2013). Simple Mathematical Law Benchmarks Human Confrontations. *Nature Scientific Reports, 3*: 3463.

Kenney, M. (2007). *From Pablo to Osama: Trafficking and Terrorist Networks, Government Bureaucracies, and Competitive Adaptation.* Pennsylvania, PA: Penn State Press.

Kirschner, M. and Gerhart, J. (2005). *The Plausibility of Life: Resolving Darwin's Dilemma.* New Haven, CT: Yale University Press.

Kurtz, C. and Snowden, D. (2003). The new dynamics of strategy: sense-making in a complex-complicated world. *IBM Systems Journal, 42*(3): 462–483.

Laland, K. (2017). *Darwin's Unfinished Symphony: How Culture Made the Human Mind.* Princeton, NJ: Princeton University Press.

Laland, K., Uller, T., Feldman, M., Sterelny, K., Müller, G., Moczek, A., Jablonka, E. and Odling-Smee, J. (2015). The extended evolutionary synthesis: its structure, assumptions and predictions. *Proceedings of the Royal Society B, 282*(1813): 20151019. DOI: 10.1098/rspb.2015.1019.

Lulham, R., Camacho Duarte, O., Dorst, K. and Kaldor, L. (2012). Designing a counterterrorism trash bin. In P. Ekblom (ed.), *Design Against Crime: Crime Proofing Everyday Objects.* Boulder, CO: Lynne Rienner.

Margulies, L. and Sagan, D. (1986). *Microcosmos: Four Billion Years of Evolution from our Microbial Ancestors.* Berkeley, CA: University of California Press.

Mesoudi, A. (2017). Pursuing Darwin's curious parallel: prospects for a science of cultural evolution. *Proceedings of the National Academy of Science, 114*: 7853–7860.

O'Doherty, S. (2008). *The Volunteer: A Former IRA Man's True Story.* Durham, CT: Strategic Book Publishing and Rights Agency.

Oppenheimer, A. R. (2009). *IRA, the Bombs AND The Bullets: A History of Deadly Ingenuity.* Dublin: Irish Academic Press.

Petroski, H. (1992). *The Evolution of Useful Things: How Everyday Artifacts – From Forks and Pins to Paper Clips and Zippers – Came to be as They are.* New York: Knopf.

Plotkin, H. (1997). *Darwin Machines and the Nature of Knowledge.* Cambridge, MA: Harvard University Press.

Popper, K. (1972). *Objective Knowledge: An Evolutionary Approach.* Oxford: Clarendon.

Roach, J. and Pease, K. (2013). *Evolution and Crime.* London: Routledge.

Ryder, C. (2005). *A Special Kind of Courage: Bomb Disposal and the Inside Story Of 321 EOD Squadron.* London: Methuen.

Sagarin, R. and Taylor, T. (eds) (2008). *Natural Security: A Darwinian Approach to a Dangerous World.* Berkeley, CA: University of California Press.

Schneier, B. (2012). *Liars and Outliers: Enabling the Trust that Society Needs to Thrive.* New York: Wiley.

Shultz, S. and Maslin, M. (2013). Early Human Speciation, Brain Expansion and Dispersal Influenced by African Climate Pulses. *PLoS ONE, 8*(10): e76750. DOI:10.1371/journal.pone.0076750.

Shover, N. (1996). *Great Pretenders: Pursuits and Careers of Persistent Thieves.* London: Westview Press/Routledge.

Stevens, M. (2016). *Cheats and Deceits. How Animals and Plants Exploit and Mislead.* Oxford: Oxford University Press.

Taylor, M. and Currie, P. (2012). *Terrorism and Affordance.* London: Continuum.

Tilley, N. (1993). After Kirkholt: theory, methods and results of replication evaluations. crime prevention Unit Paper 47. London: Home Office.

Tooby, J. and DeVore, I. (1987). The reconstruction of hominid behavioral evolution through strategic modelling. In W. Kinzey (ed.), *The Evolution of Human Behavior: Primate Models*, p. 183–227. New York: SUNY Press.

van Valen, L. (1973). A new evolutionary law. *Evolutionary Theory, 1*: 1–30.

Vermeij, G. (2008). Security, unpredictability and evolution: policy and the history of life. In R. Sagarin and T. Taylor (eds), *Natural Security: A Darwinian Approach to a Dangerous World*. Berkeley, CA: University of California Press.

Vinicius, L. (2010). *Modular Evolution. How Natural Selection Produces Biological Complexity*. Cambridge: Cambridge University Press.

Walsh, D. (2015). *Organisms, Agency, and Evolution*. Cambridge: Cambridge University Press.

Watson, R. and Szatmary, E. (2016). *Trends in Ecology and Evolution, 31*: 147–157. http://dx.doi.org/10.1016/j.tree.2015.11.009.

18

Fighting cybercrime once it switches from the online world to the real world

Gianluca Stringhini

Introduction

Cybercrime has very different characteristics compared to traditional crime: it is inherently geographically dispersed, and it goes beyond the need for victims and perpetrators to be physically located in the same place when the crime happens. The technical opportunities provided by the internet allow criminals to set up complex infrastructures for their operations that are dispersed in multiple countries and are resilient to activity by police forces geared towards stopping them. Whenever a new policy is developed that makes carrying out a specific cybercriminal operation in a certain country more difficult, criminals have the opportunity to host their operation in another country. Similarly, whenever a technical countermeasure is developed to track and block a certain cybercriminal activity, miscreants can evolve and make their operations more complex, in what can be defined as a cat-and-mouse game with security professionals and law enforcement. In this new and constantly evolving landscape, researchers and practitioners are left wondering, what is the best way to tackle cybercrime?

In this chapter I provide three case studies across a range of cybercriminal operations to show that, although criminals are free to adapt and add complexity to their operations, they are constrained by their need to make money. Monetising cybercrime usually requires criminals to switch to traditional means (bank transactions, parcel shipping), and these means typically come with physical constraints (e.g. a laptop purchased with a stolen credit card needs to be physically shipped and sold on the black market). These limitations in how cybercriminals can monetise their operations can be effectively used to curb malicious operations. We provide three examples in which looking at the monetisation part of cybercrime has been shown to be an effective and more long-term way to mitigate it. The examples are: email spam carried out by botnets, fake antivirus scams, and credit card fraud. We show that pressuring banks and credit card processors to stop processing illicit payments is an effective solution to shut down criminal operations. We also show that tracking physical people who ship stolen goods (so-called reshipping mules) and tracking parcels containing goods bought with stolen credit cards can be effective in fighting credit card fraud.

I then discuss potential new financial means that cybercriminals could use to avoid these measures. An option is turning to crypto currencies such as bitcoin. I argue that although this is feasible, it would affect criminals in two ways. First, these currencies are not commonly adopted by regular users, and this would affect the capability of criminals to make money from victims and to do business with other criminals. Second, cryptocurrencies provide anonymity, but this anonymity only lasts until such currency is converted to traditional currency, which is often a required step for successful monetisation.

Case study 1: email spam

Defined as 'unsolicited bulk email,' spam has been a nuisance for internet users since the 1970s. Early day spammers foresaw the marketing power of email and started online businesses that used electronic mail as a marketing medium for goods, some more legal than others. Such operations were usually run by a single person or a small group of people, and that worked well given the limited size of the internet at the time (McWilliams 2014). Law enforcement and internet service providers (ISPs) responded to the emerging issue of unwanted emails, by developing both legal guidelines (e.g. the CAN-SPAM Act of 2003 in the United States) and technical countermeasures to automatically detect and block unwanted email (Sahami 1998). Such technical countermeasures were pervasively deployed in email programmes and servers, making it increasingly difficult for spammers to reach victims with their content.

The increasing difficulty of successfully sending spam, together with the increasing size of the internet and the possibility of reaching billions of users and maybe selling illicit products to them created an entire ecosystem of specialised actors in the email-spam industry (Stone-Gross 2011). The main issue that cybercriminals had to solve was to reach enough computational power and network bandwidth to be able to send billions of emails. Very large numbers of messages were required because the defences deployed by users and internet service providers block the vast majority of them. To solve this problem cybercriminals started using *botnets*, networks of infected computers acting under the control of the offender to send the malicious emails (Cooke 2007). Victim computers would be infected by either luring users into clicking on deceptive content (e.g. email attachments) or by leveraging more advanced infection mechanisms that do not require any human interaction (Mavrommatis 2008). Setting up and maintaining a botnet is a complex task, and specialised cybercriminals started taking care of this process and renting a botnet to other offenders for a fee. Examples of this include the Cutwail botnet (Stone-Gross 2011).

Additional problems faced by cybercriminals include collecting a list of possible victims (i.e. email addresses) and handling the shipping of the purchased goods as well as the payments made by the users. To obtain lists of email addresses to send their spam messages, cybercriminals interact with harvesters, who specialise in collecting such addresses by crawling the web or by collecting the address books of computer users infected with malware. Stringhini et al. (2014) showed that cybercriminals that act as email harvesters participate in an underground economy, selling their lists of email addresses to multiple offenders who are interested in sending spam (from now on referred to as *spammers*). Dealing with product shipment, deliveries, payments, and chargebacks, on the other hand, is a much more complex issue. For this reason, spammers rely on *affiliate programmes* to handle these tasks (Krebs 2014). An affiliate programme is an operation, usually associated with a well-known online store, to which spammers can subscribe. Spammers will then be in charge of delivering marketing emails advertising the products on the site, and will receive a percentage on the purchases that they will attract, while the affiliate site will deal with everything else from payment to customer support to the delivery of goods (Levchenko 2011).

Most organised cybercrime originates from Russia (Krebs 2014). Taking advantage of technical expertise developed over many years and of legislation that is not as strict as that in Europe and in the United States, Russian cybercriminals have flourished in the past years. A Russian spammer wanting to start their own operation could join an online forum where services by specialised cybercriminals were offered (Stone-Gross 2011), purchase a botnet and a list of email addresses from these actors, and join an affiliate programme that takes care of providing the goods to be sold, which are often cheap prescription drugs (Levchenko 2011). Such drugs have been shown to be of particular appeal to American customers who could not afford them otherwise (Krebs 2014). Affiliate programmes are known as *Partnerka* in Russian (Samosseiko 2009), and the most successful ones in the past have been *GlavMed* and *Rx-Promotions*. Additional specialised actors in this ecosystem include internet service providers that act above the law, hosting the controlling servers of botnets without complying with takedown requests by law enforcement; payment processors who similarly close an eye on the nature of the businesses that they are working with; and manufacturing facilities that take care of producing the illicit goods and shipping them to the customer. The payment process and shipment process are particularly critical to criminals because they are key in monetising their operation. They also have the peculiar characteristic of happening in the real world (with physical payments and actual parcels being shipped), rather than only consisting of digital communications (as in the other parts of the criminal operation). For these reasons, it is easier for law enforcement to act on these elements to mitigate and block cybercriminal operations. As previous research shows, payment processors and shipping processes have been found to be the weak links in spam-related operations. In the rest of this section, we describe these examples in detail.

When dealing with criminal businesses, payment processors have to be particularly careful to remain under the radar of law enforcement and their own peers (i.e. other financial institutions), or they will be removed from the worldwide payment network and will cease doing business (Levchenko 2011). For example, the banking industry has been dealing with fraud for many decades and developed regulations and detection mechanisms to flag suspicious transactions. Adaptations of these techniques could be made to identify suspicious transactions within banks that want to cooperate. Similarly, a bank can identify fraudulent payments going from its customers to rogue banks that allow questionable companies to open accounts with them. These transactions can then be blocked or the rogue bank can be peer-pressured into stopping doing business with the criminals.

In their 2011 paper, Levchenko et al. tracked the operations of multiple cybercriminal gangs using botnets to send email spam that advertised pharmaceuticals or counterfeit goods (Levchenko 2011). They showed that each cybercriminal group would use a wide range of internet service providers, infected computers located in different countries, and domain names, to advertise the illicit goods. Targeting any of these services for mitigation would have a limited effect, because they are only used by a fraction of the criminals and it would be reasonably easy for a criminal to switch to another service. Levchenko et al. showed that shutting down the largest service with which criminals registered their website domains, for example, would have brought to a halt 35 per cent of the operations that they observed, but in a follow-up work the same authors showed that it is very easy for criminals to move to another registrar, making such countermeasures ineffective (Liu 2011). On the other hand, they show that when coming to the banks and payment processors that they do business with, all these cybercriminal operations use a much smaller range of options: for instance, the top four banks that the authors tracked were used in more than 95 per cent of all the observed operations. The fact that the number of banks willing to do business with criminals is small, together with the fact that other banks can put pressure on these misbehaving institutions to stop their endeavours identifies banks as a good point of intervention when dealing with email-spam operations.

In addition to physical payments, parcels need to be delivered for spam operations to be profitable. Interestingly, the goods that are purchased by spam victims end up actually being delivered to them, and preliminary research shows that the some of the drugs offered on websites that are advertised through email spam actually do contain the active substances that they are supposed to (Levchenko 2011; Krebs 2014). This makes sense, because reaching potential customers with spam is expensive and not very effective, and it is therefore important for spammers to make their customers happy so that they will come back in the future. Previous research showed that returning customers are key for spam operations to make a profit (McCoy 2012). To keep their customers satisfied, as with legitimate stores, spam-powered marketplaces offer customer services to deal with user complaints, and provide refunds if the customer is not satisfied with their purchase. The reason for this attention to dissatisfied customers goes beyond the need to retain customers who might, in the future, place another order. Credit card processors keep track of user complains and would stop doing business with the criminals if user complaints were not taken care of properly – for example if the number of chargebacks increased above a certain threshold (Stone-Gross 2013). For this reason, cybercriminals take great care to make sure that their customers are satisfied with the service.

The parcels containing illicit goods can be tracked and blocked by law enforcement and postal services. Previous research has found that these parcels follow identifiable patterns – for example they are always shipped from the same facility in India (Levchenko 2011). These patterns can be learned and used to track down suspicious parcels and improve border inspections. If the actual parcels never reach the customers, this will trigger a chain of chargebacks to the payment processor, which will eventually cause payment processors to freeze the criminals' accounts.

Case study 2: fake antivirus scams

Email-spam operations are not the only cybercriminal schemes requiring a switch from the online to the physical world because of monetisation needs: fake antivirus operations display similar attention to chargebacks and customer service (Stone-Gross 2013). In such schemes, users visiting a webpage are presented with a window that looks like a scan performed by an antivirus programme. Such scan tells the user that a number of malware infections have been found on her computer, and that she can remove such infections by purchasing an antivirus programme. Once downloaded, the programme claims to have removed the malicious files, and the user is likely to believe this since her computer was never infected by malware in the first place and therefore no negative effects due to malicious software (e.g. a slowdown of the computer) are visible.

Fake antivirus schemes have been shown to be very profitable by previous research (Stone-Gross 2013). Intuitively, these operations are low cost, because they do not offer anything else than useless software masked as something useful (which is referred to as *scareware* in jargon). For these reasons, criminals do not have to worry as much as with traditional malware about avoiding detection by antivirus programmes, as well as about building expensive infrastructures that are geographically dispersed and are therefore difficult to be taken down. Once again, the weak link of this cybercriminal scheme is payment networks. Fake antivirus operators need to show good will with the payment processors to avoid being disconnected, and therefore refund any user who downloaded their software and later complains that it does not work. Since the scheme falls under fraud in most legislations – after all, the criminals lure an unsuspecting victim into paying for and installing software under false pretences – payment processors can be easily identified and forced to stop doing business with criminals. As the reader can see, there is a pattern emerging, in which the common weak link of cybercriminal operations appears to be how these operations process their money.

Case study 3: credit card fraud

Another prominent example in which the need for monetisation in the real world becomes the weak link in a cybercriminal operation is credit card fraud. Stealing credit card credentials is another major focus of cybercriminal operations, for obvious reasons – owning someone else's credit card details can allow a criminal to extract money from the card by purchasing expensive goods. Nowadays cybercriminals obtain credit card credentials from victims through two main means: *information-stealing malware* and *data breaches*.

Information-stealing botnets emerged ten years ago as a new way of monetising malware as an alternative to sending spam. The idea behind these malware operations is simple: they hide on user computers monitoring the information that people input on their keyboard: user names and password credentials to websites, credit card numbers, bank account details and so on. They can then send this information to a command-and-control server managed by a criminal, who will then decide what to do with this information. For stolen account credentials, the criminal typically connects to the account and attempts to assess the value of the accounts (Bursztein 2014). The credentials will then be sold on an underground market at the established price (Stone-Gross 2011). Credit card numbers undergo a similar process, but it is more difficult to assess their value, since making purchases with them could trigger fraud protection mechanisms from the issuing banks and would render them unusable.

Due to their success, information-stealing botnets have gone through multiple technical innovations over the last ten years, to allow cybercriminals to stay under the radar and continue operating. The first popular information-stealing botnet was Zeus (Binsalleeh 2010). Zeus became popular when its source code was leaked, because this incident allowed any skilled criminal to set up their own botnet with limited effort and start stealing sensitive information from their victims. An issue with the original Zeus infrastructure was that it used a centralised command-and-control server, and it was therefore possible for law enforcement to identify and take down such control servers, effectively stopping the criminal operation. As often happens, cybercriminals adapted to this weakness of the system by improving the Zeus infrastructure, introducing a peer-to-peer control scheme that made it more difficult to identify where the control server was located. This iteration of the botnet was named Gameover Zeus (Andriesse 2013). Meanwhile, new families of information-stealing malware were developed by criminals worldwide. A famous example is Torpig, which added the use of a domain name that is changed periodically to make detection even more difficult (Stone-Gross 2009). Other examples of information-stealing malware include Dridex and Citadel.

Another common way used by criminals to obtain credit card information from victims is through data breaches. Unlike malware, in which the criminal can collect financial information from the victim's computer directly, in this case the attack happens on the systems of a server such as an online shopping site or a payment card processor. By exploiting a vulnerability in the site, the attacker is able to retrieve the payment information of its customers. Since attackers are targeting a single system, instead of hundreds of thousands of different victims, their attack vectors can be more advanced, since they can spend more effort in setting up the single attack. A prominent example of data breach is the Target one, in which more than 40 million credit card numbers were stolen (Krebs 2014).

In both cases (information-stealing malware and data breaches) in recent years we have witnessed an evolution in the techniques used by criminals both in how they get a foot into the victim's computer or organisation and in how they maintain this access for long periods of time, often defying attempts by law enforcement and practitioners to take down these operations. As with email-spam operations, however, cybercriminals have a desperate need to monetise the information that they collect through these operations. Without a way to extract value from stolen credit cards and bank accounts, cybercriminals are not able to make a profit and to sustain the cost of their operations.

Once again, monetisation of stolen-credit-card information requires a switch to the physical world. Broadly speaking, stolen cards can be monetised in two ways: by extracting money directly (e.g. by direct payments) or by purchasing goods with them. These goods will then be sold on the black market. It is quite obvious that having a single entity purchasing a large volume of goods or transferring money using multiple credit cards could be easily traced by bank fraud departments and law enforcement. Cybercriminals have therefore devised different techniques to perform and conceal these monetisation operations. In general, cybercriminals take advantage of middlemen to carry out these operations, commonly referred to as *mules*. We identify two types of mules linked to credit card monetisation: *money mules* and *reshipping mules*.

Money mules are used when money needs to be directly shipped to the criminal, and are commonly employed in bank account fraud (Florencio 2010). These people are typically recruited through online job posts, enticed by rewarding work-from-home schemes. The mule will then receive a payment from the criminal from the compromised bank account, and will be asked to send the money to another foreign account through untraceable means (e.g. Western Union). As a reward, the mule will be able to retain a fraction of the transfer amount. The mule is the one particularly at risk in this scheme, because he/she has to physically go to a payment location to make the transfer. This makes them particularly vulnerable to being identified and apprehended by law enforcement. Similarly, the payment processors can identify and block fraudulent payments going to accounts that are remitting to 'suspicious' destinations. Because of the amount of abuse present in money-transfer services, stricter regulations have been introduced. For example, to receive Western Union payments the recipient has to show proper identification to the cashier. This is a clear example of how cybercrime abuse has been limited by introducing mitigations against the way the operation is monetised in the real world.

For credit cards, the common means of monetisation is through purchasing expensive goods and selling them on the black market. Intuitively, criminals need middlemen for this too, to disguise their real location. The main method that cybercriminals use in this case is to recruit *reshipping mules* (Hao 2015). The purpose of a reshipping mule is to receive parcels at home, repackage them, and ship them to locations overseas. The criminals will then sell the stolen items on the black market. Popular items purchased in this scheme are electronics, photography items, and designer clothes.

As with email spam, the stolen-credit-card ecosystem has witnessed a specialisation of their actors, each one being very proficient in their own task. Following this trend, services specialised in managing reshipping mules have emerged. Such services take care of recruiting the mules through online job advertisements, managing the shipments, and sending them shipping labels containing the final destination to which the parcels have to be sent. The service also keeps track of the performance of the mules, marking them as 'well performing' or 'problematic'. Cybercriminals who need to monetise the stolen cards just need to sign up to the site, and are provided with a web dashboard from which they can set up their shipments and specify a location. Reshipping services typically charge their customers a flat rate, or take a percentage for each parcel sent (Hao 2015).

From the point of view of law enforcement, intercepting and blocking illicit parcels is a great opportunity to stop these operations and curb credit card fraud. Since parcels are a physical good, they can be intercepted, and the mules receiving and reshipping them can be identified and prosecuted. The key question is how to identify these parcels. When reshipping-mule operations started, the operators of these services were purchasing the shipping labels needed for the operation with stolen credit cards. Since these labels are typically purchased in bulk, if law enforcement were able to identify a purchase as being fraudulent this would allow the postal service to identify and block all the parcels that had labels from that purchase. To avoid this from happening, criminals stopped using stolen cards for their purchases of labels, reverting to legitimate white-label services which provide shipping labels at a discounted rate to businesses (Hao 2015). Still, reshipping-mule operations present anomalous traits compared to regular shipping, and these traits can be leveraged by law enforcement and postal officials to identify and apprehend the parcels containing stolen goods. For example, research showed that these parcels are in the overwhelming majority destined for the Moscow area in Russia, where they will be sold on the black market. Similarly, the parcels are usually marked as containing used goods, to avoid paying customs fees. These indicators can be used (for example by customs) to identify suspicious parcels and start inspections. For cybercriminals, adapting to these measures to evade being detected and blocked is challenging, because reshipping parcels overseas is the key way in which they monetise credit card fraud. We therefore believe that intervening at the shipping level is the correct way to fight this problem by reducing its profitability.

Another possibility is to intervene with the reshipping mules themselves. These people believe themselves to be working for a legitimate business as shipping agents, but are unknowingly participating in a crime because they are sending stolen goods overseas. Not only that, but research has shown that shipping mules are typically scammed by the site operators, who promise to pay them at the end of their first month but never do so (Hao 2015). This fact opens the possibility of running education campaigns in which potential mules are warned about the risks posed by partaking in these operations. This type of education is particularly important, because victims of these scams typically come from disadvantaged demographics who have no other chance to work (e.g. people with a criminal record, young mothers who need to stay at home, etc.).

Credit card and bank fraud are complex crimes and, as with any modern cybercriminal operations they involve many steps and many actors, which makes them difficult to track and fight. We believe that mules are the weak link in these operations, and that targeting this part of the operation can seriously damage the entire ecosystem.

Conclusion and challenges going forward

In this chapter I showed that the weak link in cybercriminal operations is often in the elements that happen in the real world, often through money payments and parcels containing stolen goods. Because of the need for cybercriminals to monetise their operations, these physical elements are difficult for them to avoid, and constitute good points at which to intervene to take the operations down. If we are able to break the link between online abuse and its monetisation in the physical world these operations will cease, since they will no longer be profitable.

In future, we might see criminals switching to less traceable monetisation techniques, such as cryptocurrencies (Meiklejohn 2013). These currencies provide some degree of anonymity, and it is therefore a natural evolution for criminals to start using them. For two reasons we do not believe, however, that switching to cryptocurrencies will solve all problems for criminals and make them untraceable and successful. First, research has shown that people (criminals or victims) are not comfortable in using cryptocurrencies, and that criminal businesses accepting only these types of payments end up being considerably less successful than others accepting traditional payments (McCoy 2016). Second, cryptocurrencies provide pseudonymity to their owners and they can be used to purchase goods that are sold on the black market or services provided by other cybercriminals, but this anonymity ceases once they get converted into traditional currency. Given the limited adoption of cryptocurrencies, this is a significant problem faced by criminals.

References

Andriesse, D., Rossow, C., Stone-Gross, B., Plohmann, D. and Bos, H. 2013. Highly resilient peer-to-peer botnets are here: an analysis of gameover zeus. In *Proceedings of the 8th International Conference on Malicious and Unwanted Software: 'The Americas' (MALWARE)* (pp. 116–123). Piscataway, NJ: IEEE.

Binsalleeh, H., Ormerod, T., Boukhtouta, A., Sinha, P., Youssef, A., Debbabi, M. and Wang, L. 2010. On the analysis of the zeus botnet crimeware toolkit. In *Proceedings of the Eighth Annual International Conference on Privacy Security and Trust (PST)* (pp. 31–38). Piscataway, NJ: IEEE.

Bursztein, E., Benko, B., Margolis, D., Pietraszek, T., Archer, A., Aquino, A., Pitsillidis, A. and Savage, S. 2014. Handcrafted fraud and extortion: Manual account hijacking in the wild. In *Proceedings of the 2014 Conference on Internet Measurement Conference* (pp. 347–358). New York: ACM.

Cooke, E., Jahanian, F. and McPherson, D. 2005. The zombie roundup: understanding, detecting, and disrupting botnets. In *Proceedings of the USENIX Workshop on Steps to Reducing Unwanted Traffic on the Internet (SRUTI)* (pp.1–6). Berkeley, CA: USENIX.

Florencio, D. and Herley, C. 2010. Phishing and money mules. In *Proceedings of the 2010 International Workshop on Information Forensics and Security (WIFS)* (pp. 1–5). Piscataway, NJ: IEEE.

Hao, S., Borgolte, K., Nikiforakis, N., Stringhini, G., Egele, M., Eubanks, M., Krebs, B. and Vigna, G. 2015. Drops for stuff: an analysis of reshipping mule scams. In *Proceedings of the 22nd ACM SIGSAC Conference on Computer and Communications Security* (pp. 1081–1092). New York: ACM.

Karami, M., Park, Y. and McCoy, D. 2016. Stress testing the booters: understanding and undermining the business of DDoS services. In *Proceedings of the 25th International Conference on World Wide Web* (pp. 1033–1043). New York: ACM.

Krebs, B. 2014. *Spam Nation: The Inside Story of Organized Cybercrime – from Global Epidemic to Your Front Door.* Naperville, IL: Sourcebooks.

Levchenko, K., Pitsillidis, A., Chachra, N., Enright, B., Félegyházi, M., Grier, C., Halvorson, T., Kanich, C., Kreibich, C., Liu, H. and McCoy, D. 2011. Click trajectories: end-to-end analysis of the spam value chain. In *Security and Privacy (SP), 2011 IEEE Symposium on Security and Privacy* (pp. 431–446). Piscataway, NJ: IEEE.

Liu, H., Levchenko, K., Félegyházi, M., Kreibich, C., Maier, G., Voelker, G.M. and Savage, S. 2011. On the effects of registrar-level intervention. In *Proceedings of the USENIX Workshop on Large Scale Exploits and Emerging Threats (LEET)* (pp. 1–6). Berkeley, CA: USENIX.

Mavrommatis, P. and Provost, N. and Abu Rajab, M. and Monrose, F. 2008. All your iframes point to us. *Proceedings of the USENIX Security Symposium* (pp. 1–15). Berkeley, CA: USENIX.

McCoy, D., Pitsillidis, A., Jordan, G., Weaver, N., Kreibich, C., Krebs, B., Voelker, G.M., Savage, S. and Levchenko, K. 2012. Pharmaleaks: understanding the business of online pharmaceutical affiliate programs. In *Proceedings of the 21st USENIX conference on Security symposium* (pp. 1–15). Berkeley, CA: USENIX.

McWilliams, B.S. 2014. *Spam Kings: The Real Story Behind the High-Rolling Hucksters Pushing Porn, Pills, and%*@)# Enlargements*. Sebastopol, CA: O'Reilly Media.

Meiklejohn, S., Pomarole, M., Jordan, G., Levchenko, K., McCoy, D., Voelker, G.M. and Savage, S. 2013. A fistful of bitcoins: characterizing payments among men with no names. In *Proceedings of the ACM SIGCOMM Internet Measurement Conference (IMC)* (pp. 127–140). New York: ACM.

Sahami, M., Dumais, S., Heckerman, D. and Horvitz, E. 1998, July. A Bayesian approach to filtering junk e-mail. In *Learning for Text Categorization: Papers from the 1998 Workshop* (Vol. 62, pp. 98–105). Menlo Park, CA: AAAI.

Samosseiko, D. 2009. The Partnerka – what is it, and why should you care. In *Proceedings of the Virus Bulletin Conference*, Geneva, September.

Stone-Gross, B., Abman, R., Kemmerer, R.A., Kruegel, C., Steigerwald, D.G. and Vigna, G. 2013. The underground economy of fake antivirus software. In *Economics of Information Security and Privacy III* (pp. 55–78). New York: Springer.

Stone-Gross, B., Holz, T., Stringhini, G. and Vigna, G. 2011. the underground economy of spam: a botmaster's perspective of coordinating large-scale spam campaigns. In *Proceedings of the USENIX Workshop on Large Scale Exploits and Emerging Threats (LEET)* (pp. 1–8). Berkeley, CA: USENIX.

Stone-Gross, B., Kruegel, C., Almeroth, K., Moser, A. and Kirda, E. 2009. Fire: finding rogue networks. In Proceedings of the Annual *Computer Security Applications Conference (ACSAC)* (pp. 231–240). Piscataway, NJ: IEEE.

Stringhini, G., Hohlfeld, O., Kruegel, C. and Vigna, G. 2014. The harvester, the botmaster, and the spammer: on the relations between the different actors in the spam landscape. In *Proceedings of the 9th ACM Symposium on Information, Computer and Communications Security* (pp. 353–364). New York: ACM.

19

The limits of anonymity in Bitcoin

Sarah Meiklejohn

Bitcoin is a decentralised virtual currency whose usage has skyrocketed since its introduction in January 2009. Participants transact bitcoins[1] using pseudonyms rather than their real-world identities, meaning that the way in which they identify themselves within the Bitcoin network is not inherently tied to their true identity. Participants can also identify themselves differently to different participants. One might thus be tempted to think of Bitcoin as the digital equivalent of cash in various illicit activities (e.g. the sale of illegal drugs on sites like Silk Road and its successors, or money laundering) that until the introduction of Bitcoin were largely carried out using cash or other opaque accounting mechanisms.

Unlike cash transactions, however, Bitcoin transactions are globally visible, meaning anyone can examine every transaction that has ever taken place; the Bitcoin ledger is thus completely transparent rather than opaque. While the senders and recipients in these transactions are identified solely using pseudonyms, there is nevertheless significant information that is revealed. In the case study described briefly below, we examine the limitations of Bitcoin anonymity and discover that the global visibility of this transaction ledger, coupled with the ability to cluster pseudonyms according to heuristics about shared ownership, allows us to identify (i.e. associate with a real-world entity or user) a significant and active slice of the Bitcoin economy. Beyond mere attribution, we also demonstrate the ability to track flows of bitcoins throughout the network, including following major Bitcoin thefts. If one can follow stolen bitcoins to the point at which they are deposited into a Bitcoin exchange (i.e. a company that trades bitcoins for fiat currency), then subpoena power would further allow one to ask the exchange for the real-world identity of the account owner associated with the deposit and thus identify the thief.

The next two sections describe the mechanics of how Bitcoin works, as well as the ecosystem of users that has developed around it. The remainder describe as a case study the ability to track money as it changes hands from one Bitcoin user to another, and the implications this has for the anonymity of these users and general crime prevention strategies.

Background on Bitcoin

Bitcoin is a form of electronic cash that was introduced by Satoshi Nakamoto (a pseudonym for the one or more unknown developers of the system) in 2008 and deployed on 3 January 2009.

Bitcoin is similar to cash, in that transactions are irreversible, and participants in transactions are not explicitly identified: both the senders and recipients in Bitcoin transactions are identified solely by pseudonym, and participants in the system can use many different pseudonyms without incurring any meaningful cost. Bitcoin has two other properties, however, that make it very unlike cash: first, it is completely decentralised, meaning a global peer-to-peer network, rather than a single central entity (such as a government) acts to regulate and generate bitcoins, and second, it provides a public transaction ledger, so while transactions operate between pseudonyms rather than explicit real-world individuals, every such transaction is visible by anyone in the world.

Ever since its introduction, Bitcoin has attracted increasing amounts of attention from potential users of the system; entrepreneurs seeking to develop further applications of Bitcoin; the media; and various international governments seeking ways to either ban or regulate Bitcoin. Much of this attention has been due to the nature of Bitcoin, and in particular to its use of pseudonyms and its public transaction ledger. The latter property has largely inspired interest in entrepreneurs, who hope to bring Bitcoin's transparency to provide insight into settings that traditionally use opaque accounting mechanisms, such as the financial sector or the administering of government benefits. The former property, on the other hand, has caused governments and law enforcement agencies to express concern that this perceived anonymity could enable money laundering or other forms of criminal activity. Finally, Bitcoin has also attracted attention from the general public due to its volatility and large growth as a currency: the price of one bitcoin was under 15 USD until mid-2012, peaked at 1,200 USD in late 2012, crashed down to 600 USD in January 2013, held relatively stable at around 200–300 USD throughout 2015, and at the time of writing (September 2018) is on the rise again at about 6,287 USD.

How Bitcoin works

Before turning to the case study, we describe the Bitcoin protocol. Bitcoin is the first proposal that achieves the two main requirements of a currency (the generation of a monetary supply and the establishment of a transaction ledger) in a completely decentralised manner, meaning every action is carried out by a global peer-to-peer network rather than by some central entity. Thus, peers serve to generate new bitcoins and to bear witness to their transfer amongst participants.

To understand how peers in the Bitcoin network can collectively generate a transaction ledger, we must first understand what a Bitcoin transaction looks like. As mentioned above, users in the Bitcoin system identify themselves using pseudonyms. Cryptographically, these pseudonyms are the result of applying a hash function to the public key of a digital signature scheme, and the owner of the pseudonym is the user who knows the secret key associated with it. Such pseudonyms can be generated with minimal computational cost, so users of the Bitcoin system can operate using many different pseudonyms. Now, suppose a user has some number of bitcoins stored with one of his pseudonyms. To send these bitcoins to some recipient, who has identified herself to him using a pseudonym, the user creates a message containing the pseudonym of this recipient and, crucially, the transaction in which the user received the bitcoins associated with his own pseudonym. Cryptographically, he then signs this message using the secret key corresponding to his pseudonym to create a signature. He then broadcasts the signature and message – which together comprise the transaction – to his peers, who in turn broadcast it to their peers.

Before broadcasting the transaction, each peer checks that the transaction is valid by checking for two things: first, that the signature verifies and thus (by the properties of the underlying cryptography) was formed correctly by the honest owner of the bitcoins and second, that no other transaction already used the same previous transaction. This first property is crucial to ensure that only the real owner of bitcoins can send them, as any other participant would have to break the underlying cryptography to do so. The second property is crucial to ensure that this transaction represents the only time the bitcoins are being spent (in cryptographic terms, to ensure that the bitcoins are not being 'double-spent'), which is why the transaction must reference the previous transaction in which the bitcoins were received, and why every peer needs to have access to the entire transaction history (or at least all transactions in which the recipient's bitcoins have not been spent already).

If a transaction is valid then it will eventually flood the network (meaning every active peer will hear about it) but it is still not clear how the peers agree upon a consistent ledger of transactions. To solve this problem, we consider special types of peers called *miners*, who group the transactions they hear about into *blocks*. New blocks reference previous blocks, so blocks form a *blockchain* and serve to timestamp the transactions they contain (i.e. the transactions contained in one block are agreed upon as having come before the transactions contained in the next block) and further vouch for their validity.

To create a consistent transaction ledger, miners must do more than simply collect transactions to form a block; otherwise, different miners could form different (and inconsistent) blocks, and there would be no obvious way for peers to decide which version of the transaction history to accept. To provide incentives for miners to perform this additional work (the nature of which we outline below) we now bring in the extra requirement of a currency, which is the generation of a monetary supply. In essence, the process of creating these blocks can also be used to create new bitcoins, and these new bitcoins can be given to the miner as a reward.

Thus, after collecting the transactions of other peers, the miner also adds to this collection a special *coin generation* transaction, in which she receives some newly minted bitcoins; the amount of bitcoins she receives is a parameter that has been agreed upon by the peer-to-peer network. In Bitcoin, this reward is further determined by the *height* of the blockchain: initially, the reward was 50 bitcoins, but at height 210,000 (i.e. after 210,000 blocks were generated, which happened on 28 November 2012), the reward halved, and will continue halving until 21 million bitcoins are generated, at which point the reward will be zero and miners will be incentivised solely by transaction fees (which will presumably increase as a result).

Once the miner has this collection of transactions, she now begins a cryptographic process in which this data (along with additional metadata, such as the previously mentioned reference to the previous block) is fed into a one-way hash function. Cryptographically, such a function can take in a large amount of data and produce a much smaller value that should be hard to predict given the input data; this last property is what is meant by referring to the hash function as 'one-way.' The miner's goal is to produce an output value that is strictly less than some target value; again, the target is a parameter that has been agreed upon by the peer-to-peer network, and is determined by the collective computational power of all peers in the network. As this collective computational power increases, it should become harder for any individual peer to produce an output value less than this target value, and this so-called *difficulty* of the network is adjusted so that the network collectively produces a new block every ten minutes.

Once the miner has computed the desired output value, this output value and the corresponding inputs (i.e. the pool of transactions) can be said to form a valid block. The miner then broadcasts this block throughout the network in a manner analogous to the broadcast of transactions, with peers checking the validity of her block by checking that applying the hash function to the input values yields an output within the target range. Because of the underlying cryptography, producing this output value should be very computationally intensive, so it should be hard to produce valid blocks, which further guarantees that few conflicting blocks should ever be produced and consistency can be achieved. (This does not tell the complete story, as it is still possible for two valid blocks to be produced at the same time by two different miners. The Bitcoin network has thus adopted the rule that the longest blockchain represents the transaction ledger, so that some blocks are ultimately *orphaned* and it is up to the discretion of peers which block to adopt in the case that two conflicting options are presented.)

To summarise, the ledger that every peer downloads when joining the Bitcoin network is the blockchain, which consists of a series of blocks, each referencing the one that preceded it. Blocks are accepted into the blockchain by *consensus*: if enough peers agree that a block is valid (e.g. its hash value is within the required target range and its coin generation transaction creates an appropriate reward for the miner), then they will choose to reference it when generating their own blocks, so that the mining of blocks (and consequent generation of bitcoins) follows a consensus-defined set of rules rather than system requirements. These blocks contain collections of transactions (which, like blocks, are validated through their acceptance by peers in the network), which specify the transfer of bitcoins from one participant, identified by pseudonym, to another.

The Bitcoin ecosystem

The Bitcoin protocol allows for the generation of bitcoins and the basic transfer of bitcoins from one participant to another, but one might naturally wonder where to spend bitcoins, or if there is any way to obtain them besides mining them oneself.

Since 2010, a variety of Bitcoin services have been introduced at an ever-increasing rate. One of the most widely used types of services, *exchanges*, allows users to exchange bitcoins for other currencies, including both fiat currencies such as dollars, and other virtual currencies such as Second Life Lindens. One can thus enter into the Bitcoin economy by simply purchasing bitcoins from an exchange, or from an individual buyer in their area using a matching service like Local Bitcoins. Most exchanges also function as banks, meaning they will store your bitcoins for you, although there are also *wallet services* dedicated to doing just that. (With all of these services one runs the risk of suffering a theft, in which someone just hacks the service and steals the holdings of all of its users; this in fact happens fairly often.)

The exchange economy is – as of early 2018 – by far the part of the Bitcoin ecosystem with the highest trading volume, as users seek to exploit the volatility of the currency to either profit directly (by buying low and selling high) or find arbitrage opportunities in which different exchanges set different exchange rates. Nevertheless, there is a range of merchants that accept bitcoins as a form of payment, and other bitcoin-based activities that users can engage with online (such as gambling).

Finally, users seeking to use Bitcoin for criminal purposes can purchase drugs and other contraband from underground marketplaces, which are often accessible only via the Tor network. The most prominent example of an underground marketplace is Silk Road, which was shut down by the FBI in October 2013, but a number of successors have arisen in the ensuing years, including ones that accept specially crafted alternative cryptocurrencies (often dubbed 'altcoins') that attempt to improve on the anonymity guarantees of Bitcoin. Criminals can also mix (i.e. launder) bitcoins with services such as Bitfog, which promise to take bitcoins and send – to the address of one's choice – new bitcoins that have no association with the ones they received.

Attributing Bitcoins to real-world owners

In spite of the concerns about Bitcoin and the regulatory scrutiny it has received, its use of pseudonyms has made gaining any real understanding of how and for what purposes Bitcoin is used a fairly difficult task, as the abstract Bitcoin protocol – when exploited to its fullest – does provide a fairly robust notion of anonymity. Nevertheless, in modern Bitcoin usage, many users rely on third-party services to store their bitcoins, and also engage in activity that does not promote the full anonymity supported by the protocol. This provides opportunities for crime prevention, namely exploiting this behaviour to erode the anonymity of the users that interact with these and other services. In doing so, we do not necessarily seek to de-anonymise individual users, but rather to de-anonymise *flows* of bitcoins throughout the network.

Our approach consists of two techniques. First, we engage in a variety of Bitcoin transactions to gain ground-truth data; e.g. by depositing bitcoins into an account at a Bitcoin exchange such as Bitstamp, we were able to tag one address as definitively belonging to that service, and by later withdrawing those bitcoins we were able to identify another. To expand on this minimal ground-truth data, we next cluster Bitcoin addresses according to two heuristics: one exploits an inherent property of the Bitcoin protocol, and another exploits an idiom of use in the Bitcoin network. By layering this clustering analysis on top of our ground-truth data collection, we transitively taint entire clusters of addresses as belonging to certain users and services; e.g. if our analysis indicated that an address we had previously tagged as belonging to Bitstamp was contained in a certain cluster, we could tag – with some reasonable level of confidence – all of the addresses in that cluster as belonging to Bitstamp as well.

As of 13 April, 2013, when we conducted this research, the blockchain contained over 16 million transactions carried out between 12 million distinct addresses. Over 11 million bitcoins had been generated (recall this is over half of all the bitcoins that will ever be generated) and those bitcoins had been spent many times over, to the point that over 1 trillion bitcoins had been transacted.

A re-identification attack

The first phase of our analysis involved interacting with many of the different types of services described earlier in order to perform our ground-truth data collection. In total, we kept accounts with 26 exchanges and ten wallet services, and made purchases with 25 different vendors, nine of which used the payment gateway BitPay. We also participated in Bitcoin's mining economy, which involved joining a 'pool' of miners who use their collective resources to mine blocks (as doing so individually requires a significant investment of computational resources); this meant purchasing an AMD Radeon HD 7970 graphics card and engaging with 11 different mining pools. We also kept accounts with five poker sites, and transacted with eight sites offering mini-games and/or lotteries. Finally, we sent bitcoins through four so-called 'mix' services, who promise to send different bitcoins from the ones that are sent to them (thus voiding the transaction history and essentially cleaning any potentially dirty bitcoins), and interacted with a handful of additional miscellaneous sites, including two donations to Wikileaks.

We engaged in 344 transactions with these services, which allowed us to definitively tag 832 addresses (recall that transactions can have arbitrarily many input addresses, which allows us to tag multiple addresses per transaction). We additionally scraped various publicly claimed addresses that we found, such as users' signatures in Bitcoin forums, although we were careful to use only tags for which we could perform some manual due diligence.

Clustering Bitcoin addresses

In theory, the use of pseudonyms within Bitcoin provides a property called *unlinkability*, which says that users' transactions using one set of pseudonyms should not be linked to their transactions using a different set of pseudonyms. In practice, however, certain properties of Bitcoin usage erode this anonymity.

Recall that, in order to create a valid Bitcoin transaction, the sender must know the private signing key corresponding to the public key in which the bitcoins are held. Now suppose that a user wishes to send 10 BTC to a merchant, but has 4 BTC in one address and 6 BTC in another. One potential way to pay the merchant would be to create a new address, send the 4 BTC and 6 BTC to this new address, and then send the 10 BTC now contained in this new address to the merchant. (In fact, this is the method that preserves the most anonymity.) Instead, the Bitcoin protocol allows for a simpler and more efficient solution: transactions can have arbitrarily many inputs, so the 4 BTC and 6 BTC addresses can be used as inputs to the same transaction, in which the receiver is the merchant.

This observation gives rise to our first clustering heuristic: if two addresses have been used as input to the same transaction, they are controlled by the same user. This heuristic is quite safe (or at least it was in April 2013), as the sender must know the private keys corresponding to all input addresses in order to form a valid transaction, and as such it has already been used in the Bitcoin literature and free tools are available online that perform this analysis.

Our second clustering heuristic expands on this first heuristic and exploits the way in which change is made. In the Bitcoin protocol, when an address receives some number of bitcoins, it has no choice but to spend those bitcoins all at once (recall that this is because each transaction must reference a previous transaction, and transactions cannot be referenced multiple times). If this number of bitcoins is in excess of what the sender wants to spend (e.g. if he has 4 BTC stored in an address and wants to send 3 BTC to a merchant), then he creates a transaction with two outputs: one for the actual recipient (e.g. the merchant receiving 3 BTC) and one *change address* that he controls and can use to receive the change (e.g. the 1 BTC left over).

This behaviour gives rise to our second clustering heuristic: the change address in a transaction is controlled by the sender. As change addresses do not a priori look any different from other addresses, significant care must be taken in identifying them. As a first step, we observe that in the standard Bitcoin client, a change address is created internally and is not even known to the user (although he can always learn it by examining the blockchain manually). Furthermore, these change addresses are used only twice: once to receive the change in a transaction, and once to fully spend their contents as the input in another transaction (in which the client will create a fresh address to receive any change).

By examining transactions and identifying the outputs that meet this pattern of one-time usage, we identify the change addresses (if more than one output meets this pattern, then we err on the side of safety and do not tag anything as a change address). Using this pattern – with a number of additional precautions, such as waiting a week to identify change addresses – we identified 3.5 million change addresses, with an estimated false positive rate of 0.17 per cent (note that the false positive rate can only be estimated, as in the absence of ground-truth data we cannot know what truly is and isn't a change address). By then clustering addresses according to this heuristic, we collapsed the 12 million public keys into 3.3 million clusters.

Putting it together

By layering our clustering analysis on top of our ground-truth data (and thus transitively tagging entire clusters that contain previously tagged addresses), we were able to identify 1.9 million public keys with some real-world service or identity, although in many cases the identity was not a real name, but rather (for example) a username on a forum. While this is a somewhat small fraction (about 16 per cent) of all public keys, it nevertheless allows us to de-anonymise significant flows of bitcoins throughout the network.

Towards this goal, we first examined interactions with known Bitcoin services. By identifying a large number of addresses for various services (e.g. we identified 500,000 addresses as controlled by Mt. Gox, the biggest exchange at the time of our analysis, and over 250,000 addresses as controlled by the underground marketplace Silk Road), we were able to observe interactions with these services, such as deposits into and withdrawals from exchanges. While this does not de-anonymise the individual participating in the transaction (i.e. we could see that a user was interacting with a service, but did not necessarily know which user), it does serve to de-anonymise the flow of bitcoins into and out of the service.

Tracking flows of Bitcoins

To demonstrate the usefulness of this type of analysis, we turned our attention to criminal activity. In the Bitcoin economy, criminal activity can appear in a number of forms, such as dealing drugs on Silk Road or simply stealing someone else's bitcoins. In this study, we followed the flow of bitcoins out of Silk Road (in particular, from one notorious address) and from a number of highly publicised thefts to see if we could track the bitcoins to known services. While some of the thieves attempted to use sophisticated mixing techniques (or possibly mix services) to obscure the flow of bitcoins, for the most part tracking the bitcoins was quite straightforward, and we ultimately saw large quantities of bitcoins flow to a variety of exchanges directly from the point of theft (or the withdrawal from Silk Road).

Our tracking technique focused on one particular idiom of use in Bitcoin that we call a 'peeling chain.' A peeling chain begins with a single address that holds a relatively large amount of bitcoins; as a concrete example, imagine that an exchange has 100 BTC stored in a single address. A smaller amount is then 'peeled' off this larger amount, creating a transaction in which a small amount is transferred to one address and the remainder is transferred to a change address; continuing with the example, this could represent a user withdrawing 1 BTC from an account, in which case the bank would peel off 1 BTC and send the remaining 99 BTC to a change address that it controls. This process is repeated for potentially many 'hops' until the larger amount is pared down to a small fraction of a bitcoin, at which point the amount remaining in the address could be aggregated with others to begin the peeling process all over again. We can repurpose our clustering heuristics to follow these peeling chains, as our ability to identify change addresses means we can isolate the 'peel' (i.e. the meaningful recipient in a transaction) and continue to follow the chain using change addresses.

Our reason for targeting exchanges was twofold. First, these are public-facing services that interact with fiat currency and its surrounding regulatory landscape; as such, they are increasingly (and necessarily) starting to implement know-your-customer (KYC) policies and are thus the likeliest service to know the real-world identity of Bitcoin users. Second, if one wants to cash out of the Bitcoin economy it is (or at least was in 2013) quite difficult to do so without using an exchange: they serve as choke points into and out of the system. Thus, while tracking stolen bitcoins to their point of deposit into an exchange does not in itself identify the thief, our analysis could be coupled with subpoena power to potentially identify the real-world owner of the account into which the stolen bitcoins were deposited.

Tracking bitcoins out of Silk Road

We first applied our tracking technique to an address believed to be associated with Silk Road. This address is one of the most well-known Bitcoin addresses: at its peak it contained 5 per cent of all generated bitcoins, receiving 613,326 BTC over a period of only eight months and then promptly emptying its contents almost immediately.

In emptying its contents, this Silk Road address sent 158,336 bitcoins to another address, which in turn sent 50,000 to each of two addresses and 58,336 to another; each of these three addresses then began a peeling chain consisting of hundreds of hops. We followed each of these chains for 100 hops and observed peels to ten different Bitcoin exchanges (including, in the first chain, 11 peels to Mt. Gox that collectively sent 492 BTC to the exchange); out of the 300 peels along the chains, 54 of them went to these exchanges. As described above, this provides an opportunity to find the real-world identity associated with this user for anyone able to subpoena these exchanges.

Tracking thefts

To ensure that our analysis could be applied more generally, we also looked at some of the major Bitcoin heists that had taken place in its history, ranging from the theft of 58,547 BTC from Bitcoinica, the largest margin-trading service and one of the most popular services in Bitcoin's history, to bitcoin-stealing malware that succeeded in stealing 3,257 BTC from various individual victims.

In examining these thefts, we observed that certain thieves attempted relatively sophisticated patterns of layering and mixing, while others made almost no attempt to hide the source of the stolen bitcoins. This setting thus provided a useful demonstration of the potential for anonymity provided by Bitcoin, and the ways in which certain usage would cause one to fall short of this potential.

Conclusions and implications for crime prevention

This study attempted to provide a characterisation of the evolving nature of Bitcoin, focusing on the rise of public-facing services and the growing gap between the potential anonymity available in the Bitcoin protocol and the actual anonymity that is achieved by its users. To this end, we developed new clustering heuristics for identifying Bitcoin addresses that belong to the same user, and used manual data collection to hand-label a small set of Bitcoin transactions; combining these two approaches allowed us to associate 1.9 million Bitcoin addresses with named individuals or services.

As acknowledged above, these techniques and the tracking technique they enable do not in themselves serve to de-anonymise individual users of Bitcoin. Rather, we argue that they enable further de-anonymisation in the cases in which certain agencies can determine – through, for example, subpoena power – the real identities of users interacting with services such as exchanges.

Thus, while this work does not in itself prevent anyone from using Bitcoin for criminal activity, the ease with which our analysis could be applied led us to conclude that using Bitcoin for money laundering or other illicit purposes did not (at least at the time of our study) seem particularly attractive. Based on the informally observed activity of thieves subsequent to our study, this deterrence seems to have served as a form of prevention, or at least as a barrier to entry, as now only those who believe themselves expert enough in the methods for achieving anonymity can safely use Bitcoin for criminal activities.

Note

1 In here and what follows, we use Bitcoin to mean the peer-to-peer network and abstract protocol, and bitcoin, or BTC, to mean the unit of currency.

20

Crime in the age of the Internet of Things

Nilufer Tuptuk and Stephen Hailes

> When wireless is perfectly applied, the whole earth will be converted into a huge brain, which in fact it is, all things being particles of a real and rhythmic whole . . . and the instruments through which we shall be able to do this will be amazingly simple compared with our present telephone. A man will be able to carry one in his vest pocket.
>
> *Nikola Tesla, 1926*

> I never think about the future – it comes soon enough
>
> *Albert Einstein, 1930*

Overview

The term *Internet of Things* (IoT) was first used by the British innovator Kevin Ashton in the late 1990s to describe a world in which computers can observe, identify and understand the physical world around them. In a presentation, Ashton explained that the networked computers of the day were reliant on data that were captured by humans through typing, recording, scanning barcodes, etc. (Ashton, 2009). The problem he saw with this was that it is error-prone since humans have limited time, attention and accuracy. As a result, Ashton envisioned a world in which computers capture the data they need without help from humans.

In reality, the conceptual beginnings of the Internet of Things lie about a decade earlier in 1988, when Mark Weiser talked about an idea he called *Ubiquitous Computing*, as detailed in his famous essay, 'The computer for the 21st century'. In this he described a vision of computing that was unlike the stereotypical desktop computer of the day. Notably, he opined that "The most profound technologies are those that disappear. They weave themselves into the fabric of everyday life until they are indistinguishable from it" (Weiser, 1999). Computing achieved this goal a decade ago: processors are now embedded in almost every device that has a power supply. These include devices in households (e.g. washing machines, dishwashers, microwave ovens), telecommunication (e.g. telephone switches, network bridges, routers, gateways), industrial automation (e.g. plant controllers, electric motors, sensors and actuators) road infrastructure (e.g. traffic control and monitoring, toll collection), medical equipment (e.g. X-ray, MRI, ultrasound, tomography, drip pumps, blood pressure monitors) and automobiles (e.g. anti-lock braking system (ABS), Electronic Stability Control (ESC), engine management). At present, about three ARM processors are shipped every year for each man woman and child on the planet; and there are several similar manufacturers (ARM, 2017). Moreover, the integration of wireless communication has happened at the hardware level – it is nearly as cheap to buy a system on a chip (SoC) combining a processor and wireless communication as it is to buy the processor on its own.

And yet, the Internet of Things is in its infancy.

Much of the reason for this lies in the vulnerability of IoT systems. In this chapter, we will examine IoT from the viewpoints of both crime that targets IoT systems, and crime that makes use of IoT systems to effect criminal intent. In terms of the former, we focus on the most probable area for deployment in the near-term – manufacturing and industry; in the latter, we consider for what kinds of crime IoT systems can most naturally be used.

Definitions

There is no universally accepted definition of IoT; instead, individual researchers and organisations have provided their own, e.g. Vermesan et al., 2009; Stankovic, 2014; and ITU, 2012. These all seek to capture a paradigm where objects ("things") communicate with other things at any time, in any place, through wireless or wired technology ("internet") with minimal human intervention, all in pursuit of a common goal. According to Borgia (2014) among key features of IoT devices are *pervasive sensing, heterogenous networks*, and *self-intelligent capabilities*.

- *Pervasive sensing* refers to the ability of a set of IoT nodes to return information about the physical environment (e.g. light, shape, position, temperature, pressure, behaviour and interactions), as measured from different points in that environment.
- Data from IoT nodes is returned across several, potentially *heterogenous networks* based on a variety of different mobile, wireless and wired standards (e.g. 3G, 4G, WLAN, WSN, BLE, Ethernet, etc.).
- *Self-intelligent capabilities* refer to the ability of networks of nodes to configure themselves autonomously, and then to self-organise and self-adapt to changes, processing incoming data to balance the desire for fidelity against a need to restrict power consumption and so a need to compress.

One of the other motivating precursors for the current research in IoT is a body of work in sensor networks. This is apparent in the above list because, missing from it, and missing from a significant part of the literature on IoT, is the entire category of actuation. An *actuator* changes something in the real world (typically they are motors or switches of some description) – they are what makes things active rather than passive and it is they that pose perhaps the most significant risk to safety.

Challenges to the adoption of IoT

There is considerable hype around the potential for IoT systems; they have been sold as possessing the potential to transform just about every aspect of life, from the home to the mining industry. However, Gartner places IoT around the peak of their hype cycle (Gartner, 2016), and this would suggest that rather soon it will enter what he calls the 'Trough of Disillusionment', as it is realised that the technology is harder to deploy than the hype suggests. In the opinion of the authors, by far the most significant reasons for delays to the widespread adoption of IoT systems are (a) challenges in security and (b) the lack of a clear value proposition.

Securing IoT systems is extremely challenging. IoT devices are resource-poor, which means that it is hard to deploy sophisticated protection mechanisms. At the same time, the availability of a wireless connection means that attackers with much greater resources can attack IoT devices directly rather than being stopped at, for example, a firewall. Moreover, new forms of attack are possible – for example, the devices themselves may be battery powered and therefore designed to use as little energy as possible to ensure that they remain active for as long as possible. This provides attackers a potential way of stopping a system from functioning. Similarly, if IoT devices have attached actuators, it is possible to cause physical damage to people or property.

The lack of a clear value proposition only applies to some sectors. Thus, for example, it is hard to see an obvious business model for use in the home, other than the relatively simple products that are currently on the market. Indeed, the connected home is also at the top of the Gartner hype cycle. There is a much clearer idea of how revenue could be generated by improving processes within areas such as energy and mining, power and utilities, automotive, industrial, hospitality, healthcare and retail. The first area in which IoT will achieve significant impact is likely to be the industrial and manufacturing sector. Interestingly, this also has a different approach to security than application areas that are rooted in the internet world: its primary defensive measure has always been security through isolation.

The first application domain

In 2013, to secure the future of Germany's manufacturing industry and so to remain as one of the most competitive high-wage economies in the world, Germany introduced the idea of Industry 4.0 (Kagermann, 2013). Sponsored by the German government, the initiative brought together 16 companies, ten institutes, two trade unions and four trade associations to examine ways in which new technologies might support highly productive, real-time, flexible manufacturing systems. In their view, this meant a move from centralised control to decentralised, self-organised networking; from pre-planned manufacturing systems to active, autonomous self-organising systems; from passive products to active products that interact with the manufacturing process; and humans, machine and resources communicating with each other naturally. By utilising IoT technology and services across the entire manufacturing process, Germany hopes to convert plants and factories into smart environments. The three goals of Industry 4.0 are (Kagermann, 2013): (i) horizontal integration through value networks, (ii) end-to-end digital integration of engineering across the entire value chain, and (iii) vertical integration and networked manufacturing systems. Wisely, as well as the technical challenges within IoT, the Industry 4.0 approach adopts a systems-of-systems viewpoint, in which IoT forms only one part; economy, society, energy and technology acceptance issues are also to be considered part of the Industry 4.0 initiative.

Germany is not alone in its vision for using IoT technology across manufacturing to strengthen its economy. Other initiatives include the Industrial Internet Consortium (IIC, 2016) in the USA, Factories of the Future under the EU Framework Programme for Research and Innovation (Commission, 2016), The European Factories of the Future Research Association (EFFRA, 2016), China's Made in China 2025 (Chang, 2015) and Japan's Industrial Value Chain Initiative (IVI, 2016). In the UK, the Engineering and Physical Sciences Research Council (EPSRC) has invested in an IoT Research Hub to drive research in IoT (EPSRC, 2016).

Security of industrial control systems

Industrial control systems (ICS) are command-and-control systems that lie at the core of both manufacturing and national critical infrastructure (CNI) systems such as gas, electricity, water treatment, telecommunications and transportation. The latter tend to be relatively well protected, but form a target for nation-state action since attacks can be launched remotely, can have effects comparable to hot warfare, and can be launched in a plausibly deniable way. Attacks on such targets are perhaps less likely to be undertaken by criminal elements since, in manufacturing, there are softer and more lucrative targets that are less likely to draw the immediate attention of government agencies. As a consequence, the remainder of this chapter will focus largely on security issues in manufacturing.

In the past, the manufacturing sector derived its security largely through isolation and obscurity: the systems used in the factories were specialist systems using sector-specific communication protocols, protected through isolation behind a physical security perimeter. Such systems were considered hard to attack because of the specialist knowledge required and the need to be physically present. If these assumptions were ever enough to discourage adversaries, they are no longer sufficient. To reduce costs, ICS have increasingly started to use general purpose computing technologies: commercial off-the-shelf (COTS) components running standard PC operating systems (typically Windows or UNIX) coupled with conventional networking, including wireless networking. The isolation between ICS and the internet-connected IT systems found in offices is being eroded with the reduction in fundamental differences between those systems. This is increasingly making them accessible to attackers. In addition, whilst these consumer-grade technologies are cheap, they have the same security problems as organisational IT services: being standard, the community of potential attackers is huge, with deep knowledge of complex modern operating systems. This allows adversaries to generate a continuous stream of novel (zero-day) attacks and, in the absence of nominated security professionals with a remit to manage systems actively, simply to launch attacks for which software security patches (software updates to fix vulnerabilities) are already available. Such security professionals have never before been needed in managing ICS, and this translates into a lack of awareness in company management that there is a need to manage what is a new and substantial risk for this industry. Moreover, the hacker community is now taking an active interest in attacking ICS. Adversaries have access to a wealth of material to improve their skills and knowledge about both conventional IT systems and, increasingly, traditional ICS. Today, hacking conferences are full of hands-on workshops and live demos aimed at allowing adversaries to improve and test skills.

Current ICS Systems

Industrial networks that are used in factories are generally hierarchical in nature, as illustrated in Figure 20.1. This architecture is motivated by the complexity of handling a large number of components whilst ensuring that timing constraints are met with high reliability. The lowest level of the automation systems is the field level, where field devices such as sensors and actuators are found; these measure or affect the underlying physical process. Signals from the sensors are transferred to controllers and control signals are sent to actuators by return, and the timing of such signals is often critical to the performance of the system and so the quality of the manufactured product. The communication protocols used here are fieldbus networks such as DeviceNet, PROFIBUS, CANOpen and LonWorks protocols (Mahalik, 2003).

The control level embodies algorithms that determine how to change actuators based on a desired outcome and the information drawn from the sensors. Again, timing is critical.

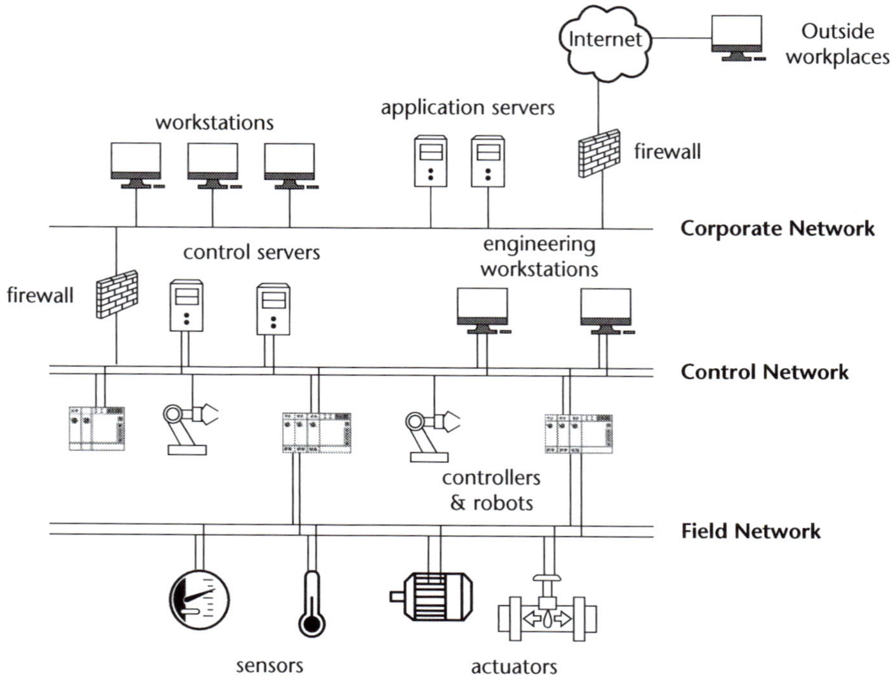

Figure 20.1 General hierarchy for industrial automation systems

The systems found at this level are programmable logic controllers (PLC), distributed control systems (DCS), supervisory control and data acquisition (SCADA) systems and human machine interfaces (HMI). In factories, production is often divided into local automation cells, where each cell is responsible for a specific part of the overall production process. These cells need to be interconnected to coordinate the production and they must be connected to operator workstations, since it is the responsibility of operators to load the algorithms, parameters and the data necessary for controlling the process, and to monitor production. The communication protocols used to achieve this include PROFIBUS, ControlNet, and Industrial Ethernet (Mahalik, 2003).

The corporate level lies at the top of the automation system. Business decisions are made at this level and production is monitored against business objectives. Consequently, enterprise management applications and servers operate here, and wide area networks such as Wide Area Ethernet are used. Security control is often provided by firewalls, which aim to protect against unauthorised access between networks.

Securing this architecture has challenges. One common feature is that most, if not all, legacy components in ICS systems were designed without reference to security because the threat landscape was very different to that of today. Because security is such a cross-cutting concern, retrofitting security to ICS designed without it has proved to be hard and error-prone. As discussed above, the introduction of new technologies means that ICS have much more in common with conventional IT systems than was the case in the past. On a positive note, this means that security comes as standard with many of those systems; on a less positive note, vulnerabilities and a community of attackers also come as standard. As first adopters, the application of IoT systems to ICS may move them back towards being more specialist, but will introduce new vulnerabilities and new complexities and will ultimately make the protection of ICS harder than it is even now.

Attacks against today's industrial control systems

In an industrial sector prone to substantial underreporting of security breaches, publicly acknowledged incidents include cyber-attacks on Estonia's national infrastructure (Lesk, 2007); the Maroochy Shire sewage-control system (Slay and Miller, 2008), which caused hundred thousands of litres of raw sewage to be spilt into the environment; the infection of the Iranian nuclear enrichment facility at Natanz (Falliere et al., 2011) which disabled Iran's nuclear programme; the attack on the Ukrainian power grid that disrupted electricity supply to the many homes (Tuptuk and Hailes, 2016); the attack on a German steel mill that caused significant physical damage (BSI, 2014); and the faulty control system of the gasoline pipeline in Bellingham (NTSB, 2002), which spilled thousands of gallons of gasoline into nearby creeks, and resulted in the deaths of three people. These incidents demonstrate the potential for a successful attack to have severe financial consequences, cause long-lasting damage to the environment, or result in injuries and loss of life.

More generally, the attacks launched to date against plants and factories had two primary motivations: exfiltration and sabotage. But to execute either, access must be gained to the system as a whole.

Exfiltration attacks involve unauthorised access that is used to harvest sensitive information about the operation of the systems and the industrial process. The information collected can be used for industrial espionage, theft of intellectual property, and to perpetrate further sabotage attacks. Some examples of exfiltration attacks are:

- *Eavesdropping attack*: By monitoring the network an adversary can intercept sensitive information about the network. The lack of security measures in industrial communication protocols means passively eavesdropping on the communication is often straightforward. Even when the network traffic is encrypted, an adversary may still obtain sensitive information such as which sensor or actuator is communicating with which controller.
- *Masquerading attack*: These attacks impersonate a system entity on a network to gain unauthorised access to steal data, spread malware and carry out other malicious activities.
- *Side-channel attack*: These attacks are carried out using a variety of techniques that monitor the physical characteristics of the system and devices such as processor's power consumption, light emissions, optical signal, traffic flow time delays, and electromagnetic, acoustic and thermal emission from hardware components (Standaert, 2010).
- *Covert-channel attack*: These attacks use legitimate channels to send and receive confidential information out of a secure environment bypassing the existing security measures (Tuptuk and Hailes, 2015).

Sabotage attacks disrupt the operation of a system with the aim of having a physical effect. Often, exfiltration attacks are used to identify suitable targets and, once these targets are known, the adversary will seek ways to prevent, delay, or corrupt the communication between sensors, actuators and controllers. Some examples of sabotage attacks are:

- *Replay attack*: In this attack, the adversary captures legitimate communication data and then later replays them to achieve a desired outcome.
- *Man-in-the-middle attack*: In this attack, the adversary sits between communicating entities and alters the communication between them. For example, it could intercept the

cryptographic key exchange protocol (many industrial control systems carry out this protocol in clear, without using encryption) between a controller and sensors, injecting a new key.

- *False data injection attack*: In this attack, the adversary injects bogus or malicious data into the system or the network, for example by modifying the payload of packets.
- *Data tampering attack*: In this attack, the adversary gains unauthorised access and modifies data in storage or in transit; for example, the data held in a server could be modified, or commands from the controller could be changed.
- *Denial-of-service (DoS) attack*: In this attack, the adversary attempts to deny the availability of resources such as a network, a system, a device, to their legitimate users. DoS attacks cause delays in actuation, sensing or control. These delays may cause operational errors, inefficiencies or cause the system to fail.
- *Distributed denial-of-service (DDoS) attack*: In this attack, the adversary uses multiple compromised devices to carry out DoS attacks. In the past few years, there has been a rise in the occurrence of malware that seeks to compromise IoT devices, and turn them into botnets (a group of internet-enabled devices that can be centrally controlled), to launch DDoS attacks. This included the high-profile IoT botnets such as Mirai (Antonakakis, et al., 2017) and Hajime (Edwards and Profetis, 2016), each of which compromised hundreds of thousands of IoT devices (e.g. printers, routers, surveillance cameras, digital video recorders, TV receivers). The resulting DDoS attacks were amongst the largest on record.

The primary reasons for these attacks are insecure communication protocols, lack of authentication or access-control mechanisms, insufficient security management and security flaws in software that are unknown to the vendors and users, known as *zero-day vulnerabilities*. Since there is, by definition, no defence against zero-day vulnerabilities (software holes that are unknown to the software vendor), they represent basic weapons with which an attacker can gain access to a system to carry out exfiltration or sabotage attacks. The number of zero-day 'exploits' has increased, possibly because the incentive for finding them is high: there is a market and buyers can pay over 100,000 USD for exploits (code that attackers use to take advantage of software vulnerabilities) (Kuehn and Mueller, 2014). As we discuss later, these exploits played an important role in targeted attacks against cyber-physical systems.

Once a particular exploit becomes known, the number of attacks using it often increases rapidly, in part because it can take a considerable amount of time for systems to be patched. Research (Bilge and Dumitras, 2012) suggests that the period of vulnerability might be as long as 312 days. Moreover, zero-day exploits also rapidly appear in *exploit toolkits* that contain pre-packaged software tools that can be used by attackers with few skills to carry out a sophisticated attack. The BlackHole exploit kit (Howard, 2012) was released in 2010, and dominated the crimeware market until 2013 with new versions and a sound business model (e.g. rentals were available from $50 a day to an annual license fee of $1,500).

To the best of our knowledge, there are no exploit kits that come with multiple pre-packaged exploits that will attack known vulnerabilities in cyber-physical systems. However, code from sophisticated (nation-state) attacks has been re-used by experts in other sophisticated attacks so we believe it simply to be a matter of time before similar user-grade tools emerge.

Attack initiation. To be able to carry out these attacks, an adversary first needs to gain access to the system. There are three common types of entries:

- *Insiders*: An insider could be a company executive, current and former employee, business partner, contractor, service provider, vendor, guest, support staff (e.g. cleaners, system

support technicians) or someone else who has a formal or informal business relationship with the organisation. Insiders may be exploited to infect the system; for example, devices that are not connected to the internet or local network can most easily be infected using removable drives (e.g. infected flash drives).
- *Social engineering techniques*: The most common social engineering attack is spear-phishing. Spear-phishing emails contain an incitement to open a malicious attachment, or click on a malicious link (for example, one that purports to be a well-reputed industry website). Spear-phishing campaigns are becoming increasingly targeted and aggressive (Symantec, 2015) and the manufacturing and utilities sector is amongst the top targets.
- *Drive-by download*: These attacks make use of the vulnerabilities in web servers, web browsers and browser plugins to install malware on to users' computers without their knowledge. In early approaches, victims' web browsers were directed to web servers hosting malicious downloads. However, to minimise traceability, most attacks seen today compromise legitimate web sites to infect users. This form of drive-by download attack is called a watering-hole attack. In a watering-hole attack the attacker observes which websites the targeted system's users (engineers and operators) visit, and they place the malware with the original software distributions or updates from a compromised vendor website.

Currently, the most common route for infection are via spear-phishing and watering-hole techniques. The introduction of IoT technology creates more points of entry, since each IoT node is potentially vulnerable, so this may change in the coming years.

Malicious actors

Industrial control systems are attractive targets for a wide variety of actors with different skills and motivations. These actors are no different to those found in the physical world. Nation-states want to keep an eye on each other; corporate rivals want trade secrets; criminals want financial gain; terrorists want violent attacks that can generate public fear; activists want to promote an ideological or political stance; insiders may want to get revenge for being passed over for a promotion; and a lone hacker may just enjoy the thrill or the notoriety. Cyberspaces have given the usual suspects the opportunity to carry out their intentions without leaving their physical spaces. It is important to understand that these actors have varying motivations and capabilities and, consequently, that some security measures aimed at one community may not reduce the risk of attack from another.

Nation-states have the capabilities and the means to finance, obtain necessary resources and people with advanced skills to carry out high-impact advanced exfiltration (espionage) and sabotage attacks. Espionage attacks are becoming widespread, targeting state secrets, patents and plans (Symantec, 2015). Carrying out an espionage attack that collects intelligence and remains present and undetected in the target infrastructure is often harder than carrying out a sabotage attack designed to cause maximum immediate damage. It is highly likely that nation-states will continue to direct most of their capabilities towards collecting intelligence rather than sabotage (Rid, 2012).

Companies are always looking for new ways to get ahead of their rivals. Industrial espionage may provide an attractive tool to achieve competitive advantage. Although organisations may have the capabilities to carry out industrial espionage, this would only be rational if the return on the investment (benefits) outweighs the potential negative consequences. In this case that could be loss of reputation or time in prison for those found guilty of commissioning the espionage.

Critical infrastructure such as utilities, telecommunication and health infrastructures might be attractive targets for *terrorist groups*. Given the asymmetric nature of terrorism, attacks on ICS provide an avenue for causing significant harm at scale, and the publicity associated with that, without a need to be physically present and without the need to assemble the resources needed to launch such an attack using conventional means. However, so far, there have been no cases (at least none reported publicly) of sabotage attacks by terrorist groups. This could be the result of either (i) a lack of capabilities such as the engineering skills needed to develop the attack, and the means of collecting the detailed target intelligence necessary to carry out a successful attack; or ii) lack of motivation, for example generating public fear and reaction might be harder this way than by suicide attacks.

Hacktivists are hacker activists who are motivated by political or social ideals. In the past their activities included blocking Lufthansa airlines website for deporting undocumented migrants out of Germany; support for Iranian dissidents; carrying out denial-of-service attacks against the Australian government for internet filtering legislation and web censorship regulations; compromising web sites and emails of oil and gas companies to protest rising oil prices; and bringing attention to other political and social causes such as the activities of WikiLeaks (Paget, 2012). Denial-of-service attacks, defacing websites, and theft and distribution of confidential information have been the primary tools of the hacktivists. Some recent large distributed denial-of-service attacks have been carried out by hacktivists (Symantec, 2015), and it is likely they will continue to carry out some of the high-profile targeted attacks in future.

Cybercriminals are typically motivated by financial gain or revenge, and their operations have become part of the daily life of businesses. Cybercriminals often use legitimate websites to install malware on their victim's devices; this includes key loggers to harvest confidential data; spyware and ransomware for blackmail; denial-of-service attacks for extortion; malware to hijack routers for ad-fraud (i.e. by subverting traffic to their customers' advertisement websites, also known as malvertising); network attached storage for cryptocurrency mining purposes. Crypto ransomware (encrypting files), has increased dramatically over recent years, overtaking the less-damaging locker-style ransomware (locking the user's computer screen). Attackers are improving their tactics for ransomware, and are now making threats to publish victim data online if the demands are not met (Mimoso, 2015), or deleting data if the victim takes too long to pay the ransom (Abrams, 2016a). In May 2017, the biggest ransomware attack seen to date, the WannaCry ransomware, infected computers in 150 countries. Once WannaCry ransomware infects a computer, it creates encrypted version of the files and deletes the originals, and then demands payment in bitcoins to release access to the files. Britain's National Health Service was probably the most affected by the attack, causing major delays and disruptions of health services, including cancelling surgical operations and suspending accident and emergency admissions (Hern and Gibbs, 2017). Other affected institutions included telecommunication company in Spain, banks in China and Russia, car factory in France, and state railway operator in Germany (Ghosh and Ashok, 2017). The ransomware exploited security vulnerabilities in older version of Microsoft operating systems, which was identified and patched by Microsoft before the attack, in March 2017. However, it seems, many failed to update their systems to protect against the ransomware.

Criminals are changing their tactics to attack organisations that are most vulnerable such as health services, where harm to patient safety is a real possibility. They are also using new propagation tactics to spread their malware. A new malware, called PopCorn Time, which was detected in December 2016 (Abrams, 2016b), uses the *carrot and stick technique*, which gives the victim the choice of paying the ransom (1 bitcoin, $898.46/£729.57), or helping to spread the malware. If two infected people pay the ransom they get the decryption key for free. Ransomware will continue to be one of the dangerous threats faced by organisations, with the average ransom demand increasing from $294 at the end of 2015 to $679 in 2016 (Symantec, 2016).

Insiders already have legitimate access to the target systems, thus they have more opportunities to carry out an attack and, by extension, to become the target of blackmail. Common insider attacks are unauthorised access to confidential data; theft of intellectual property; spreading malware and carrying out the actual attacks. The motives behind malicious insider attacks are very diverse, including financial gain, problems at work, revenge, political ideology, fear/coercion (insiders with access to sensitive data are vulnerable targets for those seeking to access this data), and merely from the thrill or the excitement of doing something not permitted. Insider attacks occur in many organisations in various forms and they only become public if legal action is taken against the attacker, which is not often the case due to concerns about negative publicity.

Lone *hackers* may break into the systems because they can, seeking entertainment, or to demonstrate their skills for self-promotion. The motivation for these attackers is often the challenge itself, and to demonstrate their skills. High-profile organisations such as utility companies and governments are attractive targets for the attackers who want to embarrass authorities and so obtain publicity.

Selected targeted attacks

The first cyber-attack against physical infrastructure may well be the attack against a Siberian gas pipeline. In 1982, during the Cold War, the CIA installed a piece of malicious software to control systems of the Urengoy–Pomary–Uzhgorod pipeline, which transports natural gas to Central and Western European markets. The software covertly changed the speeds of the pumps and valve settings to generate pressure that went above the maximum pressure with which the pipeline joints and welds were able to cope, resulting in a dramatic explosion (Russell, 2004).

Known as the Orchard operation, in 2007 there was a cyber-attack against a radar system in conjunction with a military airstrike carried out by Israel to destroy a suspected nuclear reactor being developed in the Deir ez-Zor region of Syria. Syria had one of the best, state-of-the art radar technology capabilities in the world, but they were unable to detect the Israeli warplanes. The details of the compromise are not known; however, it raised concerns about the security of the commercial off-the-shelf chips used in defence systems like the Syrian radar system, since chip manufacturers might have purposely modified the chips to have a backdoor that enabled unauthorised remote access (Adee, 2008). By sending a code to those chips, one could disrupt the operation of the radar system for a given period.

A public example of an insider attack took place in 2000 when an ex-employee of Hunter Watertech, the water treatment control system supplier to Maroochy Shire Council of South East Queensland, Australia, took control of the waste water management system of the Council (Slay and Miller, 2008). The sewage-control system had over 140 pumping stations connected by radio communication to a control centre. The disgruntled employee (contractor) exploited a vulnerability in the radio communication by masquerading as a controller and sending commands to the pumping station from this fake controller. He was able to stop pumps from running and prevent them from sending alarms to the legitimate controller, causing a release of some 800,000 litres of sewage into the environment, including onto hotel grounds, local parks and rivers, endangering public health, fish and wildlife. As this example shows, insiders can cause severe consequences, and thus it is important to ensure security is not just designed for external attacks, but is also effective against those from inside. This means it is important to protect insiders, since they can become transitional targets (Newman and Clarke, 2003), used to reach the prime target. Thus, for example, one of the biggest data breaches was carried out against the giant United States retailer Target in 2013. The attackers accessed the retailer's systems by stealing credentials from a subcontractor that was providing heating, ventilation and air conditioning (HVAC) systems for the retailer. The HVAC subcontractor had external access to the retailer's network, which the criminals exploited to infiltrate the system with malware and steal the personal information of 70 million customers, including 40 million debit and credit card accounts (Krebs, 2014). The consequences of the attack were severe, including long-term damage to share prices and revenue, resignation of the CEO and the expenditure of over $100 million to update technology (Clark, 2014).

The most sophisticated cyber-attack seen to this date against a physical infrastructure was Stuxnet (Falliere et al., 2011) (Langner, 2011) detected in 2010. Stuxnet was designed to sabotage programmable logic controllers (PLC), which are widely used in ICS, by reprogramming them to carry out malicious actions. These actions were designed to disrupt Iran's uranium enrichment facility at the Natanz plant over a long time period by shortening the lives of centrifuges and dumping enriched uranium in a waste receptacle, all without detection. Stuxnet was a highly complex piece of malware that was able to propagate stealthily between machines, including those with no internet connection, looking for specific PLCs manufactured by Siemens (PLC S7–125 and S7–417). Once it found these controllers, it injected the malicious code that disrupted the systems for small periods, misreporting sensor values to avoid detection. When not operating, it allowed the legitimate code to continue operating as normal to avoid detection and cause slow but persistent damage (Langner, 2011). Stuxnet gained access to the system by exploiting unpatched vulnerabilities (two of which were not known before); used legitimate (stolen) digital certificates from two trusted vendors; contacted command-and-control servers to receive updates (updated itself using a peer-to-peer network within a local area network); and had advanced capabilities to hide the attack to evade detection (Falliere et al., 2011). Given the complexity of the Stuxnet, the resources and the investment it required, and a sense of who might benefit from its operation, it was attributed to the United States and/or Israeli intelligence agencies.

Stuxnet was a radical departure from previous attacks. Before Stuxnet, the general perception was that ICS were hard to attack simply because they were not connected directly to the internet and they operated in isolated locations with secure physical access. Moreover, it was believed that if an attack was to happen, it would be detected in a timely manner.

In November 2014 the German government's Federal Office for Information Security (Bundesamt für Sicherheit in der Informationstechnik) published their annual report (BSI, 2014), and reported a cyber-attack on a steel mill that caused physical damage. The adversaries used spear-phishing and other sophisticated social engineering attacks to infiltrate the corporate network and, from there, propagated code to the plant network. The details of the attack are not known; however, attackers showed advanced technical skills and detailed knowledge of the industrial control systems and productions processes. The attack caused control components to fail, which led the blast furnace to become unregulated, resulting in massive damage to the plant.

Another cyber-attack that resulted in physical damage and got the world's attention was that on Ukraine's power grid in December 2015 (Tuptuk and Hailes, 2016). The attackers carried out a coordinated attack against the distribution management system. The outages resulted in several blackouts, causing 225,000 customers to lose power across Ukraine. Like the attack on the German steel mill, it is thought the attackers gained access through phishing attacks, harvested the necessary credentials, escalated privileges and moved to the target control systems (E-ISAC and SANS, 2016). The Ukrainian Security Services and the international press were quick to point at Russian state-backed hackers; however, attributing these attacks is complex, and cognitive bias might be used as a strategy to mislead investigators about the true source of the attack.

Based on the above discussion, the common steps (or, what Cornish (Cornish, 1994), would call a crime script) of targeted attacks are represented in Figure 20.2.

Pre-entry activities consist of the groundwork needed to design and implement the attack. This involves defining the objectives (identifying targets and goals), building or acquiring the necessary knowledge, skills, resources (e.g. schematics, manuals, certificates), and tools to develop the attack, and routes to infect the system. The malware is typically tested in a mirrored environment to understand the likelihood of detection. The common routes for initial infection (*entry*) include the exploitation of insiders, making use of social engineering techniques such as spear-phishing, with aggressive tactics, or subverting the supply chain (e.g. water-hole attacks in which malware is placed with the original software updates from a compromised legitimate vendor website). The *propagation* phase consists of infecting other systems and devices and escalating privileges to gain access to necessary resources (sensitive data or system of interest). Propagation is typically established by exploiting other vulnerabilities. Sometimes an attack may infect systems and simply maintain a watching presence until further instructions are received from the controller. While in the system, attack code may be able to send information and receive *updates* via the command-and-control servers. The *execution* phase consists of executing the payload to

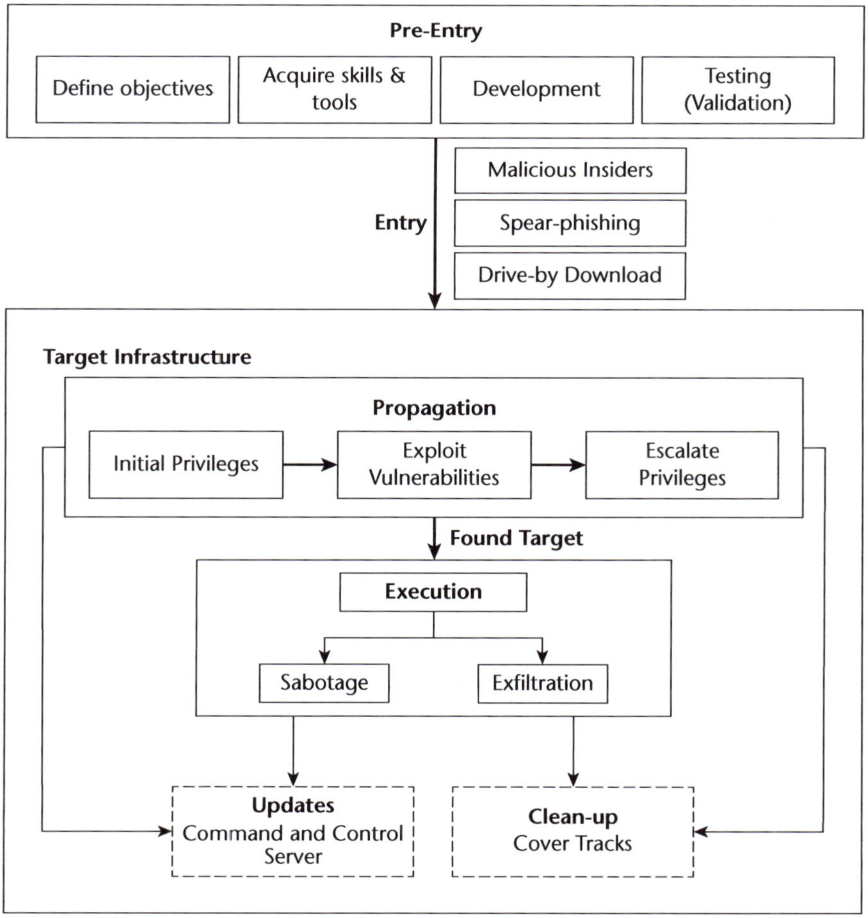

Figure 20.2 Common steps of targeted attacks

achieve the objectives of the attack: disrupt the operation of the system (sabotage) or harvest data (exfiltration). Finally, throughout the lifecycle of the attack, *clean-up* is necessary to prevent detection and extend presence within the targeted infrastructure.

Defences

There are many standards, guidelines and best practice documents provided by government and industry, aimed at managing and implementing security of ICS. Below we list a few of these; however, there are many more and a detailed list can be found in (ENISA, 2011).

The Critical Infrastructure Protection reliability standards (CIP) from the North American Electric Reliability Corporation consist of ten cyber-controls subject to enforcement to mitigate cyber-risks to the bulk electric systems: everything from physical security and electronic perimeters to incident reporting. ISA/IEC 62443 is another series of standards currently being developed to improve the security of industrial control systems. The series builds on ISA99, created by the International Society of Automation (ISA) and consists of four categories: general, policies and procedures, system, and components. These address various aspects of security, including security management, security technologies, and the secure integration of control systems. The ISO/IEC 27019 standard, which is currently under review, is aimed at the information-security management of process-control systems found within the energy sector.

Guidelines have also been issued by a whole range of organisations in the area of ICS. For example, the National Institute of Standards and Technology (NIST) provides a range of guidelines, including the NIST SP 800–82 for the management of control systems; the Centre for the Protection of National Infrastructure (CPNI) in the UK provides a collection of good-practice guidelines related to the security of ICS; and the Good Practice Guide on Cyber Security Assessments of Industrial Control Systems (CPNI, 2017), prepared jointly with the DHS, covers how to prepare and execute a cybersecurity assessment.

What organisations should do with this enormous amount of information, and how even to select the most suitable set to apply, is not clear. Achieving security through regulation with standards is complex, especially when interconnecting new technology with proprietary or legacy equipment and protocols. The experience drawn from the North American Electric Reliability Corporation shows that when security is regulated, companies start to look for ways to escape regulation, for example by removing black-start (the procedure used to restore the power in the event of a total or system wide shutdown) capabilities to avoid paying for compliance (Anderson and Fuloria, 2010).

Security of industrial control systems has received a vast amount of attention from academic research across many topics, including intrusion detection systems (Mitchell and Chen, 2014), security and risk management (Knowles et al., 2015), and testbeds (Holm et al., 2015). However, in common with most academic research that is novel, the studies are not sufficiently mature to deploy in reality. They are based on limited data, primitive testbeds for evaluation, and implementations that are not commercial grade.

Current industrial control systems, a summary

We argued above that ICS was an area in which there was a genuine business case that is likely to motivate early deployment of IoT, but that IoT introduces complexities and vulnerabilities that are likely to make security harder than it presently is. However, an analysis of current systems suggests that ICS security is important because these systems are responsible for monitoring and controlling services that are vital to the economic prosperity of nations, and the welfare of their citizens. This, and the present move towards COTS technologies, makes even existing systems attractive targets. The addition of IoT may initially make the task of attack more complex, as a result of the move away from standard internet-based COTS technologies, but its increased attack surface and plethora of resource-poor components will undoubtedly make it more vulnerable in the medium term.

Crime in cyberspace is not hugely different to traditional crime in the physical space. Criminals are motivated by the same things and they are looking for a suitable target and the absence of a capable guardian. However, physical proximity is no longer a requirement for crime in cyberspace; criminals can carry out their operations anywhere in the world without being near the victim. Crime tends to be serial (Brenner and Clarke, 2005), a one-to-one interaction in which an offender focuses on a single victim at a time, commits the crime, and then moves on to the next victim, or in some cases revisits that same victim at a later date. By contrast, cyberspace enables criminals to commit multiple crimes simultaneously at different places around the world.

The motivations for the crime and the types of crime do not change: crime is primarily focussed on financial gain or physical harm, and a working assumption is that the next wave of crime aimed at systems using IoT technology is likely to have the same motivation. In ICS systems, IoT components are likely to provide different (and easier) routes to the same kinds of attack that are now possible – primarily sabotage and exfiltration. However, more generally for IoT systems, the landscape of possible harm changes quite significantly from one in which the objective is to violate privacy or to cause damage to computer systems, to one in which the kinds of physical damage seen in attacks on ICS will be encountered more widely.

Future IoT crime

The focus of this paper has been on industrial automation, partly because it is likely to be an early adopter of IoT systems, and partly because the attacks seen against ICS speak to the possibilities for crimes in a world of internetworked actuation. The ability to launch cyber-attacks that cause physical damage has led to injuries, death, and damage to physical infrastructure, equipment and the environment. If IoT technology is to achieve its potential, then it will be embedded in many aspects of our lives, in particular healthcare, smart homes, smart cities and vehicles, where similar consequences are possible.

Healthcare: Perhaps the second most likely deployment of IoT technology is in the healthcare domain. It is already the case that embedded computing is used in devices from drip pumps and insulin pumps to robotic surgery, and it is increasingly the case that such devices are being networked, with attendant security risks. Moreover, wearable wireless sensing devices are being used for applications that range from well-being (e.g. simple step counting devices) to outpatient monitoring (e.g. for rehabilitation), as well as augmentations to social care (e.g. monitoring the elderly in their homes). It is highly probable that the trend that seeks to embed IoT-like technology in healthcare will continue largely because it has the capacity to provide data and control at a granularity that would not otherwise be possible.

Given the presence of IoT devices, given the same types of communities of attackers for ICS, and given the same kinds of vulnerability seen in ICS, we should expect that similar attacks are not only possible, but have been happening. However, the scale of the problem is not known because these events are generally made public only after the effects of an attack become apparent. So, for example, a series of high-profile ransomware attacks against hospitals across the United States took place in 2016 (Sittig and Singh, 2016). In one case (Zetter, 2016) the hospital's computers were offline for more than a week, and the officials decided to pay the ransom equivalent to $17,000 in bitcoin to regain access to their computers. In the UK, one-third of the National Health Service's trusts became victims of ransomware (Register, 2017) and the recent WannaCry ransomware attack, which happened in May 2017, demonstrates that criminals are opportunists who do not feel limited in their actions for reasons of social good. Hospitals are vulnerable targets for ransomware because they: (i) provide critical care; (ii) require access to patient data to do their work; (iii) have personnel who are security-aware, but where the focus of that awareness is typically on patient confidentiality not on these new forms of attack; and (iv) have systems, in particular the legacy systems, that were designed to operate in isolated environments with minimal requirements for security. The main lesson to take from the WannaCry ransomware is that effective information-security governance is vital for public safety. Many of Britain's National Health Service organisations were vulnerable to the WannaCry ransomware because they were using old operating systems (Windows XP, which is over 15 years old), and, failed to continue to purchase support for these.

The lack of security in personal medical devices (e.g. insulin pumps, pacemakers, implantable cardioverter defibrillators, neurostimulators, etc.), is another serious concern (Moe, 2016). Increasingly, these devices are designed to connect to the internet using wireless technology to facilitate the provision of remote healthcare. The attacks against these systems can range from determining whether someone is wearing an implant; obtaining information related to the implant (e.g. model, make); obtaining private information about the patient (e.g. identity information, medical data); changing device settings; changing treatment; and administrating inappropriate shocks (Halperin et al., 2008). Determining whether someone is wearing an implant not only endangers the privacy of the patient but can also open doors to a range of adversaries that could use this information such as future employers, insurance companies and terrorists looking for potential victims. In 2013, the former US vice-president, Dick Cheney revealed in an interview that he had disabled the wireless function of his heart implant to prevent a terrorist attack (BBC, 2013). At the time, this seemed like an exaggerated response; however, since then the US Food and Drug Administration (FDA) has issued several recall notices for medical devices (FDA, 2015, 2017) as a result of cybersecurity vulnerabilities. In these cases, there were no reports of these vulnerabilities being exploited, but, if hacked, these devices could indeed have caused harm to patients.

Autonomous vehicles: The development of fully autonomous vehicles is well underway and it is likely that we will start to see them emerge as commercial propositions in the next 10–20 years. Even now, a variety of enabling technologies that will eventually be needed for autonomous vehicles are being developed and deployed in existing vehicles, from intelligent cruise control, to lane-change warnings, to parking assist. More mundanely, even the audio systems, door mirrors or engine management systems are increasingly being controlled over networks that are local to the car – in particular using CANbus. Where those networks are connected to telemetry or mobile phone systems, there is a risk that they can be attacked and, indeed, such attacks have already been demonstrated (Greenberg, 2015b, 2016). Car manufacturers Chrysler (Greenberg, 2015a) and Mitsubishi (Bowles, 2016) recalled their cars after realising that they were vulnerable to remote attacks. Some vehicle manufacturers (e.g. Tesla and Ford Motor) have already started providing software patches (Tesla does this over-the-air; does not require owners to go to dealers) for their vehicles, and others (e.g. GM) are getting ready to do so by 2020. As vehicles become complex systems with many subsystems from many vendors and with hundreds of CPUs in each, the management of software updates will also become very complex. How the safety regulators and insurance industry will deal with these security challenges are open questions.

Since July 2016, there have been seven terrorist attacks involving driving vehicles into crowds in busy districts of European cities such as Stockholm, London and Barcelona.

These terrorist vehicle attacks have demonstrated that even a single vehicle in the hands of an attacker represents a dangerous weapon. That this might be achieved remotely and that many vehicles could be compromised simultaneously by a small team of people is particularly concerning.

Smart cities: In 1950, only 30 per cent of the world population lived in urban settlements (UN, 2015). In 2014 this had become 54 per cent, and it is expected to rise to 64 per cent by 2050, with the addition to the world's population of another 2.5 billion people. Designing smart cities (Schaffers et al., 2011) that are sustainable is becoming a necessity to cope with this dramatic growth and provide a good quality of life to their citizens. Providing utilities, housing, waste collection, lighting, parking, healthcare, education, and transport for densely settled populations can cost less and be more environmentally friendly than providing these services to a scattered rural population. IoT technologies will play an important role interconnecting devices, and achieving automation through sensing the physical environment, monitoring and controlling smart cities. However, as in other domains, it can be expected that criminals will exploit weaknesses in such systems to further their ends. Actions might include causing physical damage, obtaining a financial return through, for example, ransomware; or invading citizens' privacy. Unfortunately, again, there is a lack awareness of security in this field (ENISA, 2015).

View from the perspective of crime

So far, we have considered how new application domains for IoT technology might bring new opportunities for crime. In this brief section we draw on UK crime reporting categories to see the value of new technology from the perspective of a criminal wishing to commit a particular type of offence. At present, once somebody discovers a vulnerability, someone else will write malware to exploit that vulnerability. If vendors do not create and distribute the patches for these vulnerabilities on time, or, if they are not applied quickly enough by the owners of the devices, then these systems are available for use in all sorts of crimes and terrorism.

Table 20.1 illustrates some of the traditional offences that can be committed using IoT technology, given the vulnerabilities of existing systems. Connecting more devices will mean greater vulnerability, partly because there are more points of attack, and partly because the complexity of interactions between resource-poor devices increases with the number and variety of those devices.

Much of today's protection against IoT crime presumes either ignorance on the part of the criminal, or that the level of challenge inherent in launching an attack means that other routes to crime will be preferred. It would be unwise to continue to rely on this. As has been seen in Mexico, drug cartels have built their own private network mobile infrastructure (Johnson, 2011), and have developed better technology to monitor the location of the police than is available to the police themselves.

Conclusion

We are in the middle of a technological revolution in which embedded IoT technologies form key components of future intelligent systems that will impact many aspects of our lives. Some of these deployments are underway, and into some of the most critical infrastructure on which our society depends. These are typically areas that have not yet even been exposed to the full onslaught of internet attacks using conventional networks, which are reasonably well understood, let alone the likely attacks using IoT systems, which are not. IoT technologies are vulnerable in ways that we have yet to fully understand. If subverted, they can be used as agents of attack, as was recently seen in the IoT denial-of-service attack, or they themselves can be attacked.

Table 20.1 Some examples of future crime in IoT domains

Offence	*Offence group*	*Details*
Attempted murder	Violence against the person	Hacking personal medical devices such as insulin pumps, pacemakers, implantable cardioverter defibrillator, neurostimulator, and care-robot assistants can cause physical harm and possibly kill the patient (Finkle, 2014; Moe, 2016; Halperin et al., 2008).
Attempted murder	Violence against the person	Switching off the heating of an elderly person in winter by controlling their thermostat.
Attempted murder Interfering with a motor vehicle	Violence against the person Vehicle offence	Disabling the steering control and brakes of an autonomous car (Greenberg, 2016).
Blackmail	Theft	Extortion using ransomware to hold devices such as smart-home devices, personal medical devices, and motor vehicles, hostage at a critical time. For example, hacking the keyless door-locking systems of the vehicle to prevent the driver from opening the door.
Stalking	Violence against the person	Mobile and smart-home devices such as TV (Harris, 2015), toys (Gibbs, 2015), baby monitors (Goodin, 2015) for spying surveillance, monitoring, location tracking.
Theft from the person	Theft	Exfiltrating personal data from the personal and smart-home devices, and selling this data to interested parties.
Theft from the person	Personal theft	Utility companies cheating their customers but hacking the utility usage, e.g. keeping the heating on slightly longer than required.
Theft from an automatic machine or meter	Theft	Hacking smart-home systems and devices such as the smart meter illegally to under-report energy consumption.
Public fear, alarm or distress	Public order	Hacking smart-city transport infrastructure such as distributed attacks on road signs, traffic lights, street lighting and street lights can cause chaos (Hardy, 2016).
Possession of other weapons	Possession of weapons	Possessing and spreading malware that has the potential to carry out attacks that could cause physical damage or extortion.
Offence against the Person	Assault	Manipulating (e.g. turning them on and off) smart-home devices such as refrigerators, ovens, dishwashers, washing machines, thermostats, TV, game consoles and lighting systems.

The things that make them powerful – cheapness, simplicity, and connectivity – also make them vulnerable.

Building dependable and safe systems against misuse, faults and malicious behaviour is a complex task, and it will only become harder with IoT. Wireless technology, and the mobility it has enabled, has challenged the traditional assumptions of closed systems with clear network perimeters. Today, systems are evolving and becoming embedded in everyday objects and we are becoming increasingly reliant on them for managing and controlling critical services and delivering life-saving capabilities. Security is no longer just about information-security priorities such as confidentiality, integrity and availability. It is an engineering field, that brings together multiple disciplines to design systems that are safe to use and dependable against misuse, faults and malicious behaviour. The success of future factories, plants, smart cities, smart homes and smart healthcare relies principally on the security engineering of these systems.

Development in the IoT is a profoundly technical area of work, and causing networks of IoT nodes to operate effectively is far from simple. At present, most of the attention in IoT systems R&D is on developing functionality; far too little attention is being paid to the technical aspects of security for IoT, and even less attention is being paid to the uses to which such new technologies can be put by criminals of all descriptions. Understanding this requires a multidisciplinary team, with experts focussed on the technology, safety, the application area, and the motivations and resourcing of criminals. When things go wrong, digital forensics will need to investigate what went wrong. The establishment of a common ground between security engineering, safety engineering, crime science and forensics, is needed to provide the necessary synergy. Moreover, this needs to be done now, and it needs to be proactive: security cannot be a separate and secondary dimension that can be bought and retrofitted to systems. This has never worked effectively, and it is unlikely to start working now.

References

Abrams, L. 2016a. Jigsaw Ransomware Decrypted: Will Delete Your Files until You Pay the Ransom. Bleeping Computer. Available: www.bleepingcomputer.com/news/security/jigsaw-ransomware-decrypted-will-delete-your-files-until-you-pay-the-ransom [Accessed 12/02/2017].

Abrams, L. 2016b. New Scheme: Spread Popcorn Time Ransomware, Get Chance of Free Decryption Key. Bleeping Computer. Available: www.bleepingcomputer.com/news/security/new-scheme-spread-popcorn-time-ransomware-get-chance-of-free-decryption-key [Accessed 12/02/2017].

Adee, S. 2008. The Hunt for the Kill Switch. IEEE Spectrum. Available: http://spectrum.ieee.org/semiconductors/design/the-hunt-for-the-kill-switch [Accessed 12/02/2017].

Anderson, R. and Fuloria, S. 2010. On the Security Economics of Electricity Metering. In *Proceedings of the Ninth Workshop on the Economics of Information Security (WEIS)*, June 2010.

Antonakakis, M. et al., 2017. Understanding the Mirai Botnet. 26th Security Symposium. Vancouver, BC: USENIX Association.

ARM 2017. ARM Holdings: Q1 2017 Roadshow Slides. Cambridge: Arm Holdings. Available: www.arm.com/company/-/media/arm-com/company/Investors/Quarterly%2520Results%2520-%2520PDFs/Arm_SB_Q1_2017_Roadshow_Slides_Final.pdf [Accessed 06/09/2017].

Ashton, K. 2009. That 'Internet of Things' Thing. *RFiD Journal*. Available: www.rfidjournal.com/articles/view?4986 [Accessed 10/12/2016].

BBC 2013. Dick Cheney: Heart Implant Attack Was Credible. The British Broadcasting Corporation. Available: www.bbc.co.uk/news/technology-24608435 [Accessed 10/02/2017].

Bilge, L. and Dumitras, T. 2012. Before We Knew It: An Empirical Study of Zero-day Attacks in the Real World. In *Proceedings of the 2012 ACM Conference on Computer and Communications Security*. Raleigh, NC: ACM.

Borgia, E. 2014. The Internet of Things Vision: Key Features, Applications and Open Issues. *Computer Communications*, *54*: 1–31.

Bowles, N. 2016. Yet Another Car Can Be Hacked – This Time it's the Mitsubishi Outlander Hybrid. *The Guardian*. Available: www.theguardian.com/technology/2016/jun/06/mitsubishi-outlander-car-hacked-security [Accessed 10/02/2017].

Brenner, S. W. and Clarke, L. L. 2005. Distributed Security: Preventing Cybercrime. *The John Marshall Journal of Information Technology & Privacy Law*, *23*: 659–709.

BSI 2014. *Bericht zur Lage der IT-Sicherheit in Deutschland 2014*. Bundesamt für Sicherheit in der Informationstechnik. Available: www.bsi-fuer-buerger.de/SharedDocs/Downloads/DE/BSI/Publikationen/Lageberichte/Lagebericht2015.pdf?__blob=publicationFile&v=5 [Accessed 12/04/2016].

Chang, L. 2015. Innovation Key to Boost Manufacturing Sector. *China Daily*. Available: http://english.gov.cn/news/top_news/2015/08/04/content_281475160745630.htm [Accessed 2/01/2017].

Clark, M. 2014. Timeline of Target's Data Breach And Aftermath: How Cybertheft Snowballed For The Giant Retailer. *International Business Times*. Available: www.ibtimes.com/timeline-targets-data-breach-aftermath-how-cybertheft-snowballed-giant-retailer-1580056 [Accessed 28/12/2016].

Cornish, D. 1994. The Procedural Analysis of Offending and its Relevance for Situational Prevention. In *Crime Prevention Studies*. Monsey, NY: Criminal Justice Press.

CPNI 2017. Internet of Things and Industrial Control Systems. Centre for the Protection of National Infrastructure (CPNI). Available: www.cpni.gov.uk/internet-things-and-industrial-control-systems [Accessed 14/02/2017].

Edwards, S. and Profetis, I. 2016. Hajime: Analysis of a Decentralized Internet Worm For IoT Devices. Security Research Group, Rapidity Networks.

E-ISAC and SANS 2016. TLP: White Analysis of the Cyber Attack on the Ukrainian Power Grid. The Electricity Information Sharing and Analysis Center, The SANS Institute.

EFFRA 2016. European Factories of the Future Research Association. Available: www.effra.eu [Accessed 14/02/2017].

ENISA 2015. Cyber Security for Smart Cities: An Architecture Model for Public Transport. European Union Agency for Network and Information Security.

EPSRC 2016. New Internet of Things Research Hub Announced. The Engineering and Physical Sciences Research Council. Available: www.epsrc.ac.uk/newsevents/news/iotresearchhub [Accessed 20/12/2016].

European Commission 2016. Factories of the Future. Available: http://ec.europa.eu/research/industrial_technologies/factories-of-the-future_en.html [Accessed 28/12/2016].

Falliere, N., Murchu, L. O., and Chien, E. 2011. Symantec Security Response W32.Stuxnet Dossier. Online white paper available: www.symantec.com/content/en/us/enterprise/media/security_response/whitepapers/w32_stuxnet_dossier.pdf [Accessed 20/12/2016].

FDA 2015. Vulnerabilities of Hospira Life Care PCA3 and PCA5 Infusion Pump Systems: FDA Safety Communication. FDA US Food & Drug Administration. Available: www.fda.gov/MedicalDevices/Safety/AlertsandNotices/ucm446809.htm [Accessed 12/04/2017].

FDA 2017. Cybersecurity Vulnerabilities Identified in St. Jude Medical's Implantable Cardiac Devices and Merlin@home Transmitter: FDA Safety Communication. FDA US Food & Drug Administration. Available: www.fda.gov/medicaldevices/safety/alertsandnotices/ucm535843.htm [Accessed 12/04/2017].

Finkle, J. 2014. J and J Warns Diabetic Patients: Insulin Pump Vulnerable to Hacking. Reuters. Available: http://uk.reuters.com/article/us-johnson-johnson-cyber-insulin-pumps-e-idUKKCN12411L [Accessed 12/04/2017].

Gartner 2016. Gartner's 2016 Hype Cycle for Emerging Technologies Identifies Three Key Trends That Organizations Must Track to Gain Competitive Advantage. Gartner. Available: www.gartner.com/newsroom/id/3412017 [Accessed 12/04/2017].

Gibbs, S. 2015. Hackers Can Hijack Wi-Fi Hello Barbie to Spy on Your Children. *The Guardian*. Available: www.theguardian.com/technology/2015/nov/26/hackers-can-hijack-wi-fi-hello-barbie-to-spy-on-your-children [Accessed 12/04/2017].

Ghosh, A. and Ashok, I., 2017. Wannacry: List of Major Companies and Networks Hit by Ransomware around the Globe. *International Business Times*. Available: www.ibtimes.co.uk/wannacry-list-major-companies-networks-hit-by-deadly-ransomware-around-globe-1621587 [Accessed 05/09/2017].

Goodin, D. 2015. 9 Baby Monitors Wide Open to Hacks that Expose Users' Most Private Moments. Ars Technica. Available: http://arstechnica.com/security/2015/09/9-baby-monitors-wide-open-to-hacks-that-expose-users-most-private-moments [Accessed 10/04/2017].

Greenberg, A. 2015a. After Jeep Hack, Chrysler Recalls 1.4M Vehicles for Bug Fix. *Wired*. Available: www.wired.com/2015/07/jeep-hack-chrysler-recalls-1-4m-vehicles-bug-fix/ [Accessed 10/04/2017].

Greenberg, A. 2015b. Hackers Remotely Kill a Jeep on the Highway—With Me in It. *Wired*. Available: www.wired.com/2015/07/hackers-remotely-kill-jeep-highway/ [Accessed 12/04/2017].

Greenberg, A. 2016. *The Jeep Hackers Are Back to Prove Car Hacking Can Get Much Worse*. Wired. Available: www.wired.com/2016/08/jeep-hackers-return-high-speed-steering-acceleration-hacks [Accessed 12/04/2017].

Halperin, D., Heydt-Benjamin, T. S., Ransford, B., Clark, S. S., Defend, B., Morgan, W., Fu, K., Kohno, T., and Maisel, W. H. 2008. Pacemakers and Implantable Cardiac Defibrillators: Software Radio Attacks and Zero-Power Defenses. IEEE Symposium on Security and Privacy (SP 2008).

Hardy, I. 2016. Are Smart City Transport Systems Vulnerable to Hackers? British Broadcasting Corporation Available: www.bbc.co.uk/news/business-36854293 [Accessed 06/09/2017].

Harris, S. 2015. Your Samsung SmartTV Is Spying on You, Basically. The Daily Beast. Available: www.thedailybeast.com/articles/2015/02/05/your-samsung-smarttv-is-spying-on-you-basically.html [Accessed 04/09/2017]

Hern, A. and Gibbs, S., 2017. What is WannaCry Ransomware and Why is it Attacking Global Computers? *The Guardian*. Available: www.theguardian.com/technology/2017/may/12/nhs-ransomware-cyber-attack-what-is-wanacrypt0r-20 [Accessed 06/09/2017].

Holm, H., Karresand, M., Vidström, A. and Westring, E. 2015. A Survey of Industrial Control System Testbeds. In: Buchegger, S. and Dam, M. (eds) *Secure IT Systems: 20th Nordic Conference, NordSec 2015, Stockholm, Sweden, October 19–21, 2015, Proceedings*. Cham, Switzerland: Springer International Publishing.

Howard, F. 2012. Exploring the Blackhole Exploit Kit. SophosLabs, UK. Available: https://sophosnews.files.wordpress.com/2012/03/blackhole_paper_mar2012.pdf [Accessed 06/09/2017].

IIC 2016. Industrial Internet Innovation Forum. Industrial Internet Consortium. Available: www.iiconsortium.org/index.htm [Accessed 12/12/2016].

ITU 2012. Y.2060 Series Y: Global Information Infrastructure, Internet Protocol Aspects, Next-generation Network: Next Generation Networks – Frameworks and Functional Architecture Models, Overview of the Internet of things. International Telecommunications Union.

IVI 2016. Industrial Value Chain Initiative. IIV. Available: www.iv-i.org/en [Accessed 17/01/2017].

Johnson, R. 2011. Mexican Drug Cartels Have Built Their Own National Radio System to Communicate With Members. Business Insider. Available: www.businessinsider.com/mexican-drug-cartels-have-built-their-own-national-radio-system-to-communicate-wih-members-2011-12?IR=T [Accessed 06/09/2017].

Knowles, W., Prince, D., Hutchison, D., Disso, J. F. P. and Jones, K. 2015. A Survey of Cyber Security Management in Industrial Control Systems. *International Journal of Critical Infrastructure Protection*, *9*: 52–80.

Krebs, B. 2014. Target Hackers Broke in Via HVAC Company. KrebsonSecurity. Available: https://krebsonsecurity.com/about [Accessed 06/09/2017].

Kuehn, A. and Mueller, M. 2014. Shifts in the Cybersecurity Paradigm: Zero-Day Exploits, Discourse, and Emerging Institutions. In *Proceedings of the 2014 New Security Paradigms Workshop*. Victoria, BC: ACM.

Langner, R. 2011. Stuxnet: Dissecting a Cyberwarfare Weapon. *IEEE Security & Privacy*, *9*: 49–51.

Lesk, M. 2007. The New Front Line: Estonia under Cyberassault. *IEEE Security & Privacy*, *5*, 76–79.

Mahalik, N. P. 2003. *Fieldbus Technology*. New York: Springer-Verlag Berlin Heidelberg.

Mimoso, M. 2015. Chimera Ransomware Promises to Publish Encrypted Data. Threatpost. Available: https://threatpost.com/chimera-ransomware-promises-to-publish-encrypted-data-online/115293 [Accessed 06/09/2017].

Mitchell, R. and Chen, I.-R. 2014. A Survey of Intrusion Detection Techniques for Cyber-Physical Systems. *ACM Computing Survey*, *46*: 1–29.

Moe, M. 2016. Go Ahead, Hackers. Break My Heart. *Wired*. Available: www.wired.com/2016/03/go-ahead-hackers-break-heart [Accessed 06/09/2017].

Newman, G. R. and Clarke, R. V. 2003. *Superhighway Robbery: Preventing E-commerce Crime*. Cullompton, Devon: Willan Publishing.

NTSB 2002. Pipeline Accident Report: Pipeline Rupture and Subsequent Fire in Bellingham, Washington June 10, 1999. Washington, DC: National Transportation Safety Board.

Paget, F. 2012. White Paper: Hacktivism Cyberspace Has Become the New Medium for Political Voices. McAfee Labs.

Register. 2017. Ransomware Brutes Smacked 1 in 3 NHS Trusts Last Year. The Register. Available: www.theregister.co.uk/2017/01/17/nhs_ransomware/ [Accessed 06/09/2017].

Rid, T. 2012. Cyber War Will Not Take Place. *Journal of Strategic Studies*, *35*: 5–32.

Russell, A. 2004. CIA Plot Led to Huge Blast in Siberian Gas Pipeline. *The Telegraph*. Available: www.telegraph.co.uk/news/worldnews/northamerica/usa/1455559/CIA-plot-led-to-huge-blast-in-Siberian-gas-pipeline.html [Accessed 12/01/2017].

Schaffers, H., Komninos, N., Pallot, M., Trousse, B., Nilsson, M. and Oliveira, A. 2011. Smart Cities and the Future Internet: Towards Cooperation Frameworks for Open Innovation. In: Domingue, J et al. (eds) *The Future Internet: Future Internet Assembly 2011: Achievements and Technological Promises*. Berlin, Heidelberg: Springer Berlin Heidelberg.

Sittig, D. F. and Singh, H. 2016. A Socio-Technical Approach to Preventing, Mitigating, and Recovering from Ransomware Attacks. *Applied Clinical Informatics*, 7: 624–632.

Slay, J. and Miller, M. 2008. Lessons Learned from the Maroochy Water Breach. In Goetz, E. and Shenoi, S. (eds) *Critical Infrastructure Protection*. Boston, MA: Springer US.
Standaert, F.-X. 2010. Introduction to Side-channel Attacks. In Verbauwhede, I. M. R. (ed.) *Secure Integrated Circuits and Systems*. Boston, MA: Springer US.
Stankovic, J. A. 2014. Research Directions for the Internet of Things. *IEEE Internet of Things Journal, 1*: 3–9.
Symantec 2015. Internet Security Threat Report, Volume 20. Mountain View, CA: Symantec.
Symantec 2016. Special Report: Ransomware and Businesses. Mountain View, CA: Symantec.
Tuptuk, N. and Hailes, S. 2015. Covert Channel Attacks in Pervasive Computing. IEEE International Conference on Pervasive Computing and Communications (PerCom), 23–27 March 2015, 236–242.
Tuptuk, N. and Hailes, S. 2016. The Cyberattack on Ukraine's Power Grid Is a Warning of What's to Come. The Conversation. Available: https://theconversation.com/the-cyberattack-on-ukraines-power-grid-is-a-warning-of-whats-to-come-52832 [Accessed 13/01/2017].
UN 2015. World Urbanization Prospects: The 2014 Revision (ST/ESA/SER.A/366). United Nations, Department of Economic and Social Affairs.
Vermesan, O., Friess, P., Guillemin, P., Gusmeroli, S., Sundmaeker, H., Bassi, A., Jubert, I. S., Mazura, M., Harrison, M., Eisenhauer, M., and Doody, P. 2009. Internet of Things Strategic Research Roadmap. *Internet of Things: Global Technological and Societal Trends, 1*(2011): 9–52.
Weiser, M. 1999. The Computer for the 21st Century. *ACM SIGMOBILE Mobile Computing and Communications Review, 3*, 3–11.
Zetter, K. 2016. Why Hospitals Are the Perfect Targets for Ransomware. *Wired*. Available: www.wired.com/2016/03/ransomware-why-hospitals-are-the-perfect-targets [Accessed 14/01/2017].

21

Transdisciplinary research in virtual space

Can online warning messages reduce engagement with child exploitation material?

Jeremy Prichard, Tony Krone, Caroline Spiranovic and Paul Watters

Introduction

Human behaviour in virtual space is an increasingly important area of research. However, virtual space involves more than just people and machines. The potential of virtual space is rapidly evolving as the capacity of machines and networks develops and the ways in which people manipulate and adapt to virtual space advances. The complexity and potential value of research in this area is indicated when we consider the rapid changes wrought by the networking of machines and people; the implications of the emergence of the Internet of Things; and the amassing of big data (Dodig-Crnkovic et al. 2017; Chan & Bennett Moses 2016).

How we use virtual space occurs over a continuum between favourable use and misuse. There are many areas of widely agreed criminal misuse as well as areas where the nature of misuse is contested or where the criminality of behaviour depends on context. There is no doubt that the potential for misuse of virtual space is at least as important as beneficial use.

To understand what is happening in virtual space we must draw on the perspectives of multiple disciplines and attempt to transcend traditional disciplinary boundaries where these would otherwise constrain analysis (Gradon 2013). This chapter presents a case study of the first iteration of a research project which draws on multiple disciplinary perspectives. The project will test whether warning messages may act as a situational deterrent for those attempting to access child pornography online – referred to here as child exploitation material (CEM). As such, the project involves transdisciplinary aspects[1] and is squarely situated in the field of crime science (Gradon 2013).[2]

Hunsinger (2005) argued that researching the internet presented a number of challenges that could only be met by transdisciplinary research. Transdisciplinary research is established in other areas. For example, collaboration among health professionals has become a norm in the face of both the rapid expansion of medical expertise and the increasing challenges of population health problems (D'Amour et al. 2005). Likewise, many dimensions of crime are complex and, understandably, interdisciplinary teams form to examine this complexity and to respond to it (e.g. Farrington & Petrosino 2001).

This chapter begins with a brief discussion of 'transdisciplinary' research as one of the possible ways of classifying multiple disciplinary empirical research and considers its value within crime science. We then review some of the particular concerns for criminological research arising from the growth of information and communications technology (ICT), especially in relation to online CEM offences.

The lens of environmental criminological theory, particularly situational crime prevention, is then applied to the problem of online CEM. Through this lens, we consider whether online warning messages may act as a situational deterrent for those attempting to access CEM. The use of automated internet warnings as a potential technological crime-prevention strategy has been examined in relation to hacking (Maimon et al., 2014; Testa et al., 2017; Wilson et al., 2015). But as far as we are aware they have not been specifically evaluated for this crime type (see generally Qualye & Koukopoulos 2018).[3]

We present a case study based on early iterations of the research strategy. This reveals the importance of transdisciplinary research to bridge non-academic expertise with discipline-specific capability. We conclude with a discussion of factors required to complete transdisciplinary research successfully.

Towards 'transdisciplinary' research in crime science

Levels of collaboration may be categorised hierarchically as 'multidisciplinary', 'interdisciplinary', and 'transdisciplinary' collaboration (D'Amour et al. 2005). Multidisciplinary projects draw together discrete sub-components independently completed by collaborators from different disciplines. Interdisciplinary projects tend to require greater interdependence; collaborators work collectively on some or all project milestones, share decision-making and attempt to integrate their knowledge.

A greater level of interdependence is needed for transdisciplinary collaboration. For professional groups this is characterised by, among other things, deliberate exchanges of knowledge between collaborators and joint decision-making to the point where 'traditional discipline boundaries' are blurred (D'Amour et al. 2005: 120).

Henry (2005, 2012) invites reflection on transdisciplinary research in criminology, particularly in relation to the practical application of theory or knowledge (*praxis*). He recommends that criminologists be more willing to work not only with other academics, but any non-academic 'knowledge producers' (Henry 2012: 76) – including professionals (e.g. practitioners, agencies, professional associations) and those with experiential knowledge (e.g. clients, consumers, activists).

Cybersecurity is described by Malone and Malone (2013: 170) as a 'wicked problem' because it presents policy makers with 'incomplete, often contradictory information with an always changing, interdependent architecture'. The complexity of crime in virtual space is an important driver for transdisciplinary praxis. According to Henry (2012: 76), 'mega and complex problems such as crime require comprehensive policy and practice solutions involving collaboration among a hybrid mix of actors from different disciplines, professions, and sectors of society'. By contrast 'myopic analysis of crime from traditional disciplines' risks capturing only 'a narrow dimension of the aetiology of crime' and prescribing correspondingly narrow discipline-based policy.

Crime science, ICT and online child sexual exploitation offences

Advances in ICT have seen the emergence of whole new areas of specialised knowledge. New fields of ICT-related expertise include social media, big data, the cloud and mobile technology.

A wide variety of 'cybercrimes' now present significant challenges for ICT experts, criminologists, policymakers, law enforcement agencies (LEA) and courts (Holtfreter & Meyers 2015). Within the specialised area of cybersecurity it is recognised that 'transformational results' depend on uniting 'expertise from a range of disciplines' (Vagoun & Strawn 2015: 45; see also Jang 2013).

Online CEM is the focus of widespread concern. The Global Alliance against Child Sexual Abuse Online is a conference of ministers established in 2012 and it published a statement of commitments in 2013. This was followed by a declaration made by the ministers of 54 countries on 'Facilitating International Cooperation in Online Child Sexual Abuse Investigations' in 2014.

In addition to these developments both the US and the UK announced a joint specialised task force to combat online child exploitation material and online sexual abuse in 2013. This led to the UK government hosting a conference of government, industry and non-government organisations in 2014 to establish commitments to help eliminate online child exploitation material and other online child exploitation offending.

These developments highlight growing international recognition that collaborative responses are required to address the problem of online CEM. Criminal definitions of CEM differ across jurisdictions. In this chapter we use the core characteristics commonly used to define CEM across countries. These include the depiction of the actual sexual exploitation or abuse of children under the age of consent (taken to be 16 years, although in some countries a younger age applies) (Gillespie 2011; Clough 2012). The worst forms of CEM depict barbarous sexual torture and bestiality (Prichard & Spiranovic 2014). CEM can be produced with a digital camera or recorder anywhere in the world. CEM includes depictions of children of all ages, including infants. In fact 20 per cent of people arrested in 2009 for CEM offences in the US allegedly possessed images of children under the age of four years (Wolak, Finkelhor & Mitchell 2012).

Because there are so many ways to traffic CEM and because some of these methods are effectively invisible, estimating the size of the global CEM market is extraordinarily difficult. However, it is clear that the CEM market has rapidly expanded since the advent of digital cameras and the internet. Since 2002, the National Centre for Missing and Exploited Children has analysed over 249 million suspected CEM images in an effort to assist LEA to identify and rescue children at risk.[4] One study of peer-to-peer networks indicated that almost 245,000 computers had shared 120,418 unique files in one year in the US alone (Wolak, Liberatore & Levine 2013). A similar P2P study suggested that up to 9,700 files are trafficked daily by 2.5 million distinct peers in 100 countries (Hurley et al. 2012). In Dombert et al.'s (2016) online survey of 8,718 German men, 2.4 per cent of participants reported using CEM – 1.7 percent used CEM exclusively and 0.7 per cent in conjunction with sexual contact with children.

If these figures are contrasted with data on CEM-related arrests and prosecutions, it is clear that criminal justice systems are only dealing with a small portion of CEM offenders. McManus and Almond (2014) reported that 268 UK offenders were convicted for CEM possession in 2012 and 2013, in addition to 1,247 convictions for CEM production and distribution offences. In the US an estimated 4,901 CEM possession arrests were made in 2009 (Wolak, Finkelhor & Mitchell 2012).

Worldwide, LEAs bear the burden of responding to the CEM market and there is widespread international collaboration (Krone 2005; Acar 2017). Apart from notable cases where there is clear evidence connecting an individual to CEM offending for example, through the use of credit card records, law enforcement efforts often prioritise cases for investigation and prosecution that may lead to the identification of children depicted in CEM.[5] The next most important issue is likely to be the identification of CEM distribution networks. This is followed by other attributes of individual offending such as the scale of CEM involved, and an assessment of risk (from a policing perspective) of contact offending by a person known to be engaged with CEM images.

However, the volume of individuals distributing and accessing CEM means that LEAs will never have the capacity to *prevent* offending. Reflecting on the volume-problem, one senior Australian police officer involved in investigating online CEM suggested that LEAs 'are sipping from a fire hydrant' (DI Jon Rouse, 9 May 2014).

Prevention is not listed as a key policy of the Global Alliance Against Child Abuse Online.[6] Given the volume of material involved and the myriad opportunities for internet users to engage with CEM, the relative lack of CEM prevention policies or strategies is problematic.

It might be argued that prevention is largely irrelevant because CEM offenders are tech-savvy and highly motivated because of, among other things, the sexual gratification they derive from using CEM (e.g. Olbrycht-Palmer 2013). But in fact, research on the profiles of CEM offenders, particularly on the heterogeneity of offenders, indicates that there is a place for preventative strategies, as discussed below.

Adopting the lens of environmental criminological theory

Ekblom and Gill (2016) reviewed developments in the field of crime-script analysis for situational crime prevention. They detailed the ecological or situational and psychological factors that affect offender performance and called for cross-disciplinary study of crime opportunities and precipitators. The importance of reviewing and testing the application of criminological theory to crime in virtual space is vital to developing crime-prevention strategies for online crime.

We begin with the proposition that internet users do not need to be 'tech-savvy' to start using CEM. Non-solicited opportunities to deliberately view CEM for the first time ('onset') can occur in a wide variety of ways: mobile telephone, email, USENET groups, dedicated CEM websites, Internet Relay Chat and Peer-to-Peer (P2P) networks (Bourke & Hernandez 2009).

Regarding 'motivation', it is true that people can start viewing CEM because of pre-existing paedophilic interests. Yet, it also appears that onset may occur for people without prior sexual interest in children (e.g. see Prichard & Spiranovic 2014: 12). The compelling explanation for this phenomenon offered by situational crime perspectives rests on the fact that all criminal decision-making occurs in an interaction between *individual* and *situational* factors. Wortley and Smallbone (2012) claim that the extraordinary expansion of the CEM market has been primarily fuelled by *situational* factors – namely ready access to digital cameras and the internet – rather than an increase in *individual* factors, like paedophilia. In the internet environment, users are anonymous, have easy access to CEM and enjoy a comparatively low risk of detection provided they take basic precautions. The influence of these situational factors is clearly evidenced in the profiles of offenders prosecuted solely for accessing CEM (but not for contact child-sex offences). These offenders are remarkably heterogeneous in terms of education, employment, and family background. Their striking characteristic is their 'ordinariness, not [their] deviance' (Wortley 2012: 193).

Situational crime researchers observe from other data that previously law-abiding individuals can be 'drawn into committing specific forms of crime if they regularly encounter easy opportunities for these crimes' (Clarke 2008: 180). The risk increases when such people are aware of excuses for the crimes and they are able to entertain these excuses to justify their behaviour (Cornish & Clarke 2003). Regarding CEM, some offenders report beliefs that viewing CEM is harmless and divorced from abuse (e.g. Merdian, Wilson & Boer 2009).

It may be that community endorsement of such excuses is not uncommon, although this issue awaits future empirical assessment. McCabe (2000) surveyed 261 members of the American public who attended police-facilitated 'crime watch' meetings. Approximately one-third of the sample indicated that they thought it was legal to download CEM from a newsgroup. More recent Canadian research by Lam, Mitchell and Seto (2010) found that 6.7 per cent of participants (N=252) thought that viewing CEM was legal. Ten per cent of participants in a convenience sample of 431 Australian university students reported that there was no harm associated with just *viewing* CEM (Prichard et al. 2016). Similar logic has been used by at least one public commentator in his proposal to decriminalise CEM possession (Falkvinge 2012). Other evidence exists that CEM is sometimes normalised on mainstream and popular websites (Prichard et al. 2011) and, for example, intermingled with mainstream popular culture (TV shows, books, software, music and blockbuster movies for all ages and so forth) (Prichard et al. 2013).

Automated internet warnings as a potential technological crime-prevention strategy

Within a suite of other strategies (e.g. Quayle & Koukopoulos 2018), internet warning messages have been proposed as a useful tool to tackle CEM (e.g. Taylor & Quayle 2008). Warning messages may efficiently and economically reach a large number of potential offenders at the very time that they are contemplating accessing deviant material. According to ICT scholars, automated warnings would be practical to implement (e.g. Maimon et al. 2014). Many entities have the capacity to create internet warnings by injecting code into HTML pages and triggering a number of actions as defined in the page's java script. This could be done by domestic and international law enforcement collaborations (e.g. Virtual Global Taskforce), media and communication regulatory bodies, global search engines, internet service providers, advertising networks and P2P networks. Warning functions could also be written into software, such as internet-filtering software packages like Barracuda and Net Nanny. This would enable households and small and large institutions to activate anti-CEM warnings on their servers.

However, there is considerable uncertainty concerning the nature or tone of automated messages that will be most effective. Drawing on epidemiological studies of the effectiveness of health warnings, Williams (2005) suggests that warning messages explaining enduring harms to CEM victims would be more effective than messages emphasising the illegality of CEM (deterrence). She argues that, paradoxically, deterrence-focused messages could encourage CEM viewing by creating a challenge inviting a response from those who disagree with regulatory control or by increasing the excitement associated with using the material. Wortley and Smallbone also see value in harm-focused messages because of their capacity to prick the consciences of potential first-time offenders 'at the very moment [they are] attempting to engage in illegal activity' (2012: 120). But unlike Williams they hypothesise that deterrent messages could be equally effective, provided they concentrated on risk of detection. This is because they, like other scholars, consider that the perceived anonymity of the internet significantly increases the likelihood of disinhibited and impulsive behaviour online, including viewing CEM (e.g. Balfe et al. 2015; Merdian, Wilson & Boer 2009).

On this latter point it appears that perceptions of the risk of detection for online child groomers and CEM offenders falls along a continuum (Balfe et al. 2015). At one end, it appears the risks are well appreciated. However, at the other end of the continuum it seems that many online CEM offenders are either unaware of the risks or do not take actions to prevent detection despite an awareness of risk (Balfe et al. 2015). A study of 605 online CEM possessors arrested in 2006 found that only 3 per cent used sophisticated approaches to hide their images

(Wolak, Finkelhor & Mitchell 2011). Somewhat surprisingly only 19 per cent used a technical method of any kind to hide images.

Case study: roles for transdisciplinary research on automated warnings

Without an evidence base on the effectiveness (or otherwise) of automated warnings, little motivation exists for any agency to implement them. We suggest that transdisciplinary research, as discussed by Henry (2012), is needed to objectively determine whether automated warnings can be effective and how they ought to be designed – that is, what aspects of their appearance might influence internet users the most.

It seems that the design aspect of automated warnings is the simpler of these two broad research questions, although to date this important issue has not been considered by crime-prevention writers in relation to CEM. Research psychologist Zaikina-Montgomery (2011) drew on literature from 50 years of industrial research on successful elements of warning signs – for example on machinery and chemical products – which has shown that their effectiveness is influenced by the use of danger icons (e.g. a bolt to indicate electricity) and signal words (e.g. 'stop' and 'warning').

To assess optimum characteristics of online warnings for children about legal pornography, Zaikina-Montgomery asked adolescents and adults to rate how hypothetical internet users might perceive warnings which differed according to their use of colour, icons and signal words. Zaikina-Montgomery's results indicated that icons, signal words and messages have main effects as well as interaction effects (i.e. the effect of signal words is moderated by type of icon and message).

This laboratory method could be adapted to address the issue of CEM. For example, adult participants could be asked to rate how hypothetical internet users who are contemplating viewing CEM for the first time might perceive automated warnings, thereby examining the effects of colour, icons and signal words. Although such laboratory research would be a useful first step, the more difficult research question is how to *objectively* test the influence of automated warnings. The obvious disadvantage of laboratory studies is that they do not reflect a real-life online setting.

Criminologists have in fact mimicked real-life online settings in the past (Maimon at al. 2014; Testa et al. 2017; Wilson et al. 2015), but not in relation to CEM. Broadhurst and Jayawardena (2011) operated fake child-identities in online social networking platforms to study the behaviour of persons with a potential sexual interest in children. Demetriou and Silke (2003) were interested in measuring users' willingness to engage in low-level deviant decision-making. They developed a games website that contained fake links to adult pornography, among other things. Over 88 days the website recorded the proportion of visitors to the site (N=803) that attempted to access the links to pornography (N=483). In terms of experimental research on warning messages in a cybercrime setting, Testa et al. (2017) explored the effect of warning messages detailing sanction threats on dissuading system trespasses from further illegal access of a (honeypot) computer system.

Wortley and Smallbone (2012: 108) speculated what Demetriou and Silke (2003) might have found if their experiment had included a fake CEM link. However, they recognised that such an experiment would face considerable ethical barriers.

Our 2012 pilot study attempted to grapple with this issue by drawing on expertise in criminal law. We concluded that, among other ethical problems, any participant who clicked on a fake CEM link could be guilty of attempting to access the material depending on the laws of their home country. Consequently, we decided to create a free games website like Demetriou and Silke's (2003) containing a fake link to legal pornography.

This material purported to show pornographic images of women who were in fact adults *and* who appeared to be adults, but nonetheless pretended to be under age. In this way we developed a legal proxy for CEM that explicitly eroticised adult-minor relationships. Legal forms of this sort of pornography, generically called 'barely legal' and 'teen', are relatively popular and widely available (Jensen 2010).

Legal forms of 'teen' pornography may carry a higher deviant status than mainstream pornography. For instance Dines (2009: 124) refers to legal 'teen' pornography as 'pseudo-child pornography'. The pilot study was approved by a registered ethics committee.[7] Although the study involved deception and covert observation of participants without their consent, the committee determined that the project adhered to internationally recognised norms of research ethics because:

(a) The fake links purportedly led to legal pornography
(b) Our ICT procedure sufficiently protected participants' anonymity
(c) The research was for the public benefit – namely, attempting to find new strategies to reduce demand for CEM.

However, the distinguishing feature of this pilot study was not the fake link per se, but rather a double-blind randomised controlled experiment with naïve participants to examine the effect of automated warnings. The study was designed to test whether automated warnings increased desistance – in other words whether they had a significant effect in dissuading participants from attempting to enter the pornographic website.

Participants who clicked on the fake pornography link were randomly allocated to one of three conditions. The experimental groups received automated warnings. One message described the harmfulness of viewing legal 'teen' pornography (harm) and the other stated that the material might be illegal (deterrence). By incorporating two types of messages the study also aimed to directly address disagreement in the CEM literature about the usefulness of deterrent-focused automated messages (Williams 2005; Wortley & Smallbone 2012).

After cancelling the warnings, participants in both groups arrived at what appeared to be the entrance to the pornographic website where they had the option of 'exiting' and returning to the previous page or 'entering', which triggered an error message indicating temporary malfunction of the site. Control participants were directed to the entrance site without an automated warning. The control condition included the 'enter/exit' option which served as an indicator of the persistence or desistence of participants.

The demographics of the participants was unknown. However, the design of the website was oriented towards young male internet users, since this group appears most likely to repeatedly encounter opportunities to view CEM without searching for it (e.g. Prichard et al. 2013; Svedin, Åkerman & Priebe 2013).

This means that while our results are not as generalisable as a representative sample, they are superior to a convenience sample. Moreover, the efficacy of our data is reinforced by our double-blind randomised controlled design with naïve online participants. It should be mentioned here that ICT procedures within this study prevented double counting (internet users could only enter the experiment once) and also excluded false data being generated by web crawlers and User_Agents, like *Googlebot*.

The study was run in 2012 and was valuable as a proof of concept inasmuch as all features of the website and experiment functioned properly. However, the study revealed the difficulty of attracting and maintaining the interest of internet users drawn to a site that gives no outward indication of it containing sexually oriented material. The experimental website required sufficient 'online presence' to generate enough user interaction to test the fake link. The number of visits to the website over five months was too small and users did not explore the site and no visitors clicked on the experimental fake link.

In the early 2000s Demetriou and Silke (2003) were able to secure their sample size over 88 days without any advertising and by designing their website in-house. It is now very difficult to attract internet traffic and to maintain users' interest so that they explore website functions; web traffic can be lost very quickly without an attractive and fashionable layout (e.g. Hui, Wong & Fu 2015).

Our reaction to this additional layer of complexity has been to broaden our scope from being *interdisciplinary* (ICT, crime science, law) to *transdisciplinary*. We recognise that the success of our project depends on non-academic skills – namely contemporary, artistic web design and website advertising – and that these skills are accessible in the commercial sector. Our collaboration with the commercial sector is integral to our ongoing research.

We are encouraged by industry support for the research aims and willingness to design a website that attracts and retains young males. Our industry partner is contractually bound to monthly participant recruitment targets (measured by unique clicks on the experimental fake link). In the next iteration additional collaborations will be established with a wider range of experts to ensure we address wider design and content issues to maximise website interest and exploration.

Conclusion

The case for prevention strategies to respond to the CEM market is clear. Reliance on law enforcement alone is not working adequately and may be even less effective in the future (see for example, Bailey 2018). Arrests and convictions capture a small portion of users of CEM globally and with the global CEM market expected to expand further in the future, alternative responses to curb or even prevent the production of CEM are needed. Many law-abiding people have repeated opportunities to view CEM for the first time. The numbers of such people that choose to do so appears significant enough to help fuel the growth of the CEM market. Part of the reason that many previously law-abiding people choose to view CEM for the first time is due to situational factors and cues in the online environment which suggest the permissibility of deviant behavior, and promote perceptions of user anonymity. Our research goal is to assess if and how automated warning messages can reduce the numbers of these new entrants to the CEM market. If warning messages even have a relatively small effect they may still be worth implementing because they are cost-effective and may alleviate some pressure on LEA and criminal justice systems.

We are hardly the first group of researchers to find benefit in collaborating across disciplines. However, our experience to date underscores that complex 21st-century crimes, like CEM, require innovative responses. And 'transdisciplinary' collaboration increases the potential for innovation because it brings together different forms of knowledge – including non-academic expertise – and ways of interpreting information that can produce results that would not be possible with traditional approaches.

Acknowledgements

This project was partly funded by the Australian Government through the Australian Research Council (Project ID DP160100601).

Notes

1 As described by Laycock (2014: 394) crime science is 'the systematic application of scientific principles to the control of crime (including disorder, organised crime and terrorism)'.
2 See Frodeman et al. (2017) for a discussion of multidisciplinary research (involving the juxtaposition of disciplines), interdisciplinary research (with the integration of perspectives), and transdisciplinary research (which involves creating a new and overarching synthesis).
3 Steel's (2015) analysis of the prevalence of CEM-related queries on search engines (July 2013-July 2014) was not able to differentiate between the effect of warning messages and blocking strategies.
4 National Center for Missing and Exploited Children, *Key Facts*, www.missingkids.com/KeyFacts (accessed 18/02/2015).
5 For example, the Queensland Police Service is reported to prioritise CEM cases where a child is considered to be at risk (Queensland Sentencing Advisory Council 2017: 24).
6 European Commission, Migration and Home Affairs, http://ec.europa.eu/dgs/home-affairs/what-we-do/policies/organized-crime-and-human-trafficking/global-alliance-against-child-abuse/index_en.htm (accessed 18/02/2015).
7 Approval #H0012409 2012, University of Tasmania Social Sciences Human Research Ethics Committee.

References

Acar, K. V. 2017, 'Organizational aspect of the global fight against online child sexual abuse'. *Global Policy, 8*(2) 259–262.

Bailey, S. 2018, 'National Police Chiefs' Council – written evidence'. Home Affairs Committee Policing for the Future Inquiry, PFF0013, 8 May 2018.

Balfe, M., Gallagher, B., Masson, H., Balfe, S., Brugha, R. & Hackett, S. 2015, 'Internet child sex offenders' concerns about online security and their use of identity protection technologies: a review', *Child Abuse Review, 24*, 427–439.

Broadhurst, R. & Jayawardena, K. 2011, 'Online social networking and pedophilia: an experimental research 'sting', *Cyber Criminology*. Hoboken, NJ: CRC Press, 79–102.

Chan, J. & Bennett Moses, L. 2016, 'Is Big Data challenging criminology?', *Theoretical Criminology, 20*(1), 21–39.

Clarke, R. 2008, 'Situational crime prevention', in R. Wortley & L. Mazerolle (Eds), *Environmental Criminology and Crime Analysis*. Cullompton, UK: Willan Publishing, 178–195.

Cornish, D. & Clarke, R. 2003, 'Opportunities, precipitators and criminal decisions: a reply to Wortley's critique of situational crime prevention', *Crime Prevention Studies, 16*, 41–96.

Clough, J. 2012, 'Lawful acts, unlawful images: the problematic definition of 'child'pornography', *Unlawful Images: The Problematic Definition of 'Child' Pornography, 38*(3), 213–245.

D'Amour, D., Ferrada-Videla, L., Rodriguez, & Beaulieu, M. 2005, 'The conceptual basis for interprofessional collaboration: core concepts and theoretical frameworks', *Journal of Interprofessional Care, 19*, 116–131.

Demetriou, C. & Silke, A. 2003, 'A criminological internet 'sting' – experimental evidence of illegal and deviant visits to a website trap', *British Journal of Criminology, 43*(1), 213–222.

Dines, G. 2009, 'Childified women: how the mainstream porn industry sells child pornography to men', in S. Olfman (Ed.), *The Sexualization of Childhood*. Westport, CT: Praeger, 121–142.

Dodig-Crnkovic, G., Kade, D., Wallmyr, M., Holstein, T. & Almér, A. 2017, 'Transdisciplinarity seen through information, communication, computation, (inter)-action and cognition', in M. Burgin & W. Hofkirchner (Eds), *Information Studies and the Quest for Transdisciplinarity*, World Scientific Series in Information Studies: Volume 9. Singapore: World Scientific Publishing Company.

Dombert, B., Schmidt, A. F., Banse, R., Briken, P., Hoyer, J., Neutze, J. & Osterheider, M. 2016. 'How common is men's self-reported sexual interest in prepubescent children?' *The Journal of Sex Research, 53*(2), 214–223.

Ekblom, P. & Gill, M. 2016, 'Rewriting the script: cross-disciplinary exploration and conceptual consolidation of the procedural analysis of crime', *European Journal on Criminal Policy and Research, 22*(2), 319–339.

Falkvinge, R. 2012, 'Three reasons possession of child porn must be re-legalised in the coming decade', http://beforeitsnews.com/eu/2012/09/three-reasons-child-porn-must-be-re-legalized-in-the-coming-decade-2449306.html (accessed 18/02/15).

Farrington, D. & Petrosino, A. 2001, 'The Campbell Collaboration Crime and Justice Group', *The Annals of the American Academy of Political and Social Science*, *578*(1), 35–49.

Frodeman, R., Thompson Klein, J. & Dos Santos Pacheco, R. 2017, *The Oxford Handbook of Interdisciplinarity*, Second Edition. Oxford: Oxford University Press.

Gillespie, A. A. 2011, *Child Pornography: Law and Policy*. London: Routledge.

Gradon, K. 2013, 'Crime science and the internet battlefield: securing the analog world from digital crime', *IEEE Security & Privacy*, September–October, 93–95.

Henry, S. 2005, 'Disciplinary hegemony meets interdisciplinary ascendancy: can interdisciplinary/integrative studies survive, and if so, how?', *Issues in Integrative Studies*, *23*, 1–37.

Henry, S. 2012, 'Expanding our thinking on theorizing criminology and criminal justice? The place of evolutionary perspectives in integrative criminological theory', *Journal of Theoretical and Philosophical Criminology*, *4*(1), 62–89.

Holtfreter, K. & Meyers, T. 2015, 'Challenges for cybercrime theory, research, and policy, in G. Lajeunesse (Ed.), *The Norwich Review of International and Transnational Crime*. Norwich, UK: Norwich University.

Hui, A., Wong, P. & Fu, K. 2015, 'Evaluation of an online campaign for promoting help-seeking attitudes for depression using a facebook advertisement: an online randomized controlled experiment', *JMIR Mental Health*, *2*(1), e5.

Hunsinger, J. 2005, 'Toward a Transdisciplinary Internet Research', *The Information Society*, *21*(4), 277–279.

Hurley, R. C. et al. 2012, Measurement and analysis of child pornography trafficking on gnutella and emule, University of Massachusetts. https://web.cs.umass.edu/publication/docs/2012/UM-CS-2012-016.pdf (accessed 18/02/2015).

Jang, Y. J. 2013, 'Harmonization among national cyber security and cybercrime response organizations: new challenges of cybercrime' (arXiv preprint). arXiv:1308.2362.

Jensen, R. 2010, 'A content analysis of youth sexualized language and imagery in adult film packaging, 1995–2007', *Journal of Children and Media*, *4*(4), 371–386.

Jones, H., Maimon, D. & Ren, W. 2017, 'Sanction threat and friendly persuasion effects on system trespassers' behaviour during a system trespassing event', in T. Holt (Ed.), *Cybercrime Through an Interdisciplinary Lens*. London: Routledge, 164–180.

Krone, T. 2005, 'International police operations against online child pornography', *Trends and Issues in Crime and Criminal Justice*, *296*, 1–6.

Lam, A., Mitchell, J., & Seto, M. C. (2010). Lay perceptions of child pornography offenders. *Canadian Journal of Criminology and Criminal Justice*, *52*(2), 173–201.

Laycock, G. 2014, 'Crime science and policing: lessons of translation', *Policing: A Journal of Policy and Practice*, *8*(4), 393–401.

Maimon, D., Alper, M., Sobesto, B. & Cukier, M. 2014, 'Restrictive deterrent effects of a warning banner in an attacked computer system', *Criminology*, *52*(1), 33–59.

Malone, E. & Malone, M. 2013, 'The "wicked problem" of cybersecurity policy: analysis of United States and Canadian policy response', *Canadian Foreign Policy Journal*, *19*(2) 158–177.

McCabe, K. A. (2000). Child pornography and the Internet. *Social Science Computer Review*, *18*(1), 73–76.

McManus, M. A. & Almond, L. 2014, 'Trends of indecent images of children and child sexual offences between 2005/2006 and 2012/2013 within the United Kingdom', *Journal of Sexual Aggression*, *20*(2), 142–155.

Merdian, H., Wilson, N. & Boer, D. 2009, 'Characteristics of Internet sexual offenders: a review', *Sexual Abuse in Australia and New Zealand*, *2*(1), 34–47.

Olbrycht-Palmer, M. 2013, 'The Pirate party and Coalition agree: internet censorship is not the answer', *The Guardian*, 06/09/2013. www.theguardian.com/commentisfree/2013/sep/06/pirate-party-censorship-australia (accessed 22/01/2014).

Prichard, J. & Spiranovic, C. 2014, Child Exploitation Material in the Context of Institutional Child Sexual Abuse. Royal Commission into Institutional Responses to Child Sexual Abuse, Sydney.

Prichard, J., Spiranovic, C., Gelb, K., Watters, P. & Krone, T. 2016, 'Tertiary education students' attitudes to the harmfulness of viewing and distributing child pornography', *Psychiatry, Psychology and Law*, *23*(2), 224–239.

Prichard, J., Spiranovic, C., Watters, P. & Lueg, C. 2013, 'Young people, child pornography, and subcultural norms on the internet', *Journal of the American Society for Information Science and Technology*, *64*(5), 992–1000.

Prichard, J., Watters, P. & Spiranovic, C. 2011, 'Internet subcultures and pathways to the use of child pornography', *Computer Law & Security Review*, *27*(6), 585–600.

Quayle, E. & Koukopoulos, N. 2018, 'Deterrence of online child sexual abuse and exploitation', *Policing: A Journal of Policy and Practice*, pay028, 1–18.

Queensland Sentencing Advisory Council, 2017, Classification of child exploitation material for sentencing purposes. Consultation paper, QSAC, Brisbane.

Rouse, J. 2014, Personal communication, 9/5/2014.

Steel, C. M. 2015. 'Web-based child pornography: the global impact of deterrence efforts and its consumption on mobile platforms'. *Child Abuse & Neglect*, *44*, 150–158.

Taylor, M. & Quayle, E. 2008, 'Criminogenic qualities of the internet in the collection and distribution of abuse images of children', *The Irish Journal of Psychology*, *29*(1–2), 119–130.

Testa, A., Maimon, D., Sobesto, B. & Cukier, M. 2017, 'Illegal roaming and file manipulation on target computers: assessing the effect of sanction threats on system trespassers' online behaviors', *Criminology & Public Policy*, *16*(3), 689–726.

Vagoun, T. & Strawn, G. 2015, 'Implementing the Federal cybersecurity R&D strategy', *Computer*, April, 45–55.

Williams, K. 2005, 'Facilitating safer choices: use of warnings to dissuade viewing of pornography on the internet', *Child Abuse Review*, *14*(6), 415–429.

Wilson, T., Maimon, D., Sobesto, B. & Cukier, M. (2015). 'The effect of a surveillance banner in an attacked computer system: additional evidence for the relevance of restrictive deterrence in cyberspace'. *Journal of Research in Crime and Delinquency*, *52*(6), 829–855.

Wolak, J., Finkelhor, D. & Mitchell, K. 2011, 'Child pornography possessors: trends in offender and case characteristics', *Sexual Abuse: A Journal of Research and Treatment*, *23*(1), 22–42.

Wolak, J., Finkelhor, D. & Mitchell, K. 2012, Trends in arrests for child pornography possession: the third national juvenile online victimization study (NJOV-3). Durham, NH: University of New Hampshire.

Wolak, J., Liberatore, M. & Levine, B. 2013, 'Measuring a year of child pornography trafficking by us computers on a peer-to-peer network', *Child Abuse & Neglect*, *38*(2), 347–356.

Wortley, R. 2012, 'Situational prevention of child abuse in the new technologies', in E. Quayle & K. Ribisl (Eds), *Understanding and Preventing Online Sexual Exploitation of Children*. London: Routledge, 188–204.

Wortley, R. & Smallbone, S. 2012, *Internet Child Pornography: Causes, Investigation, and Prevention*. Oxford: Praeger.

Zaikina-Montgomery, H. 2011, 'The dilemma of minors' access to adult content on the internet: A proposed warnings solution', University of Nevada. http://digitalscholarship.unlv.edu/thesesdissertations/944 (accessed 07/07/2018).

22

Those who do big bad things still do little bad things

Re-stating the case for self-selection policing

Jason Roach

Introduction

Traditionally, police have identified serious offenders either from information supplied by the public, forensic techniques, or by the targeting of known offenders. This last is commonly referred to as 'the usual suspects' method of criminal investigation, whereby a case is constructed against 'known offenders' (McConville, Sanders, and Leng, 1991), principally those who have "built up a set of previous convictions and have been well known to the local police" (Maguire, 2008, p. 435). It is common, for example in the case of sex offences, for those on the 'sex offenders register' to feature highly in the initial attempt to generate leads.

The usual suspect approach neglects recent recruits to active criminality and targets those who have desisted from crime (Townsley and Pease, 2003). The usual suspects approach requires accurate knowledge of active offenders and their offending patterns. Absent that, it may waste police time, or worse, lead to justified complaints of harassment. Put simply, although the usual suspects approach can (and does) lead to known suspects being appropriately identified for specific crimes some of the time, it needs to be used cautiously. There is a complementary (yet seldom used) more morally defensible way with which to identify serious offenders: *self-selection policing* (SSP) (Roach and Pease, 2016; Roach 2007a, 2007b). Setting out what it is, why it has failed to be universally adopted by police in England and Wales, and why it should be, constitutes the main purpose of this chapter.

Self-selection policing seeks to identify those minor, often routine, offences which are indicative of more serious current criminality (Roach and Pease, 2016; Roach, 2007a, 2007b). It is based upon the simple premise that 'those who do big bad things also do little bad things' (Roach, 2007a) and that increased police scrutiny of certain minor offences will help identify active offenders responsible for more serious crime (but not specific serious crimes which they are investigating). By *certain minor offences*, I mean those which are committed most frequently by serious offenders. This does not include all minor offending, of course, as many minor offences are also committed by those who are not serious criminals.

Roach and Pease (2016) argue that satisfactory answers to the following four questions are required to warrant pursuing self-selection as an approach in policing.

1 *Why and how should it work?* (What theoretical and empirical support is there in the criminological, crime science, and psychology literature?)
2 *Which minor offences work best*? (What supporting case study research identifies SSP *'trigger offences'*?)
3 What are the practical, logistical, ethical and institutional barriers to implementing the SSP approach? (Why has SSP not become part of routine policing in the UK?)
4 *What should the future be for SSP?* (For both empirical research and police policy and practice).

Structured around these four questions, this chapter re-visits the case for self-selection policing. It argues that SSP deserves more attention from police, crime scientists and criminologists and needs to be incorporated widely in to police thinking and routine practice. For both of these goals to be realised however, certain barriers and hurdles in police thinking, policing policy and practice need to be acknowledge. Some suggestions for overcoming them are made at the end of the chapter.

Why and how should self-selection policing work?

To suitably address the wider 'why and how SSP should work' questions, three pivotal premises must first be supported (Roach and Pease, 2016). That:

1 Active, serious offenders are 'criminally versatile'
2 Active, serious offenders do not stop at committing minor offences
3 Identifiable links exist between active serious offenders and specific minor offences.

We will deal briefly with each in turn, starting with the most important: whether those who do big bad things are likely to also do little bad things (Roach, 2007a).

The case for the crime-versatile serious offender

On the subject of whether offenders are offence 'specialist' or 'versatile', David Farrington and colleagues summed up in 1988 the general findings of all the criminal-careers research to date beautifully: 'There is a small but significant degree of specialisation, superimposed on a great deal of versatility' (Farrington, Snyder, and Finnegan, 1988, p. 483). The evidence since 1988 does not appear to indicate a change in the offence versatility of most criminals (e.g. Cunliffe and Shepherd, 2007; Roach and Pease, 2013). Indeed, even those often assumed to be the most specialised of offenders appear not to be so. Take, for example, sexual offenders whose perceived specialisation is reflected in the raft of dedicated legislation in the UK which has been introduced to deal with them (e.g. the Sex Offenders Act 1997, the Children (Protection from Offenders) Regulation 1997, and provision in the more generically prescribed Crime and Disorder Act of 1998). It appears that many within this group of offenders are not specialists. In their study of the criminal careers of over 7,000 UK sex offenders, Soothill et al. (2000) found evidence for differences in offence specialisation and versatility between different groups of sex offenders. Soothill et al. (2000) suggest that with regard to criminal careers, criminologists must recognise that offending specialisation and generalisation (versatility) exist at two levels; sex offenders may be specialists, generalists, or both, suggesting that thinking of offence specialisation or versatility is a false dichotomy.

Blumstein, Cohen, Roth, and Visher's classic work *Criminal Careers and Career Criminals* (1986a, 1986b) provided the first major empirical demonstration of how limited was the degree of specialisation in most criminal careers, with other work of the same era confirming the central finding of offence versatility (e.g. Farrington, 1986; Blumstein, Cohen, Das, and Moitra, 1988; Gottfredson and Hirschi, 1990). The same conclusion holds whether self-report, arrest or conviction data are examined (e.g. Soothill, Fitzpatrick, and Francis, 2009; Harris, Smallbone, Dennison, and Knight, 2009) and is consistent with more recent research into the varied criminal histories of 'stranger sexual killers' (Greenall and Wright, 2015).

Persistent offenders, in particular, have been found to be versatile in their offending (Blumstein et al., 1988; Cohen and Felson, 1979, 1986; Farrington, 1988; Gottfredson and Hirschi, 1990; Kempf, 1987; LeBlanc and Frechette, 1989; Mazerolle et al., 2000; Tarling, 1993). Terri Moffitt and colleagues have identified two types of offenders: the 'adolescence limited' group, typically constituting young males who will eventually grow up and out of low-level rule breaking; and the smaller (but arguably more significant) 'life-course persistent' group, whose members continue to offend throughout their lives, with their criminal careers only curtailed by periods of incarceration or their offending cut short by death. Moffitt identifies this group to be particularly criminally versatile (Moffitt, 1997, 1999, 2003; Piquero and Moffitt, 2004). Additonally, Alex Piquero (2000) found that frequent violent offenders were indistinguishable from non-violent offenders in respect of their future criminal careers, where, contrastingly, Deane, Armstrong and Felson (2005) found them more likely to commit further violent offences than their non-violent counterparts. Both studies nonetheless showed substantial offence versatility.

To restate the argument so far for offence versatility: although problems associated with calculating the degree of offence specialisation within a criminal career are acknowledged (see e.g. Fisher and Ross, 2006, p. 154), the consistent conclusion which must be drawn from the criminal-careers literature is that offenders are in the main offence versatile, particularly those deemed 'life-course persistent' (Moffitt, 1997, 1999, 2003; Piquero and Moffitt, 2004) with only modest levels of offence specialisation. As this group presumably commits less serious as well as serious crimes according to the criminal-careers literature, the first premise of self-selection policing appears to be supported. But what about hard case evidence that serious offenders commit minor offences? I start with the arguably anecdotal and unempirical.

The most sensational demonstrations of the versatility of serious offenders are instances where notorious repeat killers and rapists have been uncovered, not so much as a direct result of long and protracted high-profile police investigations, but because they have committed offences of a much more routine and less serious nature. A famous English example concerns the notorious eighteenth-century highwayman (armed robber) Richard 'Dick' Turpin, wanted for a string of crimes including murder. Turpin was apprehended and imprisoned for the lesser offence of stealing a horse, but the authorities were not aware of the significance of this arrest for several weeks. When they finally realised he was Turpin, he was hanged as a murderer.

Here are a few more contemporary examples, from Schechter and Everitt's *The A to Z Encyclopedia of Serial Killers* (2006).

- UK serial killer Peter Sutcliffe (aka the Yorkshire Ripper), murderer of at least 13 women, was identified because he was found to have false number plates on his car. Presumably, he committed this minor offence to maintain anonymity from the manhunt launched to identify him.
- US convicted killer Charles Manson was arrested after police were called to his house on suspicion of him having committed offences of criminal damage.

- The serial killer 'Son of Sam' David Berkowitz was arrested after a parking ticket put him at the scene of one of his horrendous crimes.
- When US multiple killer Daniel Rifkin was stopped by police for a minor traffic violation, the body of his thirteenth victim was found in the boot of his car.

There are numerous additional examples of serious criminals being identified by dint of the minor offences they have committed. In 2013, for example, five men from the West Midlands of the UK were convicted of preparing an act of terrorism.[1] They had planned to set off a bomb at a rally organised by the English Defence League, in Dewsbury, West Yorkshire. The men had travelled in two cars with the intent of killing, but had arrived late, after the rally had finished. On their way back home, one of the cars was stopped for not having valid insurance (identified by a police Automatic Number Plate Recognition System on the M11). As a consequence, the car was impounded and when later searched, police found a bomb and several guns in the boot.

Theoretical grounds for expecting self-selection policing to work comes readily from crime science, particularly from environmental criminology.

- **Rational choice perspective** predicts that individuals will offend if they consider expected benefits to exceed the costs and risks. Active serious offenders are highly unlikely to cavil at committing minor offences as minor crime generally carries little risk of serious punishment. Put another way, those who take large risks to commit serious crimes are not likely to be deterred by small-risk minor crimes.
- **Routine activity approach** (aka RAT) lends strong support to the self-selection approach by identifying environments and situations as important in crime commission, with versatile offenders demonstrating a heterogeneity in their offences, acting (or not) on opportunities as they present themselves rather than as dedicated crime specialists. Cohen and Felson (1979), although initially concerned with crimes of a predatory nature, go on to make little distinction between a routine activities explanation of serious and minor offending, their theory being one for all crime.

To summarise the discussion of why and how self-selection policing works, theoretical support and empirical evidence have been presented to support the first two of our pivotal premises that;

1. Active, serious offenders are crime-versatile (evidenced by the majority of criminal-careers research and supported theoretically by Moffitt's taxonomy, routine activity theory, and rational choice theory).
2. Active, serious offenders will not stop at committing minor offences (evidenced in the criminal-careers literature and in the identification of numerous notorious violent offenders).

Which minor offences work best? In search of SSP 'trigger' offences

While sensational accounts of serial murders identified by the commission of a minor offence are all well and good, admittedly they are not exactly empirical evidence to support the self-selection policing approach. In this section the handful of SSP studies to date (although admittedly some are not badged as such) are briefly outlined. They are presented here as indications of what could be done with SSP research in the future.[2] We begin with those that can be badged as self-selection now, but were not so at the time, some occurring before the term was coined by Chenery, Henshaw and Pease in 1999 (discussed later).

Self-selection policing: the beginning of empirical research support

Here are a few early examples of self-selection policing extracted from the literature.

- Kelling and Coles (1995) discovered that a substantial minority of 'Squeegee merchants'[3] in New York also had outstanding warrants for felony offences. Thus, when an officer served a DAT[4] for squeegeeing[5] and the offender did not appear, then that officer could make an immediate arrest, and jail time would follow. With punishment swift and certain, squeegeeing died out in a matter of weeks (Kelling and Coles, 1995, p. 143).
- The New York Transit Police found that by preventing individuals from jumping ticket turnstiles to avoid paying, a general drop in crime in the subway and on trains occurred. The fall in crime was attributed to fare evaders also being those who committed many of the other offences (Maple, 1999). Turnstile jumpers therefore were self-selecting themselves as likely candidates for more serious types of criminality.
- In her study of burglary, Jacqui Schneider found an unanticipated but identifiable link between shoplifting and burglary, and she concluded that shop theft played an instrumental role in the offending patterns of prolific burglars (Schneider, 2005). Interviews conducted with 50 prolific burglars revealed that 44 (88 per cent) admitted to committing shop theft. Of these, 26 did so daily and a further eight did so 'several times a week'. Only six burglars claimed they had never stolen from shops, leading Schneider to conclude, "that shop thieves be policed as though they were burglars on their day off rather than shop thieves pure and simple" (2005, p. 3).

These three research studies have several important implications for the self-selection policing approach, as they provide empirical support, first to the perception of the versatile offender; second to the notion that serious offenders will not cavil at minor offences; and third that a considered minor offence such as shoplifting is indicative of active serious criminality, such as burglary. Indeed, Schneider's study suggests that those who commit burglary self-select for increased police scrutiny by virtue of committing much more frequent thefts from shops. Indeed, increased and justifiable police scrutiny of the lives of known, seemingly low-level offenders should pay dividends in identifying many as 'part-time burglars'. Shop theft here should be seen as a trigger offence for identifying burglars, with the bonus of often being a far easier crime to detect (Schneider, 2005).

The bulk of SSP trigger offences thus far identified by empirical research have related to 'driving' (sometimes called 'motoring') offences. As such, they warrant the next section to themselves.

Driving offences and serious criminals

One early piece of UK-based research, and a classic study that demonstrates the promise of the self-selection policing approach for uncovering serious criminality, stems from a pioneering local study of illegal parking in disabled bays (Chenery, Henshaw and Pease, 1999). The findings indicated that one in five individuals who had committed this minor offence had outstanding warrants for the arrest of the registered keeper of the vehicle, or possessed other characteristics which would have 'excited immediate police attention', when compared with 2 per cent for legally parked adjacent cars (Chenery, Henshaw and Pease, 1999). Parking in disabled bays (when adjacent bays were available) was identified in this study as an indicator of active serious criminality and the link between this type of minor offence and concurrent serious criminality established.

The link driving offences and criminality is by no means a recent discovery. Willett's 1964 book *Criminal on the Road* was one of the first to focus on those who commit traffic offences and the types of other offences they might be committing. However, it was not until Gerry Rose's study in 2000 (research dedicated to the criminal histories of a large number of serious road-traffic offenders) was conducted. Rose explored the hypothesis that those committing such offences were no more criminal than the average motorist, based on the findings of a small study conducted by Steer and Carr-Hill (1967). This entailed investigation of the nature of serious traffic offending and the extent to which it is "interwoven with mainstream criminal offending" (Rose, 2000, p. 67).

Rose divided a large sample of UK serious traffic offenders into three groups; drink-drivers, disqualified drivers, and dangerous drivers, based on current convictions and incidents. As a group, serious traffic offenders were found to be predominantly white males. The age profiles of *dangerous drivers* and *disqualified drivers* were found to be similar to those of more mainstream offenders, with some 60–75 per cent aged between 18 and 32 years (although those in the drink-driver category were older). Those from lower social groups were more likely to have committed vehicle licence and car insurance offences. Risk factors such as family, schooling and peer groups were found to correlate significantly with serious traffic offences, mirroring mainstream offending (Rose 2000).

Rose also found areas of consistency with previous studies. Steer and Carr-Hill (1967), for example, had found a distinction between *dishonest offenders* and *driving offenders*, with the 'dishonest' group' including disqualified drivers and those driving without a licence or insurance. However, Rose found that Steer and Carr-Hill's 'driving offenders' were not simply 'unlucky' members of the public, but were more likely to have also been serious mainstream offenders. For example, drink-drivers were estimated to be twice as likely to have criminal records as members of the wider population, with dangerous and reckless drivers more likely to be involved in concurrent criminality, especially car theft.

Rose's findings are also consistent with Suggs's (1998) study of motor offenders (including theft of vehicles and driving while disqualified) who attended several vehicle maintenance projects run by the then National Probation Service. Suggs's results showed that the motoring offenders were far from being 'crime specialists', but had convictions for serious mainstream offences such as theft (75 per cent), burglary (60 per cent) and violence against the person (30 per cent). Reconvictions (over a two-year period) commonly included non-motoring offences such as theft (39 per cent), burglary (25 per cent) and violence against the person (15 per cent). Tangentially, Smerdon and South (1997) found in a small study of people that had driven without motor insurance, that 'Kevin', a principal focus of the case study research, had been arrested for an incident of robbery soon after they had interviewed him.

Wellsmith and Guille (2005) examined the suitability of parking fixed-penalty notices (FPN) as indicative of concurrent criminality. Recorded single offences were found to be unreliable indicators of serious offending. However, repeat FPN offences were modestly associated with concurrent criminality relative to a random group selected from an electoral role.

Townsley and Pease (2003) attempted to draw on self-selection in 'Operation Safeground'. Alongside Merseyside Police, the DVLA and a local taxi association, a vehicle inspection programme was introduced where over the course of a four-hour period on a selected day, any driver seen not wearing a seatbelt would be pulled over. Where the 'non-use of seatbelt' self-selection trigger was used for private vehicles (n=62), 3 per cent of drivers were immediately arrested, 14.5 per cent were found to have committed a Vehicle Excise License offence (VEL) and 11 per cent were issued a dangerous 'un-roadworthy vehicle' prohibition notice. A staggering 50 per cent of taxis (and private-hire cars) stopped during the operation were issued with vehicle defect and stop notices, where the licensed-for-private-hire plate was removed until such time as the vehicle was deemed 'roadworthy'.

By way of comparison, an operation was conducted that did not deploy the non-use of seatbelt self-selection trigger, where officers stopped all vehicles of a specific age, at a specific time of day (selected their likelihood of theft by police estimation). Those found to have other offences amounted to approximately 5 per cent, demonstrating that the non-use-of-seat-belt trigger had a much greater hit rate than random stop checks by at least a factor of ten (Townsley and Pease, 2003).

To complete the review of the driving related self-selection research that has been published to date, two more studies warrant mentioning. First, an incidental finding from Roach's (2007a) prison visitor study was that 25 per cent of drivers issued with Home Office Road Traffic 1 (HO/RT1) failed to produce (i.e. did not comply). The HO/RT1 required them to produce their documents (e.g. driver's licence and insurance certificate) on request or at a police station for checking within 28 days (the time period has recently been reduced to seven days). This raises the question why so many failed to produce the necessary documents. Was it because they had something to hide? Did it display a general contempt for criminal justice? In short, was it that the 'little bad thing' of failing to produce could be a flag for the 'big bad things' which they were also engaging in. To explore these hypotheses further, a dedicated analysis of over 120 HO/RT1 issued on a specific date was conducted (Roach, 2007b). The findings showed that those who did not or only partially complied with the HO/RT1 (referred to as 'no shows') were found to be significantly more likely than those that complied (referred to as 'shows') to have a criminal record. 'No shows' were also more likely to have offence histories which comprised two or more offences than were the 'shows' (indeed many had three or more crimes recorded). 'No shows' were also found to have committed more serious (often violent) offences than the HO/RT1 'show' group. Lastly, and most significantly, the results of regression analysis indicated that the 'no shows' offended more recently than 'shows', with many committing a serious offence(s) within a six-month period of being issued with the HO/RT1.

Second, in a study of 50 people convicted of driving while disqualified, Roach (2017) found that they had a total of 704 recorded convictions between them, with an average of 14 recorded offences per disqualified driver (range= 0–84 offences, SD = 17.63 offences). Of the 50 disqualified drivers, 43 (86 per cent) had previous criminal convictions for offences other than the index offence of driving while disqualified that had flagged them for this study. The range of offence types found (i.e. category versatility) for each of the 43 criminal careers when discounting the original index offence of driving while disqualified, ranged from one to ten different offence categories from 12 possible (mean = 4.9 and SD=2.8).[6] Moreover, 60 per cent had convictions for between four and ten other types of offence categories, indicating that those with a conviction for disqualified driving were likely to be very crime-versatile, with their offending more generalist and more reminiscent of mainstream offenders than simply a discrete category of driving offenders, albeit a serious driving offence (Roach, 2017). Driving whilst disqualified appears therefore to be a promising SSP tool for uncovering versatile criminality.

Let me rehearse the argument for employing the self-selection policing approach before moving to speculating why it has not been more widely adopted in practice. Research has shown that using offender self-selection can identify active serious offenders at a greater hit rate than picking individuals randomly (e.g. Roach, 2007b; Wellsmith and Guille, 2005; Townsley and Pease, 2003; Maple, 1999; Chenery et al., 1999). The fundamental principle established in this chapter is that career criminals commit a wide spectrum of offences that range in both seriousness and frequency. By focusing police attention on those who frequently commit common minor offences, attention is also placed on those who engage in active serious criminality.

Some specific minor offences, if they could be discerned reliably from the pool of minor offences, could be used to uncover such offenders. The value of self-selection is that by virtue of the commission of a minor offence, the offender makes him or herself justifiably eligible for official police attention. Wellsmith and Guille (2005) suggest that for SSP 'trigger offences' to be chosen they must fulfil three criteria:

- Their acceptability in themselves for police attention
- Their empirical association with further and future criminality
- Their unobtrusiveness in use, since the majority of those targeted will not be active serious criminals.

In the next section I suggest why the initial enthusiasm for SSP shown more than a decade ago has neither resulted in the adoption of SSP tactics by police nor translated into an active research programme to identify new and robust 'trigger offences'. In a spirit of optimism, the chapter concludes with some comments on how barriers to SPP thinking and implementation can be overcome and what a dedicated research programme might look like.

So what's the problem? Barriers to adopting self-selection policing

The primary barriers to the implementation of SSP over the past decade can be roughly categorised into three distinct sets of issues: *perceptions of offending patterns, police policy and practice,* and the *lack of a dedicated research programme.* I will take each in turn.

Perceptions of offending patterns

Research evidence supporting SSP and people's perceptions of criminal versatility are rarely the same. There are many reasons to hypothesise that people will tend to overstate the homogeneity of criminal careers (i.e. the degree of offence specialisation) rather than overstate heterogeneity (offence versatility). The very language we use to categorise offenders often implies homogeneity; for example, when we speak of burglars, robbers, fraudsters and paedophiles, rather than, of 'offenders whose most recent crime was burglary'. The very existence of a vocabulary of this kind suggests that offenders are framed in these more circumscribed ways (Roach and Pease, 2013). The popularity of perceiving serious offenders to be 'crime specialists' is reflected in popular crime programmes and literature, exemplified by colourful characters like the Victorian gentleman 'safe-breaker' Raffles (Hornung, 1899).

Such an overestimation of offence specialisation across a criminal career may of course be a result of the 'representativeness heuristic identified' (Kahneman, Slovic and Tversky, 1982) whereby often information of little or partial relevance is used as a basis for making decisions (e.g. Bar-Hillel, 1982; Kahneman, 2011). In this context an individual with a conviction for a sexual offence is likely to be considered to pose a danger to children by many who live close by.

One important manifestation of the representativeness heuristic is 'confirmation bias', whereby initial partially or non-relevant information (in this case the prior officially processed offence) restricts an investigator's search space inappropriately. For example, those with convictions for burglary may not be considered as suspects for a robbery. Confirmation bias is implicated in many cases of criminal investigative failure (Rossmo, 2009).

Evidence suggests that police, too, also tend to overestimate offence homogeneity. In a study on police estimates of next offences in criminal careers, Roach and Pease (2013) found overwhelmingly that police participants considered an individual's previous offence types as the best predictor of their future types of offending, irrespective of the type of offence history presented. Put simply, whatever the first offence type, participants predicted that most likely next offence would be of the same type (e.g. for an offender with a previous offence of robbery, the most likely next offence prediction was robbery). Indeed, for the vast majority of offenders and offence types, the average for participant predictions of offence homogeneity was in excess of 50 per cent, where comparison with re-conviction studies estimated a more modest 30 per cent (e.g. Cunliffe and Shepherd, 2007). Roach and Pease (2013) note some difficulties with directly comparing participant predictions of offence homogeneity using 'official' re-conviction data; for example, the lack of detail with regard to first offence and second offence across individual offence categories. However, those data, complementing the findings of criminal-careers research more generally, find offence homogeneity to be relatively low (Cunliffe and Shepherd, 2007; Farrington, 1988; Roach and Pease, 2013) and nowhere near the levels perceived by police.

Why has this been a likely barrier to the adoption of the SSP approach? A police overestimation of offence homogeneity, with particular regard to serious criminals, appears to be pervasive with specialist squads and teams organised to combat criminals according to the type of crimes they commit (e.g. robbery squads) and can be construed to some degree to be suitable evidence that police do not see serious offenders as generalists (Roach and Pease, 2013). If indeed the overestimation of offence homogeneity is a collective police perspective then this poses a significant problem for policing methods which seek to identify active, serious offenders from their versatile offending patterns, especially more minor infractions of the law: the essence of self-selection policing. Here, those who do 'big bad things' are flagged up to police by the 'little bad things' that they do' (Chenery, Henshaw and Pease, 1999; Roach, 2007a, 2007b; Roach and Pease, 2016), which is clearly at odds with police perception of serious offenders and their homogenous offending found by the Roach and Pease (2013) study. Offence homogeneity appears to be pervasive with specialist squads and teams organised to combat criminals according to the type of crimes they commit.

For many forces then, misperceptions of offending patterns are likely to have had a negative influence on whether to adopt SSP (or not) over the past decade. The same appears to equally dominate the thinking around policing policy.

Police policy and practice

The police have limited resources and they can be tempted to prioritise the investigation of more serious crimes and to pay cursory attention to minor ones. Indeed, in the UK the approach was endorsed in a major review of policing in the 21st century (Flanagan 2008), which suggested that the police should focus their work on combating major threats such as terrorism. Doing so would mean, for example, brief investigations and collection of few details of minor crimes.

In accordance with Flanagan's line, police services have developed screening polices, such as the following, which prioritise some crimes over others.[7] The crime-screening decision-making processes and the prioritisation of the crime for the allocation of resources for investigation will depend on the category to which a crime is allotted. What is of most interest is that although serious and priority crimes are 'prioritised', minor 'non-priority offences' are totally disregarded unless there appears what are termed 'special aggravating features' (such as repeat victimisation or evidence of victimisation). Crimes are therefore screened and then categorised into discrete categories, with serious and minor offenders constructed as homologous and distinct groups. Such an explicit crime-screening policy reflects a lack of awareness of the links between serious offenders and minor offences. The low priority given to most minor offences suggests that most will fail to make it through the screening process, with only serious offences investigated and serious offenders targeted.

The reader is (hopefully) now persuaded that serious offenders are often offence-heterogeneous. Such screening policies are the antithesis of self-selection policing, whereby many possible self-selection opportunities for identifying serious offenders are foregone, simply because police policy and guidance assumes that minor offences are committed only by minor offenders. It suffices to say here that these are only the two main ways UK police policy guidance (and thinking) is currently working against it. Small wonder then that initial enthusiasm for it more than a decade ago, has dissolved. So how can these barriers in thinking and police policy be overcome if SSP is to flourish? Some brief suggestions comprise the remainder of the chapter.

The future for self-selection policing?

In order for self-selection policing to become part of routine police practice, several changes would have to be made. Although the challenges are by no means small, they are achievable.

First, a sea change in thinking about criminal careers and offending patterns is required. When one understands that the main purpose of self-selection is to identify active *serious* offenders, then it no longer appears to clash with current police policy. When being considered by the police, therefore, the contribution of self-selection policing to the serious-crime agenda is crucial. As discussed, possibly the largest obstacle to self-selection is the tendency of police to overestimate offence homogeneity. If this obstacle is universal (Roach and Pease, 2013) then it must be overcome before self-selection can be accepted. The writer surmises that this will only be achieved if more research evidence demonstrating offence-heterogeneity is presented to strengthen the case and if officers (particularly new recruits) are educated otherwise

With regard to the wider topic of offender self-selection, acknowledgement must be given that many experienced and astute police officers already have an intuitive sense of the potential of offender self-selection. However, the argument here is as follows:

1 The minor offences which are chosen to trigger special attention should be based on research establishing the extent and nature of links with more serious offending. This removes subjectivity from the enforcement process.
2 A process should be established whereby the intuitions of police officers are made external and available, and tested against the evidence.

In short, offender self-selection is not so much about rediscovering one aspect of the craft of policing as it is about evidencing and quantifying links between offences of which some experienced officers have a sense, and discarding those police intuitions which are unfounded. Many police officers will think SSP intuitively, but they will not be familiar with the term.

The second suggestion involves a sea change in approach but links to the first suggestion. Despite the growing volume of criminological research suggesting that offenders tend to be offence-heterogeneous (e.g. Farrington et al., 2006; Soothill et al., 2000; Farrington and Hawkins, 1991), little attention is paid generally by criminologists to the possible significance of minor offences. As discussed, criminal career research neglects the importance of minor offences in a career, preferring to treat minor offences as markers of onset and evidence of de-escalation of seriousness, temporary or otherwise. To the writer's knowledge, self-selection policing is not mentioned in any of the leading texts in criminology, crime science, or policing (e.g. Maguire, Morgan and Reiner, 2012; Newburn, 2012; Newburn and Neyroud, 2008; Newburn, Williamson, and Wright, 2007; Smith and Tilley, 2005).

It is hoped that with the development of a growing body research dedicated to self-selection this situation will change. What is needed most, perhaps, is a programme of research which explores in more detail the links between serious and minor offending, and identifies reliable and robust trigger offences. The writer is currently researching the criminal histories and offending patterns of disqualified drivers, minor offences most likely to be committed by those planning to execute acts of terrorism, and cruelty to animals as triggers for serious, concurrent criminality. But more needs to be done.

Finally, here are six points that may contribute to the acceptance and implementation of self-selection policing. If those who do big bad things are still doing little bad things, then an evidence-based programme of research will provide police with an additional weapon with which to identify them. What is needed:

1 **A dedicated research programme to investigate the major–minor offending link**. There is a multitude of potential minor offences which could act as markers for serious offender identification. Vigorous research is needed to discover the most reliable and robust.
2 **A re-framing of minor offences as significant**. Evidence is still growing in support of serious offenders displaying crime versatility, especially with regard to committing both serious and minor infractions of the law. By committing minor offences, serious offenders are self-selecting for increased police attention, which can be used to uncover more serious criminality.
3 **An acceptance that self-selection policing does not discriminate**. The beauty of this approach is that it does not seek to identify via discriminatory practice, such as offender profiling; it is focused instead on actions (i.e. the breaking of a law, however minor).
4 **Educate officers about SSP and its potential**. Most frontline officers have less than five years' worth of experience in the service. When the significant number of recent recruits to the extended police family are added, the urgent need to provide as much know-how as possible becomes apparent. As offender self-selection knowledge grows it provides much-needed know-how for the inexperienced. For example, if a list of minor offences that warrant increased perpetrator scrutiny can be given, this would have big implications (e.g. for the application of police resources). The illegal parking in disabled bays study (Chenery et al., 1999) suggests a need for a closer working relationship between police and traffic wardens in order to identify 'wanted' and serious offenders more effectively.
5 **Ensure that SSP trigger offences are publicly acceptable and do not breach rights**. An important learning point is that any such indicator-offence needs to be both of minimal inconvenience and justifiable to the public. Generally, people do not object to obtrusive measures such as being searched at a prison, provided they clearly understand the reasons for it. Offender self-selection is about identifying those minor offences which best indicate that more serious offending might be present, whilst remembering that most minor offences will be committed by minor offenders. The best trigger offences will be the least obtrusive, as with the disabled bays study where the illegal parkers were not aware they were the subject of increased interest. In this case, the number of false negatives either does not matter (because no inconvenience has been caused) or actually contribute to the safety of others; for example, using mobile phones while driving and not wearing seat belts are triggers where advice given to those who are not involved in crime is in any case in the driver's best interests (Townsley and Pease, 2003).
6 **Develop an SSP 'evidence-base'**. Only thoroughly researched, robust trigger offences should be rolled-out into police practice. Modern senior police officers are most likely to be persuaded by developments founded in strong research evidence.

And finally, a few potential SSP trigger offences being looked at currently include animal cruelty offences and common minor offences committed by those planning terrorist attacks. Any additional suggestions you might have will be gratefully received.

Notes

1 See www.bbc.co.uk/news/uk-22344054 (accessed on 26 August, 2015).
2 The reader is directed to Roach and Pease (2016) for a more detailed exploration of these research studies.
3 'Squeegee merchant' refers to those individuals who undertake unsolicited cleaning of drivers' car windscreens while at traffic lights and in traffic jams.
4 Desk Appearance Ticket – usually entailing an appearance at a police station to pay a fine.
5 Forgive me if I have made this word up, but it would get a decent score at scrabble!
6 See Roach (2017) for a listing of the 12 offence categories mimicking those used by the UK National Crime Agency.
7 For example, see Cambridge police policy guidance found at www.cambs.police.uk/about/foi/policies/Crime%20Screening%20Policy%20_09.10.06_.pdf (accessed 3 February, 2018).

References

Bar-Hillel, M. (1982) Studies of representativeness. In D. Kahneman, P. Slovic and A. Tversky, *A. Judgement Under Uncertainty: Heuristics and Biases*. Cambridge: Cambridge University Press.

Blumstein, A., Cohen, J., Roth, J. A. and Visher, C. A. (eds) (1986a) *Criminal Careers and 'Career Criminals', Vol. I.* Washington, DC: National Academy Press.

Blumstein, A., Cohen, J., Roth, J. A. and Visher, C.A. (eds) (1986b) *Criminal Careers and 'Career Criminals', Vol. II.* Washington, DC: National Academy Press.

Blumstein, A., Cohen, J., Das, S. and Moitra, S.D. (1988) Specialisation and seriousness during adult criminal careers. *Journal of Quantitative Criminology*, *4*: 303–345.

Chenery, S., Henshaw, C. and Pease, K. (1999) Illegal parking in disabled bays: a means of offender targeting, policing and reducing crime. Briefing note 1/99. London: Home Office.

Clarke, R. V. G. (1980) Situational crime prevention: theory and practice. *British Journal of Criminology*, *20*(2): 136–147.

Clarke, R. V. G. (1997) (ed.) *Situational Crime Prevention: Successful Studies* (2nd edition). Albany, NY: Harrow and Heston.

Clarke, R. V. G. and Felson, M. (1998). Opportunity makes the thief. Practical theory for crime prevention. Police Research Paper 98. Policing and Reducing Crime Unit, Research, Development and Statistics Directorate, UK Home Office. Also found at http://webarchive.nationalarchives.gov.uk/20110218135832/rds.homeoffice.gov.uk/rds/prgpdfs/fprs98.pdf (accessed 08/10/2015).

Cohen, L. and Felson, M. (1979). Social change and crime rate trends: a routine activity approach, *American Sociological Review*, *44*: 588–608.

Cohen, L. and Felson, M. (2008) The routine activity approach. In R. Wortley, and L. Mazerolle (eds) *Environmental Criminology and Crime Analysis*. Collumpton, UK: Willan Publishing.

Cornish, D. B. (1994) The procedural analysis of offending, and its relevance for situational prevention. In R. V. Clarke (ed.) *Crime Prevention Studies*, Volume 3. Monsey, NY: Criminal Justice Press.

Cornish, D. B. and Clarke, R. V. (1986) (eds) *The Reasoning Criminal*. New York: Springer-Verlag.

Cornish, D. B. and Clarke, R. V. (2006). The rational choice perspective. In S. Henry and M. M. Lanier (eds) *The Essential Criminology Reader*. Boulder, CO: Westview Press.

Cornish, D. B. and Clarke, R.V. (2008) The rational choice perspective. In R. Wortley and L. Mazerolle (eds) *Environmental Criminology and Crime Analysis*. Uffculme: Willan Publishing.

Cunliffe, J. and Shepherd, A. (2007) Re-offending of adults: results from the 2004 cohort. Home Office Statistical Bulletin 06/04. London: Home office.

Deane, G., Armstrong, D. P. and Felson, R. B. (2005). An examination of offense specialization using marginal logit models. *Criminology*, *43*(4), 955–988.

Farrington, D. P. (1986). Age and Crime. *Crime and Justice*, 7: 189–250.

Farrington, D. P., Coid, J. W., Harnett, L., Jolliffe, D., Soteriou, N., Turner, R. and West, D. J. (2006) *Criminal* careers and life success: new findings from the Cambridge Study in Delinquent Development.

Home Office Findings Paper 281. London: Home Office. Also found at www.crim.cam.ac.uk/people/academic_research/david_farrington/hofind281.pdf (accessed 08/10/2015).

Farrington, D. P. and Hawkins, J. D. (1991) Predicting participation, early onset, and later persistence in officially recorded offending. *Criminal Behaviour and Mental Health, 1*: 1–33.

Farrington, D. P., Snyder, H. N. and Finnegan, T. A. (1988) Specialisation in juvenile court careers, *Criminology, 26*: 461–487.

Felson, M. (1994) *Crime and Everyday Life*. Thousand Oaks, CA: Pine Forge Press.

Felson, M. (1998). *Crime and Everyday Life* (2nd edition). Thousand Oaks, California: Pine Forge Press.

Fisher, G. and Ross, S. (2006). Beggarman or thief: methodological issues in offender specialisation research. *Australian and New Zealand Journal of Criminology, 39*: 151–171.

Flanagan, R. (2008) A review of policing – final report. Independent Review of Policing, found at http://webarchive.nationalarchives.gov.uk/20080910134927/police.homeoffice.gov.uk/publications/police-reform/review_of_policing_final_report (accessed 08/10/2015).

Gottfredson, M. and Hirschi, T. (1990) *A General Theory of Crime*. Stanford, CA: Stanford University Press.

Greenall, P. V. and Wright, M. (2015) Exploring the criminal histories of stranger sexual killers. *The Journal of Forensic Psychiatry and Psychology, 26*(2): 249–259.

Harris, D. A., Smallbone, S., Dennison, S. and Knight, R. A. (2009) Specialisation and versatility in sexual offenders referred for civil commitment. *Journal of Criminal Justice, 37*(1): 37–44.

Hornung, E. W. (1899) *The Amateur Cracksman*. New York: Schriber's.

Innes, M. (2007). Investigation order and major crime inquiries. In T. Newburn, T. Williamson, and A. Wright (eds) *Handbook of Criminal Investigation*. Cullompton: Willan Publishing, pp. 255–75.

Kahneman, D., Slovic, P. and Tversky, A. (1982) *Judgement Under Uncertainty: Heuristics and Biases*. Cambridge: Cambridge University Press.

Kelling, G. and Coles, C. (1995) *Fixing Broken Windows*. New York: Free Press.

Kempf, K. (1987) Specialisation and the criminal career. *Criminology, 25*(2): 399–420.

LeBlanc, M. and Frechette, M. (1989) *Male Criminal Activity from Childhood Through Youth: Multilevel and Developmental Perspectives*. New York: Springer-Verlag.

Maguire, M. (2008) Criminal investigation and crime control, in, T. Newburn (ed.) *Handbook of Policing* (2nd Edition). Cullompton, UK: Willan Publishing.

Maguire, M., Morgan, R. and Reiner, R. (eds) (2012). *The Oxford Handbook of Criminology* (5th Edition) Oxford: Oxford University Press.

Maple, J. (1999) *Crime Fighter*. New York: Broadway Books.

Mazerolle, P., Brame, R., Paternoster, R., Piquero, A. and Dean, C. (2000) Onset age, persistence, and offending versatility: comparisons across gender. *Criminology, 38*: 1143–1172.

McConville, M., Sanders, A. and Leng, R. (1991) *The Case for the Prosecution*. London: Routledge.

Moffitt, T. E. (1997) Adolescent-limited and life-course persistent offending: a complementary pair of developmental theories. In T. Thornberry (ed.) *Developmental Theories of Crime and Delinquency. Advances in Criminological Theory*. Abingdon, UK: Transaction Publishers.

Moffitt, T. E. (1999) Life-course persistent and adolescence-limited antisocial behaviour: a developmental taxonomy. *Psychological Review, 100*: 674–701.

Moffitt, T. E. (2003) life-course-persistent and adolescent-limited antisocial behavior. In B. B. Lahey, T. E. Moffitt and A. Casp (eds) *Causes of Conduct Disorder and Juvenile Delinquency*. New York. The Guilford Press.

Newburn, T. (2008) (ed.) *Handbook of Policing* (2nd edition). Cullompton, UK: Willan Publishing.

Newburn, T. (2012) *Criminology* (2nd edition). London: Routledge.

Newburn, T. and Neyroud, P. (2008) *Dictionary of Policing*. Cullompton, UK: Willan Publishing.

Newburn, T., Williamson, T. and Wright, A. (2007) (eds) *Handbook of Criminal Investigation*. Cullompton, UK: Willan Publishing.

Piquero, A. (2000) Frequency, specialisation, and violence in offending careers. *Journal of Research in Crime and Delinquency, 37*: 392–418.

Piquero, A. and Moffitt, T. (2004) Life-course persistent offending. In J. Adler (ed.) *Forensic Psychology: Concepts, Debates and Practice*. Cullompton, UK: Willan Publishing, pp. 177–193.

Roach, J. (In press). Self-selection policing and the disqualified driver. *Policing: A Journal of Policy and Practice* (advanced access paw056). https://doi.org/10.1093/police/paw056.

Roach, J. (2007a) Those who do big bad things also usually do little bad things: identifying active serious offenders using offender self-selection. *International Journal of Police Science and Management, 9*(1): 66–79.

Roach, J. (2007b) HO/RT1culture: cultivating police use of Home Office Road Traffic 1 form to identify active serious offenders. *International Journal of Police Science and Management*, *9*(4), 357–370.
Roach, J. (2012) Terrorists, affordance and the over-estimation of offence homogeneity. In M. Taylor and P. M. Currie (eds) *Terrorism and Affordance*. London: Continuum.
Roach, J. and Pease, K. (2013) Police overestimation of criminal career homogeneity. *Journal of Investigative Psychology and Offender Profiling*, *11*: 164–178.
Roach, J., and Pease, K. (2016) *Self-Selection Policing: Theory, Research and Practice*. London: Palgrave Macmillan.
Rose, G. (2000) The criminal histories of serious traffic offenders. Home Office Research Study Number 206. London: Home Office.
Schechter, H. and Everitt, D. (2006) *The A to Z Encyclopedia of Serial Killers*. New York: Simon and Schuster.
Schneider, J. L. (2005). The link between shoplifting and burglary: the booster burglar. *British Journal of Criminology*, *45*: 395–401.
Smerdon, J., & South, N. (1997). Deviant Drivers and'Moral Hazards': Risk, No-insurance Offending and Some Suggestions for Policy and Practice. *International Journal of Risk Security and Crime Prevention, 2*, 279–290.
Smith, M. J. and Tilley, N. (eds) (2005) *Crime Science: New Approaches to Preventing and Detecting Crime*. Cullompton, UK: Willan Publishing.
Soothill, K., Fitzpatrick, C. and Francis, B. (2009) *Understanding Criminal Careers*. Cullompton, UK: Willan Publishing.
Soothill, K., Francis, B., Sanderson, B. and Ackerley, E. (2000) Sex offenders: specialists, generalists or both? *British Journal of Criminology*, *40*: 56–67.
Steer, D. J. and Carr-Hill, R. A. (1967). The Motoring Offender-Who Is He?. *Criminal Law Review*, 214.
Suggs, D. (1998). Motor projects in England and Wales: an evaluation. Home Office Research, Development and Statistics Directorate, Research Findings Number 81. London: Home Office.
Tarling, R. (1993) *Analysing Offending: Data, Models and Interpretations*. London: HMSO.
Townsley, M. and Pease, K. (2003) Two go wild in Knowsley: analysis for evidence-led crime reduction. In, K. Bullock and N. Tilley (eds) *Problem-Orientated Policing*. Cullompton, UK: Willan Publishing.
Wellsmith, M. and Guille, H. (2005) Fixed penalty notices as a means of offender selection. *International Journal of Police Science and Management*, 7(1): 36–44.
West Midlands Police (1997) Annual Report. Found at www.west-midlands.police.uk/pdfs/publications/annual-reports/.pdf (accessed 17/4/2005).
Willett, Terence C. (1964). *Criminal on the Road*. Tavistock Publ.

23

Agent-based decision-support systems for crime scientists

Daniel Birks and Michael Townsley

Introduction

Crime events are the output of a complex system. Where and when crime does and does not occur, by whom it is carried out, and against whom/what it is perpetrated, are all the result of interconnected, interdependent, and situated interactions, amongst multiple, heterogeneous, adaptive actors and the environment within which they are situated. These interactions of crime commission (and control), and the mechanisms that underlie them are consistently difficult to observe or control in service of the scientific method. Academically, this limits theoretical advancement. But more importantly, we would argue, it constrains efforts to respond to crime, disrupt ongoing events, and better understand those offences that have occurred previously to facilitate future prevention.

In this chapter we discuss computational analytic methods that embrace this complexity and aim to explore it, with the hope of increasing our understanding of crime, and informing what we might do about it. Drawing on research from the field of distributed computing, and emboldened by a range of other social sciences with compatible goals, in the last decade crime scientists have begun to apply computational models to better understand how the actions and interactions of individuals influence complex social systems, the crime opportunities and events they give rise to, and the effectiveness of potential responses to them.

Computational models allow researchers to construct simplified versions of real-world systems by encoding them as computer programs. These computational models encompass suites of data objects, algorithms and logical dependencies that collectively provide a caricature of the system of interest that is easier to both observe and manipulate than the system they seek to emulate (Townsley & Birks, 2008).

Such models have supported research in a range of natural and social sciences when empirical research is infeasible or prohibitively expensive. One particular approach, the individual- or agent-based model (ABM), is seeing a considerable upswell in application. ABMs allow researchers to construct synthetic environments and populate them with virtual decision makers (referred to as agents) designed to represent key societal actors. These agents are imbued with behaviours that reflect theoretical proposition and/or previous empirical insight. Once a model is constructed it can be used to conduct simulated experiments whereby populations of agents are instantiated in some particular configuration, and the aggregate outcome patterns (e.g. patterns of crime) that result from their repeated interactions observed. Within this burgeoning field of computational criminology, ABMs have been productively constructed to study a diverse range of crime problems and responses to them (see for example, Birks et al., 2012, 2014; Birks & Davies, 2017; Bosse et al., 2010; Brantingham & Tita, 2008; Groff, 2007, 2008; Hill et al., 2013; Malleson et al., 2012; Marchione et al., 2014; Wang et al., 2008; Weisburd et al., 2017).

This approach to understanding crime events and patterns departs from a range of other quantitative modelling techniques that typically operate in a 'top-down' analytic fashion, inferring individual-level explanations from observed aggregate associations (e.g. affluence and crime). By contrast, ABMs allow researchers to explore crime events from the bottom-up, casting crime as the emergent outcome of a series of lower-order interactions. By doing so, individual crime-event actors, their characteristics and calculi are formalised, and by running the model one is able to assess if proposed individual-level mechanisms are capable of generating plausible outcome patterns. In this way, ABMs provide the means to assess whether a proposed decision calculus is sufficient to generate known societal phenomena (Epstein, 1999). This approach is nothing more than a formalised version of asking, 'if people do behave this way, what would we expect to observe?' By comparing the outcomes of these models to what is known about the real system, the validity of underlying theory is thus assessed (Birks et al., 2012).

Modelling the connection between individual behaviour and crime events confers several inherent analytic advantages in examining the complex social systems that produce and shape crime problems. First, it permits the explicit modelling of heterogonous populations. Agents within an ABM are represented as instantiations of an agent class or template that contains individual characteristics and behaviours that can be set on a per-agent basis. Thus, realistically diverse populations of actors can be modelled. This approach overcomes traditional analytical assumptions that often enforce population homogeneity in order to manage analytical tractability. Second, by modelling the repeated interaction of agents over time, ABMs permit the exploration of longitudinal processes. Agent behaviours can be constructed to represent feedback-driven processes where events at t_1 influence or inform events at t_{1+n}. Thus, agents can 'learn' from experience and adapt to previous events. By extension, ABMs are capable of providing insight into collective, temporally bounded phenomena such as tipping points and phase changes. Third, as agents are situated and interact in some form of simulated environment (real or abstract), ABMs provide a platform for modelling situated interactions, which in turn can inform cognitively bounded decision calculi – thus circumnavigating assumptions of complete actor knowledge that are implicit in other statistical models (e.g. discrete choice). Finally, and perhaps most importantly, ABMs provide researchers with an instrument that enables absolute observation and manipulation at all scales – from the inner workings of an agent's decision calculus to environmental configuration and aggregate societal outcome. Thus, an ABM provides a Petri dish of sorts for examining social systems – enabling the equivalent of an in-vitro form of social science.

By constructing agents that represent potential offenders, victims and crime controllers, and examining their interaction, ABMs allow researchers to understand what configurations of behavioural and environmental conditions are capable of generating particular patterns of crime, and, in turn, to construct and estimate the effectiveness of crime-control strategies that might be implemented to respond to them. ABMs thus provide computational laboratories in which researchers can prototype, test, and refine both criminological theory, and proposed intervention – free from ethical and logistical constraints and prior to the carrying out of necessary, but likely costly, empirical investigation.

In this chapter we focus on the application of ABMs for the latter purpose – as a means to investigate the likely impacts of differing crime-control strategies. In doing so, we aim to demonstrate how ABM can be productively used in the field of crime science as a means to support decision-making in complex systems. Following this rationale, the remainder of the chapter begins by briefly describing the notion of ABMs as a method for decision support. Subsequently, we describe an example ABM of police resource deployment and present a series of illustrative experiments run using it. We conclude by discussing some of the insights gleaned from this simple model and highlighting several potential fruitful areas of research where we believe ABM may be productively incorporated into key crime science problem areas.

Agent-based decision-support systems

One important area where ABM may offer policymakers and other decision makers unique insight over other analytical methods is in the estimation of likely impacts of different intervention strategies (Groff & Birks, 2008). In this section we briefly argue why ABMs have the potential to provide policymakers in particular with more insight into proposed interventions and problems, with a view to developing policy and practice in a scientific, evidence-based manner.

As we see it, policymakers have three primary objectives: (i) identifying substantive social problems, (ii) understanding the underlying causes of said problems, and (iii) activating the most effective means for addressing them. In the interests of space, we assume the first two of these tasks are appropriately conducted (our policymaker has been able to locate a substantive social problem and that research has identified some underlying cause for the problem). The challenge now is to identify the most effective way of tackling the underlying cause(s).

Spoiler alert: this aim is considerably easier to state than it is to accomplish. A number of fundamental constraints obscure the task. First, context plays such an important role in effective practice. Often, interventions work for particular people in particular situations (Pawson & Tilley, 1997). The policymaker needs to consider different contexts and the degree to which these might frustrate or facilitate the intended mechanisms to be activated. While some advice does exist (Laycock, 2002), much of this boils down to having comprehensive domain knowledge and a coherent mental model of how the world works. In our view, the sheer range of potential contexts makes this an overwhelmingly difficult task.

The second constraint is scale. Some social problems can be tackled in a demonstration or pilot project. But many cannot. Social marketing, for instance, relies on wide-scale network effects, which will be outside the financial reach of most pilot schemes. An action research paradigm might provide some effective evidence, but even the most promising intervention can become diluted when mainstreamed.

The third constraint is unintended consequences, about which many thinkers have written. For instance, Robert Merton (1936), credited with popularising the term 'unintended consequences' in the 20th century, cited more than a dozen highly influential theorists who have written on the topic, including the likes of Hegel, Weber, Marx and Adam Smith. Until recently, much of this literature has consisted of examples of policy failure, and reads like an 'if only we knew then what we know now, the unforeseen could be avoided' fable. While a catalogue of case studies is useful for illustrative purposes, ensuring that we learn from our mistakes requires uncommon discipline.

Our contention is that because ABMs can be used to construct artificial societies, they can represent a policy-prototyping environment for policy and decision makers. They are not bound by the financial, ethical or logistical constraints of the real world, so problems of scale can be avoided. Provided individual-level dynamics are understood and can be formalised (i.e. the calculus of individual actors can be explicitly expressed), then ABMs offer policymakers a unique scenario-testing environment. With the help of domain experts, ABMs can operationalise contextual features and unintended consequences.

Thus, we envisage ABMs as a decision-support tool for crime scientists in understanding crime problems, and for policy and decision makers in providing a platform where competing strategies can be explored with respect to efficacy, unintended consequences, and dose-response outcomes.

Such models can operate at varying levels of abstraction, from the very abstract – for example, understanding how particular tactics may disrupt the formation of particular types of hot spots – to the very applied – for example, examining responses to an empirically plausible distribution of calls for service (which we explore later in the chapter). Where a particular ABM is located on this spectrum is dictated by the data available to construct and calibrate the model, and our understanding of the system to be modelled. If the target system is sufficiently understood, ABMs can be constructed emulating a range of potential intervention strategies and then the model used to generate outputs in a range of circumstances.

To illustrate this potential we now present a simple ABM used to explore the effectiveness of varying police call-for-service response strategies. The point here is not to present the most elaborate or useful model but instead to demonstrate key processes involved in the construction of ABM, and demonstrate how we envisage they may support decision-making in the field of crime science.

An illustrative example: prototyping strategies for call-for-service despatch

The problem

A core task of the police is to respond to calls for service (CFS). On a day-to-day basis, police agencies receive large volumes of CFS that require police attendance. Responding to CFS requires that police identify and prioritise an ongoing volume of service requests and subsequently, allocate and despatch resources to attend to those requests.

The effectiveness of these response strategies can be measured in multiple ways: time taken to respond to incidents; the number of responders required to do so (and their associated costs); the proportion of time (thus efficiency) responders spend responding; and so on. Moreover, there are also safety-focused characteristics that will equally need to be assessed, such as shift length, average number of incidents responded to per shift, etc. Finally, there are likely a number of constraints that cannot be violated, such as a government-mandated maximum-response times.

Moreover, the characteristics of any particular strategy can be defined over an array of potential variables. These include the number of response vehicles available at any given time, the spatial configuration of locations from which these responders are despatched, the method by which equally categorised events are responded to, strategies responders might employ when not responding to minimise subsequent response times, and costs, etc.

If we take these few proposed strategy characteristics it is easy to see a constellation of potential strategy configurations rapidly emerge. To illustrate, the hypothetical strategy characteristics depicted in Table 23.1 produce a total of 8,000 (100 × 2 × 4 × 10) unique response strategies.

Relating this vast array of resource configurations to a large number of potential outcome conditions is difficult for a range of reasons:

(1) Exhaustively assessing all possible despatch configurations is logistically infeasible
(2) Some configurations may be infeasible to test – i.e. moving despatch locations repeatedly

Table 23.1 Illustrative response-strategy parameters

Strategy element	*Description*	*Hypothetical possible values*
Number of responders	The number of responders available to respond at any time	0–100
Incident prioritisation	How currently active CFS are allocated to responders	First-in-first-out (FIFO) Nearest
Idling strategy	A navigation strategy for responders not currently responding to an event	(1) Static; (2) Random walk; (3) Global hotspot surveillance; (4) Local hotspot surveillance
Spatial configuration of despatch locations	The locations from which responders are despatched	10 Unique spatial configurations

(3) Empirically assessing the effectiveness of some despatch configurations may be potentially unethical
(4) Optimising configuration to favour particular outcome variables (such as average response time, or resourcing costs) is a multiple-constraints problem.

Here, like others (Zhang & Brown, 2013), we propose that one potential way to explore how despatch configurations are related to effectiveness is to construct an ABM to prototype potential configurations and estimate their likely effectiveness across a range of metrics. To illustrate this assertion, we now present a simple model of police despatch, its key components, and describe several key experiments carried out using it.

The model

We envisage an abstract urban environment in which a police agency despatches response vehicles to attend to CFS. We model hypothetical, but empirically plausible, distributions of CFS, and provide the researcher with a range of despatch configuration options that allow us to examine a wide range of strategies, and a range of output metrics against which these are assessed for effectiveness.

The model environment

The environment in which the simulation takes place is represented as a simple two-dimensional lattice. In the version of the model presented here, this lattice consists of 2,500 distinct locations (or cells) arranged in a 50 × 50 lattice. Each cell represents a 1,000 m by 1,000 m area. Assuming an average responder speed of 60 kmph we infer a response vehicle can traverse a single cell in 1 minute. This dictates that each simulation cycle is equivalent to 1 minute of real time, by extension there are 1,440 cycles per 24-hour period in our simulated world.

Calls for service

We simulate CFS as a series of discrete events that are probabilistically generated each time a simulation is run. We aim to provide a simple approximation of real-world CFS. In our example model CFS have three attributes: (a) occurrence time, (b) occurrence location, (c) occurrence duration.

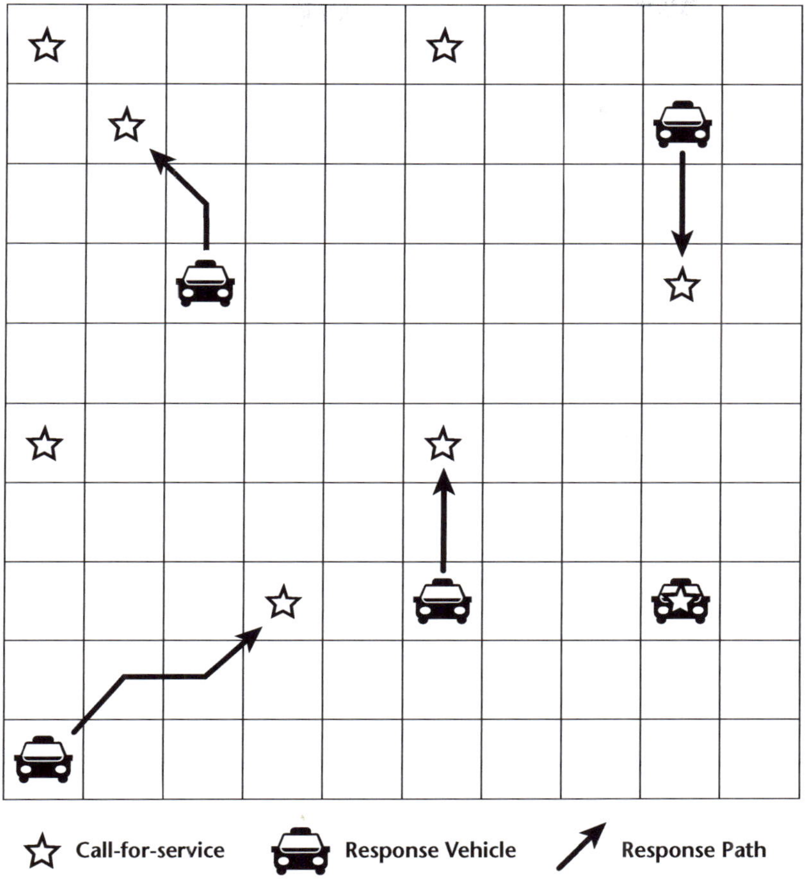

Figure 23.1 Example model environment[1]

As a simulation progresses, the following actions are taken each cycle, to generate CFS.

(1) Draw the number of CFS to be generated from a Poisson distribution with lambda λ. We experimentally manipulate λ to generate three distinct demand models (see below).
(2) For each CFS generated we probabilistically determine if the call is a unique incident (*p(0.5)*) or is clustered in close proximity to a previous CFS (*p(0.5)*). The former are simply positioned at a random location in the environment, the latter are positioned somewhere within a three-cell radius of a currently active CFS. These simple rules create a distribution of CFS that is spatially and temporally concentrated.
(3) For each CFS generated we also probabilistically determine the duration of time required to attend to the incident in cycles once a responder arrives. This duration is again drawn from Poisson distribution such that duration = Poisson (3) + 1. Thus, most incidents can be responded to in a short period of time but some require more resources.

Given that the model is generating a hypothetical distribution of CFS we also generate three unique call-demand scenarios – low, medium and high. This is done by manipulating λ as follows: low demand (= 0.5), medium demand (= 0.75) high demand (= 1.5). These values of λ equate to the generation of roughly 500, 1,000, and 2,000 CFS over a 24-hour period respectively. In addition, we assume that all CFS must be responded to within a two-hour window (120 cycles) from generation or they are deemed as failed responses.

Responders

We simulate a population of response vehicles as agents. These vehicles can move freely around the environment from cell to cell. Each cycle, each responder is able to move a single cell from its current location in any of the eight cardinal directions. Once allocated and travelling to an incident, a responder agent simply takes the shortest path from its current location to the allocated CFS. When a responder agent moves we assume it consumes one unit of fuel. Responder agents can thus be in one of three states: (i) travelling to an incident, (ii) attending an incident, and (iii) idling. This latter state reflects when a responder is currently not assigned a CFS.

Response-strategy parameters

We explore the impact of three distinct response-strategy parameters: the number of responders, incident prioritisation, and idling strategy. Each of these response parameters is now described.

Number of responders: One obvious property of a response strategy is the number of responder vehicles available at any given time. This characteristic simply defines the number of responder agents that are instantiated when a simulation is initialised that can be used to investigate the impact of varying resourcing commitments on CFS response. Here we explore five configurations of 10, 20, 30, 40 and 50 vehicles.

Incident prioritisation: The prioritisation of a CFS is a key parameter associated with response strategies. The prioritisation strategy defines how CFS are allocated to responders. We explore two distinct models of incident prioritisation.

(1) *FIFO*: a simple first-in-first-out queue system, such that incidents are responded to in the order that they are received. Once an incident is at the top of the queue, the closest non-responding vehicle is allocated to respond to it.
(2) *Nearest*: allocates a non-responding vehicle to the nearest incident to their current location, ignoring the order in which incidents were received (note, in the event of multiple incidents in the same proximity to a single responder, incidents are selected at random).

Idling strategy: Depending upon current demand there are times throughout the day that responders are not responding to CFS. The idling-strategy parameter dictates the spatial strategies responders in this state should adopt. We explore four distinct strategies that are adopted in the absence of a current incident:

(1) *Static*: non-responding vehicles remains stationary until allocated to a new CFS.
(2) *Random walk*: non-responding vehicles move randomly throughout the environment until allocated to a new CFS.
(3) *Global hotspot surveillance – global*: non-responding vehicles move toward the location that has received the greatest number of CFS over the last 24 hours.
(4) *Local hotspot surveillance*: non-responding vehicles move toward the location that has received the greatest number of CFS over the last 24 hours within ten cells of their current location.

Experimental setup

Having constructed the model we now present a series of illustrative simulation experiments that seek to assess the impact of the different strategies described above on several outcome measures.

Following the description above the independent variables (IVs) for all simulation runs are as follows: number of responders, prioritisation strategy and idling strategy. Manipulating these IVs we also explore outcomes across low, medium and high-demand scenarios. This configuration produces a 3 (*demand scenario*) × 5 (*number of responders*) × 2 (*prioritisation strategy*) × 4 (*idling strategy*) *factorial experimental design*, and thus 120 unique demand–response configurations. Due to the model's probabilistic nature, for each configuration we run 100 simulations (of 1,440 cycles – i.e. 24 simulated hours). In each simulation we use a unique random seed value, thus ensuring the distribution of CFS is unique (just like each day in the real world). This results in the model being used to run 12,000 simulations. Finally, we aggregate the outcome measures across 100 simulations of each of the 120 unique demand–response configurations.

Model output data

In each simulation we record the following data relating to each CFS incident:

(1) The response vehicle allocated to that incident
(2) The number of cycles it took from initiation of the event and when the responder reached the incident.

In addition, for each response vehicle we also record:

(1) The number of cycles spent responding or idling
(2) The quantity of fuel consumed (under the assumption that one unit of fuel is consumed when the vehicle moves a single cell).

From these data we collate the following summary statistics associated with the effectiveness of each response strategy: (1) the proportion of incidents responded to within a two-hour window, (2) the average response time per incident, (3) the average cost of response per incident (calculated by summing fuel consumed by all responders over the 24-hour period, divided by the total number of incidents responded to), (4) the global proportion of responder-time spent responding or idle.

Findings

To summarise, our simulation has three contexts (high, medium or low CFS demand). The model allows a patrolling strategy to be formulated by combining three input parameters: (1) the number of responders; (2) how responders are allocated CFS; and (3) what responders do when there are no calls to respond to. If this were a game, the player would have three dials from which to generate a response strategy, of which there are 40 possible patrol strategies. Assessing the effectiveness of these strategies we have five metrics that are analogous to key performance indicators: (1) proportion of incidents attended within two hours, (2) response time, (3) total fuel consumed, (4) fuel consumed per incident, and (5) percentage of time spent travelling or idling.

Tables 23.2, 23.3 and 23.4 in the Appendix depict the relationship between the number of responders, prioritisation strategy, idling strategy and the outcome measures discussed above over all three CFS demand scenarios (Low – Table 23.2, Medium – Table 23.3, High – Table 23.4).

While a full and systematic exploration of the model outcomes are beyond the scope of this chapter, below we discuss some key insights that can be gleaned regarding the three response-strategy parameters explored. These 'qualitative' insights demonstrate how an ABM provides us with an understanding of the dynamics of the system being modelled.

Model insights

Number of responders

Examining manipulations to the number of responders illustrates several key outcomes. First, the potentially intuitive assertion that response times are linearly related to the number of responding vehicles does not bear out. Figure 23.2 illustrates that in each of the three demand scenarios there is a critical value of responders required in order to ensure that all incidents are responded to within the specified two-hour time window. In the low- and medium-demand models 20 responders are required, in the high-demand scenario, 40. However, after these critical values there is a distinct drop in the advantages gained from the cost of additional responders. To illustrate, in the medium-demand scenario, increasing the number of responders from 30 to 40 or 50 requires considerably more resources but results in a reduction in average response times in the order of one minute per additional ten responders.

Interestingly, Figure 23.3 illustrates that under the *Static* idling strategy where greater numbers of responders do not largely impact on response times, they do minimise the fuel expended

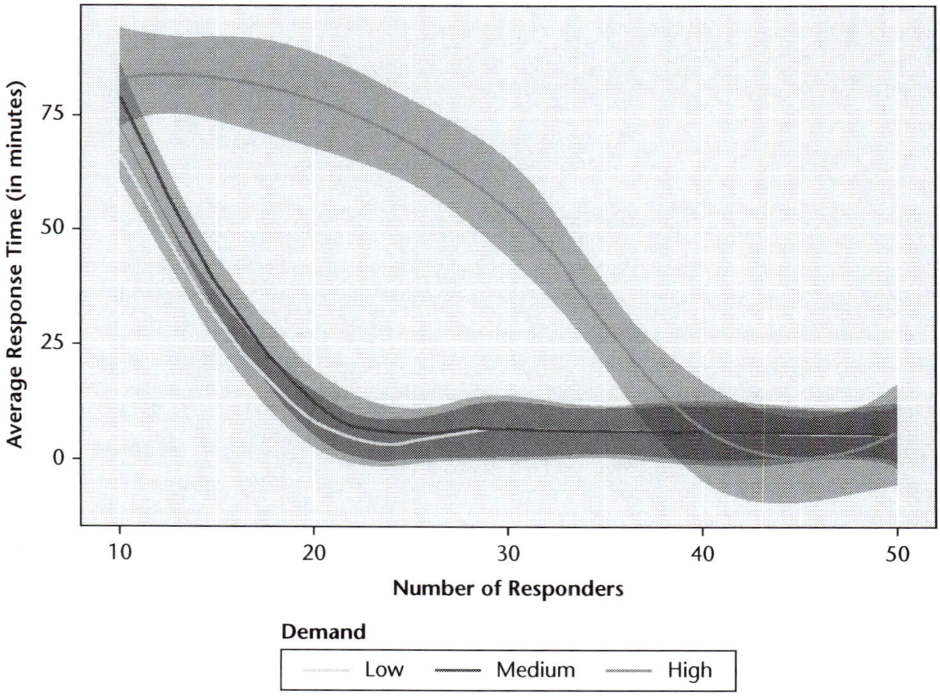

Figure 23.2 Relationship between number of responders and average response time, by demand scenario

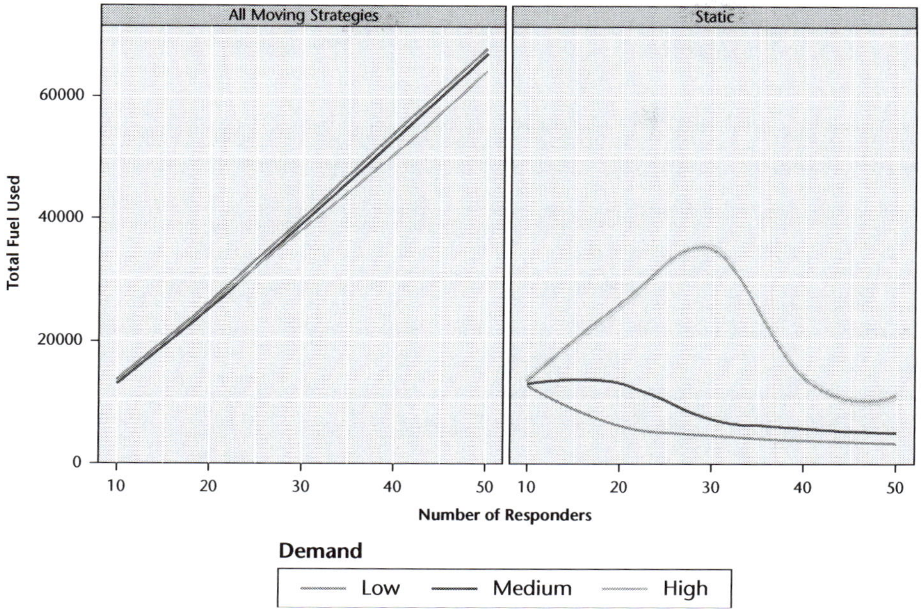

Figure 23.3 Relationship between number of responders and fuel usage, by demand scenario

by responders, although obviously not the human resources. This finding is a result of the fact that a smaller number of responders are required to traverse the environment more than a larger number of dispersed responders.

Finally, Figure 23.4 shows that in the models where all incidents are responded to within the two-hour time window the proportion of time spent actually responding by responders is sub-optimal. For example, in the low-demand scenario, tenresponders spend almost all their time (~98 per cent) responding to incidents but still fall just short of responding to all in the two-hour window. By contrast, 20 responders respond to all incidents considerably quicker (roughly ten times on average) but need spend only a quarter of their time responding in order to do so.

Prioritisation strategies

Examining the impact of the incident-prioritisation strategy reveals one interesting, and largely unexpected, outcome. Figure 23.5 illustrates that in demand scenarios where there are sufficient responders to respond to all incidents within the two-hour time window there are no substantive differences between the *FIFO* and *Nearest* strategies. However, when responders are overstretched to the point that not all incidents can be responded to within the two-hour time window, the *Nearest* strategy produces consistently lower average responses times and higher rates of response within the two-hour time window.

To illustrate, with only ten responders in the medium-demand scenario, the *FIFO* prioritisation strategy produces a mean response time of just over 100 minutes and a response rate 44 per cent, whereas the same number of responders adopting the *Nearest* prioritisation strategy on average respond to incidents in 60 minutes at a response rate of 55 per cent. Examining this disparity in efficiency over the numerous model configurations indicates that the *Nearest* prioritisation strategy produces the most significant advantages over *FIFO* when resources are scarcest. Visual examination of single simulation runs indicate that this phenomenon is likely

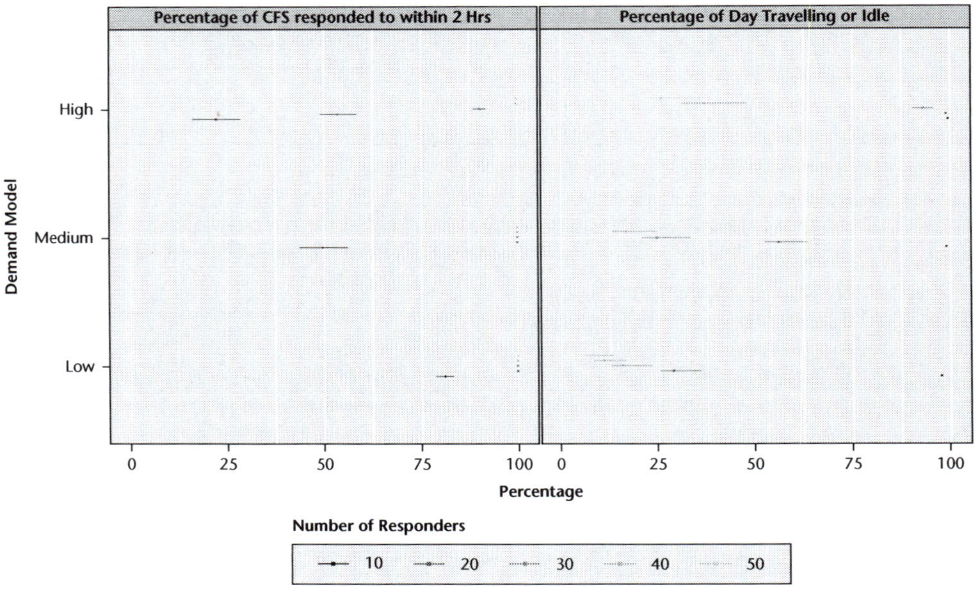

Figure 23.4 Relationship between number of responders, percentage of calls responded to within two hours, and percentage of time spent travelling/idle, by demand scenario

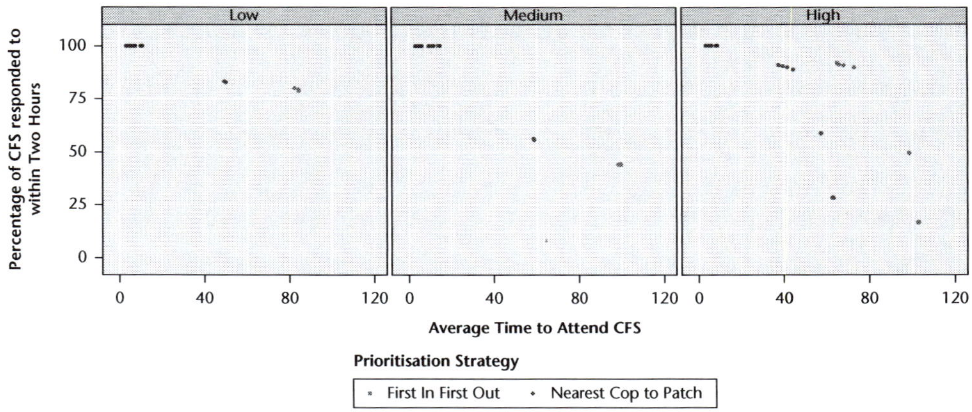

Figure 23.5 Relationship between number of responders, percentage of calls responded to within two hours, and average response time, by prioritisation strategy and demand scenario

caused by responders following the *FIFO* strategy increasingly playing 'catch up' as the simulated day progresses.

Idling strategies

Finally we examine the impacts of the four proposed idling strategies on effectiveness. This examination reveals several key insights. First, intuitively, when the percentage of time that responders spend responding is high, idling strategies have little impact on effectiveness.

This is simply a result of the fact that response vehicles spend very little time idling in order to pursue any of the selected strategies. Second, and likely more interestingly, while there is a very small advantage in response times associated with the *Random walk* over the *Static* strategy, the increased cost in fuel consumption is substantive. Both hotspot surveillance strategies prove to increase response times and fuel consumption. While this result may to some degree be a product of the distribution of CFS generated, using the current model it seems that the *Static* strategy whereby response vehicle remain stationary when not responding strikes a good balance between response times and resource consumption.

Discussion

In this chapter we sought to demonstrate how ABM might be productively used in supporting the decisions of crime scientists and practitioners who seek to devise responses to crime problems that are the product of a complex system. In doing so, we presented an illustrative model of police deployment, outlining its key components, and a series of simulated experiments carried out using it. It is our hope that this model not only provides an example of the type of research problem ABM are capable of supporting, but also the types of insights their application may provide.

While ABMs do not seek to replace existing analytical methods, they do provide new means to support theoretical and empirical efforts, especially in areas of research where a more 'traditional' approach is hampered by logistical and ethical constraints. The model we constructed and utilised here demonstrated a range of overarching findings that were not immediately apparent when considering the CFS problem, and that would likely be difficult to predict through logistically feasible empirical methods.

These findings mirror the difficulties associated with identifying crime-reduction techniques that work across diverse settings. It is our hope that ABMs such as the one presented here may offer some insight into the complex systems that generate crime events. Moreover, by providing the means to prototype candidate-response strategies, ABMs can identify those that are likely to be most fruitful with respect to disrupting said events. Subsequently, we might reasonably suggest that these strategies be field tested in an operational setting, with results from these trials informing both responses, and where appropriate new models.

In addition, our model demonstrates that in complex domains the task of devising appropriate crime-control strategies must be viewed as multiple-constraints problems.

Here we propose the ABM offers a unique means to cheaply and easily estimate the impact of differing strategies on these constraints. Ultimately however, it will be up to those at the coalface to decide which constraints are currently most important.

In concluding, we note an observation, which we consistently make in conceiving, designing and constructing ABM of crime problems. The construction of the model is, in and of itself, a powerful tool for promoting the rigour with which one considers a particular problem. To construct an ABM, one must be capable of effectively translating a mental model of the world into a computational one – this process rapidly uncovers any weaknesses in one's understanding and conception of the world. It is this process that 'enforces a scientific habit of mind' (Epstein, 2008, 1.16) – a disposition that all problem-oriented crime scientists should strive to maintain.

Note

1 Car icon made by Freepik from www.flaticon.com.

References

Birks, D. & Davies, T. (2017). Street network structure and crime risk: an agent-based investigation of the encounter and enclosure hypotheses. *Criminology, 55*(4), 900–937.

Birks, D., Townsley, M., & Stewart, A. (2012). Generative models of crime: using simulation to test criminological theory. *Criminology, 50*, 221–254.

Birks, D., Townsley, M., & Stewart, A. (2014). Emergent regularities of interpersonal victimization: an agent-based investigation. *Journal of Research in Crime and Delinquency, 51*(1), 119–140.

Bosse, T., Elffers, H., & Gerritsen, C. (2010). Simulating the dynamical interaction of offenders, targets and guardians. *Crime Patterns and Analysis, 3*(1), 51–66.

Brantingham, P. & Brantingham, P. (2004). Computer simulation as a tool for environmental criminologists. *Security Journal, 17*(1), 21–30.

Brantingham, P., Glasser, U., Kinney, B., Singh, K., & Vajihollahi, M. (2005a). A computational model for simulating spatial and temporal aspects of crime in urban environments. *IEEE International Conference on Systems, Man, and Cybernetics, 4*, 3667–3674.

Brantingham, P., Glasser, U., Kinney, B., Singh, K., & Vajihollahi, M. (2005b). Modelling urban crime patterns: viewing multi-agent systems as abstract state machines. *Proceedings of the 12th International Workshop on Abstract State Machines*, 101–117.

Brantingham, P. J. & Tita, G. (2008). Offender mobility and crime pattern formation from first principles. In L. Liu & J. Eck (Eds). *Artificial Crime Analysis Systems: Using Computer Simulations and Geographic Information Systems* (pp, 193–208). Hershey, PA: IGI Global.

Eck, J., & Liu, L. (2008). Contrasting simulated and empirical experiments in crime prevention. *Journal of Experimental Criminology, 4*, 195–213.

Epstein, J. M. (1999). Agent-based computational models and generative social science. *Complexity, 4*(5), 41–57.

Epstein, J. M. (2008). Why model? *Journal of Artificial Societies and Social Simulation, 11*(4), 12.

Groff, E. (2007). Simulation for theory testing and experimentation: an example using routine activity theory and street robbery. *Journal of Quantitative Criminology, 23*(2), 75–103.

Groff, E. (2008). Adding the temporal and spatial aspects of routine activities: a further test of routine activity theory. *Security Journal, 21*(1–2), 95–116.

Groff, E. & Birks, D. 2008. Simulating crime prevention strategies: a look at the possibilities. *Policing: A Journal of Policy and Practice, 1*(0): 1–10.

Hill J. F., Johnson S. J., & Borrion H. (2013). Potential uses of computer agent-based simulation modeling in the evaluation of wildlife poaching, In A. Lemieux (Ed.) *Situational Prevention of Poaching*. London: Routledge.

Laycock, G. (2002). Methodological issues in working with policy advisers and practitioners. In N. Tilley (Ed.) *Analysis for Crime Prevention*, Volume 13 of Crime Prevention Studies (pp. 205–237) Monsey, NY: Criminal Justice Press.

Malleson, N. & Brantingham, P. L. (2009). Prototype burglary simulations for crime reduction and forecasting. *Crime Patterns and Analysis, 2*(1), 47–65.

Malleson, N., See, L., Evans, A., & Heppenstall, A. (2012). Implementing comprehensive offender behaviour in a realistic agent-based model of burglary. *Simulation, 88*(1), 50–71.

Marchione, E., Johnson, S., & Wilson, A. (2014). Modelling maritime piracy: a spatial approach. *Journal of Artificial Societies and Social Simulation, 17*(2), 9. http://jasss.soc.surrey.ac.uk/17/2/9.html. DOI: 10.18564/jasss.2477.

Melo, A., Belchior, M., & Furtado, V. (2006). Analyzing police patrol routes by simulating the physical reorganization of agents. In *Multi-Agent-Based Simulation VI* (pp. 99–114). Berlin, Heidelberg: Springer.

Merton, R. K. (1936) The unanticipated consequences of purposive social action. *American Sociological Review, 1*(6), 894–904. DOI :10.2307/2084615.

Pawson, R. & Tilley, N. (1997). *Realistic Evaluation*. New York: Sage Publications.

Townsley, M. & Birks, D. J. (2008). Building better crime simulations: systematic replication and the introduction of incremental complexity. *Journal of Experimental Criminology, 4*(3), 309–333.

Wang, X., Liu, L., & Eck, J. (2008). Crime simulation using GIS and artificial intelligent agents. In L. Liu & J. Eck (Eds) *Artificial Crime Analysis Systems: Using Computer Simulations and Geographic Information Systems* (pp. 209–225). Singapore: Idea Group Inc.

Weisburd, D., Braga, A. A., Groff, E. R., & Wooditch, A. (2017). Can hot spots policing reduce crime in urban areas? an agent-based simulation. *Criminology, 55*(1), 137–173.

Zhang, Y. & Brown, D. E. (2013). Police patrol districting method and simulation evaluation using agent-based model & GIS. *Security Informatics, 2*(1), 1–13.

Appendix

Table 23.2 Low-demand scenario

Idling strategy	*Number of responders*	*Prioritisation strategy*	*Mean response time (minutes)*	*Fuel per incident*	*% of time spent responding*	*% incidents responded to in 2 hours*	*Total fuel consumed*	*Total person minutes*
Static	10	FIFO	82.63	17.48	98.07	80.02	12,557.22	14,400
		Nearest	50.35	17.25	98.03	82.78	12,442.35	14,400
	20	FIFO	7.31	8.30	26.37	100	5,968.79	28,800
		Nearest	7.35	8.34	26.45	100	6,005.13	28,800
	30	FIFO	4.85	5.83	13.20	100	4,172.67	43,200
		Nearest	4.86	5.85	13.36	100	4,223.71	43,200
	40	FIFO	3.77	4.75	8.54	100	3,416.78	57,600
		Nearest	3.81	4.79	8.65	100	3,470.54	57,600
	50	FIFO	3.13	4.11	6.20	100	2,970.67	72,000
		Nearest	3.12	4.10	6.18	100	2,963.85	72,000
Random walk	10	FIFO	82.58	17.92	97.92	79.86	12,823.18	14,400
		Nearest	50.16	17.64	97.96	82.62	12,708.69	14,400
	20	FIFO	7.07	36.03	25.75	100	25,892.56	28,800
		Nearest	7.01	36.13	25.56	100	25,873.93	28,800
	30	FIFO	4.69	55.20	13.04	100	39,811.16	43,200
		Nearest	4.67	55.47	12.96	100	39,804.99	43,200
	40	FIFO	3.71	74.82	8.49	100	53,789.20	57,600
		Nearest	3.74	74.67	8.55	100	53,772.74	57,600
	50	FIFO	3.15	93.58	6.26	100	67,788.63	72,000
		Nearest	3.15	94.46	6.20	100	67,792.82	72,000
Local hotspot surveillance	10	FIFO	84.43	17.82	98.06	78.70	12,844.25	14,400
		Nearest	49.87	17.69	97.97	83.15	12,697.79	14,400
	20	FIFO	8.12	36.23	28.53	100	26,116.70	28,800
		Nearest	8.16	36.56	28.38	100	26,114.60	28,800
	30	FIFO	6.20	55.37	15.51	100	39,651.11	43,200
		Nearest	6.29	55.27	15.73	100	39,824.78	43,200
	40	FIFO	5.58	75.16	10.89	100	54,228.52	57,600
		Nearest	5.59	74.43	10.86	100	53,540.12	57,600
	50	FIFO	5.25	94.84	8.32	100	68,206.09	72,000
		Nearest	5.32	93.47	8.37	100	66,982.65	72,000
Global hotspot surveillance	10	FIFO	84.31	17.88	97.95	79.33	12,834.49	14,400
		Nearest	49.32	17.74	97.46	83.19	12,713.80	14,400
	20	FIFO	11.10	36.77	36.04	100	26,432.62	28,800
		Nearest	11.10	36.76	36.16	100	26,508.56	28,800
	30	FIFO	10.58	55.89	23	100	40,302.53	43,200
		Nearest	10.72	55.91	23.21	100	40,264.72	43,200
	40	FIFO	10.52	76.02	17.07	100	54,623.38	57,600
		Nearest	10.51	75.91	17.04	100	54,510.74	57,600
	50	FIFO	10.30	94.89	13.45	100	68,399.13	72,000
		Nearest	10.22	95.43	13.33	100	68,673.30	72,000

Table 23.3 Medium-demand scenario

Idling strategy	*Number of responders*	*Prioritisation strategy*	*Mean response time (minutes)*	*Fuel per incident*	*% of time spent responding*	*% incidents responded to in 2 hours*	*Total fuel consumed*	*Total person minutes*
Static	10	FIFO	100.07	12.04	99.39	43.84	13,020.19	14,400
		Nearest	59.16	11.70	99.36	55.52	12,646.96	14,400
	20	FIFO	11.79	11.93	54.23	100	12,902.39	28,800
		Nearest	11.75	11.80	53.90	99.92	12,802.63	28,800
	30	FIFO	5.52	6.50	21.85	100	7,034.40	43,200
		Nearest	5.51	6.50	21.70	100	6,988.62	43,200
	40	FIFO	4.09	5.08	13.53	100	5,487.14	57,600
		Nearest	4.09	5.08	13.49	100	5,470.79	57,600
	50	FIFO	3.33	4.31	9.62	100	4,654.03	72,000
		Nearest	3.34	4.32	9.66	100	4,672.67	72,000
Random walk	10	FIFO	99.98	12.18	99.35	44.22	13,113.06	14,400
		Nearest	59.24	11.80	99.39	55.80	12,731.23	14,400
	20	FIFO	11.09	23.13	52.80	100	25,076.08	28,800
		Nearest	11.64	23.14	53.97	99.98	25,078.83	28,800
	30	FIFO	5.24	35.91	21.11	100	38,780.47	43,200
		Nearest	5.26	35.91	21.15	100	38,787.99	43,200
	40	FIFO	3.98	48.96	13.29	100	52,727.23	57,600
		Nearest	3.98	49.18	13.23	100	52,756.45	57,600
	50	FIFO	3.29	61.93	9.55	100	66,706.65	72,000
		Nearest	3.30	61.84	9.59	100	66,728.86	72,000
Local hotspot surveillance	10	FIFO	99.75	12.11	99.37	44.38	13,098.84	14,400
		Nearest	59.01	11.83	99.33	56.09	12,734.83	14,400
	20	FIFO	11.64	23.42	54.59	100	25,258.76	28,800
		Nearest	11.80	23.33	55.12	99.98	25,202.58	28,800
	30	FIFO	6.49	36.31	24.22	100	39,083.31	43,200
		Nearest	6.57	36.12	24.40	100	38,846.46	43,200
	40	FIFO	5.71	48.49	16.72	100	52,622.33	57,600
		Nearest	5.71	49.25	16.57	100	53,060.16	57,600
	50	FIFO	5.37	62.40	12.65	100	66,979.88	72,000
		Nearest	5.30	62.16	12.58	100	66,815.66	72,000
Global hotspot surveillance	10	FIFO	98.75	12.11	99.29	44.10	13,114.14	14,400
		Nearest	59.08	11.80	99.29	56.01	12,726.43	14,400
	20	FIFO	14.13	23.52	61.43	100	25,473.57	28,800
		Nearest	14.81	23.49	63.43	99.93	25,479.60	28,800
	30	FIFO	10.12	36.52	33.52	100	39,397.15	43,200
		Nearest	10.12	36.72	33.46	100	39,550.43	43,200
	40	FIFO	9.73	49.92	24.25	100	53,832.60	57,600
		Nearest	9.94	49.24	24.66	100	53,146.09	57,600
	50	FIFO	9.60	63.05	19.11	100	67,970.63	72,000
		Nearest	9.71	62.70	19.28	100	67,561.66	72,000

Table 23.4 High-demand scenario

Idling strategy	*Number of responders*	*Prioritisation strategy*	*Mean response time (minutes)*	*Fuel per incident*	*% of time spent responding*	*% incidents responded to in 2 hours*	*Total fuel consumed*	*Total person minutes*
Static	10	FIFO	103.38	6.21	99.78	16.68	13,416.61	14,400
		Nearest	63.45	5.90	99.76	28.37	12,718.40	14,400
	20	FIFO	99.36	11.93	99.34	49.18	25,781.04	28,800
		Nearest	57.80	11.64	99.26	58.53	25,136.13	28,800
	30	FIFO	68.45	16.21	93.20	90.77	35,055.16	43,200
		Nearest	40.09	15.87	92.09	90.38	34,394.02	43,200
	40	FIFO	5.40	6.37	32.48	100	13,718.66	57,600
		Nearest	5.35	6.32	32.51	100	13,682.65	57,600
	50	FIFO	4.01	4.99	21.61	100	10,769.12	72,000
		Nearest	3.98	4.96	21.52	100	10,706.71	72,000
Random walk	10	FIFO	103.64	6.19	99.77	16.66	13,439.73	14,400
		Nearest	63.20	5.92	99.78	28.54	12,747.80	14,400
	20	FIFO	99.04	12	99.24	49.34	25,953.29	28,800
		Nearest	57.97	11.80	99.28	58.60	25,342.12	28,800
	30	FIFO	65.37	17.48	92.48	91.78	37,696.93	43,200
		'Nearest'	38.15	17.39	90.40	90.93	37,497.77	43,200
	40	FIFO	5.14	23.10	31.54	100	49,741.53	57,600
		Nearest	5.13	23.04	31.55	100	49,709.89	57,600
	50	FIFO	3.82	29.42	21.04	100	63,588.69	72,000
		Nearest	3.82	29.55	20.97	100	63,608.41	72,000
Local hotspot surveillance	10	FIFO	103.47	6.21	99.78	16.71	13,438.69	14,400
		Nearest	63.04	5.89	99.77	28.25	12,752.64	14,400
	20	FIFO	99.46	12.05	99.26	49.24	25,967.70	28,800
		Nearest	57.79	11.80	99.28	58.54	25,351.24	28,800
	30	FIFO	66.28	17.53	93.25	91.29	37,803.79	43,200
		Nearest	41.98	17.45	93.98	89.99	37,676.71	43,200
	40	FIFO	6.40	23.16	36.46	100	49,980.82	57,600
		Nearest	6.42	23.09	36.66	100	49,958.88	57,600
	50	FIFO	5.38	29.63	25.79	100	63,884.92	72,000
		Nearest	5.45	29.56	26.02	100	63,736.18	72,000
Global hotspot surveillance	10	FIFO	103.16	6.22	99.75	16.45	13,454.27	14,400
		Nearest	63.20	5.89	99.75	28.42	12,745.03	14,400
	20	FIFO	99.32	12.02	99.28	49.34	25,962.72	28,800
		Nearest	57.69	11.72	99.22	58.46	25,332.02	28,800
	30	FIFO	73.33	17.60	95.70	89.81	37,937.27	43,200
		Nearest	44.72	17.51	95.99	88.82	37,784.29	43,200
	40	FIFO	9.40	23.55	47.87	100	50,854.94	57,600
		Nearest	9.37	23.61	47.67	100	50,975.89	57,600
	50	FIFO	8.86	29.81	36.59	100	64,442.82	72,000
		Nearest	8.82	29.81	36.43	100	64,407.39	72,000

24

Economic efficiency and the detection of crime

A case study of Hong Kong policing

Matthew Manning and Gabriel T. W. Wong

Society's goal of preventing crime has been propelled forward with the emergence of innovative scientists who focus explicitly on crime rather than criminality. Prevention techniques developed or adapted by this group have been shown to deliver immediate and sustainable reductions in crime. Context, however, is important as dynamic and highly variable environments are amenable to minor changes that may influence the outcomes of a policy or intervention. As promising as these techniques are, their effectiveness will always be measured against efficiency both within and between environments. Put simply, policy is shaped by assumptions that pitch inputs against expected outputs or outcomes.

In terms of economic analysis, cost–benefit analysis often comes to mind when we think about inputs (costs) and outcomes (benefits). Economics, however, can contribute more than this! In this chapter we demonstrate, using Hong Kong policing data, how an applied micro-economics technique ('data envelopment analysis') can be applied to identify the relative performance of organisational policing units where the presence of multiple inputs and outputs makes comparisons difficult. The technique addresses key policy requirements regarding the efficacy of crime prevention across districts with slight contextual variation.

Introduction

Criminologists' clear focus on crime and the criminal justice system is underpinned by a rich theoretical tradition which has identified potential causal mechanisms for the actions of both offenders and criminal justice agents. In addition, they understand the criminal justice system and the data issues faced by researchers. Economists' contributions to the study of crime and the agencies that attempt to prevent and control it would have been hamstrung had it not been for the tireless work of criminologists.

Bushway and Reuter disaggregate economists' contributions to crime and justice research in terms of: (1) theory – for example, economists' work on perceptual deterrence with an emphasis on the centrality of time discounting (e.g. Nagin, 1978, 1998; Paternoster, 1987); (2) technique – for example, specialised techniques used by econometricians, in particular, James Heckman's approaches to problems of selection (see Bushway, Johnson, & Slocum, 2007) and cost–benefit analysis (e.g. Aos, Phipps, Barnoski, & Lieb, 2001; Bowles & Pradiptyo, 2004); and (3) substantive expertise – for instance, economists' study of illegal markets, particularly drug markets (e.g. Cameron & Williams, 2001; Petrie, Pepper, & Manski, 2001; Reuter & Greenfield, 2001).

In this chapter we focus exclusively on technique.[1] Instead of adopting techniques that are well documented and understood by criminologists (e.g. multivariate time series analysis or cost–benefit analysis), we employ a less commonly used and understood technique, 'data envelopment analysis' (DEA) to examine the relative efficiency of organisational policing units in Hong Kong. Our goal is to show how DEA can be used to provide information to police and policy makers to help transform policing inputs (e.g. human resources) to produce more efficient and effective outcomes (e.g. detection of crime).

What follows is a brief discussion of: concepts relating to economic efficiency; a technique that measures economic efficiency; the method employed in this study; results; and the implications of DEA for the development of police management policies and procedures.

Economic concepts relating to efficiency

Measuring efficiency has two elements – technical efficiency and allocative efficiency. Technical efficiency refers to an organisation's ability to maximise output (e.g. rate of crime detection) with a limited set of inputs (e.g. police strength). Allocative efficiency reflects the ability of an organisation to optimise their use of inputs given their respective prices relative to a set of comparable organisational entities (Stone, 2002). The achievement of overall economic efficiency (EE) involves both technical and allocative efficiency. The 'production possibilities frontier' (PPF) is utilised to identify combinations of outputs that can theoretically be achieved by employing the same or similar amount of input. Before discussing how to measure efficiency we introduce a few important economic concepts.

Comparative advantage

Comparative advantage refers to the ability to produce a particular good or service at a lower opportunity cost[2] than others. That is, an organisation has a comparative advantage if the things that must be foregone to produce the goods or services are assessed to be of less value than those to be produced (Manning, Johnson, Tilley, Wong, & Vorsina, 2016). Within an organisation, specialisation amongst employees may also produce comparative advantage.

Division of labour

Economists use the term division of labour to describe situations where each worker specialises in separate tasks so the group can thereby achieve comparative advantage and produce outputs in an economically efficient manner (Hill, 2004). The benefits of specialisation through division of labour are deemed to allow: (1) tasks to be assigned according to individual preferences and abilities in accordance with the law of comparative advantage; (2) employees who perform the same task again and again to become better at it; (3) time lost to be reduced as employees work on tasks in which they have specialised knowledge and ability; and (4) the development and introduction of new techniques or tools that will permit employees, who specialise in the production of a given output or activity, to become more productive.

Production possibilities frontier (PPF)

Factors of production (i.e. the inputs that are used in the production of goods or services - land, labour and capital) and how they are used (which includes specialisation and division of labour) are essential to the effectiveness and efficiency of outputs or outcomes (e.g. reducing crime). The production possibility frontier (PPF) shows the various combinations of outputs that could be produced using the same fixed total amount of each of the inputs or factors of production. In the context of crime, this could comprise the amount of crime prevented (output or outcome) from a combination of interventions (inputs), or the number of interventions of a particular type implemented.

The PPF illustrated in Figure 24.1 shows the opportunity cost of a decision between two alternative choices (this could relate to, for example, two different types of crime prevention). The dots labelled A, B, X and Z show the combinations that can be made with respect to two fictitious options (1 and 2). Any points on the PPF line (Points A and B) are said to be efficient and an indication that scarce resources are being fully employed. These organisations are considered to be 'allocative efficient'. Any point inside the PPF (e.g. point X) is said to be inefficient because output could be produced more efficiently using existing resources or factors of production. Any point outside the PPF frontier (e.g. point Z) is impossible given current resource limitations. Only increases in technology will allow this point to be reached – this would be shown as an outward shift in the PPF curve (dotted curve line). The PPF also assists in making decisions regarding whether or not to specialise or how changes can be made to improve the economic viability of an activity.

The use of the PPF to illustrate the opportunity cost of a change in the quantity of output produced for a given intervention can be shown as a movement from point A to point B. The result is a loss of output of 25 Option 2s (from 65 to 40). Thus, the opportunity cost of this

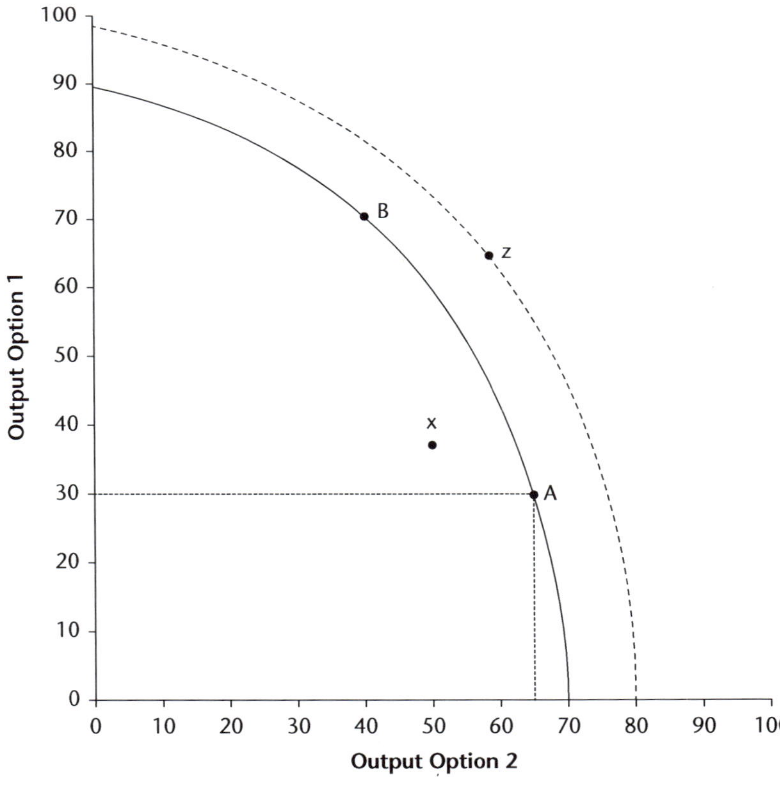

Figure 24.1 Production possibilities frontier

decision is 25 Option 2s. As a crude crime-reduction example such as responding to alcohol-related violence, the intervention (labelled A, B, X or Z in Figure 24.1) might represent a number of proactive police patrols routinely deployed to geographic hotspots of crime and outputs of the intervention might be detection rate of violence (Output option 1) and enhancement of sense of safety (Output option 2). The PPF, therefore, provides a systematic way – both conceptually and empirically – of estimating the impact of different allocation combinations. Of course, the scales on the x and y axes will be determined by the alternatives considered, as will the shape of the PPF, but the principle remains the same.

Measuring relative efficiency

Shortcomings of standard economic approaches

Standard economic approaches (e.g. cost–benefit analysis (CBA)) used to assess the relationship between costs and benefits are unable to answer some questions. CBA, for example, is unable to fully identify the mechanisms and underlying contextual conditions which drive the efficiency of the most economically efficient intervention (i.e. the intervention that is determined to be the most efficient within the sample). Without the PPF, it is not possible to set the given efficiency of an intervention against alternative possibilities. Hence, standard economic-analysis approaches do not show how programmes can be modified to improve their PPF or reach the PPF of the benchmark intervention. Caro et al. (2010) and Url (2001) therefore suggest that standard economic analyses (e.g. CBA) should be complemented with frontier methods such as DEA.

Models of efficiency

Input-oriented models

The input-oriented model allows us to measure technical efficiency attempts to estimate how inputs can be reduced to produce the same amount of output. Figure 24.2 provides an example that involves a police intervention with two inputs (i.e. number of detectives (x^1) and number of uniform police officers (x^2)) to produce one output (i.e. reduction of alcohol-related violence (y) – assuming constant returns-to-scale[3]). The fully efficient intervention represented by point F, which lies on the isoquant SS', provides a measure of technical efficiency (TE). If an intervention employs a quantity of inputs (defined by point P) to produce an output, technical inefficiency can be identified as the distance FP. This represents the amount by which the intervention could proportionately reduce the inputs without a reduction in output. Typically, this measure is expressed as a ratio:

$$\mathrm{TE}_1 = 0F/0P \tag{1}$$

where, TE is equal to 1 minus $FP/0P$. The efficiency score will always lie between zero and 1 (where zero indicates full inefficiency and 1 indicates full efficiency). This score provides a measure of the relative technical efficiency of the intervention. When the price ratio is known, an evaluator can measure the allocative efficiency, which is represented by the line AA' in Figure 24.2. Allocative efficiency is defined as a ratio:

$$\mathrm{AE}_1 = 0G/0F \tag{2}$$

where the distance between *GF* represents the reduction in costs that could theoretically be achieved if the inputs are reduced to an efficient point (*F'* in Figure 24.2). Finally, the combination of AE and TE produce a measure of overall EE. This is defined as a ratio:

$$EE_1 = TE_1 \text{ x } AE_1 = (0F/0P) \times (0G/0F) = (0G/0P) \quad (3)$$

where the distance between *GP* in Figure 24.2 represents an opportunity for reducing costs but not at the expense of outputs. A more comprehensive discussion of the proofs and theorems that underpins DEA can be found in Stone (2002).

Output-oriented models

The output-oriented model assesses by how much an output can be proportionally increased leaving inputs unchanged. Figure 24.3 provides a scenario in which an inefficient intervention, represented by a decreasing returns-to-scale technology[4] (*f*(*x*)), operating at point *P*. TE in Figure 24.3 is represented by the ratio:

$$TE = CP/CD \quad (4)$$

Figure 24.4 presents a scenario that involves two outputs (y1 and y2) and one input (x1). Assuming constant returns-to-scale, line *ZZ'* represents the unit PPF and point *A* highlights the inefficient intervention. Note that point A lies beneath the PPF (i.e. below the upper bound of the production possibilities) and the distance *AB* indicates technical inefficiency. This distance represents the amount by which outputs could be increased without the use of additional inputs. Output-oriented technical efficiency is presented as a ratio:

$$TE_o = 0A/0B \quad (5)$$

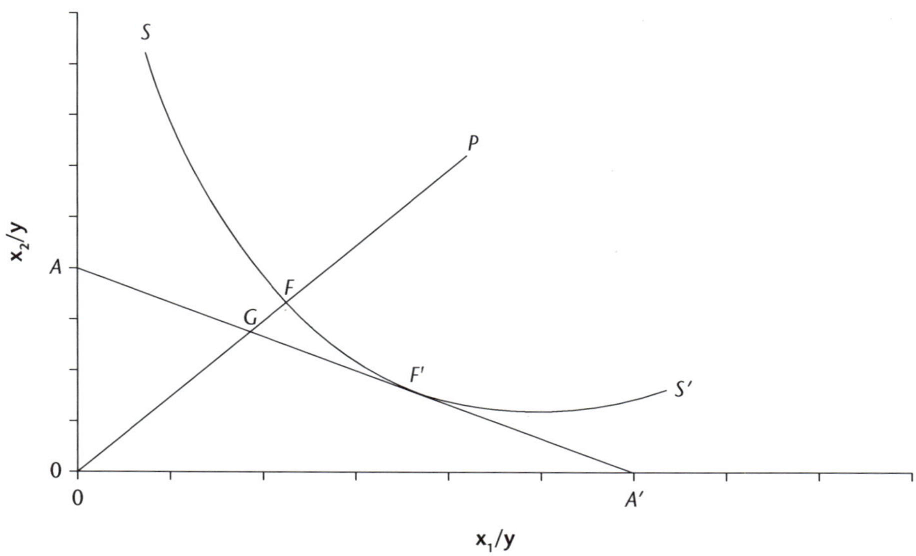

Figure 24.2 Illustration of input-oriented model

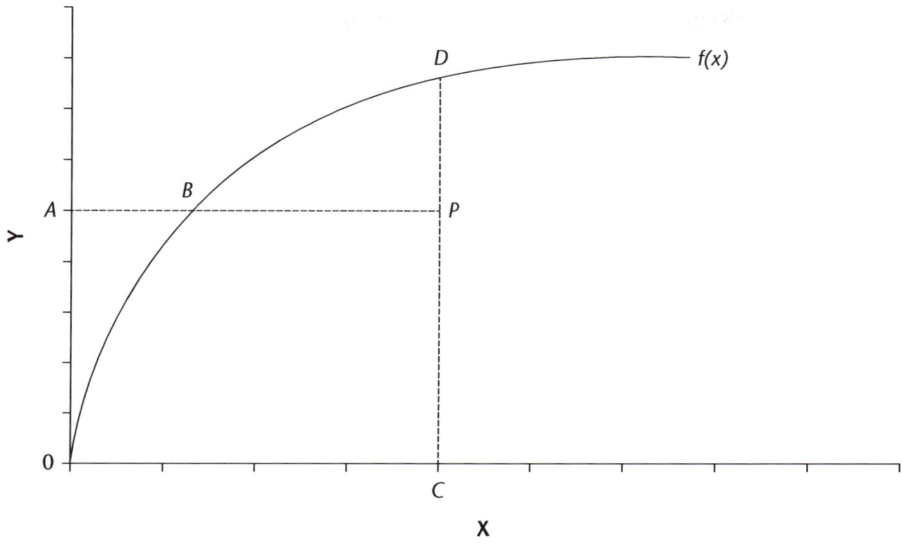

Figure 24.3 Illustration of the decreasing returns-to-scale technology

Drawing on price information, we can then produce the isorevenue line *DD'* and calculate allocative efficiency by the ratio:

$$AE_o = 0B/0C \tag{6}$$

Overall EE is represented by the following equation:

$$EE_o = TE_o \times AE_o = (0A/0B) \times (0B/0C) = (0A/0C) \tag{7}$$

Similar to the efficiency score produced in the input-oriented model the estimate is bounded by zero and one.

In summary, frontier analysis helps find out: (1) whether the allocation of resources in an organisation is efficient (through the use of input-/output-oriented models); and (2) how efficiency can be improved (by enhancing technical efficiency) (Manning et al., 2016).

Data envelopment analysis

DEA provides a mathematical programming approach to the construction of production frontiers that measure the relative efficiency of similar organisational entities, known as decision-making units (DMUs). Basic models of DEA require a choice of inputs or outputs orientation (i.e. minimisation of inputs to achieve given levels of output or maximisation of outputs given the level of inputs utilised) and an assumption on the scale of input/output conversion (constant returns-to-scale (CRS) or variable returns-to-scale (VRS)). The original DEA-CCR model (Charnes, Cooper, & Rhodes, 1978) assumes a CRS – that is, one unit of input results in one unit of output. With an alternative set of assumptions, the DEA-BCC model (Banker, Charnes, & Cooper, 1984) adopts the VRS allowing the generation of DMU-specific scale-efficiency information for each DMU on the frontier. This can be characterised as either increasing returns-to-scale

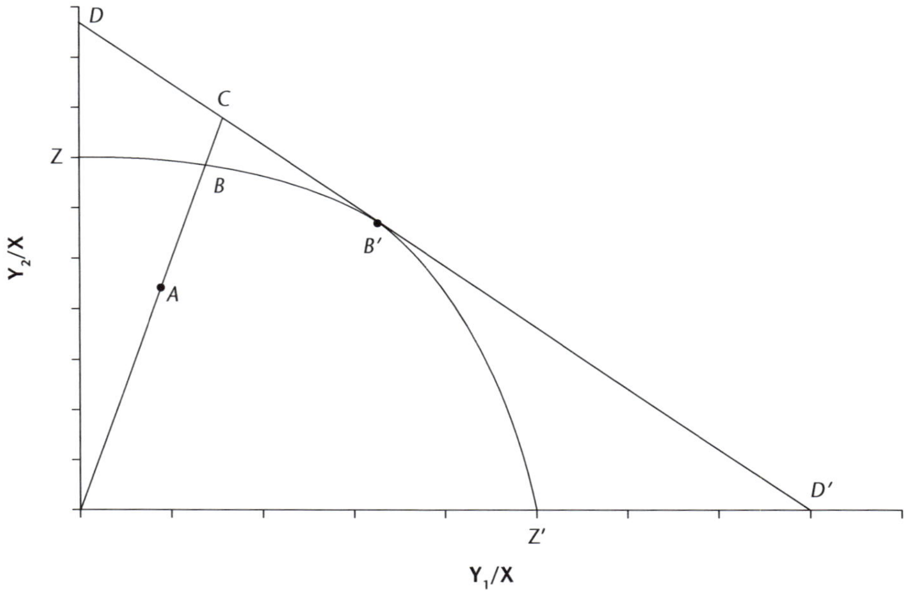

Figure 24.4 Illustration of output-oriented model

(IRS) (i.e. one unit of input results in more than one unit of output) or decreasing returns-to-scale (DRS) (i.e. one unit of input results in less than one unit of output). Such information allows the most productive scale size and allocative efficiency to be identified.

Police forces across the world are now beginning to see the benefits of examining the efficiency of their operations. DEA, in this context, has been undertaken in England and Wales (Drake & Simper, 2000, 2001, 2002, 2003, 2004, 2005a, 2005b; Thanassoulis, 1995), Spain (Diez-Ticio & Mancebon, 2002; García-Sánchez, Rodríguez-Domínguez, & Parra Domínguez, 2013; García-Sánchez, 2007, 2009), Belgium (Verschelde & Rogge, 2012), Portugal (Barros, 2006; Carlos Pestana Barros, 2007), the United States (Ferrandino, 2012; Goltz, 2006; Gorman & Ruggiero, 2008; Moore, Nolan, & Segal, 2005; Nyhan & Martin, 1999), Australia (Carrington, Puthucheary, Rose, & Yaisawarng, 1997; Hughes & Yaisawarng, 2004), Taiwan (Sun, 2002; Wu, Chen, & Yeh, 2010), Ankara (Akdogan, 2012), Israel (Hadad, Keren, & Hanani, 2013) and India (Verma & Gavirneni, 2006).

Choice of input and output variables used in DEA

Outputs of the police production process

Outputs of the police production process can be put into two broad categories – the control of crime and the maintenance of social order. This study focuses on outcomes related to crime detection.

Number of arrests and clear-ups are commonly used as output variables. These can be presented in absolute terms (i.e. the number of arrests/offence cleared) or in relative terms (i.e. the arrest/clear-up rates in relation to recorded crimes). Analysts may also distinguish crime types. With regards to arrests and clear-ups/detection, arrests have been deemed the worse option.

Diez-Ticio and Mancebon (2002), for example, identify two key limitations – the first relates to the potential inclusion of wrongfully arrested individuals or arrests of guilty individuals without sufficient evidence for conviction and sanction. The second relates to the risk that might manipulate data by making false (single or multiple) arrests rather than detecting crime. Because of these potential limitations, we used detection rate as the output variable.

Inputs of the police production process

There are two key types of input factors that affect the police production process: (1) resources (e.g. land, labour and capital); and (2) contextual conditions (e.g. population size, geographical size of the district). Resources tend to be under the control of the policing agency, while contextual factors tend to lie outside the control of the policing agency. The methodological foundations for DEA require that inputs satisfy the assumption of perfect substitutability – that is, a level of output (e.g. crime clear-up rates) may be produced using only each individual input or an infinite combination of all inputs (Kirigia, 2013).

With regards to resources, labour – as in the strength of police (sworn officers and civilians) and capital equipment (e.g. number of premises, vehicles and information systems etc.) are commonly included in efficiency analysis models. Depending on the type of model, these resources may be priced as expenses (for cost-efficiency analysis) or quantified as functional inputs such as labour force (for allocative efficiency analysis). In the former, where the analyst attempts to evaluate the relative cost-efficiency of a DMU (e.g. police station) in relation to the benchmark DMU/s, the expenditure/s are commonly captured under categories including, total department costs, employment costs, premises-related expenses, transport-related expenses and capital and other costs. In the latter, the unit used for each labour and capital input may vary. Earlier models (e.g. Barros, 2007; Carrington et al., 1997; Diez-Ticio & Mancebon, 2002; Gorman & Ruggiero, 2008; Hughes & Yaisawarng, 2004; Moore et al., 2005; Sun, 2002; Thanassoulis, 1995) have used the total number of police officers to quantify labour. Some of these studies calculate the ratio of the total number of police officers to total population of the district for the input.

Police strength may be disaggregated. One distinction is between sworn police and civilian/non-sworn police officers. Sworn positions include uniformed police officers who are responsible for general law enforcement duties such as regular patrols and response to calls for service, and detectives who investigate criminal cases. There may be other grouping methods to accommodate a range of specialised units, but the simple division between uniformed police officers and detectives allows analysts to distinguish the labour inputs according to their contribution to capturing offenders. Distinctions by functions, however, are not widely applied in the existing DEA models of police efficiency. This may be due to data limitations, where detailed information about the police strength in each DMU is not available, and/or because all police officers are deemed equally involved in producing outputs and outcomes. Civilian or non-sworn positions may include a range of roles from crime analysts, who translate crime data into information (e.g. crime trends and patterns), to forensic scientists who collect and analyse trace evidence. Since civilian officers, by the nature of their duties, are often considered to be less directly involved in the production process of crime clearance, they are sometimes treated as a separate labour input or omitted from the DEA model.

Capital inputs such as vehicles, evidence-gathering equipment, detection materials and premises represent the technology and non-human resources that are available for the police to generate outputs such as detecting crime or arresting offenders. One of the most commonly used capital inputs in allocative efficiency analysis is the number of vehicles available. Most capital inputs may be captured using policing expenditure budgets.

Contextual or external factors provide a picture of the underlying context in which the production process takes place. The inclusion of these variables may help explain why similar DMUs (in the sense that they use similar volumes of resource) have different relative efficiency scores. The general public can influence the production of detections, thus efficiency, in various ways. First, other things being equal, population size can be expected to correlate with the demand for police services, which may or may not be crime-related. Therefore, police stations located in a highly populated district are likely to spend additional resources dealing with police tasks that are not directly related to combating crime. Second, a larger population makes the identification and detection of suspected offenders more difficult. Typically, the probability of arrest falls when the population in an area increases. Finally, the general public may contribute to detection by collaborating with the police. Morris and Heal (1981) note that the public need to report crimes to the police for their detection. Assuming that the public's willingness and ability to report crimes do not differ across districts, the population size of the district may serve as an approximation of the public's contribution to the police production process.

Another contextual factor that varies across districts is the prevalence of crime. This input may be included in output-oriented DEA models for allocative efficiency of resources. Production models (e.g. Barros, 2006, 2007; Drake & Simper, 2005a, 2005b; García-Sánchez et al., 2013; Hadad et al., 2013; Sun, 2002) that take account of the number of various criminal activities that are recorded allow the analyst to evaluate the DMU's clear-up efficiency with regards to the given level of crime problem and volume of inputs used. This variable, when included as a direct input for the assessment of police efficiency, however, may violate the assumption of perfect substitutability and produce an inaccurate estimation of efficiency (Diez-Ticio & Mancebon, 2002). Specifically, the number of offences recorded often has a complementary relationship with the number of police, in that it may affect citizens' dispositions to report crime. It is suggested, therefore, that the influence of the prevalence of crime/level of crime in the district be captured under the crime clear-up rate/detection rate as the output in a DEA model.

Method

This study represents the first empirical examination of police efficiency in Hong Kong using an output-oriented DEA method. The study illustrates how DEA was employed to examine police efficiency and how results can be used from a macro level (i.e. to inform policy decision-making) and micro level (i.e. shape policing operations and interventions).

The case study: police efficiency in Hong Kong

Administrative data from the Hong Kong Police Force (Force from hereon) were used in this study. The selected variables for our DEA model include three inputs (number of uniformed police officers, number of detectives and population size of the district) and three outputs (detection rate of violent crimes, burglaries, and other crimes). Other potentially relevant variables such as information on the number of civilian officers and capital equipment employed were not included in this DEA analysis due to lack of data. Cost data of the DMUs (e.g. budget expenditure) were not available in publicly accessible administrative statistics and, therefore, could not be included in the analysis.

Background and contextual setting

The Force is responsible for maintaining a safe and stable society by: upholding the rule of law; maintaining law and order; preventing and detecting crime; safeguarding and protecting life and property; and working in partnership with the community and other agencies (Hong Kong Police Force, 2017). The Force is divided into several branches for the day-to-day policing in six regions, which include five land regions (Hong Kong Island, Kowloon East, Kowloon West, New Territories North and New Territories South) and the marine region. This study includes only policing across the land regions.

This study focuses on 18 (out of 21) districts. These 18 districts provide services to 98.9 per cent of all the population, and deal with more than 97 per cent of all the recorded crimes in Hong Kong. Table 24.1 gives an overview.

Results

Model selection

The relevance of the included input variables in the theoretical model for evaluating the efficiency of the selected DMUs (18 districts) is examined. Table 24.2 shows the included variables in each model and the percentage of DMUs whose efficiency scores change by more than 10 per cent when compared to the base model (Model 1). Our production model is extended stepwise by including an additional variable in each step.

Table 24.1 Characteristics of the Hong Kong police district in 2014

DMU	*Estimated population*	*Violence/ population in the district *100,000*	*Burglary/ population in the district *100,000*	*Other crimes/ population in the district *100,000*	*Detection rate of violent crime*	*Detection rate of burglary*	*Detection rate of other crime*
Central	104,900	390.85	82.94	2,297.43	0.62	0.25	0.32
Wanchai	154,400	373.70	64.77	1,950.78	0.65	0.27	0.44
Western	422,900	113.27	28.85	453.06	0.63	0.19	0.37
Eastern	587,800	88.30	14.46	527.39	0.55	0.20	0.39
Wong Tai Sin	469,500	132.27	31.52	590.84	0.69	0.07	0.37
Sau Mau Ping	361,500	141.91	18.81	622.96	0.62	0.10	0.42
Kwun Tong	717,100	117.14	26.64	537.86	0.53	0.12	0.35
Yau Tsim	122,200	600.65	139.93	3,214.40	0.57	0.15	0.40
Mongkok	191,400	410.66	155.17	2,252.35	0.54	0.13	0.44
Sham Shui Po	423,700	194.71	70.33	847.53	0.58	0.08	0.39
Kowloon City	387,600	139.32	46.70	623.32	0.63	0.12	0.36
Yuen Long	582,000	174.74	39.86	728.52	0.65	0.14	0.43
Tuen Mun	496,700	118.99	22.95	549.63	0.63	0.11	0.45
Tai Po	577,200	125.95	29.97	625.09	0.64	0.14	0.36
Tsuen Wan	291,600	151.92	29.49	733.88	0.63	0.27	0.42
Sha Tin	663,400	83.66	19.14	455.53	0.66	0.19	0.44
Kwai Tsing	493,200	109.49	20.68	467.36	0.69	0.17	0.49
Lantau	110,900	156.00	58.61	652.84	0.78	0.08	0.48
Mean		201.3	50.05	1,007.27	0.63	0.15	0.41
Excluded samples							
Border	39,100	243.0	125.3	1,355.5	0.75	0.08	0.48
Marine region	37,700	114.1	10.6	220.2	0.81	0.25	0.71
Airport	N/A	N/A	N/A	N/A	0.73	N/A	0.76

Table 24.2 Results of the model selection procedure

Variable	*Model 1 (base case)*	*Model 2*	*Model 3*	*Model 4*
Detection rate of crimes in district (DRC)	x	x	x	x
Number of detectives in district (D)	x	x	x	x
Number of uniformed police in district (UPO)		x		x
Population size of district (POP)			x	x
Percentage of DMUs whose efficiency scores change is ≥ 10%	N/A	50	11.11	55.55

Model 1 includes the number of detectives in the district (D). The input variable has been extended in step 1 with the addition of the number of uniformed police in the district (UPO) (Model 2). The extra variable was found to significantly contribute to the explanation of efficiency in crime detections. The input variable, population size of the district (POP), was introduced in Model 3. This was found to have a significant but smaller impact on efficiency in overall crime detections when compared to Model 2. The total model (Model 4), which employs all input variables highlights that the use of all inputs substantially contributes to the explanation of efficiency of crime detections.

Table 24.3 presents the results of the analysis of overall, technical, and scale efficiencies, as well as returns-to-scale results for the 18 police districts examined. Results indicate that 72.2 per cent of the evaluated DMUs are found to be overall inefficient with an average overall

Table 24.3 Efficiency of the 18 police districts

DMU	*Efficiency measures (%)*			*RTS*
	Overall efficiency	*Technical efficiency*	*Scale efficiency*	
Central	100	100	100	CRS
Wanchai	100	100	100	CRS
Western	75.3	91.2	82.6	DRS
Eastern	68.4	85.9	79.6	DRS
Wong Tai Sin	36.8	88.7	41.5	DRS
Sau Mau Ping	55.4	85.7	64.6	DRS
Kwun Tong	42.3	73.5	57.5	DRS
Yau Tsim	85.8	90.6	94.8	DRS
Mongkok	66.6	93.1	71.6	DRS
Sham Shui Po	100	100	100	DRS
Kowloon City	43.8	84.7	51.8	CRS
Yuen Long	41.3	90.4	45.7	DRS
Tuen Mun	51.8	91.7	56.5	DRS
Tai Po	52.4	89.2	58.8	DRS
Tsuen Wan	100	100	100	DRS
Sha Tin	59.3	95.6	62.1	CRS
Kwai Tsing	69	100	69	DRS
Lantau	100	100	100	DRS
Mean	69.4	92.2	74.2	CRS

Notes: CRS = constant returns-to-scale; DRS = decreasing returns-to-scale efficiency score of 69.34. In addition, 66.7 per cent of the 18 DMUs are technically inefficient with an average technical efficiency score of 92.24. Approximately 72.2 per cent were scale inefficient with an average scale-efficiency score of 74.23. Regarding the number of DMUs in each returns-to-scale category, there are five DMUs with constant returns-to-scale (CRS) and 13 DMUs with decreasing returns-to-scale (DRS).

Five out of the 18 DMUs are found to be overall efficient. They include Central, Wanchai, Sham Shui Po, Tsuen Wan and Lautau. These five DMUs are also scale and technically efficient. The Kwai Tsing district is found to be technically efficient but not overall or scale-efficient. The average scale-efficiency score of 74.2 suggests that there is further potential for efficiency improvement (approximately 25.8 per cent) if the DMU is to operate with CRS. Since these 18 DMUs are experiencing DRS, their performance could be improved by evolving their input-output combination and decreasing their current operating input levels.

Peer references

The reference sets and the number of times that a benchmark DMU is used as an indicator of efficient production or good performance for less efficient DMUs are reported in Table 24.4. The most frequently reported benchmark peers are Lantau, Wanchai and Kwai Tsing. These DMUs are similar in that they have a relatively high detective to population ratio, uniformed police to population ratio and high detection rates of the crime types examined.

Slack analysis

Results from the slack analysis (Table 24.5) reveal information on what areas and by how much could inefficient police districts improve so that they can be as efficient as their benchmark peers.

Table 24.4 Reference sets for the DMUs

DMU	*BCC model reference set with weights*	*Frequency of being chosen as a peer reference*
Central		1
Wanchai		10
Western	Wanchai (0.672); Lantau (0.328)	0
Eastern	Wanchai (0.640); Kwai Tsing (0.360)	0
Wong Tai Sin	Wanchai (0.036); Lantau (0.964)	0
Sau Mau Ping	Lantau (0.413); Kwai Tsing (0.587)	0
Kwun Tong	Wanchai (0.286); Lantau (0.442); Kwai Tsing (0.272)	0
Yau Tsim	Wanchai (0.283); Central (0.170); Lantau (0.547)	0
Mongkok	Wanchai (0.267); Kwai Tsing (0.180); Lantau (0.553)	0
Sham Shui Po		0
Kowloon City	Wanchai (0.311); Lantau (0.689)	0
Yuen Long	Wanchai (0.251); Kwai Tsing (0.357); Lantau (0.392)	0
Tuen Mun	Lantau (0.214); Kwai Tsing (0.786)	0
Tai Po	Wanchai (0.441); Lantau (0.559)	0
Tsuen Wan		0
Sha Tin	Lantau (0.179); Wanchai (0.456); Kwai Tsing (0.365)	0
Kwai Tsing		7
Lantau		11

Table 24.5 Slacks for each input and output for the inefficient DMUs

DMU	*Inputs*			*Outputs*		
	D	*UPO*	*POP*	*DRV*	*DRB*	*DRO*
Central	0	0	0	0	0	0
Wanchai	0	0	0	0	0	0
Western	8.478	143.486	282,747.605	0	0	0.047
Eastern	3.478	50.408	311,463.504	0.023	0	0
Wong Tai Sin	83.777	373.653	357,042.114	0	0	0.056
Sau Mau Ping	21.764	24.035	26,341.151	0	0.009	0
Kwun Tong	64.646	181.166	489,788.354	0	0	0
Yau Tsim	111.490	327.061	0	0.089	0	0
Mongkok	99.975	99.909	0	0.146	0	0
Sham Shui Po	0	0	0	0	0	0
Kowloon City	58.987	318.761	263,160.176	0	0	0.042
Yuen Long	99.707	331.966	323,689.383	0	0	0
Tuen Mun	52.399	0	85,263.584	0.017	0.023	0
Tai Po	86.302	203.875	447,112.569	0	0	0.053
Tsuen Wan	0	0	0	0	0	0
Sha Tin	35.689	189.661	392,975.432	0	0	0
Kwai Tsing	0	0	0	0	0	0
Lantau	0	0	0	0	0	0
Mean	40.37	124.67	165,532.44	0.015	0.00	0.011
Number of DMUs with slacks	12	11	10	4	2	4

Notes: D = number of detectives; UPO = number of uniformed police officers; POP = population size; DRV= detection rate of violent crime; DRB = detection rate of burglary; and DRO = detection rate of other crime

For output measures, the highest number of non-zero slacks comes from the detection rate of violent crimes and other offences, while the detection rate of burglary has the lowest number of non-zero slacks. In order to be economically efficient, four DMUs could increase their detection rate of violent crimes and other offences by 0.015 and 0.011, respectively. Further, two DMUs could increase their detection rate of burglary by 0.002.

For DMUs which are inefficient or weakly efficient (i.e. having slacks in inputs but not outputs) under the output-oriented VRS frontier model (i.e. being technically but not overall efficient) (e.g. Eastern in 2011), our results highlight estimated reductions in inputs which need to be accompanied by the estimated increases (for those who are inefficient) or maintenance (for those who are weakly inefficient) in detection rates if a police district were to achieve scale-efficiency (i.e. both technical and overall efficient). Holding the level of police services constant, a number of inefficient DMUs could modify the ratio of detectives per crimes reported. With regards to input measures, the number of detectives has the highest number of non-zero slacks, while the population size, as a proxy of the public's contribution to crime detection activities, has the lowest number of non-zero slacks. Holding the level of police services constant, 12 DMUs could reduce the number of detectives by an average of 40; 11 DMUs could reduce the number of uniformed police officers by an average of 125; and 10 DMUs could reduce their population in the district by an average of 165,532 residents without reducing outputs.

For an inefficient DMU to become fully efficient, it has to comply with the slack movement – that is, convert inputs into outputs based on the estimated reductions in inputs and increases in outputs, while simultaneously trying to achieve its optimal targeted input-output levels.

Information on such target levels and the percentage change when compared to the original input-output levels are provided in Table 24.6. For example, Kwun Tong district could improve its input-output conversion and reduce the number of detectives by 41.44 per cent, the number of uniformed police officers by 29.08 per cent and the public participation in crime detection activities by 68.3 per cent. These reductions in inputs would theoretically allow this DMU to become as scale-efficient as its peer references. However, caution is required in interpreting results on public participation in crime detection. Population size in the district, as a proxy of such contribution, is beyond the control of the police force. The target population sizes indicate reductions in reliance on public voluntary support and participation if a police district is to be efficient.

Conclusion

In this chapter, a simplified frontier-analysis method using a non-parametric distance function approach (DEA) was employed to evaluate the relative efficiency of DMUs (police districts) in the Hong Kong Police Force. We purposefully employed a very simple model for exposition purposes. For more detailed results, a sophisticated model may be employed. For example, this may involve a Malmquist productivity index or window analysis to examine efficiencies over time. Our results reveal a considerable divergence in efficiency rates across the DMUs

Table 24.6 Target inputs and outputs levels for the inefficient DMUs

DMU	*Target inputs (% change)*			*Target outputs (% change)*		
	D	*UPO*	*POP*	*DRV*	*DRB*	*DRO*
Western	106.52	448.51	140152.40	0.69	0.21	0.45
	(–7.37%)	(–24.24%)	(–66.86%)	(9.60%)	(9.80%)	(22.37%)
Eastern	129.52	564.59	276,336.50	0.66	0.23	0.46
	(–2.62%)	(–8.20%)	(–52.99%)	(20.55%)	(16.50%)	(16.31%)
Wong Tai Sin	49.22	282.35	112,457.90	0.78	0.08	0.47
	(–62.99%)	(–56.96%)	(–76.05%)	(12.86%)	(13.02%)	(27.91%)
Sau Mau Ping	88.24	475.97	335,158.90	0.73	0.13	0.49
	(–19.78%)	(–4.81%)	(–7.29%)	(16.75%)	(26.29%)	(16.68%)
Kwun Tong	91.35	441.83	227,311.70	0.72	0.16	0.47
	(–41.44%)	(–29.08%)	(–68.30%)	(35.95%)	(36.30%)	(35.91%)
Yau Tsim	82.51	415.94	122,200.00	0.72	0.16	0.44
	(–57.47%)	(–44.02%)	(0.00%)	(26.03%)	(10.12%)	(10.43%)
Mongkok	83.03	405.10	191,400.00	0.73	0.15	0.47
	(–54.63%)	(–19.78%)	(0.00%)	(34.32%)	(7.66%)	(7.37%)
Kowloon City	74.01	354.24	124,439.80	0.74	0.14	0.46
	(–44.35%)	(–47.36%)	(–67.89%)	(18.07%)	(18.08%)	(29.92%)
Yuen Long	94.29	462.03	258,310.60	0.71	0.16	0.47
	(–51.40%)	(–41.81%)	(–55.62%)	(10.69%)	(10.38%)	(10.63%)
Tuen Mun	102.60	545.00	411,436.40	0.71	0.15	0.49
	(–33.81%)	(0.00%)	(–17.17%)	(11.72%)	(28.91%)	(9.11%)
Tai Po	85.70	388.13	130,087.40	0.72	0.16	0.46
	(–50.17%)	(–34.44%)	(–77.46%)	(12.16%)	(12.10%)	(26.72%)
Sha Tin	113.31	518.34	270,424.60	0.69	0.20	0.47
	(–23.95%)	(–26.79%)	(–59.24%)	(4.60%)	(4.78%)	(4.71%)

within the Force. Approximately 72 per cent of the police districts are overall inefficient relative to their efficient peers. The efficiency rates suggest that it should be possible to achieve an improvement in the observed outputs (crime detection rates) via contraction of identified inputs. According to the results of our slack analysis, police managers should focus on modifying the use of discretionary inputs (number of detectives and uniformed police) and enhance their input-output conversion so that they can achieve CRS.

So why is this evidence important? The delivery of better and more efficient policing services can be achieved by employing methods that complement traditional economic analyses. Police managers and policymakers can objectively address key policy questions related to the efficiency of alternative policing/service delivery options and potentially optimise their production process when there are multiple inputs and outputs to consider. Additionally, legitimacy of policing can be enhanced when there is evidence behind the decisions made. For example, inefficient DMUs have the empirical evidence to support the redistribution of police patrols to highly populated areas where there is a greater concentration of crime.

Finally, this evidence can identify future areas that may be examined to allow for the introduction of new technologies to move the PPF outward, thus detecting more crime. As stated above, it is possible to extend this research by investigating productivity changes using panel data (e.g. window analysis) and examining the impact of non-discretionary (e.g. environmental and external) factors on the production process.

Notes

1 Readers interested in a full review of economists' contribution of the study of crime and its prevention are encouraged to read Bushway and Reuter (2008).
2 Costs are perceived as opportunity costs. That is, if the input is not used in one context it could be used in another (Manning, 2014). In other words, the opportunity cost of using an input is its value in its best alternative use.
3 One unit of input results in one unit of output.
4 One unit of input results in less than one unit of output.

References

Akdogan, H. (2012). The efficiency of police stations in the city of Ankara: an application of data envelopment analysis. *Policing*, *35*(1), 25–38.

Aos, S., Phipps, P., Barnoski, R., & Lieb, R. (2001). The Comparative Costs and Benefits of Programs To Reduce Crime. Version 4.0. Olympia, WA: Washington State Institute for Public Policy.

Banker, R. D., Charnes, A., & Cooper, W. W. (1984). Some models for estimating technical and scale inefficiencies in data envelopment analysis. *Management Science*, *30*(9), 1078–1092.

Barros, C. P. (2006). Productivity growth in the Lisbon police force. *Public Organization Review*, *6*(1), 21–35.

Barros, C. P. (2007). The city and the police force: analysing relative efficiency in city police precincts with data envelopment analysis. *International Journal of Police Science & Management*, *9*(2), 164–182.

Bowles, R., & Pradiptyo, R. (2004). Reducing burglary initiative: an analysis of costs, benefits and cost effectiveness. London, UK: Home Office, Research, Development and Statistics Directorate.

Bushway, S., Johnson, B., & Slocum, L. A. (2007). Is the magic still there? The use of the Heckman two-step correction for selection bias in criminology. *Journal of Quantitative Criminology*, *23*(2), 151–178.

Bushway, S., & Reuter, P. (2008). Economists' contribution to the study of crime and the criminal justice system. *Crime and Justice*, *37*(1), 389–451.

Cameron, L., & Williams, J. (2001). Cannabis, alcohol and cigarettes: substitutes or complements? *Economic Record*, 77(236), 19–34.

Caro, J. J., Nord, E., Siebert, U., McGuire, A., McGregor, M., Henry, D., . . . Kolominsky-Rabas, P. (2010). The efficiency frontier approach to economic evaluation of health-care interventions. *Health Economics*, *19*(10), 1117–1127.

Carrington, R., Puthucheary, N., Rose, D., & Yaisawarng, S. (1997). Performance measurement in government service provision: the case of police services in New South Wales. *Journal of Productivity Analysis, 8*(4), 415–430.

Charnes, A., Cooper, W. W., & Rhodes, E. (1978). Measuring the efficiency of decision making units. *European Journal of Operational Research, 2*(6), 429–444.

Coase, R. H. (1978). Economics and contiguous disciplines. *The Journal of Legal Studies*, 7, 201–211.

Coelli, T. (1996). *A Guide to DEAP Version 2.1: A Data Envelopment Analysis (Computer) Program*. Armidale, NSW: University of New England.

Diez-Ticio, A., & Mancebon, M.-J. (2002). The efficiency of the Spanish police service: an application of the multiactivity DEA model. *Applied Economics, 34*(3), 351–362.

Drake, L., & Simper, R. (2000). Productivity estimation and the size-efficiency relationship in English and Welsh police forces: an application of data envelopment analysis and multiple discriminant analysis. *International Review of Law and Economics, 20*(1), 53–73.

Drake, L., & Simper, R. (2001). The economic evaluation of policing activity: an application of a hybrid methodology. *European Journal of Law and Economics, 12*(3), 173–192.

Drake, L., & Simper, R. (2002). X-efficiency and scale economies in policing: a comparative study using the distribution free approach and DEA. *Applied Economics, 34*(15), 1859–1870.

Drake, L., & Simper, R. (2003). The measurement of English and Welsh police force efficiency: a comparison of distance function models. *European Journal of Operational Research, 147*(1), 165–186.

Drake, L., & Simper, R. (2004). The economics of managerialism and the drive for efficiency in policing. *Managerial and Decision Economics, 25*(8), 509–523.

Drake, L. M., & Simper, R. (2005a). The measurement of police force efficiency: an assessment of U.K. Home Office police. *Contemporary Economic Policy, 23*(4), 465–482.

Drake, L. M., & Simper, R. (2005b). Police efficiency in offences cleared: An analysis of English 'Basic Command Units'. *International Review of Law and Economics, 25*(2), 186–208.

Ferrandino, J. (2012). The comparative technical efficiency of Florida campus police departments. *Criminal Justice Review, 37*(3), 301–318.

García-Sánchez, I.-M. (2007). Evaluating the effectiveness of the Spanish police force through data envelopment analysis. *European Journal of Law and Economics, 23*(1), 43–57.

García-Sánchez, I.-M. (2009). Measuring the efficiency of local police force. *European Journal of Law and Economics, 27*(1), 59–77.

García-Sánchez, I., Rodríguez-Domínguez, L., & Parra Domínguez, J. (2013). Evaluation of the efficacy and effectiveness of the Spanish security forces. *European Journal of Law and Economics, 36*(1), 57–75.

Goltz, J. W. (2006). Police organizational performance in the state of Florida: Confirmatory analysis of the relationship of the environment and design structure to performance. PhD, University of Central Florida Orlando, FL.

Gorman, M. F., & Ruggiero, J. (2008). Evaluating US state police performance using data envelopment analysis. *International Journal of Production Economics, 113*(2), 1031–1037.

Hadad, Y., Keren, B., & Hanani, M. Z. (2013). Combining data envelopment analysis and Malmquist Index for evaluating police station efficiency and effectiveness. *Police Practice and Research, 16*(1), 5–21.

Hill, L. (2004). Division of labour. Paper presented at the Australasian Political Studies Association Conference, Adelaide, SA: University of Adelaide.

Hong Kong Police Force. (2017). Force vision, common purpose and values. Retrieved from www.police.gov.hk/ppp_en/01_about_us/vm.html.

Hughes, A., & Yaisawarng, S. (2004). Sensitivity and dimensionality tests of DEA efficiency scores. *European Journal of Operational Research, 154*(2), 410–422.

Kirigia, J. M. (2013). Introduction to health services production and cost theory. In J. M. Kirigia (Ed.), *Efficiency of Health System Units in Africa: A Data Envelopment Analysis* (pp. 69–136). Nairobi: University of Nairobi Press.

Manning, M. (2014). Cost–benefit analysis. In G. Bruinsma & D. Weisburd (Eds.), *Encyclopedia of Criminology and Criminal Justice* (pp. 641–651). New York: Science + Business Media.

Manning, M., Johnson, S., Tilley, N., Wong, G. T. W., & Vorsina, M. (2016). *Economic Analysis and Efficiency in Policing, Criminal Justice and Crime Reduction: What Works?* London: Palgrave Macmillan.

Moore, A., Nolan, J., & Segal, G. F. (2005). Putting out the trash: measuring municipal service efficiency in US cities. *Urban Affairs Review, 41*(2), 237–259.

Morris, P., & Heal, K. (1981). Crime control and the police: a review of research. Home Office Research Study No. 67. London: HM Stationery Office.

Nagin, D. (1978). General deterrence: a review of the empirical evidence. In A. Blumstein, J. Cohen, & D. Nagin (Eds.), *Deterrence and Incapacitation: Estimating the effects of Criminal Sanctions on Crime Rates*. Washington DC: National Academy Press.

Nagin, D. (1998). Criminal deterrence research at the outset of the twenty-first century. *Crime and Justice, 23*, 1–42.

Nyhan, R. C., & Martin, L. L. (1999). Assessing the performance of municipal police services using data envelopment analysis: an exploratory study. *State & Local Government Review, 31*(1), 18–30.

Paternoster, R. (1987). The deterrent effect of the perceived certainty and severity of punishment: A review of the evidence and issues. *Justice Quarterly, 4*(2), 173–217.

Petrie, C., Pepper, J., & Manski, C. (2001). *Informing America's Policy on Illegal Drugs: What We Don't Know Keeps Hurting Us*. Washington, DC: National Academies Press.

Reuter, P., & Greenfield, V. (2001). Measuring global drug markets. *World Economics, 2*(4), 159–173.

Stone, M. (2002). How not to measure the efficiency of public services (and how one might). *Journal of the Royal Statistical Society: Series A (Statistics in Society), 165*(3), 405–434.

Sun, S. (2002). Measuring the relative efficiency of police precincts using data envelopment analysis. *Socio-Economic Planning Sciences, 36*(1), 51–71.

Thanassoulis, E. (1995). Assessing police forces in England and Wales using data envelopment analysis. *European Journal of Operational Research, 87*(3), 641–657.

Url, N. D. (2001). Technical efficiency, allocative efficiency, and the implementation of a price cap plan in telecommunications in the United States. *Journal of Applied Economics, 4*(1), 163–186.

Verma, A., & Gavirneni, S. (2006). Measuring police efficiency in India: an application of data envelopment analysis. *Policing: An International Journal of Police Strategies & Management, 29*(1), 125–145.

Verschelde, M., & Rogge, N. (2012). An environment-adjusted evaluation of citizen satisfaction with local police effectiveness: evidence from a conditional data envelopment analysis approach. *European Journal of Operational Research, 223*(1), 214–225.

Wong, K. C. (2015). HKP reform: the 1950s. In K. C. Wong (Ed.), *Policing in Hong Kong: History and Reform* (pp. 341–434). Boca Raton, FL: CRC Press.

Wu, T.-H., Chen, M.-S., & Yeh, J.-Y. (2010). Measuring the performance of police forces in Taiwan using data envelopment analysis. *Evaluation and Program Planning, 33*(3), 246–254.

25

No need for X-ray specs

Through-the-wall radar for operational policing

Kevin Chetty

Introduction

In the late 1880s, German physicist Heinrich Hertz applied the mathematical theories of James Clark Maxwell's work on electromagnetic radiation (Maxwell, 1873) to prove the existence of what we now know as radio waves. However, it was not until the early 20th century that radio waves found any useful practical applications when Guglielmo Marconi's pioneering work in wireless telegraphy (Marconi, 1897) allowed him to demonstrate the first transatlantic radio communication, which subsequently led to the 1909 Nobel Prize in Physics. At around the same time Marconi was experimenting with radio waves for wireless telegraphy, German inventor Christian Hülsmeyer built his *Telemobilscope* (Hülsmeyer, 1904) – a simple ship-detection device intended to help avoid collisions in fog. This technique of RAdio Detection And Ranging of objects (RADAR) represented the beginning of a new era of remote sensing that to this day has many important applications worldwide.

In the mid- to late 20th century, radar technology experienced a sustained and rapid growth within the military for applications in maritime and airborne surveillance, although its use for civilian applications was rather limited, focussing primarily on weather forecasting, air traffic control and aerial mapping. However, over the last few decades, the increase in low-cost computational power and commercial-off-the-shelf (COTS) hardware has driven the growth of radar technology in both civilian and domestic use. Applications range from safety systems such as: collision avoidance for boats and bikes (Hovenden, July 2015), and autonomous cars (Guizzo, 2011), right through to everyday smart objects that are controlled using human gestures (Baldwin, 2015; Pu et al., 2013). Radar systems are even being used as tools to study geophysical effects like the melting of the Antarctic ice shelf (Brennan et al., 2014) and avalanche flows (Keylock et al., 2014), and to identify debris falling on railway tracks (Coxworth, 2012)

The adoption of radar technology by the police and security services over the last decade has been especially noteworthy and various types of radar systems are now well established in the policing toolkit. These systems include: *ground penetrating radars* (Science, 2013) that can quickly search large areas for buried evidence such as bodies, weapons and other contraband; *perimeter surveillance radars* (Caris et al., 2015) for monitoring activity around, and breaches into, restricted areas within critical infrastructures; and imaging radars such as *holographic* and *ultrawideband* systems

(Skolnik, 1980) for detecting concealed objects under clothing. Speed cameras which employ *Doppler radars* to monitor roadway violations are an example of a large-scale adoption of radar technology by the police authorities. In 2014 it was estimated that there were 3,500 fixed installations and 2,500 handheld units being used across the UK.

This chapter is concerned with the use of through-the-wall (TTW) radar in operational policing. Firstly, in 'Radar fundamentals' I describe some basic technical principles that lay the groundwork for a non-specialist reader to understand the radar concept of operation. 'Sensing through a wall' then introduces the sub-field of TTW radar and outlines how major challenges to enable TTW 'vision' are addressed using well-established radar systems and techniques. This treatise also includes an overview of the latest breakthroughs that are expected to be integrated in the next generation of commercial TTW systems. TTW radar technology was originally developed for the military, and battlefield applications can have significantly different system requirements than those needed for operational policing. 'Through-the-wall radar in operational policing', therefore, outlines how TTW radar can meet the capability requirements for five scenarios within the context of operational policing: (1) building sweep (2) surprise entry (3) emergency planning (4) strategic planning, and (5) search and rescue. The subsequent discussion focuses on the importance of TTW radar in bringing about strategic operational benefits and discusses important ethical and legal issues which arise through the use of TTW technology in law enforcement. Finally, 'Through-the-wall passive radar' describes a novel TTW radar technology we are developing in the emerging field of 'passive radar', and 'Summary' provides a recap of the chapter.

Radar fundamentals

Radio waves lie in the lowest-frequency band of the electromagnetic spectrum and are defined as having frequencies between 10,000 Hertz (Hz) and 100,000,000,000 Hz (or 100 GHz) – see Table 25.1. The lowest-frequency radio waves are able to travel far distances, penetrate numerous materials, and can even bounce off the ionosphere to overcome problems associated with the curvature of the earth. As their frequency increases, propagating radio waves are subject to higher levels of attenuation – a process in which signal power is lost through both scattering and absorption. High-frequency radio waves therefore travel shorter distances and are less penetrative. However the amount of information which they can carry, as well as their precision for detecting objects is superior. Figure 25.1 shows the different levels of attenuation experienced by radio or radio-frequency (RF) waves as a function of frequency for three materials. Like all forms of electromagnetic radiation, RF waves travel at the speed of light, which is approximately 300,000,000 m/s.

Radars are used to survey an area of interest by transmitting a probing RF signal towards it. The signal is then scattered in all directions by physical objects in that space, so by detecting these reflections the radar is able to identify the presence of the objects, and in some cases gauge further information about them. In outdoor scenarios these physical objects (or targets)

Table 25.1 The electromagnetic spectrum

Frequency					
0 Hz	10^{10}Hz	10^{15}Hz	10^{16}Hz	10^{18}Hz	10^{20}Hz
Radio and Microwaves	**Infrared Radiation**	**Visible Light**	**Ultraviolet Radiation**	**X-Rays**	**Gamma Rays**

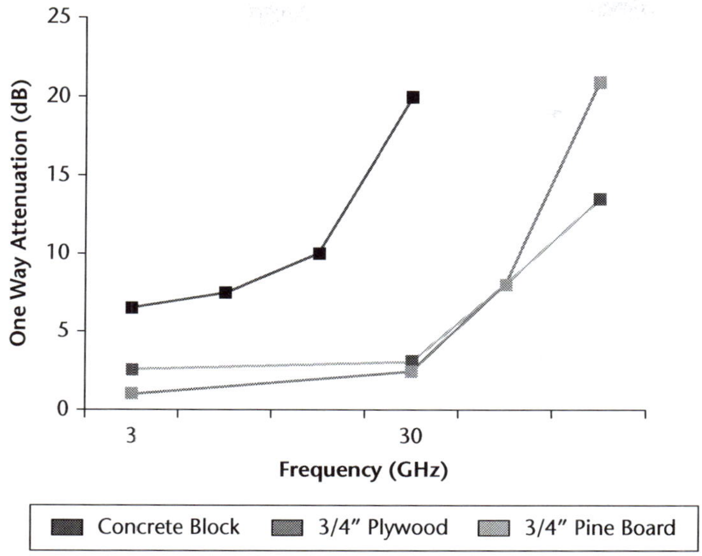

Figure 25.1 Attenuation properties of common building materials. (Image from Frazier, L.M. Feb. 18, 1997. *Radar Surveillance through Solid Materials*. Bellingham, WA: SPIE, 2938: pp. 139–146)

include trees, vehicles, aircraft and buildings; while in an indoor setting, targets may include people, small objects, the furniture and walls. The ability of the targets to reflect the RF signal back in the direction of the radar is known as its radar cross-section (RCS) and is dependent on a number of factors including the type of RF signal transmitted, and the shape, size, material and orientation of the target. The transmitted signal may be a continuous radio wave or pulsed (repetitive with a finite duration). If a pulsed signal is used, then the time-of-flight between transmission and reception of the echo can be used to give an indication of the distance (or range) of the target from the radar. The distance accuracy (or range resolution) of the system is dependent on the frequency capacity of the transmitted signal, a property known as the *bandwidth*, and this can vary from millimetre precision (high-bandwidth signals) to kilometre accuracy (low-bandwidth signals). When a target of interest is in motion (e.g. a flying aircraft or person moving around inside a room) a phenomenon known as the Doppler effect (Gill, 1965) acts to shift the frequency of the reflected signal by an amount proportional to the speed of the target. Detecting these small frequency changes allows the radar to distinguish between stationary and moving targets, and to determine their corresponding velocities. All radar systems draw on a vast pool of signal-processing techniques in order to understand the recorded signal data and achieve the desired functionality of the radar.

Sensing through a wall

A special case of radar detection occurs where an opaque barrier (such as a wall) exists between the radar and target of interest, and this adds a significant level of complexity to the radar-sensing scenario. Unfortunately the radar operator cannot simply turn up the signal transmission power to circumvent the wall as the power of the initial reflection resulting from the signal encountering the wall as it also penetrates through it will increase linearly and put a strain on the sensitivity of the radar for detecting the smallest target echoes (a term known as the *dynamic range*). Additionally, this high-strength *primary wall reflection* may saturate the receiver electronics in the radar.

Once the RF signal has breached the wall and interacted with the target (losing a significant amount of energy in the process), there is still the added complication of a portion of the reflected signal returning back to the receiver having to again penetrate through the wall. These processes result in the reflected target signal being many orders of magnitude weaker than the original transmitted signal. Operation of a TTW radar therefore typically requires that the system is placed directly on the wall to ensure minimal loss of signal power.

TTW radar systems have by no means reached their full potential and there is an ongoing requirement for improvements in the technology to enhance its utility for existing applications in security, surveillance, and search and rescue, as well as to find new and novel applications. To that end, many of the challenges which arise in TTW detection scenarios have been and continue to be addressed by the academic research community. TTW radar research brings together many different areas from the field of electrical engineering including radar hardware and RF circuits, signal and data processing, image formation and sharpening, antenna development, and electromagnetic wave propagation. It also draws on numerous research disciplines ranging from communications and computer science, to medicine and materials. In order to give the reader a sense of current capabilities and future possibilities, the following sections summarise the state-of-the-art in TTW radar technology and outline where important advancements are being made.

Radar systems and waveforms

The vast majority of TTW radar systems employ transmission waveforms that are either based on short ultrawideband (UWB) pulses (Nag et al., 2002) or longer continuous waves (CW) (Skolnik, 1980). CW waveforms are characterised as being always 'on', and have many typologies. In their most basic form CW radars transmit a stable frequency continuous wave which allows the application of Doppler processing techniques for sensing moving targets. However they are not able to accurately determine target ranges, so are only used in *Doppler radar* for detecting motion. Frequency-modulated continuous waveforms (FMCW) where the instantaneous frequency changes linearly across the waveform overcomes this ranging issue and has been investigated for TTW applications (Maaref et al., 2009). Similarly stepped-CW systems which transmit short CW bursts at progressively higher frequencies (Greneker Iii, 1998) and frequency-hopping radars which have the agility to move their operational frequencies back and forth (Hunt, 2009) have also been examined for application to TTW radar.

UWB radars (Sisma et al., 2008) have emerged as the technology-of-choice for TTW systems. They differ from conventional narrowband radar systems by transmitting signals across much wider frequencies, using transmission pulses which have very short durations (typically less than one nanosecond). These high-bandwidth RF signals give high resolution combined with good material penetration. UWB radars are defined as having a minimum bandwidth of 25 per cent the transmission frequency, which must also be at least 500 MHz. So, for example, a TTW radar which transmits an RF signal with a 4 GHz centre frequency would be required to have a minimum 1 GHz bandwidth to be classed as UWB. In addition to the superior range resolutions which are achievable with UWB waveforms, they are also scattered well by targets of differing scales, giving rise to improved target-recognition capabilities compared to narrowband systems. Disadvantages include the high costs of electronic components suitable for UWB radar, and the requirement to have expensive wideband antennas.

Target identification and localisation

The reflected signals detected by a TTW radar originate from numerous sources that include the initial wall it encounters and, on the other side of the wall, objects such as tables, chairs and other types of furniture, other walls, and people. To discriminate people from other signal scatterers, TTW radars make use of the fact that people are non-stationary and therefore induce a Doppler shift on the original transmitted signal, which can also give an indication of the speed of a target. Once target movement has been identified its location can then be determined. Two positioning measures are: (i) the axial range and (ii) the angle of the target to the radar. The axial range is simply the distance d between the radar and the target of interest and is determined by the time-of-flight between transmission of the signal, and reception of its echo. As described in 'Radar fundamentals', d has an associated uncertainty with it termed 'the range resolution' ΔR, which is given by equation (1)

$$\Delta R = c/2B \qquad (1)$$

where c is the speed of light and B is the bandwidth of the signal. In addition to the range resolution, an angular uncertainty in this measurement exists, as d can be any position on an iso-range contour within the beamwidth of the antenna as shown in Figure 25.2. This angular uncertainty can be minimised by using a narrower beamwidth antenna, for which the trade-off is a smaller surveillance coverage cell, or by employing direction finding (DF) techniques (Schell and Gardner, 1993) which typically require additional antennas and/or receiver channels, and thus increases the complexity of the radar system.

In many real-world situations there will be more than one person *in-theatre* so the ability to detect multiple targets within the surveillance cell of the radar is an important function. However, two targets separated by a distance less than the range-resolution capability of the radar cannot be distinguished from one another and would appear to the radar as a single target. In the case of a conventional radar system, which typically transmits signals of around 50 MHz bandwidth, equation (1) predicts a range resolution of 3 m which for certain operational

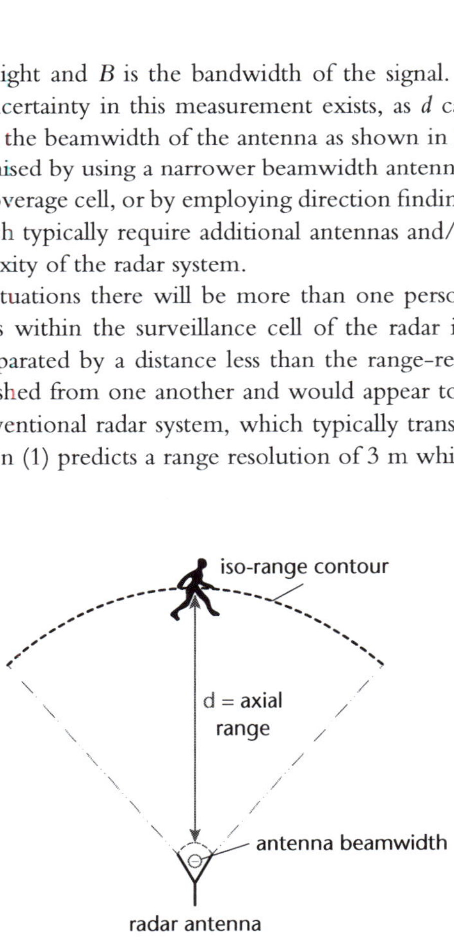

Figure 25.2 The distance *d* between the radar antenna and target of interest is determined by the time-of-flight between transmission and reception of the radar signal. However, within the beamwidth Θ of the transmitting antenna the target may be located at any point on an iso-range contour (at which every point has a distance *d*). This represents the angular uncertainty of the radar measurement.

applications would be rather coarse. However, the more complex and expensive UWB systems (which have minimum bandwidths of 500 MHz) would give better than 0.3 m range resolution.

Detection and localisation capabilities in TTW radar can be classified as either 0-, 1-, 2- or 3-dimensional (0D, 1D, 2D, 3D respectively). Zero-dimensional systems are simply motion detectors and do not output any range or angular information relating to the targets. These systems are typically simple CW radars. 1D systems are able to range targets but not localise them by an angle. The range-only capability of 1D systems allows the radar to distinguish between different targets (within the systems-range resolution) and coarsely assist with identifying if a target is within a specific area of a room, an adjacent room or further in the building. One-dimensional systems also usually consist of a single transmitter and a single receiver antenna. Antenna arrays used in 2D and 3D systems offer the ability to perform beamforming and DF capabilities. DF techniques are used to estimate range, direction and other parameter information of a target signal as it enters a receiver channel. There are numerous applications outside TTW radar research that require target positions to be derived and these have given rise to vast collections of DF strategies and algorithms.

3.3 Mapping building interiors

Two-dimensional and 3D systems are capable of imaging the structural features of a building and typically employ synthetic aperture radar (SAR) techniques. Compared to 1D systems, 2D systems such as those developed by Lin (Lin-Ping et al., 2005) and Nag (Nag et al., 2002) give improved localisation capabilities by measuring range and angular target information but are, however, subject to distortion effects arising from the projection of targets onto a 2D plane. Three-dimensional approaches such as those discussed in Ahmad and Amin (2008) are aimed at obtaining a volumetric representation of the scene of interest in range, and both azimuth and elevation angles, and can overcome the distortions associated with the 2D representation. However, they are expensive and are typically mounted on vehicles for real-world deployment.

Detection through multiple walls

In everyday domestic locations such as homes, offices, commercial buildings, shopping malls, supermarkets, nightclubs, etc. where TTW technology could be used by the police, the areas which require surveying are divided into different rooms. It is therefore a desirable capability for the TTW radar to be able to detect people not just in a single site obfuscated by a wall, but in adjacent or deeper areas which are also separated by a physical barrier. In these situations the radar signal may have to penetrate different types of materials, ranging from external brick walls to interior walls composed of plasterboard, wooden panels or breeze blocks. As mentioned in 'Radar fundamentals', the main challenge posed by the presence of a barrier is its ability to significantly reduce the power of the radar signal through attenuation. Penetration through multiple walls therefore severely degrades the sensitivity of radar for detecting targets. Furthermore, as shown in Figure 25.1 there is frequency dependence in the way different materials attenuate RF signals, making it difficult to tune TTW radar to operate optimally for all conditions. Some prototype TTW radars are beginning to employ dual- or tri-band architectures (Amin, 2011), or frequency-hopping techniques (Dona, 2013) in order to optimally adapt their operational parameters for improved sensitivity. These systems are also being aided by improvements in software-defined systems and reconfigurable hardware (Yunqiang & Fathy, 2009,) which are low-cost and can be bought off-the-shelf.

Activity recognition

When monitoring an area with a radar, there are numerous other non-stationary targets in addition to humans which could register as a 'detected person'. False alarms may arise from:

- Animals, e.g. cats and dogs
- Mechanical motions from machines, e.g. air conditioning units, fans, and washing machines
- Unmanned vehicles, e.g. micro-drones and radio controlled cars
- Objects falling over, possibly due to gunfire, vibrations from music, etc.
- Objects swaying in the wind.

It is therefore highly advantageous for a TTW radar to be able to discriminate humans from moving animals and objects. An emerging area receiving significant interest in TTW radar research is the use of micro-Doppler signature analysis, which allows for a more complete description of the dynamic properties of targets, and can be used for example to identify different types of human movements (Chen et al., 2014) and also to distinguish people from other moving targets such as animals or the blades of a fan.

Micro-Doppler is an additional effect to the main 'bulk' Doppler motion, whereby component motions on the main body of movement, such as rotations (e.g. the swinging limbs of a person) induce further Doppler frequency perturbations around the main Doppler shift. These perturbations, or micro-Doppler signatures, are characteristic to particular types of movement (Smith et al., 2010) and can therefore be used to provide extra information about the targets of interest, using classification techniques (Balleri et al., 2011).

Identifying the periodic frequency modulations around the bulk Doppler motion which represents a micro-Doppler signature is very much a challenge that falls in the domain of signal processing and machine learning. As micro-Doppler is essentially a temporal effect, the corresponding signal processing is based around a group of techniques known as joint time-frequency methods, the most common being the short-time Fourier Transform (STFT) (Allen, 1977). The spectrogram which is output from STFT illustrates how the reflected target frequency changes as a function of time. The spectrograms in Figure 25.3 show the micro-Doppler signature of a person as they are (a) walking, (b) running, and (c) shadow boxing. These signatures are generated from the swinging motions of the arms and legs, and swaying of the torso.

Recognising micro-Doppler signatures involves the application of algorithms that separate features according to their energy distribution. Examples include principal-component analysis

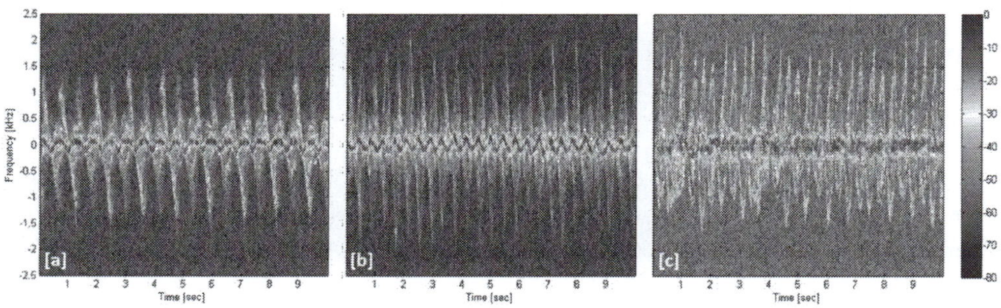

Figure 25.3 Spectrograms showing the radar micro-Doppler signature of a person as they are (a) walking, (b) running and (c) shadow boxing. These measurements were taken at University College London

and empirical-mode decomposition (Fairchild and Narayanan, 2014). Modelling approaches to investigate human micro-Doppler involve treating a person as a number of rigid body parts connected together by hinge joints, which when moving together may be considered as a series of non-rigid motions due to their complex articulation (Amin, 2011). Ram et al. (2010) present a simulation tool for generating micro-Doppler signatures of humans moving behind walls. Their approach entails combining standard human-modelling techniques with finite-difference time-domain simulations, and is validated by experimental data. The results suggest that although the returned signal power is severely compromised by the wall, the effect on the micro-Doppler signature is minimal.

Tracking

Tracking the movement of people as they move around a building from room to room could offer a wealth of information to aid tactical decision-making. Radar-tracking approaches associate consecutive observations of the same target into tracks which contain information about the target's position, heading and speed, and are informed by some model of the target's movement. However, unlike vehicle tracking where the motion of targets can, to a certain extent, be anticipated, the unpredictability in the way in which a person may move around a room or building is detrimental to a tracker, thus there are only a few studies to date concerned with target tracking of people. In recent years, though, many new radar target-tracking approaches have emerged in the literature (Yuan et al., 2011) and are now being investigated for the through-wall scenarios (Gennarelli et al., 2015, Xiaoli et al., 2014).

Signs-of-life detection

Detecting signs of life is an emerging capability in radar that focuses on identifying either the very small movements of a person's chest during breathing, or the beating of the heart itself. The high-range resolutions of UWB radars, or the superior motion sensitivity of Doppler radars are typically chosen for this job (Othman et al., 2013). In addition, narrow beamwidth antennas are used to avoid RF illumination of moving people and objects outside the area of interest. Furthermore, narrowbeam antennas have high sensitivities, a term known as 'antenna gain'.

TTW signs-of-life detection is becoming an area of increasing interest and Adib et al. (2015) have shown that their radar system named *vital radio* can detect chest-wall movements of a person standing still, immediately next to a wall. Moreover, the high motion sensitivity of an emerging radar technology termed *wireless passive radar* which we are developing in our lab (Chetty et al., 2012) is also showing the ability to detect signs of life through a wall (see 'Through-the-wall passive radar').

Through-the-wall radar in operational policing

The presence of obscuring barriers such as walls, doors and even curtains can severely impede the ability of the police to develop situational awareness in operational scenarios such as when planning to storm a building during hostage situations, or when monitoring criminals or terrorists cells over longer-term surveillance operations. However, the high cost of even the most basic handheld commercial TTW radar systems restricts their use to high-priority events, which limits their widespread application for tackling common low-level crime. A report released by the US Department of Justice in May 2014 estimated that unit costs of commercial TTW radar systems can range from $6,000 to around $50,000 (Ericson et al., 2014).

The use of TTW radar by the police globally has largely been kept confidential, although media-reported activity seems to be concentrated in the US. This secrecy is partly due to the high-profile or high-risk-to-life situations which TTW technology has typically been designed for, as well as the ethical issues surrounding its use. In January 2015, American newspaper *USA Today* reported that at least 50 US law enforcement agencies secretly equipped their officers with TTW radar 'with little notice to the courts or public' (Heath, 2015). Data documenting the number of systems currently owned by police forces globally and the frequency of their use is therefore very limited.

TTW systems used in law enforcement typically originate from the military and are not designed to meet the exact requirements for the policing operations within which they are expected to be deployed. For example, most TTW radars used in the defence industry only have a real-time output and cannot record, time-stamp or geocode the measured data – features which could be valuable for the prosecution in a criminal trial. Additionally, many existing systems require a skilled operator who can manipulate various radar parameters and clearly interpret the results. This does not easily translate to operation by an untrained police officer.

In this section, the current and future capabilities of TTW radar systems described in 'Sensing through a wall' are assessed against key practical and technical requirements in five exemplar police operational scenarios where TTW has brought or could bring a number of benefits. Table 25.2 illustrates the five scenarios and the essential and desirable requirements for each.

Scenario A: building sweep

Sweeping a building is a task that usually needs to be carried out rapidly and over many areas to identify if a person or people are present, e.g. when scanning a building for an intruder, looking for people trapped during a fire, or when searching hidden areas in a kidnapping. In these circumstances it is essential that the radar has some basic movement-detection capability, and is

Table 25.2 Through-the-wall system requirements for various scenarios within operational policing

Key: ✓✓= Essential ✓= Desireable X= Not required	*POLICE OPERATIONAL SCENARIOS*				
	[A] Building Sweep	*[B] Forced Entry*	*[C] Emergency Planning*	*[D] Strategic Planning*	*[E] Search & Rescue*
Examples	*Burglary in progress Hidden person search*	*House raid*	*Terrorist takeover*	*Hostage situation Snatch & grab mission*	*Building collapse*
Target identification	✓✓	✓✓	✓✓	✓✓	✓
Target localisation	X	✓✓	✓✓	✓✓	✓
Interior mapping	X	X	✓✓	✓✓	X
Multiple wall detection	✓	X	✓	✓✓	X
Activity classification	X	✓	✓	✓✓	X
Tracking	X	X	X	✓✓	X
Signs of life detection	✓	X	✓	✓	✓✓
Rapidly deployed	✓✓	✓✓	✓✓	X	✓✓
Mobile and lightweight	✓✓	✓✓	✓	X	X
Low cost	✓✓	✓✓	X	X	✓

lightweight and mobile. For increased functionality, the ability to traverse multiple barriers for a wide-area search would also be desirable. Moreover, to be viable for tackling large-scale, low-level crimes such as burglary or hunting a fugitive, a TTW system would have to be low-cost and useable with only some basic operator training. A commercial system which meets many of these requirements is the *Range-R* radar: a handheld TTW motion detector that weighs 0.5 kg, operates over 15 m and costs around £5,000 per unit.

Scenario B: forced entry

Forcing entry into a building, especially domestic dwellings, is frequently carried out in law enforcement to gather evidence and make arrests, and in 2014 it was reported that the Special Weapons and Tactics (SWAT) division in the USA carried out more than 80,000 house raids (Whitehead, 2013). Tools used to gain entry through doors include battering rams, axes, and devices that leverage the door itself, whilst in larger operations forcing entry into a building can be achieved through the use of explosives. In all of the above cases there exists a danger zone around the entry point which is blind to the police but where there is a high risk of injury or even death. TTW radars could therefore be used to ensure that no one is present within the danger zone immediately around the entry point. Barriers will typically involve doors that are composed of wood or high-density plastic, or brick walls. Important requirements include target localisation to ensure any targets detected are clear of the high-risk zone; target discrimination to distinguish people from animals such as dogs and cats; rapid and mobile deployment, and for regular use in tasks such as house raids; low-cost operation to ensure the systems can be economically rolled-out on a large scale.

Scenarios C and D: emergency and strategic planning

TTW sensing could aid the police in situations that require varying degrees of operational planning. These include both time-critical emergency scenarios where information needs to be acquired quickly, and events where time is available to build up a more detailed picture of theatre dynamics. Emergency situations constitute terrorist takeovers like the attacks seen in the Westgate shopping mall, Kenya; the Bataclan Theatre in Paris, France; and the Radisson Blu Hotel in Bamako, Mali. Here, the ability to quickly identify the positions of people over large areas offers significant operational advantage. Activity recognition to possibly distinguish between those who are moving around and making overt gestures, and those who are crouched or lying down in a submissive manner would also be highly advantageous, as would mapping a building interior to produce a 2D image of its layout prior to storming the building. However, both the time and complexity associated with these tasks means that they may not be achievable in emergencies but more suited to cases such as snatch-and-grab missions where the extra time available facilitates strategic operational planning. Furthermore, target tracking could be exploited to keep ongoing logs of who are victims and who are assailants, e.g. by following a hostage taker after identifying them through a window, or by making them answer a landline telephone.

TTW radars with the localisation, recognition, imaging, and tracking capabilities described would be considered as specialised and complex systems. They would therefore not be suitable for applications that have low-cost, lightweight, mobile and easy-to-use requirement specifications. However for scenarios 2 and 3, a vehicle-mounted TTW radar system operated by numerous people (possibly within the vehicle) seems feasible for the application.

Scenario F: search and rescue

The collapse of buildings is a relatively common occurrence around the world and can be caused by terrorist attacks, natural disasters such as earthquakes, landslides and monsoon rains, or simply a lack of structural integrity. The police and other first responders typically employ trained dogs to search for victims but this has a number of disadvantages such as a limited amount of time each dog can be effective. For a TTW radar to be of any use by the police in these situations, the essential requirements are to identify signs of life, and to be lightweight and rapidly deployable. As described in 'Signs-of-life detection', detecting heartbeats and chest-wall movements associated with breathing are at the cutting edge of radar systems and their use for search and rescue is at an early stage, with systems now only coming onto the market. One of these is the portable FINDER device (Finding Individuals for Disaster and Emergency Response) (Buck, 2015), which has been developed by teams based at the Jet Propulsion Laboratory and NASA in the US. Initial testing showed that the system can detect a human heartbeat buried beneath 30 feet of crushed materials, hidden behind 20 feet of solid concrete. In April 2015 the early prototype of FINDER (Figure 25.4) deployed in the aftermath of the Gorkha earthquake in Nepal was able to locate four men who had been buried under three f of mud and rubble for four days (Gough, 2015).

Civil liberties and the law

The use of TTW radar technology in law enforcement raises many legal and privacy issues, and there have been a number of court cases in the US where lawyers have questioned whether the technology can lawfully be used to scan a person's home. In 2001, police in Oregon used a thermal-imaging device to scan Danny Lee Kyllo's home to record how much heat was emanating from it, and were able to determine hotspots that were consistent with high intensity lights

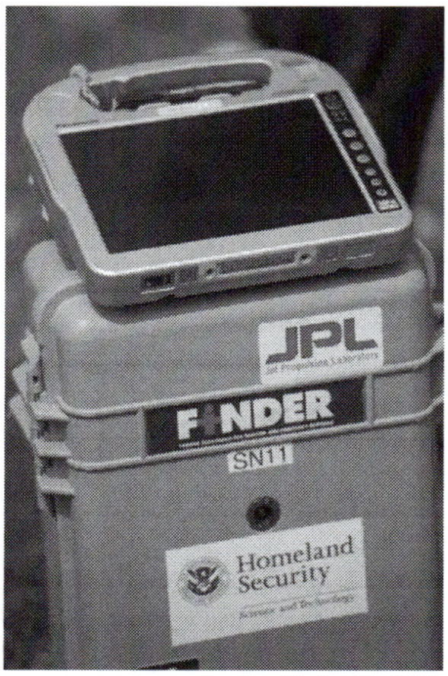

Figure 25.4 Finding Individuals for Disaster and Emergency Response – FINDER radar

used for marijuana growth. A warrant was then issued to search the home which then led to Kyllo being indicted on a federal drug charge. Kyllo unsuccessfully tried to suppress the drugs evidence seized from his home by arguing that the use of the thermal-imaging device was an invasion of his privacy. However, the US Supreme Court (2001) did rule that the search was unconstitutional and a violation of the Fourth Amendment, meaning that thermal cameras to monitor scan people's home could no longer be used without a warrant. Moreover, the court specifically noted that that ruling would apply to TTW-based radar systems that were being developed at the time.

More recently, in December 2014, the US Marshals Service tracked fugitive Steven Denson to a house in Wichita and used the Range-R TTW radar (Figure 25.5) to identify his presence in the building before apprehending him. Denson was also found in possession of two illegal firearms but attempted to overturn the additional gun charge, again arguing invasion of privacy. Though unsuccessful, his case led to significant national scrutiny and public debate. The Judge, Neil Gorsuch (Louwagie, 2014) stated:

> We have little doubt that the radar device deployed here will soon generate many questions for this court and others . . . New technologies bring with them not only new opportunities for law enforcement to catch criminals, but also new risks for abuse and new ways to invade constitutional rights.

Christopher Soghoian, the American Civil Liberties Union's principal technologist described TTW radar as being among the most intrusive tools which the police possess, and said 'The idea that the government can send signals through the wall of your house to figure out what's inside is problematic' (Lee, 2015). USA Today, which first reported the case, said that agencies including the FBI and the US Marshals Service, had been using radars since 2012. The Marshals Service had spent at least $180,000 (£118,000) on them, it said. But none of the agencies has made any public disclosure about how or when the devices would be used.

Through-the-wall passive radar

An emerging class of radar are 'passive' systems which use opportunistic transmissions (i.e. signals which are already present in the atmosphere) to detect targets (Howland, 2005). These can include signals originating from FM and TV base stations (Griffiths and Long, 1986, Howland et al., 2005) , GSM cell-phone towers (Zemmari et al., 2014), and wireless local area networks (WLAN) such as those created by Wi-Fi access points (Chetty et al., 2009). At UCL we have been developing a passive wireless movement detection (PWMD) radar that harnesses existing wireless network or mobile device signals to detect and classify human motions through walls. The PWMD platform (Figure 25.5) is built around a software-defined radio (SDR) hardware core, which is flexible and adaptable for use with many different signal sources, including WiMAX, Z-wave, Bluetooth, DAB and LTE.

Wireless Fidelity, or Wi-Fi networks have experienced a global and rapid rollout over the last few decades. An important benefit which a TTW Wi-Fi-based passive radar offers over its 'active' radar counterparts is that Wi-Fi access points are typically already located within building interiors and therefore are not subject to the loss in power experienced by active systems as they penetrate through a wall into the building. Passive radars also have excellent motion sensitivity. Two main disadvantages though are that: (i) the Wi-Fi signals transmitted are not under the control of the radar operator, and therefore not optimised for the application, and (ii) the requirement for passive systems to have two synchronised receiver channels: one *reference*

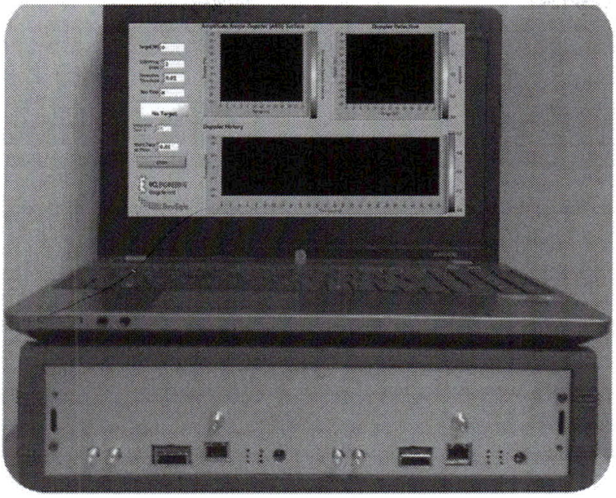

Figure 25.5 UCL's passive wireless movement detector

channel to monitor the communication signals emanating from the transmitters of opportunity, and one *surveillance channel* to record the reflections from the target of interest. The signals detected by both channels must be cross-correlated to produce range and Doppler information about the target.

A series of experiments were conducted to demonstrate the ability of the PWMD system for detecting targets through walls (Chetty et al., 2014), and were carried out within the bricked pavilion structure shown in Figure 25.6. Measurements were taken as a person moved around within the coverage area of the Wi-Fi access point whilst both the reference and surveillance receivers were located on the other side of the wall. The result shown in Figure 25.7 illustrates the detection of a person walking in the surveillance cell. Note that in this case the target velocity (plotted in terms of a Doppler shift) has a negative value as the person was walking away from

Figure 25.6 Experimental test site for demonstrating the through-wall detection capability of UCL's passive wireless movement detector

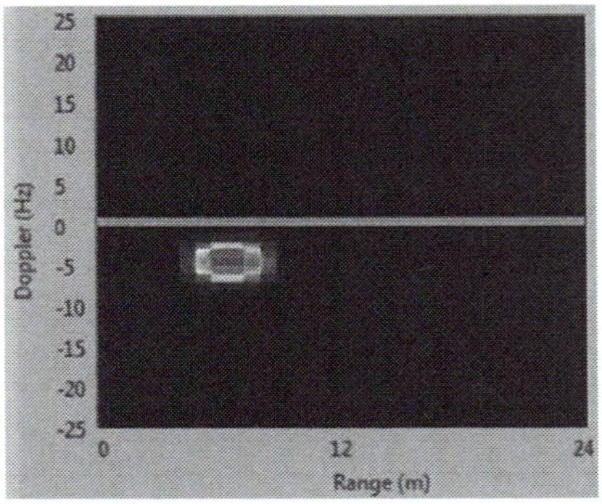

Figure 25.7 Detection of a person through a wall in the experimental test scenario. The Doppler shift on the y-axis indicates the velocity of the target, and the x-axis shows the range of the target from the surveillance receiver

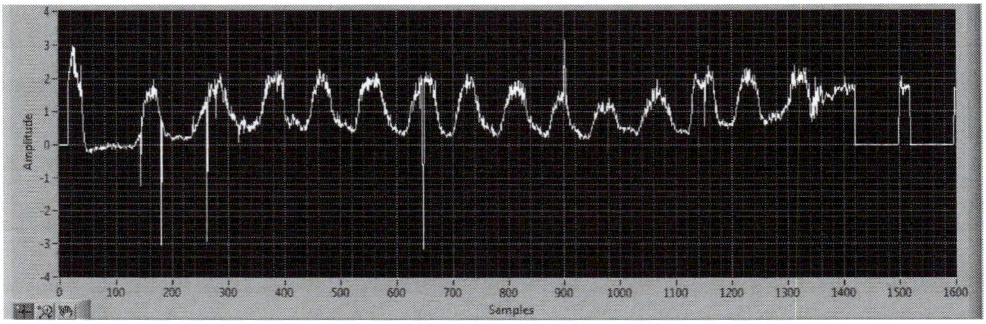

Figure 25.8 Through-wall breathing detection using UCL's passive wireless movement detector. The trace shows a sine wave pattern which corresponds to the target inhaling and exhaling

the surveillance receiver. Signs-of-life detection using the PWMD have also been examined in a similar TTW scenario and Figure 25.8 shows the detection results of the Doppler changes that occur with chest movements during breathing.

Summary

Detecting people and mapping interior structures through walls is a complex and challenging problem that has found a niche in the field of radar, but which also draws on numerous other disciplines as well as different sub-fields within electronic engineering. TTW radar is an example of a battlefield technology that is finding its way into civilian policing. However, the majority of systems have not been designed to match specific requirements in operational policing, and are used rather secretively to minimise public criticism and legal violations.

This chapter provides non-specialist readers with a grounding in the physics and engineering principles are the foundations of radar, and describes the added complexities when a wall barrier is introduced into surveillance and monitoring scenarios. It also summarises the state-of-the-art systems and outlines potential future capabilities which are currently being developed in both academia and industry for integration into the next generation of TTW systems. Armed with this background knowledge, five scenarios were defined in order to perform a critical analysis of how current and future TTW systems could be exploited for the benefit of operational policing. The main outcomes suggest that TTW radar could be a valuable technology in the policing toolkit but its embodiment would have to cover a few bespoke systems: from low-cost, mobile and lightweight radars – with basic motion-detection and ranging abilities for wide-scale deployment across the police to tackle frequent low-level crimes – right through to complex systems that are less manoeuvrable but are able to build up a fuller, more detailed picture of obscured areas in order to address more serious cases of criminality and urgent high-priority incidents. Furthermore, the way in which TTW radars are deployed and operate will need to match existing legislation, and ideally foster public acceptance in order to maximise their acceptability and effectiveness for tackling crime.

References

Adib, F., Mao, H., Kabelac, Z., Katabi, D. & Miller, R. C. 2015. Smart Homes that Monitor Breathing and Heart Rate. *Proceedings of the 33rd Annual ACM Conference on Human Factors in Computing Systems.* Seoul, Republic of Korea: ACM.

Ahmad, F. & Amin, M. G. 2008. Multi-location wideband synthetic aperture imaging for urban sensing applications. *Journal of the Franklin Institute, 345*, 618–639.

Allen, J. B. 1977. Short term spectral analysis, synthesis, and modification by discrete Fourier transform. *IEEE Transactions on Acoustics, Speech and Signal Processing, 25*, 235–238.

Amin, M. 2011. *Through-the-Wall Radar Imaging.* Boca Raton, FL: CRC Press.

Baldwin, R. 2015. Google's Project Soli to bring gesture control to wearables [online]. Engadget. Available: www.engadget.com/2015/05/29/atap-project-soli [accessed Feb 2016].

Balleri, A., Chetty, K. & Woodbridge, K. 2011. Classification of personnel targets by acoustic micro-doppler signatures. *Radar, Sonar & Navigation, IET, 5*, 943–951.

Brennan, P. V., Lok, L. B., Nicholls, K. & Corr, H. 2014. Phase-sensitive FMCW radar system for high-precision Antarctic ice shelf profile monitoring. *Radar, Sonar & Navigation, IET, 8*, 776–786.

Buck, J. 2015. DHS successfully transistions search and rescue tool that pinpoints buried victims. NASA Headquarters Press Office.

Caris, M., Johannes, W., Stanko, S. & Pohl, N. 2015.Millimeter wave radar for perimeter surveillance and detection of MAVs (micro aerial vehicles). *Radar Symposium (IRS)*, 16th International, 24–26 June 2015, 284–287.

Chen, V. C., Tahmoush, D. & Miceli, W. 2014. *Micro-Doppler Signatures – Review, Challenges, and Perspectives.* Institution of Engineering and Technology.

Chetty, K., Bo, T. & Woodbridge, K. 2014 Data processing for real-time wireless passive radar. Radar Conference, 2014, IEEE, 19–23 May, 0455–0459.

Chetty, K., Smith, G., Hui, G. & Woodbridge, K. 2009. Target detection in high clutter using passive bistatic WiFi radar. Radar Conference, 2009 IEEE, 4–8 May, 1–5.

Chetty, K., Smith, G. E. & Woodbridge, K. 2012. Through-the-wall sensing of personnel using passive bistatic wifi radar at standoff distances. *IEEE Transactions on Geoscience and Remote Sensing, 50*, 1218–1226.

Coxworth, B. 2012. Radar system could detect people who fall onto train tracks [online]. Gizmag. Available: www.gizmag.com/radar-train-subway-platforms/21028 [accessed Feb 2016].

Dona, G. 2013. Frequency Hopped UWB radar for through-the-wall breathing detection and area surveillance tracking. In *14th International Radar Symposium (IRS).* https://ieeexplore.ieee.org/document/6581687.

Ericson, L., Hayes, J., Huffman, C., Fuller, J. & Libonati, V. 2014. *Through-the-Wall Sensors (TTWS) for Law Enforcement: Use Case Scenarios.* Fairmont, VA: ManTech, for National Institute of Justice.

Fairchild, D. P. & Narayanan, R. M. 2014. Classification of human motions using empirical mode decomposition of human micro-Doppler signatures. *Radar, Sonar & Navigation, IET, 8*, 425–434.

Gennarelli, G., Vivone, G., Braca, P., Soldovieri, F. & Amin, M. G. 2015. Multiple extended target tracking for through-wall radars. *IEEE Transactions on Geoscience and Remote Sensing, 53*, 6482–6494.

Gill, T. P. 1965. *The Doppler Effect: An Introduction to the Theory of the Effect*. London: Logos Press.
Gough, M. 2015. NASA radar detects heartbeats under rubble, saves four men in Nepal [online]. Science Alert. Available: www.sciencealert.com/nasa-radar-detects-heartbeats-under-rubble-saves-four-men-in-nepal [accessed May 2018].
Greneker III, E. F. 1998. Radar flashlight for through-the-wall detection of humans. In *Proceedings Volume 3375, Targets and Backgrounds: Characterization and Representation IV*. https://doi.org/10.1117/12.327172.
Griffiths, H. D. & Long, N. R. W. 1986. Television-based bistatic radar. *Communications, Radar and Signal Processing, IEE Proceedings F, 133*, 649–657.
Guizzo, E. 2011. How Google's self-driving car works [online]. IEEE. Available: http://spectrum.ieee.org/automaton/robotics/artificial-intelligence/how-google-self-driving-car-works [accessed Feb 2016].
Heath, B. 2015. New police radars can 'see' inside homes. *USA Today* (Jan. 19).
Hovenden, C. 2015. First ride with the new Garmin Varia range of 'smart' cycling devices [online]. *Cycling Weekly*, July. Available: www.cyclingweekly.co.uk/news/latest-news/first-ride-with-new-garmin-varia-range-of-smart-cycling-devices-182166 [accessed Feb 2016].
Howland, P. 2005. Editorial: passive radar systems. *Radar, Sonar and Navigation, IEE Proceedings, 152*, 105–106.
Howland, P. E., Maksimiuk, D. & Reitsma, G. 2005. FM radio based bistatic radar. *Radar, Sonar and Navigation, IEE Proceedings, 152*, 107–115.
Hülsmeyer, C. 1904. The Telemobiloscope. *Electrical Magazine*. London.
Hunt, A. R. 2009. Use of a frequency-hopping radar for imaging and motion detection through walls. *IEEE Transactions on Geoscience and Remote Sensing, 47*, 1402–1408.
Keylock, C. J., Ash, M., Vriend, N., Brennan, P. V., Mcewaine, J. N. & Sovilla, B. 2014. Looking inside an avalanche using a novel radar system. *Geology Today, 30*, 21–25.
Kyllo v. United States (99–8508) 533 U.S. 27. 2001. United States Supreme Court.
Lee, L. 2015. Radar that 'sees' through walls raises privacy concerns [online]. BBC News. Available: www.bbc.co.uk/news/technology-30904218 [accessed May 2018].
Lin-Ping, S., Chun, Y. & Qing Huo, L. 2005. Through-wall imaging (TWI) by radar: 2-D tomographic results and analyses. *IEEE Transactions on Geoscience and Remote Sensing, 43*, 2793–2798.
Louwagie, L. 2014. Police radar carries risk of abuse, court says [online]. Courthouse News Service. Available: www.courthousenews.com/2014/12/31/police-radar-carries-risk-of-abuse-court-says.htm [accessed May 2018].
Maaref, N., Millot, P., Pichot, C. & Picon, O. 2009. A study of UWB FM-CW radar for the detection of human beings in motion inside a building. *IEEE Transactions on Geoscience and Remote Sensing, 47*, 1297–1300.
Marconi, G. 1897. Transmitting electrical signals. United States patent application. July 13, 1897.
Maxwell, J. C. 1873. *A Treatise on Electricity and Magnetism*, Oxford: Clarendon Press.
Nag, S., Barnes, M. A., Payment, T. & Holladay, G. 2002. Ultrawideband through-wall radar for detecting the motion of people in real time. *Radar Sensor Technology and Data Visualization*. Orlando, FL. SPIE, 48–57.
Othman, M. A., Sinnappa, M., Azman, H., Aziz, M. Z. A. A., Ismail, M. M., Hussein, M. N., Sulaiman, H. A., Misran, M. H., Said, M. A. M., Ramlee, R. A., Jack, S. P. & Ahmad, B. H. 2013. 5.8 GHz microwave Doppler radar for heartbeat detection. In *2013 23rd International Conference Radioelektronika*. https://ieeexplore.ieee.org/document/6530947.
Pu, Q., Gupta, S., Gollakota, S. & Patel, S. 2013. Whole-home gesture recognition using wireless signals. *Proceedings of the 19th Annual International Conference on Mobile Computing*. Miami, FL: ACM.
Ram, S. S., Christianson, C., Youngwook, K. & Hao, L. 2010. Simulation and analysis of human micro-Dopplers in through-wall environments. *IEEE Transactions on Geoscience and Remote Sensing, 48*, 2015–2023.
Schell, S. V. & Gardner, W. A. 1993. High-Resolution Direction Finding. In Bose, N. K. & Rao, C. R. (eds) *Handbook of Statistics*. Amsterdam: Elsevier Science Publishers.
Sisma, O., Gaugue, A., Liebe, C. & Ogier, J.-M. 2008. UWB radar: vision through a wall. *Telecommunication Systems, 38*, 53–59.
Skolnik, M. I. 1980. *Introduction to Radar Systems*. New York: McGraw-Hill.
Smith, G. E., Woodbridge, K., Baker, C. J. & Griffiths, H. 2010. Multistatic micro-Doppler radar signatures of personnel targets. *Signal Processing, IET, 4*, 224–233.
Whitehead, J. W. 2013. Are police in America now a military, occupying force? [online]. The Rutherford Institute. Available: www.rutherford.org/publications_resources/john_whiteheads_commentary/are_police_in_america_now_a_military_occupying_force [accessed May 2018].

Xiaoli, C., Leung, H. & Mao, T. 2014. Multitarget detection and tracking for through-the-wall radars. *IEEE Transactions on Aerospace and Electronic Systems*, *50*, 1403–1415.

Yuan, H., Savelyev, T. & Yarovoy, A. 2011. Two-stage algorithm for extended target tracking by multistatic UWB radar. In *Proceedings of 2011 IEEE CIE International Conference on Radar*. https://ieeexplore.ieee.org/abstract/document/6159660.

Yunqiang, Y. & Fathy, A. E. 2009. Development and implementation of a real-time see-through-wall radar system based on FPGA. *IEEE Transactions on Geoscience and Remote Sensing*, *47*, 1270–1280.

Zemmari, R., Broetje, M., Battistello, G. & Nickel, U. 2014. GSM passive coherent location system: performance prediction and measurement evaluation. *Radar, Sonar & Navigation, IET*, *8*, 94–105.

26

Electronic noses

The chemistry of smell and security

William J. Peveler and Ivan P. Parkin

This chapter describes the use of smell in detecting and preventing crime, and in particular the development of electronic noses (e-noses) for this purpose. The sense of smell and its relevance to crime and security are described, followed by an introduction to the design and applications of e-noses. Finally an in-depth case study of explosives detection with e-noses is presented.

What do we want to smell and why?

Smell is a powerful sense and many illicit materials or criminal activities can be detected *via* their associated odours. The nose is called on frequently in crime prevention to warn and inform practitioners of risks (for example, entering a potentially explosive methamphetamine lab) and crimes (perhaps alcohol on the breath or a rotting cadaver). The advantage of smell is that it allows us to detect things that may not be immediately visible to the naked eye, and it is often hard to contain or conceal smells (Pearce et al. 2002).

We perceive odour from the interaction between the vapour form of a substance – a volatile organic compound (VOC) – and the receptors of the olfactory bulb in the nose. Whilst the nature of these interactions is still the subject of great debate (Block et al. 2015; Brookes et al. 2007; Hettinger 2011), the result is the stimulation of a set of these olfactory receptors, triggering a response that the brain interprets as a smell or odour.

How much a VOC smells depends on how much vapour it produces and the sensitivity of the olfactory receptors to that vapour. The amount of vapour produced by a VOC at room temperature is called the 'vapour pressure' and typically given in Pascals (Pa), where the smaller the number, the less vapour is emitted. The larger the vapour pressure of a VOC, the greater the concentration of vapour generated in air at room temperature. Concentrations of odour are normally expressed as parts per million (ppm) or parts per billion (ppb), where 1 ppb is equivalent to 1 mg in 1,000,000 litres (very approximately one drop in an Olympic size swimming pool) and 1 ppm is 1,000 times more concentrated.

Many VOCs, such as putrescine in Table 26.1, are detectable by the human nose at their typical concentrations in the air because they have a high vapour pressure, or because our olfactory bulb is very sensitive to even small amounts, and they are deemed to have a detectable odour-threshold value (OTV). Humans are capable of detecting certain VOCs at concentrations as low as 10 ppb

Table 26.1 A selection of chemical odorants (VOCs) and their typical concentrations based on vapour pressures. DMDNB is 2,3-dimethyl-2,3-dinitrobutane, and is used in the US to tag military explosives. DNT is the breakdown product of TNT and is a key odorant in many kinds of explosives, due to its much higher vapour pressure.

VOC	*Odorant in . . .*	*Vapour pressure (in Pa at 25°C)*
Ethanol	Alcohol	5,950
Putrescine	Decaying bodies	310
Methyl benzoate	Cocaine	40
DMDNB	Plastic explosives	0.28
Dinitrotoluene (DNT)	High explosives	0.049
Trintirotoluene (TNT)	High explosives	0.0001

(for example, hydrogen sulphide – rotten eggs), but we cannot smell many compounds in everyday situations, because their vapour pressures are low and so the concentrations generated fall below the human OTV – there is simply not enough smell for us to be able to detect, or our noses are not responsive enough – examples include DMDNB in Table 26.1 (Leonardos et al. 1969).

To detect these hard-to-smell VOCs, canine noses are commonly applied, and less commonly rats, mice or bees have been demonstrated as potential chemical detectors (Furton & Myers 2001; McCabe et al. 2012). Detection dogs (sniffer dogs) are extensively used to locate concealed drugs, explosives or people. The canine nose is exquisitely sensitive and able to detect certain substances at one part in a trillion (0.001 ppb). This is because some breeds of dog have up to 220 million odour-receptor cells in their olfactory bulb, comprising some 50 per cent of their nasal area, compared to an average 5 million odour-receptor cells in a human. Furthermore, olfactory processing has been shown to take up almost one-eighth of a dog's brain (Furton et al. 2015). This is manifested, for example, in the ability of dogs to detect the compounds used to tag military explosives, DMDNB, at less than 0.5 ppb (Johnston 1999). Humans can only smell these same materials at thousands of ppb or higher.

As with the human nose however, dogs are still not sensitive to all substances, and require thorough training and expert handling for most effective application.

There are also other considerations when applying the canine nose to detect illicit materials. For example, dogs and their noses tire, thus they may only work a certain number of hours in a shift, because as they tire they lose their effectiveness and accuracy (Porritt et al. 2015). Furthermore, although dogs can indicate the source of an odour, they can provide little information on what that substance might be, other than something that they have been trained to detect. Thus, if a new threat emerges, the dog must be retrained with the smell of that item or material, limiting their usefulness in detecting "emerging threats" or non-standard contraband.

This also means that we do not know what the 'odour handle' for many substances is – for example it is known that dogs do not necessarily detect drug compounds themselves, but the smell of the solvents and decomposition products from the drug manufacture process. For example, methyl benzoate has been shown to be a key chemical signal for cocaine and piperonal is being investigated as a VOC odour for MDMA (ecstasy) (Furton et al. 2002; Furton et al. 2015). These odour signals can be very variable between batches, formulations and countries of origin, so it is hard to train for reliably.

To investigate this phenomenon, much analytical work has been done on the VOCs that are produced by drugs, explosives or other criminal objects or activities (Rosier et al. 2015). A discussion on the smells of explosives is presented later as a case study.

With better understanding of what VOCs law enforcement and security personnel need to detect, much work has gone into the development of "electronic noses" or "e-noses", by chemists and electronic engineers. These are machines capable of detecting a threat by sampling the air and performing some chemical test on what is present, to read out information to the operator, creating an artificial nose. Although they often cannot achieve the high sensitivity of a well-trained canine, e-noses can achieve satisfactory ppb detection levels of key odours. They have the advantage of not tiring, so can be run continuously, and can provide real-time information on any threats or illicit materials they might detect. Their small size and low power requirements make them easily portable, and thus available to a first responder at any time, even potentially in covert situations.

Networks of such sensors can also be set up across large areas to monitor the local atmosphere, and paired with CCTV and other imaging techniques to indicate the presence of, and identify, stationary and mobile threats (Swedish Defence Research Agency n.d.).

E-noses can be easily "retrained" to detect new odours simply and rapidly by uploading a few new files to their on-board database, and one device has the potential to act as, for example, a drugs dog, explosive dog, and cadaver dog all in one box.

To date, e-noses have been developed to detect drugs (Haddi et al. 2011) and explosives, alcohol, or contraband substances (Pardo et al. 2003). As well as their application for the detection of these specific odours of interest, e-noses can also be used to detect the absence of key smells, and have been applied to the differentiation of genuine and counterfeit high-value materials, such as wines and spirits or perfumes (Berna 2010).

The metrics used to assess an e-nose are its sensitivity and specificity to the target odours. The sensitivity is equivalent to the OTV – how little of an odour is required to trigger a response. The specificity is how well the e-nose can detect and report a target odour in the presence of other competing odours that may trigger a false positive.

How to build an e-nose

Workers in the field of chemistry have been building sensors and detection systems for vapours for many years. However, it is important to note the difference between a sensor and a test. A test is applied once and then read out, giving a snapshot in time, and may either need to be processed for re-use, or may simply be discarded. A good e-nose is a sensor – it gives real-time output in a continuous and re-usable fashion (Wolfbeis 2013).

The e-nose comes in many shapes and sizes, but has a few basic requirements beyond sensitive and specific odour-sensing element(s). These are: portability, air-sampling capability and an on-board computer to analyse the sensor signals and read out information to the operator on the presence or absence of any materials of interest (Figure 26.1). If we are interested in building a sensing network, then portability is less of a concern, but as a general rule these devices are designed to be as light and easy to carry as possible, for use by first responders and the military.

Air sampling – sniffing

The air sampler is a system that takes in air from the surroundings and passes it in a controlled way over the sensing elements. Relying on natural air currents reduces the volume of air that can be effectively sampled, effectively lowering sensitivity, and the variation in the natural flow of air may produce spurious readings from the sensor by preventing vapour samples moving over the sensors in a consistent fashion.

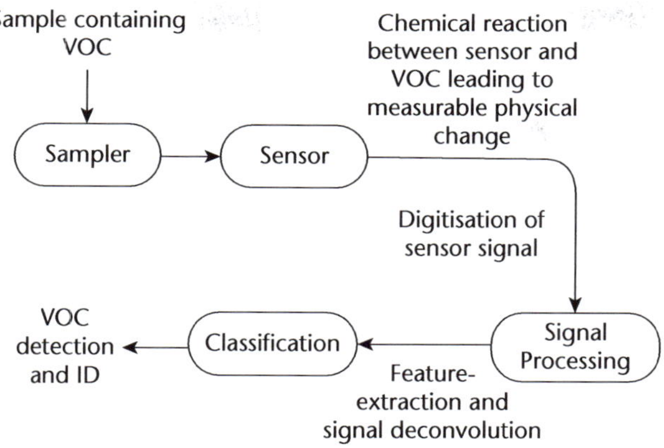

Figure 26.1 Scheme of an e-nose. A sampler sniffs the air and passes the sample over the sensor(s). Signals from the sensor(s) are then processed by a computer to provide information on the VOCs/threats present. Classification could occur locally on-board the device, or remotely

Two methods of sampling are routinely used. The first is constant flow, whereby a fan draws air in a steady stream over the sensor elements at a set rate. The rate of air intake affects how much air the device can sample, but the more air sampled, the less time a sample can dwell on the sensor, potentially lowering overall sensitivity.

The second method is pre-concentration, where a fan draws a set volume of air into a storage device, trapping any odorants, and this sample is then desorbed over the sensor. This latter method has the advantage of concentrating small amounts of material from large volumes of air, potentially improving the sensitivity of the e-nose. It can also then be adapted to sniff solid samples such as swabs used in airport baggage screening. However the downside to this system is lower throughput and non-continuous sensing, increasing the chance that a short-lived odour might be missed.

Odour sensing – smelling

The sensor elements are the heart of the e-nose – some chemical interaction must occur between the sensor and the odour of interest, and this affects a measurable response. The technical term for this process is *transduction*. The method of transduction can vary greatly, but in most e-noses it is a modification of the electrical, optical or physical properties of the sensor.

The construction of an e-nose sensor element can follow two models to obtain the desired sensitivity and specificity. The first is to use an instrumental technique that detects a signal associated with a particular molecule, such as its mass, charge or optical properties (examples include mass spectrometry, ion-mobility spectrometry or infrared spectroscopy) and compares the properties of an unknown sample with that of a database to obtain a match. This relies on highly specific molecular properties, but often utilises well-characterised laboratory techniques (Caygill et al. 2012).

The second approach uses a cross-reactive sensing array, mimicking the mammalian nose – rather than measuring exactly the properties of the unknown odour, with a single highly specific sensor it measures how it interacts across an array of different sensors and then matches this sensory pattern with a stored library of patterns (Albert et al. 2000). This approach can improve

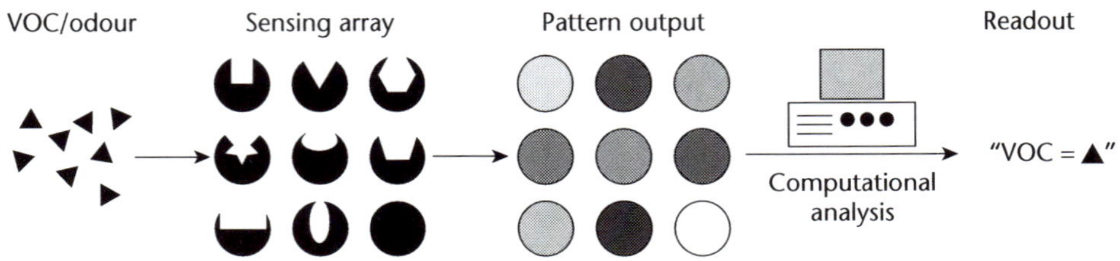

Figure 26.2 Schematic of array-based sensing illustrating the use of non-specific binding of a VOC, to generate specific patterns to that VOC, which can be analysed and identified by a computational approach

specificity and allows for the creation of a device that can sense a wide variety of odours with simple technology (Utriainen et al. 2008; ICX Technologies 2011).

Three examples of e-nose sensor technology are discussed here, the first two are array-based approaches, and the third is a more specific approach.

Electrochemical gas sensors have been researched since the 1960s, and are used widely for environmental monitoring, both in the home and work place (detecting toxic gases such as carbon monoxide) or outdoors for pollution monitoring (nitrous oxides, ozone, etc.). However, they have only recently started to be targeted towards security applications, such as detecting drugs or explosives, and although the technology is simple and lightweight, sensitivity and especially specificity must still be improved. The sensors comprise a material suspended between two electrodes. A current is passed across this material and the resistance is measured. On binding a molecule from the vapour, the resistive properties of the sensor change and this change can be related back to the vapour being sensed. Advances in electrochemical gas sensors include the use of improved semiconducting metal-oxide materials, and the application of nanomaterials such as gold nanoparticles or carbon nanotubes as the sensing material (Hernández et al. 2014; Schnorr et al. 2013).

A second technology is fluorescent polymer-based sensing, which has been developed from the work of Swager et al. at the Massachusetts Institute of Technology. This new class of polymer fluoresces when irradiated with an ultraviolet (UV) light source. Air is drawn over the illuminated polymers, and on contact with certain molecules of interest the fluorescence is quenched. This quenching can be measured easily, and small amounts of VOC cause large fluorescence quenching (see the explosives case study). The structure of the polymer can be varied to target certain different vapours, and the amount of fluorescence quenching can be related to the concentration of the vapour present. Recent advances have focussed on the development of lasing polymers to improve sensitivity further, and extending the range of materials that can be detected with this technique (Yang & Swager 1998; Swager 1998).

A final technology of note is the use of mass to sense and differentiate different odour molecules with the application of mass spectrometry or ion-mobility spectrometry (IMS). The latter method works by drawing in a sample of vapour, ionising the molecule in an electric field, and then passing it down a charged tube. The rate of travel of the molecule down the tube is linked to its intrinsic charge and mass, and can be related back to the components of the original vapour that was sampled. This technique requires more advanced machinery but much research has led to reliable, portable units that can differentiate complex mixtures well, and are highly sensitive – thus IMS is a current standard technology used by the military (Eiceman & Stone 2004).

Odour analysis – recognition and action

Once a signal has been generated by the sensor elements, it must be converted into information that is of use to the operator, such as an identification or a warning. This is achieved by processing the transduced sensor signal and comparing it to a library of previously classified (known) signals, using pattern-recognition tools, to generate a match for the substance detected. The library can be easily updated with any new materials/odours of interest, and doesn't require extensive retraining. If the pattern is not well matched to the library, the operator could receive an indicator of similarity to other patterns, giving him/her a selection of best guesses and a guide on how certain each guess is.

Pattern recognition is performed using mathematical formulae termed 'machine-learning' algorithms. These are algorithms that, on being given a set of training data, where the sensing signal is linked to the material being detected, generate a mathematical model of the data. When a signal is processed that has an unknown provenance, it is compared to the model, and matched on the basis of similarity to known materials. There are many kinds of algorithm that can achieve this process, such as linear discriminant analysis (LDA), support vector machines (SVM) or principal component analysis (PCA) (Diehl & Anslyn 2013).

Case study – sniffing out explosives

As already suggested above, one case where e-noses are starting to be widely used in conjunction with traditional canines is in the detection of explosives. Explosives present a particular challenge because the explosive materials themselves demonstrate low vapour pressures (Table 1 e.g. trinitrotoluene: TNT) – that is, they are not very smelly. Thus practitioners in this area require high sensitivity from an e-nose, good understanding and detection capabilities for associated odours that might be more easily detected, and selectivity over everyday vapours, such as perfumes, car fumes, etc. that might mask the explosive signal. Several tools have been developed to address this, ranging from robust and extensively trialled technologies, based on the principles described above, to new potentially more sensitive and selective technologies that are just leaving the laboratory (Peveler et al. 2016, 2017).

It is important that explosives sensors can detect and differentiate a variety of threats. The first targets are conventional high explosives such as TNT, RDX or PETN, present in unexploded munitions, landmines, and IEDs created from conventional munitions. The second is the broad variety of homemade explosives that can be concocted from strong oxidants such as hydrogen peroxide and perchlorate (bleach) in combination with various other materials such as acetone.

The VOCs that can be targeted by an explosives e-nose include the materials used to prepare the explosive, such as more smelly starting materials (acetone, ammonia) or by-products of the manufacturing process (DNT contamination in TNT, cyclohexanone leftovers in RDX). Other targets are the plasticisers used to bind different explosives together (2-ethyl-1-hexanol in C4 compositions – (Kranz et al. 2014)) and the chemicals deliberately added to aid in the vapour detection of explosive materials (DMDNB).

The most prolific e-nose technology used against explosives is IMS, which is widely used on the ground by the military and by civilian first responders. It has been shown to be effective at detecting both small quantities of pure explosive, as well as other relevant VOCs (Eiceman & Schmidt 2009; Eiceman & Stone 2004). The original IMS technology relied on radioactive sources to ionise the intake sample, which had the disadvantages of procuring, safely storing, and disposing of the source. Recent advances have focussed on developing an electrospray technique that uses a high voltage instead of the radioactive source, although this requires increased battery power, reducing portability (Reid Asbury et al. 2000).

The fluorescent sensing of explosives has become a very important topic of research after the development of the FIDO instrument (ICX Technologies 2011; Andrew & Swager 2007), using fluorescent polymers to detect trace levels of nitro-aromatic explosives, and more recently RDX (Gopalakrishnan & Dichtel 2013). Work then focussed on creating polymers that responded to more than the (highly limited) amount of explosive odour in the air, and targeted the more smelly companion odours that indicate explosives, as discussed above (Thomas et al. 2005; Rochat & Swager 2014). There is now much research into other fluorescent materials, beyond polymers, that might be more sensitive or more selective, such as nanostructured materials (Jurcic et al. 2015; Diehl & Anslyn 2013; Germain & Knapp 2009).

Recent innovation in electrochemical sensing of explosives has focussed on the creation of miniature and low-cost e-noses for detecting VOCs linked to explosives. It has been shown that an array of millimetre-sized sensors based on metal oxides can detect DMDNB, 2-ethyl-1-hexanol and ammonia with good specificity, due to the array approach and advanced pattern-recognition software (Peveler et al. 2013). A drawback of this system is the requirement to heat the sensors to high temperatures for optimal sensitivity, requiring extra power and limiting portability. Now work is focussed on attaining similar levels of sensitivity and specificity at room temperature to address this issue (Evans et al. 2014).

Finally, it is worth warning against a set of technologies that purport to be e-noses for explosives, but are nothing of the sort. In recent years, due to the high levels of IED attacks in civilian and military locales, various companies have started to manufacture and sell divining-rod-like devices, claimed to be able to detect trace explosives. There is no scientifically valid method in which these devices could operate, and first responders and military personnel must be cautioned against relying on such technologies, and putting themselves and others in danger (Rhykerd et al. 1999).

Scope for the future

E-noses are already starting to become widely used tools by the military and civilian first responders. The IMS and FIDO systems were routinely used by the US and UK military in Afghanistan and Iraq in conjunction with explosives dogs, and the MOD and UK police forces have invested in such tools. E-noses can be especially powerful in combination with other techniques, such as X-ray or THz scanning of people and cargoes, as sniffing can be built into scanners, and does not take up any extra time above the normal scan routine.

Developments in the e-nose field now focus on creating new sensing techniques, using novel materials and engineering developed in laboratories around the world, as well as working with the existing technologies to make instruments smaller, lighter and more sensitive and more specific to their targets. New sensor materials are being developed almost daily, but much work must go into taking the most promising of these forward and applying them with the appropriate engineering, and the best data processing, to develop better e-noses.

The odours that can be targeted by e-noses also need to evolve. Much work has gone into developing e-noses for conventional military explosives (TNT, C4), and popular narcotics (cocaine, methamphetamine). However, emerging threats must not be overlooked and there is now a move towards the smelling of peroxide explosives (Burks & Hage 2009), emerging narcotics, and even trying to build an e-nose to detect concealed persons (Giannoukos et al. 2018). These areas bring with them a whole new set of challenges, such as high variability in the odours given off, and ever more complex ways of hiding or masking these odours, meaning sensitivity must increase.

E-noses are a rapidly expanding area of scientific research and a potentially highly useful tool for the practitioner. By combining the needs of the practitioner with the knowledge of the researcher it should be possible to improve their capabilities to assist in the prevention of crime and protection of life.

References

Albert, K. J. et al., 2000. Cross-reactive chemical sensor arrays. *Chemical Reviews, 100*(7), pp. 2595–2626.

Andrew, T. L. & Swager, T. M., 2007. A fluorescence turn-on mechanism to detect high explosives RDX and PETN. *Journal of the American Chemical Society, 129*(23), pp. 7254–7255.

Berna, A., 2010. Metal oxide sensors for electronic noses and their application to food analysis. *Sensors, 10*(4), pp. 3882–3910.

Block, E. et al., 2015. Implausibility of the vibrational theory of olfaction. *Proceedings of the National Academy of Sciences, 112*(21), pp. E2766–E2774.

Brookes, J. C. et al., 2007. Could humans recognize odor by phonon assisted tunneling? *Physical Review Letters, 98*(3), p. 038101.

Burks, R. M. & Hage, D. S., 2009. Current trends in the detection of peroxide-based explosives. *Analytical and Bioanalytical Chemistry, 395*(2), pp. 301–313.

Caygill, J. S., Davis, F. & Higson, S. P. J., 2012. Current trends in explosive detection techniques. *Talanta, 88*, pp. 14–29.

Diehl, K. L. & Anslyn, E. V., 2013. Array sensing using optical methods for detection of chemical and biological hazards. *Chemical Society Reviews, 42*(22), pp. 8596–8611.

Eiceman, G. A. & Schmidt, H., 2009. Advances in ion mobility spectrometry of explosives. In M. Marshall & J. C. Oxley (eds) *Aspects of Explosives Detection*. Oxford: Elsevier, pp. 171–202.

Eiceman, G. A. & Stone, J. A., 2004. Peer reviewed: ion mobility spectrometers in national defense. *Analytical Chemistry, 76*(21), pp. 390 A–397 A.

Evans, G. P. et al., 2014. Single-walled carbon nanotube composite inks for printed gas sensors: enhanced detection of NO_2, NH_3, EtOH and acetone. *RSC Advances, 4*(93), pp. 51395–51403.

Furton, K. G. & Myers, L. J., 2001. The scientific foundation and efficacy of the use of canines as chemical detectors for explosives. *Talanta, 54*(3), pp. 487–500.

Furton, K. G. et al., 2002. Identification of odor signature chemicals in cocaine using solid-phase micro-extraction-gas chromatography and detector-dog response to isolated compounds spiked on US paper currency. *Journal of Chromatographic Science, 40*(3), pp. 147–155.

Furton, K. G. et al., 2015. Advances in the use of odour as forensic evidence through optimizing and standardizing instruments and canines. *Philosphical Transactions of the Royal Society B, 370*(1674), p. 20140262.

Germain, M. E. & Knapp, M. J., 2009. Optical explosives detection: from color changes to fluorescence turn-on. *Chemical Society Reviews, 38*(9), pp. 2543–2555.

Giannoukos, S., Agapiou, A. & Taylor, S., 2018. Advances in chemical sensing technologies for VOCs in breath for security/threat assessment, illicit drug detection, and human trafficking activity. *Journal of Breath Research, 12*(2), p. 027106.

Gopalakrishnan, D. & Dichtel, W. R., 2013. Direct detection of RDX vapor using a conjugated polymer network. *Journal of the American Chemical Society, 135*(22), pp. 8357–8362.

Haddi, Z. et al., 2011. A portable electronic nose system for the identification of cannabis-based drugs. *Sensors and Actuators B: Chemical, 155*(2), pp. 456–463.

Hernández, P. T. et al., 2014. Assessing the potential of metal oxide semiconducting gas sensors for illicit drug detection markers. *Journal of Materials Chemistry A, 2*(23), pp. 8952–8960.

Hettinger, T. P., 2011. Olfaction is a chemical sense, not a spectral sense. *Proceedings of the National Academy of Sciences, 108*(31), pp. E349–E349.

ICX Technologies, 2011. *Fido Explosives Detectors Technical Overview*. PDF online: www.flir.ca/threatdetection/display/?id=65350.

Johnston, J. M., 1999. Canine detection capabilities: operational implications of recent R & D findings. Institute for Biological Detection Systems.

Jurcic, M. et al., 2015. The vapour phase detection of explosive markers and derivatives using two fluorescent metal–organic frameworks. *Journal of Materials Chemistry A, 3*(12), pp. 6351–6359.

Kranz, W. et al., 2014. On the smell of composition C-4. *Forensic Science International, 236*(0), pp. 157–163.

Leonardos, G., Kendall, D. & Barnard, N., 1969. Odor threshold determinations of 53 odorant chemicals. *Journal of the Air Pollution Control Association, 19*(2), pp. 91–95.

McCabe, K. J., Wingo, R. M. & Haarmann, T. K., 2012. Method for training honeybees to respond to olfactory stimuli and enhancement of memory retention therein. USPO Patent US20120264353A1.

Pardo, M. et al., 2003. Detection of contraband food products with a hybrid chemical sensor system. *Proceedings of IEEE Sensors Conference*, 2003 (pp. 1073–1076). DOI: 10.1109/ICSENS.2003.1279108.

Pearce, T. C. et al. (eds) 2002. *Handbook of Machine Olfaction*. Weinheim, FRG: Wiley-VCH Verlag GmbH & Co. KGaA.

Peveler, W. J. et al., 2013. Detection of explosive markers using zeolite modified gas sensors. *Journal of Materials Chemistry A, 1*(7), pp. 2613–2620.

Peveler, W. J. et al., 2016. Multichannel detection and differentiation of explosives with a quantum dot array. *ACS Nano, 10*(1), pp. 1139–1146.

Peveler, W. J., Jaber, S. B. & Parkin, I. P., 2017. Nanoparticles in explosives detection – the state-of-the-art and future directions. *Forensic Science, Medicine, and Pathology, 10*, pp. 1–7.

Porritt, F. et al., 2015. Performance decline by search dogs in repetitive tasks, and mitigation strategies. *Applied Animal Behaviour Science, 166*, pp. 112–122.

Reid Asbury, G., Klasmeier, J. & Hill Jr., H. H., 2000. Analysis of explosives using electrospray ionization/ion mobility spectrometry (ESI/IMS). *Talanta, 50*(6), pp. 1291–1298.

Rhykerd, C. L. et al., 1999. Guide for the selection of commercial explosives detection systems for law enforcement applications. Washington, DC: US Department of Justice.

Rochat, S. & Swager, T. M., 2014. Fluorescence sensing of amine vapors using a cationic conjugated polymer combined with various anions. *Angewandte Chemie International Edition in English, 53*(37), pp. 9792–9796.

Rosier, E. et al., 2015. The search for a volatile human specific marker in the decomposition process. *PLOS ONE, 10*(9), p. e0137341.

Schnorr, J. M. et al., 2013. Sensory arrays of covalently functionalized single-walled carbon nanotubes for explosive detection. *Advanced Functional Materials, 23*(42), pp. 5285–5291.

Swager, T. M., 1998. The molecular wire approach to sensory signal amplification. *Accounts of Chemical Research, 31*(5), pp. 201–207.

Swedish Defence Research Agency, EMPHASIS. foi.se. Available at: www.foi.se/en/Customer--Partners/Projects/EMPHASIS/EMPHASIS [accessed May 7, 2015].

Thomas III, S. W., et al., 2005. Amplifying fluorescent polymer sensors for the explosives taggant 2,3-dimethyl-2,3-dinitrobutane (DMNB). *Chemical Communications, 36*, pp. 4572–4574.

Utriainen, M. et al., 2008. *Novel Hand-Held Chemical Detector with Micro Gas Sensors*. Article in M. Utrianinen, ed. Oslo: Nordic Innovation Centre.

Wolfbeis, O. S., 2013. Probes, sensors, and labels: why is real progress slow? *Angewandte Chemie International Edition in English, 52*(38), pp. 9864–9865.

Yang, J.-S. & Swager, T. M., 1998. porous shape persistent fluorescent polymer films: an approach to TNT sensory materials. *Journal of the American Chemical Society, 120*(21), pp. 5321–5322.

27

Understanding forensic trace evidence

Ruth M. Morgan, James C. French and Georgina E. Meakin

Introduction

Trace materials (including both particulate matter and residues) can offer vital intelligence for investigations, and evidence for crime reconstructions. Understanding the source of that material can be very important. However, understanding how that material behaves in different environments and under different conditions is fundamental, if the significance or meaning of the material is to be established in a transparent and evidence-based manner. This is an area that is currently under-researched. However, developing the understanding of trace evidence dynamics is critical for the development of forensic science (French et al. 2014; Morgan et al. 2014a; Brayley-Morris et al. 2015).

Evidence dynamics, a term first articulated by Chisum and Turvey (2000), addresses the variables that may change, relocate, obscure, contaminate or obliterate trace physical evidence. Such variables may be environmental, a function of time, and/or anthropogenic, and are at work during the generation, transfer and collection of trace evidence. Therefore, understanding the context (both general and case specific) of trace materials in a forensic case is important for accurate source and activity-level inferences to be made. An important aspect of this understanding is establishing empirical evidence bases that can offer the foundation for balanced, logical, transparent and robust interpretations of trace evidence. However, it is only in recent years that studies have begun to be published within the forensic science literature that address the need for experimental studies which can contribute to the empirical evidence bases required (Morgan et al. 2009).

The transfer and persistence of evidence is a key part of the 'journey' forensic materials take in their transition from 'material' to 'evidence/intelligence'. Experimental studies have a significant role to play in building our understanding of how these processes work in different contexts. If an understanding of the nature of trace material transfer and persistence is identified for a given forensic material, it becomes possible to begin to assign significance and weight to a particular form of forensic evidence/intelligence in a specific case. A key attribute of this process that has been identified empirically in the last five years is the prevalence of multiple transfers of evidence and their redistribution within a system (whether that system be an item of clothing or an entire crime scene) (Morgan et al. 2010; French et al. 2012; Meakin and Jamieson 2013). Understanding the extent to which such multiple transfers occur is critical for inferences of the significance of that evidence in a specific context as outlined in the examples presented in the section 'Examples'.

The role of experimental studies is therefore significant in establishing baselines and providing empirical evidence bases upon which inferences can be based. Whilst it is important to establish the source of a trace, understanding the transfers and preservation history of the trace is arguably equally, if not of more importance, for inferring the meaning of that particular trace in a specific case context.

This chapter provides examples of three different forms of trace evidence, DNA, gunshot residue (GSR) and sediments, each representing the diverse areas of forensic enquiry. Each example illustrates the type of questions forensic scientists seek to answer in crime reconstructions. Each example also outlines the role experimental studies can play in establishing the empirical evidence bases that enable the forensic scientist to understand the evidence dynamics of specific forensic trace materials and to make inferences about the meaning of that trace in a specific case.

Examples

DNA

The cells that make up our bodies contain smaller substructures, one of which, the nucleus, houses the DNA that is routinely targeted in forensic DNA profiling. Most cells have a nucleus (with the notable exception of red blood cells) and it is DNA from these cells that can be recovered from a crime scene. Traditionally, a detectable body fluid, such as blood or semen, was required for sufficient cells to be recovered to give a good-quality profile. However, with increasing sensitivity of profiling methods, it is now possible to obtain reliable DNA profiles for which the biological source of those cells is unknown, be it a body fluid or indeed any other tissue such as skin.

When the biological source of the DNA recovered is unknown, the DNA is commonly referred to as 'trace DNA' or 'touch DNA' (Meakin and Jamieson 2013). However, the term 'touch DNA' has led to the common misconception that DNA recovered from a surface got there via that surface being touched. The term 'trace DNA' allows for the fact that DNA can be transferred by other means, such as being deposited by speaking or coughing within the vicinity of an item, although there is little published research on transfer via these activities. These instances of transfer are referred to as direct, or primary, transfer, and once DNA is deposited on a surface, that DNA can also be transferred onward to another surface, a process referred to as indirect transfer. Such transfer can be via one intermediary surface ('secondary transfer'), two intermediary surfaces ('tertiary transfer'), or potentially via more surfaces. Whether the surface on which the DNA is deposited is a person or an object, that DNA is potentially available for onward transfer.

There are two purposes in recovering trace DNA from a crime scene; one is to try to identify the individual(s) from whom the DNA has originated in order to identify possible suspects, and the second is to try to use the locations and proportions of DNA found to assess whether the individual(s) identified actually had anything to do with the crime that was committed. In order to assess the latter, it is imperative that forensic experts consider issues of transfer (how did it get there), persistence (how long has it been there) and preservation (would it have survived the circumstances in question) in order to interpret the meaning and importance of finding trace DNA at a crime scene.

Indirect DNA transfer

a) The issue

It is now well established by empirical studies that indirect DNA transfer can occur in casework-relevant scenarios (several such studies are reviewed in Meakin and Jamieson 2013, and van Oorschot et al. 2010). However, many experiments demonstrating indirect transfer used items that had been cleaned of DNA, but in casework, items are unlikely to be free of DNA before coming into contact with DNA from the offender. Given that the average person sheds approximately 400,000 skin cells per day (Wickenheiser 2002), surfaces are likely to already have a background layer of DNA present, particularly regularly used items such as clothing and some types of weapons. This raises the question of whether indirectly transferred DNA can still be detected on a surface if a background layer of DNA is already present. A study by Meakin et al. (2015) is presented here that examined this issue by investigating whether DNA transferred indirectly via a handshake could be detected on knife handles that had been artificially set up as 'regularly used'.

b) The experiment and results

Volunteers each used a set of knives in a prescribed manner twice a day over a period of two days. On the following three consecutive days, each of these 'regular users' shook hands with another person ('handshaker') for ten seconds and then immediately, without touching anything else, repeatedly stabbed one of their own regularly used knives into a foam block for 60 seconds (Figure 27.1a). DNA was recovered from the knife handles using mini-tapes (adhesive pieces of tape, Figure 27.1b) and analysed to generate DNA profiles. In three of the four pairings of volunteers, complete and partial profiles matching those of the regular user and handshaker respectively, at ratios of ~10:1, were recovered from the knife handles (Figure 27.1c). Unknown DNA, not from the volunteers or the laboratory staff, was also recovered from the knife handles (Figure 27.1c). This second pairing included the repeated detection of DNA that could be attributed to the profile of the regular user's partner. For the fourth pairing, only complete single-source DNA profiles matching the profile of the regular user were recovered.

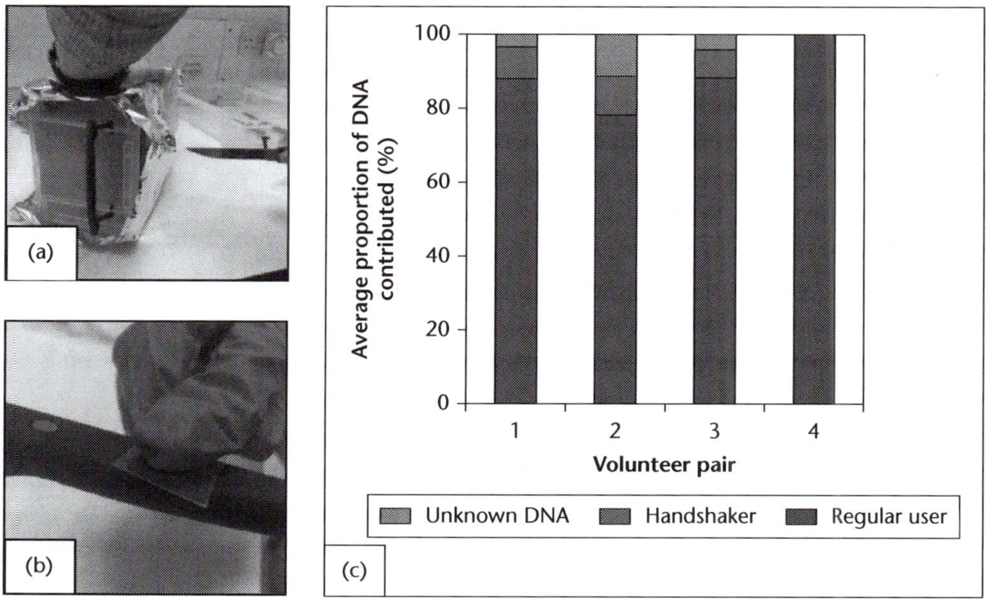

Figure 27.1 The stabbing of regularly used knives into a foam block following a handshake (a), the recovery of DNA from the knife handles using mini-tapes (b) and the DNA contributions observed in the profiles obtained from the knife handles (c)

c) The implications
The results of this study demonstrate that indirectly transferred DNA can still be detected when a background layer of DNA is present (Meakin et al. 2015, 2017a). In casework, it is therefore possible that DNA from a person who has not touched the item of interest could be recovered from that item, potentially falsely implicating that person. Whilst this study only examined the detection of DNA immediately following the secondary transfer event (the handshake), the finding of DNA from other individuals not associated with the experiment illustrates that DNA can be readily indirectly transferred and subsequently detected. This was of particular note regarding the finding of DNA that could be identified as having come from the romantic partner of one of the volunteers, even though the partner had never been in the laboratory (Meakin et al. 2015, 2017a). When evaluating the findings of trace DNA in casework, forensic experts must therefore consider issues of transfer to ensure that any opinion formed on how the DNA got to be on the item of interest is scientifically sound. This is crucial to ensure that the interpretation of the DNA evidence does not falsely implicate someone in a crime.

Persistence of DNA

a) The issue
When trace DNA is recovered from a surface of interest at a crime scene, it is important to consider whether the DNA was deposited at the time the crime occurred. Mixed DNA profiles, that is, DNA from more than one person, are commonly recovered from items that are used in the commission of a crime, thus raising the question of how to assess which DNA came from the person that used the item most recently. While it is common to assume that the main profile of these mixtures comes from the last person to touch the item, there are instances observed where the last person to touch the surface is not the main contributor (Goray and van Oorschot 2015). This is of particular concern regarding regularly used items that are likely to have a background layer of DNA present (as described above), and that therefore potentially lead to more instances of mixtures in which the main contributor is not that of the most recent user. Furthermore, when it comes to clothing, whilst some casework scientists in the UK opine that the main profile is likely to be that of the wearer (Casey et al. 2016), clarification is required as to whether that means the most recent wearer or the regular wearer, which may not be the same person depending on the case circumstances (Meakin and Jamieson 2016). A preliminary study described here, using T-shirts worn by the regular wearer and then by someone else, examined whether the method used to recover DNA could assist in assessing which DNA profile came from which wearer (Meakin et al. 2014).

b) The experiment and results
T-shirts that had been regularly worn and washed over a period of two years were worn for a day by the regular user, and then worn by a second individual on the consecutive day. Samples for DNA analysis were recovered from inside the sleeves of the T-shirts by using mini-tapes or by cutting out a small section of the material. The majority of the DNA in the mixed profiles obtained was attributed to the regular wearer, although an increased contribution of DNA from the most recent wearer was detected using mini-tapes (Figure 27.2).

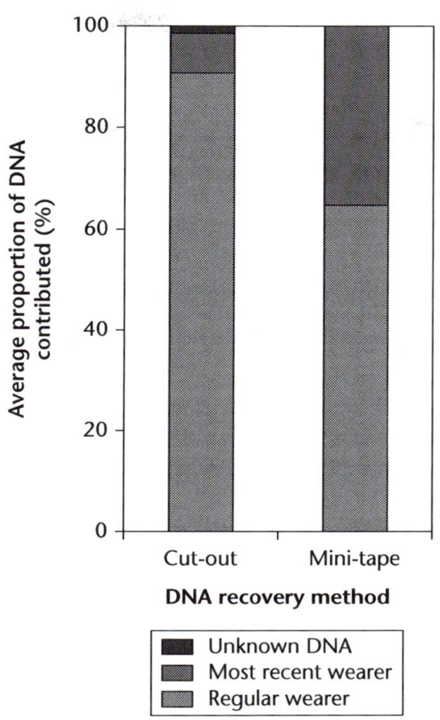

Figure 27.2 The DNA contributions observed in DNA profiles recovered from regularly used T-shirts that were first worn by the regular wearer and then by a second individual.

c) The implications

These results and other work (van Oorschot et al. 2014; Oldoni et al. 2016) indicate that DNA from a regular user/wearer of an item can persist to give the major contribution to mixed profiles recovered, even after a subsequent person uses the item. However, further work on this topic has shown that whether the major contribution comes from the regular wearer or most recent wearer will depend on the ability of each of the wearers to shed their DNA (Meakin et al. 2017b). It is therefore important that forensic experts consider the research available on the persistence, and transfer, of DNA when evaluating whether the DNA found was deposited prior to, during, or since the crime occurred. The preliminary study presented here also suggests that the way in which DNA is recovered from an item might assist in helping to recover more of the DNA from the most recent user, although further research is on-going to verify and expand these findings (Meakin et al. 2017b).

Preservation of DNA

a) The issue

After a crime, the offender or indeed the victim may try to destroy evidence linking them to the crime. When investigating a case in which it is suspected that this has happened, it is important to consider the preservation of DNA to assess whether time and money should be spent in trying to recover DNA evidence. One example of note is a common occurrence in sexual assault cases involving internal child sex trafficking. It is known that victims can hide their semen-stained clothing for several months before laundering them, such that when these items are seized during a criminal investigation, they are not routinely examined due to the assumption that the time delay and washing would result in no detectable DNA. A study by Brayley-Morris et al. 2015 is presented here that examined whether viable DNA profiles could be recovered from laundered semen stains where there had been a significant time lag since semen deposition.

b) The experiment and results

T-shirts that can be worn as part of a UK school uniform were stained with 1 ml fresh semen, stored in a wardrobe for eight months, and then washed at 30°C or 60°C with non-biological or biological detergent. A subset of the T-shirts were also washed multiple times at 30°C with non-biological detergent. High quantities of DNA (6–18 μg), matching the DNA profile of the semen donor, were recovered from the semen-stained sites of all the T-shirts that had been laundered, irrespective of wash conditions (Figure 27.3a) or number of washes (Figure 27.3b).

c) The implications

This study demonstrates that DNA can be recovered from semen stains on clothing, even after several months and after the clothing has been washed (Brayley-Morris et al. 2015). It emphasises the need to recover clothing of sexual assault victims and examine them for semen and DNA evidence, regardless of the time lag since the sexual offence took place and the number of times the clothing might be presumed to have been washed. This provides an example of how research on the preservation of DNA can be used to inform whether attempts should be made to detect potential DNA evidence during a criminal investigation.

Gunshot residue

Gunshot residue (GSR), or firearm discharge residue (FDR), is produced when a firearm is discharged and is composed of material from the propellant and priming compounds, as well

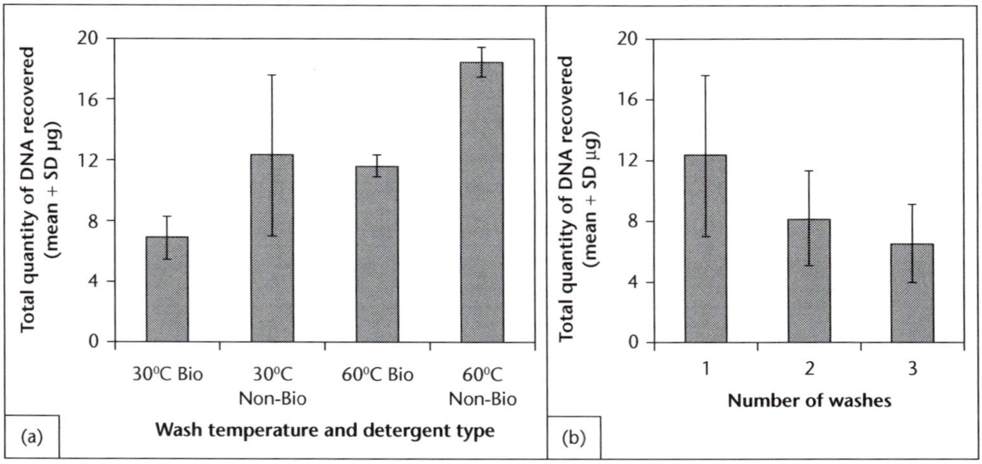

Figure 27.3 The quantities of DNA recovered from semen-stained sites of T-shirts that had been laundered at different temperature with different detergents (a) and laundered multiple times at 30°C with non-biological detergent (b). Taken and adapted from Brayley-Morris et al. 2015.

as other material from the bullet and the firearm itself. These components form particles that typically have diameters of 1–10μm, but can measure in excess of 30μm or 100μm. The particles are often spherical and their elemental composition is derived from the elements present in the primer. Often, GSR particles contain lead, barium, and antimony, while other primers do not contain lead and result in GSR particles with different elemental combinations (see Wallace 2008 for a comprehensive review). The most established analytical method for GSR identification is SEM-EDX (see Romolo and Margot 2001; Dalby et al. 2010 for a detailed review of analysis methods). Certain other environmental materials and practices can produce particles similar to GSR (see, for example, Garofano et al. 1999; Torre et al. 2002) and therefore, the presence of GSR particles must be determined according to the ASTM standard (ASTM 2010).

The recovery and identification of GSR particles in a forensic investigation can be crucial to the investigation and reconstruction of incidents involving firearms. GSR particles can be attributed to particular ammunition types and shooting distances and angles can be determined by interpreting the distribution of particles. The presence on GSR on the hands of a suspect can indicate that the suspect has discharged a firearm or has come into contact with a firearm, or has been in the presence of a discharge. Maitre et al. (2017) and Blakey et al. (2018) provide comprehensive reviews of the published literature on GSR and discuss the interpretation of this form of trace evidence in detail.

The notion of secondary transfer has been explored in relation to other types of forensic evidence (see Grieve et al. 1989; van Oorschot and Jones 1997; French et al. 2012, for example). Secondary transfers involve the transfer of material from one surface to another, via an intermediary surface. The result is that trace material is present on a surface which has had no direct contact with the surface from which the material originated. Conceivably, tertiary transfers may result from a further contact.

The possibilities of indirect GSR transfer are under-researched and it is not known whether, and in what quantities, GSR might be transferred to a person through indirect contact. Understanding the transfer and deposition properties of GSR and generating empirical data on these mechanisms is crucial to ensuring the accurate interpretation of GSR which is recovered from a suspect in casework. If such mechanisms are effective in depositing GSR and are not acknowledged in casework scenarios, the potential for misinterpretation may arise and ultimately, the possibility of misidentifying the suspect may result.

Transfer of GSR

a) The issue

Two questions were posed and addressed through an experimental study:

- To what extent can GSR be transferred and deposited through mechanisms other than discharging a firearm?
- What might be the implications of these mechanisms for crime reconstruction and evidence interpretation?

b) The experiments and results

Three experiments were designed to address these questions (as reported in French et al. 2014; French and Morgan 2015, and presented in Table 27.1). For all experiments, test firings were

Table 27.1 Outline of the experimental scenarios

	Experimental scenario			
	1 (Secondary transfer)	*2 (Tertiary transfer)*	*3 (Firearm handling)*	*4 (Bystander)*
Rounds fired per run	5	5	5	5
Description	Following the discharge, the shooter shook hands with a participant who was not present during the shooting	Following the discharge, the shooter shook hands with a participant who then shook hands with another	Following the discharge, the shooter passed the firearm to a participant who was not present during the shooting	During the discharge, a bystander stood with their hands by their sides a distance of 1 m behind the shooter
Sample taken	Handshake recipient	Second handshake recipient	Firearm handler	Bystander
Runs	3	3	3	3

carried out using a SIG Sauer P226 self-loading pistol and five rounds of 9 mm ammunition. The hands of participants were sampled and these samples were analysed for the presence of GSR using SEM-EDX with an automated search and detection software package. Participants were control sampled, prior to each experiment to ensure that no GSR was present. All control samples tested negative for the presence of GSR.

Table 27.2 presents the GSR particle counts from the transfer recipients in each run of each scenario. The results confirm that in each run of each scenario a transfer or deposition of GSR particles resulted from the mechanism that was being investigated. Secondary transfers to an individual, through contact with a shooter or through contact with a discharged firearm were observed. Meanwhile, tertiary transfers through contact with two intermediaries were also observed. Finally, GSR was recovered from bystanders, who made no contact with any other participants or surfaces. Of the four mechanisms, secondary transfers via the shooter resulted in the largest quantities of material being recovered (88, 30 and 129 particles in runs one, two and three, respectively). However, as many as 86 particles were recovered following the handling of the firearm in run one of scenario three. It is clear that the amount of transfer and deposition varied from run to run; this was not unexpected as it is known that the initial quantities of GSR that can be recovered from the shooter are variable (Matricardi and Kilty 1977; Lindsay et al. 2011; French et al. 2014).

Table 27.2 GSR particles recovered from the subject in runs 1–3 of experimental scenarios one, two, three and four (from French et al. 2014 and French and Morgan 2015)

	Experimental scenario			
	1 (Secondary transfer)	*2 (Tertiary transfer)*	*3 (Firearm handling)*	*4 (Bystander)*
Run 1	88	18	86	21
Run 2	30	22	18	36
Run 3	129	12	14	28

c) The implications

It is notable that in each run of each experiment, a significant quantity of GSR was recovered. This has a number of potential implications for the use of GSR evidence in the investigation of firearms crime. From the point of view of a scene of a crime examiner who is collecting material at the scene of a crime, it is clear from the experimental data that we might expect to recover GSR from surfaces other than the hands of the shooter. Therefore, sampling from bystanders and other surfaces and individuals is recommended in the interests of recovering as much GSR as possible and of enabling accurate crime reconstruction. Meanwhile, the propensity of GSR to undergo successive transfer highlights the risk of unwanted contamination when, for example, officers are arresting suspects or handling firearms or exhibits. Such transfers should be guarded against.

Crucially, these results have ramifications for the interpretation of GSR that is recovered from a suspect. Clearly, the data suggest that, under certain circumstances, the presence of (moderate) quantities of GSR evidence may not result from the discharge of a firearm by the suspect. Instead, the transfer and deposition properties of GSR observed in these experiments suggest that alternative means of transfer and deposition might be proffered as reasonable explanations for the presence of material. Therefore, when determining the probability that a certain quantity of GSR is observed, given that suspect X was the shooter, it is necessary to acknowledge that there are scenarios in which we might expect to observe GSR evidence, given that the suspect was not the shooter and was, perhaps, in (indirect) contact with a shooter after the event, or was involved in disposing of or concealing the firearm, for example. The generation of empirical data such as those presented in Table 2 is an important step in the process of interpreting evidence within a Bayesian paradigm (Cook et al. 1998a, 1998b; Evett et al. 2000) that is underpinned by principles of balance, logic and robustness.

Sediments

Soils and sediments are highly environmentally specific and can offer both spatial and temporal indicators that can be valuable for crime reconstructions. Such sediments have physical (mineralogy, particle size, colour), chemical (salinity, pH, elemental profiles) and biological (pollen, diatoms) components (Bull and Morgan 2007). There are many examples in the published literature and in casework of sediments being a form of evidence and/or intelligence that can provide indications of provenance and journey histories of critical exhibits such as footwear and vehicles (Ruffell and McKinley 2008).

Understanding the transfer and persistence of sediments in different environments and during different activities is important for establishing an evidence base that can provide the foundations for robust interpretation of what the presence of a particular trace in a particular place means, and the significance of its presence in the specific case context (Morgan al. 2009). The role of experimental studies is therefore an important step for ensuring the robust and transparent interpretation of trace forensic materials (as outlined in the Introduction). To illustrate the role of experimental studies in achieving this type of robust interpretation, an example of this approach for the pollen component of soils/sediments is presented here.

The distribution of pollen in domestic dwellings

a) The issue

A significant body of published literature has addressed the environmental specificity of pollen assemblages in different environments (Bryant et al. 1990; Mildenhall 2006; Montali et al.

2006; Mildenhall et al. 2006). The application of these findings have been used extensively in the crime reconstructions of outdoor scenes (Horrocks and Walsh 1999; Brown 2002) but until recently, the use of pollen assemblages to characterise indoor locations has only been addressed for medical and occupational health issues (Emberlin et al. 2004), rather than for forensic reconstruction purposes.

Establishing how geoforensic indicators (such as pollen) accumulate in an indoor environment offers insights into where pollen may collect and accumulate. Understanding where the richest sources of pollen are likely to be indicates which surfaces are most likely to lead to a transfer if a contact is made by an offender. Furthermore, it may also indicate the type of profile that an indoor setting may have in comparison to an outdoor location in the close vicinity, offering the means to distinguish between contact being made outside and inside the dwelling.

b) The experiment and results

A series of experimental studies were designed to assess these questions concerning the spatial distribution of pollen in indoor settings (Morgan al. 2014a):

- How and where do geoforensic indicators (pollen) accumulate in indoor environments?
- Is the geoforensic indicator profile of an indoor environment distinct from an outdoor location of close proximity?

The results demonstrated that when cut flowers were displayed in a room in a domestic dwelling a distinctive pollen assemblage profile was created. The highest pollen counts were observed within 0.8 m of the flowers over the duration of each experiment (up to 17 days of continuous observations). Once the flowers were removed from the room, the deposited pollen grains remained in the room for at least a further 20 days in the study. It is therefore likely that rooms in domestic dwellings will build up distinctive pollen assemblages indicative of the cut flowers that may have been displayed in the preceding days, weeks and even months before a forensic event. Indeed these pollen grains are present on a wide variety of surfaces within the room (both soft furnishing and hard surfaces) increasing the likelihood of transfer of the pollen onto shoes or clothing taking place if any contact within the room is made. It was also identified that the indoor profiles created over time were often distinctive to the outdoor environments due to the non-native flowering plants displayed in the indoor setting reflecting that cut flowers are often imported and are therefore not indicative of the local environs.

c) The implications

This study indicated that it is possible to develop an understanding of where pollen evidence is most likely to be, and what kind of assemblage is likely to be present, at the critical locations within a domestic dwelling where contact may be made with an offender (such as a door handle or table surface). This result contributes to an empirical evidence base to guide investigators in the collection of representative comparator samples from the scene for comparison with an exhibit, such as a glove or item of clothing, belonging to the suspect. It also informs the 'collection of evidence procedures' to ensure that valuable evidence/intelligence is not missed on an important exhibit, such as clothing or footwear, as this may offer both source and activity level indications for a reconstruction. Finally, understanding the type of assemblage of pollen that is likely to be present within a domestic dwelling and how it may differ from other domestic dwellings (or indeed outside the dwelling in question) is significant. This finding offers the potential to build an empirical foundation that can be used to base the interpretation of pollen evidence recovered from clothing, vehicles or footwear to assess the source of that profile. It is therefore possible to offer insights into the significance of that profile as evidence/intelligence within the context of a specific case.

The preservation of pollen after fire

a) The issue

Whilst understanding the source assemblage within a specific crime scene is important for being able to infer a source of a comparator sample, it is also critical to understand how such trace materials may change over time (in terms of quantity and identifiable characteristics), particularly if those traces are exposed to efforts to destroy the trace evidence, such as washing or burning. Furthermore, identifying the degree to which a form of trace evidence may persist through washing and burning can offer evidence-based indicators for the best places to collect samples from particular exhibits (such as in the washing machine filter or under the inner sole of a shoe after washing), and whether such forms of evidence remain viable for analysis and subsequent interpretation.

b) The experiment and results

A series of experimental studies were designed to assess the degree to which pollen grains were preserved after exposure to fire conditions (Morgan et al. 2014b). The experimental studies replicated the exposure of pollen in sediments to vehicle fires. A classification system was devised to characterise the pollen grains to establish the degree to which the heat had changed the morphology of the grains and therefore the ability of an examiner to identify the pollen (see Table 27.3). Pollen grains assigned classification 1 had retained their shape and texture, a classification 2 indicated that the grains were still identifiable but exhibited some signs of thermal stress such as a partial distortion of the shape of the grain, classification 3 indicated that the grains were significantly distorted and often conglomerated and a classification of 4 indicated that the pollen was unidentifiable and therefore unsuitable for forensic analysis.

The results indicated that whilst the persistence of different pollen types varied when exposed to high temperatures for between 30 seconds and 24 hours, it was possible to identify all the pollen morphologies after 30 minutes of exposure to 400°C. After shorter times of heat exposure, the threshold for successful identification was higher (500°C after five minutes of exposure). With lower temperatures, pollen morphologies were still identifiable after 18 hours of exposure (lily pollen was preserved after 18 hours at 300°C, and daffodil pollen at 200°C).

c) The implications

It has been identified that peak temperatures in vehicle fires are often below the critical heat thresholds identified in these experiments (Morgan et al. 2008). Therefore pollen in vehicles, particularly when it is present in the footwells or wheel arches, has the potential to be preserved in a viable form for subsequent collection and morphological analysis. This has significant implications for the collection stage of a forensic investigation, ensuring that samples are collected even when arson has taken place, but has also demonstrated the impact of heat on the morphology of the pollen grains tested in these experiments (see Table 27.3). Being able to demonstrate

Table 27.3 Morphological characteristics of pollen grains exposed to heat. (Morgan et al. 2014b)

Pollen type	*Classification 1*	*Classification 2*	*Classification 3*
Lily			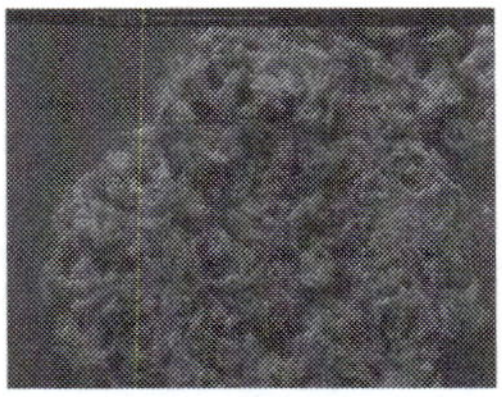
Daffodil			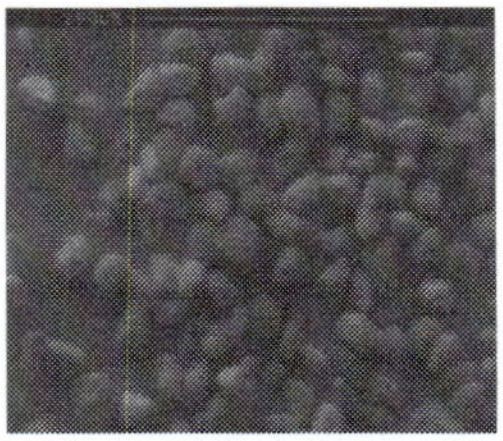
Tulip			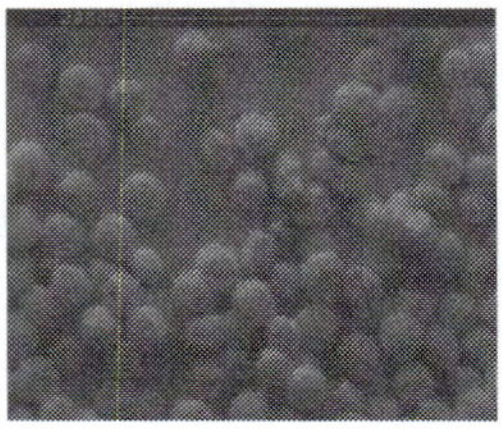

in court what a viable and non-viable pollen grain looks like is important for establishing the strength of pollen evidence that has been recovered from a vehicle or building fire. This finding also reduces the conjecture surrounding the heat threshold achieved in a particular fire as the morphological characteristics of the pollen grains can be demonstrated to be visually viable or not for comparison purposes on the basis of these findings.

Summary

The dynamics of trace evidence is an important concept to incorporate into the practice and understanding of each phase of the forensic science process (collection, analysis, interpretation and presentation of evidence). This chapter has demonstrated that experimental studies can make an important contribution to establishing empirical evidence bases that can form the foundation for evidence-based trace material collection, analysis, and interpretation. Whilst it is acknowledged that experimental studies are generally restricted in their scope and can only account for a limited number of variables, they have a significant and demonstrable role to play in the development of evidence bases for understanding what trace evidence means in a particular scenario.

An appreciation of the importance of trace evidence dynamics is timely, given the scientific (NAS report 2009), legal (Law Commission Report 2011), economic (Science and Technology Committee Report 2012) and political (Annual Report of the Chief Scientific Advisor 2015) challenges that are facing the forensic sciences. The interpretation of evidence has never been more scrutinised and a case can be made for the development of evidence bases that incorporate both experimental findings and the experience of experts, which can offer the transparency and accuracy in evidence interpretation that is needed if forensic science is to continue to aid the justice system.

The implications of such an approach are wide reaching, and have relevance for both investigators and the courts. Producing reliable intelligence and evidence to investigators is vital if forensic evidence is to aid investigations. Only when forensic science can offer transparency in how intelligence/evidence has been interpreted can investigators be equipped to assess the significance of the evidence/intelligence in a specific case context. This transparency is also important within the court systems. It is likely that in the future Daubert admissibility style tests will be brought into more justice systems (Law Commission 2011), and it has been argued that only with established empirical evidence bases can forensic evidence be demonstrated to have the validity that such tests require (Morgan et al. 2014b). Ensuring forensic evidence is presented in court in such a way that a judge and/or jury can identify how the significance and weight of the evidence have been established is critical to achieve transparency in the decision making that takes place during the trying of a case.

References

Annual Report of the Government Chief Scientific Advisor (2015) Forensic science and beyond: authenticity, provenance and assurance, evidence and case studies. Available at: www.gov.uk/government/publications/forensic-science-and-beyond.

ASTM (2010) E1588–10e1. *ASTM Standard Guide for Gunshot Residue Analysis by Scanning Electron Microscopy/Energy Dispersive X-Ray Spectrometry*. West Conshohocken, PA: ASTM International. DOI: 10.1520/C0033-03.

Blakey, L., Sharples, G., Chana, K., and Birkett, J. (2018) Fate and behaviour of gunshot residue – a review. *Journal of Forensic Sciences 63*(1): 9–19.

Brayley-Morris, H., Sorrell, A., Revoir, A. P., Meakin, G. E., Court, D. S., and Morgan, R. M. (2015) Persistence of DNA from laundered semen stains: implications for child sex trafficking cases. *Forensic Science International: Genetics 19*: 165–171.

Brown, A. G. Smith, A., and Elmhurst, O. (2002) The combined use of pollen and soil analyses ina search and subsequent murder investigation. *Journal of Forensic Sciences* 47(3): 614–618.

Bryant, V. M., Jr, Jones, J. G., and Mildenhall, D. C. (1990) Forensic palynology in the United States of America. *Palynology 14*: 193–208.

Casey, D. G., Clayson, N., Jones, S., Lewis, J., Boyce, M., Fraser, I., Kennedy, F., and Alexander, K. (2016) A response to Meakin and Jamieson DNA transfer: review and implications for casework. *Forensic Science International: Genetics 21*: 117–118.

Chisum, W. J. and Turvey, B. (2000) Evidence dynamics: Locard's exchange principle & crime reconstruction. *Journal of Behavioral Profiling*, *1*(1).

Cook, R, Evett, I., Jackson, G., Jones, P., and Lambert, J. (1998a) 'A Model For Case Assessment And Interpretation'. *Science and Justice 38*(3): 151–156.

Cook, R., Evett, I., Jackson, G., Jones, P., and Lambert, J. (1998b) A hierarchy of propositions: deciding which level to address in casework. *Science and Justice 38*(4): 231–239.

Dalby, O., Butler, D., and Birkett, J. (2010) Analysis of gunshot residue and associated materials - A review. *Journal of Forensic Sciences 55*(4): 924–943.

Emberlin, J., Adams-Groon, B., Treu. R., and Carswell, F. (2004) Airborne pollen and fungal spores in florist shops in Worcester and in Bristol, UK: a potential problem for occupational health *Aerobiologia 20*(2): 153–160.

Evett, I., Jackson, G., and Lambert, J. (2000) More on the hierarchy of propositions: exploring the distinction between explanations and propositions. *Science and Justice 40*(1): 3–10.

French, J. C., Morgan, R. M., Baxendell, P., and Bull, P. A. (2012) Multiple transfers of particulates and their dissemination within contact networks. *Science and Justice 52*(1): 33–41.

French, J. C., Morgan, R., and Davy, J. (2014) The secondary transfer of gunshot residue: An experimental investigation carried out with SEM-EDX analysis. *X-Ray Spectrometry 43*(1): 56–61.
French, J. C. and Morgan, R. (2015) An experimental investigation of the indirect transfer and deposition of gunshot residue: further studies carried out with SEM-EDX analysis. *Forensic Science International 247*: 14–17.
Garofano, L., Capra, M., Ferrari, F., Bizzaro, G., Di Tullio, D., Dell'Olio, M., and Ghitti, A. (1999) Gunshot residue: further studies on particles of environmental and occupational origin. *Forensic Science International 103*(1): 1–21.
Goray, M. and van Oorschot, R.A.H. (2015) The complexities of DNA transfer during a social setting. *Legal Medicine 17*: 82–91.
Grieve, M., Dunlop, J., and Haddock, P. (1989) Transfer experiments with acrylic fibres. *Forensic Science International 40*(3): 167–277.
Horrocks, M. and Walsh, K. A. J. (1999) Fine resolution of pollen patterns in limited space: differentiating a crime scene from an alibi scene seven metres apart. *Journal of Forensic Science 44*(2): 417–420.
House of Commons Science and Technology Committee (2013) Forensic science 2nd report of session 2012–2013. Available at: www.publications.parliament.uk/pa/cm201314/cmselect/cmsctech/610/610.pdf.
Law Commission. (2011) Law Comm. No 325. Expert evidence in criminal proceedings in England and Wales. Available at: www.lawcom.gov.uk/wp-content/uploads/2015/03/lc325_Expert_Evidence_Report.pdf.
Lindsay, E., McVicar, M., Gerard, R., Randall, E., and Pearson, J. (2011) Passive exposure and persistence of gunshot residue (GSR) on bystanders to a shooting: comparison of shooter and bystander exposure to GSR. *Canadian Society of Forensic Science Journal 44*(3): 89–96.
Maitre, M., Kirkbride, K., Horder, M., Roux, C., and Beavis, A. (2017) Current perspectives in the interpretation of gunshot residues in forensic science: a review. *Forensic Science International 270*: 1–11.
Matricardi, V. and Kilty, J. (1977) Detection of gunshot residue particles from the hands of a shooter. *Journal of Forensic Sciences 22*(4): 725–738.
Meakin, G. and Jamieson, A. (2013) DNA transfer: review and implications for casework. *Forensic Science International: Genetics 7*: 434–443.
Meakin, G. and Jamieson, A. (2016) A response to a response to Meakin and Jamieson DNA transfer: review and implications for casework. *Forensic Science International: Genetics 22*: e5–e6.
Meakin, G. E., Boccaletti, S. and Morgan, R.M. (2014) DNA as trace evidence: developing the empirical foundations for interpretation. Australian and New Zealand Forensic Science Society 22nd International Symposium on the Forensic Sciences. Adelaide, Australia.
Meakin, G. E., Butcher, E. V., van Oorshchot, R. A. H, and Morgan, R. M. (2015) The deposition and persistence of indirectly-transferred DNA on regularly-used knives. *Forensic Science International: Genetics Supplement Series 5*: e498–e500.
Meakin, G. E., Butcher, E. V., van Oorshchot, R. A. H, Morgan, R. M. (2017a) Trace DNA evidence dynamics: an investigation into the deposition and persistence of directly- and indirectly-transferred DNA on regularly-used knives. *Forensic Science International: Genetics 29*: 38–47.
Meakin, G. E., Jacques, G. S., and Morgan, R. M. (2017b) the effects of recovery method and sampling location on DNA from regularly-worn hoodies subsequently worn by a different individual. 27th Congress of the International Society for Forensic Genetics. Seoul, South Korea.
Mildenhall, D. C. (2006) Hypericum pollen determines the presence of burglars at the scene of a crime: an example of forensic palynology. *Forensic Science International 163*(3): 231–235.
Mildenhall, D. C., Wiltshire, P. E. J. And Bryant, V. M. (2006) Forensic palynology: why do it and how it works. *Forensic Science International 163*(3): 163–172.
Montali, E., Mercuri, A. M., Grandi, G. T., and Accorsi, C. A. (2006) Towards a 'crime pollen calendar' – pollen analysis on corpses throughout one year. *Forensic Science International 163*(3): 211–223.
Morgan, R. M., Allen, E., King, T., and Bull, P. A. (2014a) The spatial and temporal distribution of pollen in a room: Forensic implications. *Science and Justice 54*(1): 49–56.
Morgan, R. M., Cohen, J., McGookin, I., Murly-Gotto, J., O Connor, R., Muress, S., Freudiger-Bonzon, J. and Bull, P. A. (2009). The relevance of the evolution of experimental studies for the interpretation and evaluation of some trace physical evidence. *Science and Justice 49*(4): 277–285.
Morgan, R. M., Flynn, J., Sena, V., Bull. P. A. (2014b) Experimental forensic studies of the preservation of pollen in vehicle fires *Science and Justice 54*(2): 141–145.

Morgan, R. M., French, J. C., O'Donnell, L., and Bull, P. A. (2010) The reincorporation and redistribution of trace geoforensic particulates on clothing: An introductory study. *Science and Justice 50*(4): 195–199.

Morgan, R. M., Gibson, A., Little, M., Hicks, L., Dunkerley, S., and Bull, P. A. (2008) The preservation of quartz grain surface textures following vehicle fire and their use in forensic enquiry. *Science & Justice 48*(3): 133–140.

Oldoni, F., Castella, V., Hall, D. (2016) Shedding light on the relative DNA contribution of two persons handling the same object. *Forensic Science International: Genetics 24*: 148–157.

Romolo, F. and Margot, P. (2001) Identification of gunshot residue: a critical review. *Forensic Science International 119*(2): 195–211.

Ruffell, A. and McKinley, J. (2008) *Geoforensics*. Hoboken, NJ: Wiley-Blackwell.

Taroni, F., Aitken, C., Garbolino, P., and Biedermann, A. (2006) *Bayesian Networks and Probabilistic Inference in Forensic Science*. Chichester, UK: John Wiley.

Torre, C., Mattutino, G., Vasino, V., and Robino, C. (2002) Brake linings: a source of non-GSR particles containing lead, barium and antimony. *Journal of Forensic Sciences 47*(3): 494–504.

van Oorschot, R. and Jones, M. (1997) DNA fingerprints from fingerprints. *Nature 387*: 767.

van Oorschot, R. A. H., Ballantyne, K. N., and Mitchell, R. J. (2010) Forensic trace DNA: a review. *Investigative Genetics 1*.

van Oorschot, R. A. H., Glavich, G., and Mitchell, R.J. (2014) Persistence of DNA deposited by the original user on objects after subsequent use by a second person. *Forensic Science International: Genetics 8*(1): 219–225.

Wallace, J. (2008) *Chemical Analysis of Firearms, Ammunition, and Gunshot Residue*. Boca Raton, FL: CRC Press.

Wickenheiser, R. A. (2002) Trace DNA: a review, discussion of theory, and application of the transfer of trace quantities of DNA through skin contact. *Journal of Forensic Sciences 47*(3): 442–450.

28

Interpretation of forensic science evidence at every step of the forensic science process

Decision-making under uncertainty

Ruth M. Morgan, Helen Earwaker, Sherry Nakhaeizadeh, Adam J. L. Harris, Carolyn Rando, and Itiel E. Dror

Introduction

The endeavour of forensic science is to provide evidence-based forensic reconstructions that can assist in both the detection and prevention of crime. These reconstructions are products of the entire forensic science process, which include the activities that occur at the crime scene, laboratory analysis, interpretation of that analysis and the presentation of those findings to investigators as intelligence and/or in court as legal evidence. There is a growing awareness and understanding that human involvement in decision-making is impacted by many psychological factors (Edmond et al. 2016), and that decision-making is an integral part of the forensic science process (Morgan 2017a, 2017b; Dror 2018). Uncertainty is present in much of this decision-making due to the nature of the reconstruction process where evidence is partial and probabilistic, and where there is often no definitive, known 'ground truth'.

There is a significant body of published research addressing the uncertainty inherent in making inferences for forensic reconstructions (Aitken and Taroni 2004; Taroni et al. 2006; Robertson et al. 2016; Biedermann et al. 2016). So far the research has mainly focussed on quantifying this uncertainty and assessing probability using statistical methods. However, the human decision-making element that is integral to every stage of the forensic science process has not yet been fully taken into account. For example, the decisions made at the crime scene, such as where to look for evidence and what trace to sample, will have a significant impact on what analysis is subsequently undertaken in the laboratory. The questions asked at the crime scene likewise affect the type of analysis undertaken on exhibits, and the order in which such analyses are undertaken. Therefore, whilst existing published work that addresses inference approaches has provided valuable insights concerning the interpretation stage of the forensic science process, we have not yet managed to achieve generalisable and holistic approaches that take into account the impact of decision-making mechanisms at every stage of the forensic science process which can be applied to the highly complex and case specific instances of forensic investigation and crime reconstructions (Morgan 2017a, 2017b).

In recent years there has been an increased research focus on the role of human cognition and the presence of cognitive biases in the interpretation of forensic science evidence within many of the forensic science domains (Found, 2015; Kassin et al. 2013; Edmund et al. 2016). Understanding cognitive influences on human decision-making at each stage of the forensic science process is critical to identifying the best approaches for holistic forensic reconstruction (Roux et al. 2012; Morgan 2017a). Cognitive influences affect the way in which inferences are drawn and conclusions reached throughout the processes involved in forensic reconstructions. However, inferences and conclusions may also be affected by the way information and evidence are recognised, perceived and observed in the first place (Dror 2016).

This chapter outlines the decision-making that takes place at four key points of the forensic science process (crime scene, evidence analysis, evidence interpretation, and the judicial arena) and highlights some of the cognitive influences that can be in play at each stage. In this way, it is illustrated that a holistic approach is valuable for addressing the impacts of human cognition in the inference and forensic-reconstruction process.

Cognition and decision-making in the forensic process; crime scene to court

The importance of taking a holistic approach to interpretation within forensic science

Figure 28.1 represents the progression of forensic evidence from the time a crime is committed to the point that a judicial outcome is reached, depicting the key stages of decision-making within the forensic process and their relationship to selected decision areas within policing. It is important to highlight the linear yet iterative nature of the forensic process; each subsequent process (and decision) is reliant upon the outcome of a previous process (or decision). Thus, it is vital that decision-making and interpretation is acknowledged as occurring throughout the forensic process from the outset of a forensic investigation. A decision made early in the process will impact subsequent decisions in an investigation (Dror et al. 2017, Nakhaeizadeh et al. 2017) and has the potential to impact the judicial outcome of the case. There is therefore a need to develop a scientific approach to the forensic process as a whole and also within each stage of the forensic process that provides a clear basis for how inferences are made and conclusions reached. Considering the forensic process in this way highlights the need for an approach to forensic investigation that goes beyond the analysis that takes place in the laboratory and demonstrates the importance of having an awareness of the opportunities that all personnel involved within the forensic process have to make decisions and interpret intelligence and/or evidence. This chapter focuses on the stages directly related to the collection, analysis, interpretation and presentation of forensic evidence, whilst acknowledging that there are critical decisions being made concurrently in the investigation of a crime within the policing sphere, as illustrated in Figure 28.1.

Challenges of decision-making at the crime scene

At a crime scene many decisions need to be made, often within a highly emotive, pressured, and uncertain environment. Upon arrival at a scene, a crime scene examiner must consider a number of factors in order to inform the strategy for processing the scene. A determination of the type of crime committed (and sometimes whether a crime has been committed at all), and the resources available to deal with this type of crime will heavily influence subsequent

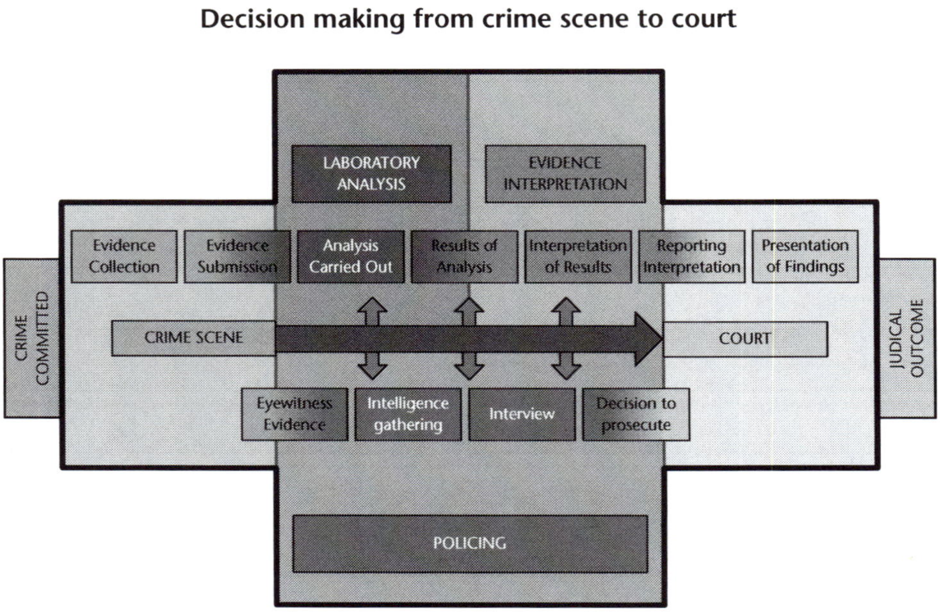

Figure 28.1 The forensic science process and the decision-making that occurs from crime scene to court

decision-making. Decisions at this early stage may include determining the position of cordons at the crime scene, for example, if a bike has been stolen from a shed, an appropriate cordon may be around the shed itself, whereas, if a murder has taken place in the shed it is likely that an appropriate cordon is a much wider area. Other decisions will include the number of crime scene examiners needed to process the scene and the attendance of any specialist practitioners (for example pathologists or entomologists). Background information relating to the alleged offence is often provided, but it may also be the role of the examiner to determine appropriate questions to ask of witnesses or victims so as to target an appropriate search for evidence at the scene. All of these aspects combine to influence the creation of a context-dependant strategy which is bespoke to that scene. Within the confines of the agreed strategy the examiner must decide which items of evidence to recover. This requires the examiner to make a decision about the possible relevance of the item to the events being investigated and to make a determination of the types and value of any potential forensic evidence identified on these items.

The aforementioned decisions are fundamental to the collection of the most appropriate and valuable exhibits and samples in a specific case. If relevant information is not recovered at this stage, or if evidence recovered does not maintain continuity and integrity, then this evidence will be lost to the investigative process (Weston 1998). As such, it is crucial that these decisions are made logically and in an evidence-based manner as much as possible.

However, the context in which these important decisions are made may have the potential to leave Scene of Crime Officers (SOCOs) vulnerable to 'cognitive contamination' (Dror 2014) For example, it is commonplace that before an officer arrives at a crime scene, they will already have been provided with information concerning the alleged crime and activities at the scene.

Such information prior to arriving at the crime scene can potentially lead to belief perseverance in the crime scene examiner (Burke 2005). This is manifested in the tendency to accept new information that conforms to a pre-existing belief (here the original case scenario) and to discount the value of evidence contrary to the original account. This effect has been identified within other police investigator roles (Ask et al. 2008). Equally, examiners will often be provided with an account of the crime by a victim or witness. Whilst this account may be important to direct an evidence-recovery strategy, it can also impart potentially irrelevant information in a highly emotive way, adding an increased emotional context to the investigation, which has the potential to influence subsequent scene processing (Van den Eeden 2016).

In addition, the experience of a crime scene examiner may have an impact upon the way in which they perceive and thus process the crime scene. It was found that novice crime-scene examiners (university students) focussed their attention when appraising a scene by considering the items present, whereas experts (operational crime-scene examiners) concentrated on assessing the potential evidential value of items present as a result of potential subsequent analysis (Baber and Butler 2012). This contrast in approach suggests the potential for individual differences between examiners according to their experience, but also highlights the added degree of complexity and interpretation that expertise brings. Thus, the role of expertise and experience is significant and can have an impact on the way that different actors within the investigation engage with contextual information and the inference process (Doak and Assimakopoulos 2007; Gobet 2015), potentially adding complexity to the decision-making process. Given the importance of selecting or collecting exhibits in a manner that does not adversely impact future analyses at the laboratory stage (such as understanding the requirements of different chemical treatments in a fingerprint laboratory to ensure that an exhibit is on an appropriate substrate, or using the appropriate swabbing technique when taking a DNA sample), there is a vulnerability to cognitive overloading at the crime scene through the requirement to have a working knowledge of the science surrounding the subsequent evidence analysis.

Further research is required to determine more fully the effects of 'cognitive contamination' (Dror 2016; Dror et al. 2017) on crime scene management, and to explore in more detail decision-making mechanisms at the crime scene. Such empirical research has a fundamental contribution to make in the creation of a more informed and balanced approach to information management within crime scene investigation. The decisions made at the crime scene stage of the forensic process are critical given the impact they can have on subsequent stages of the forensic process from both bias cascade and bias snowball effects (Dror et al. 2017). Therefore, understanding where critical decisions are being made at the crime scene allows for evidence-based approaches to minimise and mitigate the impact of unwarranted influences on the decision-making process, not only at the crime scene but also throughout the entire forensic process.

Decisions required during laboratory analysis

Forensic evidence recovered from the crime scene is often submitted to a police force evidence recovery laboratory or to an external provider for further specialist analysis. The analysis undertaken will vary according to the evidence type recovered. Examples of laboratory analysis include DNA analysis, chemical analysis of drugs samples, toxicological analysis, and the chemical visualisation of latent fingermarks. Laboratory analysis is similar to the field of crime scene examination in that there is a paucity of research that addresses decision-making and cognition during this stage of the forensic process. While there are well-documented quality standards and processes for laboratory analyses of trace evidence and exhibits, it is important to be aware of the decisions required of the forensic scientist throughout the analysis process.

Indeed, many factors can influence the decisions made by laboratory analysts when dealing with casework (Dror 2016). Many decisions must be made within the laboratory (such as what is the best test(s) to conduct, and in what order) and there is considerable interaction between the human analyst and the forensic evidence. In the lab, similar questions are addressed to those posed at the scene. For example, it may be necessary to determine the most appropriate areas of an exhibit for sampling, to consider activity level and case context (Morgan et al. 2018), and to assess the quality of the trace material. One example is the analysis of fingermarks.

A case study of decision-making within the analysis of fingermark evidence

Fingerprint enhancement laboratories routinely fulfil the vital role of chemically enhancing latent fingermarks on crime scene exhibits and submitting developed ridge detail to the Fingerprint Bureau for comparison against a known suspect. Due to the resource constraints placed upon police in-house forensic services it would be quixotic for laboratory practitioners to submit all developed ridge detail, instead they must filter the developed marks, ideally submitting marks which are of sufficient quality for use by fingerprint examiners and discarding (not capturing) marks which are of insufficient quality. Fingermark enhancement laboratory practitioners are routinely trained in selecting and carrying out chemical and physical development techniques to enhance latent fingermarks on a variety of surface types; however, they are not routinely trained in aspects of fingerprint analysis or quality assessment. As such, laboratory practitioners lack the training input given to examiners, yet they are required to quality assess a mark to conform to the quality threshold of an examiner (Earwaker et al. 2015a). There are therefore significant decisions being made about the viability of marks within the laboratory processes and analysis.

Initial research was undertaken to establish the efficiency of the process of mark submission from the enhancement laboratory to the Bureau (Earwaker et al. 2015b). This study utilised the usability determinations of fingerprint examiners as a benchmark to assess the 'correctness' of decisions made by practitioners to either submit or discard a fingermark. To achieve this benchmark, fingerprint examiners were given a series of images of developed fingermarks alongside a series of inked ten prints from the same source. Examiners were asked if they could identify each of the mark photographs, given the good quality set of ten prints provided. Where agreement between the examiners was reached on the usability of the mark photographs in the identification process these were selected as the 'experimental marks'. Half of the experimental marks had been agreed as being of insufficient quality whilst the other half were deemed to be of sufficient quality to use to identify. Laboratory practitioners were provided with these experimental fingermark images and were instructed to look at each in turn and state whether or not they would submit each mark to the bureau. The submission decisions made by the laboratory practitioners were compared to the usability determination made by the examiners. Decisions to submit an identifiable mark and to discard a non-identifiable mark were classed as 'correct' practitioner decisions whilst decisions to submit a no identifiable mark were 'false positives' and decisions to discard an identifiable mark were 'false negatives'.

Results indicate that there are discrepancies in laboratory fingermark submission and fingerprint examiner usability determinations in the more challenging marks (see Table 28.1), reflecting that there were false positive (poor quality marks submitted to the bureau) as well as false negative (good quality marks discarded) decisions. Experimentally, 34 per cent of submission decisions made by laboratory practitioners did not match the usability determinations of the examiners, with 20 per cent of decisions to submit unusable fingermarks, and 14 per cent of decisions to discard useable fingermarks.

Table 28.1 Percentage of false negative and false positive decision outcomes within the fingermark submission process (adapted from Earwaker et al. 2015b)

Participating practitioner	*Percentage of marks discarded that were of sufficient quality (false negatives)*	*Percentage of marks submitted that were of insufficient quality (false positives)*	*Did false positive submission fall above or below Metropolitan Police Service maximum false positive submission threshold of 20%*
A	45.45 (N=33)	28.57 (N=7)	Above maximum threshold
B	30.00 (N=20)	30.00 (N=20)	Above maximum threshold
C	25.00 (N=20)	25.00 (N=20)	Above maximum threshold
D	20.00 (N=25)	0.00 (N=15)	Below maximum threshold
E	35.71 (N=28)	16.67 (N=12)	Below maximum threshold
F	37.04 (N=27)	23.08 (N=18)	Above maximum threshold
G	38.46 (N=13)	44.44 (N=27)	Above maximum threshold
H	45.16 (N=31)	33.33 (N=9)	Above maximum threshold
I	20.00 (N=10)	40.00 (N=30)	Above maximum threshold
J	11.11 (N=9)	38.71 (N=31)	Above maximum threshold
K	0.00 (N=1)	48.72 (N=39)	Above maximum threshold

This study highlights the importance of considering the chain of forensic evidence recovery as a holistic process which is not limited to the comparison of a crime scene and suspect trace. Crucial decisions concerning the recovery of forensic evidence are being made in the laboratory setting, which could rule out the possibility of further evidentially beneficial interpretation. Whilst this study focussed upon the analysis and mark quality assessment processes carried out within a fingermark recovery enhancement laboratory, it is important to note that similar quality assessment decisions are made on a routine basis by scene of crime examiners.

Decision-making in the interpretation of evidence

The stage of interpreting forensic evidence is most commonly associated with subjective decision-making and, consequently, the fallibility of human decision makers (Kassin et al. 2013). Such interpretations commonly involve the comparison of a trace from an exhibit/victim/suspect with a control sample or the comparison of a crime scene and suspect pattern (for example fingermarks lifted from a crime scene to fingerprints taken from a suspect, or tool marks left at a scene compared to a tool), which is a subjective determination (Dror 2014; PCAST Report 2016). A notable exception is the comparison of suspect and crime scene DNA samples, where population frequency databases are available; however this process still requires the interpretation of profiles within the forensic context (Meakin and Jamieson 2013), and complex DNA, such as mixtures, involves subjective judgements which are susceptible to bias (Dror and Hampikian 2011).

Studies conducted to assess the processes and identify the influences on the interpretation of forensic evidence have been undertaken within a number of forensic domains. For example, the effect of contextual information has been shown in the fingerprint domain where decisions are made by examiners as to whether or not a fingermark and fingerprint originate from the same source (Dror and Charlton 2006; Dror, Charlton and Péron 2006; Dror et al. 2011). In many of these experiments, the majority of experts reached different conclusions on previously assessed fingermark comparisons, and were inconsistent in their analysis when provided with new contextual information (Dror et al. 2005; Dror and Charlton 2006), showing potential for confirmation and contextual biases. Findings from other studies within fingerprint comparison also found that even without the context of the comparison print there was still a lack of consistency in analysing some latent marks (Schiffer and Champod 2007; Langenburg et al. 2009; Dror et al. 2011). Not only was this reflected by inconsistency between different experts, but also the same experts at different times were inconsistent within their own analysis (Dror et al. 2011; Dror 2016). In addition, studies have also shown that the position of matching prints in the 'line up' affected the way in which fingerprint examiners assessed the print, highlighting the degree of false exclusions and inconclusive identifications across a series of mark evaluations where in an experimental study it was found that of 55,200 comparisons, 1,516 were considered to be 'errors' (Dror et al. 2012).

Similarly, empirical studies addressing confirmation bias and contextual effects have also been conducted within the domains of DNA (Dror and Hampikian 2011), handwriting and document examinations (Found and Ganas 2013), footwear impressions (Kerstholt et al. 2007), bullet comparison (Kerstholt et al. 2010), forensic anthropology (Nakhaeizadeh 2014a; Nakhaeizadeh et al. 2017), and bloodstain analysis (Laber et al. 2014) where different effects have been highlighted in each forensic discipline. In addition, the potential for contextual influences has also been discussed and identified within forensic entomology (Archer and Wallman 2016), bite mark comparisons (Page et al. 2011; Osborne et al. 2014) and fire-scene examinations (Bieber 2012).

A case study of contextual effects in the interpretation of forensic anthropology evidence

Studies within the domain of forensic anthropology have demonstrated empirically that the contextual information provided to the participants prior to their assessments can affect their evaluations and interpretations when establishing a biological profile on human remains (Klales and Lesciotto 2016; Nakhaeizadeh et al. 2017; Nakhaeizadeh et al. 2014a). In the Nakhaeizadeh et al. (2014a) study, three groups of participants were asked to examine an ambiguous skeleton and assess the sex, ancestry and age at death using traditional visual methods. The study identified that there was a significant difference between the three groups and demonstrated that when participants in each group were given contextual information prior to their analysis of the skeletal remains, their assessments were affected by the context they had been given. For example, in the assessment of sex of a female skeleton, the group that received contextual information that the remains were female were in agreement 100 per cent of the time in concluding the remains to be female. However, in the group that received contextual information that the remains were male, only 14 per cent indicated the correct decision that the remains were female (72 per cent indicated the skeletal remains to be from a male, and 14 per cent were undetermined in their conclusion (see Figure 28.2)). Similar results were also observed in the assessment of ancestry and age at death.

It is, however, important to acknowledge that context may affect the interpretation process but not necessarily the ultimate decision-making outcome of the forensic examiner. It is in ambiguous cases where the impact on the final decision-making is more likely. For example, a study by Kerstholt et al. (2010) addressed whether providing additional contextual information could affect experts when observing similarities between two bullets. They demonstrated that the context provided had no effect on the final conclusion reached by the expert. Such a null finding was also the case in a study on footwear analysis where the manipulation of the context had no effect on the evaluations of the experts (Kerstholt et al. 2007). Although these studies did not show a confirmation bias effect on forensic experts, it is important to note the argument that what is considered as 'influential' has been argued to depend on the nature of the task, the

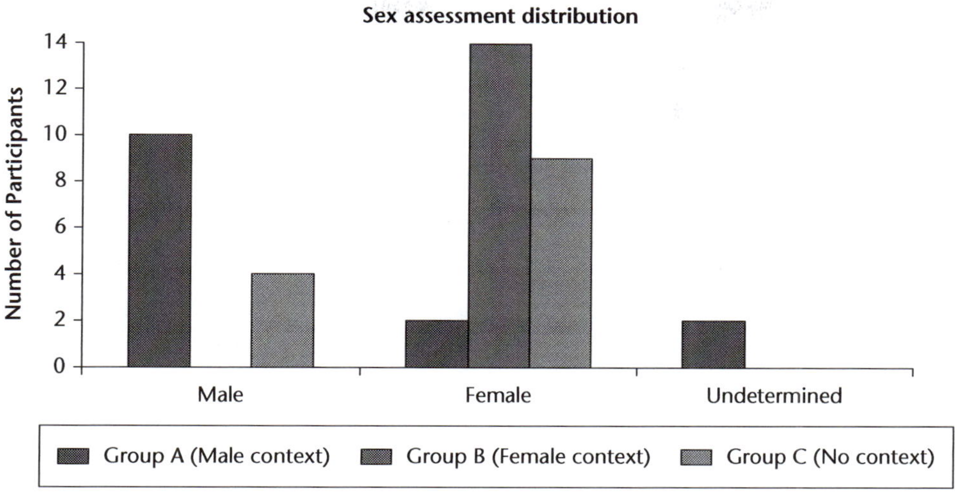

Figure 28.2 Sex assessment of remains from the Nakhaeizadeh et al. (2014a) study

level of ambiguity of the evidence characteristics being interpreted, as well as the difficulty of the judgement, and the strength of the context in which the decision is made, and, of course, whether the participants actually believe the contextual information (Kunda 1990; Dror 2016; Dror 2014; Nakhaeizadeh et al. 2017).

Demonstrating the fallibility of forensic interpretations (as exemplified in the empirical studies mentioned above) does not suggest that forensic expert judgement is universally irrational. These studies do, however, indicate situations in which the information present in the decision-making setting may influence a decision. It is important to be aware that there are various factors that will determine the strength and impact of the influences on the perception and observation of the evidence, as well as on the way inferences and conclusions are reached (Dror 2016).

Challenges for the presentation of evidence in court (admissibility of evidence, expert witnesses, jury decision-making, judge decision-making/sentencing)

Decision research within psychology and social science has demonstrated that perceptions and understandings are highly related to our emotional state and that these have a significant impact upon the way information is processed and interpreted (Byrne and Eysenck 1993; Dror et al. 2005). For example, mock juror studies have demonstrated that emotional state can influence verdict outcomes with results indicating that presenting emotionally disturbing evidence can influence the verdict of mock jurors in favour of a conviction (Bright and Goodman-Delahunty 2006). Similarly, the information presented to jurors in the courtroom is integrated with their individual prior knowledge and beliefs, especially when it comes to their general awareness of the criminal justice system and forensic evidence, which may be of varying degrees of accuracy (Smith et al. 2011) and can lead to unrealistic expectations (the so-called 'CSI effect') (Durnal 2010).

Equally, jurors are often asked to agree upon a verdict after the outcome is known and the events have occurred, which makes them susceptible to what is known as hindsight bias (Hawkins and Hastie 1990). Hindsight bias is the tendency for the inclination that an uncertain outcome often seems more likely after it is known that the outcome has occurred, despite there being little if any objective basis for such predictions. The role of memory reconstruction plays a significant role in hindsight bias. Psychological research has demonstrated that when searching memories, people tend to misrecall events (Klayman 1995). One study by Carli (1999) presented participants with a case situation of a romantic encounter. The participants were divided into a feedback group and a non-feedback group. The feedback group was told that the romantic encounter led to rape and the results demonstrated that it was difficult for the feedback group to disregard the event outcome when asked a week later to describe the romantic encounter. The feedback group was more likely than the non-feedback group to misrecall the details of the romantic encounter in a way more consistent with the rape outcome. Similarly, mock juror studies have recognised that jurors tend to be unable to ignore evidence that has been ruled inadmissible in court and tend to be subject to the effects of hindsight bias (Hawkins and Haiste 1990).

There is a growing debate concerning how scientific conclusions based on relevant evidence should be communicated in court in a manner that can be understood by laypeople. The value of probability frameworks (such as the likelihood ratio or verbal expressions of significance) as tools to offer a consistent and understandable format for the preparation and presentation of opinions in forensic science is increasingly being recognised by the forensic science community (Arscott et al. 2017; Howes 2015; Cook et al. 1998; Willis et al. 2015; Marquis et al. 2016). Although uptakes of these approaches have varied considerably amongst disciplines and jurisdictions, the debate about how to present the results of complex forensic analysis in court has, as yet, not fully incorporated the body of empirical evidence conducted within the field of psychology and judgement and decision-making. Studies have repeatedly shown that people have difficulties understanding probabilistic and statistical estimations (Gigerenzer and Edwards 2003). Verbal equivalents to communicate statistical data have been suggested; however this can also create problems as studies suggest that the meaning attributed to a single word could vary for each person and also depends in what context it is presented (e.g. Beyth-Marom 1982; Budescu and Wallsten 1995; Villejoubert et al. 2009; de Keijser and Elffers 2012; see also Martire et al. 2013, 2014).

There is therefore arguably a clear need to develop approaches that can incorporate the evidence in a particular case and illustrate how the significance and relationships between those different forms of evidence affect the inferences required for accurate forensic-reconstruction inferences. There are promising approaches, such as Bayes Nets (Taroni et al. 2006; Fenton et al. 2016) which offers a graphical approach to understanding the relationships between different forms of evidence and contribution of these forms of evidence to influencing the probability. Initial work highlights the potential to offer a transparent approach to illustrating the foundation upon which inferences may be made (such as Smit et al. 2016) and how ultimate conclusions of probability are reached.

Summary

Decision-making under conditions of uncertainty is present at every stage of the forensic process. The holistic and interactive nature of the different parts of the forensic science process as presented in this chapter (summarised in Figure 28.1), illustrates that decisions are not made in isolation. There is the potential for decisions and inferences made at one stage to impact a later stage and therefore, the ultimate judicial outcome of a case (Dror et al. 2017). It is therefore important to build the management of context effects on decision-making into every stage of the forensic process, not just the 'interpretation' stage.

Given the importance of decision-making to forensic reconstructions, there have been calls to develop standardised, and in some cases, automated approaches for interpreting evidence. It is, however, important to recognise and value the role of human decision-making in addressing forensic evidence in specific cases (Roux et al. 2012; Margot 2011; Morgan 2017a). Robust forensic interpretation requires both an evidence base and expertise of the decision maker in order to incorporate the specific variables and conditions of each case (Morgan 2017b) and provide a robust, transparent forensic reconstruction.

It is therefore important to develop approaches that present evidence in a manner that clearly incorporates an understanding of all the decisions that have been made during the forensic process. If this can be achieved, the degree to which prior decisions may have an influence on the conclusion being presented will be apparent, and judgement of the significance and/or weight of that conclusion more accurately assessed. Such an approach will also reveal the basis for the inference that is being presented and ensure that the conclusion is presented appropriately and is not overstated.

Understanding the decisions that are made throughout the forensic process is critical to ensuring that the interpretation of forensic science evidence is context sensitive and transparently presented to the trier of fact. Forensic evidence must always be approached within the context of the case in question and the different impinging variables incorporated into the decision-making that leads to the inferences that are presented. The role of human cognition in this process is complex, multi-layered and critical at every stage, and therefore only with a better understanding of where and when decisions are being made, what cognitive influences are impinging on those decisions and a fully articulated understanding of the basis upon which those decisions are made, will our ability to interpret what forensic science evidence means when it is identified be realised.

References

Aitken, C. G. and Taroni, F. (2004). Uncertainty in forensic science. *Statistics and the Evaluation of Evidence for Forensic Scientists*, Second Edition, pp. 1–34. Chichester, UK: John Wiley & Sons.

Archer, M. S. and Wallman, J. F. (2016). Context effects in forensic entomology and use of sequential unmasking in casework. *Journal of Forensic Sciences*, *61*(5), 1270–1277.

Arscott, E., Morgan, R., Meakin, G., and French, J. (2017). Understanding forensic expert evaluative evidence: a study of the perception of verbal expressions of the strength of evidence. *Science & Justice*, *57*(3), 221–227.

Ask, K., Rebelius, A., and Granhag, P. A. (2008). The 'elasticity' of criminal evidence: a moderator of investigator bias. *Applied Cognitive Psychology*, *22*(9), 1245–1259.

Baber, C. and Butler, M. (2012). Expertise in crime scene examination: comparing search strategies of expert and novice crime scene examiners in simulated crime scenes. *Human Factors: The Journal of the Human Factors and Ergonomics Society*, *54*(3), 413–424.

Beyth-Marom, R. (1982). How probable is probable? A numerical translation of verbal probability expressions. *Journal of Forecasting*, *1*, 257–269.

Bieber, P. (2012). Measuring the impact of cognitive bias in fire investigation. In *International Symposium on Fire Investigation*. Columbia, MD, 3–15 July 2012, pp. 3–15

Biedermann, A., Bozza, S., Taroni, F., and Aitken, C. (2016). The consequences of understanding expert probability reporting as a decision. *Science & Justice*, *57*, 80–85.

Bright, D. A. and Goodman-Delahunty, J. (2006). Gruesome evidence and emotion: anger, blame, and jury decision-making. *Psychiatry, Psychology & Law*, *11*(1), 154–166.

Budescu, D. V. and Wallsten, T. S. (1995). Processing linguistic probabilities: general principles and empirical evidence. *Psychology of Learning and Motivation*, *32*, 275–318.

Burke, A. S. (2005). Improving prosecutorial decision making: some lessons of cognitive science. *William and Mary Law Review*, *47*(5), 1587–1633.

Byrne, A. and Eysenck, M. W. (1993). Individual differences in positive and negative interpretive biases. *Personality and Individual Differences*, *14*(6), 849–851.

Carli, L. L. (1999). Cognitive reconstruction, hindsight, and reactions to victims and perpetrators. *Personality and Social Psychology Bulletin, 25*(8), 966–979.
Cook, R., Evett, I. W., Jackson, G., Jones, P. J., and Lambert, J. A. (1998). A model for case assessment and interpretation. *Science & Justice, 38*(3), 151–156.
Crispino, F., Ribaux, O., and Margot, P. (2011). Forensic science – a true science? *Australian Journal of Forensic Sciences, 43*(2–3), 157–176.
de Keijser, J. and Elffers, H. (2012). Understanding of forensic expert reports by judges, defense lawyers and forensic professionals. *Psychology, Crime & Law, 18*(2), 191–207.
Doak, S. and Assimakopoulos, D. (2007) How do forensic scientists learn to become competent in casework reporting in practice: A theoretical and empirical approach. *Forensic Science International, 167*(2–3), 201–206.
Dror, I. E. (2014). Practical solutions to cognitive and human factor challenges in forensic science. *Forensic Science Policy & Management: An International Journal, 4*(3–4), 105–113.
Dror, I. E. (2016). A hierarchy of expert performance (HEP). *Journal of Applied Research in Memory and Cognition, 5*(2), 121–127.
Dror, I. E. (2018). Biases in Forensic Experts. *Science, 360*(6386), 243.
Dror, I. E., Champod, C., Langenburg, G., Charlton, D., Hunt, H., and Rosenthal, R. (2011). Cognitive issues in fingerprint analysis: inter- and intra-expert consistency and the effect of a 'target' comparison. *Forensic Science International, 208*(1–3), 10–17.
Dror, I. E., Charlton, D., and Péron, A.E. (2006). Contextual information renders experts vulnerable to making erroneous identifications. *Forensic Science International, 156*(1), 74–78.
Dror, I. E. and Charlton, D. (2006). Why experts make errors. *Journal of Forensic Identification, 56*(4), 600–616.
Dror, I. E. and Hampikian, G. (2011). Subjectivity and bias in forensic DNA mixture interpretation. *Science and Justice, 51*(4), 204–208.
Dror, I. E., Morgan, R. M., Rando, C, Nakhaeizadeh, S. (2017). the bias snowball and the bias cascade effects: two distinct biases that may impact forensic decision-making. *Journal of Forensic Sciences, 62*(3), 832–833.
Dror, I. E., Peron, A. E., Hind, S. L., and Charlton, D. (2005). When emotions get the better of us: the effect of contextual top-down processing on matching fingerprints. *Applied Cognitive Psychology, 19*(6), 799–809.
Dror, I. E., Wertheim, K., Fraser-Mackenzie, P., and Walajtys, J. (2012). The impact of human-technology cooperation and distributed cognition in forensic science: biasing effects of AFIS contextual information on human experts. *Journal of Forensic Sciences, 57*(2), 343–352.
Durnal, E. (2010). Crime Scene Investigation (as seen on TV). *Forensic Science International, 199*(1–3), 1–5.
Earwaker, H, Charlton D, and Bleay, S. (2015a). *Fingerprinting – the UK Landscape: Processes, Stakeholders, and Interactions.* Horsham, UK: Forensic Science Knowledge Transfer Network.
Earwaker, H., Morgan, R. M., Harris, A. J. L., and Hall, L. J. (2015b). Fingermark submission decision-making within a UK fingerprint laboratory. *Science & Justice, 55*(4), 239–247.
Edmond, G., Towler, A., Growns, B., Ribeiro, G., Found, B., White, D., Ballantyne, K., Searston, R. A., Thompson, M. B., Tangen, J. M., and Kemp, R. I. (2016). Thinking forensics: cognitive science for forensic practitioners. *Science and Justice, 57*, 144–154.
Fenton, N. E., Neil, M., Lagnado, D., Marsh, W., Yet, B., and Constantinou, A. (2016). How to model mutually exclusive events based on independent causal pathways in Bayesian network models. *Knowledge-Based Systems, 113*, 39–50.
Found, B. (2015). Deciphering the human condition: the rise of cognitive forensics. *Australian Journal of Forensic Sciences, 47*(4), 386–401.
Found, B. and Ganas, J. (2013). The management of domain irrelevant context information in forensic handwriting examination casework. *Science and Justice, 53*(2), 154–158.
Gigerenzer, G. and Edwards, A. (2003). Simple tools for understanding risks: from innumeracy to insight. *BMJ, 327*(7417), 741–744.
Gobet, F. (2015) *Understanding Expertise: A Multidisciplinary Approach.* London: Palgrave Macmillan.
Hawkins, S. A. and Hastie, R. (1990). Hindsight: biased judgments of past events after the outcomes are known. *Psychological Bulletin, 107*(3), 311–327.
Howes, L. M. (2015). The communication of forensic science in the criminal justice system: a review of theory and proposed directions for research. *Science & Justice, 55*(2), 145–154.

Kahneman, D. and Klein, G. (2009). Conditions for intuitive expertise: a failure to disagree. *American Psychologist, 64*(6), 515.

Kassin, S. M., Dror, I. E., and Kukucka, J. (2013). The forensic confirmation bias: problems, perspectives, and proposed solutions. *Journal of Applied Research in Memory and Cognition, 2*(1), 42–52.

Kerstholt, J., Elkelboom, A., Dijkman, T., Stoel, R., Hermsen, R., and van Leuven, B. (2010). Does suggestive information cause a confirmation bias in bullet comparisons? *Forensic Science International, 198*(1–3), 138–142.

Kerstholt, J. H., Paashuis, R., and Sjerps, M. (2007). Shoe print examinations: effects of expectation, complexity and experience. *Forensic Science International, 165*(1), 30–34.

Klayman, J. (1995). Varieties of confirmation bias. *Psychology of Learning and Motivation, 32*, 385–418.

Klales, A. R. and Lesciotto, K. M. (2016). The 'science of science': examining bias in forensic anthropology. In *American Association of Forensic Science Annual Meeting*, 188–189.

Kunda, Z. (1990). The case for motivated reasoning. *Psychological Bulletin, 108*, 480–498.

Laber, T., Kish, P., Taylor, M., Owens, G., Osborne, N., and Curran, J. (2014). Reliability assessment of current methods in bloodstain pattern analysis. Washington, DC: National Institute of Justice, US Department of Justice. Available at: www.ncjrs.gov/pdffiles1/nij/grants/247180.pdf.

Langenburg, G., Champod, C., and Wertheim, P. (2009). Testing for potential contextual bias effects during the verification stage of the ACE-V methodology when conducting fingerprint comparisons. *Journal of Forensic Sciences, 54*(3), 571–582.

Margot, P. (2011). Forensic science on trial – what is the law of the land? *Australian Journal of Forensic Sciences, 43*(2–3), 89–103.

Marquis, R., Biedermann, A., Cadola, L., Champod, C., Gueissaz, L., Massonnet, G., and Hicks, T. (2016). Discussion on how to implement a verbal scale in a forensic laboratory: benefits, pitfalls and suggestions to avoid misunderstandings. *Science and Justice, 56*(5), 364–370.

Martire, K. A., Kemp, R. I., Watkins, I., Sayle, M. A., and Newell, B. R. (2013). The expression and interpretation of uncertain forensic science evidence: verbal equivalence, evidence strength, and the weak evidence effect. *Law and Human Behaviour, 37*(3), 197–207.

Martire, K. A., Kemp, R. I., Sayle, M. A., and Newell, B. R. (2014). On the interpretation of likelihood ratios in forensic science evidence: presentation formats and the weak evidence effect. *Forensic Science International, 240*, 61–68

Meakin, G. and Jamieson, A. (2013). DNA transfer: review and implications for casework. *Forensic Science International: Genetics*, 7(4), 434–443.

Morgan, R. M. (2017a). Conceptualising forensic science and forensic reconstruction; Part I: a conceptual model. *Science and Justice, 57*(6), 455–459.

Morgan, R. M. (2017b). Conceptualising forensic science and forensic reconstruction; Part II: the critical interaction between research, policy/law and practice. *Science and Justice, 57*(6), 460–467.

Morgan, R. M., French, J. C., and Meakin, G. E. (2019). Understanding forensic trace evidence. In R. Wortley et al. (eds) *Handbook of Crime Science*. Abingdon, UK: Routledge.

Nakhaeizadeh, S., Dror, I., and Morgan, R. M. (2014a). Cognitive bias in forensic anthropology: visual assessment of skeletal remains is susceptible to confirmation bias. *Science & Justice, 54*(3), 208–214.

Nakhaeizadeh, S., Hanson, I., and Dozzi, N. (2014). The power of contextual effects in forensic anthropology: a study of biasability in the visual interpretations of trauma analysis on skeletal remains. *Journal of Forensic Sciences, 59*(5), 1177–1183.

Nakhaeizadeh, S., Rando, C., Dror, I. E., and Morgan, R. M. (2017). Cascading bias of initial exposure to information at the crime scene to the subsequent evaluation of skeletal remains. *Journal of Forensic Sciences, 63*(2), 403–411.

Osborne, N. K., Woods, S., Kieser, J., and Zajac, R. (2014). Does contextual information bias bitemark comparisons? *Science & Justice, 54*(4), 267–273.

Page, M., Taylor, J., and Blenkin, M., (2012). Context effects and observer bias –implications for forensic odontology. *Journal of Forensic Sciences, 57*(1), 108–112.

PCAST Report to the President. (2016). Forensic science and the criminal courts: ensuring scientific validity of feature comparison methods. Available at www.whitehouse.gov/sites/default/files/microsites/ostp/PCAST/pcast_forensic_science_report_final.pdf.

Robertson, B., Vignaux, G. A., and Berger, C. E. (2016). *Interpreting Evidence: Evaluating Forensic Science in the Courtroom*. Chichester, UK: John Wiley & Sons.

Roux, C., Crispino, F., and Ribaux O. (2012). From forensics to forensic science. *Current Issues in Criminal Justice, 24*(1), 7–24.

Saks, M. J., Risinger, D. M., Rosenthal, R., and Thompson, W. C. (2003). Context effects in forensic science: a review and application of the science of science to crime laboratory practice in the United States. *Science & Justice, 43*(2), 77–90.

Schiffer, B. and Champod, C. (2007). The potential (negative) influence of observational biases at the analysis stage of fingermark individualisation. *Forensic Science International, 167*(2–3), 116–120.

Smit, N. M., Lagnado, D. A., Morgan, R. M., and Fenton, N. E. (2016). Using Bayesian networks to guide the assessment of new evidence in an appeal: a real case study. *Crime Science, 5*, 9–21.

Taroni, F., Aitken, C., Garbolino, P., and Biedermann, A. (2006). *Bayesian Networks and Probabilistic Inference in Forensic Science*. Hoboken, NJ: Wiley-Blackwell.

Taroni, F., Bozza, S., Biedermann, A., Garbolino, P., and Aitken, C. (2010). *Data Analysis in Forensic Science: A Bayesian Decision Perspective* (Vol. *88*). Chichester, UK: John Wiley & Sons.

van den Eeden, C. A. J., de Poot, C. J., and van Koppen, P. J. (2016). Forensic expectations: investigating a crime scene with prior information. *Science and Justice, 56*(6), 475–481.

Villejoubert, G., Almond, L., and Alison, L. (2009). Interpreting claims in offender profiles: the role of probability phrases, base-rates and perceived dangerousness. *Applied Cognitive Psychology, 23*, 36–54.

Weston, N. (1998). The crime scene. In P. White (ed.) *The Essentials of Forensic Science*. London: Royal Society of Chemistry.

Willis, S., Mc Kenna, L., Mc Dermott, S., O' Donnell, G., Barrett, A., Rasmusson, B., Höglund, T., Nordgaard, A., Berger, C., Sjerps, M., Molina, J. J. L., Zadora, G., Aitken, C., Lovelock, T., Lunt, L., Champod, C., Biedermann, A., Hicks, T., and Taroni, F. (2015). ENFSI guideline for evaluative reporting in forensic science. www.enfsi.eu/news/enfsi-guideline-evaluative-reporting-forensic-science.

Wilson, M. (2011). Quality assurance standards for forensic analysis of evidence. In J. B. Cliff, H. W. Kreuzer, C. J. Ehrhardt, and D.S. Wunschel (eds) *Chemical and Physical Signatures for Microbial Forensics*. New York: Springer.

29

Better preparation for the future – don't leave it to chance

Dick Lacey

Introduction

A lot has been written about the future. This article starts from the premise that the future is not pre-determined; observation would suggest that it is pretty safe to say that nobody is able to accurately predict it. Among other things, bookmakers make money because people cannot accurately predict the outcome of sporting events and many publications carry horoscopes which are widely read even if not believed. Maybe it fuels our optimism to learn that we will 'learn something to our advantage on Tuesday'. On a more serious note, and despite some people claiming they saw it all coming, the Arab Spring, the taking down of the Berlin Wall and the global financial crash all came as something of a surprise. One thing is certain however, and that is that whatever it holds for us, the future will happen. This short note provides an introduction to the ideas and methods that enable us to prepare better and anticipate future developments that are going to affect us. In government and large corporations, this activity goes by a number of names that include 'foresight' and 'horizon scanning' (Habbegger, 2009). These terms are not always well defined and very often embrace a host of techniques that can help us become more future-aware; more strategic in our planning; more resilient to change; and help us to intervene early if necessary. A salutary example of how technology can change peoples' thinking in relatively short timescales is the growth of social media.

It is difficult to predict where social media will go in the future. The growth of the internet has been remarkable and the statistics are quite startling (Regan, 2015). There are now over 3 billion internet users in the world and of these 2.2 billion are active users of social media. Different numbers are given by different analysts but one thing is agreed and that is that these numbers are accelerating. Clearly this growth needs to be recognised in many strategies developed by large corporations and governments.

In a review conducted in 2012 by the Chairman of the Joint Intelligence Committee, John Day for the British Government, horizon scanning was defined as:

> A systematic examination of information to identify potential threats, risks, emerging issues and opportunities, beyond the Parliamentary term, allowing for better preparedness and the incorporation of mitigation and exploitation into the policy making process.
>
> *(Cabinet Office, 2013, p. 2)*

This is one of a number of definitions of horizon scanning; there are many more (e.g. Pearson, 2015). There does not seem a lot of point in a short article getting bogged down in definitions so, for the purposes here we will use John Day's definition.

Future planning - beware the dystopian view

> If you want a picture of the future, imagine a boot stamping on a human face—for ever.
>
> *George Orwell,* 1984

There are many dystopian views of the future, of which the George Orwell quote above provides a vivid example. It makes for good science fiction: law being enforced by heartless robots and the like and, very often, future scenarios descend into 'gloom and doom' territory. However, to try and understand the future, it is very useful to look back and see what the world was like say ten years ago, twenty years ago and so on. As Confucius said, 'Study the past if you would define the future'.

Take the example of changes in life-expectation. There has been a dramatic increase seen in all countries since industrialisation (Roser, n.d.). A similar trend is seen in the increase in literacy rates in selected countries over a similar time period. These examples are only indicative. A closer examination of the data shows that in some countries life expectancy decreases on a short timescale; Russia during the First World War, for example, but the overwhelming trend in both sets of data is upwards.

These two examples illustrate that the future is not always a nightmare scenario; especially when one examines trends rather than one-off events. It is often said that the world has got smaller. News travels fast, ideas are disseminated quickly, and advances in science and technology have brought immense benefits to the whole of the planet notwithstanding that wealth is very unevenly distributed. Diseases have been treated or even eradicated, new agricultural practices have been adopted, and between 1990 and 2000, 1.6 billion people gained access to electricity (Badger, 2013).

These are global trends. They drive the way the future will happen. There are an enormous number of drivers and it is not always possible to identify and measure their relative importance. In the area of space travel, it was quite fashionable in the 1950s and 1960s, with the excitement surrounding early manned space flight, to predict that there would be bases on the moon by the 1980s and Mars by the year 2000. This did not happen and will probably not happen for a good number of years. However, predictions made about computing and the power of computers are way off-target. There is little or no mention of anything that looks like the World Wide Web.

Even in the mid-1990s, predictions were being made about the directions the web was taking which way off the mark (see, for example, O'Toole, 2014). This example serves to show that predicting the future is fraught with difficulty. Horizon scanning is not about prediction. It is about looking at what is plausible in the future what the consequences might be and how we can be better prepared. The next section describes some of the tools available.

Tools for futures planning

Horizon scanning is intimately related to the management of risk. There are both strategic tools that help us build resilience and mitigate problems. Indeed some of the diagrams and charts that are used in horizon scanning are very similar to those used in risk management (International Organisation for Standarization, n.d.). However, the tools developed for horizon scanning are relatively new in their development and allow considerable flexibility. Horizon scanning requires imagination and the development of scenarios and storyboards is a very powerful way of envisioning a plausible future. The UK government has developed a toolkit for developing strategic futures (Government Office for Science, 2017) and they are worth examining further. Other more comprehensive tools for futures thinking can be found at the Millennium Project (n.d.). Some of the main toolkits are described below.

Delphi

Delphi should be used at the beginning of a project and involves interacting with a large group of external experts. A set of predefined questions is used to elicit informed views on when events are likely to happen and what the underlying influences are, in an iterative process. Initially, the questions are circulated to the expert panel who respond in confidence. The responses are then analysed for the range of opinion. This analysis is fed back to the panel, some of whom may want to modify their initial responses. It is common to form a second panel of stakeholders to consider these later iterations.

Horizon scanning

Not to be confused with the often-used global term for futures analysis, Horizon scanning should be used at the beginning of a project: it examines evidence and issues that are starting to emerge. This is something most of us do naturally but formalising it can pay big dividends. It is advisable to structure horizon scanning around a framework. One common framework is PESTLE (which can also be called STEEP, STEEPLE or PESTELO). These are all acronyms for elements that make up the external environment (Societal, Political, Technological, Environmental, Economic, Legal, Ethical and Organisational). It is usual to look in 0–2, 2–5 and 5+ year timeframes. These studies can be completed by individuals and can form an excellent basis for discussing the future.

Three horizons

This is a graphical approach that can be used to illustrate how the importance of issues will change with time. Projections are created by plotting the results of horizon-scanning exercises according to time and impact. The near future can be quite clear as the direction of travel is well defined. Further in the future, some current, very weak signals of trends may prove to have great importance. For example, only recently has the problem of plastics in the ocean gained widespread recognition, although the dangers of plastic pollution have been long identified (see, for example, Hester and Harrison, 2011).

Seven questions

This technique is used to draw key information from senior and important stakeholders. This should also be used at the beginning of a project. The technique was pioneered by Shell and the seven questions reproduced here are taken from Ringland and Schwartz (1998) although good variations have been developed by SAMI Consulting (n.d.).

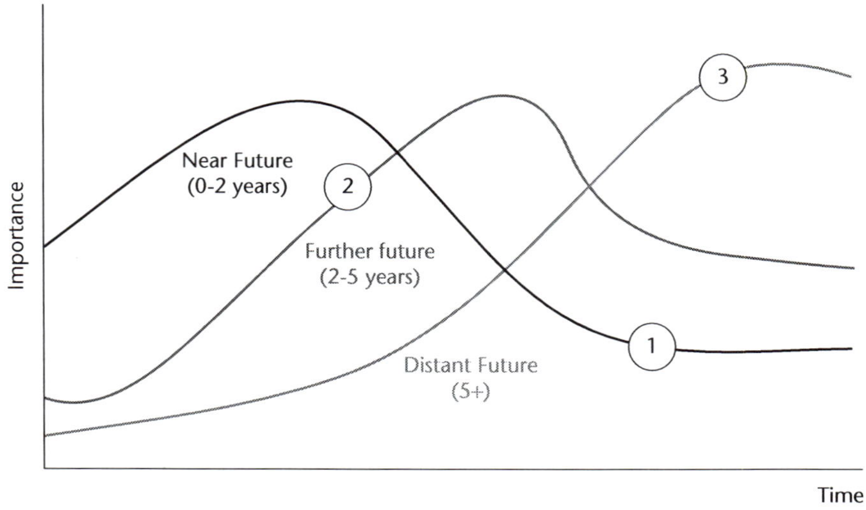

Figure 29.1 Horizons approach representation (taken from *The Futures Toolkit*, 2017)

1 What would you identify as the critical issue for the future?
2 If things went well, being optimistic but realistic, talk about what you would see as a desirable outcome?
3 If things went wrong, what factors would you worry about?
4 Looking at internal systems, how might these need to be changed to help bring about the desired outcome?
5 Looking back, what would you identify as the significant events which have produced the current situation?
6 Looking forward, what would you see as priority actions which should be carried out soon if you were responsible?
7 If all constraints were removed and you could direct what is done, what more would you wish to include?

These questions can be modified to suit particular needs.

Causal layered analysis (CLA)

This technique was pioneered by Inayatullah (2014) and examines situations at a number of levels. Initially, it looks at the headlines (referred to in the literature as the litany), which can often be sensationalist and politically motivated. It then moves deeper and examines things at a systems level, usually through the use of data and via more considered analysis. Below this level is the world view. This, to a certain extent, is what the man on the street thinks about the issues in hand. It can bring in ideas of rights, responsibilities and so forth. The fourth level is probably the hardest to grasp. In the literature, this is referred to as myth or metaphor. These are reflective of the deep rooted, emotive almost subconscious thinking that can affect our world view. This is not an easy technique to use but it can be very powerful. It is probably best illustrated by an example: The issue of mass migration.

The headlines are quite sensational, 'X thousand migrants camped at Calais', '250,000 migrants wait to enter the EU' and so on. At the next level, we might ask, why do these people

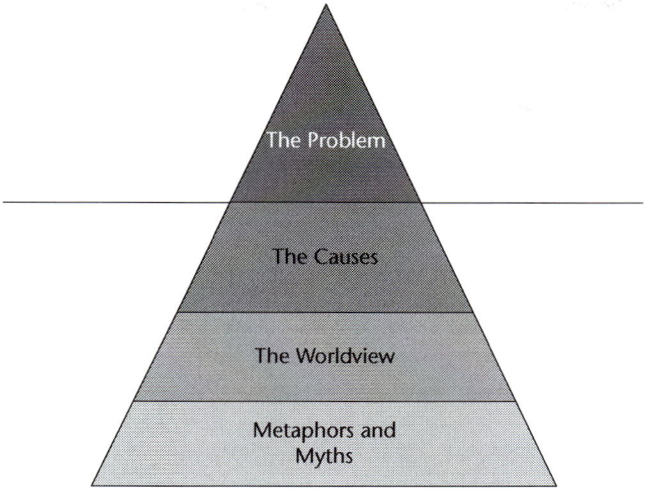

Figure 29.2 Schematic diagram of the CLA method

want to come to Europe? It could be that they are escaping from oppressive regimes in their countries of origin or that there is no work in their country or they are experiencing famine and need to be fed. What about the attitude of the target countries? Some say they are welcome because we need the labour and others are trying to prevent as much migration as they can. Some countries are in-between. At the third level there is the view of the migrants that Europe is like some sort of Shangri-La where work is plentiful and everybody leads a good life. There is the view of the host country inhabitants who could say there is no work for migrants and they are only trying to gain entry to take advantage of the health service and the benefit system. The fourth layer could include attitudes towards migrant groups in the past; the inability or unwillingness of some groups to integrate, the differences in religion, social attitudes, family and even food.

By examining the situation in a vertical and horizontal way, a much richer picture emerges and planning should be fuller and better informed. The CLA methodology is illustrated in Figure 29.2.

Figure 29.2 is based on a number of illustrations. Very often the pyramid is represented as an iceberg and like an iceberg 90 per cent of the issue is not immediately visible. The problem can be ongoing; the timescales to change the causes can be of the order of years; the worldview somewhat longer and the metaphors and myths are a deep rooted part of our society so change very slowly.

It should be remembered that futures analysis produces changing outputs. It is not an exercise that, once completed, can be put on a shelf and forgotten. It will need to be modified as new signals and additional information become apparent.

Some worked scenarios

Let us look at a couple of examples in some detail. There is no doubt that the degree of autonomy becoming available in the production of motor vehicles is growing dramatically: the Google self-drive car has completed over one million miles and currently drives around the streets of Mountain View in California. There are a number of reviews of the self-drive car, usually written by motoring journalists, that describe the experience as boring, mainly because the car has been taught to behave very safely and there is nothing for the driver to do. For instance, when the lights change to green, the car waits for a second before pulling away as many accidents happen by people jumping red lights.

Most of the big car companies plan to have self-drive vehicles available by 2020 but these are vehicles that are equipped to drive on the roads as they are now. Imagine what the world would be like if not only the cars but the entire traffic infrastructure, such as traffic lights, road signs, satellite navigation, and collision-warning systems were all connected and talking to each other without the intervention or even the knowledge of the driver. This is where the Internet of Things meets the roads (Government Office for Science, 2014).

This scenario presents a very different picture. Here the cars really do drive themselves. There is little (possibly no) passenger intervention and being a vehicle passenger will be much more akin to being on a train. This will have a number of societal advantages. Older people will be able to remain mobile for longer (important in an ageing society). Safe speed limits should be able to be dramatically increased for self-drive vehicles, and policing the roads will not have to be performed in the way that it is now. Accidents should be a thing of the past. However, there are some problems. Some people enjoy driving and will want to carry on so doing. How will those cars (which in the not-too-far future will be in the minority) be integrated with the self-drive majority? Will children be allowed in such vehicles on their own? What does this mean for offences such as drunken driving? These are all questions which will require legislation and probably some fundamental rethinking on road transport.

What does this do for car ownership? If a car can drive itself to a location with no driver whatsoever, then one can envisage a service where, in the future, cars are not owned but leased at the time needed. Sure, we lose the ability to jump in a car to pop to the supermarket to collect things we may have forgotten but the supermarket could probably deliver that stuff to you anyway, potentially by a driverless vehicle or a drone.

Where there are new ideas there are new ways of making money and where money can be made, crime will follow. If such a service outlined above becomes reality then the potential for scamming and running false accounts will need to be addressed. Will it be possible to hijack rides and get somebody else to pay for your travel? The leasing companies will need to have good computer security to prevent such incidents and almost certainly encryption of data will become the norm. There are strong indicators for this as these types of problem are already being seen in services such as banking and communications as they have become more automated.

Another very serious consideration is the security of the 'internet of the roads' infrastructure. If this could be hacked, it would be open to potential organised crime and terrorist use. Imagine holding a whole country to ransom simply because one had the wherewithal to bring the transport system to a standstill.

There is a move to having more and more technology worn on the person. What other technologies could be worn? Some suggestions are clothing that harvests power from our movements and allows charging of our electronic devices; the migration of the mobile phone to wrist-worn technology (this is already happening); clothes that automatically warm and cool us; clothes that allow us to display messages and clothes that monitor and report the state of our well-being.

There have been attempts to introduce augmented or enhanced reality via devices such as Google Glass (Naughton, 2017). So far, this has not been entirely successful but other big players are active in this area and in all probability it will become established in the next few years.

How about wearable technology that can change your mood (Venkataramanan, 2015)? A British start-up company has developed a product called Doppel, which they claim can change you mood in a similar way to music.

It is highly probable that we will be wearing more and more technology in the next few years. Will this lead to a similar phenomenon to the phone theft that was seen when mobile phones first became popular and is reportedly still increasing now in an environment of falling crime? What prevention strategies could be adopted to prevent this happening?

Conclusion

Hopefully this short article has shown the importance of futures analysis and horizon scanning. It is appearing in a book about crime science and any crime prevention strategy would benefit from horizon-scanning activity as hopefully the two examples given illustrate. By the time you read this it will already be out of date. Technology is moving at a frantic rate and is accelerating. We cannot predict the future but we do not just have to leave it to chance.

References

Badger, E. (2013). Where a billion people still live without electricity. Citylab. www.citylab.com/life/2013/06/where-billion-people-still-live-without-electricity/5807.

Cabinet Office (2013). Review of cross-government horizon scanning. London: Gov.UK. www.gov.uk/government/uploads/system/uploads/attachment_data/file/79252/Horizon_Scanning_Review_20121003.pdf.

Government Office for Science (2014). Internet of Things: making the most of the second digital revolution. Gov. UK. https://assets.publishing.service.gov.uk/government/uploads/system/uploads/attachment_data/file/409774/14-1230-internet-of-things-review.pdf.

Government Office for Science (2017). The futures toolkit: tools for thinking and foresight across UK Government. Gov. UK. https://assets.publishing.service.gov.uk/government/uploads/system/uploads/attachment_data/file/674209/futures-toolkit-edition-1.pdf.

Habegger, B. (2009). *Horizon Scanning in Government.* Zurich: Centre for Security Studies.

Hester , R. E. and Harrison, R. M. (eds) (2011). *Marine Pollution and Human Health.* London: Royal Society of Chemistry.

Inayatullah, S. (2014). Causal layered analysis defined. *The Futurist, 48*(1), 26.

International Organization for Standardisation (n.d.). ISO31000 – Risk management. www.iso.org/iso-31000-risk-management.html.

Millenium Project (n.d.). Global futures studies and research. www.millennium-project.org.

Naughton, J. (2017). The rebirth of Google Glass shows the merit of failure. *The Guardian*, 23 July. www.theguardian.com/commentisfree/2017/jul/23/the-return-of-google-glass-surprising-merit-in-failure-enterprise-edition.

O'Toole, J. (2014). 5 predictions for the Web that were WAY off. *CNN Tech.* http://money.cnn.com/2014/03/11/technology/web-predictions.

Pearson, T. (2015). Defining 'horizon scanning'? Simplexity analysis. www.simplexityanalysis.com/blog/2015/6/23/defining-horizon-scanning.

Regan, K. (2015). 10 amazing social media growth stats from 2015. *Social Media Today.* www.socialmediatoday.com/social-networks/kadie-regan/2015-08-10/10-amazing-social-media-growth-stats-2015.

Ringland, G. & Schwartz, P. P. (1998). *Scenario Planning: Managing for the Future.* Chichester, UK: John Wiley & Sons.

Roser, M. (n.d.). Life expectancy. https://ourworldindata.org/life-expectancy.

SAMI Consulting (n.d.). The SAMI seven questions. www.samiconsulting.co.uk/training/sevenquestions.html.

Venkataramanan, M. (2015). The Doppel writstband can literally change your mood. *Wired.* www.wired.co.uk/article/doppel-wristband.

White, S. (2013). Social media growth 2006 to 2012. All Things Marketing. http://dstevenwhite.com/2013/02/09/social-media-growth-2006-to-2012.

30
Future crime

Shane D. Johnson, Paul Ekblom, Gloria Laycock, Michael J. Frith, Nissy Sombatruang and Erwin Rosas Valdez

Introduction

The nature of crime is clearly changing. To illustrate, consider findings from the Crime Survey of England and Wales (ONS, 2017). For the first time, this sweep of the survey included questions about cybercrime. And while it only included questions about a handful of such offences, it suggested that at least half the crimes committed in the recall year, that were included in the survey,[1] involved the misuse of computers. As much cybercrime will go unnoticed, and many types of online offending were not considered in the survey, this is likely to be an underestimate of the scale of offending. While many new forms of offending will be facilitated by the internet, new forms of crime opportunity will not be limited to the kinds of offending we commonly associate with the term cybercrime and it is hence important to think more broadly than this.

The Dawes Centre for Future Crime at UCL was established in October 2016 with the dual aim of identifying new forms of offending and developing informed strategies to address them. As part of the activity of the Centre, a scoping study was conducted to examine how developing technologies might create new opportunities for crime, or inform approaches to combat them. Three exercises were undertaken. The first involved a search of key science and technology publications to identify emerging technologies with potential implications for crime. The second involved a systematic review of research conducted across UCL – a multi-faculty university – for which the crime implications of developing technologies were explicitly discussed. The third focused on research conducted at UCL on developing technologies for which there were latent crime implications that had not been discussed by the authors.

In this chapter, we discuss the findings from these studies. This is intended to illustrate some of the emerging technologies that might facilitate new forms (or more likely methods) of offending and to highlight the diversity of academic disciplines and university departments that currently contribute to work in these areas, and will need to do so in the future. Many of the lines of enquiry that will be covered are rarely discussed in mainstream criminology journals, if at all. It is not our aim to explain why this is the case, but to highlight the need for a broader perspective and an explicitly multidisciplinary approach to research focused on offending if we are to address future and emerging crime threats.

Managing expectations

Before proceeding it is worth noting that predicting the future is fraught with difficulty and subject to error, both in terms of trends that were not anticipated and false positives. For example, in 1957 Alex Lewyt, president of the Lewyt Vaccuum Company apparently predicted that within ten years nuclear-powered vacuum cleaners would probably be a reality. As far as we are aware, this prediction did not come to pass. Accordingly, it is important to manage expectations. Equally, however, it is important to stress that without such exercises we risk repeating errors of the past. To elaborate, and as has been discussed elsewhere (Ekblom, 1997; Pease, 1997), where innovation and change are concerned, a common story has played out time and again. That is, when new technologies or services are introduced their benefits are reaped and uptake increases. However, as crime prevention is often overlooked, or inadequate attention given to it, there frequently follows a crime harvest, whereby offenders exploit the crime opportunities that the new product or service affords. Examples include vehicle crime (Laycock, 2004) and robbery at ATMs (Guerette and Clarke, 2003) in the 1980s, credit card theft in the 1990s (Levi, 2000) and mobile phone theft in the 2000s (Mailey et al., 2008). In all of these cases, criminals exploited vulnerabilities associated with these products and services and rates of crime increased. Each of these problems could have been anticipated but if they were, they were not addressed until after the crime problems emerged.

Another issue to raise at this point is that the aim of the work discussed in this chapter was to examine the future crime potential of a wide array of developing technologies, as opposed to a specific class of technology. As such, we do not report detailed analyses of background changes or other factors that would be considered in a PESTLE analysis, or the other types of horizon-scanning exercises discussed in Chapter 29. Such exercises should be conducted for particular classes of technology, but they are not reported here. The final point to make is that the research reported here was completed at the beginning of 2017 and we live in a time of rapid technological change. As such, some of the technologies may have advanced substantially by the time this chapter is published or read.

The rest of the chapter is organised as follows. In the next section, we discuss how the theories that underpin much research in crime science (e.g. see Chapter 1; see also Bruinsma and Johnson, 2018) can contribute to thinking about the future and how they were used to identify emerging technologies with potential crime implications. We go on to describe the methodology employed in our systematic review of research conducted at UCL and summarise key findings of the review. Then we briefly discuss some of the developing technologies with implications for crime that were identified over the course of the project. We close by discussing crime prevention and the roles that different actors might play in preventing future crime.

Looking to the future through a crime-science lens

In this section, we briefly summarise some of the theoretical perspectives commonly used in crime-science research that informed our scanning work. Most of these are discussed in more detail in other chapters of this book (including Chapter 1) and hence we highlight only their core features and how they can inform thinking about crime futures.

1 **Routine activity perspective** (Cohen and Felson, 1979; Pease, 1997; Felson and Eckert, 2015) – is an ecological model of crime occurrence that considers how everyday routine activities bring together a likely (capable, motivated) offender, with a suitable target, absent capable guardians. A key aspect of the perspective is that changes to the activity of any one

of these elements (not just offenders) can influence the likelihood of crime occurrence. Consequently, we can ask of any technological or social change, 'how might this innovation or change affect the routine activities of likely offenders, suitable targets and capable guardians to that bring them together or keep them apart?'

2 **Rational choice perspective** – is a psychological/economic/opportunity model of offender decision-making (Cornish and Clarke, 2017). It considers an offender's response to perceived risk, effort and reward from a contemplated criminal act, or wider criminal involvement choice, based on 'opportunity structure'. From this perspective, it is assumed that offenders will more likely engage in crime when they perceive the rewards to outweigh the risk and effort involved. We can ask, 'how might an innovation/change influence actual and/or perceived risk, effort and reward for a given opportunity or wider criminal involvement choice?' We can also ask what new crime opportunities a particular technology might create.
3 **Crime-pattern theory** – is traditionally a geographical approach to understanding offender activity spaces and movement patterns and how this shapes their perception and awareness of local environments and the crime opportunities they offer (Brantingham, Brantingham and Andresen, 2017). We can ask, 'how might innovation/change affect offenders' ability to move within, spot opportunities and get to know risks in their activity space?' We can also ask 'how might that activity space itself change with (for example) the introduction of new transit systems, the use of mobile navigation applications that direct people through areas they would otherwise not visit, or as a consequence of receiving data on the activity of places?' Further, we might consider 'how might offenders develop activity spaces in virtual or other environments made accessible by new technology (e.g. unmanned aerial vehicles make airspace – and the third dimension – easily accessible to people)?'
4 **Crime precipitators** – is a psychological approach that considers the role of factors in or near the immediate crime situation which influence the motivation/emotion of offenders, making their search for, or exploitation of, criminal opportunities more likely. For example, situational precipitators, such as environmental cues, events or influences can prompt, pressure, permit or provoke criminal behaviour (Wortley, 2008, 2017). We can ask, 'how might innovation/change influence the nature, strength and patterns in situational precipitators, or the susceptibility of offenders to them?'
5 **Twenty-five techniques of situational prevention** – is an extensive catalogue of practical techniques (e.g. Clarke and Eck, 2003; www.popcenter.org/25techniques/) organised around various situational prevention principles relating to the above perspectives (risk, effort, reward to offender; excuses and provocations). We can ask, 'how might innovation/change enable or constrain the successful operation or implementation of each of these categories of preventive technique, or individual exemplars?'
6 The **conjunction of criminal opportunity** (CCO: Ekblom, 2011 and http://5isframework.wordpress.com) – is an integrated suite of 11 immediate causes of criminal events, and counterpart intervention principles; CCO merges situational prevention perspectives along with various offender-oriented approaches. These causes and interventions could change in the future and thus offer broad leads to systematically envisaging crime/security possibilities. We can ask, 'how might innovation/change affect each of these immediate causes of criminal events and how they interact? And how might it affect the scope for intervention in those causes?'
7 **Misdeeds and security framework** – is a 'think thief' approach to distinguishing several broad ways in which products, places, procedures and systems can feature in criminal action (Misappropriated, Mistreated, Mishandled, Misbegotten, Misused, Misbehaved

with, Mistaken) and security counterparts (see Ekblom, 2005, 2017). We can ask 'how might innovation/change enable or constrain Mistreatment, Misuse etc by offenders?'

8 **Risk and protective factors** – frameworks such as CRAVED (Clarke, 1999) have been developed to inform understanding of what makes a product 'hot' (i.e. targets at high risk of theft/misappropriation). Hot products are considered to be those that are Concealable, Removable, Available, Valuable, Enjoyable and Disposable and we can ask 'how might innovation/change affect these risk factors, or the capabilities/intent of offenders who might target them?'

Identifying developing technologies of interest

The first part of the work involved the identification of developing technologies that might have crime implications. The aim of the exercise was not to develop a list for which there would be consensus across researchers, but to identify a broad list of developing technologies. To do this, the second author scanned key science and technology publications over a six-month period and considered articles through the lens of the perspectives described above. The Science Daily,[2] BBC technology[3] and BBC science and environment web pages[4] were scanned on a near-daily basis, while the *New Scientist* magazine was read on a weekly basis and the UK Engineering and Physical Sciences Research Council (EPSRC) *Pioneer* magazine read every quarter. The frequency of scanning reflected the rate of publication for these different sources.

Science Daily and the BBC websites produce daily updated listings of science and technology news items and feature articles across the full spectrum of disciplines and domains, including relevant social sciences. Science Daily is based on edited publicity accompanying scientific journal articles supplied by source institutions, usually with links to the formal publications themselves. As such, it provides substantial coverage of current activity in the science and technology domains. *New Scientist* similarly provides links from both news items and specially commissioned feature articles which cover topics in depth and combine several sources.

To supplement this systematic search, sources including *The Daily Telegraph, The Economist, The Independent, WIRED* and *Nature* were sampled on a more ad-hoc basis, sometimes in the process of following up source material from the news feeds. All of the articles surveyed were coded in a number of ways, but most importantly in terms of if they had potential crime and security implications. Inevitably, the approach taken was somewhat subjective since only one of the authors engaged in this task. However, the use of the above frameworks was intended to structure the process. The final outcome of this exercise was a set of keywords regarding developing technologies with implications for crime (available upon request) to inform a search for articles published by staff at UCL.

UCL systematic review

As discussed above, two systematic searches of research published at UCL were conducted to identify (separately) work on developing technologies that explicitly discussed crime and work which did not, but for which there may be crime/security implications in the future. To conduct the two searches, all research outputs published over the four-year period January 2013 to December 2016 listed in the UCL Research Publications Service [RPS] repository were extracted for analysis – a total of 89,299 items. Of these, 16,144 did not meet the inclusion criteria for the two literature searches and were removed during one of four stages of sifting. Details of the reasons for removing outputs are shown in Figure 30.1. In total, 73,155 outputs were eligible for further examination.

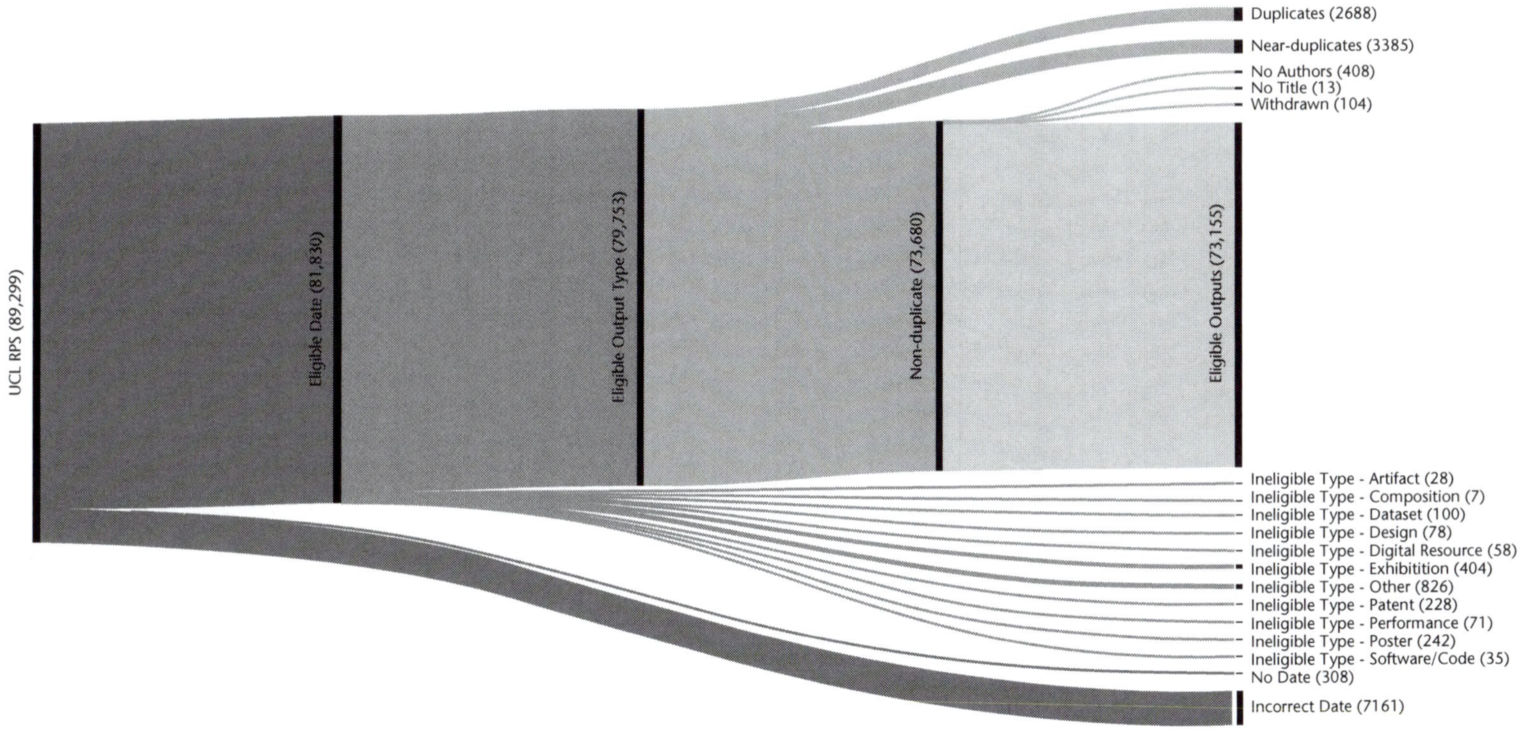

Figure 30.1 Sankey diagram showing the literature selection process and the inclusion and exclusion of research outputs

Search 1: research that explicitly mentions crime

The titles, abstracts, keywords and notes of each of the 73,155 outputs described above were systematically searched to find outputs (that were directly) related to crime, using the following set of 16 keywords:

- aggress* (for aggression, aggressive, etc.)
- assault
- burglar
- crime
- forensic
- malicious
- murder
- offend* (for offender, offending, etc.)
- police/policing
- rob/robber
- secur* (for secure, security etc.)
- theft
- threat
- victim
- violen* (for violence, violent, etc.)

Note that the character '*' is a wildcard, so that variants of the word stem searched for would be identified (e.g. offend* would identify terms such as offend, offender and offending)

Outputs that contained one or more of the keywords were identified as potentially relevant and inspected further. The term 'disorder' was originally included as a keyword. However, pilot testing revealed that it identified a large number of outputs (3,000+) that were unrelated to crime (e.g. articles concerned with topics such as psychological disorders but not crime). As such, this keyword was excluded.

In total, 1,839 outputs were identified that contained one or more of the crime keywords. Of these, 223 involved staff or students from the UCL Department of Security and Crime Science (DSCS). These were excluded from what follows – as we were primarily interested in articles published in other academic departments – and hence a total of 1,616 outputs remained.

The titles, abstracts and keywords for each of the remaining outputs were then reviewed by one of three research assistants (RAs) to assess its likely relevance. As with the previous exercise, this involved some degree of subjectivity (see below), but was completed using clear inclusion and exclusion criteria (available upon request). Chief amongst these was that the article should discuss a developing technology – defined as a new or in-development technology that has the potential to be involved in the commission, prevention or detection of crime in the next five years. Moreover, inter- and intra-rater exercises conducted for a sample of articles showed that the RAs' judgements were in close agreement – both with each other and with themselves at different stages of the review process. Following this exercise, a total of 274 articles were identified for the purposes of the review.

Figure 30.2 is a network graph that shows how research activity concerned with developing technology that has implications for crime (explicitly noted in the abstract, title or keywords) was distributed across UCL. Each green dot represents a research output, while each blue dot represents the academic department from which the lead author of the output is located. It is evident from Figure 30.2 that there are concentrations of activity within some UCL departments (and researchers within those departments). This is particularly the case for computer science, which is to be expected and welcomed, given that data from the CSEW suggest that at least half of all crime is now online. However, it is also clear that relevant research is conducted across a wide array of UCL departments, highlighting the fact that numerous disciplines can contribute to our understanding of crime and security and that there is a need to break down disciplinary silos.

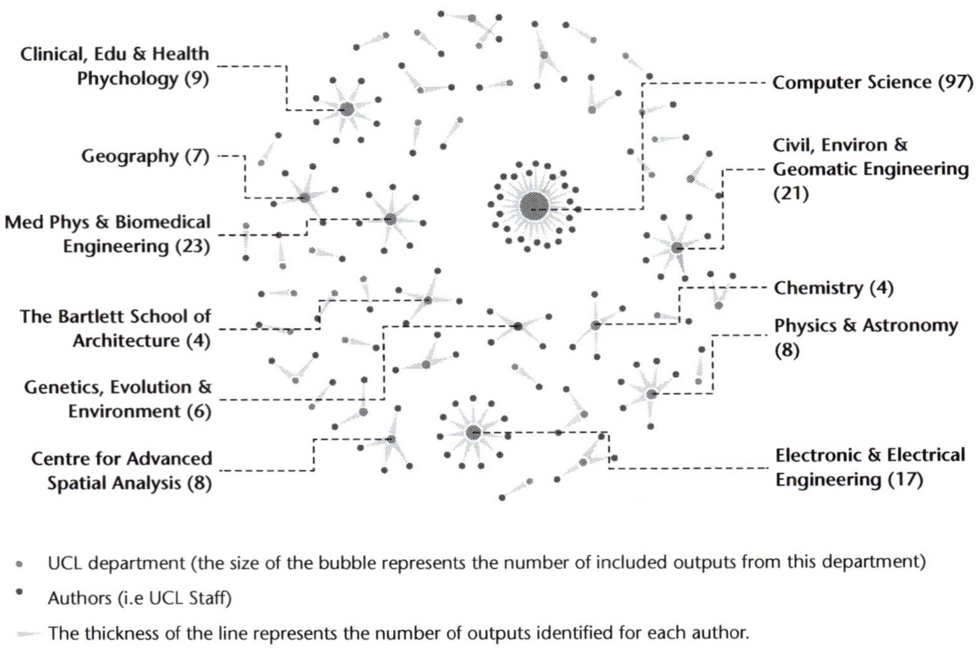

Figure 30.2 Network graph showing research activity concerned with crime and technology across UCL departments

Emerging themes

In this section, we draw out some of the general themes that emerged from the literature identified. These were identified through an iterative 'thematic analysis' and represent a mixture of broad crime types (e.g. cybercrime), targets, techniques, technologies and approaches. The 274 outputs were grouped into 13 overall themes which are listed in Table 30.1, along with the number of outputs associated with each theme.

Of these, outputs were further classified as those that were rated to be of most relevance to the future-crimes agenda. Forty-six articles met this criterion. Focusing on these outputs, Figure 30.3 shows the themes identified (green dots) and the home departments (blue dots) of the lead authors (some of which are labelled for the purposes of illustration). The nodes in the network are proportionately scaled to reflect the volume of outputs associated with a specific theme, and the number of outputs authored by staff in a particular department. The links between themes and departments are also proportionately shaded to indicate which departments contributed most to each theme. Again, a clear trend that emerges is that while there are concentrations of research activity for each theme in particular departments, work is conducted across a number of departments, highlighting the multidisciplinary nature of work on these issues.

It is beyond the scope of the current chapter to discuss each of the themes identified and the research associated with them. Instead, we offer a brief discussion of some of these to illustrate the type of work underway and how the technology might create new crime opportunities or ways to address them.

A total of 127 outputs were identified as being relevant to the theme of cyber-security, including 26 that were assessed as being highly relevant to the future-crimes agenda. These can be further divided into sub-categories to include research that has examined privacy and two-step

Table 30.1 The number of publications by theme

Theme	*All outputs*	*Highly relevant outputs*
Cyber-security	127	26
Scanning technology	29	9
Forensics	22	2
Other	15	3
Spatial analysis	15	0
Policing	13	4
Health & safety	10	0
Smart technology	9	1
Wildlife & environmental crime	9	0
Terrorism	8	1
Critical infrastructure security	7	1
Neuroscience	5	0
Virtual reality	5	0

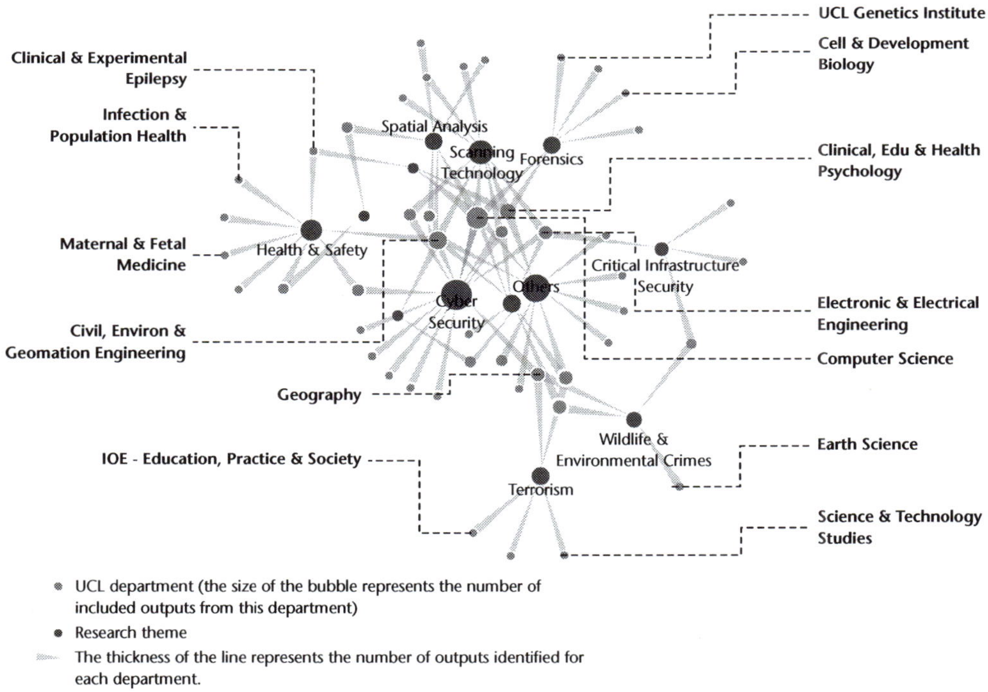

Figure 30.3 Network graph showing research activity by research themes and the UCL departments involved

authentication systems for government services (Brandao et al., 2015), the security of cloud computing (Jeuk et al., 2013), the application of cryptography to secure phone calls (Murdoch, 2016), the security of cryptocurrencies such as Bitcoin (e.g. Courtois et al., 2014) methods for quickly updating the security of networked computers (e.g. Forrester et al., 2016), the security of web browsers (e.g. Yang et al., 2013), patterns of contagion in cyber-attacks (Pym et al., 2012[5]) and the security of 5G networks (Wang et al., 2016).[6]

Many of these topics reflect emerging technologies associated with online activity that have the potential to be transformational in the future and to affect people's routine activities and hence opportunities for crime. Considering money, for example, cryptocurrencies such as Bitcoin have been used by criminals on the darknet for some time due to the fact that they are pseudonymous and have no central controller, which provides benefits to those who wish to conceal their identity and deal in illegal products or services. However, cryptocurrencies are increasingly used by legitimate businesses such as Microsoft, and travel companies such as Expedia,[7] as well as smaller businesses in urban settings. As their legitimate use increases, this may create new opportunities for offending. When introduced, 5G technology will lead to (for example) massive increases in the bandwidth available for internet-connected devices. Other research concerned with online activity discussed the trade-offs between the usability of online security techniques and the security they afford (Sasse and Smith, 2016) and why online security warnings fail (Sasse, 2015).

A second theme that emerged concerned scanning technologies. This included research on automated methods of analysing X-ray images of cargo (Jaccard et al., 2016; Rogers et al., 2017) to verify the content of containers, and a novel system for detecting illicit drugs in fast-parcel environments (Drakos, 2015). Other work involved the use of nanomaterials for the detection of illicit materials such as explosives (Peveler, 2015), and electromagnetic imaging systems for detecting materials through metallic enclosures (Darrer et al., 2015). Like most of the cyber-crime examples above, the research associated with this theme has developed in response to the crime opportunities afforded by changes, in this case changes to the ways in which goods are moved. For example, the growth in online shopping and increased competition in the delivery sector has created an environment of large volumes of 'fast' parcels which, while convenient for consumers, create new opportunities for crime and challenges for law enforcement as checking the volumes of parcels now delivered throughout the world is an immense challenge.

Search 2: Research with latent crime implications

The aim of the second search was to identify research on developing technologies that might have implications for crime in the future, but for which these implications are not acknowledged – at least not in the title, abstracts, keywords or notes of the articles. The absence of a discussion of crime in these articles is to be expected, as the researchers who undertook the studies generally work in other disciplines, and crime will be but one of many practical implications of their work. The aim of the research was thus to tease out some of these implications.

As with the first exercise, we systematically searched the 73,155 outputs described above. This time, however, we searched the articles using the set of 76 technology-related keywords identified as part of our first strand of work. As with the crime keyword search, some of the keywords initially used led to the identification of a large number of outputs (1,000+) that pilot testing (of a sample of around 5 per cent of them) suggested were entirely unrelated to crime. These keywords[8] were therefore excluded. In addition, outputs that had been identified in the crime keyword search were excluded from what follows to avoid duplication.

In total, 3,251 outputs were identified that contained one or more of the technology-related keywords. As with the first search, each of the outputs was reviewed by one of the RAs and retained or discarded according to whether it met our inclusion criteria.[9] A total of 304 publications remained after completion of this exercise.

Figure 30.4 shows how research activity of this kind is distributed across UCL. In this case, because of the focus of the keyword search, the network graph includes outputs from

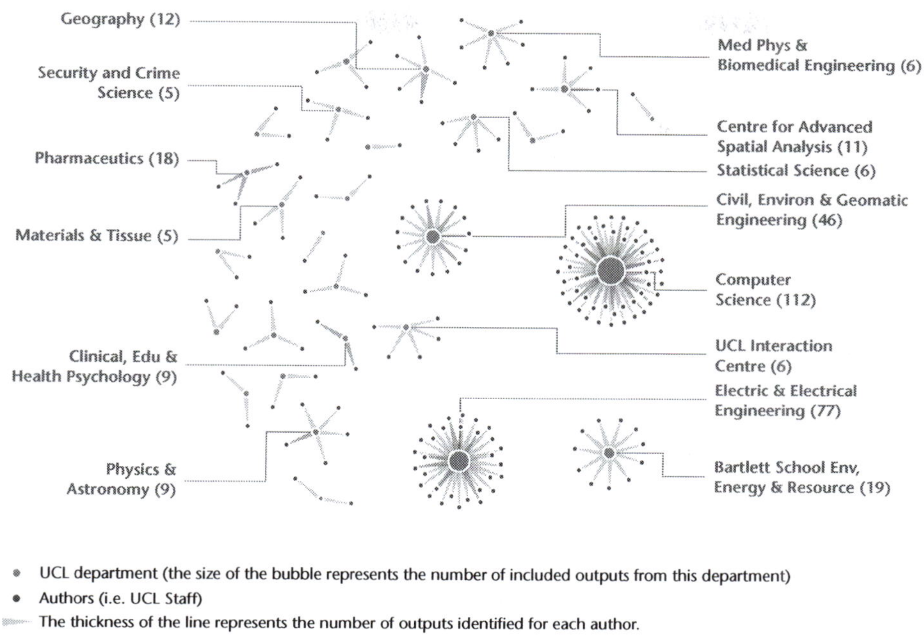

Figure 30.4 Network graph showing research activity concerned with developing technology with implications for crime across UCL departments

the Department of Security and Crime Science (SCS) as well as other UCL departments. There are some similarities between Figures 30.2 and 30.4. That is, activity is concentrated in some departments but is also clearly evident across the university. However, there are differences. For example, the Department of Electronic and Electrical Engineering features more prominently in Figure 30.4 than Figure 30.2 (accounting for 77 and 17 outputs across the two figures, respectively). Moreover, the Departments of Pharmaceutics and Materials and Tissue feature in Figure 30.4 but not in its counterpart. The number of relevant outputs identified as being of particular relevance also tended to be higher per department for this search than the earlier one. One interpretation of this is that, in the future, research on crime will need to become increasingly multidisciplinary.

Emerging themes

An iterative 'thematic analysis' of the 304 outputs revealed a total of 18 'overall' themes of research. These are shown in Figure 30.5 (green dots) along with the home departments (blue dots) of the lead authors.

In Table 30.2, we provide a further synthesis of topics and highlight ten example areas that were perceived by the authors of this chapter as being particularly relevant, either because they might facilitate crime or help to prevent it. It is beyond the scope of this chapter to discuss each theme in detail and hence their identification is simply intended to illustrate the diversity of issues and some of the implications. With this in mind, in each case we do provide a pen picture to illustrate some of the issues. To supplement this, we take two related themes and elaborate on these a little.

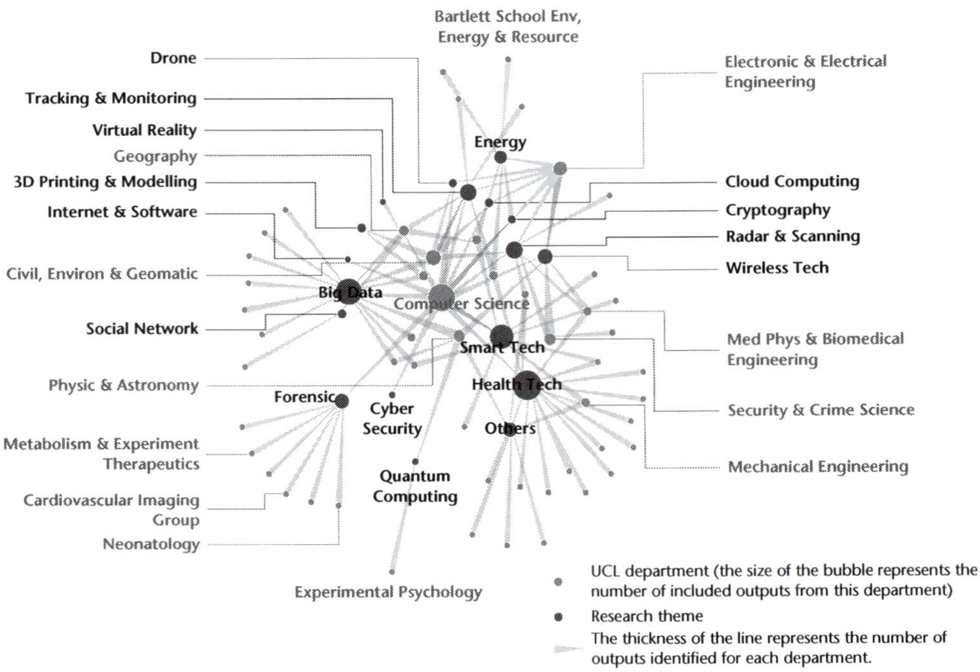

Figure 30.5 Network graph showing research activity by research themes and the UCL departments involved

Table 30.2 A sample of emerging technologies with implications for crime

Topics
1 Crime, place and the internet
In cities, analysis shows that crime clusters spatially, with around 20 per cent of places accounting for 80 per cent of problems. This has informed successful crime prevention. We can ask, while cybercrime does not occur at physical locations in the same way, does it cluster in other ways that might inform our understanding of (cyber)crime and its prevention?
2 Radar and scanning
As legitimate parcels are moved with increasing speed to meet consumer demand (across and within country borders), this provides opportunities for the movement of illegal goods. Advances in sensor technology increase what (e.g. counterfeit drugs) can be detected in containers, parcels and so on, while advances in artificial intelligence (AI) can increase the speed with which data obtained from sensors can be analysed and made sense of. In concert, such technologies may play an important role in reducing the crime opportunities that fast parcels offer criminals.
3 Social networks and monitoring technology
Advances in mobile technology and sensing enable people's physical and online activity to be tracked and correlated in real time. This could be used for criminal purposes (e.g. stalking), but could also be used to 'nudge' positive behaviour, or scan for emerging problems.
4 Internet of Things – industrial and domestic devices/autonomous vehicles, smart cities
Electronic devices, buildings and other physical infrastructure are increasingly internet-enabled. This presents opportunities to enhance people's quality of life, make our roads safer and run our cities more efficiently and sustainably. However, absent adequate security, connected infrastructure may be vulnerable to cyber-attack.

5 Smart technology and artificial intelligence

Advances enable artificial systems to learn rather than follow instructions. This revolution, along with the proliferation of 'smart devices' which enable sensing at low cost (e.g. Amazon Alexa) dramatically increases their potential for positive and criminal applications (see below).

6 Wireless technology

Next generation wireless technologies (e.g. 5G) are intended to enable faster data transfer, minimise energy consumption and allow wireless energy transfer. Ambient signals can also be used to detect and track activity in enclosed spaces.

7 Nano materials

Nano materials (including graphene) have tiny components. Their structural properties enable the manufacture of lightweight, resilient materials which can have embedded sensors. Such materials, which can be manufactured to meet specific functional requirements, have clear implications for combating crime. Examples would include lightweight but super-strong protective clothing for police officers.

8 Synthetic biology including CRISPR

CRISPR allows DNA editing and the manipulation of biological circuits. Current applications are in medicine and crops, possible applications include DNA as a storage medium. The potential implications are profound. Example crimes include gene doping and narcotic-crop mutation, while genetic tagging may help track and prevent the theft of industrial material.

9 Blockchain

The blockchain is an electronic, open, distributed ledger system used to verify and record transactions securely. It is perhaps best known as being the technology that underpins cryptocurrencies, including Bitcoin. It may fundamentally change economic and other transaction-based systems (e.g. land and property registration systems), making them more secure. It may also have applications in securing evidence in (digital) investigations. However, vulnerabilities might be exploited and, as cryptocurrencies are pseudonymous, they can and have facilitated cybercrime.

10 Quantum computing

Quantum computing would enable complex computations (currently intractable) to be completed efficiently. Effects would be pervasive as current methods of encryption (which secure the internet) would be threatened. Quantum cryptography would address this.

Smart technology

As discussed in Chapter 20, smart technology (also called the Internet of Things, or IoT) refers to products which are internet-connected, incorporate sensors and may have actuators that can make physical changes to the environment within which they are located. Such devices are often designed with the goal of improving people's quality of life and domestic examples can range from smart watches/activity trackers, to health monitors (e.g. heart-rate monitors), to internet-connected fridges, to smart energy meters, to home security systems. Most devices collect and transmit data, which could include indicators of health, physical activity or other forms of data. As such, the security of these technologies is important as they may store and/or transmit sensitive information such as people's daily routines, leaving them vulnerable to crime. Unfortunately, at present the security of many such devices is notoriously weak (e.g. DCMS, 2018). As the number of devices increases – industry experts estimate that by 2020 there will be around 20 billion devices (e.g. Gartner, n.d.) – so too will the opportunity for criminal activity that exploits them.

Insecurities in the IoT pose substantial risks to national infrastructure, as discussed in Chapter 20. Considering the risks posed by the IoT from a routine activity perspective, devices can send and receive data about people's movements and actions. Such data might be exploited by offenders to commit crimes such as burglary and other offences for which guardianship is an important deterrent, or it may facilitate domestic abuse in which coercive control and stalking play an important role (e.g. Dragiewicz et al., 2018). In terms of crime opportunity more generally, the proliferation of devices in people's homes and critical infrastructure suggests that the potential for their exploitation is huge and the implications alarming.

On a more positive note, researchers (Hunter, 2016) at UCL have looked at the possibility of developing automated persuasion systems (APS) that would run on mobile devices to encourage behaviour-change in individuals. As such devices become ever more pervasive so too does the opportunity to engage people with APS to affect their behaviour – in other words, the solution can scale up in step with the problem. In the context of crime, the authors discuss possible applications for the prevention of anti-social behaviour to include violence, sexism and trolling. Similarly, work by Lathia et al. (2013) has looked at how smartphones can unobtrusively sense human behaviour and how this might be applied to monitor and change it (through feedback). Extrapolating from these papers, an interesting application would be in the prevention of high-harm crimes such as domestic abuse. For instance, for offenders wanting to desist from behaviours such as stalking, smart sensing could be used to detect when an offender is at risk of committing abuse and an APS used to discourage this.

A different possible application comes from an anecdotal example of a case of domestic abuse.[10] During the incident, the abuser accused the victim of calling the Sherriff's office. Accidentally, their home smart speaker misheard his accusation, believing him to ask *it* to call the Sheriff's office. It did so, and officers were promptly dispatched to deal with the incident. We might ask whether such technology could and should be used in this kind of capacity in the future to prevent crime or detect offenders? In considering such questions, due care and attention does, of course, need to be given to ethical implications, and to opportunities to abuse such safeguarding. For example, while the type of artificial intelligence employed in such systems is advancing, there have already been demonstrations of how – through what are known as adversarial perturbations – these systems can be tricked in ways that would be impossible for a human to detect (e.g. Carlini and Wagner, 2018).

Smart cities

A related theme concerns smart cities. The smart-city concept takes the beneficial principles of smart devices and applies them at scale to make the running of cities more efficient, and in many cases more sustainable. Smart connectivity has the potential to impact on all aspects of city functioning, and cities around the world are already trialling smart technology to include everything from smart bins to smart traffic management.

In the smart city, transportation too is likely to change significantly both for service providers and ordinary citizens. For example, already we are seeing the emergence of Mobility as a Service (MaaS), which may ultimately reduce or eliminate the need for (most) individuals to own their own vehicles. The operating model of MaaS is to provide users with transportation for whole (door-to-door) journeys specified via a mobile phone application. Parts of the journey may involve rail, parts might involve taxis, or driving a rental car (according to the user's preferences), with the service seamlessly (in theory at least) providing the user with access to an efficient combination of various forms of transport, none of which the user needs to own.

While such services will have enormous benefits for the environment and people's mobility, some thought should go into how they will impact on our routine activities and if these changes are likely to create or disrupt opportunities for crime.

A perhaps more obvious concern regarding smart cities is their resilience to attack. In 2017, we saw that the operation of one-third of hospital trusts in the UK was adversely affected following cyber-attacks in the form of *Wannacry* (Ehrenfeld, 2017; Mayor, 2018). Wannacry is a type of ransomware that in this case was used by offenders to take over hospital systems and encrypt patient data, making it unavailable to hospital staff until ransoms were paid. In many cases, the attacks resulted in significant disruptions to patient treatment and care. This type of offending was (in part) made possible by the existence of cryptocurrencies, which are a form of non-fiat currency underpinned by a blockchain. While cryptocurrencies have many positive aspects (Brito and Castillo, 2013), they are transacted pseudonymously, which means offenders using them can conceal their identity in ways that they cannot so easily do using more traditional banking systems (but see, Meiklejohn et al., 2013). The use of cryptocurrencies in this context serves to highlight the importance of how *convergences* of technology – as opposed to single technologies – can make crime more likely: that is, while hospitals may have been vulnerable to attack before, absent cryptocurrencies it would have been difficult for offenders to extract ransoms at scale and with such little effort. In the language of the rational choice perspective, these technologies have tipped the balance of risk, effort and reward, creating new crime opportunities that are attractive to offenders.

As with wearable devices, smart cities do of course offer considerable potential for law enforcement and the prevention of crime more generally. For example, at present, law enforcement agencies take advantage of sensors in the environment in the form of CCTV cameras. These can provide surveillance capabilities to help in the detection or prevention of crime (Welsh and Farrington, 2009). The camera streams that are currently routinely available to the police are limited to those on their networks. However, as more cameras become internet-connected, so too does the potential network of cameras that could easily be used to prevent crime. This raises the question of how the other sensors that might form part of smart-city infrastructure could inform law enforcement activity? This will require careful consideration to avoid an Orwellian nightmare, but if done in an ethically appropriate manner that is seen as legitimate by the public whom the police serve, and with suitable checks and balances, the opportunities to protect our cities are substantial. Issues of provenance and verification will, of course, be important too as the potential to interfere with or inject data into networks will offer further opportunities for crime.

Discussion

In scanning the literature, we employed a range of theoretical frameworks such as the routine activity and rational choice perspectives to inform our thinking. In doing so, we identified various ways in which developing technologies might increase opportunities for crime. Of course, these approaches also provide a framework for thinking about what to do about the types of problems identified. Perhaps the most obvious is the application of situational crime prevention (e.g. Clarke, 1995). Initially developed to address everyday urban crime problems such as burglary and theft, it has since been developed for the application to acts of terrorism (Clarke and Newman, 2006) and cybercrime (Newman and Clarke, 2013). In summary form, as discussed in Chapter 1, the approach currently comprises 25 techniques intended to increase the effort (e.g. car immobilisers), increase the risks (e.g. CCTV on public transport), reduce the rewards (e.g. graffiti cleaning), reduce provocations (e.g. separate enclosures for rival teams at football stadia), or remove excuses (e.g. breathalysers in pubs) for crime (Clarke and Eck, 2003; www.popcenter.org/25techniques). In thinking about what to do about emerging crime problems, or how to enhance existing approaches to crime prevention with developing technologies, this would seem like a good place to start, and researchers are encouraged to do so.

The problem-analysis triangle (Scott et al., 2008; see also Chapter 1), related to routine activities, also provides a framework for thinking about how to address future crime problems and, in particular, who might need to be engaged to address them. As discussed in elsewhere in this book and the introduction to this chapter, the roles of the victim, offender and capable guardians are central to the routine activity perspective – crime is less likely in the presence of the latter and (generally impossible in) the absence of the former.

Guardians can take many forms, and include anyone or anything whose presence can deter crime. In considering new and emerging crime, we may need to think carefully about this role. The police will undoubtedly always be relevant, but they will not have the capability to address all future crime issues and nor will they be best placed to do so. Cybercrime provides a contemporary example for thinking about the changing shape of guardianship. In this context, guardians would include anti-virus software and home routers – the latter providing a gateway between home networks and the internet. Anti-virus software is imperfect and is generally of little value against zero-day attacks (when virus or malware patterns are unknown), but it does serve a guardian function by protecting against those infections that *are* known. What of routers? Are these as secure as they could be? In considering this question, Szewczyk and Macdonald (2017) suggest that the architects of router communication technology overlooked one thing – security. They thus acted as what are referred to as 'crime promoters' in the conjunction of criminal-opportunity framework described above. This refers to people, organisations or designers who inadvertently, carelessly or deliberately increase the likelihood of crimes committed by other people, e.g. by supplying vulnerable targets or useful resources for offending. Thinking about crime promoters draws explicit attention to how developing technologies, goods and services might contribute to future crime problems and emphasises the role that those other than the police might play in making crime more or less likely. Returning to the example of routers, as with many products and services, Szewczyk and Macdonald (2017) suggest that a focus on function took primacy over security. This will need addressing going forwards, but similar thinking will be required for new technologies.

The routine activity perspective has developed over time to incorporate other actors whose influence can affect the likelihood of crime occurrence. These include place managers (Madenson and Eck, 2018) who are responsible for the way in which particular facilities are managed, the policies that are practised, and the extent to which staff and those who use the facilities comply with them. In the context of future crime, we can ask what role place managers can play in reducing the likelihood that offenders will exploit new crime opportunities. This might include, for example, ensuring that managers of community synthetic biology laboratories[11] (see Table 30.2) set and enforce clear rules to ensure that those who use them do not engage in criminal activity.

The role of place managers may, however, need some rethinking in the context of smart cities. For example, as our environments become more automated and self-organising, will the role of individuals as place managers slowly (or rapidly) decline? While such futures may seem a long way off, consider that in shops, self-service checkouts have existed for some time. This removes a form of guardianship and perhaps it is not surprising that the evidence (e.g. Taylor, 2016) suggests their introduction has been accompanied by an increase in shop theft. Consider further that Amazon GO (in Seattle) and AliBaba (in China) are already testing the next generation of shopping environments in which customers (who register for the service via a smartphone application) do not even need to use a checkout but can, in the case of Amazon GO, simply pick up items and leave the store, with their accounts being charged automatically.

If the role of people as place managers does decline, attention will need to be given to how the role that they have fulfilled to date can be incorporated into smart systems of place management. If it does not, consideration will need to be given as to how place managers can and should exert an influence over smart systems to make crime less likely. It seems probable that – at least in the near future – some environments will become increasingly automated, while others will continue to be managed by people. If this is the case, then both issues will need consideration. In the last resort, human managers will be needed to cope with the adaptive nature of offenders when this exceeds the capability of any automated security system (e.g. Ekblom, 2017).

Another important type of actor that forms part of the problem-analysis triangle is the handler – a person who can directly influence the activity of a likely offender. Handlers usually have some form of emotional attachment to an offender such as a parent, friend or sibling (Sampson et al., 2010). Guardians, handlers and place managers are all forms of controllers (ibid.), and each can influence the likelihood of crime by protecting victims, discouraging offenders from offending and by making places safer, respectively. A further iteration of these ideas (ibid.) identifies *super controllers* as a set of actors who have a more indirect influence on the crime equation but who can have a broader impact on incentivising or enforcing approaches to crime prevention. These include regulators, the media and mass markets. Super controllers can exert their influence on all actors in a variety of ways. For instance, regulators can set standards for the manufacture of products or services to make them less criminogenic and enforce compliance with these standards. Apropos future and emerging crime, consider that at present there is no regulation regarding the security standards that consumer IoT devices should meet. As such, many devices have little to no security, making them vulnerable to attack and criminal exploitation.[12] In most countries, regulations exist to ensure that vehicles are roadworthy and safe to drive, and hence we might ask why similar regulation does not exist for IoT and similar products. Efforts are now underway by a number of governments (e.g. DCMS, 2018) to address this problem but this will take time and we have already seen criminal exploitation of the insecurities that these devices possess. The action is hopefully not too late, but it certainly could have started sooner. When considering developing technologies, or new services, it therefore seems important to consider the role that super controllers can and should play in ensuring that (at least) those that will become ubiquitous do not facilitate crime and are secure by design (for an extended discussion of such issues, see Clarke, 2005). The challenge is to find ways to turn them from potential crime promoters, into active and competent crime preventers.

Regulation will not always be the answer, but super controllers will still have a role to play. To take an example, consider vehicle crime in the UK in the 1990s. At that time, the theft of vehicles was soaring, which was unsurprising since vehicle security was woefully inadequate despite calls for this to be addressed. To encourage industry to respond, the UK Home Office published the Car Theft Index (see Laycock, 2003), which provided consumers with information on the rate at which different makes and models of vehicles were stolen (given the number that were on the road in the UK). Simple in its construction, it had the potential to influence both consumer choice and the industry who, presumably, would want to avoid reputational damage. Its publication was one of the factors that led to the industry quickly improving vehicle security, and it serves as an example of how super controllers can exert an influence using data and evidence (plus consumer and reputational pressure) as opposed to legislation.

In this chapter, we focused on how developing technologies might generate new opportunities for the commission or prevention of crime. However, technology is not the only thing that will influence the shape of crime in the future. Broader policy changes, societal preferences, and demographic change (to name a few) can act as externalities that have the potential to influence future crime patterns. If we are to anticipate future crime opportunities and address them, all of these changes will need consideration, as will their convergence with changes in technology. As discussed throughout this chapter and the introduction to this handbook, identifying these influences, understanding them and finding solutions to the problems that may follow will require a multidisciplinary approach, as embodied by the aspiration of crime science.

Notes

1 It is important to note that not all crime is covered in the survey, including that against shops and other businesses.
2 www.sciencedaily.com.
3 www.bbc.co.uk/news/technology.
4 www.bbc.co.uk/news/science_and_environment.
5 The most recent version of the paper is Baldwin et al. (2017).
6 Interestingly, this research employs statistical models that have been used to study the near-repeat phenomenon in the context of urban crime (e.g. Mohler et al., 2010).
7 www.expedia.com/Checkout/BitcoinTermsAndConditions.
8 Specifically, 'optic' and 'brain AND (reading OR control)' which led to the identification of articles concerned with topics such as eye conditions and scans of abnormal brain functionality, respectively.
9 To be included, the main criteria that articles needed to address was that they were concerned with a developing technology that has plausible implications for crime, and for the application of the research to be plausibly realised within the next five years.
10 www.independent.co.uk/life-style/gadgets-and-tech/news/man-beat-girlfriend-murder-threat-alexa-gadget-call-police-google-home-bernalillo-county-sheriff-new-a7835366.html. Last accessed 25 June 2018.
11 www.nature.com/scitable/blog/bio2.0/synthetic_biology_at_home.
12 For examples, see https://krebsonsecurity.com/tag/iot/; https://krebsonsecurity.com/2017/10/reaper-calm-before-the-iot-security-storm/; https://arstechnica.com/information-technology/2016/01/how-to-search-the-internet-of-things-for-photos-of-sleeping-babies.

References

Baldwin, A., Gheyas, I, Ioannidis, C., Pym, D., and Williams, J. (2017). Contagion in cyber security attacks. *Journal of the Operational Research Society*, *68*(7), 780–791.

Brandão, L. T., Christin, N., and Danezis, G. (2015). Toward mending two nation-scale brokered identification systems. *Proceedings on Privacy Enhancing Technologies*, *2015*(2), 135–155.

Brantingham, P. J., Brantingham, P. L., and Andresen, M. (2017). The geometry of crime and crime pattern theory. In R. Wortley and M. Townsley (eds) *Environmental Criminology and Crime Analysis* (2nd edition). London: Routledge.

Brito, J. and Castillo, A. (2013). *Bitcoin: A Primer for Policymakers*. Mercatus Center at George Mason University.

Carlini, N. and Wagner, D. (2018). Audio adversarial examples: targeted attacks on speech-to-text. arXiv preprint, arXiv:1801.01944.

Clarke, R. V. (1995). Situational crime prevention. *Crime and Justice*, *19*, 91–150.

Clarke, R. (1999). Hot products: understanding, anticipating and reducing demand for stolen goods. Police Research Series Paper 112. London: Home Office.

Clarke, R. V. and Newman, G. R. (2005). Security coding of electronic products. *Crime Prevention Studies*, *18*, 231.

Clarke, R. V. G. and Newman, G. R. (2006). *Outsmarting the Terrorists*. Westport, CT: Praeger.

Cohen, L. and Felson, M. (1979). Social change and crime rate changes: a routine activities approach. *American Sociological Review*, *44*, 588–608.

Cornish, D. and Clarke, R. (2017). The rational choice perspective. In R. Wortley and M. Townsley (eds) *Environmental Criminology and Crime Analysis* (2nd edition). London: Routledge.

Courtois, N. T., Valsorda, F., and Emirdag, P. (2014). Private key recovery combination attacks: on extreme fragility of popular bitcoin key management, wallet and cold storage solutions in presence of poor RNG events. Available at https://eprint.iacr.org/2014/848.

Darrer, B. J., Watson, J. C., Bartlett, P. A., and Renzoni, F. (2015). Electromagnetic imaging through thick metallic enclosures. *AIP Advances*, *5*(8), 087143.

Dragiewicz, M., Burgess, J., Matamoros-Fernández, A., Salter, M., Suzor, N. P., Woodlock, D., and Harris, B. (2018). Technology facilitated coercive control: domestic violence and the competing roles of digital media platforms. *Feminist Media Studies*, *4*, 609–625.

Drakos, I. (2015). Optimisation of illicit drug detection using X-ray diffraction: drug identification using low angle X-ray scatter–DILAX III. Doctoral dissertation, University College London.

Ehrenfeld, J. M. (2017). Wannacry, cybersecurity and health information technology: A time to act. *Journal of Medical Systems*, *41*(7), 104.

Ekblom, P. (1997). Gearing up against crime: a dynamic framework to help designers keep up with the adaptive criminal in a changing world. *International Journal of Risk Security and Crime Prevention*, *2*, 249–266.

Ekblom, P. (2005). How to police the future: scanning for scientific and technological innovations which generate potential threats and opportunities in crime, policing and crime reduction. In M. Smith and N. Tilley (eds) *Crime Science: New Approaches to Preventing and Detecting Crime*. Cullompton, UK: Willan Publishing.

Ekblom, P. (2011). *Crime Prevention, Security and Community Safety Using the 5Is Framework*. Basingstoke, UK: Palgrave Macmillan.

Ekblom, P. (2017). Technology, opportunity, crime and crime prevention – current and evolutionary perspectives. In B. Leclerc and E. Savona (eds) *Crime Prevention in the 21st Century*. New York: Springer.

Felson, M. and Eckert, M. (2015). *Crime and Everyday Life* (5th edition). London: Sage.

Foerster, K. T., Schmid, S., and Vissicchio, S. (2016). Survey of consistent network updates. arXiv preprint, arXiv:1609.02305.

Hunter, A. (2016). Computational Persuasion with Applications in Behaviour Change. In the annual proceedings of *Computational Models of Argument*, January, pp. 5–18.

Jaccard, N., Rogers, T. W., Morton, E. J., and Griffin, L. D. (2016). Tackling the X-ray cargo inspection challenge using machine learning. In *Anomaly Detection and Imaging with X-Rays (ADIX)* (Vol. 9847, p. 98470N). International Society for Optics and Photonics.

Jeuk, S., Zhou, S., and Rio, M. (2013). Tenant-id: tagging tenant assets in cloud environments. In *IEEE/ACM International Symposium on Cluster, Cloud and Grid Computing (CCGrid)*, May 13, 2013 (pp. 642–647). Piscataway, NJ: IEEE.

Lathia, N., Pejovic, V., Rachuri, K. K., Mascolo, C., Musolesi, M., and Rentfrow, P. J. (2013). Smartphones for large-scale behavior change interventions. *IEEE Pervasive Computing*, *12*(3), 66–73.

Levi, M. (2000). The prevention of plastic and cheque fraud: a briefing paper. London: Home Office.

Mailley, J., Garcia, R., Whitehead, S., and Farrell, G. (2008). Phone theft index. *Security Journal*, *21*(3), 212–227.

Mayor, S. (2018). Sixty seconds on . . . the WannaCry cyberattack. *British Medical Journal*, *361*: k1750.

Meiklejohn, S., Pomarole, M., Jordan, G., Levchenko, K., McCoy, D., Voelker, G. M., and Savage, S. (2013). A fistful of bitcoins: characterizing payments among men with no names. *In Proceedings of the 2013 Conference on Internet Measurement Conference*, October (pp. 127–140). New York: ACM.

Murdoch, S. J. (2016). Insecure by design: protocols for encrypted phone calls. *Computer*, *49*(3), 25–33.

Newman, G. R. and Clarke, R. V. (2013). *Superhighway Robbery*. Abingdon, UK: Routledge.

ONS (Office for National Statistics) (2017). Crime Survey in England and Wales. Office for National Statistics. Available online at: www.ons.gov.uk/peoplepopulationandcommunity/crimeandjustice/bulletins/crimeinenglandandwales/yearendingmar2017#what-is-happening-to-trends-in-crime.

Pease, K. (1997). Predicting the future: the roles of routine activity and rational choice theory. In G. Newman, R. V. G. Clarke, and S. G. Shosham (eds) *Rational Choice and Situational Crime Prevention: Theoretical Foundations*. Aldershot, UK: Dartmouth Publishing.

Peveler, W. J. R. (2015). Development of nanomaterial-based sensors for the detection of explosives. Doctoral dissertation, University College London.

Pym, D. J., Williams, J., Ioannidis, C., Gheyas, I. A., and Baldwin, A. (2012). Contagion in cybersecurity attacks. In *11th Annual Workshop on the Economics of Information Security*. Berlin, 25–26 June.

Rogers, T. W., Jaccard, N., Morton, E. J., and Griffin, L. D. (2017). Automated X-ray image analysis for cargo security: critical review and future promise. *Journal of X-ray Science and Technology*, *25*(1), 33–56.

Sampson, R., Eck, J. E., and Dunham, J. (2010). Super controllers and crime prevention: a routine activity explanation of crime prevention success and failure. *Security Journal*, *23*(1), 37–51.
Sasse, A. (2015). Scaring and bullying people into security won't work. *IEEE Security and Privacy*, *13*(3), 80–83.
Sasse, M. A., and Smith, M. (2016). The security-usability tradeoff myth. *IEEE Security & Privacy*, *14*(5), 11–13.
Scott, M., Eck, J. E., Knutson, J., and Goldstein, H. (2008). Problem-oriented policing and environmental criminology. In: R. Wortley and L. Mazerolle (eds) *Environmental Criminology and Crime Analysis*. Cullompton, UK: Willan Publishing, pp. 221–246.
Szewczyk, P., and Macdonald, R. (2017). Broadband Router Security: History, Challenges and Future Implications. *Journal of Digital Forensics, Security and Law*, *12*(4), 6.
Taylor, E. (2016). Supermarket self-checkouts and retail theft: the curious case of the SWIPERS. *Criminology & Criminal Justice*, *16*(5), 552–567.
Welsh, B. C. and Farrington, D. P. (2009). Public area CCTV and crime prevention: an updated systematic review and meta-analysis. *Justice Quarterly*, *26*(4), 716–745.
Wang, L., Wong, K. K., Elkashlan, M., Nallanathan, A., and Lambotharan, S. (2016). Secrecy and energy efficiency in massive MIMO aided heterogeneous C-RAN: a new look at interference. *IEEE Journal of Selected Topics in Signal Processing*, *10*(8), 1375–1389.
Wortley, R. (2017). Situational precipitators of crime. In R. Wortley and M. Townsley (eds) *Environmental Criminology and Crime Analysis* (2nd edition). London: Routledge.

31

Future directions for crime science

Richard Wortley, Aiden Sidebottom, Nick Tilley and Gloria Laycock

Introduction

This handbook was conceived as a manifesto for crime science. We set out to describe the origins, development and key characteristics of crime science (Chapter 1), demonstrate how different disciplines can contribute to a better understanding of and response to crime (Chapters 2 to 13) and to showcase examples of crime science in action (Chapters 14 to 30). The chapters that make up this handbook thus cover a very wide range of topics. This is deliberate. Part of our intention was to highlight the diversity of research that falls under our definition of crime science. In this sense, the range of activities contained herein are illustrative rather than exhaustive, designed to convey a sense of what it means to do crime science, without trying to cover all research possibilities.

In this final chapter we present promising avenues for further work, as we see them. Our suggestions are necessarily cautious: it will be for future crime scientists to shape what is achieved. Moreover, some of that will be influenced by future scientific, technological, societal, environmental, and political developments that are currently unknowable. These challenges notwithstanding, in the remainder of this chapter we identify three potential areas for further work: academic developments; extending the range and depth of research topics; and old crimes and new methods. Each area has several suggested sub-topics, which again are illustrative rather than exhaustive.

Academic developments

Academics develop new techniques and theories as an integral part of their job. It is no surprise therefore that this activity should continue. In the sections below we suggest some of the areas in which crime science specifically might focus its academic endeavour.

The relationship between opportunity and criminal careers

In Chapter 1 we described how the roots of crime science can be traced back to environmental criminology. Thus, much crime science (as illustrated in many of the chapters in this handbook), like environmental criminology, focusses on the *crime event* rather than the sources of *criminality*. For many crime scientists this is because they are primarily interested in reducing crime and there is extensive evidence to suggest that the immediate environment can be changed in ways that make crime less likely.

A preoccupation with crime does not preclude insight on criminals, however, nor deny the fundamental fact that crime occurs as the result of a person-situation interaction. Take the so-called 'international crime drop'. We remarked earlier that crime rates for many offences have been dropping since the early to mid-1990s in most western societies (Farrell, Tilley & Tseloni, 2014). This has been associated with a striking change in the age–crime curve, most especially for what had been high-volume property crimes such as vehicle theft and burglary (Farrell, Laycock & Tilley, 2015). The adolescent spikes for these offences have dropped dramatically over time (for example, see Matthews & Minton, 2018; Payne et al., 2018). The age–crime curve has been flattening (although it remains far from flat). This means that fewer people are being drawn into criminal careers. For those interested in criminal careers and in reducing youth criminality, this is of fundamental importance. It suggests a research agenda better to understand: 1) whether and how changing opportunities, brought about largely by improvements in the quality and extent of security as well as routine activities, have interacted with recruitment patterns of young people into criminal activities, and 2) whether and how this process has then fed into wider changes in patterns of longer-term criminal involvement.

There is much interesting and challenging work to be undertaken in relation to this. It includes, for example, a) modelling changes in opportunity and criminal involvement across different settings and crime types (including possible displacement to online offending), b) assembling and analysing data on offending patterns as they can be discerned from criminal-justice records to reconstruct (changing) criminal-career patterns by time, place and sub-group, c) re-analysing available data from longitudinal studies with a specific focus on identifying and explaining changing patterns of opportunity and criminal involvement, and d) initiating fresh primary studies with a specific focus on variations in opportunity and involvement in criminal behaviour.

None of these suggestions should be taken to disparage existing criminological research that aims to map out and understand criminal careers. It is only to note that crime scientists have important contributions to make to that work by focusing on the links between crime-event opportunity (in contrast to social opportunity which has long been a focus of criminological enquiry) and criminal careers. The practical importance is obvious. If there is indeed a link, and it can be understood, given the relatively straightforward task of opportunity reduction we may have a powerful method of addressing youth criminality that is less focussed on the biological and social sources of criminality, which are generally much more difficult to manipulate in the short term than crime-event opportunity structures and also raise serious ethical issues.

Development of big-data analytics for crime science

'Big data' is the ubiquitous, albeit somewhat vague term used to describe extremely large, unprocessed datasets that promise new ways to explore trends and patterns in human behaviour. Big data has already had a major influence on many aspects of modern life. Retailers, for example, routinely sift through social media data in an effort to work out what items are 'trending' so as to make predictions about what customers might want from their next purchase. Energy companies likewise employ sophisticated analytical software to determine patterns in customer usage data so as to optimise their responses to energy surges. Big data may also have implications for how we conceive of and practice science. According to Anderson (2008), the era of big data may usher in the disappearance of the scientific method, whereby the traditional hypothesise-model-test approach is replaced by the use of supercomputers and machine learning techniques to analyse huge swathes of data so as to detect reliable patterns and associations, some of which may not have been predicted.

There can be little doubt that big data will have a significant effect on both crime and efforts to control it. It is already happening. There are now countless examples of how big data managed by governments and businesses has been hacked, breached and compromised. On the other hand, police services and other criminal-justice agencies are increasingly using big-data analytical techniques to determine ways to better allocate resources and reduce wastage. There is much important work to be done to harness the potential of big data better to understand and respond to crime (Sanders & Sheptycki, 2017; Williams, Burnap & Sloan, 2017). This relates both to improvements in explanations of the nature and patterns of crime, such as the analyses of mobile phone records to determine individual-level movement patterns (see Gonzalez, Hidalgo and Barabasi, 2008), and to the prediction of crime occurrences. The latter call for work to develop, test and implement algorithms that use past incidents of crime to estimate those places where crime is most likely to occur in the immediate future (Perry, 2013). We contend that crime scientists are well placed to contribute to this line of research, in part because of the clear need for collaborative work with those skilled in areas of computer and data science.

That contribution may take several forms. One caveat to unfettered enthusiasm for big-data analysis is to note the potential danger of using data with inbuilt prejudices (such as biases in some police data toward the criminalisation of racial minorities) to further entrench these prejudices (Bayne, 2017; Ferguson, 2017; Shapiro, 2018). As alluded to in Chapter 1, crime science must remain mindful of the fact that much work carried out in the interests of crime reduction carries ethical considerations. It is an important caveat which is easy to overlook as novel and valuable analyses emerge. That said, the most critical and potentially ethically problematic use of big-data analytics arises when attempting to predict the past, present or future criminality of individuals (see Harcourt, 2005 for an early and critical discussion of the trend toward actuarialism in criminal justice). The use of such data for prevention purposes, as we discuss the term here, is, we would contend, less of an ethical challenge since it does not threaten the liberty or treatment of individuals. individuals. Just the same, care must always be taken to balance crime prevention benefits against potential negative side-effects.

The challenge of bringing disciplines together

As the case of big data illustrates, the implementation of technology does not occur in a vacuum. It involves both technical and societal considerations. The headlong rush to big-data analytics and the ethical issues this raises provide but one example of the crucial need for social and data scientists (in this case) to talk to one another. And of course this principle extends to many other areas of crime control. We outlined in Chapter 1 (Wortley et al.) the case for breaking down disciplinary silos and we need not rehearse the arguments here. In this volume we have explicitly sought contributions from disciplines including those not traditionally associated with crime research.

But in truth, most of the contributions in this volume showed what individual disciplines could contribute to the crime problem in general (Section 1) or to specific crime types (Section 2). They were at best demonstrations of multidisciplinarity in crime science. One chapter that took on the issue of disciplinary integration as its central theme was Prichard et al. (Chapter 21). They describe a project developed by a team of researchers with backgrounds in computer science, psychology, crime science and law. The project involved the creation of a dummy website purporting to offer 'barely legal' pornography images. As individuals sought out the website they encountered a warning message designed to deter them from progressing. The authors make the case that this innovative project would simply not have been possible without the combined expertise of the collaborators.

As noted in Chapter 1, disciplinary integration is difficult to achieve. True progress towards disciplinary integration may not occur until the structural impediments – e.g., the disciplinary structure of university departments and research funding bodies - are removed. But our experience at the Jill Dando Institute is that disciplinary collaboration is possible and is enormously rewarding. The JDI is fundamentally problem-focussed; it comprises academics from many disciplines but has the single goal of finding ways to reduce crime. Having a shared mission is crucial in getting people working together. We have made progress towards greater disciplinary integration but we acknowledge that there is still a long way to go before the benefits of collaborative research are fully exploited.

Extending the range and depth of research topics

Crime science, as with most criminology, has focussed so far on a quite narrow range of high-volume offence types that are typically committed by disadvantaged young males (burglary, theft, street crime, sexual assault and so on). One consideration when collating Section 2 (Crime science in action) of this handbook was to present a range of research case studies that highlight neglected and/or emerging crime problems. But we have only scratched the surface of possibilities. Here, we suggest some of the crime challenges that future work might address.

The glocalisation of crime and crime opportunities

'Glocalisation' is used here to refer to the trend toward the attenuation of the local (although not its disappearance) and the rise of the global, with some interaction and interdependency between the one and the other. In relation to crime this means that some theories may need revision or replacement. The routine activities approach, for example, stresses the convergence in space and time of likely offenders, suitable targets and the absence of capable guardianship. Environmental criminology stresses the spatial configuration of cities, the routine movements of likely offenders, and the geographic availability of crime targets as drivers of crime-opportunity-awareness spaces and hence crime-distribution patterns. While the local still functions as a source of crime patterns, with the emergence of information technologies in particular, the global has taken on major importance. Cyberspace, cyber traffic, and consequential cyber-opportunity awareness are now important sources of crime patterns (Hartel & Junger, Chapter 12; Stringhini, Chapter 18; Johnson et al., Chapter 30). These still surface, of course, in local space in the form of property and personal crimes but crime targets, crime opportunities, crime scripts, and crime resources now reside in cyber/global as well as local spaces.

One future direction for crime science concerns the adaptation of theory and formulation of crime-prevention strategies better to speak to the cyber/global nature of crime as well as the physical/local, and the inevitable intersection of the two. Initial forays look promising. In a recent study, Sidebottom and Tilley (2017) demonstrated how the high levels of concentration found to characterise crime patterns in physical space were also observed when analysing the distribution of crime in cyberspace, specifically online romance scams across dating websites. Put differently, just as crime is shown to be heavily concentrated in a small number of physical places, so too were a small number of online spaces (dating websites) found to account for a disproportionate number of all reported romance scams.

Preventing organised crime and terrorism

Research specifically on the prevention of organised crime and terrorism has been relatively sparse in the criminological literature. We have attempted to redress this neglect with several chapters in this volume devoted to these topics (Lavorgna, Chapter 15; Marchment & Gill, Chapter 16; Ekblom & Gill, Chapter 17). But there is much more that can be done. Taking a specific form of organised crime – trafficking in human organs – as an example, a number of potentially fruitful questions arise: what are the patterns in terms of place, time, movement, victim, incentives, etc. (for example where, when and how are organs sourced for trafficking, how are they transported, how does their identity get changed, and who knows and does not know about the provenance of the trafficked organs?). What are the recurrent sources of opportunity as the offences unfold (for example, what types of hospital with what management structures allow organs to be taken in ways that are of low-enough risk and high-enough reward for those implicated to take part, and how and by what relationships are prospective 'donors' identified and how are they paid for the organs taken?). What measures put in place, where and when, could block opportunities by increasing risk, reducing reward, increasing difficulty, reducing excuses, and removing prompts and provocations. Would it be, for example, at the point at which potential 'donors' are identified; in the surgery involved in removing the organ; in transporting it, or in re-presenting the trafficked organ to the surgeon and other health workers transferring it to the recipient?

There is a substantial crime-science research agenda that will draw on a wide range of disciplines, depending on the specific organised crimes of interest. In relation to organ trafficking, expertise in management, medicine, economics, psychology, sociology, and international development might all have a contribution to make in helping understand the ways in which patterns of organ trafficking are produced and in figuring out promising ways of reducing opportunities for it.

What goes for organ trafficking in terms of required details of analysis prior to identifying potential intervention strategies goes, of course, for other forms of organised crime. There is an enormous research-and-policy agenda ripe for exploitation in the interests of harm reduction.

White-collar crime

Very substantial harms are caused by offences that are undertaken by the relatively 'respectable', rich and powerful. Those committing such crimes may include public servants such as police officers, professional workers such as doctors, accountants and solicitors, politicians at all levels from all parties and across jurisdictions, and those involved in running private-sector organisations.

Just as the fundamental attribution error can lead to blindness to the importance of situations in producing patterns of volume crime so too it can do the same for white-collar crimes committed by the relatively powerful. Here, the notion that the offences are committed by a few exceptional bad apples, who need to be identified and rooted out, diverts attention from situations that enable or encourage patterns of criminal behaviour and what can be done to reduce the opportunities that are exploited. This should be a fruitful focus for future crime-science research.

Counterfeit medicines in low-income countries

Counterfeit medicines are a common and costly problem, particularly in low-income settings. They can take several forms, from drugs which contain none of the required active pharmaceutical ingredients to cocktails of harmful substances. In 2011, the World Economic Forum reported that the market for fake medicines was worth an estimated US$200 billion, second only to the illicit drug trade.

To date, much of the research into counterfeit medicines has focussed on the extent and correlates of the problem, and the harms it generates (see Crews, Kenny, O'Flynn & Speller, 2018). Less research has examined patterns of counterfeiting with a view to informing preventive efforts. Products are not stolen with equal frequency. The acronym CRAVED (Concealable, Removable, Available, Valuable, Enjoyable and Disposable) attempts to identify those features that are attractive to offenders and which make certain items more susceptible to theft (Clarke, 1999). Equally we could ask whether certain types of medicines are more likely to be counterfeited than others, perhaps reflecting the demand of the local population or the ease with which the product and packaging of a given drug can be copied. This sort of target-oriented research is standard fare for crime scientists, but has not yet been systematically applied to the problem of fake drugs in resource-limited settings. We think it should be.

This speaks to a broader point. As should be clear from reading this chapter so far, despite significant gaps in our knowledge, we have made huge progress in controlling crime and understanding the mechanisms through which this has been achieved. These mechanisms apply in the context of the leading, largely western democracies. Whether the same mechanisms and thus prevention techniques can be applied in areas of economic underdevelopment, or in countries where there are significant issues of corruption and disorder remains to be seen. Our opening premise is that they can because they are based on some fundamental attributes of human nature – human behaviour being the product of internal dispositions and situational forces. However, we are also acutely aware of the practical challenges of doing crime prevention, where issues of implementation are legion and which can affect the activation and sustenance of said preventive mechanisms. There is much to be gained from a systematic programme of work centred on the generalisability of preventive mechanisms and the extent to which (and how) they can be triggered in diverse, atypical conditions.

Old crimes, new opportunities

One of the insights on which crime science draws is that opportunity is a major driver of crime. This leads to the realisation not only that new technologies and major social changes will lead to changes in crime, but also that something can be done to reduce those opportunities and thus reduce crime. Here we look at how some of the major developments we are now seeing have already led to changes in the crime profile and discuss how expected future developments might play out.

Thefts of intangibles and their prevention

Targets of property crime have traditionally been things such as cars, cameras and computers, but consumption now includes intangibles such as online pornography, bank deposits, cryptocurrencies, music, film, computer games, e-books, and pay-per-view television. Crime science to date has focussed most of its attention on physical objects, which have fundamentally different crime-target attributes, require different crime skills and present distinctive preventive challenges. CRAVED still applies to intangibles, but what makes intangibles concealable, removable, available, valuable, enjoyable and disposable is different and presents distinctive preventive challenges. Making their theft or illicit use more risky, less rewarding, and more difficult is likely to require attention from IT specialists as well as crime scientists, as is the challenge of issuing timely rule reminders and the reduction of prompts and provocations. The previously described project by Prichard et al. (Chapter 21) is an example of using automated warning messages to deter individuals contemplating accessing child-sexual-exploitation material, and this strategy might usefully be applied in other areas of online deviant behaviour.

Global shifts

Current predictions are that there will be major changes in the global climate, in migration patterns and in population dynamics. These changes will alter the opportunity patterns for crime and thus change the nature of crime itself. As with the technological developments discussed above, pre-empting the expected shifts in opportunities for crime, and attempting to block them, would be a sensible policy option.

A good example of what we have in mind is the growth in people trafficking across the Mediterranean Sea following the political turmoil in North Africa and Syria. Migration of large numbers of citizens, either because of war, collapsing economies, or both, was predictable, as was the emergence of organised crime groups offering illegitimate routes to Europe. Waiting until the trafficking routes are established and the organised criminals are organised before reacting should be avoided if possible.

Technological development, crime foresight and crime pre-emption

A theme that has been developed throughout this volume is that science and technology have transformed the nature of the crime and security threats that we face, and also the way that we need to respond to these threats. Several chapters are concerned with how recent technologies and innovations are exploited for criminal gain, be it bitcoins (Meiklejohn, Chapter 19) or the Internet of Things (Tuptuk & Hailes, Chapter 20). Other chapters centre on ways to better forecast and respond to the crime risks associated with new and emergent technologies (Johnson, Chapter 30; Lacey, Chapter 29). The advent of the internet provides the most dramatic example of these developments. The very features of the internet that make it such a powerful tool for performing legitimate tasks also provide opportunities for offenders to exploit it for criminal and terrorist purposes, while we are only beginning to see the emergence of crimes associated with the IoT (Ng, 2018; SafeGadget, 2018). But it is not just the digital revolution that has changed the crime and security landscape. As Johnson et al. (Chapter 30) outline, crime opportunities are also presented by developments in, for example, nanotechnology, bioscience, robotics and cybernetics. There is a steady flow of new weapons, materials, and devices (drones, 3D printers, driverless cars) that can potentially be exploited for criminal activities. In response, we must anticipate the criminogenic threats posed by new technologies, and develop new expertise and adopt new strategies to counter such threats.

Aside from the obvious technical challenges these new crimes present, requiring as they do collaboration between law enforcement personnel and those with the necessary technical skills, a feature of many technology-assisted crimes is the anonymity it offers many offenders, a development that fundamentally challenges the traditional criminal-justice paradigm of arrest, punish and rehabilitate. This in turn has implications for the type of crime research that is required.

Take, for example, what has occurred in the case of child-exploitation material (CEM) (see Wortley & Smallbone, 2012). During the 1960s and 1970s the US (among other western counties) experienced a mini boom in hard-copy CEM in the form of (largely) imported books, photos and films. This sparked a concerted effort by law enforcement and customs agencies to stem the tide through a range of traditional law-enforcement activities – introduction of new legislation, more vigorous enforcement, higher prosecution rates, tightening the importation of material from overseas, and so on. These efforts had considerable success, and by 1980 the largest-selling CEM magazine in the US was reckoned to sell just 800 copies. In 1982, a report by a subcommittee of the US Congress concluded that 'As a result of the decline in commercial child pornography, the principal Federal agencies responsible for laws covering the distribution of child pornography . . . do not consider child pornography a high priority'. Nine months later, in January 1983, the internet protocols were signed and changed everything.

Today, CEM distributed via the internet is a serious international problem with active offenders estimated in the millions. The internet has created a pool of offenders who in pre-internet times would never have had the opportunity to access CEM, and perhaps would never have even thought to do so. A tiny fraction of these offenders are ever caught and brought before the justice system. While it is technically possible to trace many (but by no means all) offenders, it is practically impossible to do so. The effort required to identify offenders (e.g., via an IP address), coupled with the sheer volume of offenders, overwhelms police resources. Moreover, offenders may be located anywhere in the world, outside the jurisdiction of the investigating agency. This situation is forcing a shift away from offender-focussed law enforcement to the adoption of new techniques aimed at countering and disrupting the online behaviour of 'anonymous' offenders. The strategies available to apply to the problem are necessarily situational (e.g. increasing the effort to access CEM – see Wortley & Smallbone, 2012). Likewise, traditional psychological theories and approaches focussed on describing the offender's psychological profile are of little practical value if the offender is never caught. Where psychology (and other social sciences) can be of value is: 1) to understand the way that offenders interact with technology – for example, the search strategies they use to locate material, their perceptions of risk, and the efforts they make to avoid detection – so that countermeasures can be devised, 2) to help law-enforcement agencies triage their work load so that they can reliably allocate resources to the riskiest and most serious cases and 3) to contribute to the task of forecasting the nature and spread of child-sexual-exploitation crimes as new technologies come online.

The same issue applies to a greater of lesser degree to other cyber-enabled crimes – cyber-bullying, fraud, internet scams and so on – where identifying, let alone catching offenders, is in most cases not feasible. The crime science model, with its emphasis on here-and-now prevention and broadly-based interdisciplinarity, is ideally placed to help counter the crime threats that these new technologies may pose.

Conclusion

We began this volume with an introductory chapter tracing the development of crime science and setting out its key characteristics. In this final chapter we have speculated on some promising ways ahead for the field. We have been cautious in our predictions, and mindful that there are countless pathways upon which crime science might advance. Of what we are certain, however, is that crime science provides a valuable blue-print for responding to the crime problem we face today and those that are now emerging.

References

Anderson, C. (2008) The end of theory: the data deluge makes the scientific method obsolete. *Wired Magazine*, *16*(7), 16–17.

Brayne, S. (2017) Big data surveillance: the case of policing. *American Sociological Review*, *82*(5), 977–1008.

Clarke, R. (1999) Hot products: understanding, anticipating and reducing demand for stolen goods. London: Home Office, Policing and Reducing Crime Unit, Research, Development and Statistics Directorate.

Crews, C., Kenny, P. S., O'Flynn, D., & Speller, R. D. (2018) Multivariate calibration of energy-dispersive X-ray diffraction data for predicting the composition of pharmaceutical tablets in packaging. *Journal of Pharmaceutical and Biomedical Analysis, 151*, 186–193.

Farrell, G., Laycock, G., & Tilley, N. (2015) Debuts and legacies: the crime drop and the role of adolescence-limited and persistent offending. *Crime Science, 4*(1), 16.

Farrell, G., Tilley, N., & Tseloni, A. (2014) Why the crime drop? *Crime and Justice, 43*, 421–490.

Ferguson, A. G. (2017) *The Rise of Big Data Policing: Surveillance, Race, and the Future of Law Enforcement*. New York: New York University Press.

Gonzalez, M. C., Hidalgo, C. A., & Barabasi, A. L. (2008) Understanding individual human mobility patterns. *Nature, 453*(7196), 779.

Harcourt, B. E. (2005) *Against Prediction: Sentencing, Policing, and Punishing in an Actuarial Age*. University of Chicago Public Law & Legal Theory Working Paper No. 94.

Matthews, B. & Minton, J. (2018) Rethinking one of criminology's 'brute facts': the age–crime curve and the crime drop in Scotland. *European Journal of Criminology, 15*(3), 296–320.

Ng, A. (15 March 2018) IoT attacks are getting worse – and no one's listening. C/Net. March 15. www.cnet.com/news/iot-attacks-hacker-kaspersky-are-getting-worse-and-no-one-is-listening.

Payne, J., Brown, R., & Broadhurst, R. (2018) Where have all the young offenders gone? Examining changes in offending between two NSW birth cohorts. *Trends and Issues in Crime and Criminal* Justice No. 553. Canberra: Australian Institute of Criminology.

Perry, W. L. (2013) *Predictive Policing: The Role of Crime Forecasting in Law Enforcement Operations*. Santa Monica, CA: Rand Corporation.

SafeGadget (1 January 2018) Hacked Internet of Things database. SafeGadget. www.safegadget.com/139/hacked-internet-things-database.

Sanders, C. B. & Sheptycki, J. (2017) Policing, crime and 'big data'; towards a critique of the moral economy of stochastic governance. *Crime, Law and Social Change, 68*(1–2), 1–15.

Shapiro, A. (2018) The Rise of big data policing: surveillance, race, and the future of law enforcement. *Surveillance & Society, 16*(1), 123–126.

Sidebottom, A. & Tilley, N. (2017) Designing crime against systems: introducing leaky systems. In N. Tilley & A. Sidebottom (eds) *Handbook of Crime Prevention and Community Safety*. London: Routledge.

Williams, M. L., Burnap, P., & Sloan, L. (2017) Crime sensing with big data: the affordances and limitations of using open-source communications to estimate crime patterns. *The British Journal of Criminology, 57*(2), 320–340.

Wortley, R. & Smallbone, S. (2012) *Internet Child Pornography: Causes, Investigation and Prevention*. Santa Barbara, CA: Praeger.

Index

Printed in Great Britain
by Amazon

67595364R00280